Frommer's®
New York City

My New York City
by Brian Silverman

NEW YORKERS ARE GREAT COMPLAINERS. WE LIKE TO BITCH AND MOAN.
And this is a good thing. Our grumbling keeps us on our toes.

We're also initially suspicious of the new—of invasions to our beloved landscape. When the twin towers of the World Trade Center were constructed, many of us saw them as a blight on the city's famous skyline. Compared with treasures like the Empire State Building and the Chrysler Building, they were abominations. Generations later, we mourn their loss not just because of the lives that went down with them, but because they'd become part of our spiritual landscape, symbols of our sheer brashness, our restless energy, our drive.

What makes New York a true original, however, is not one building or museum but the sum of it all, including the people. Las Vegas can create an instant New York on the Strip, but it's a fantasy—you need New Yorkers to make New York. The city, and the spirit it embodies, just cannot be duplicated. I have no complaints about that.

Here are some of the places I like to go back to over and over. You won't want to miss them either.

CENTRAL PARK (left) I'm very fortunate to live with my family near Central Park. It's like having our own personal nature preserve—except that we share it with thousands of others. Central Park is one of the best places in the city for people-watching, especially during summer. The parade of bikers, joggers, roller-bladers, and strollers is a source of endless amusement. And the park has so many routes I never get never bored. Pictured here is the Mall, with its wide walkway and overarching elms.

THE ROSE CENTER FOR EARTH AND SPACE (above) City icons don't develop overnight. But as soon as this giant glass cube opened 5 years ago, it was an instant hit. Inside, a four-story-high planetarium offers one of the most technologically advanced sky shows on the planet. This futuristic structure, draped in the largest suspended glass curtain wall in the U.S., is the perfect complement to the dusty dinosaurs inside the American Museum of Natural History, the building both share.

SUBWAY MUSICIANS (left) Most of us who live in New York spend a good deal of time taking the subways. It's the fastest and cheapest way to get around and not as complicated as it might seem. Rushing like rats through the stations to make connections, we're cheered on by sounds of music, even if we stop only long enough to drop a quarter in a cup. What makes the beat so special is that you never know when or where you'll hear it, or what it might be. Here, a jazz duo has found an impromptu stage to show off their stuff.

CENTRAL PARK RESERVOIR (below) Also known as the Jacqueline Kennedy Onassis Reservoir, this is my favorite place for a jog. I'm not alone: The 1½-mile jogging track around the reservoir is packed with joggers in the morning and after work. What makes it so special are the views. As you circle east you see the stately apartment buildings of Fifth Avenue. From the north end you can see the Manhattan skyline to the south. The view west reveals the majestic Art Deco apartment buildings that line Central Park West.

GRAND CENTRAL STATION (above) No, it's not a planetarium, it's the "sky ceiling" in the main concourse of the magnificently restored Grand Central Station. The ceiling, lit greenish-blue, depicts the constellations of the winter sky above New York. Be careful staring up; you might get trampled by one of the thousands of commuters who rush through here each day. Grand Central is a pleasure even if you're not catching a train—you could spend hours shopping at the upscale food market, visiting the New York Transit Museum Store, noshing on the dining concourse, or slurping oysters at the landmark Oyster Bar.

LOUIS ARMSTRONG'S BATHROOM (right) This mirrored bathroom happens to be in the former house of jazz great Louis Armstrong. Armstrong could have lived anywhere, but he chose an unassuming house in the blue-collar neighborhood of Corona, Queens. Now a museum, the house has been preserved exactly as it was when his wife passed away in 1983.

© Serge Hambourg/Louis Armstrong House & Archives

A FOODIE'S TOWN I admit it, I love food, and New York has tremendous variety. Other city greenmarkets are more convenient to my home, but none matches this one in **UNION SQUARE (left)**, not only for the scene but for the variety. The best time to visit is in the summer and fall, when the produce—apples, lettuces, corn, you name it—from local farms is bountiful. The dominant color on a brisk fall day? Pumpkin orange. When I want the best Southern fried chicken in the city, I head to the **M&G DINER (bottom left)** on 125th Street. Waiting on line for smoked fish at **ZABAR'S (upper right)** on a Sunday morning is an Upper West Side tradition. I love walking in Chinatown, where everything is right out on the street, from bootleg DVDs to boxes of ginseng. But what I love best about Chinatown are the countless restaurants, the vegetable markets, and the **FISH MARKETS (bottom right)**, where the catch is so fresh it's still flapping on ice.

FLATIRON BUILDING (left) This architectural icon is one of the most recognizable structures in the world. It was built in 1902 to fill the awkward triangular property created by the intersection of Broadway and Fifth Avenue. Fronted with limestone and terra cotta, it measures just 6 feet across at its narrow end. It's a beauty to look at, but don't bother going inside; I've been there many times (my wife had an office there), and it's not worth the interminable wait for the out-dated elevators.

YANKEE STADIUM (below) Rome may have its Colosseum, but New York has Yankee Stadium. There is no more famous sports arena in America than "The House that Ruth Built." You may be from Boston or Chicago and hate the Yankees, but don't hold that against Yankee Stadium. If you're here in the off-season, you can still go for a tour and wander amid the ghosts of all-time greats like Ruth, Gehrig, DiMaggio, and Mantle.

WALDORF-ASTORIA (above) I'm a sucker for old-time, early-20th-century New York hotels. Thankfully, quite a few of these "grande dames" are still around. The Waldorf, comprising one square block and 1,000 rooms, just might be the grandest of them all. This is where kings stay when they come to town; where the president lays his head; and where Secret Service agents of all nationalities are a regular sight. The Waldorf also has fine shops, three restaurants, and four bars.

MUSEUM OF MODERN ART (right) The old MoMA was indistinguishable among the faceless towers on 53rd Street. Following a $425-million reno-vation, MoMA is now as close to a work of art as a museum can be—It's stunning both inside and out. Anyone who claims a love of modern art has to come here to enjoy one of the greatest collections of 20th-century art in the world.

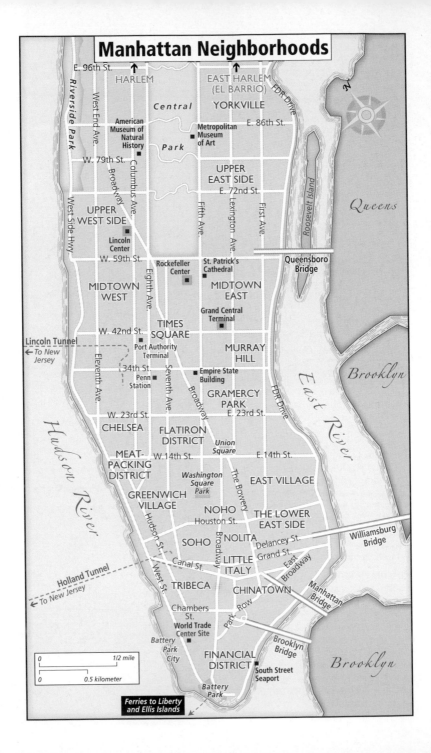

Manhattan Neighborhoods

Central Park

ℹ Information
Ⓜ Subway stop

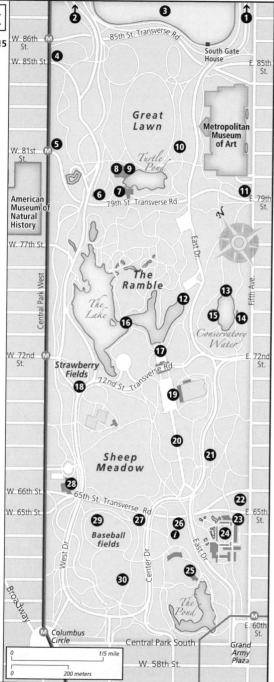

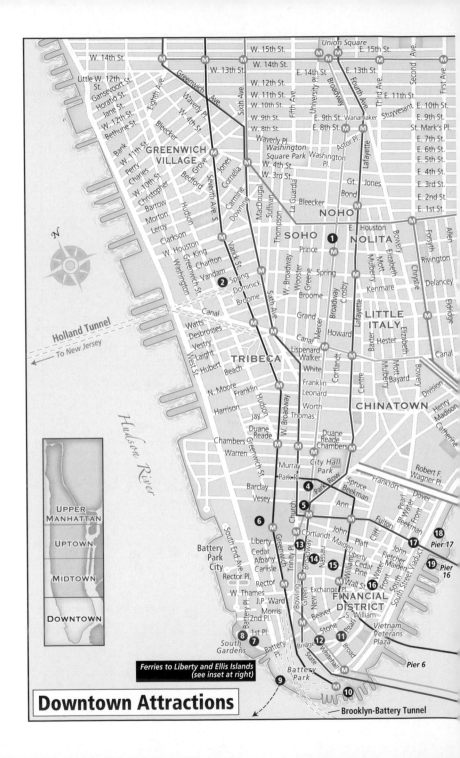

Downtown Attractions

W. 14th St.

Little W. 12th St.
Gansevoort St.
Horatio St.
Jane St.
W. 12th St.
Bethune St.

Bank
W. 11th St.
Perry
Charles
W. 10th St.
Christopher
Barrow
Morton
Leroy
Clarkson
W. Houston
King
Charlton
Vandam
Spring
Dominick
Broome

Watts
Desbrosses
Vestry
Laight
Hubert
Beach
N. Moore
Franklin
Harrison
Jay
Duane Reade
Chambers
Warren

GREENWICH VILLAGE

Eighth Ave.
Greenwich Ave.
Waverly Pl.
W. 4th St.
Bleecker
Grove
Bedford
Jones
Cornelia
Carmine
Downing
MacDougal
Sullivan
Thompson
La Guardia
Washington
Hudson
Greenwich St.
Washington
West St.

TRIBECA

W. 15th St.
W. 13th St.
W. 14th St.
W. 12th St.
W. 11th St.
W. 10th St.
W. 9th St.
W. 8th St.
Waverly Pl.
Washington Square Park
W. 4th St.
W. 3rd St.
Bleecker

Union Square
E. 15th St.
E. 14th St.
E. 13th St.
E. 11th St.
E. 10th St.
E. 9th St.
St. Mark's Pl.
E. 7th St.
E. 6th St.
E. 5th St.
E. 4th St.
E. 3rd St.
E. 2nd St.
E. 1st St.

Sixth Ave.
Fifth Ave.
University Pl.
Broadway
Fourth Ave.
Third Ave.
Second Ave.
First Ave.
Wanamaker
Stuyvesant
Astor Pl.
Lafayette
Gt. Jones
Bond

NOHO

SOHO
Prince
Spring
Broome
Grand

NOLITA
Bowery
Elizabeth
Mott
Mulberry
Crosby
Kenmare

Forsyth
Allen
Rivington
Delancey
Eldridge

E. Houston

LITTLE ITALY
Baxter
Hester
Elizabeth
Mott
Mulberry
Bayard
Bowery

Canal
Lispenard
Walker
White
Franklin
Leonard
Worth
Thomas

Canal
Howard
Cortlandt
Centre
Division

CHINATOWN
Henry
Madison
Catherine

Duane
Reade
Chambers
Murray
Park Pl.
Barclay
Vesey

City Hall Park
Park Row
Spruce
Beekman
Ann
Frankfort
Dover
Pearl
Water
Front
Robert F. Wagner Pl.

Liberty
Cedar
Albany
Carlisle
Rector Pl.
Rector
W. Thames
J.P. Ward
Morris
2nd Pl.
1st Pl.

Battery Park City
South End Ave.
Battery Pl.

Cortlandt
John
Platt
Cliff
Maiden
Nassau
Liberty
Cedar
Pine
Wall St.
Exchange Pl.
New
Beaver
Stone
S. William
Broad
Whitehall
State
Bridge

Fulton
John
Fletcher
Maiden
Front
Water
South
William
Pearl
FINANCIAL DISTRICT
Beaver
Vietnam Veterans Plaza

Pier 17
Pier 16
Pier 6
South Street Viaduct

Hudson River

Holland Tunnel
To New Jersey

South Gardens

Battery Park

Ferries to Liberty and Ellis Islands
(see inset at right)

Brooklyn-Battery Tunnel

N

❶ ❷ ❸ ❹ ❺ ❻ ❼ ❽ ❾ ❿ ⓫ ⓬ ⓭ ⓮ ⓯ ⓰ ⓱ ⓲ ⓳

UPPER MANHATTAN
UPTOWN
MIDTOWN
DOWNTOWN

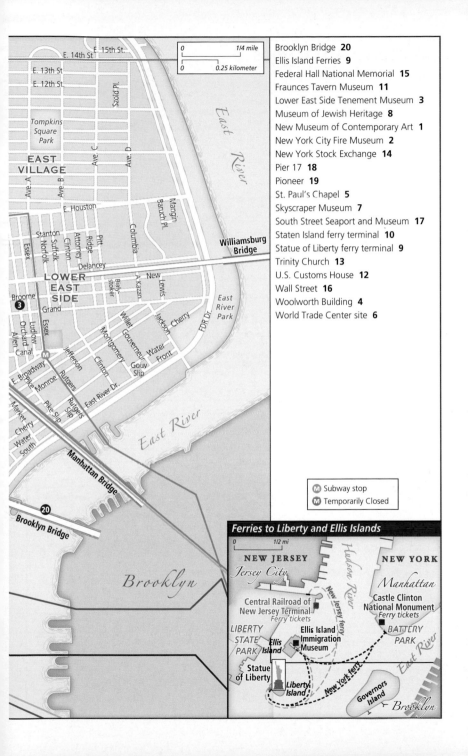

Brooklyn Bridge **20**
Ellis Island Ferries **9**
Federal Hall National Memorial **15**
Fraunces Tavern Museum **11**
Lower East Side Tenement Museum **3**
Museum of Jewish Heritage **8**
New Museum of Contemporary Art **1**
New York City Fire Museum **2**
New York Stock Exchange **14**
Pier 17 **18**
Pioneer **19**
St. Paul's Chapel **5**
Skyscraper Museum **7**
South Street Seaport and Museum **17**
Staten Island ferry terminal **10**
Statue of Liberty ferry terminal **9**
Trinity Church **13**
U.S. Customs House **12**
Wall Street **16**
Woolworth Building **4**
World Trade Center site **6**

Ⓜ Subway stop
Ⓜ Temporarily Closed

Ferries to Liberty and Ellis Islands

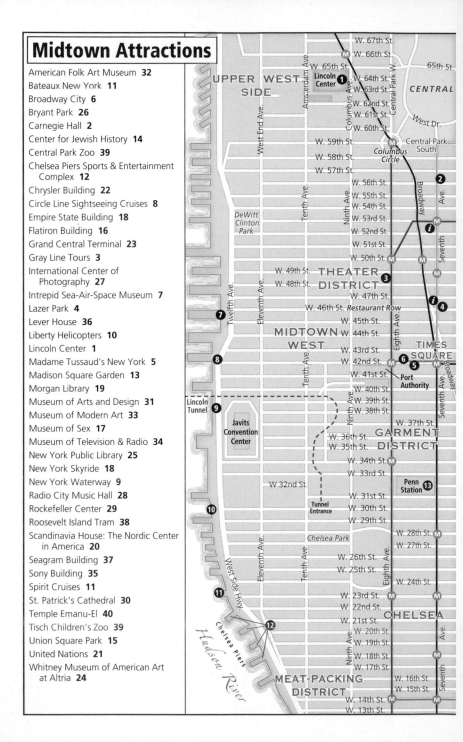

Midtown Attractions

American Folk Art Museum **32**
Bateaux New York **11**
Broadway City **6**
Bryant Park **26**
Carnegie Hall **2**
Center for Jewish History **14**
Central Park Zoo **39**
Chelsea Piers Sports & Entertainment
    Complex **12**
Chrysler Building **22**
Circle Line Sightseeing Cruises **8**
Empire State Building **18**
Flatiron Building **16**
Grand Central Terminal **23**
Gray Line Tours **3**
International Center of
    Photography **27**
Intrepid Sea-Air-Space Museum **7**
Lazer Park **4**
Lever House **36**
Liberty Helicopters **10**
Lincoln Center **1**
Madame Tussaud's New York **5**
Madison Square Garden **13**
Morgan Library **19**
Museum of Arts and Design **31**
Museum of Modern Art **33**
Museum of Sex **17**
Museum of Television & Radio **34**
New York Public Library **25**
New York Skyride **18**
New York Waterway **9**
Radio City Music Hall **28**
Rockefeller Center **29**
Roosevelt Island Tram **38**
Scandinavia House: The Nordic Center
    in America **20**
Seagram Building **37**
Sony Building **35**
Spirit Cruises **11**
St. Patrick's Cathedral **30**
Temple Emanu-El **40**
Tisch Children's Zoo **39**
Union Square Park **15**
United Nations **21**
Whitney Museum of American Art
    at Altria **24**

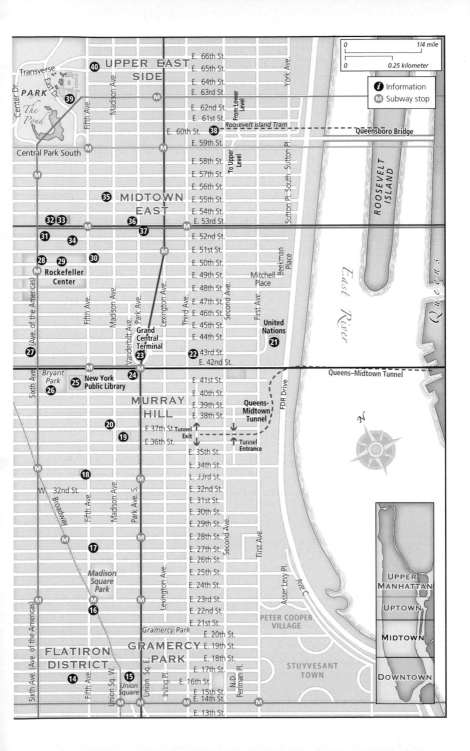

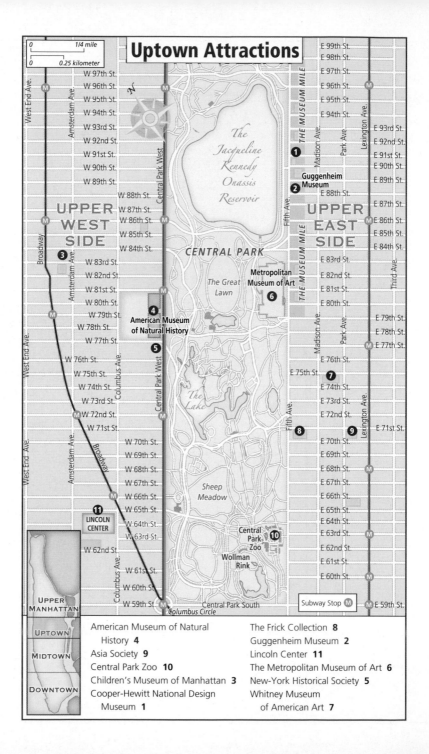

Uptown Attractions

0   1/4 mile

0   0.25 kilometer

W 97th St.
W 96th St.
W 95th St.
W 94th St.
W 93rd St.
W 92nd St.
W 91st St.
W 90th St.
W 89th St.
W 88th St.
W 87th St.
W 86th St.
W 85th St.
W 84th St.
W 83rd St.
W 82nd St.
W 81st St.
W 80th St.
W 79th St.
W 78th St.
W 77th St.
W 76th St.
W 75th St.
W 74th St.
W 73rd St.
W 72nd St.
W 71st St.
W 70th St.
W 69th St.
W 68th St.
W 67th St.
W 66th St.
W 65th St.
W 64th St.
W 63rd St.
W 62nd St.
W 61st St.
W 60th St.
W 59th St.

West End Ave.
Amsterdam Ave.
Broadway
Central Park West
Columbus Ave.

UPPER WEST SIDE

American Museum of Natural History ❹ ❺

LINCOLN CENTER ⓫

Columbus Circle

The Jacqueline Kennedy Onassis Reservoir

CENTRAL PARK

The Great Lawn

The Lake

Sheep Meadow

Central Park Zoo ❿
Wollman Rink

Central Park South

E 99th St.
E 98th St.
E 97th St.
E 96th St.
E 95th St.
E 94th St.
E 93rd St.
E 92nd St.
E 91st St.
E 90th St.
E 89th St.
E 88th St.
E 87th St.
E 86th St.
E 85th St.
E 84th St.
E 83rd St.
E 82nd St.
E 81st St.
E 80th St.
E 79th St.
E 78th St.
E 77th St.
E 76th St.
E 75th St.
E 74th St.
E 73rd St.
E 72nd St.
E 71st St.
E 70th St.
E 69th St.
E 68th St.
E 67th St.
E 66th St.
E 65th St.
E 64th St.
E 63rd St.
E 62nd St.
E 61st St.
E 60th St.
E 59th St.

THE MUSEUM MILE

Fifth Ave.
Madison Ave.
Park Ave.
Lexington Ave.
Third Ave.

❶
Guggenheim Museum ❷

Metropolitan Museum of Art ❻

UPPER EAST SIDE

❼
❽ ❾

Subway Stop Ⓜ

UPPER MANHATTAN
UPTOWN
MIDTOWN
DOWNTOWN

American Museum of Natural History **4**
Asia Society **9**
Central Park Zoo **10**
Children's Museum of Manhattan **3**
Cooper-Hewitt National Design Museum **1**

The Frick Collection **8**
Guggenheim Museum **2**
Lincoln Center **11**
The Metropolitan Museum of Art **6**
New-York Historical Society **5**
Whitney Museum of American Art **7**

Frommer's®

New York City

2008

by Brian Silverman

Here's what the critics say about Frommer's:

"Amazingly easy to use. Very portable, very complete."
                                                    —*Booklist*

"Detailed, accurate, and easy-to-read information for all price ranges."
                                                    —*Glamour Magazine*

"Hotel information is close to encyclopedic."
                                                    —*Des Moines Sunday Register*

"Frommer's Guides have a way of giving you a real feel for a place."
                                                    —*Knight Ridder Newspapers*

BICENTENNIAL
1807
WILEY
2007
BICENTENNIAL
Wiley Publishing, Inc.

About the Author

Brian Silverman is a freelance writer whose work has been published in *Saveur, The New Yorker, Caribbean Travel & Life, Islands, Four Seasons.* Among the many topics he writes about are food, travel, sports, and music. He is the author of numerous books including *Going, Going, Gone: The History, Lore, and Mystique of the Home Run,* and the *Twentieth Century Treasury of Sports.* For Frommer's, he has written Complete, Portable, and Budget guides to New York City, as well as *New York City For Dummies.* He lives in Manhattan with his wife and children.

Published by:

Wiley Publishing, Inc.

111 River St.
Hoboken, NJ 07030-5774

ISBN: 978-0-470-14439-8

Editor: Kathleen Warnock
Production Editor: Jana M. Stefanciosa
Cartographer: Guy Ruggiero
Photo Editor: Richard Fox
Anniversary Logo Design: Richard Pacifico
Production by Wiley Indianapolis Composition Services

Front cover photo: Chrysler Building seen from below
Back cover photo: Greenwich Village clothing store, apartments above

For information on our other products and services or to obtain technical support, please contact our Customer Care Department within the U.S. at 800/762-2974, outside the U.S. at 317/572-3993 or fax 317/572-4002.

Wiley also publishes its books in a variety of electronic formats. Some content that appears in print may not be available in electronic formats.

Manufactured in the United States of America

5 4 3 2

Contents

4 Suggested New York City Itineraries   63

5 Getting to Know New York City   74

6 Where to Stay   109

7 Where to Dine   155

8   Exploring New York City   225

9   Shopping   305

10 New York City After Dark   343

Index   390

List of Maps

Acknowledgments

My editor, Kathleen Warnock, with her guidance and support, helps make working on this book a pleasure rather than a chore and for that I am very thankful. I'd also like to thank Michelle Krumland for her tireless fact-checking of this very fact-filled book.

—Brian Silverman

An Invitation to the Reader

In researching this book, we discovered many wonderful places—hotels, restaurants, shops, and more. We're sure you'll find others. Please tell us about them, so we can share the information with your fellow travelers in upcoming editions. If you were disappointed with a recommendation, we'd love to know that, too. Please write to:

Frommer's New York City 2008
Wiley Publishing, Inc. • 111 River St. • Hoboken, NJ 07030-5774

An Additional Note

Please be advised that travel information is subject to change at any time—and this is especially true of prices. We therefore suggest that you write or call ahead for confirmation when making your travel plans. The authors, editors, and publisher cannot be held responsible for the experiences of readers while traveling. Your safety is important to us, however, so we encourage you to stay alert and be aware of your surroundings. Keep a close eye on cameras, purses, and wallets, all favorite targets of thieves and pickpockets.

Other Great Guides for Your Trip:

Frommer's New York City Day by Day
Pauline Frommer's New York City
New York City For Dummies
Frommer's New York City with Kids
Frommer's Memorable Walks in New York
Suzy Gershman's Born to Shop New York
Frommer's NYC Free & Dirt Cheap
Frommer's Portable New York City

Frommer's Star Ratings, Icons & Abbreviations

Every hotel, restaurant, and attraction listing in this guide has been ranked for quality, value, service, amenities, and special features using a **star-rating system.** In country, state, and regional guides, we also rate towns and regions to help you narrow down your choices and budget your time accordingly. Hotels and restaurants are rated on a scale of zero (recommended) to three stars (exceptional). Attractions, shopping, nightlife, towns, and regions are rated according to the following scale: zero stars (recommended), one star (highly recommended), two stars (very highly recommended), and three stars (must-see).

In addition to the star-rating system, we also use **seven feature icons** that point you to the great deals, in-the-know advice, and unique experiences that separate travelers from tourists. Throughout the book, look for:

Finds	Special finds—those places only insiders know about
Fun Fact	Fun facts—details that make travelers more informed and their trips more fun
Kids	Best bets for kids and advice for the whole family
Moments	Special moments—those experiences that memories are made of
Overrated	Places or experiences not worth your time or money
Tips	Insider tips—great ways to save time and money
Value	Great values—where to get the best deals

The following **abbreviations** are used for credit cards:

AE	American Express	DISC	Discover	V	Visa
DC	Diners Club	MC	MasterCard		

Frommers.com

Now that you have this guidebook to help you plan a great trip, visit our website at **www. frommers.com** for additional travel information on more than 3,500 destinations. We update features regularly to give you instant access to the most current trip-planning information available. At Frommers.com, you'll find scoops on the best airfares, lodging rates, and car rental bargains. You can even book your travel online through our reliable travel booking partners. Other popular features include:

- Online updates of our most popular guidebooks
- Vacation sweepstakes and contest giveaways
- Newsletters highlighting the hottest travel trends
- Online travel message boards with featured travel discussions

What's New in New York City

The year 2007 might be remembered as the year of breaking ground. Ground was broken for numerous new hotels (see below) and soaring condos throughout the city. But more importantly, ground was broken at the former World Trade Center Site for the proposed Freedom Tower and what was just an empty hole for 5 years; now signs of progress can be seen. Still, it won't be until late 2009 at the earliest before completion of the Tower and the 9/11 Memorial.

Ground was also broken in the Bronx, where a new **Yankee Stadium** is being built adjacent to the historic "House that Ruth Built." Will this be the "House that Jeter Built?" The new stadium is scheduled to open for the 2009 season.

Not to be outdone by the Yankees, the Mets also broke ground on their own new stadium in Flushing, Queens next to the crumbling **Shea Stadium** it will replace. The new stadium should also to be ready for the 2009 season.

Though they haven't actually broken ground, an arena-naming ceremony was held in late 2006 in Brooklyn on the site over the Atlantic Yards at Atlantic Avenue where the New Jersey Nets, who will become the **Brooklyn Nets,** will build their new arena called Barclays Center (named after the British bank) . . . that is if owner/developer Bruce Ratner can hold off the protests of community activists who feel a basketball arena will destroy their neighborhood.

Here are some other recent changes in the Big Apple:

ACCOMMODATIONS With a record 44 million visitors to New York City in 2006 and a forecast of 45.5 million for 2007, hotel rooms are in demand, and a slew are scheduled to open in 2007 and 2008.

Many will be in areas not known for hotels including Noho, which will feature **The Bowery Hotel** (✆ 212/505-9100; www.theboweryhotel.com), owned by the proprietors of The Maritime Hotel, at 335 Bowery. The Bowery will feature loft-style rooms and offer modern conveniences such as flat screen HDTVs combined with old world ambience.

Despite numerous delays, TriBeCa will finally get its signature hotel when actor Robert DeNiro's $43-million, 83-room **Downtown Hotel** in his beloved TriBeCa opens late in 2007.

Jason Pomeranc, the owner of **60 Thompson** (p. 118), has two new hotel ventures: the 90-room **6 Columbus Circle,** which, despite numerous delays, just might be open by the time you read this, and the 112-room **Allen Street,** an ambitious Lower East Side project scheduled to open by the end of 2007.

After more than 2 years of renovations, **The Plaza** (✆ 212/546-5380) is scheduled to reopen in late 2007, albeit a bit smaller, with 350 rooms and 150 new residential units (starting price: $1.5 million!).

There hadn't been a new hotel opening in Brooklyn since 1998, but by 2008 there will be two major new Brooklyn hotels: the 93-room **Smith Hotel,** 75

Smith Street, at Atlantic Avenue, in Carroll Gardens and the 200-room **Starwood Aloft** in downtown Brooklyn. Both claim that they will open by the end of 2007, but 2008 seems more realistic.

RESTAURANTS New Yorkers crave red meat, or one would assume with the opening of countless new steakhouses including **Kobe Club, Quality Meats, Benjamin Steakhouse, Harry's Steaks, and Porter House New York** (see chapter 7 for detailed information on those).

But it wasn't just steak. New York welcomed the arrival of two renowned European chefs. The notorious super chef Gordon "Hell's Kitchen" Ramsey from London opened his restaurant **Gordon Ramsay at The London** in **The London NYC hotel,** 151 W. 54th St (✆ 212/468-8888; www.gordonramsay.com) and quickly earned two stars from the *New York Times* and Joël Robuchon from Paris opened **L'Atelier de Joël Robuchon** in the **Four Seasons Hotel** 57 E. 57th St. (✆ 212/350-6658) and earned three stars from the *Times.*

At **the Ritz-Carlton New York-Central Park,** chef Laurent Tourondel of BLT fame (BLT Fish, BLT Steak, BLT Prime) will open **BLT Market** which will feature a rotating seasonal menu.

New York has thousands of pizzerias so a new one would not attract much attention. To counter that, **Nino's Bellisima,** 890 Second Avenue (at 47th St.; ✆ 212/355-5540) made a splash by offering a $1,000 pizza., the most expensive ever in New York topped with lobster and six kinds of caviar. I wonder if they will sell it by the slice?

The TriBeCa favorite, **Landmarc** (p. 162) helmed by Marc Murphy has moved up in many ways when in the Spring of 2007 a 300-seat branch on the third floor of the Time Warner Center (third floor, ✆ 212/823-6123) on Columbus Circle opened as part of the Center's prestigious "Restaurant Collection" which includes Masa, Per Se, Café Gray, and Porter House New York.

ATTRACTIONS No definitive location has been found yet, but lower Manhattan will be the home for the new **National Sports Museum (✆ 212/837-7950;** www.thesportsmuseum.com), and the museum will be the home for the Heisman Trophy. It will also be the home of the **Billie Jean King International Women's Sports Center,** a hall of fame for women in sports.

Museum Mile will extend a bit further north on Fifth Avenue when the 90,000 square-foot $80 million **Museum of African Art** is built between 109th and 110th streets. The Museum will be housed below 115 luxury condominiums and offer 16,000 square feet of exhibition space. Construction of the Museum is scheduled for the end of 2009.

As part of improvements to Battery **Park,** an ambitious project called **Sea Glass: The Carousel** is underway. The Carousel will be an aquatic-themed ride featuring sea creatures and a ride-the-waves turntable. Kids will love it; adults bring the Dramamine. The Carousel is scheduled to debut in 2008.

The beloved *U.S.S. Intrepid* **Sea, Air & Space Museum** was towed away for much-needed renovations in late 2006. The World War II vessel will be refurbished over the next 2 years including opening now-hidden areas of the ship to the public. While in dry dock, the ship will be repainted in classic battleship gray, and many of the military aircraft on its flight deck will be restored. Pier 86 will be rebuilt as well. The ship should return and reopen by fall of 2008.

In 2007 the new home of the *New York Times* on the corner of Eighth Avenue and 41st Street is scheduled to open. Within that building will be two new performance and banquet venues, The Stage and The Hall called **The TimesCenter.** Designed by Italian architect, Renzo

Lady Liberty Changes Ferries

Hornblower Yachts (the same company that runs the Alcatraz ferry in San Francisco), will take over the ferries and tours to the Statue of Liberty in late 2007, replacing the Circle Line (which held the franchise for many years). If you're going to be visiting Lady Liberty toward the end of the year, go to **www.statue cruises.com** for more information. Before then, you can still get information and book tickets at **www.circlinedowntown.com**.

Piano, The Stage will be used for lectures, concerts, and live broadcasts while The Hall will be used for banquets and receptions.

Over in Coney Island, 2007 is set to be the last season for beloved amusement park Astroland. New owners have purchased the site, and say they will keep the famed Cyclone rollercoaster (a National Historic Landmark), but plan on constructing a new amusement, retail and residential project on the site.

AFTER DARK   After many lives, legendary rock and roll club, **CBGB** finally expired in 2006, rising rents and gentrification also claimed the music club **Tonic** and dance club **Crobar.**

But when one legend fades, another rises from the ashes. **Minton's Playhouse,** in Harlem was the gathering spot for some of jazz's greatest artists. During the dark days of New York in the 1970's, Minton's closed and over the years efforts were made by many to resurrect it. Finally, in 2006, the club re-opened now called the **Uptown Jazz Lounge at Minton's Playouse,** 208 W,

118th St (© **212/864-8346;** www. uptownatmintons.com) and though the physical improvements were slap dash, the jazz is still straight ahead and first rate. And that's all that matters.

Can New York get any funnier? With the addition of a big new comedy club, **Comix,** 353 W. 14th St (at 9th Avenue) © **212/524-2500;** www.comixny.com, apparently it can. And the club is in the fashionista-magnet Meatpacking District, an area that, in this writer's opinion, could certainly use a few laughs.

A little bit north of the Meatpacking District, near the proposed "Highline" park in west Chelsea which will be constructed on an unused elevated railway line, the area lost a grand old music/disco venue in the **Roxy,** but there's a glittering new music venue in the neighborhood: the **Highline Ballroom,** at 431 W. 16th St, between 9th and 10th Aves., © **212/ 414-5994;** www.highlineballroom.com. It opened with a bang in spring 2007, as the hub of the "Highline Festival," curated by David Bowie, featuring such acts as Lou Reed and Tommy Ramone.

1

The Best of the Big Apple

We New Yorkers have heard the proud refrain from local politicos many times: how New York is better than ever. The FBI has rated New York as the safest big city in the United States. It's cleaner than it ever was. The number of hotels, restaurants, and clubs keeps growing and gets better every year. This rebirth has helped bring in over 44 million tourists in 2006 and even more are projected in the next few years. Everything seems rosy. Why then, are some of us worried about our city? With this boom, those of us who have been here a long time and have seen the changes from a city in need to what it is today, fret that this renaissance is one without character. We worry that with a Starbucks on every corner and new, glass and steel condos sprouting like mushrooms at the expense of an old favorite bookstore or our local Cuban/Chinese joint, that we are slowly losing our identity; the fear being that we will become like everycity USA.

But change is inevitable. "Of the city's five boroughs, Manhattan, in particular, refuses to remain as it was. It is dynamic, not static. What seems permanent when you are twenty is too often a ghost when you are thirty," Pete Hamill writes in his book *Downtown: My Manhattan.*

And the longer you live in this town, the more ghosts you will encounter. But New Yorkers adapt . . . sometimes painfully. Hamill explains: "The New York version of nostalgia is not simply about lost buildings or their presence in the youth of the individuals who lived with them. It involves an almost fatalistic acceptance of the permanent presence of loss. Nothing will ever stay the same . . . . Irreversible change happens so often in New York that the experience affects character itself. New York toughens its people against sentimentality by allowing the truer emotion of nostalgia. Sentimentality is always about a lie. Nostalgia is about real things gone."

So though we might mourn loss, we also anticipate and expect change—it's part of our way of life. We know that a restaurant, show, club, or store might be the hottest thing now, but a couple months later, the next one has opened or been discovered and that once hot spot quickly becomes passé.

But some icons and institutions are so entrenched in our daily lives that we could never accept their loss. What would we do without that reassuring sight of the Lady in the harbor or the gleaming spire of the Empire State Building? Or the perfect pizza? Or a Sunday in Central Park? Or the rumbling of the trains beneath the earth? Or the sounds of jazz from a Village club? So while New York is ever-changing, as long as its core remains the same we might complain a bit, but we aren't going anywhere.

1 Most Unforgettable New York City Experiences

- **Sailing to the Statue of Liberty,** on Liberty Island in New York Harbor. If you have time to do only one thing on your visit to New York, sail to the Lady in the harbor. No other monument embodies the nation's—and the

New York Metropolitan Area

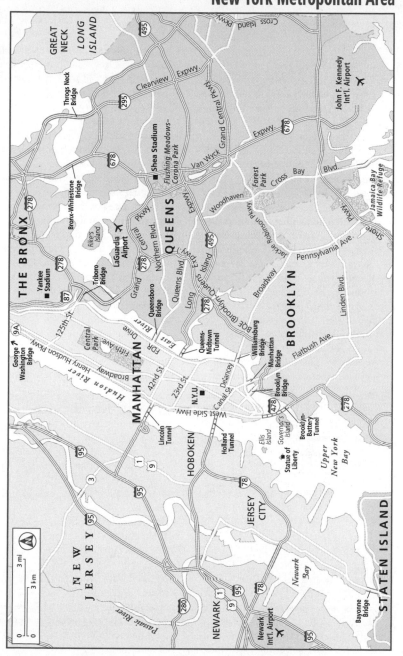

world's—notion of political freedom and economic potential more than Lady Liberty. It is also the ultimate symbol of New York, the personification of the city's vast diversity and tolerance. See p. 244.

- **Visiting the Empire State Building Observatory at Dusk:** Like the Statue of Liberty, the Empire State Building, once again the tallest building in New York, is one of the city's definitive icons. Arrive at dusk and watch the lights of the city come on. It's pure magic. See p. 238.

- **Walking the Brooklyn Bridge:** Manhattan has five major bridges connecting the island to other shores, and the most historic and fascinating is the Brooklyn Bridge. For a close-up look at what was a marvel of civic engineering when it was built in 1883, and a true New York experience, walk across from Manhattan to Brooklyn. See p. 236.

- **Taking the subway to Yankee Stadium for a Yankee game:** It doesn't sound very intriguing, does it? Good or bad, there's nothing like being crammed into a subway car packed with rabid Yankee fans. And it's an experience you'll not soon forget. See p. 247.

- **Jogging around the Central Park Reservoir:** Okay, you don't even have to jog it. You can walk the jogging path around the Jacqueline Kennedy Onassis Reservoir and take in the beauty of Central Park, the views of Central Park West, Fifth Avenue, and especially the skyline of midtown Manhattan. See p. 271.

- **Sunday Morning in New York:** This might not sound so unforgettable, but to experience the city minus the noise and activity is something special. I've noticed quite a few tourists, usually jet-lagged Europeans, wandering the parks and streets early Sunday mornings.

- **Walking 125th Street:** Take a walk across this famous Harlem boulevard and your senses will be overwhelmed with the music, the variety of stores, the restaurants, the stalls selling everything from homemade CDs to bean pies, and the street prophets and musicians. The energy is relentless.

2 New York's Best Events & Seasons

- **Best Parade: West Indian–American Day Carnival and Parade.** Held on Eastern Parkway in Brooklyn, this is the biggest parade in New York. The music (calypso, soca, reggae, and Latin), the costumes, and the Caribbean food make this unforgettable. If you're lucky enough to be in town on Labor Day, don't miss it. See p. 34.

- **Best Season in New York: Christmas.** Christmas trees on Park Avenue, the big snowflake on 57th and Fifth, the trees at Rockefeller Center and Lincoln Center, the menorah at Grand Army Plaza at Fifth and 59th Street, the decorations in department store windows, restaurants, and hotels. And even though the crowds, especially around Midtown and Rockefeller Center, might bring out the Scrooge in you, the atmosphere is almost always festive and like no other time of year.

- **Best Time of Year to Come to New York: Summer.** Most people prefer the temperate days of fall to visit New York, and that's when the city is most crowded. But my personal favorite season is summer, when the streets are empty, restaurants and shows are easier to get into, and free outdoor cultural events abound.

- **Best Day to Come to New York: New Year's Day.** The holidays are over. You've had enough festivity—see above. You've wisely skipped the insanity of New Year's Eve and arisen fresh and (relatively) sober. Get out on the town early; you'll have the city practically to yourself.

3 New York's Best Museums

- **Best Overall Museum: American Museum of Natural History.** You can spend your entire visit to New York at this 4-square-block museum; there is that much to see. From the famed dinosaur halls to the Hall of Ocean Life, the Museum of Natural History houses the world's greatest natural science collection. See p. 235.
- **Best Art Museum: Metropolitan Museum of Art.** Not just the best art museum in New York, but the best in North America. The number of masterworks is mind-boggling. See p. 239.
- **Best-Looking Museum: Museum of Modern Art.** Though the sight of the Guggenheim is the most memorable, MoMA's $450-million renovation makes it the classiest- and coolest-looking museum, inside and out, in town. See p. 241.
- **Best New York Museum about New York: Museum of the City of New York.** Start here before you tour New York and get a feel of what the city is like from past to present. There are always fascinating exhibits. See p. 256.
- **Best Home Posing as a Museum: The Louis Armstrong House Museum.** This unassuming house in Queens was Satchmo's home for almost 30 years and it's been preserved almost exactly as it was when he died in 1971. See p. 300.

4 Best New York City Structures

- **Best Historic Building: Grand Central Terminal.** Despite all the steel-and-glass skyscrapers in New York, there are still many historic marvels standing, and the best is this Beaux Arts gem. This railroad station, built in 1913, was restored in the 1990s to recapture its brilliance. Even if you don't have to catch a train, make sure you visit. See p. 238.
- **Best Skyscraper: The Chrysler Building.** There is no observation deck, but this Art Deco masterpiece is best viewed from outside or from other observation decks like the Empire State Building. See p. 261.
- **Most Impressive Place of Worship: Cathedral of St. John the Divine.** Construction began on the world's largest Gothic cathedral in 1892 and it's still going on. But this is one structure that benefits from being a work-in-progress.

5 Best Parks in New York City

- **Best Park: Central Park.** One of the world's greatest urban refuges—a center of calm and tranquillity amongst the noise and bustle that is Manhattan. See p. 268.
- **Runners-Up for Best Park: Riverside Park.** This 4-mile-long park along the Hudson River is a welcome alternative to the sometimes-overcrowded Central Park. **Battery Park.**

At the island's southern tip, walk the promenade and marvel at the harbor with Lady Liberty standing sentinel. See p. 273.

6 Best Places in New York to Take the Kids

• **Central Park.** With its lovely carousel, a zoo, two ice-skating rinks, and numerous playgrounds and ball fields, Central Park is a children's wonderland. See p. 268.

• **Bronx Zoo Wildlife Conservation Park.** This is one of the great zoos in the world—and you don't have to be a kid to love it. See p. 289.

• **New York Hall of Science.** This Queens museum in Flushing Meadows-Corona Park has hands-on exhibits that thrill children from preschool and up. And after the museum the park offers a carousel, zoo, and boat and bike rentals. See p. 287.

7 Best Places to Stroll in New York

• **The Upper West Side.** With museums, parks, some old buildings and brownstones, inexpensive restaurants, and a residential feel, this is my favorite neighborhood to stroll.

• **Greenwich Village.** With its historic streets, hidden cafes, cozy restaurants, and eccentric characters, Greenwich Village is a constant, but pleasant, barrage on the senses.

• **Chinatown.** With the relentless activity and crowded sidewalks, Chinatown might not seem like ideal strolling territory, but it's so colorful, it's worth braving the mobs.

8 Best Things to Do for Free (or Almost) in New York

• **Ride the Staten Island Ferry.** The Staten Island Ferry is used daily by thousands of commuters. Ride with them for a great view of the Statue of Liberty, Ellis Island, New York Harbor, and the lower Manhattan skyline. You really can't beat the price: It's free. See p. 244.

• **Attend a Gospel Service.** All around New York you'll find Sunday gospel services, but for some special soul-stirring, head to Harlem and the **Abyssinian Baptist Church** or Brooklyn and the **Brooklyn Tabernacle.** Services are free but when the basket is passed, don't be stingy. See p. 265 and 294.

• **Visit Free Museums.** Believe it or not, there are museums in New York that don't charge admission. Two of my favorites are the **National Museum of the American Indian** and the **Federal Hall National Memorial.** See p. 256 and 264.

• **Take in a Game at the West 4th Street Basketball Courts,** West 4th Street and Sixth Avenue. I don't know what's more entertaining: the moves on the court or the inventive, trash talk accompanying the games.

9 Best Offbeat New York Experiences

• **Visit the Little Italy of the Bronx.** With the demise of Little Italy in Manhattan, the area centered around Arthur Avenue, known as the Little Italy of the Bronx, is the place to go for old-fashioned Italian charm, food, and ambience. Though it still qualifies as offbeat, word is out about Arthur Avenue.

- **Museum of Sex.** How many cities can claim their own Museum of Sex? Not too many! We got your Museum of Sex right here . . . but you must be 18 or older to enter. See p. 253.
- **Roosevelt Island Tram.** Impress your family and friends with a little-known but spectacular view of the skyline by taking them on the Roosevelt Island Tram. During the 4-minute ride, you will be treated to a gorgeous view down the East River with views of the United Nations and the Queensboro, Williamsburg, Manhattan, and Brooklyn bridges. On a clear day you might even spot Lady Liberty. See p. 243.

- **Bike Along the Hudson River.** If walking is not enough exercise for you, a good alternative is to rent a bike and ride the length of Manhattan via the work-in-progress **Hudson River Park.** As of this writing, you can bike from Battery Park to Fort Tryon Park near the George Washington Bridge. There are detours along the way, which occasionally take you off the paths. For bike-rental info, see p. 272.
- **Ride the International Express.** The no. 7 train is sometimes known as the "International Express." Take it through the borough of Queens and you will pass one ethnic neighborhood after another, from Indian to Thai, from Peruvian to Columbian, from Chinese to Korean.

10 Best Way to Spend a Day in a Borough Other Than Manhattan

- **In the Bronx:** Spend the morning at the **Bronx Zoo Wildlife Conservation Park** (p. 289) or the **New York Botanical Gardens** (p. 289) and then head to **Arthur Avenue,** the Little Italy of the Bronx (see "Best Offbeat New York Experiences," above), for an authentic Italian feast.
- **In Brooklyn:** You can take a look at what's on at the always exciting **Brooklyn Museum of Art** (p. 294), then get some fresh air with a stroll in nearby, lovely **Prospect Park** (p. 296). Cap it off with a sandwich and a slice of cheesecake at **Junior's** (p. 222) on Flatbush Avenue. Or, head for **Coney Island,** whose face will change forever within the life of

this book. Go in the summer, hit the beach, the amusement park, the Aquarium, Nathan's Famous hot dogs, and/or maybe a Cyclones baseball game. It's a schlep, but one you will never forget. See. p. 294

- **In Queens:** Take the 7 train, the **International Express** (see "Best Offbeat New York Experiences," above), to the **Queens Museum of Art** (p. 301), on the grounds of the 1964 World's Fair, or the **Louis Armstrong House Museum** (p. 300). On your way back, stop for a meal at any of the ethnic restaurants you will find within close proximity of the no. 7 train.

11 Best Splurge Hotels in Manhattan

- **Ritz-Carlton New York, Central Park,** 160 Central Park South (© **212/308-9100**). The combination of a great location across from

Central Park, large well-outfitted rooms, and excellent Ritz-Carlton service is as good as it gets. See p. 127.

- **The Mercer,** 147 Mercer St. (© **888/ 918-6060** or 212/966-6060). The best of the hip, downtown hotels, The Mercer is in the heart of SoHo. The high-ceilinged, loftlike rooms and suites, some with fireplaces, all with ceiling fans and luxurious bathrooms, are spectacular. See p. 117.
- **The Peninsula-New York,** 700 Fifth Ave. (© **800/262-9467** or 212/956-2888). The combination of old-world elegance and 21st-century technology is best realized in this practically perfect hotel. See p. 141.
- **The Ritz-Carlton New York, Battery Park,** 2 West St. (© **212/344-0800**). For magnificent views of New York Harbor and all its treasures, not to mention impeccable service on every level, it's hard to top this Ritz. See p. 113.
- **Trump International Hotel & Tower,** 1 Central Park West (© **212/ 299-1000**). Suites are huge and

overlook Central Park. Service is so good they treat you like the Donald here. The great **Jean-Georges** restaurant offers room service, and guests have use of an excellent fitness club and pool. See p. 148.

- **The Carlyle: A Rosewood Hotel,** 35 E. 76th St. (© **800/227-5737** or 212/744-1600). You are in rarefied territory when you stay in The Carlyle. Service is white-gloved and rooms are sumptuous. Many have incredible views of the city and Central Park. And don't forget **Café Carlyle** for cabaret and **Bemelmans Bar** for a cocktail. See p. 153.
- **The Lowell,** 28 E. 63rd St. (© **212/ 838-1400**). Although smaller and more intimate than The Carlyle, The Lowell is just as elegant and romantic. Rooms are all unique; many have fireplaces while some have good-size terraces. See p. 154.

12 Best Moderately Priced Hotels in Manhattan

- **Casablanca Hotel,** 147 W. 43rd St. (© **888/922-7225 or 212/869-1212**). In the Theater District, the Casablanca not only offers clean, well-outfitted rooms at value rates, it also includes extras like complimentary breakfast, bottled water, free high-speed Internet, and a lovely roof deck perfect for a cocktail on a balmy evening. See p. 133.
- **Inn on 23rd Street,** 131 W. 23rd St. (© **877/387-2323** or 212/463-0330). You cannot do better than this charming inn for top-notch quality and extras. Rooms are rustic and

uniquely designed but all have up-to-date amenities. Breakfast is complimentary and served in a lovely library. See p. 122.

- **Sofitel New York,** 45 W. 44th St. (© **212/354-8844**). This relatively new hotel exudes old-world (French) elegance. And you should be able to score some good weekend packages on the Internet. See p. 132.
- **Hotel Metro,** 45 W. 35th St. (© **800/356-3870** or 212/947-2500). You'll find good deals and lots of extras at this Midtown hotel that's popular with Europeans. See p. 135.

13 Best Hotels for Families

- **Hotel Beacon,** 2130 Broadway (© **800/572-4969** or 212/787-1100). Not only is this hotel a great deal—you can get good-size suites for

much less than in Midtown—the Upper West Side, with its parks, the Museum of Natural History, and fun, inexpensive restaurants, is a great neighborhood for children. See p. 149.

- **Doubletree Guest Suites Times Square,** 1568 Broadway (© **800/222-TREE** or 212/719-1600). This hotel boasts an entire floor of childproof suites, complete with living rooms for spreading out and kitchenettes for preparing light meals. Also just a block from kid-friendly chain restaurants and the Toys "R" Us superstore. See p. 129.

14 Best Incentives for Hotel-Hopping

- **Best Hotel Suite: Townhouse Suite in the Kitano New York,** 66 Park Ave. (© **212/885-7000**). Each of the three one-bedroom suites in the townhouse that is part of this hotel features a hallway leading to a sunken living room with original art, a state-of-the-art stereo system, and a tea maker with green tea. See p. 144.
- **Best Inexpensive Hotel Restaurant: Burger Joint** in **Le Parker Meridien,** 118 W. 57th St. (© **800/543-4300** or 212/245-5000). Hidden off the lobby, this unnamed joint has been discovered by savvy locals, so the lines are long, but worth it. The burgers are fabulous (see "Best Burger," below) and under $6. See p. 130.
- **Best Hotel Bar: Bemelmans Bar** in **The Carlyle,** 35 E. 76th St. (© **800/227-5737** or 212/744-1600). Named after illustrator Ludwig Bemelmans, who created the *Madeline* books and painted the mural in the bar, this romantic, charming bar features white-gloved service and classic cocktails. For more on Bemelmans, see p. 383.

- **Best Hotel for a Romantic Tryst: Hotel Elysée,** 60 E. 54th St. (© **800/535-9733** or 212/753-1066). This lovely old hotel, a favorite of mid-20th-century writers and actors, is discreetly dwarfed between two mammoth office buildings and is the perfect romantic hideaway in the middle of Manhattan. See p. 143.
- **Best Hotel Renovation: Gramercy Park Hotel,** 2 Lexington Ave. (© **212/920-3300**). Hotelier Ian Schrager and artist Julian Schnabel have taken a rundown 1925-built legend and restored it to a unique look. There's so much for the eye here that it will feel like you are staying in an eclectic museum. See p. 123.
- **Best Hotel Swim-Up Bar: Hotel QT,** 125 W. 45th St. (© **212/354-2323**). New in 2005, this moderately priced addition to the Times Square hotel scene was a welcome one. There is much to like about the Hotel QT, but I love the fact that it has a swimming pool—in the lobby—with a swim-up bar. You can't ask for much more in the middle of Manhattan. See p. 136.

15 The Most Unforgettable Dining Experiences in New York

- **Chanterelle,** 2 Harrison St. (© **212/966-6960**). You'll be made to feel special here, from the impeccable, personalized service in a simple but lovely room to the exquisitely prepared food. Other restaurants try, but this is how it's supposed to be done. See p. 161.

- **The River Café,** 1 Water St., Brooklyn (© **718/522-5200**). At the foot of the Brooklyn Bridge in Brooklyn, there is no better dining view of Manhattan. Go at twilight as the lights of downtown begin to flicker on. Though the food at restaurants with views is usually not great, you won't be disappointed by the fare here. See p. 220.

- **Aquavit,** 65 E. 55th St. (ⓒ 212/ 307-7311). Though its new digs are not nearly as charming as its former town-house setting, the service and the food are as good as ever. See p. 200.

- **Big Wong King,** 67 Mott St. (ⓒ 212/ 964-0540). Come here for the true Chinatown experience. You'll share tables with Chinese families, order bowls of *congee* with fried crullers, plates of stir-fried vegetables, and platters of roast pork and duck. I guarantee it will be unforgettable. See p. 166.

16 Best New Restaurants

- **A Voce,** 41 Madison Ave. (ⓒ 212/ 545-8555). Chef Andrew Carmellini serves a delicious combination of rustic and innovative Italian in a sleek, Madison Square Park space. See p. 185.
- **Kefi,** 222 W. 79th St. (ⓒ 212/873-0200). In the space that formerly held Onera, chef Michael Psilakis has gone from nouveau Greek to traditional with stunning results. You won't believe basic Greek *taverna* food could be so good. See. p. 212.
- **Porter House New York,** 10 Columbus Circle. (ⓒ 212/823-9500). In a year when new steakhouses were a dime a dozen, this one in the Time Warner Center and helmed by chef Michael Lomonaco distinguished itself far ahead of the pack. See p. 208.

17 Best Bites for All Appetites

- **Best BBQ: RUB,** 208 W. 23rd St. (ⓒ 212/524-4300). Co-owner Paul Kirk brings his Kansas City pit prowess to New York with mouthwatering results. Try the "Taste of the Baron," a little bit of everything for a big crowd. See p. 183.
- **Best for Breakfast: Good Enough to Eat,** 483 Amsterdam Ave. (ⓒ 212/ 496-0163). They've been lining up on Amsterdam Avenue every weekend for over 20 years for chef/owner Carrie Levin's bountiful home-cooked breakfasts. But why wait on line? You're on vacation, go during the week. See p. 214.
- **Best for Brunch: Norma's,** at Le Parker Meridien hotel, 118 W. 57th St. (ⓒ 212/708-7460). Though I am not a devotee of brunch (see box "Breakfast, Not Brunch," on p. 215), I make an exception for Norma's. Skip the traditional breakfast items and go for creative interpretations like the asparagus-and-seared-rock-lobster omelet. See p. 195.
- **Best Jewish Deli: Katz's Delicatessen,** 205 E. Houston St. (ⓒ 212/ 254-2246). This is the choice among those who know their kreplach, knishes, and pastrami. No cutesy sandwiches named for celebrities here—just top-notch Jewish classics. See p. 170.
- **Best Burger: Burger Joint,** at Le Parker Meridien hotel, 118 W. 57th St. (ⓒ 212/708-7414). Who woulda thunk that a fancy hotel like Le Parker Meridien would be the home to a "joint" that serves great burgers at great prices? See p. 202.
- **Best Pizzeria: Patsy's Pizzeria,** 2287 First Ave. (ⓒ 212/534-9783). This great East Harlem pizzeria has been cranking out coal-oven pizza since 1932. You can also order by the slice here, but only do so if the pie is fresh out of the oven. See p. 197.

- **Best 20th-Century Steakhouse: Frankie & Johnnie's,** 32 W. 37th St. (© **212/997-8940**) and 269 W. 45th St. (© **212/997-9494**). Whether you choose the former speakeasy that is the original location in the Theater district or the newer branch in the late actor John Barrymore's former townhouse, your steak, particularly the house sirloin, will remind you why Frankie & Johnnie's has been around since 1926. See p. 191.
- **Best 21st Century Steakhouse: Porter House New York.** See "Best New Restaurants" above.
- **Best Mutton Chop: Keens Steakhouse,** 72 W. 36th St. (© **212/947-3636**). Of course, it might be the *only* restaurant in New York that offers a mutton chop, but that's not the only reason to head to Keens. The other "chops" are first-rate and the rooms—there are several—are like museum pieces without a museum's stuffiness. See p. 192.
- **Best for Families: Virgil's Real BBQ,** 152 W. 44th St. (© **212/921-9494**). In kid-friendly Times Square, Virgil's, in a sense, is a theme restaurant, the theme being barbecue, but they do an excellent job of it. It's loud, colorful, and has great options for children. See p. 195.
- **Best Cheap Meal: Gray's Papaya,** 2090 Broadway (© **212/799-0243**). Though the $2.45 "recession special"—two hot dogs and a fruit drink—is almost a $1 increase from the previous recession, it's still a

bargain. But is it any good? Witness the lines out the door every day for lunch. See p. 165.
- **Best Ice Cream: Brooklyn Ice Cream Factory,** Fulton Ferry Landing Pier, Brooklyn (© **718/246-3963**). The perfect reward after a brisk walk across the Brooklyn Bridge. Rich homemade ice cream with a view of the Manhattan skyline; a tough combination to beat. See p. 222.
- **Best Bagel: Absolute Bagels,** 2788 Broadway (© **212/932-2052**). They're not huge like some bagels these days, but they are always hot and baked to perfection. See p. 189.
- **Best Soul Food: Charles' Southern Style Kitchen,** 2841 Eighth Ave. (© **877/813-2920** or 212/926-4313). Not only does this Harlem restaurant serve the best soul food in the city, it offers the best buffet. For $9.95 on weekdays and $12 on weekends, the down-home offerings will tempt you to make any number of visits to the buffet line. See p. 220.
- **Best New/Old Dining Room: Country,** 90 Madison Ave. (© **212/889-7100**). Designed by architect David Rockwell, the upstairs restaurant in the Carlton Hotel is a marvel with restored mosaic tiles, dramatic chandeliers, nooks overlooking the hotel lobby, and most impressive, a gorgeous Tiffany skylight dome that had been hidden for years and was uncovered during the renovation. See p. 201.

18 Best Shopping in New York

- **Best Store: Saks Fifth Avenue.** Not as overwhelming as other department stores, Saks is consistently good. And don't miss those window displays at Christmas. See p. 316.

- **Best Clothes Store: Barneys.** This store is the pinnacle, with prices to match. See p. 314.

- **Best Shopping Zone: Soho, NoHo, and Nolita.** All three neighborhoods are within walking distance of one another and feature the newest, trendiest boutiques. See chapter 10.

- **Best Old World Food Store: DiPalo's Dairy.** This 1910-originated store is one of the last vestiges of Old Little Italy, and is still in the DiPalo family. See. p. 328.

19 Best Culture & Nightlife in New York

- **Best Performance Space: Carnegie Hall.** One of the world's great performance spaces, with an array of world-class talent on display almost every night. See p. 356.

- **Best Free Cultural Event: Shakespeare in the Park.** Imagine Shakespeare performed by stars, under the stars, in Central Park. No wonder it has become a New York institution. See p. 360.

- **Best Children's Theater: Paper Bag Players.** For children ages 4 to 9, this group performs in the winter and offers tales told in imaginative and original ways. See p. 348.

- **Best Jazz Club: The Village Vanguard.** The acoustics and sightlines aren't great, but you can't do better for consistent good-quality jazz. See p. 369.

- **Best Rock Club: Mercury Lounge.** This venue is intimate but not obscure. The Merc is the best for hard-edged rock 'n' roll. See p. 365.

- **Best Comedy Club: Gotham Comedy Club.** Comfortable and sophisticated, this is where the best come to hone their acts. See p. 370.

- **Best Cocktail: Pegu Club,** 77 W. Houston, 2nd floor. Leave it to that supreme mixologist Audrey Saunders to open a club where the cocktails are unbeatable. Everything is top label and all juices and mixers are freshly made. See p. 375.

- **Best Pub: Ear Inn.** An old hanger-on in chic SoHo, this old joint continues to survive amongst the lush lounges that surround it. See p. 375.

- **Best Dive Bar: Subway Inn.** Sure, I know you came to New York to go to a dive bar. Enter the Subway Inn, and it's as if you stepped into a 1940s film noir—minus the cigarette smoke, of course. See p. 381.

- **Best Bar with a View: Rise Bar,** in the Ritz-Carlton Battery Park Hotel. With views of Lady Liberty, New York Harbor, and incredible sunsets, this bar is worth seeking out even if you're not staying here. See p. 376.

- **Best Exclusive Bar: Rose Bar,** in the Gramercy Park Hotel. This magnificent room with its Schnabel originals, incredible sound system, lush seating, beautiful people, and very expensive cocktails is worth groveling to enter. See p. 381.

2

A Traveler's Guide to New York City Architecture

by Lisa Torrance Duffy

New York City contains a wealth of architectural styles, from modest row houses to ornate churches to soaring skyscrapers. Constructed over 300 years, these buildings represent the changing tastes of the city's residents from Colonial times to the present. A brief look at the city's most popular styles provides a unique perspective on the city's past, present, and future.

For the locations of the buildings mentioned in this chapter, see p. 17.

1 New York Architecture

GEORGIAN (1700–76)

This style reflects Renaissance ideas made popular in England, and later in the United States, through the publication of books on 16th-century Italian architects. The most-studied Italian of this period was **Andrea Palladio** (1508–80), who had freely adapted classical Roman forms. Georgian houses are characterized by a formal arrangement of parts employing a symmetrical composition enriched with classical details, such as columns and pediments. In the United States, the style was seen as an appropriate expression of the relative prosperity and security of the colonies. It was a sharp contrast to the unadorned Colonial style that preceded it.

St. Paul's Chapel

Georgian buildings share the following characteristics:

- A formal, symmetrical arrangement
- A roof with four uniformly pitched sides
- A *balustrade* (a railing with balusters, or posts)
- A central projecting pavilion topped by a *pediment* (a low-pitched triangular feature) and supported by colossal columns or *pilasters* (rectangular columns projecting only slightly from a wall)
- A transom light above the front door
- Palladian windows (see illustration)
- *Quoins* (cornerstones in a distinctive material)
- Double-hung sash windows

Pediment

Palladian Window   Quoins

St. Paul's Chapel, on Broadway between Vesey and Fulton streets (1764–66, Thomas McBean), the only pre-Revolutionary building remaining in Manhattan, is an almost perfect example of the Georgian style, with a pediment, colossal columns, Palladian window, quoins, and balustrade above the roof line (see illustration). Although it's a 20th-century reconstruction of a formal English house built here in 1719, **Fraunces Tavern,** 54 Pearl St., is another fine example of the style.

FEDERAL (1780–1820)

Federal was the first truly American architectural style. It was an adaptation of a contemporaneous English style called Adamesque, created by Scotsman **Robert Adam** (1728–92), which included ornate, colorful interior decoration. Federal combined Georgian architecture with the delicacy of the French rococo and the classical architecture of Greece and Rome. The overall effect is one of restraint and dignity, and may appear delicate when compared to the more robust Georgian style. Federal was popular with successful merchants throughout the cities and towns of the eastern seaboard. Its connection to the prosperous empires of Rome and Greece was seen as an appropriate reference for the young United States.

Typical Federal Exterior

In New York, the Federal style was popular for row houses (see illustration) built after the 1811 creation of the city's grid pattern of avenues and streets. These houses often share the following features:

- A height of two or three stories
- Prominent end chimneys
- A red brick exterior
- A steeply pitched roof
- *Dormers* (upright windows projecting from a sloping roof) with pediments
- Double-hung sash windows, often with a flat *lintel* (horizontal member over a window, which carries the weight of the wall above it; commonly of stone)
- An elaborate doorway with sidelights and a fan or transom light (see illustration)
- Pilasters or columns flanking the doorway
- Delicate, exterior ornament of Roman origin, such as swags, urns, sheaths of wheat, and garlands
- A high basement

Federal Doorway

New York Architecture

In the **West Village,** near and along Bedford Street between Christopher and Morton streets, are more original Federal-style houses than anywhere else in Manhattan. House nos. 4 through 10 (1825–34) on Grove Street, just off Bedford, present one of the most authentic groups of late Federal–style houses in America. Notice the pedimented dormers and doors surrounded by pilasters and transom lights. Local carpenters created these buildings from plan books, probably published in England. In adapting the styles, they pared down the detail from the more delicate Adamesque in order to adapt to the needs—and pocketbooks—of their American merchant and craftsman clients.

GREEK REVIVAL (1820–60)

The Greek Revolution in the 1820s, in which Greece won its independence from the Turks, recalled to American intellectuals the democracy of ancient Greece and its elegant architecture, created around 400 B.C. At the same time, the War of 1812 diminished American affection for the British influence, including the still-dominant Federal style. With many believing America to be the spiritual successor of Greece, the use of classical Greek forms, particularly the Greek temple front, came to dominate residential, commercial, and government architecture. The style was so popular it came to be known as the National Style, and was used for numerous state capitols, as well as the U.S. Capitol in Washington, D.C.

Because ancient Greek structures did not use arches, the arched entrances and elliptical fanlights so popular in the Federal style were abandoned. The Greek Revival is most distinguished by a Greek temple front with the following:

- Classical orders specifying the use of three different column types: Corinthian, Ionic, or Doric (see illustration)
- A full *entablature* (a set of roof parts, usually supported by a column, consisting of an architrave, frieze, and cornice)
- A low-pitch pediment
- White exteriors (it was not known at this time that ancient Greek buildings had been polychrome)

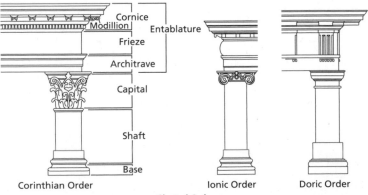

Classical Orders

In New York, Grecian columns and orders were used mostly to decorate entrances on row houses, but whole buildings were also created. Perhaps the city's finest Greek Revival building is **Federal Hall National Memorial** (1834–42), at 26 Wall St., at Nassau Street, the site where George Washington took his presidential oath in 1789 (see illustration). The structure has a Greek temple front, with Doric columns and a simple pediment, resting on a high base, called a *plinth,* with a steep flight of steps.

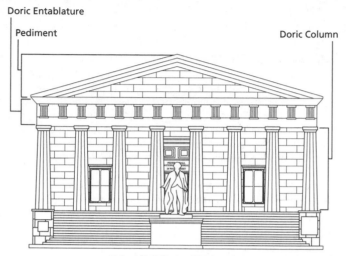

Federal Hall National Memorial

The Row (1832–33, with later alterations), nos. 1 through 11 on Washington Square North, is an imposing block front of early-19th-century town houses. Note the stately entranceways with carved wooden and marble columns; the brickwork, called Flemish Bond, which alternates long and short brick in each row; and the Greek motifs, such as obelisks, lyres, and honeysuckle adornments, called *anthemia.*

GOTHIC REVIVAL (1830–60)

The term *Gothic Revival* refers to a literary and aesthetic movement of the 1830s and 1840s that occurred in England and later in the United States. A pervasive current within this movement was known as Romanticism. Adherents believed that the wickedness of modern times could benefit with a dose of "goodness" presumed to have been associated with the Christian medieval past. Architecture was chosen as one of the vehicles to bring this message to the people. The revival style was used for everything from timber cottages to stone castles and churches. Some structures had only one or two Gothic features, most commonly a steeply pitched roof or pointed arches, whereas other buildings, usually churches, were accurate copies of English Gothic structures.

A derivative style called **Victorian Gothic** (1860–90) became popular after the Civil War. Influenced by the writings of English theorist **John Ruskin** (1819–1900), this style is distinguished by contrasting colors of brick and stone in bold polychromatic patterns and decorative bands. This more freewheeling interpretation of the Gothic was well suited to the florid decorative approach of the late 19th century.

Gothic Window

Gothic Revival is characterized by the following:

- Asymmetry
- Pointed arches
- Large pointed windows with tracery and colored glass (see illustration)
- Steeply pitched roofs
- A curvilinear gingerbread trim along the eaves (on houses)
- Towers
- *Battlements* (a fortified wall with alternate solid parts and openings; used for defense or a decorative motif)
- An overall picturesque quality

Trinity Church, at Broadway and Wall Street (Richard Upjohn, 1846), is one of the most celebrated, authentic Gothic Revival structures in the United States. Here you see all the features of a Gothic church: a steeple, battlements, pointed arches, Gothic tracery, stained-glass windows, *flying buttresses* (an external bracing system for supporting a roof or vault), and medieval sculptures. This was the tallest building in the area until the late 1860s.

The **Jefferson Market Library,** at 425 Sixth Ave. (Frederich Clarke Withers and Calvert Vaux, 1874–77), is a magnificent structure in the Victorian Gothic mode. Built as a courthouse, the asymmetrical structure sports striking bands of red brick and white stone, stained-glass windows, pointed arches, and a dramatic clock tower.

ITALIANATE (1840–80)

The architecture of Italy served as the inspiration for this building style, which could be as picturesque as the Gothic or as restrained as the classical. This adaptability made it immensely popular in the 1850s. In New York, the style was used for urban row houses and commercial buildings. The development of cast iron at this time permitted the inexpensive mass production of decorative features that few could have afforded in carved stone. This led to the creation of cast-iron districts in nearly every American city, including New York.

Rival Revivals: Architectural Styles in the Late 19th Century

On the eve of the Civil War, the United States was a country of diverse tastes, interests, and cultures, and its differences were reflected in the country's architectural styles. During the latter half of the 19th century, several modes—including Victorian Gothic, Italianate, Renaissance Revivals, Second Empire, and even the exotic Moorish and Egyptian Revivals—coexisted. What these styles share is a certain eclecticism and picturesqueness. Mid-century architects reasoned that no age had produced the perfect architectural expression, so why not borrow freely from the best of the past and even mix different styles on the same building?

Although some of these styles were popular, none became dominant. In the 1870s in Chicago, technological advancements and imaginative design were coming together to create the world's first skyscrapers—*the* style that would one day dominate New York and the country's other urban areas.

Italianate buildings often have a formal symmetry accentuated by pronounced moldings and decorative details. The commercial buildings resemble Italian palaces and tend to be rectangular buildings of several, spacious stories well suited to their original purposes as work spaces. The facades usually have the following features:

- A flat or low-pitched roof
- A bracketed cornice and an elaborate entablature
- Windows rounded at the top (flattened arches above windows are common, too)
- Large moldings over windows, called *hood moldings*
- Columns or pilasters flanking, or separating, windows
- Decorative keystones
- Quoins
- Balustrades
- Belt courses or entablatures at each story
- Vertical rows of windows and horizontal belt courses giving the building a very regular, compartmentalized look

New York's **SoHo–Cast Iron Historic District** has 26 blocks jammed with cast-iron facades, many in the Italianate manner. The single richest section is **Greene Street** between Houston and Canal streets. Stroll along here and take in building after building of sculptural facades. At Greene and Broome streets is the **Gunther Building** (Griffith Thomas, 1871), a fine example of the Italianate. The most celebrated building in SoHo is the **Haughwout Store** (John P. Gaynor, 1857), at the corner of Broadway and Broome streets, a New York version of a Venetian palace (now housing a Staples store, of all things). The handsome facade with cast iron on two sides has a window arrangement—two small, Corinthian columns supporting an arch over each window—based directly on a 15th-century, Italian design (see illustration).

Haughwout Store

EARLY SKYSCRAPER (1880–1920)

The invention of the skyscraper can be traced directly to the use of cast iron in the 1840s for storefronts, such as those seen in New York's SoHo. Experimentation with cast and wrought iron in the construction of interior skeletons eventually allowed buildings to rise higher. (Previously, buildings were restricted by the height supportable by their load-bearing walls.) In Chicago, important technical innovations—involving safety elevators, electricity, fireproofing, foundations, plumbing, and telecommunications—combined with advances in skeletal construction to create a new building type, the skyscraper. These buildings were spacious, cost-effective, efficient, and quickly erected—in short, the perfect architectural solution for America's growing downtowns.

Solving the technical problems of the skyscraper did not resolve how the building should look. Most solutions relied on historical precedents, including decoration reminiscent of the Gothic, Romanesque (a style characterized by the use of rounded arches), or Beaux Arts.

Other features of the early skyscrapers include the following:

- A rectangular shape with a flat roof
- Tripartite division of the facade, similar to that of a column, with a *base* (usually of two stories), *shaft* (midsection with a repetitive window pattern), and *capital* (typically an elaborate, terra-cotta cornice)
- Exterior expression of the building's interior skeleton through an emphasis on horizontal and vertical elements
- Use of *terra cotta,* a light and fireproof material that could be cast in any shape and attached to the exterior

New York's early skyscrapers relied heavily on historical decoration. A good early example in the Beaux Arts mode is the **American Surety Company,** at 100 Broadway (Bruce Price, 1895). The triangular **Flatiron Building,** at Fifth Avenue and 23rd Street (Daniel H. Burnham & Co., 1902), has strong tripartite divisions and Renaissance Revival detail. And, finally, the later **Woolworth Building** (Cass Gilbert, 1913), on Broadway at Park Place, dubbed the "Cathedral of Commerce," is a neo-Gothic skyscraper with flying buttresses, spires, sculptured gargoyles, and pointed arches.

SECOND RENAISSANCE REVIVAL (1890–1920)

Buildings in this style show a definite studied formalism. A relative faithfulness to Italian Renaissance precedents of window and doorway treatments distinguishes it from the much looser adaptations of the Italianate. Scale and size, in turn, set the Second Renaissance Revival apart from the first, which occurred from 1840 to 1890. The grand buildings of the Second Renaissance Revival, with their textural richness, well suited the tastes of New York's wealthy Gilded Age. The style was used for banks, swank town houses, government buildings, and private clubs.

Typical features include the following:

- A cubelike structure with a massive, imposing quality
- Symmetrical arrangement of the facade, including distinct horizontal divisions
- A different stylistic treatment for each floor; with different classical orders, finishes, and window treatments on each level
- Use of *rustication* (masonry cut in massive blocks and separated from each other by deep joints) on the lowest floor
- Quoins
- The indication of additional floors with small windows

- The mixing of Greek and Roman styles on the same facade (Roman arches and arcades may appear with Greek-style pedimented or straight-headed windows)
- A projecting cornice supported by large brackets
- A balustrade above the cornice

New York's Upper East Side has two fine examples of this building type, each exhibiting most of the style's key features: the **Racquet and Tennis Club,** 370 Park Ave. (McKim, Mead & White, 1918), based on the style of a Florentine palazzo; and the **Metropolitan Club,** 1 East 60th St. (McKim, Mead & White, 1891–94).

BEAUX ARTS (1890–1920)

This style takes its name from the Ecole des Beaux-Arts in Paris, where a number of prominent American architects (including **Richard Morris Hunt** [1827–95], **John Mervin Carrère** [1858–1911], and **Thomas Hastings** [1860–1929], to name only a few) received their training, beginning around the mid-19th century. These architects adopted the academic design principles of the Ecole, which emphasized the study of Greek and Roman structures, composition, and symmetry, and the creation of elaborate presentation drawings. Because of the idealized origins and grandiose use of classical forms, the Beaux Arts in America was seen as the ideal style for expressing civic pride.

> **Impressions**
> New York is the perfect model of a city, not the model of a perfect city.
> —Lewis Mumford

Grandiose compositions, an exuberance of detail, and a variety of stone finishes typify most Beaux Arts structures. Particular features include the following:

- A pronounced cornice and ornate entablature topped by a tall parapet, balustrade, or attic story
- Projecting pavilions, often with colossal columns grouped in pairs
- Windows framed by freestanding columns, a sill with a balustrade, and/or entablatures with pediments or decorative keystones
- Grand staircases
- Grand arched openings
- Classical decoration: freestanding statuary, ornamental panels, swags, medallions
- A heavy *ashlar* (squared stone) base

New York has several exuberant Beaux Arts buildings, exhibiting the style's key features. The **New York Public Library,** at Fifth Avenue and 42nd Street (Carrère & Hastings, 1911), is perhaps the best example. Others of note are **Grand Central Terminal,** at 42nd Street and Park Avenue (Reed & Stem and Warren & Whetmore, 1903–13), and the **U.S. Customs House** (Cass Gilbert, 1907) on Bowling Green between State and Whitehall streets.

INTERNATIONAL STYLE (1920–45)

In 1932, the Museum of Modern Art hosted its first architecture exhibit, titled simply "Modern Architecture." Displays included images of International Style buildings from around the world, many designed by architects from Germany's Bauhaus, a progressive design school. The structures all shared a stark simplicity and vigorous functionalism, a definite break from historically based, decorative styles.

The International Style was popularized in the United States through the teachings and designs of **Ludwig Mies van der Rohe** (1886–1969), a German émigré based in Chicago. Interpretations of the "Miesian" International Style were built in most U.S. cities, including New York, as late as 1980. In the 1950s, erecting an office building in this mode made companies appear progressive. In later decades, after the International Style was a corporate mainstay, the style took on conservative connotations.

Features of the International Style as popularized by Mies include the following:

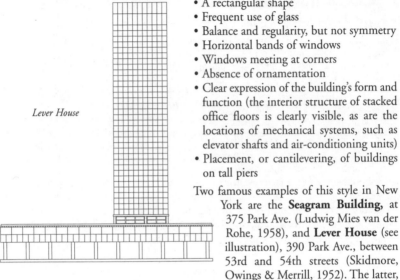

Lever House

- A rectangular shape
- Frequent use of glass
- Balance and regularity, but not symmetry
- Horizontal bands of windows
- Windows meeting at corners
- Absence of ornamentation
- Clear expression of the building's form and function (the interior structure of stacked office floors is clearly visible, as are the locations of mechanical systems, such as elevator shafts and air-conditioning units)
- Placement, or cantilevering, of buildings on tall piers

Two famous examples of this style in New York are the **Seagram Building,** at 375 Park Ave. (Ludwig Mies van der Rohe, 1958), and **Lever House** (see illustration), 390 Park Ave., between 53rd and 54th streets (Skidmore, Owings & Merrill, 1952). The latter, designed by a firm that made "Miesian" architecture a corporate staple, is credited for popularizing the use of plazas and glass curtain walls. Another well-known example is the Secretariat building in the **United Nations** complex, at First Avenue and 46th Street (1947–53), designed by an international committee of architects.

ART DECO (1925–40)

Art Deco is a decorative style that took its name from a Paris exposition in 1925. The jazzy style embodied the idea of modernity. One of the first widely accepted styles not based on historic precedents, it influenced all areas of design from jewelry and household goods to cars, trains, and ocean liners.

Art Deco buildings are characterized by a linear, hard edge, or angular composition, often with a vertical emphasis and highlighted with stylized decoration. The New York zoning law of 1916, which required setbacks in buildings above a certain height to ensure that light and air could reach the street, gave the style its distinctive profile. Other important features include the following:

- An emphasis on geometric form
- Strips of windows with decorated *spandrels* (the horizontal panel below a window) that added to the sense of verticality

- Use of hard-edged, low-relief ornamentation around doors and windows
- Frequent use of black and silver tones
- Decorative motifs of parallel straight lines, zigzags, chevrons (see illustration), and stylized florals

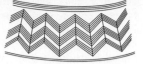

Chevron

Despite the effects of the Depression, several major Art Deco structures were built in New York in the 1930s, often providing crucial jobs. **Rockefeller Center** (Raymond Hood, 1932–40), a complex sprawling from 48th to 50th streets between Fifth and Sixth avenues, includes 30 Rockefeller Plaza, a tour de force of Art Deco style, with a soaring, vertical shaft and aluminum details. The **Chrysler Building,** Lexington Avenue at 42nd Street (William Van Alen, 1930), is a towering tribute to the automobile (see illustration). The Chrysler's needlelike spire with zigzag patterns in glass and metal is a distinctive feature on the city's skyline. The famous **Empire State Building,** Fifth Avenue at 34th Street (Shreve, Lamb & Harmon, 1931), contains a black- and silver-toned lobby among its many Art Deco features.

ART MODERNE (1930–45)

Art Moderne strove for modernity and an artistic expression for the sleekness of the machine age. Unbroken horizontal lines and smooth curves visually distinguish it from Art Deco and give it a streamlined effect. It was popular with movie theaters, and was often applied to cars, trains, and boats to suggest the idea of speed.

The key features of art moderne buildings are as follows:

- A flat roof
- Soft or rounded corners
- Smooth wall finish without surface ornamentation
- Horizontal bands of windows creating a distinctive streamlined or wind-tunneled effect
- Ornamentation of mirrored panels, cement panels, and perhaps low-relief metal panels around doors and windows
- Aluminum and stainless steel for door and window trim, railings, and balusters
- Metal or wood doors may have circular windows or patterns with circular and angular outlines

Chrysler Building

The **Majestic Apartments,** at 115 Central Park West (Irwin S. Chanin, 1930), has futuristic forms and wide banks of windows that wrap around corners. **Radio City Music Hall,** on Sixth Avenue at 50th Street (Edward Durrell Stone and Donald Deskey, 1932), has a sweeping Art Moderne marquee.

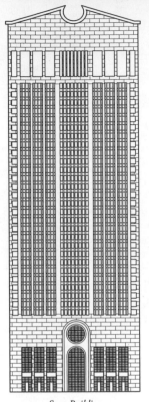

Sony Building

POSTMODERN (1975–90)

After years of steel-and-glass office towers in the International Style, Postmodernism burst on the scene in the 1970s with the reintroduction of historical precedents in architecture. With many feeling that the office towers of the previous style were too cold, Postmodernists began to incorporate classical details and recognizable forms into their designs—often applied in outrageous proportions.

Characteristics of postmodern skyscrapers tend to include the following:

• An overall shape (or incorporation) of a recognizable object, not necessarily associated with architecture

• Classical details, such as columns, domes, or vaults, often oversize and used in inventive ways

• A distinctive profile in the skyline

• A use of stone, rather than glass

The **Sony Building,** at 550 Madison Ave. (Philip Johnson/John Burgee, 1984), brings the distinctive shape of a Chippendale cabinet to the New York skyline. The **Morgan Bank Headquarters,** 60 Wall St. (Kevin Roche, John Dinkeloo & Assocs., 1988), resembles a classical column, with modern interpretations of a base, shaft, and capital. The base of the column mirrors in style the facade of the 19th-century building across the street.

3

Planning Your Trip to New York City

1 Visitor Information

Before you leave home, your best information source (besides this book, of course) is **NYC & Company,** the organization that fronts the New York Convention & Visitors Bureau (NYCVB), 810 Seventh Ave., New York, NY 10019. You can call © **800/NYC-VISIT** to request the *Official NYC Guide* detailing hotels, restaurants, theaters, attractions, events, and more. The guide is free and will arrive in 7 to 10 days. (*Note:* I've received complaints that they sometimes take longer.)

You can find a wealth of free information on the bureau's website, **www.nycvisit.com**. To speak with a live travel counselor, call © **212/484-1222,** which is staffed weekdays from 8:30am to 6pm EST, weekends from 8:30am to 5pm EST.

For visitor-center and information-desk locations once you arrive, see "Visitor Information" in chapter 5.

FOR U.K. VISITORS The **NYCVB Visitor Information Center** is at 36 Southwark Bridge Rd., London, SE1 9EU (© **020/7202 6367**). You can order the Official NYC Visitor Kit by sending an A5-size self-addressed envelope and 72p postage to the above address. For New York–bound travelers in London, the center also offers free one-on-one travel-planning assistance.

2 Entry Requirements

ENTRY REQUIREMENTS
PASSPORTS

For information on how to get a passport, go to **"Passports"** in the **"Fast Facts"** section of Chapter 5—the websites listed provide downloadable passport applications as well as the current fees for processing passport applications. For an up-to-date, country-by-country listing of passport requirements around the world, go to the "Foreign Entry Requirement" Web page of the U.S. State Department at **http://travel.state.gov**. International visitors can obtain a visa application at the same website. *Note:* Children are required to present a passport when entering the United States at airports. More information on obtaining a passport for a minor can be found at **http://travel.state.gov**.

VISAS

For information on how to get a Visa, go to **"Visas"** in the **"Fast Facts"** section of chapter 5.

The U.S. State Department has a **Visa Waiver Program (VWP)** allowing citizens of the following countries (at press time) to enter the United States without a visa

U.S. Entry: Passport Required

New regulations issued by the Homeland Security Department now require virtually every air traveler entering the U.S. to show a passport—and future regulations will cover land and sea entry as well. As of January 23, 2007, all persons, including U.S. citizens, traveling by air between the United States and Canada, Mexico, Central and South America, the Caribbean, and Bermuda are required to present a valid passport. Similar regulations for those traveling by land or sea (including ferries) are expected as early as January 1, 2008.

for stays of up to 90 days: Andorra, Australia, Austria, Belgium, Brunei, Denmark, Finland, France, Germany, Iceland, Ireland, Italy, Japan, Liechtenstein, Luxembourg, Monaco, the Netherlands, New Zealand, Norway, Portugal, San Marino, Singapore, Slovenia, Spain, Sweden, Switzerland, and the United Kingdom. Canadian citizens may enter the United States without visas; they will need to show passports and proof of residence, however. *Note:* Any passport issued on or after October 26, 2006, by a VWP country must be an **e-Passport** for VWP travelers to be eligible to enter the U.S. without a visa. Citizens of these nations also need to present a round-trip air or cruise ticket upon arrival. E-Passports contain computer chips capable of storing biometric information, such as the required digital photograph of the holder. (You can identify an e-Passport by the symbol on the bottom center cover of your passport.) If your passport doesn't have this feature, you can still travel without a visa if it is a valid passport issued before October 26, 2005, and includes a machine-readable zone, or between October 26, 2005, and October 25, 2006, and includes a digital photograph. For more information, go to **www.travel.state.gov/visa**.

Citizens of all other countries must have (1) a valid passport that expires at least 6 months later than the scheduled end of their visit to the United States, and

2) a tourist visa, which may be obtained without charge from any U.S. consulate.

As of January 2004, many international visitors traveling on visas to the United States will be photographed and fingerprinted on arrival at Customs in airports and on cruise ships in a program created by the Department of Homeland Security called **US-VISIT.** Exempt from the extra scrutiny are visitors entering by land or those (mostly in Europe) that don't require a visa for short-term visits. For more information, go to the Homeland Security website at **www.dhs.gov/dhspublic**.

MEDICAL REQUIREMENTS

Unless you're arriving from an area known to be suffering from an epidemic (particularly cholera or yellow fever), inoculations or vaccinations are not required for entry into the United States.

If you have a medical condition that requires **syringe-administered medications,** carry a valid signed prescription from your physician; syringes in carry-on baggage will be inspected. Insulin in any form should have the proper pharmaceutical documentation. If you have a disease that requires treatment with **narcotics,** you should also carry documented proof with you—smuggling narcotics aboard a plane carries severe penalties in the U.S.

For **HIV-positive visitors,** requirements for entering the United States are somewhat vague and change frequently.

For up-to-the-minute information, contact **AIDSinfo** (© **800/448-0440** or 301/519-6616 outside the U.S.; www.aidsinfo.nih.gov) or the **Gay Men's Health Crisis** (© **212/367-1000;** www.gmhc.org).

CUSTOMS

For information on what you can bring into and take out of the U.S., go to "**Customs**" in the "**Fast Facts**" section of chapter 5.

3 When to Go

Summer or winter, rain or shine, there's always great stuff going on in New York City, so there's no real "best" time to go.

Culture hounds might come in fall, winter, and early spring, when the theater and performing-arts seasons reach their heights. During summer, many of the top cultural institutions, especially Lincoln Center, offer free, alfresco entertainment. Those who want to see the biggest hits on Broadway usually have the best luck getting tickets in the slower months of January and February.

Gourmands might find it easiest to land the best tables during July and August, when New Yorkers escape the city on weekends. If you prefer to walk every city block to take in the sights, spring and fall usually offer the mildest and most pleasant weather.

New York is a nonstop holiday party from early December through the start of the New Year. Celebrations of the season abound in festive holiday windows and events like the lighting of the Rockefeller Center tree and the Radio City Christmas Spectacular—not to mention those terrific seasonal sales that make New York a holiday shopping bonanza.

However, keep in mind that hotel prices go sky high (more on that below), and the crowds are almost intolerable. If you'd rather have more of the city to yourself—better chances at restaurant reservations and shows, easier access to museums and other attractions—choose another time of year to visit.

MONEY MATTERS   Hotel prices have gone up the past couple of years and bargains are harder to find. Therefore, if money is a big concern, you might want to follow these rough seasonal guidelines.

Bargain hunters might want to visit in winter, between the first of the year and early April. Sure, you might have to bear some cold weather, but that's when hotels are suffering from the post-holiday blues, and rooms often go for a relative song—a song in this case meaning a room with a private bathroom for as little as $150. AAA cardholders can do even better in many cases (generally a 5%–10% savings if the hotel offers a AAA discount). However, be aware that the occasional convention or event, such as February's annual Fashion Week, can sometimes throw a wrench in your winter savings plans.

Spring and fall are traditionally the busiest and most expensive seasons after holiday time. Don't expect hotels to be handing you deals, but you may be able to negotiate a decent rate.

The city is drawing more families these days, and they usually visit in the summer. Still, the prospect of heat and humidity keeps some people away, making July and the first half of August a cheaper time to visit than later in the year; good hotel deals are often available.

During the Christmas season, expect to pay top dollar for everything. The first 2 weeks of December—the shopping weeks—are the worst when it comes to scoring an affordable hotel room; that's when shoppers from around the world converge on the town to catch the holiday spirit and spend, spend, spend. But Thanksgiving can be a great time to come, believe it or not: Business travelers have gone home, and the holiday shoppers haven't yet arrived. It's a little-known secret that most hotels away from the Thanksgiving Day Parade route have empty rooms, and they're usually willing to make great deals to fill them.

WEATHER Many consider that long week or 10 days that arrive each summer between mid-July and mid-August, when temperatures go up to around 100°F (38°C) with 90% humidity, as New York's worst weather. But don't get put off by this—summer has its compensations, such as wonderful free open-air concerts and other events, as I've mentioned—but bear it in mind. But if you are at all temperature sensitive, your odds of getting comfortable weather are better in June or September.

Another period when you might not like to stroll around the city is during January or February, when temperatures are commonly in the 20s (below 0 Celsius) and those concrete canyons turn into wind tunnels. The city looks gorgeous for about a day after a snowfall, but the streets soon become a slushy mess. Again, you never know—temperatures have regularly been in the 30s and mild 40s (single digits Celsius) during the past few "global warmed" winters. If you hit the weather jackpot, you could have a bargain bonanza (see "Money Matters," above).

Fall and spring are the best times in New York. From April to June and September to November, temperatures are mild and pleasant, and the light is beautiful. With the leaves changing in Central Park and just the hint of crispness in the air, October is a fabulous time to be here—but expect to pay for the privilege.

If you want to know what to pack just before you go, check the Weather Channel's online 10-day forecast at **www.weather.com**; I like to balance it against CNN's online 5-day forecast at **www.cnn.com/weather**. You can also get the local weather by calling © **212/976-1212**.

New York's Average Temperature & Rainfall

	Jan	Feb	Mar	Apr	May	June	July	Aug	Sept	Oct	Nov	Dec
Daily Temp. (°F)	38	40	48	61	71	80	85	84	77	67	54	42
Daily Temp. (°C)	3	4	9	16	22	27	29	29	25	19	12	6
Days of Precipitation	11	10	11	11	11	10	11	10	8	8	9	10

NEW YORK CITY CALENDAR OF EVENTS

The following information is always subject to change. Confirm information before you make plans around a specific event. Call the venue or the NYCVB at © 212/484-1222, go to **www.nycvisit.com**, or buy a copy of **Time Out New York** when you arrive for the latest details.

January

New York National Boat Show. Slip on your Top-Siders and head to the **Jacob K. Javits Convention Center** for the boat show, which promises a leviathan fleet of boats and marine products from the world's leading manufacturers. Call © 212/984-7000 or visit www.boatshows.com or www.javitscenter.com. First or second week in January.

Restaurant Week. Twice a year some of the best restaurants in New York offer three-course prix-fixe meals at *almost* affordable prices. At lunch, the deal is $24.07 (as in 24/7), while dinner is $35. Some restaurants in 2007 included stalwarts such as Esca, LeCirque, Union Square Café, and Devi. Call © 212/484-1222 for info or visit www.nycvisit.com. Late January.

February

Chinese New Year. Every year, Chinatown rings in its own New Year (based on a lunar calendar) with 2 weeks of celebrations, including parades with dragon and lion dancers, plus vivid costumes of all kinds. The parade usually winds throughout Chinatown along Mott, Canal, and Bayard streets, and along East Broadway. Call the NYCVB hot line at ✆ **212/484-1222** or the Asian American Business Development Center at ✆ **212/966-0100.** Chinese New Year falls on February 7 in 2008, and it's the Year of the Rat.

Westminster Kennel Club Dog Show. The ultimate purebred-pooch fest. Some 30,000 dog fanciers from the world over congregate at **Madison Square Garden** for the 130th "World Series of Dogdom." All 2,500 dogs are American Kennel Club Champions of Record, competing for the Best in Show trophy. Check the website **www. westminsterkennelclub.org** for further info. Tickets are available after January 1 via **Ticketmaster** (✆ **212/307-7171;** www.ticketmaster.com). February 11 and 12, 2008.

March

Triple Pier Antiques Show. The city's largest and most comprehensive antiques show takes place over 2 consecutive weekends, as more than 600 dealers exhibit their treasures, ranging from jewelry to home furnishings, on three piers along the Hudson River between 48th and 51st streets. **Pier 88** features 20th-century modern collectibles; **Pier 90** has all manner of Americana, including country rustic, folk art, and Arts and Crafts; and **Pier 92** houses 18th- and 19th-century formal European antiques. Call ✆ **212/255-0020** for this year's dates, plus a calendar of additional shows. Usually mid-March, and again in mid-November.

St. Patrick's Day Parade. More than 150,000 marchers join in the world's largest civilian parade, as Fifth Avenue from 44th to 86th streets rings with the sounds of bands and bagpipes. The parade usually starts at 11am, but go extra early if you want a good spot. Call ✆ **212/484-1222.** March 17.

Easter Parade. This isn't a traditional parade, *per se*: There are no marching bands, no baton twirlers, no protesters. Once upon a time, New York's gentry came out to show off their tasteful but discreet toppings. Today, if you were planning to slip on a tasteful little number—say something delicately woven in straw with a simple flower or two that matches your gloves—you will *not* be the grandest lady in this springtime hike along Fifth Avenue from 48th to 57th streets. It's more about flamboyant exhibitionism, with hats and costumes that get more outrageous every year—and anybody can join right in for free. The parade generally runs Easter Sunday from about 10am to 3 or 4pm. Call ✆212/484-1222. March 23, 2008.

April

New York International Auto Show. Here's the irony: You don't need a car in New York, yet this is the largest car show in the U.S. Held at the Javits Center, many concept cars show up that will never roll off the assembly line but are fun to dream about. Call ✆ **718/ 746-5300** or visit www.autoshowny. com or www.javitscenter.com. The show ran from April 6–15 in 2007.

Tribeca Film Festival. Conceived in 2002 by the unofficial mayor of TriBeCa, Robert De Niro, the festival has grown in popularity and esteem every year. In 2007, the 12-day festival featured over 250 films and included special events like a Family Festival Street Fair. Call ✆ **212/941-2400** or visit www.tribecafilmfestival.org. Last week in April.

May

Bike New York: The Great Five Boro Bike Tour. The largest mass-participation cycling event in the United States attracts about 30,000 cyclists from all over the world. After a 42-mile ride through the five boroughs, finalists are greeted with a traditional New York–style celebration of food and music. Call © **212/932-BIKE** (2453) or visit www.bikenewyork.org to register. First or second Sunday in May.

Ninth Avenue International Food Festival. Street fairs are part of the New York landscape each summer, but this is one of the best. You can spend the day sampling Italian sausages, homemade pierogi, spicy curries, and other ethnic dishes. Street musicians, bands, and vendors add to the festive atmosphere stretching along Ninth Avenue from 37th to 57th streets. Call © **212/484-1222.** Early to mid-May.

Fleet Week. About 10,000 Navy and Coast Guard personnel are "at liberty" in New York for the annual Fleet Week at the end of May. Usually from 1 to 4pm daily, you can watch the ships and aircraft carriers as they dock at the piers on the west side of Manhattan, tour them with on-duty personnel, and watch some dramatic exhibitions by the U.S. Marines. Even if you don't take in any of the events, you'll know it's Fleet Week because those 10,000 sailors invade Midtown in their starched white uniforms. It's wonderful—just like *On the Town* come to life. Call © **212/245-0072** or visit www.fleetweek.com (your best source for a full list of events) or www.intrepidmuseum.org. Late May.

June

Belmont Stakes. The third jewel in the Triple Crown is held at **Belmont Park Race Track** in Belmont, Long Island. If a Triple Crown winner is to be named, it will happen here. For information, call © **516/488-6000** or visit www.nyra.com. Early June.

Museum Mile Festival. Fifth Avenue from 82nd to 104th streets is closed to cars from 6 to 9pm as 20,000-plus strollers enjoy live music, from Broadway tunes to string quartets; street entertainers; and free admission to nine Museum Mile institutions, including the Metropolitan Museum of Art and the Guggenheim. Call © **212/606-2296** or any of the participating institutions for details. Usually the second Tuesday in June.

Parades Around Town. During the summer there is a parade for almost every nationality or ethnicity. June is the month for (among others) the sometimes raucous but usually very colorful **Puerto Rican Day Parade** and the **Lesbian and Gay Pride Week and March,** where Fifth Avenue goes wild as the gay/lesbian community celebrates with bands, marching groups, floats, and plenty of panache. The parade starts on upper Fifth Avenue around 52nd Street and continues into the Village, where a street festival and a waterfront dance party with fireworks cap the day. Call © **212/807-7433** or check www.hopinc.org. Mid- to late June.

SummerStage. A summer-long festival of outdoor performances in **Central Park,** featuring world music, pop, folk, and jazz artists ranging from Steve Earle to Craig David to Basement Jaxx to the New York Grand Opera to the Chinese Golden Dragon Acrobats. Shows are often free, but some big-name shows (referred to as "fundraisers") require tickets. Call © **212/360-2756** or visit www.summerstage.org. June through August.

Shakespeare in the Park. The Delacorte Theater in **Central Park** is the setting for first-rate free performances under the stars—including at least one Shakespeare play each season—often with stars on the stage. For details, see "Park It! Shakespeare, Music & Other Free Fun," in chapter 10. Call ℂ 212/ 539-8500 or visit www.publictheater. org. June through August.

Restaurant Week. Late June. (see "January," above).

July

Independence Day Harbor Festival and Fourth of July Fireworks Spectacular. Start the day amid the crowds at the Great July Fourth Festival in lower Manhattan, and then catch Macy's fireworks extravaganza (one of the country's most fantastic) over the East River (the best vantage point is from FDR Dr., which closes to traffic several hours before sunset). Call ℂ 212/484-1222 or Macy's Visitor Center at 212/494-2922. July 4.

Lincoln Center Festival 2008. This festival celebrates the best of the performing arts from all over—theater, ballet, contemporary dance, opera, nouveau circus performances, even puppet and media-based art. Recent editions have featured performances by Ornette Coleman, the Royal Opera, the Royal Ballet, and the New York Philharmonic. Schedules are available in mid-March, and tickets go on sale in May or early June. Call ℂ 212/546-2656 or visit www.lincolncenter.org. Throughout July.

Midsummer Night's Swing. Dancing duos head to the **Lincoln Center's Josie Robertson Plaza** for evenings of big-band swing, salsa, and tango under the stars to the sounds of top-flight bands. Dance lessons are offered with purchase of a ticket. Call ℂ 212/875-5766 or visit www.lincolncenter.org. July and August.

Mostly Mozart. World-renowned ensembles and soloists (Alicia de Larrocha and André Watts have performed in the past) are featured at this month-long series at **Avery Fisher Hall.** Schedules are available in mid-April, and tickets in early May. Call ℂ 212/875-5030 or 212/546-2656 for information, 212/721-6500 to order tickets, or visit www.lincoln center.org. Late July through August.

August

Lincoln Center Out of Doors. This series of free music and dance performances is held outdoors on the plazas of **Lincoln Center.** Call ℂ 212/875-5766 or 212/546-2656 or visit www. lincolncenter.org for the schedule (usually available in mid-July). Throughout August.

Harlem Week. The world's largest black and Hispanic cultural festival actually spans almost the whole month to include the Black Film Festival, the Harlem Jazz and Music Festival, and the Taste of Harlem Food Festival. Expect a full slate of music, from gospel to hip-hop, and lots of other festivities. Call ℂ 212/484-1222. Throughout August.

New York International Fringe Festival. Held in a variety of downtown venues and park spaces for a crowd looking for the next underground hit, this arts festival presents alternative as well as traditional theater, musicals, dance, comedy, and all manner of performance. Hundreds of events are held at all hours over about 10 days. The quality can vary wildly (lots of performers use Fringe as a workshop to develop their acts and shows), and some performances really push the envelope. Nonetheless, you'd be surprised at how many shows are actually *good*. Call ℂ **888/FRINGE-NYC** or 212/279-4488; to purchase tickets, 800/ 965-4827 or visit www.fringenyc.org. Late August.

U.S. Open Tennis Championships.
The final Grand Slam event of the tennis season is held at the Arthur Ashe Stadium at the USTA National Tennis Center, the largest public tennis center in the world, at **Flushing Meadows Park** in Queens. Tickets go on sale in May or early June. The event sells out immediately because many tickets are held by corporate sponsors who hand them out to customers. (It's worth it to check the list of sponsors to determine if anyone you know has a ticket connection.) You can usually buy scalped tickets outside the complex (an illegal practice, of course), which is right next to Shea Stadium. The last few matches of the tournament are the most expensive, but you'll see a lot more tennis early on, when your ticket allows you to wander the outside courts and view several matches. Call ✆ **866/OPEN-TIX** (it's always busy) or 718/760-6200 well in advance; visit www.usopen.org or www.usta.com for information. Two weeks around Labor Day.

September

West Indian–American Day Parade.
This annual Brooklyn event is New York's largest and best street celebration. Come for the extravagant costumes, pulsating rhythms (soca, calypso, reggae), bright colors, folklore, food (jerk chicken, oxtail soup, Caribbean soul food), and two million hip-shaking revelers. The route can change from year to year, but it usually runs along Eastern Parkway from Utica Avenue to Grand Army Plaza (at the gateway to Prospect Park). Call ✆ **718/467-1797;** www.wiadca.org. Labor Day.

Broadway on Broadway. This free alfresco afternoon show features the songs and casts from nearly every Broadway show, on a stage in the middle of Times Square. Call ✆ **212/768-1560** or visit www.timessquarenyc.

org and click on "Events." Sunday in mid-September.

New York Film Festival. Legendary hits *Pulp Fiction* and *Mean Streets* both had their U.S. premieres at the Film Society of Lincoln Center's 2-week festival, a major stop on the filmfest circuit. Schedules in recent years have included advance looks at *Pan's Labyrinth, Volver,* and *The Queen.* Screenings are held in various Lincoln Center venues; advance tickets are a good bet always, and a necessity for certain events (especially evening and weekend screenings). Call ✆ **212/875-5166** (for recorded information), 212/875-5050 for box office information, or check out www.filmlinc.com. Two weeks from late September to early October.

BAM Next Wave Festival. One of the city's most important cultural events takes place at the **Brooklyn Academy of Music.** The months-long festival showcases experimental new dance, theater, and music by both renowned and lesser-known international artists. Recent performances have included Astor Piazzolla's *Maria de Buenos Aires* (featuring Piazzolla disciple Gidon Kremer), the 25th anniversary of the Kronos Quartet, and choreographer Bill T. Jones's *We Set Out Early . . . Visibility Was Poor* (set to the music of Igor Stravinsky, John Cage, and Peteris Vask). Call ✆ **718/636-4100** or visit www.bam.org. September through December.

October

Feast of St. Francis. Animals from goldfish to elephants are blessed as thousands of *Homo sapiens* look on at the **Cathedral of St. John the Divine.** A magical experience—pets, of course, are welcome. A festive fair follows the blessing and music events. Buy tickets in advance because they can be hard to get. For tickets call ℂ **866/468-7691,** visit www.ticketweb.com; or call the cathedral's box office at ℂ **212/662-2133** or visit www.stjohndivine.org. First Sunday in October.

Ice-Skating. Show off your skating style in the limelight at the diminutive **Rockefeller Center** rink (ℂ **212/332-7654;** www.rockefellercenter.com), open from mid-October to mid-March or early April (you'll skate under the magnificent Christmas tree for the month of Dec). In Central Park, try **Wollman Rink** on the east side of the park between 62nd and 63rd streets (ℂ **212/439-6900;** www.wollmanskatingrink.com), and **Lasker Rink,** midpark between 106th and 108th streets (ℂ **917/492-3857**). Both Central Park skating rinks usually close in early April.

The Pond in Bryant Park. The season here is a short one—from October to mid-January—but the skating is free. Call ℂ **212/768-4242** or visit www.bryantpark.org.

Big Apple Circus. New York City's homegrown, not-for-profit performing-arts circus is a favorite with children and anyone who's young at heart. Big Apple is committed to maintaining the classical circus tradition with sensitivity and only features animals that have a traditional working relationship with humans. A tent is pitched in **Damrosch Park** at **Lincoln Center.** Call ℂ **800/922-3772** or visit www.bigapplecircus.org. Late October through January.

Greenwich Village Halloween Parade. This is Halloween at its most outrageous. You may have heard Lou Reed singing about it on his classic album *New York*—he wasn't exaggerating. Drag queens and assorted other flamboyant types parade through the Village in wildly creative costumes. The parade route has changed over the years, but most recently it has started after sunset at Spring Street and marched up Sixth Avenue to 23rd Street or Union Square. Call the *Village Voice* Parade hot line at ℂ **212/475-3333,** ext. 14044, visit www.halloween-nyc.com, or check the papers for the exact route so you can watch—or participate, if you have the threads and the imagination. October 31.

November

The Chocolate Show. This burgeoning 4-day event devoted to chocolate takes place each year about 2 weeks before Thanksgiving and is open to the public. The event is at the Metropolitan Pavilion in Chelsea and features booths representing over 50 of the world's best chocolate makers, tastings, demonstrations, and activities for children. For info, call **866/CHOC-NYC** or 212/889-5112 or visit www.chocolateshow.com. Call for 2008 dates.

New York City Marathon. Some 30,000 runners from around the world participate in the largest U.S. marathon, and more than a million fans cheer them on as they follow a route that touches all five New York boroughs and finishes at Central Park. Call ℂ **212/423-2249** or 212/860-4455, or visit www.nyrrc.org, where you can find applications. First Sunday in November. November 4, 2007.

Radio City Music Hall Christmas Spectacular. A rather gaudy extravaganza, but lots of fun. Starring the Radio City Rockettes and a cast that includes live animals (just try to picture the camels sauntering into the Sixth Ave. entrance!). For information, call ℂ **212/247-4777** or visit www.radiocity.com; buy tickets at the box office or via Ticketmaster's **Radio City Hot Line** (ℂ **212/307-1000**), or visit www.ticketmaster.com. Throughout November and December.

Triple Pier Antiques Show. The city's largest antiques show takes place over 2 consecutive weekends, usually before Thanksgiving; for details, see "March," above. Call ☎ 212/255-0020 or visit www.stellashows.com for this year's dates.

Macy's Thanksgiving Day Parade. The procession from Central Park West and 77th Street and down Broadway to Herald Square at 34th Street continues to be a national tradition. Huge hot-air balloons in the forms of Rocky and Bullwinkle, Snoopy, the Pink Panther, Bart Simpson, and other cartoon favorites are the best part. The night before, you can usually see the big blow-up on Central Park West at 79th Street; call in advance to see if it will be open to the public. Call ☎ 212/484-1222 or Macy's Visitor Center at ☎ 212/494-2922. November 23, 2007.

The Nutcracker. Tchaikovsky's holiday favorite is performed by the New York City Ballet at **Lincoln Center.** The annual schedule is available beginning in mid-July, and tickets usually go on sale in early October. Call ☎ 212/870-5570 or go online to www.nycballet.com. Late November through early January.

Lighting of the Rockefeller Center Christmas Tree. The annual lighting ceremony is accompanied by ice skaters, singing, entertainment, and a *huge* crowd. The tree stays lit 24/7 until after the New Year. Call ☎ 212/332-6868 or visit www.rockefellercenter.com. Late November or early December.

December

Holiday Trimmings. Stroll down festive Fifth Avenue and you'll see a 27-foot sparkling snowflake floating over the intersection outside **Tiffany's,** the **Cartier** building ribboned and bowed in red, wreaths warming the necks of

the **New York Public Library's** lions, and fanciful figurines in the windows of **Saks Fifth Avenue** and **Lord & Taylor.** Madison Avenue between 55th and 60th streets is also a good bet; **Sony Plaza** usually displays something fabulous, as does **Barney's New York.** Throughout December.

Christmas Traditions. In addition to the **Radio City Music Hall Christmas Spectacular** and the New York City Ballet's staging of *The Nutcracker* (see "November," above), traditional holiday events include *A Christmas Carol* at **The Theater at Madison Square Garden** (☎ 212/465-6741 or www.thegarden.com, or ☎ 212/307-7171 or www.ticketmaster.com for tickets), usually featuring a big name to draw in the crowds. At **Avery Fisher Hall** is the National Chorale's singalong performances of Handel's *Messiah* (☎ 212/875-5030; www.lincolncenter.org) for a week before Christmas. Don't worry if the only words you know are "Alleluia, Alleluia!"—a lyrics sheet is given to ticket holders. Throughout December.

Lighting of the Hanukkah Menorah. Everything is done on a grand scale in New York, so it's no surprise that the world's largest menorah (32 ft. high) is at Manhattan's **Grand Army Plaza,** Fifth Avenue and 59th Street. Hanukkah celebrations begin at sunset, with the lighting of the first of the giant electric candles. December 5, 2007.

New Year's Eve. The biggest party of all is in **Times Square,** where raucous revelers count down the year's final seconds until the ball drops at midnight at 1 Times Sq. This one, in the cold surrounded by thousands of drunks, is a masochist's delight. Call ☎ 212/768-1560 or 212/484-1222 or visit www.timessquarenyc.org. December 31.

Runner's World **Midnight Run.** Enjoy **fireworks** followed by the New York Road Runners Club's annual run in **Central Park,** which is fun for runners and spectators alike; call ☎ **212/860-4455** or visit www.nyrrc.org. December 31.

Brooklyn's fireworks celebration. Head to Brooklyn for the city's largest New Year's Eve **fireworks** celebration at Prospect Park. Call ☎ **718/965-8999** or visit www.prospectpark.org. December 31.

New Year's Eve Concert for Peace. The Cathedral of St. John the Divine is known for its annual concert, whose past performers have included the Manhattan School of Music Chamber Sinfonia, Tony Award–winning composer Jason Robert Brown *(Parade),* American soprano Lauren Flanigan, and the Forces of Nature Dance Company. Call ☎ **212/316-7540** for information, 212/662-2133 for tickets, or go online to www.stjohndivine.org. December 31.

4 Getting There

BY PLANE

Three major airports serve New York City: **John F. Kennedy International Airport** (☎ **718/244-4444**) in Queens, about 15 miles (1 hr. driving time) from midtown Manhattan; **LaGuardia Airport** (☎ **718/533-3400**), also in Queens, about 8 miles (30 min.) from Midtown; and **Newark International Airport** (☎ **973/961-6000**) in nearby New Jersey, about 16 miles (45 min.) from Midtown. Information about all three airports is available online at **www.panynj.gov**; click on the "All Airports" tab on the left.

Even though LaGuardia is the closest airport to Manhattan, it has a bad reputation for delays and terminal chaos, in both ticket-desk lines and baggage claim. You may want to use JFK or Newark instead. (JFK has the best reputation for timeliness among New York–area airports.)

Almost every major domestic carrier serves at least one of the New York–area airports; most serve two or all three. Among them **American** (☎ 817/967-2000; www.aa.com), **Continental** (☎ 800/525-3273; www.continental.com), **Delta** (☎ 800/221-1212; www.delta.com), **Northwest** (☎ 800/225-2525; www.nwa.com), **US Airways** (☎ 800/428-4322; www.usairways.com), and **United** (☎ 800/864-8331; www.united.com).

In recent years, there has been rapid growth in the number of start-up, no-frills airlines serving New York. You might check out Atlanta-based **AirTran** (☎ 800/AIRTRAN; www.airtran.com), Chicago-based **ATA** (☎ 800/225-2995; www.ata.com), Denver-based **Frontier** (☎ 800/432-1359; www.flyfrontier.com), Milwaukee- and Omaha-based **Midwest Airlines** (☎ 800/452-2022; www.midwest

---

Tips **Choosing Your NYC-Area Airport**

It's more convenient to fly into Newark than JFK if your destination is Manhattan, and fares to Newark are often cheaper than those to the other airports. Newark is particularly convenient if your hotel is in Midtown West or downtown. Taxi fare into Manhattan from Newark is roughly equivalent to the fare from JFK—both now have AirTrains in place (see "Getting Into Town from the Airport," below), but the AirTrain to Newark from Manhattan is quicker.

airlines.com), or Detroit-based **Spirit Airlines** (© 800/772-7117; www.spirit air.com). The JFK-based cheap-chic airline **jetblue** ✈ (© 800/JETBLUE; www.jetblue.com) has taken New York by storm with its low fares and classy service to cities throughout the nation. The nation's leading discount airline, **Southwest** (© 800/435-9792; www.iflyswa.com), flies into MacArthur (Islip) Airport on Long Island, 50 miles east of Manhattan.

FLYING FOR LESS: TIPS FOR GETTING THE BEST AIRFARE

• Passengers who can book their ticket either **long in advance or at the last minute,** or who **fly midweek** or **at less-trafficked hours** may pay a fraction of the full fare. If your schedule is flexible, say so, and ask if you can secure a cheaper fare by changing your flight plans.

• Search **the Internet** for cheap fares. The most popular online travel agencies are **Travelocity.com** (www. travelocity.co.uk); **Expedia.com** (www.expedia.co.uk and www.expedia. ca); and **Orbitz.com**. In the U.K., go to **Travelsupermarket** (© 0845/ 345-5708; www.travelsupermarket. com), a flight search engine that offers flight comparisons for the budget airlines whose seats often end up in bucket-shop sales. Other websites for booking airline tickets online include **Cheapflights.com**, **SmarterTravel. com**, **Priceline.com**, and **Opodo** (www.opodo.co.uk). Meta search sites (which find and then direct you to airline and hotel websites for booking) include **Sidestep.com** and **Kayak.com**—the latter includes fares for budget carriers like jetBlue and Spirit as well as the major airlines. **Site59.com** is a great source for last-minute flights and getaways. In addition, most **airlines** offer online-only fares that even their phone agents know nothing about. British travelers should check **Flights International** (© 0800/0187050; www.flights-international.com) for deals on flights all over the world.

• Watch local newspapers for **promotional specials** or **fare wars,** when airlines lower prices on their most popular routes. Also keep an eye on price fluctuations and deals at websites such as **Airfarewatchdog.com** and **Farecast.com**.

• **Consolidators,** also known as bucket shops, are wholesale brokers in the airline-ticket game. Consolidators buy deeply discounted tickets ("distressed" inventories of unsold seats) from airlines and sell them to online ticket agencies, travel agents, tour operators, corporations, and, to a lesser degree, the general public. Consolidators advertise in Sunday newspaper travel sections (often in small ads with tiny type), both in the U.S. and the U.K. They can be great sources for cheap international tickets. On the down side, bucket shop tickets are often rigged with restrictions, such as stiff cancellation penalties (as high as 50% to 75% of the ticket price). And keep in mind that most of what you see advertised is of limited availability. Several reliable consolidators are worldwide and available online. **STA Travel** (www. statravel.com) has been the world's leading consolidator for students since purchasing Council Travel, but their fares are competitive for travelers of all ages. **Air Tickets Direct** (© 800/778-3447; www.airtickets direct.com) is based in Montreal and leverages the currently weak Canadian dollar for low fares; they also book trips to places that U.S. travel agents won't touch, such as Cuba.

• Join **frequent-flier clubs.** Frequent-flier membership doesn't cost a cent, but it does entitle you to free tickets or upgrades when you amass the airline's required number of frequent-flier points. You don't even have to fly to earn points; **frequent-flier credit cards** can earn you thousands of miles for doing your everyday shopping. But keep in mind that award seats are limited, seats on popular routes are hard to snag, and more and more major airlines are cutting their expiration periods for mileage points—so check your airline's frequent-flier program so you don't lose your miles before you use them. *Inside tip:* Award seats are offered almost a year in advance, but seats also open up at the last minute, so if your travel plans are flexible, you may strike gold. To play the frequent-flier game to your best advantage, consult the community bulletin boards on **FlyerTalk** (www.flyertalk.com) or go to Randy Petersen's **Inside Flyer** (www.insideflyer.com). Petersen and friends review all the programs in detail and post regular updates on changes in policies and trends.

ARRIVING AT THE AIRPORT
IMMIGRATION & CUSTOMS CLEARANCE   Foreign visitors arriving by air, no matter what the port of entry, should cultivate patience and resignation before setting foot on U.S. soil. U.S. airports have considerably beefed up security clearances in the years since the terrorist attacks of 9/11, and clearing Customs and Immigration can take as long as 2 hours.

People traveling by air from Canada, Bermuda, and certain Caribbean countries can sometimes clear Customs and Immigration at the point of departure, which is much faster.

GETTING INTO TOWN FROM THE AIRPORT
Since there's no need to rent a car in New York, you're going to have to figure out how you want to get from the airport to your hotel and back.

For transportation information for all three airports (JFK, LaGuardia, and Newark), call **Air-Ride** (© **800/247-7433**), which offers 24-hour recorded details on bus and shuttle companies and car services registered with the New York and New Jersey Port Authority. Similar information is available at **www.panynj. gov/airports**; click on the airport at which you'll be arriving.

The Port Authority runs staffed Ground Transportation Information counters on the baggage-claim level at each airport where you can get information and book various kinds of transport. Most transportation companies also have courtesy phones near the baggage-claim area.

Generally, travel time between the airports and midtown by taxi or car is 45 to 60 minutes for JFK, 20 to 35 minutes for LaGuardia, and 35 to 50 minutes for Newark. Always allow extra time, especially during rush hour, peak holiday travel times, and if you're taking a bus.

SUBWAYS & PUBLIC BUSES   For the most part, your best bet is to stay away from the MTA when traveling to and from the airport. You might save a few dollars, but subways and buses that currently serve the airports involve multiple transfers, and you'll have to drag your luggage up and down staircases. On some subways, you'd be traveling through undesirable neighborhoods. Spare yourself the drama.

The only exception to this rule that I feel somewhat comfortable with is the subway service to and from JFK, which connects with the new AirTrain (see the box "AirTrains: Newark & JFK—The Very Good & the Not-So-Very Good," below). The subway can actually be more reliable than taking a car or taxi at the height of rush hour, but *a few words of warning:* This isn't the right option for you if you're bringing more than a single piece of luggage or if you have a sizable family in tow, since there's a good amount of walking and some stairs involved in the

An Airport Warning

Never accept a car ride from the hustlers who hang out in the terminal halls. They're illegal, don't have proper insurance, and aren't safe. You can tell who they are because they'll approach you with a suspicious conspiratorial air and ask if you need a ride. Not from them, you don't. Sanctioned city cabs and car services wait outside the terminals.

trip, and you'll have nowhere to put all those bags on the subway train. And *do not* use this method if you're traveling to or from the airport after dark or too early in the morning—it's just not safe. For additional subway information, see "Getting Around," in chapter 5.

TAXIS Despite significant rate hikes the past few years, taxis are still a quick and convenient way to travel to and from the airports. They're available at designated taxi stands outside the terminals, with uniformed dispatchers on hand during peak hours at JFK and LaGuardia, around the clock at Newark. Follow the GROUND TRANSPORTATION or TAXI signs. There may be a long line, but it generally moves pretty quickly. Fares, whether fixed or metered, do not include bridge and tunnel tolls ($4–$6) or a tip for the cabbie (15%–20% is customary). They do include all passengers in the cab and luggage—never pay more than the metered or flat rate, except for tolls and a tip (8pm–6am a $1 surcharge also applies on New York yellow cabs). Taxis have a limit of four passengers, so if there are more in your group, you'll have to take more than one cab. For more on taxis, see "Getting Around," in chapter 5.

- **From JFK:** A flat rate of $45 to Manhattan (plus tolls and tip) is charged. The meter will not be turned on and the surcharge will not be added. The flat rate does not apply on trips from Manhattan to the airport.
- **From LaGuardia:** $17 to $27, metered, plus tolls and tip.

- **From Newark:** The dispatcher for New Jersey taxis gives you a slip of paper with a flat rate ranging from $30 to $38 (toll and tip extra), depending on where you're going in Manhattan, so be precise about your destination. New York yellow cabs aren't permitted to pick up passengers at Newark. The yellow-cab fare from Manhattan to Newark is the meter amount plus $15 and tolls (about $45–$55, perhaps a few dollars more with tip). Jersey taxis aren't permitted to take passengers from Manhattan to Newark.

PRIVATE CAR & LIMOUSINE SERVICES Private car and limousine companies provide convenient 24-hour door-to-door airport transfers for roughly the same cost of a taxi. The advantage they offer over taking a taxi is that you can arrange your pickup in advance and avoid the hassles of the taxi line. Call at least 24 hours in advance (even earlier on holidays), and a driver will meet you near baggage claim (or at your hotel for a return trip). You'll probably be asked to leave a credit card number to guarantee your ride. You'll likely be offered the choice of indoor or curbside pickup; indoor pickup is more expensive but makes it easier to hook up with your driver (who usually waits in baggage claim bearing a sign with your name on it). You can save a few dollars if you arrange for an outside pickup; call the dispatcher as soon as you clear baggage claim and then take your luggage out to the designated waiting area, where you'll wait for the driver to come around, which can take anywhere from 10 minutes to a half-hour. Besides the wait, the other disadvantage of this option is that curbside can be chaos during prime deplaning hours.

Vehicles range from sedans to vans to limousines and tend to be relatively clean and comfortable. Prices vary slightly by company and the size of car reserved, but expect a rate roughly equivalent to taxi fare if you request a basic sedan and have only one stop; toll and tip policies are the same. (*Note:* Car services are not subject to the flat-rate rule that taxis have for rides to and from JFK.) Ask when booking what the fare will be and if you can use your credit card to pay for the ride so there are no surprises at drop-off time. There may be waiting charges tacked on if the driver has to wait an excessive amount of time for your plane to land

when picking you up, but the car companies will usually check on your flight beforehand to get an accurate landing time.

I've had the best luck with **Carmel** (② **800/922-7635** or 212/666-6666) and **Legends** (② **888/LEGENDS** or 888/888-8884; www.legendslimousine.com); **Allstate** (② **800/453-4099** or 212/333-3333) and **Tel-Aviv** (② **800/222-9888** or 212/777-7777) also have reasonable reputations. (Keep in mind, though, that these services are only as good as the individual drivers—and sometimes there's a lemon in the bunch. If you have a problem, report it immediately to the main office.)

These car services are good for rush hour (no ticking meters in rush-hour traffic), but if you're arriving at a quieter time of day, taxis work fine.

⎛Tips Getting Through the Airport

- Arrive at the airport at least 1 hour before a domestic flight and 2 hours before an international flight. You can check the average wait times at your airport by going to the TSA **Security Checkpoint Wait Times** site (waittime/tsa.dhs.gov).
- Know what you can carry on and what you can't. For the latest updates on items you are prohibited to bring in carryon luggage, go to **www.tsa.gov/travelers/airtravel**.
- Beat the ticket-counter lines by using the self-service electronic ticket kiosks at the airport or even printing out your boarding pass at home from the airline website. Using curbside check-in is also a smart way to avoid lines.
- Bring a current, government-issued photo ID such as a driver's license or passport. Children under 18 do not need government-issued photo IDs for flights within the U.S., but they do need passports for international flights.
- Help speed up security before you're screened. Remove jackets, shoes, belt buckles, heavy jewelry, and watches and place them either in your carryon luggage or the security bins provided. Place keys, coins, cellphones, and pagers in a security bin. If you have metallic body parts, carry a note from your doctor. When possible, pack liquids in checked baggage.
- Use a TSA-approved lock for your checked luggage. Look for Travel Sentry certified locks at luggage or travel shops and Brookstone stores (or online at www.brookstone.com)

AirTrains: Newark & JFK—The Very Good & the Not-So-Very Good

First the very good: A few years back, a new rail link revolutionized the process of connecting by public transportation to New York's notoriously underserved airport: the brand-new **AirTrain Newark,** which now connects Newark Airport with Manhattan via a speedy monorail/rail link.

Even though you have to make a connection, the system is fast, pleasant, affordable, and easy to use. Each arrivals terminal at Newark Airport has a station for the AirTrain, so just follow the signs once you collect your bags. All AirTrains head to **Newark International Airport Station,** where you transfer to a **NJ Transit** train. NJ Transit will deliver you to New York Penn Station at 33rd Street and Seventh Avenue, where you can get a cab to your hotel.

The trip from my apartment on Manhattan's Upper West Side to the Newark Alitalia terminal, for example, was under a half-hour and only cost me $14 ($12 for the AirTrain link via Penn Station plus $2 for the subway to get to Penn Station). That's a savings of at least $35 if I took a cab, not to mention the time I saved. NJ Transit trains run two to three times an hour during peak travel times (once an hour during early and late hours); you can check the schedules on monitors before you leave the airport terminal, and again at the train station. Tickets can be purchased from vending machines at both the air terminal and the train station (no ticket is required to board the AirTrain). The one-way fare is $11 (children under 5 ride free). (On your return trip to the airport, the AirTrain is far more predictable, time-wise, than subjecting yourself to the whims of traffic.)

Note that travelers heading to points beyond the city can also pick up Amtrak and other NJ Transit trains at Newark International Airport Station to their final destinations.

PRIVATE BUSES & SHUTTLES Buses and shuttle services provide a comfortable and less expensive (but usually more time-consuming) option for airport transfers than do taxis and car services.

Super Shuttle serves all three airports; **New York Airport Service** serves JFK and LaGuardia; **Olympia Trails and Express Shuttle USA** serves Newark. These services are my favorite option for getting to and from Newark during peak travel times because the drivers usually take lesser-known streets that make the ride much quicker than if you go with a taxi or car, which will virtually always stick to the traffic-clogged main route.

The familiar blue vans of **Super Shuttle** (© **212/258-3826;** www.supershuttle. com) serve all three area airports, providing door-to-door service to Manhattan and points on Long Island every 15 to 30 minutes around the clock. As with Express Shuttle, you don't need to reserve your airport-to-Manhattan ride; just go to the ground-transportation desk or use the courtesy phone in baggage claim and ask for Super Shuttle. Hotel pickups for your return trip require 24 to 48 hours' notice; you can make your reservations online. Fares run $13 to $22 per person, depending on the airport, with discounts available for additional persons in the same party.

Now the not-so-very good: A few bumpy years after opening in 2003, after years of anticipation and $1.9 billion, AirTrain JFK is beginning to operate more efficiently. Though you can't beat the price—only $7 if you take a subway to the AirTrain, $12 if you take the Long Island Rail Road—you won't save much on time getting to the airport. From midtown Manhattan, the ride can take anywhere from 40 minutes to an hour, depending on your connections. The ride takes approximately 90 minutes and the connections are murky. Only a few lines connect with the AirTrain: the A, E, J, and Z; the E, J, Z to Jamaica Station and the Sutphin Blvd.–Archer Ave. Station; and the A to Howard Beach/JFK Airport Station. The MTA is working hard to clear up the confusion, and though they are contemplating adding connections to the AirTrain in lower Manhattan sometime in the next decade, there's not much they can do now to speed up the trip.

A word of warning for both AirTrains: If you have mobility issues, mountains of luggage that will make connections difficult, or a bevy of small children to keep track of, skip the AirTrain. You'll find it easier to rely on a taxi, car service, or shuttle service that can offer you door-to-door transfers.

For more information on AirTrain Newark, call (✆ **888/EWR-INFO** or go online to **www.airtrainnewark.com**. For connection details, click on the links on the AirTrain website or contact **NJ Transit** (✆ **800/626-RIDE**; www. njtransit.com) or **Amtrak** (✆ **800/USA-RAIL**; www.amtrak.com).

For more information on AirTrain JFK, go online to www.airtrainjfk.com. For connection details, click on the links on the AirTrain website or the MTA site, www.mta.nyc.ny.us/mta/airtrain.htm.

New York Airport Service (✆ **718/ 875-8200**; www.nyairportservice.com) buses travel from JFK and LaGuardia to the Port Authority Bus Terminal (42nd St. and Eighth Ave.), Grand Central Terminal (Park Ave. between 41st and 42nd sts.), and to select Midtown hotels between 27th and 59th streets, plus the Jamaica LIRR Station in Queens, where you can pick up a train for Long Island. Follow the GROUND TRANSPORTATION signs to the curbside pickup or look for the uniformed agent. Buses depart the airport every 20 to 70 minutes (depending on your departure point and destination) between 6am and midnight. Buses to JFK and LaGuardia depart the Port Authority and Grand Central Terminal on the Park Avenue side every 15 to 30 minutes, depending on the time of day and the day of the week. To request direct shuttle service from your hotel, call the above number at least 24 hours in advance. One-way fare for JFK is $15, $27 round-trip; to LaGuardia it's $12 one-way and $21 round-trip.

Olympia Airport Express (✆ **212/ 964-6233**; www.coachusa.com/olympia) provides service every 15 to 30 minutes (depending on the time of day) from Newark Airport to Penn Station (the pickup point is the northwest corner of

34th St. and Eighth Ave., and the drop-off point is the southwest corner), the Port Authority Bus Terminal (on 42nd St. between Eighth and Ninth aves.), and Grand Central Terminal (on 41st St. between Park and Lexington aves.). Passengers to and from the Grand Central Terminal location can connect to Olympia's Midtown shuttle vans, which service select Midtown hotels. Call for the exact schedule for your return trip to the airport. The one-way fare runs $13, $22 round-trip; seniors and passengers with disabilities ride for $6.

BY CAR

From the **New Jersey Turnpike** (I-95) and points west, there are three Hudson River crossings to the city's West Side: the **Holland Tunnel** (lower Manhattan), the **Lincoln Tunnel** (Midtown), and the **George Washington Bridge** (Upper Manhattan). From **upstate New York,** take the **New York State Thruway** (I-87), which crosses the Hudson River on the Tappan Zee Bridge and becomes the **Major Deegan Expressway** (I-87) through the Bronx. For the East Side, continue to the Triborough Bridge and then down the FDR Drive. For

---

If You're Flying into MacArthur Airport on Southwest

Southwest Airlines is one of several carriers flying into the New York area via Long Island's MacArthur Airport, 50 miles east of Manhattan. If you're on one of these flights (because the price was *sooooo* low), here are your options for getting into the city:

Colonial Transportation (© 631/589-3500; www.colonialtransportation.com), **Classic Transportation** (© 631/567-5100; www.classictrans.com), and **Legends** (© 888/LEGENDS or 888/888-8884; www.legendslimousine.com) will pick you up at Islip Airport and deliver you to Manhattan via private sedan, but expect to pay about $125 plus tolls and tip for door-to-door service (which kind of defeats the purpose of flying a budget airline). Be sure to arrange for it at least 24 hours in advance.

For a fraction of the cost, you can catch a ride aboard a **Hampton Jitney** coach (© 631/283-4600; www.hamptonjitney.com) to various drop-off points on Midtown's east side. The cost is $27 per person, plus a minimal taxi fare from the terminal to the Hampton Jitney stop. Hampton Jitney can explain the details and arrange for taxi transport.

Colonial Transportation (© 631/589-3500; www.colonialtransportation.com) also offers regular shuttle service that traverses the 3 miles from the airport to the Ronkonkoma Long Island Rail Road station, where you can pick up an LIRR train to Manhattan. The shuttle fare is $5 per person, $1 for each additional family member accompanying a full-fare customer. From Ronkonkoma, it's about a 1½-hour train ride to Manhattan's Penn Station; the one-way fare is $13 at peak hours, $9.50 off-peak (half-fare for seniors 65 or older and kids 5–11). You can also catch the Suffolk County Transit bus no. S-57 between the airport and the station Monday to Saturday for $1.50. Trains usually leave Ronkonkoma once or twice every hour, depending on the day and time. For more information, call © 718/217-LIRR or visit www.mta.nyc.ny.us/lirr.

For additional options and the latest information, call © 631/467-3210 or visit www.macarthurairport.com.

Getting to the Other Boroughs & the 'Burbs

If you're traveling to a borough other than Manhattan, call **ETS Air Service** (© **718/221-5341**) for shared door-to-door service. For Long Island service, call **Classic Transportation** (© **631/567-5100**; www.classictrans.com) for car service. For service to Westchester County or Connecticut, contact **Connecticut Limousine** (© **800/472-5466** or 203/878-2222; www.ctlimo.com) or **Prime Time Shuttle of Connecticut** (© **800/377-8745**; www.primetimeshuttle.com).

If you're traveling to points in New Jersey from Newark Airport, call **Olympic Airporter** (© **800/822-9797** or 732/938-6666; www.olympicairporter.com) for Ocean, Monmouth, Middlesex and Mercer counties, plus Bucks County, Pennsylvania; or **State Shuttle** (© **800/427-3207** or 973/729-0030; www.stateshuttle.com) for destinations throughout New Jersey.

Additionally, **New York Airport Service** express buses (© **718/875-8200**; www.nyairportservice.com) serve the entire New York metropolitan region from JFK and LaGuardia, offering connections to the Long Island Rail Road; the Metro-North Railroad to Westchester County, upstate New York, and Connecticut; and New York's Port Authority terminal, where you can pick up buses to points throughout New Jersey.

---

the West Side, take the Cross Bronx Expressway (I-95) to the Henry Hudson Parkway or the Taconic State Parkway to the Saw Mill River Parkway to the Henry Hudson Parkway south.

From **New England,** the **New England Thruway** (I-95) connects with the **Bruckner Expressway** (I-278), which leads to the Triborough Bridge and the FDR Drive on the East Side. For the West Side, take the Bruckner to the Cross Bronx Expressway (I-95) to the Henry Hudson Parkway south.

Note that you'll have to pay tolls along some of these roads and at most crossings. If your state has an E-ZPass program, your pass will allow you to go through the designated E-ZPass lanes.

Once you arrive in Manhattan, park your car in a garage (expect to pay $20–$45 per day) and leave it there. Don't use your car for traveling within the city. Public transportation, taxis, and walking will easily get you where you want to go without the headaches of parking, gridlock, and dodging crazy cabbies.

BY TRAIN

Amtrak (© **800/USA-RAIL;** www.amtrak.com) runs frequent service to New York City's **Penn Station,** on Seventh Avenue between 31st and 33rd streets, where you can get a taxi, subway, or bus to your hotel. To get the best rates, book early (as much as 6 months in advance) and travel on weekends.

If you're traveling to New York from a city along Amtrak's Northeast Corridor—such as Boston, Philadelphia, Baltimore, or Washington, D.C.—Amtrak may be your best travel bet now that they've rolled out their new high-speed Acela trains. The Acela Express trains cut travel time from D.C. down to 2½ hours, and travel time from Boston to a lightning-quick 3 hours.

5 General Travel Resources

MONEY & COSTS

It's always advisable to bring money in a variety of forms on a vacation: a mix of cash, credit cards, and traveler's checks. You should also exchange enough petty cash to cover airport incidentals, tipping, and transportation to your hotel before you leave home, or withdraw money upon arrival at an airport ATM.

You never have to carry too much cash in New York, and while the city's pretty safe, it's best not to overstuff your wallet (although always make sure you have at least $20 in taxi fare on hand).

ATMS

In most Manhattan neighborhoods, you can find a bank with **ATMs** (automated teller machines) every couple of blocks. Many small stores and delis have ATMs with varying fees to withdraw money from your bank account or credit card. The **Cirrus** (✆ **800/424-7787;** www. mastercard.com) and **PLUS** (✆ **800/843-7587;** www.visa.com) networks span the country; you can find them even in remote regions. Go to your bank card's website to find ATM locations at your destination. Be sure you know your daily withdrawal limit before you depart.

Note: Many banks impose a fee every time you use a card at another bank's ATM, and that fee is often higher for international transactions (up to $5 or more) than for domestic ones (where they're rarely more than $2). In addition, the bank from which you withdraw cash may charge its own fee. To compare banks' ATM fees within the U.S., use **www.bankrate.com**. Visitors from outside the U.S. should also find out whether their bank assesses a 1% to 3% fee on charges incurred abroad.

CREDIT CARDS & DEBIT CARDS

Credit cards are the most widely used form of payment in the United States: **Visa** (Barclaycard in Britain), **Master-Card** (EuroCard in Europe, Access in Britain, Chargex in Canada), **American Express, Diners Club,** and **Discover.** They also provide a convenient record of all your expenses, and offer relatively good exchange rates. You can withdraw cash advances from your credit cards at banks or ATMs, but high fees make credit-card cash advances a pricey way to get cash.

It's highly recommended that you travel with at least one major credit card. You must have a credit card to rent a car, and hotels and airlines usually require a credit card imprint as a deposit against expenses.

ATM cards with major credit card backing, known as **"debit cards,"** are now a commonly acceptable form of payment in most stores and restaurants. Debit cards draw money directly from your checking account. Some stores enable you to receive cash back on your debit-card purchases as well. The same is true at most U.S. post offices.

⟨Tips Easy Money

If you're coming to New York from another country, you'll avoid lines at airport ATMs by exchanging at least some money—just enough to cover airport incidentals and transportation to your hotel—before you leave home.

When you change money, ask for some small bills or loose change. Petty cash will come in handy for tipping and public transportation. Consider keeping the change separate from your larger bills, so that it's readily accessible and you'll be less of a target for theft.

TRAVELER'S CHECKS

Though credit cards and debit cards are more often used, traveler's checks are still widely accepted in the U.S. Foreign visitors should make sure that traveler's checks are denominated in U.S. dollars; foreign-currency checks are often difficult to exchange.

You can buy traveler's checks at most banks. Most are offered in denominations of $20, $50, $100, $500, and sometimes $1000. Generally, you'll pay a service charge ranging from 1% to 4%.

The most popular traveler's checks are offered by **American Express** (℃ **800/807-6233;** ℃ **800/221-7282** for card holders—this number accepts collect calls, offers service in several foreign languages, and exempts Amex gold and platinum cardholders from the 1% fee.); **Visa** (℃ **800/732-1322**)—AAA members can obtain Visa checks for a $9.95 fee (for checks up to $1,500) at most AAA offices or by calling ℃ **866/339-3378;** and **MasterCard** (℃ **800/223-9920**).

Be sure to keep a copy of the traveler's checks serial numbers separate from your checks in the event that they are stolen or lost. You'll get a refund faster if you know the numbers.

Another option is the new **prepaid traveler's check cards,** reloadable cards that work much like debit cards but aren't linked to your checking account. The **American Express Travelers Cheque Card,** for example, requires a minimum deposit ($300), sets a maximum balance ($2,750), and has a one-time issuance fee of $14.95. You can withdraw money from an ATM ($2.50 per transaction, not including bank fees), and the funds can be purchased in dollars, euros, or pounds. If you lose the card, your available funds will be refunded within 24 hours.

TRAVEL INSURANCE

The cost of travel insurance varies widely, depending on the cost and length of your trip, your age and health, and the type of trip you're taking, but expect to pay between 5% and 8% of the vacation itself. You can get estimates from various providers through **InsureMyTrip.com.** Enter your trip cost and dates, your age, and other information, for prices from more than a dozen companies.

For **U.K. citizens,** insurance is always advisable when traveling in the States. Travelers or families who make more than one trip abroad per year may find an annual travel insurance policy works out cheaper. Check **www.moneysuper market.com,** which compares prices across a wide range of providers for single- and multi-trip policies.

Most big travel agents offer their own insurance and will probably try to sell you their package when you book a holiday. Think before you sign. **Britain's Consumers' Association** recommends that you insist on seeing the policy and reading the fine print before buying travel insurance. **The Association of British Insurers** (℃ **020/7600-3333;** www.abi.org.uk) gives advice by phone and publishes *Holiday Insurance,* a free guide to policy provisions and prices. You might also shop around for better deals: Try **Columbus Direct** (℃ **0870/033-9988;** www.columbusdirect.net).

TRIP-CANCELLATION INSURANCE

Trip-cancellation insurance will help retrieve your money if you have to back out of a trip or depart early, or if your travel supplier goes bankrupt. Trip cancellation traditionally covers such events as sickness, natural disasters, and State Department advisories. The latest news in trip-cancellation insurance is the availability of **expanded hurricane coverage** and the **"any-reason"** cancellation coverage—which costs more but covers cancellations made for any reason. You won't get back 100% of your prepaid trip cost, but you'll be refunded a substantial portion. **TravelSafe** (℃ **888/885-7233;**

www.travelsafe.com) offers both types of coverage. Expedia also offers any-reason cancellation coverage for its air-hotel packages.

For details, contact one of the following recommended insurers: **Access America** (© 866/807-3982; www.accessamerica.com); **Travel Guard International** (© 800/826-4919; www.travelguard.com); **Travel Insured International** (© 800/243-3174; www.travelinsured.com); and **Travelex Insurance Services** (© 888/457-4602; www.travelex-insurance.com).

MEDICAL INSURANCE

Although it's not required of travelers, health insurance is highly recommended. Most health insurance policies cover you if you get sick away from home—but check your coverage before you leave.

International visitors should note that unlike many European countries, the United States does not usually offer free or low-cost medical care to its citizens or visitors. Doctors and hospitals are expensive, and in most cases will require advance payment or proof of coverage before they render their services. Good policies will cover the costs of an accident, repatriation, or death. Packages such as **Europ Assistance's "Worldwide Healthcare Plan"** are sold by European automobile clubs and travel agencies at attractive rates. **Worldwide Assistance Services, Inc.** (© 800/777-8710; www.worldwideassistance.com) is the agent for Europ Assistance in the United States.

Though lack of health insurance may prevent you from being admitted to a hospital in nonemergencies, don't worry about being left on a street corner to die: The American way is to fix you now and bill the living daylights out of you later.

INSURANCE FOR BRITISH TRAVELERS Most big travel agents offer their own insurance and will probably try to sell you their package when you book a holiday. Think before you sign. **Britain's Consumers' Association** recommends

that you insist on seeing the policy and reading the fine print before buying travel insurance. **The Association of British Insurers** (© 020/7600-3333; www.abi.org.uk) gives advice by phone and publishes *Holiday Insurance,* a free guide to policy provisions and prices. You might also shop around for better deals: Try **Columbus Direct** (© 0870/033-9988; www.columbusdirect.net).

Canadians should check with their provincial health plan offices or call **Health Canada** (© 866/225-0709; www.hc-sc.gc.ca) to find out the extent of their coverage and what documentation and receipts they must take home in case they are treated in the United States.

LOST-LUGGAGE INSURANCE

On flights within the U.S., checked baggage is covered up to $2,500 per ticketed passenger. On flights outside the U.S. (and on U.S. portions of international trips), baggage coverage is limited to approximately $9.07 per pound, up to approximately $635 per checked bag. If you plan to check items more valuable than what's covered by the standard liability, see if your homeowner's policy covers your valuables, get baggage insurance as part of your comprehensive travel-insurance package, or buy Travel Guard's "BagTrak" product.

If your luggage is lost, immediately file a lost-luggage claim at the airport, detailing the luggage contents. Most airlines require that you report delayed, damaged, or lost baggage within 4 hours of arrival. The airlines are required to deliver luggage, once found, directly to your house or destination free of charge.

HEALTH
STAYING HEALTHY

If you get sick, consider asking your hotel concierge to recommend a local doctor—even his or her own. This will probably yield a better recommendation than any toll-free telephone number would.

Avoiding "Economy-Class Syndrome"

Deep-vein thrombosis, or as it's known in the world of flying, "economy-class syndrome," is a blood clot that develops in a deep vein. It's a potentially deadly condition that can be caused by sitting in cramped conditions—such as an airplane cabin—for too long. During a flight (especially a long-haul flight), get up, walk around, and stretch your legs every 60 to 90 minutes to keep your blood flowing. Other preventative measures include frequent flexing of the legs while sitting, drinking lots of water, and avoiding alcohol and sleeping pills. If you have a history of deep-vein thrombosis, heart disease, or another condition that puts you at high risk, some experts recommend wearing compression stockings or taking anticoagulants when you fly; always ask your physician about the best course for you. Symptoms of deep-vein thrombosis include leg pain or swelling, or even shortness of breath.

There are also several walk-in medical centers, like **DOCS at New York Healthcare,** 55 E. 34th St., between Park and Madison avenues (© **800/673-3627**), for non-emergency illnesses. The clinic, affiliated with Beth Israel Medical Center, is open Monday through Thursday from 8am to 8pm, Friday from 8am to 7pm, Saturday from 9am to 3pm, and Sunday from 9am to 2pm.

The **NYU Downtown Hospital** offers physician referrals at © **888/698-3362.** You can also try the emergency room at a local hospital. Many hospitals also have walk-in clinics for emergency cases that are not life-threatening; you may not get immediate attention, but you won't pay the high price of an emergency-room visit. We list hospitals and emergency numbers under "Fast Facts: New York City," p. 103.

If you suffer from a chronic illness, consult your doctor before your departure. For conditions like epilepsy, diabetes, or heart problems, wear a **MedicAlert identification tag** (© **888/633-4298;** www.medicalert.org), which will immediately alert doctors to your condition and give them access to your records through MedicAlert's 24-hour hot line.

Pack **prescription medications** in their original containers in your carry-on luggage. Also bring along copies of your prescriptions in case you lose your pills or run out. Don't forget an extra pair of contact lenses or prescription glasses.

If you have dental problems on the road, a service known as **1-800-DENTIST** (© **800/336-8478**) will provide the name of a local dentist.

SAFETY
STAYING SAFE

The FBI consistently rates New York City as one of the safest large cities in the United States, but it is still a large city and crime most definitely exists. Here are a few tips for staying safe in New York:

- Trust your instincts, because they're usually right.
- You'll rarely be hassled, but it's always best to walk with a sense of purpose and self-confidence. Don't stop in the middle of the sidewalk to pull out and peruse your map.
- Anywhere in the city, if you find yourself on a deserted street that feels unsafe, it probably is; leave as quickly as possible.
- If you do find yourself accosted by someone with or without a weapon, remember to keep your anger in check and that the most reasonable response (maddening though it may be) is not to resist.

6 Specialized Travel Resources

TRAVELERS WITH DISABILITIES

New York is more accessible to travelers with disabilities than ever before. The city's bus system is wheelchair friendly, and most of the major sightseeing attractions are easily accessible. Even so, **always call first** to be sure that the places you want to go to are fully accessible.

Most hotels are ADA-compliant, with suitable rooms for wheelchair-bound travelers as well as those with other disabilities. But before you book, **ask lots of questions based on your needs.**

Many city hotels are in older buildings that have had to be modified to meet requirements; still, elevators and bathrooms can be on the small side, and other impediments may exist. If you have mobility issues, you'll probably do best to book one of the city's newer hotels, which tend to be more spacious and accommodating. At **www.access-able.com** (see below), you'll find links to New York's best accessible accommodations (click on "World Destinations"). Some Broadway theaters and other performance venues provide total wheelchair accessibility; others provide partial accessibility. Many also offer lower-priced tickets for theatergoers with disabilities and their companions, though you'll need to check individual policies and reserve in advance. **Hospital Audiences, Inc.** (© 212/ 575-7676; www.hospitalaudiences.org) arranges attendance and provides details about accessibility at cultural institutions as well as cultural events adapted for people with disabilities. Services include "Describe!," which allows visually impaired theatergoers to enjoy theater events; and the invaluable **HAI Hot Line** (© 212/575-7676), which offers accessibility information for hotels, restaurants, attractions, cultural venues, and much more. This nonprofit organization also publishes *Access for All*, a guidebook on accessibility, available free-of-charge on the website, www.hospitalaudiences.org.

Another terrific source for travelers with disabilities who are coming to New York City is **Big Apple Greeter** (© 212/ 669-8159; www.bigapplegreeter.org). All of its employees are extremely well versed in accessibility issues. They can provide a resource list of city agencies that serve those with disabilities, and sometimes have special discounts available to theater and music performances. Big Apple Greeter even offers one-to-one tours that pair volunteers with visitors with disabilities; they can even introduce you to the public transportation system if you like. Reserve at least 1 week ahead.

GETTING AROUND Super Shuttle-Express Shuttle USA (© 800/451-0455 or 212/315-3006; www.supershuttle.com) operates minibuses with lifts from Newark airports to Midtown hotels by reservation; arrange pickup 3 or 4 days in advance. **Olympia Trails** (© 877/894-9155 or 212/964-6233; www.coachusa. com/olympia provides service from Newark Airport, with half-price fares for travelers with disabilities (be sure to pre-purchase your tickets to guarantee the discount fare, as drivers can't sell discounted tickets). Not all buses are appropriately equipped, so call ahead for the daily schedule of accessible buses (press "0" to reach a real person).

Taxis are required to carry people who have folding wheelchairs and service dogs. However, don't be surprised if they don't run each other down trying to get to you; even though you shouldn't have to, you may have to wait a bit for a friendly (or fare-desperate) driver to come along.

Public buses are an inexpensive and easy way to get around New York. All buses' back doors are supposed to be equipped with wheelchair lifts (though the city has had complaints that not all are in working order). Buses also "kneel," lowering their front steps for people who have difficulty boarding. Passengers with disabilities pay half-price fares ($1). The **subway** isn't yet fully wheelchair accessible, but a list of about 30 accessible subway stations and a guide to wheelchair-accessible subway itineraries is on the MTA website. Call (C) **718/596-8585** for bus and subway transit info or go online to www.mta. nyc.ny.us/nyct and click on the wheelchair symbol.

You're better off not trying to rent your own car to get around the city. But if you consider it the best mode of transportation for you, **Wheelchair Getaways** ((C) **800/642-2042** or 800/344-5005; www.wheelchairgetaways.com) rents specialized vans with wheelchair lifts and other features for travelers with disabilities throughout the New York metropolitan area.

Organizations that offer a vast range of resources and assistance to disabled travelers include **MossRehab** ((C) **800/CALL-MOSS;** www.mossresourcenet.org); the **American Foundation for the Blind (AFB;** (C) **800/232-5463;** www.afb.org); and **SATH (Society for Accessible Travel & Hospitality;** (C) **212/447-7284;** www.sath.org). **AirAmbulanceCard.com** is now partnered with SATH and allows you to preselect top-notch hospitals in case of an emergency.

Access-Able Travel Source ((C) **303/ 232-2979;** www.access-able.com) offers a database on travel agents from around the world with experience in accessible travel; destination-specific access information; and links to such resources as service animals, equipment rentals, and access guides.

Many travel agencies offer customized tours and itineraries for travelers with disabilities. Among them are **Flying Wheels Travel** ((C) **507/451-5005;** www.flying wheelstravel.com); and **Accessible Journeys** ((C) **800/846-4537** or 610/521-0339; www.disabilitytravel.com).

Flying with Disability (www.flying-with-disability.org) is a comprehensive information source on airplane travel. **Avis Rent a Car** ((C) **888/879-4273**) has an "Avis Access" program that offers services for customers with special travel needs. These include specially outfitted vehicles with swivel seats, spinner knobs, and hand controls; mobility scooter rentals; and accessible bus service. Be sure to reserve well in advance.

Also check out the quarterly magazine **Emerging Horizons** (www.emerging horizons.com), available by subscription ($16.95 year U.S.; $21.95 outside U.S).

The "Accessible Travel" link at **Mobility-Advisor.com** (www.mobility-advisor.com) offers a variety of travel resources to disabled persons.

British travelers should contact **Holiday Care** ((C) **0845-124-9971** in UK only; www.holidaycare.org.uk) to access travel information and resources for disabled and elderly people.

GLBT TRAVELERS

Gay and lesbian culture is as much a part of New York's basic identity as yellow cabs, high-rises, and Broadway theater. Indeed, in a city with one of the world's largest, loudest, and most powerful GLBT populations, homosexuality is squarely in the mainstream. So city hotels tend to be neutral on the issue, and gay couples shouldn't have a problem. Check out "The Gay & Lesbian Scene" in chapter 10 for nightlife suggestions.

All over Manhattan, but especially in neighborhoods like the **West Village** (particularly Christopher St., famous the world over as the main drag of New York gay-male life) and **Chelsea** (especially Eighth Ave. from 16th to 23rd sts., and W. 17th to 19th sts. from Fifth to Eighth aves.), shops, services, and restaurants have a lesbian and gay flavor. The **Oscar Wilde Bookshop,** 15 Christopher St. ((C) **212/ 255-8097;** www.oscarwildebooks.com), is the city's best gay and lesbian bookstore and a good source for information on the city's gay community.

The **Lesbian, Gay, Bisexual & Transgender Community Center,** familiarly known as "The Center," is at 208 W. 13th St., between Seventh and Eighth avenues (© **212/620-7310;** www. gaycenter.org). The center is the meeting place for more than 400 lesbian, gay, and bisexual organizations. You can check the online events calendar, which lists hundreds of happenings—lectures, dances, concerts, readings, films—or call for the latest. Their site offers links to gay-friendly hotels and guesthouses in and around New York, plus tons of other information; the staff is also friendly and helpful in person or over the phone.

Other good sources for lesbian and gay events are the two free weekly newspapers, *Gay City News* (www.gaycitynews.com) and the *New York Blade* (www.nyblade. com), and the free glossy magazines *HX* (www.hx.com), *Next* (www.nextmagazine. com) and *GONYC* (www.gomag.com), which is lesbian-oriented. You'll also find lots of information on their websites.

The weekly *Time Out New York* (www.timeoutny.com) boasts a terrific gay and lesbian section. The Center (see above) publishes a monthly guide listing many events (also listed on its website).

In addition, there are lesbian and gay musical events, such as performances by the **New York City Gay Men's Chorus** (© 703/647-8020; www.nycgmc.org); health programs sponsored by the **Gay Men's Health Crisis (GMHC;** © 800/ AIDS-NYC or 212/807-6655; www. gmhc.org); the **Gay & Lesbian National Hot Line** (© 212/989-0999; www. glnh.org), offering peer counseling and information on upcoming events; and many other organizations.

The **International Gay and Lesbian Travel Association (IGLTA;** © 800/448-8550 or 954/776-2626; www.iglta.org) is the trade association for the gay and lesbian travel industry, and offers an online directory of gay- and lesbian-friendly travel businesses and tour operators.

Many agencies offer tours and travel itineraries specifically for gay and lesbian travelers. **Above and Beyond Tours** (© **800/397-2681;** www.abovebeyond tours.com) are gay Australia tour specialists. San Francisco–based **Now, Voyager** (© **800/255-6951;** www.nowvoyager. com) offers worldwide trips and cruises and **Olivia** (© **800/631-6277;** www. olivia.com) offers lesbian cruises and resort vacations.

Gay.com Travel (© **800/929-2268** or 415/644-8044; www.gay.com/travel or www.outandabout.com) is an online successor to the popular *Out & About* print magazine. It provides regularly updated information about gay-owned, gay-oriented, and gay-friendly lodging, dining, sightseeing, nightlife, and shopping establishments in every important destination worldwide. British travelers should click on the "Travel" link at **www. uk.gay.com** for advice and gay-friendly trip ideas.

The Canadian website **GayTraveler (gaytraveler.ca)** offers ideas and advice for gay travel all over the world.

The following travel guides are available at bookstores, or you can order them online: *Spartacus International Gay Guide, 35th Edition* (Bruno Gmünder Verlag; www.spartacusworld.com/ gayguide) and *Odysseus: The International Gay Travel Planner, 17th Edition* (www.odyusa.com); and the *Damron* guides (www.damron.com), with annual books for gay men and lesbians.

SENIOR TRAVEL

Members of **AARP,** 601 E St. NW, Washington, DC 20049 (© **888/687-2277;** www.aarp.org), get discounts on hotels, airfares, and car rentals. AARP offers members a wide range of benefits, including *AARP: The Magazine* and a newsletter. Anyone over 50 can join.

New York subway and bus fares are half-price ($1) for people 65 and older. Many museums and sights (and some theaters and performance halls) offer discounted admittance and tickets to seniors, so don't be shy about asking. Always bring an ID card, especially if you've kept your youthful glow.

Many hotels offer senior discounts; **Choice Hotels** (which include Comfort Inns, some of my favorite affordable Midtown hotels; see chapter 7, "Where to Stay"), for example, gives 30% off their published rates to anyone over 50, provided you book your room through their nationwide toll-free reservations number (that is, not directly with the hotels or through a travel agent). For a complete list of Choice Hotels, visit **www.hotelchoice.com.**

Many reliable agencies and organizations target the 50-plus market. **Elderhostel** (℃ 800/454-5768; www.elderhostel.org) arranges worldwide study programs (including some in New York City) for those aged 55 and over.

Recommended publications offering travel resources and discounts for seniors include: the quarterly magazine *Travel 50 & Beyond* (www.travel50andbeyond.com) and the bestselling paperback *Unbelievably Good Deals and Great Adventures That You Absolutely Can't Get Unless You're Over 50 2005–2006, 16th Edition* (McGraw-Hill), by Joann Rattner Heilman.

FAMILY TRAVEL

To locate accommodations, restaurants, and attractions that are particularly kid-friendly, refer to the "Kids" icon throughout this guide.

For more extensive recommendations, you might want to purchase a copy of *Frommer's New York City with Kids,* an entire guidebook dedicated to family visits to the Big Apple.

Good bets for the most timely information include the "Weekend" section of Friday's *New York Times,* which has a section dedicated to the week's best kid-friendly activities; the weekly *New York* magazine, which has a full calendar of children's events in its listings section; and *Time Out New York,* which also has a weekly kids section with a bit of an alternative bent. The *Big Apple Parents' Paper* is usually available, for free, at children's stores and other locations in Manhattan; you can also find good information from the folks behind the paper at **www.parentsknow.com.**

The first place to look for **babysitting** is in your hotel (better yet, ask about babysitting when you reserve). Many hotels have babysitting services or will provide you with lists of reliable sitters. If this doesn't pan out, call the **Baby Sitters' Guild** (℃ 212/682-0227; www.babysittersguild.com). The sitters are licensed, insured, and bonded, and can even take your child on outings.

Familyhostel (℃ 800/733-9753; www.learn.unh.edu/pcw/index.php) takes the whole family, including kids ages 8 to 15, on moderately priced U.S. and international learning vacations. Lectures, field trips, and sightseeing are guided by a team of academics.

Recommended family travel websites include **Family Travel Forum** (www.familytravelforum.com), a comprehensive site that offers customized trip planning; **Family Travel Network** (www.familytravelnetwork.com), an online magazine providing travel tips; **TravelWithYourKids.com** (www.travelwithyourkids.com), a comprehensive site written by parents for parents offering advice for long-distance and international travel with children.

AFRICAN-AMERICAN TRAVELERS

Black Travel Online (www.blacktravelonline.com) posts news on upcoming events and includes links to articles and travel-booking sites. **Soul of America**

(www.soulofamerica.com) is a comprehensive website, with travel tips, event and family-reunion postings, and sections on historically black beach resorts and active vacations.

Agencies and organizations that provide resources for black travelers include: **Rodgers Travel** (© 800/825-1775; www. rodgerstravel.com), the **African American Association of Innkeepers International** (© 877/422-5777; www.africanamerican inns.com), and **Henderson Travel & Tours** (© 800/327-2309 or 301/650-5700; www.hendersontravel.com), which has specialized in trips to Africa since 1957. For more information, check out the following collections and guides: *Go Girl: The Black Woman's Guide to Travel & Adventure* (Eighth Mountain Press), a compilation of travel essays by writers including Jill Nelson and Audre Lorde; *The African American Travel Guide,* by Wayne Robinson (Hunter Publishing; www.hunterpublishing.com); *Steppin' Out,* by Carla Labat (Avalon); *Travel and Enjoy Magazine* (© 866/266-6211;

www.travelandenjoy.com); and *Pathfinders Magazine* (© 877/977-PATH; www. pathfinderstravel.com), which includes articles on everything from Rio de Janeiro to Ghana as well as information on upcoming ski, diving, golf, and tennis trips.

STUDENT TRAVEL

The **International Student Travel Confederation (ISTC;** www.istc.org) was formed in 1949 to make travel around the world more affordable for students. Check out its website for comprehensive travel services information and details on how to get an **International Student Identity Card (ISIC),** which qualifies students for substantial savings on rail passes, plane tickets, entrance fees, and more. It also provides students with basic health and life insurance and a 24-hour helpline. The card is valid for a maximum of 18 months. You can apply for the card online or in person at **STA Travel** (© 800/781-4040 in North America; www. statravel.com), the biggest student travel agency in the world; check out the website

---

Frommers.com: The Complete Travel Resource

It should go without saying, but we highly recommend **Frommers.com**, voted Best Travel Site by *PC Magazine*. We think you'll find our expert advice and tips; independent reviews of hotels, restaurants, attractions, and preferred shopping and nightlife venues; vacation giveaways; and an online booking tool indispensable before, during, and after your travels. We publish the complete contents of over 128 travel guides in our **Destinations** section covering nearly 3,800 places worldwide to help you plan your trip. Each weekday, we publish original articles reporting on **Deals and News** via our free **Frommers.com Newsletter** to help you save time and money and travel smarter. We're betting you'll find our new **Events** listings (http://events. frommers.com) an invaluable resource; it's an up-to-the-minute roster of what's happening in cities everywhere—including concerts, festivals, lectures and more. We've also added weekly **Podcasts, interactive maps,** and hundreds of new images across the site. Check out our **Travel Talk** area featuring **Message Boards** where you can join in conversations with thousands of fellow Frommer's travelers and post your trip report once you return.

to locate STA Travel offices worldwide. If you're no longer a student but are still under 26, you can get an **International Youth Travel Card (IYTC)** from the same people, which entitles you to some discounts. **Travel CUTS** (℡ 800/592-2887; www.travelcuts.com) offers similar services for both Canadians and U.S. residents. Irish students may prefer to turn to **USIT** (℡ 01/602-1904; www.usit.ie), an Ireland-based specialist in student, youth, and independent travel.

7 Staying Connected

TELEPHONES

Generally, hotel surcharges on long-distance and local calls are astronomical, so you're better off using your **cellphone** or a **public pay telephone.** Many convenience groceries and packaging services sell **prepaid calling cards** in denominations up to $50; for international visitors these can be the least expensive way to call home. Many public pay phones at airports now accept American Express, MasterCard, and Visa credit cards. **Local calls** made from pay phones in most locales cost either 25¢ or 35¢ (no pennies, please).

Most long-distance and international calls can be dialed directly from any phone. **For calls within the United States and to Canada,** dial 1 followed by the area code and the seven-digit number. **For other international calls,** dial 011 followed by the country code, city code, and the number you are calling.

Calls to area codes **800, 888, 877,** and **866** are toll-free. However, calls to area codes **700** and **900** (chat lines, bulletin boards, "dating" services, and so on) can be very expensive—usually a charge of 95¢ to $3 or more per minute, and they sometimes have minimum charges that can run as high as $15 or more.

For **reversed-charge or collect calls,** and for person-to-person calls, dial the number 0 then the area code and number; an operator will answer, and you should specify whether you are calling collect, person-to-person, or both. If your operator-assisted call is international, ask for the overseas operator.

For **local directory assistance** ("information"), dial 411; for long-distance information, dial 1, then the appropriate area code and 555-1212.

CELLPHONES

Just because your cellphone works at home doesn't mean it'll work everywhere in the U.S. (thanks to our nation's fragmented cellphone system). It's a good bet that your phone will work in major cities, but take a look at your wireless company's coverage map on its website before heading out; T-Mobile, Sprint, and Nextel are particularly weak in rural areas. If you need to stay in touch at a destination where you know your phone won't work, **rent** a phone that does from **InTouch USA** (℡ 800/872-7626; www.intouchglobal.com) or a rental car location, but beware that you'll pay $1 a minute or more for airtime.

If you're not from the U.S., you'll be appalled at the poor reach of our **GSM (Global System for Mobile Communications) wireless network,** which is used by much of the rest of the world. Your phone will probably work in most major U.S. cities; it definitely won't work in many rural areas. To see where GSM phones work in the U.S., check out www.t-mobile.com/coverage. And you may or may not be able to send SMS (text messages) home.

INTERNET/E-MAIL
WITHOUT YOUR OWN
COMPUTER

To find cybercafés in New York City, check **www.cybercaptive.com** and **www.cybercafe.com**. (We also recommend some places in the box below).

Most major airports have **Internet kiosks** that provide basic Web access for a per-minute fee that's usually higher than cybercafe prices. Steer clear of them if you can. Check out copy shops like **Kinko's** (FedEx Kinkos), which offers computer stations with fully loaded software (as well as Wi-Fi), though Kinkos generally doesn't have the cheapest 'net access in town.

WITH YOUR OWN COMPUTER

More and more hotels, resorts, airports, cafes, and retailers are going Wi-Fi (wireless fidelity), becoming "hotspots" that offer free high-speed Wi-Fi access or charge a small fee for usage. Wi-Fi is found in campgrounds, RV parks, and in some places, even covers entire towns. Most laptops sold today have built-in wireless capability. To find public Wi-Fi

---

Where to Check Your E-mail in the City That Never Sleeps

If your hotel doesn't offer free access to its business center or a terminal in the lobby to check your email (and many do), where can you go to check it if you don't have a computer with you?

All branches of the **New York Public Library** (www.nypl.org) feature computers that offer free access to the Internet, electronic databases, library catalogs and Microsoft Office.

More free access is available at the **Times Square Visitors Center,** 1560 Broadway, between 46th and 47th streets (© **212/768-1560**; daily 8am–8pm), has computer terminals that you can use to send e-mails courtesy of Yahoo!; you can even send an electronic postcard with a photo of yourself home to Mom.

Open 24/7 in the heart of Times Square, **easyInternetcafé** ✹, 234 W. 42nd St., between Seventh and Eighth avenues (© **212/398-0775**; www.easy everything.com/map/nyc1.html), is the first stateside branch of a worldwide chain of Internet cafes. Boasting flat-screen monitors and a superfast T-3 connection, this mammoth place makes accessing the Internet cheap through the economy of scale: Access is available for as little as $1, and the length of time that buck buys you fluctuates depending on the occupancy at the time you log on. This will generally work out to the cheapest Web time you can buy in the city.

CyberCafe (www.cyber-cafe.com)—in Times Square at 250 W. 49th St., between Broadway and Eighth Avenue (© **212/333-4109**), and in SoHo at 273 Lafayette St., at Prince Street (© **212/334-5140**)—is more expensive at $6.40 per half-hour, with a half-hour minimum (you're billed $3.20 for every subsequent 15 min.). But their T1 connectivity gives you superfast access, and they offer a full range of other cyber, copy, fax, and printing services.

FedEx Kinko's (www.kinkos.com) charges 30¢ per minute ($15 per hour) and there are dozens of locations around town. In addition, an increasing number of delis and copy shops frequently stick an "Internet" sign in the window, and you can log on in a unit wedged into a corner next to the ATM for a couple bucks, while you drink your genuine New York City deli coffee.

Online Traveler's Toolbox

Veteran travelers usually carry some essential items to make their trips easier. Following is a selection of handy online tools to bookmark and use.

- **Airplane Food** (www.airlinemeals.net)
- **Airplane Seating** (www.seatguru.com; and www.airlinequality.com)
- **Foreign Languages for Travelers** (www.travlang.com)
- **Maps** (www.mapquest.com)
- **Subway Navigator** (www.subwaynavigator.com)
- **HopStop.com** (www.hopstop.com) Helps you navigate public transit in NYC, Washington, Boston, Chicago, and San Francisco.
- **Time and Date** (www.timeanddate.com)
- **Travel Warnings** (http://travel.state.gov, www.fco.gov.uk/travel, www.voyage.gc.ca, www.dfat.gov.au/consular/advice)
- **Universal Currency Converter** (www.xe.com/ucc)
- **Visa ATM Locator** (www.visa.com), **MasterCard ATM Locator** (www.mastercard.com)
- **Weather** (www.intellicast.com and www.weather.com)

hotspots at your destination, go to **www.jiwire.com**; its Hotspot Finder holds the world's largest directory of public wireless hotspots.

For dial-up access, most business-class hotels in the U.S. offer dataports for laptop modems, and a few thousand hotels in the U.S. and Europe now offer free high-speed Internet access.

Wherever you go, bring a **connection kit** of the right power and phone adapters, a spare phone cord, and a spare Ethernet network cable—or find out if your hotel supplies them to guests.

8 Packages for the Independent Traveler

Package tours are simply a way to buy the airfare, accommodations, and other elements of your trip (such as car rentals, airport transfers, and sometimes even activities) at the same time and often at discounted prices.

One good source of package deals is the airlines themselves. Most major airlines offer air/land packages, including **American Airlines Vacations** (© 800/321-2121; www.aavacations.com), **Delta Vacations** (© 800/654-6559; www.deltavacations.com), **Continental Airlines Vacations** (© 800/301-3800; www.covacations.com), and **United Vacations** (© 888/854-3899; www.united vacations.com). Several big **online travel agencies**—Expedia, Travelocity, Orbitz, Site59, and Lastminute.com—also do a brisk business in packages.

Travel packages are also listed in the travel section of your local Sunday newspaper. Or check ads in the national travel magazines such as *Arthur Frommer's Budget Travel Magazine*, *Travel & Leisure*, *National Geographic Traveler*, and *Condé Nast Traveler*.

Tips Ask Before You Go

Before you invest in a package deal or an escorted tour:

- Always ask about the **cancellation policy.** Can you get your money back? Is there a deposit required?
- Ask about the **accommodations choices and prices** for each. Then look up the hotels' reviews in a Frommer's guide and check their rates online for your specific dates of travel. Also find out what types of rooms are offered.
- Request a complete **schedule.** (Escorted tours only.)
- Ask about the **size** and demographics of the group. (For escorted tours only.)
- Discuss what is included in the **price** (transportation, meals, tips, airport transfers, and so on). (For escorted tours only.)
- Finally, look for **hidden expenses.** Ask whether airport departure fees and taxes, for example, are included in the total cost—they rarely are.

---

9 Escorted General-Interest Tours

Escorted tours are structured group tours with a group leader. The price usually includes everything from airfare to hotels, meals, tours, admission costs, and local transportation.

Despite the fact that escorted tours require big deposits and predetermine hotels, restaurants, and itineraries, many people derive security and peace of mind from the structure they offer. Escorted tours—whether they're navigated by bus, motor coach, train, or boat—let travelers sit back and enjoy the trip without having to drive or worry about details. They take you to the maximum number of sights in the minimum amount of time with the least amount of hassle. They're particularly convenient for people with limited mobility and they can be a great way to make new friends.

On the downside, you'll have little opportunity for serendipitous interactions with locals. The tours can be jam-packed with activities, leaving little room for individual sightseeing, whim, or adventure—plus they often focus on the heavily touristed sites, so you miss out on many a lesser-known gem.

AQ: Give us a couple of firms that offer tours to New York City. Or go to specific NYC events.

---

10 Tips on Accommodations
SURFING FOR HOTELS

In addition to the online travel booking sites **Travelocity, Expedia, Orbitz, Priceline,** and **Hotwire,** you can book hotels through **Hotels.com; Quikbook** (www.quikbook.com); and **Travelaxe** (www.travelaxe.net).

HotelChatter.com is a daily webzine offering smart coverage and critiques of hotels worldwide. Go to **TripAdvisor.com**

or **HotelShark.com** for helpful independent consumer reviews of hotels and resort properties.

It's a good idea to **get a confirmation number** and **make a printout** of any online booking transaction.

Tips for Digital Travel Photography

- **Take along a spare camera—or two.** Even if you've been anointed the "official" photographer of your travel group, encourage others in your party to carry their own cameras and provide fresh perspectives—and backup. Your photographic "second unit" may include you in a few shots so you're not the invisible person of the trip.

- **Stock up on digital film cards.** At home, it's easy to copy pictures from your memory cards to your computer as they fill up. During your travels, cards seem to fill up more quickly. Take along enough digital film for your entire trip or, at a minimum, enough for at least a few days' of shooting. At intervals, you can copy images to CDs. Many camera stores and souvenir shops offer this service, and a growing number of mass merchandisers have walk-up kiosks you can use to make prints or create CDs while you travel.

- **Share and share alike.** No need to wait until you get home to share your photos. You can upload a gallery's worth to an online photo sharing service. Just find an Internet café where the computers have card readers, or connect your camera to the computer with a cable. You can find online photo sharing services that cost little or nothing at **www.clickherefree.com**. You can also use America Online's Your Pictures service, or commercial enterprises that give you free or low-cost photo sharing: Kodak's EasyShare gallery (**www.kodak.com**), Yahoo! Photos (**www.photos.yahoo.com**), Snapfish (**www.snapfish.com**), or Shutterfly (**www.shutterfly.com**).

- **Add voice annotations to your photos.** Many digital cameras allow you to add voice annotations to your shots after they're taken. These serve as excellent reminders and documentation. One castle or cathedral may look like another after a long tour; your voice notes will help you distinguish them.

- **Experiment!** Travel is a great time to try out new techniques. Take photos at night, resting your camera on a handy wall or other support as your self-timer trips the shutter for a long exposure. Try close-ups of flowers, crafts, wildlife, or maybe the exotic cuisine you're about to consume. Discover action photography—shoot the countryside from trains, buses, or cars. With a digital camera, you can experiment and then erase your mistakes.

—From Travel Photography Digital Field Guide, 1st edition
(Wiley Publishing, Inc., 2006)

SAVING ON YOUR HOTEL ROOM

The **rack rate** is the maximum rate that a hotel charges for a room. Hardly anybody pays this price, however, except in high season or on holidays. To lower the cost of your room:

- **Ask about special rates or other discounts.** You may qualify for corporate, student, military, senior, frequent flier, trade union, or other discounts.
- **Dial direct.** When booking a room in a chain hotel, you'll often get a better deal by calling the individual hotel's reservation desk rather than the chain's main number.
- **Book online.** Many hotels offer Internet-only discounts, or supply rooms to Priceline, Hotwire, or Expedia at rates much lower than the ones you can get through the hotel itself.
- **Remember the law of supply and demand.** Resort hotels are most crowded and therefore most expensive on weekends, so discounts are usually available for midweek stays. Business hotels in downtown locations are busiest during the week, so you can expect big discounts over the weekend.
- **Look into group or long-stay discounts.** If you come as part of a large group, you should be able to negotiate a bargain rate. Likewise, if you're planning a long stay (at least 5 days), you might qualify for a discount. As a general rule, expect 1 night free after a 7-night stay.
- **Sidestep excess surcharges and hidden costs.** Many hotels have the unpleasant practice of nickel-and-diming its guests with opaque surcharges. When you book a room, ask what is included in the room rate, and what is extra. Avoid dialing direct from hotel phones, which can have exorbitant rates. And don't be tempted by the room's minibar offerings: Most hotels charge through the nose for water, soda, and snacks. Finally, ask about local taxes and service charges, which can increase the cost of a room by 15% or more.

LANDING THE BEST ROOM

Somebody has to get the best room in the house. It might as well be you. You can start by joining the hotel's frequent-guest program, which may make you eligible for upgrades. A hotel-branded credit card usually gives its owner "silver" or "gold" status in frequent-guest programs for free. Always ask about a corner room. They're often larger and quieter, with more windows and light, and they often cost the same as standard rooms. When you make your reservation, ask if the hotel is renovating; if it is, request a room away from the construction. Ask about nonsmoking rooms, rooms with views, and rooms with twin, queen- or king-size beds. If you're a light sleeper, request a quiet room away from vending machines, elevators, restaurants, bars, and discos. Ask for a room that has been most recently renovated or redecorated.

If you aren't happy with your room when you arrive, ask for another one. Most lodgings will be willing to accommodate you.

11 Recommended Books, Films & Music

BOOKS

For the definitive history of the birth of New York City to the end of the 19th century, there is no better read than the Pulitzer Prize–winning *Gotham: A History of New York City to 1898*, by Edwin R. Burrows and Mike Wallace (Oxford University Press). Another recommended historical look at the growth of New York City, this one told in a breezy narrative tone, is *The Epic of New York City: A Narrative History,* by Edward Robb Ellis (Kodansha).

Luc Sante's *Low Life: Lures and Snares of Old New York* (Vintage Departures) details the bad old days of brothels, drug dens, and gambling saloons in New York in the early 20th century—it's a lively, fascinating read.

One of master biographer Robert Caro's early works, *The Power Broker: Robert Moses and the Fall of New York* (Random House) focuses on how the vision of master dealmaker Robert Moses transformed New York to what it became in the second half of the 20th century.

The 2004-published *Downtown,* by Pete Hamill (Little Brown & Co.), is as concise a history of the area to the south of Times Square as you will find—and told in Hamill's typically breezy and gritty style, while Hamill's 2003-novel *Forever,* chronicles the three centuries of a man who has been given the gift of eternal life as long as he never leaves the island of Manhattan. In *The Great Bridge: The Epic Story of the Building of the Brooklyn Bridge* (Simon & Schuster), author David McCullough devotes his estimable talents to the story of the building of the Brooklyn Bridge.

The companion to the PBS Series (see below) *New York,* by Ric Burns, Lisa Ades, and James Sanders (Knopf), uses lavish photographs and illustrations to show the growth of New York City.

My all-time favorite book about New York is a children's classic called *This Is New York* (Universe Publishing), written and illustrated by M. Sasek in 1960. The book was recently reissued and, with an update added, is as fresh as it was all those years ago.

If the city is looking a little too clean and well scrubbed for you, pick up a copy of the new anthology *Manhattan Noir* (Akashic Books, 2006).

FILMS

There are not many places as cinematic as New York City. Filmmakers sometimes think of the city as a character unto itself. The list of movies in which New York plays a crucial role are too many to mention, but here are some of the top New York City movies that are worth renting before you visit.

Possibly the best New York City promotional film is the musical **On the Town,** with Gene Kelly and Frank Sinatra, about three sailors with 24 hours' leave spent exploring Gotham. Shot on location, all the landmarks were captured in beautiful Technicolor.

Woody Allen is known as a New York filmmaker and proudly shoots almost all his films in the city. One of his best—and a good, but maybe a bit dated, look at neurotic New York—is *Annie Hall.*

Following in Woody Allen's footsteps are director Rob Reiner and writer Nora Ephron, who made *When Harry Met Sally.* It's sort of a poor-man's *Annie Hall* but a gorgeous cinematic tribute to New York. The famous "I'll have what she's having" scene was filmed in **Katz's Delicatessen** (p. 170).

"I love this dirty town," says Burt Lancaster in the gritty, crackling *Sweet Smell of Success.* In the beautifully photographed black-and-white movie, Lancaster plays malicious gossip columnist J. J. Hunsecker, and Tony Curtis is perfectly despicable as the groveling publicist Sidney Falco.

Another filmmaker always identified with New York is Martin Scorsese. He has made many films where New York plays a central role, from *Mean Streets* to *Gangs of New York,* which was actually filmed in Italy. But the one film in which New York is a character, and not a very flattering one, is *Taxi Driver.* The Academy Award–nominated 1976 movie about an alienated and psychotic taxi driver is tough and bloody, but to see images of seedy Times Square as it was before its recent reincarnation, there is no better film.

The best history of New York on video is the Ric Burns documentary *New York*, which aired on PBS. The seven-disc, 14-hour DVD (also available on VHS) is a must-see for anyone interested in the evolution of this great city.

Suggested New York City Itineraries

I've lived in New York for more than half my life and I still haven't seen it all. That's not because I don't want to, it's just there is so much to see. So it's understandable if you feel a bit overwhelmed by all the options. Seeing the best of New York requires endurance, patience, perseverance, good walking shoes, a $7 daily MetroCard Fun Pass (p. 96), and a map of the subway system. For some attractions—like the Empire State Building or a Broadway play—you should score tickets *before* you come to New York to avoid long lines or a disappointing shutout. Besides your own two feet, the subway will be your best bet to cover the most ground. I also recommend a few bus routes that will not only get you to some of New York's best attractions, but will also act as your own tour bus on which you'll see sights on the way.

1 The Best of NYC in 1 Day

If you want to have any chance of seeing the best of New York in just 1 day, you need to get an early start. You also need a plan of attack. You don't want to waste time zigzagging around the city to various attractions. So I recommend taking on New York by thirds. On the first third, we will concentrate on the best of midtown Manhattan. **Start:** *Pier 83 on 42nd St.*

❶ Circle Line Sightseeing Cruise 𝒜𝒜

By starting your day on the water on this 2-hour half-island cruise, you'll get a good overview of Manhattan. You'll pass by the Statue of Liberty and Ellis Island; see the lower Manhattan skyline; head up the East River, where you will go under the Brooklyn, Manhattan, and Williamsburg bridges; and view the United Nations and the East Side skyline, including the Empire State and Chrysler buildings. See p. 278.

Afterwards, take the M42 42nd Street crosstown bus to Fifth Avenue, where you'll come to the:

❷ New York Public Library 𝒜𝒜

You'll recognize this building by the lion sculptures guarding its gates. Step inside for more grandeur, especially the incredible **Main Reading Rooms,** where you might want to take a break and read the paper (if you have time). While you're here, take a look at the library's backyard, **Bryant Park.** If there are tents up, it means you're here during one of the two Fashion Weeks. Or between November and January, **The Pond** ice skating rink will be up. See p. 262.

❸ Grand Central Terminal 𝒜𝒜

Before stepping into this magnificent working train station, take a look east toward Lexington Avenue and then crane your neck up. You'll see my favorite skyscraper, the **Chrysler Building** 𝒜𝒜. Okay, now enter Grand Central, where approximately 500,000 commuters dash through daily. I hope it's not rush hour . . . but even if it is, you really won't have to worry about colliding with a commuter: The building and the stupendous main concourse were constructed so cleverly that despite the perceived chaos, people rarely bump into each other. You'll want to spend hours examining the beautiful detail throughout the terminal, but you don't have hours to spare. A walk through the main concourse and a look at the sky ceiling will be evidence enough. See p. 238.

---

4 GRAND CENTRAL TERMINAL
You're hungry now and the choices in the Grand Central Terminal dining concourse are plentiful and good. Chow down on anything from Indian food to pizza. Or opt for a heartier (and more expensive!) lunch at the legendary **Oyster Bar & Restaurant** or upstairs overlooking the concourse at **Michael Jordan's—The Steakhouse.** See p. 205 and 184.

---

5 Empire State Building 𝔊𝔊𝔊
It's an 8-block walk down Fifth Avenue from Grand Central Station to the Empire State Building. Let's hope it's a beautiful day because I want your view from the top of this historic structure, the tallest building in New York, to be pristine. You already have your tickets (don't you?), so you don't have to wait at the ticket booth (see box on p. 236 for details). The elevator will zip you up to the 86th story, where you will get a panoramic view of Manhattan. See p. 239.

Take the B or D train uptown to Seventh Avenue. Walk east across 53rd Street to the:

6 Museum of Modern Art 𝔊𝔊
Yes, the $20 suggested admission is outrageous, but this is New York and you are getting used to outrageous. And you'll forget about the admission charge once you peruse the exhibits in this beautiful museum. Airy and expansive, with sky-lit,

open galleries along with smaller, intimate rooms, the museum is one of a kind. See p. 241.

7 Rockefeller Center 𝔊𝔊
A short walk from MoMA is the Rockefeller Center complex. If you are here during the Christmas holidays, you'll fight the crowds for a glimpse of the Christmas tree and the skaters in the small rink. If your timing is right, you might be able to squeeze in the 70-minute NBC Studio Tour. If not, you'll see **Radio City Music Hall** 𝔊 and **30 Rockefeller Plaza** 𝔊. If you did not have advance tickets for the Empire State Building and the line was much too long, take the elevator up 70 floors to **Top of the Rock** 𝔊𝔊 for, arguably, as good a view as you would have at the Empire State Building. Across the street (Fifth Ave.) you'll see **St. Patrick's Cathedral.** See p. 241.

8 Fifth Avenue
Is a street an attraction? When it's one of the most famous in the world, it is. Walk north up Fifth Avenue from Rock Center and pass big-name stores like Saks Fifth Avenue, Henri Bendel, the NBA Store, Tiffany & Co., Cartier, Bergdorf Goodman, FAO Schwarz, and The Apple Store. You'll also see Trump Tower from the popular *Apprentice* TV series. At 59th Street you'll see the ornate Plaza Hotel, which, after extensive renovations will reopen as a hotel/condo in 2008. Across the street you'll see the southern end of Central Park. See p. 89.

---

9 KING COLE BAR
Now would be a good time to rest your legs as well as your senses. Head back down Fifth Avenue a few blocks to the lounge at the St. Regis Hotel. This is where the Bloody Mary was supposedly invented, and it's the perfect place for a late-afternoon or early-evening cocktail. 2 E. 55th St., at Fifth Avenue. ℭ **212/753-4500.** See p. 383.

The Best of NYC in 1 Day

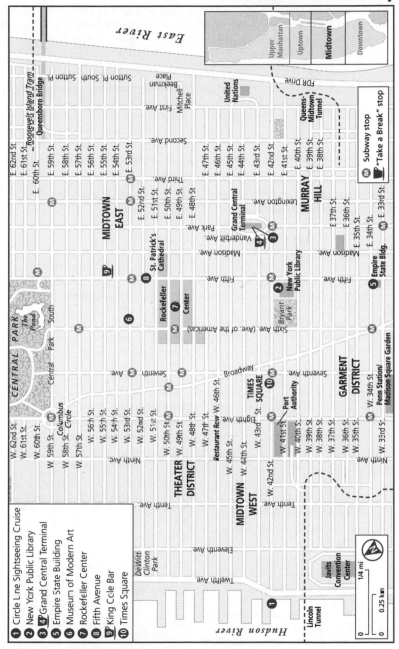

1 Circle Line Sightseeing Cruise
2 New York Public Library
3 Grand Central Terminal
5 Empire State Building
6 Museum of Modern Art
7 Rockefeller Center
8 Fifth Avenue
9 King Cole Bar
10 Times Square

65

⑩ Times Square

You've got tickets for a Broadway show, so before you head into the theater, this is your chance to see what Times Square is all about. The lights are blinding, the crowds are thick, and the noise is infernal, but that's Times Square. There's nowhere like it in the world. But don't linger too long! Broadway curtains rise promptly! See p. 245.

2 The Best of NYC in 2 Days

On your second day, you'll head downtown and explore the city where it began. You'll wander through streets that are as old as any in New York, and some that are curiously towered by ultramodern, gleaming steel-and-glass skyscrapers. Again, you'll want to get a very early start because there is so much to see and always too little time. *Start: Subway: 1 to South Ferry or 4 or 5 to Bowling Green.*

❶ Statue of Liberty 𝕲𝕲𝕲

You saw Lady Liberty on your Circle Line half-island tour yesterday, but now you want to get up close and personal with her. Ferries leave from Battery Park every half-hour beginning at 8:30am. On Liberty Island, you can take one of two tours. The Promenade Tour takes visitors through the monument lobby, past the original torch to the Statue of Liberty exhibit for a 20- to 30-minute ranger-guided tour and then outdoors to the lower promenade. The Observatory Tour incorporates the promenade tour and makes a visit to the pedestal observation platform where you can view the statue's interior framework through a new glass ceiling portal. See p. 244.

❷ Ellis Island 𝕲𝕲

Your Statue of Liberty ferry ticket also includes a stop at Ellis Island; ferries to Ellis Island leave Liberty Island every half-hour. The Immigration Museum is one of the most touching in the city. Incredible, personal details of the immigrant experience are on display, from personal letters and jewelry to battered valises. You could spend all day, but you don't have time! Wander through the Registry room and you'll hear the echoes of hundreds of different languages of immigrants who came through these doors to a better life. See p. 237.

❸ Wall Street

Back in Manhattan, the walk up to the Financial District is not long. Along the way you'll see structures such as **Castle Clinton National Monument,** the remnants of a fort built in 1808 to defend New York Harbor against the British, and the impressive **U.S. Customs House,** which houses the Museum of the American Indian, part of the Smithsonian Institution. Once on Wall Street, stop for a photo-op at the **Federal Hall National Memorial,** with the statue of George Washington in front, and the **New York Stock Exchange,** across the street. Unfortunately, the exchange is no longer open for tours, but if you are a person of some significance, they might let you ring the opening day's bell. See p. 245.

Take the free Downtown Connection bus that travels from Battery Park to South Street Seaport with stops along the way including one at Wall Street. See chapter 5 for details.

❹ South Street Seaport

Here the streets are really old—so old they are rough with cobblestones. This is a 17th-century historic district with restored 18th- and 19th-century buildings still standing. The interesting South Street Seaport Museum will fill you in on more of the 11 square blocks of seafaring history. Also part of the seaport complex is Pier 17, a historic barge that now is the

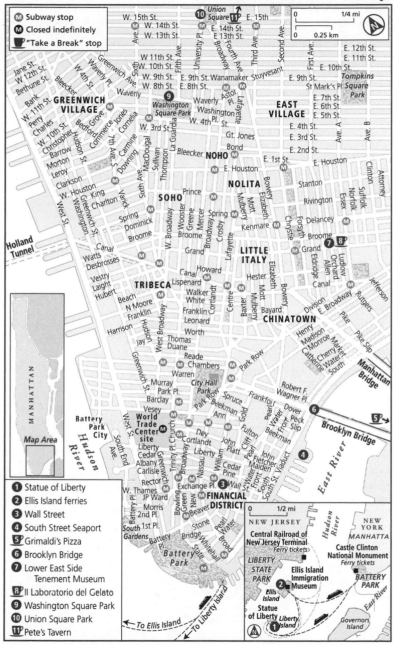

Subway stop

Closed indefinitely

"Take a Break" stop

MANHATTAN

Map Area

1 Statue of Liberty
2 Ellis Island ferries
3 Wall Street
4 South Street Seaport
5 Grimaldi's Pizza
6 Brooklyn Bridge
7 Lower East Side
   Tenement Museum
8 Il Laboratorio del Gelato
9 Washington Square Park
10 Union Square Park
11 Pete's Tavern

67

home to various stores that you are probably very familiar with. See p. 259.

Take the A or C train at Broadway–Nassau Street toward Brooklyn and get off at High Street, the first stop in Brooklyn.

🍵 GRIMALDI'S PIZZERIA

You are now in Brooklyn and probably very hungry. You'll need nourishment for your next adventure, and where better than this famed pizzeria, in the shadow of the Brooklyn Bridge? 19 Old Fulton St., between Front and Water streets. ℂ **718/858-4300.** See p. 196.

---

❻ Brooklyn Bridge 𝕉𝕉𝕉

You have been well fed, so now you have the energy to make the approximately half-hour stroll back to Manhattan across one of the greatest suspended bridges in the world. The view of the Manhattan skyline is spectacular—make sure you have plenty of room in the card of your digital camera. See p. 236.

❼ Lower East Side Tenement Museum 𝕉

When you visited Ellis Island, you learned about the immigrants' struggles to gain entry into this country. Now visit the prototype of a Lower East Side tenement where many of those immigrants lived. The only way to see the museum is by guided tour, which takes place every 40 minutes on weekdays and every half-hour on weekends. See p. 251.

🍵 IL LABORATORIO DEL GELATO

Just across the street from the Lower East Side Tenement Museum is a wonderful ice-cream-and-gelato shop where you can experience a multitude of homemade ice cream and sorbet flavors. Pick up a cone or cup for the walk to the subway. 95 Orchard St., between Broome and Delancey streets. ℂ **212/343-9922.**

Take the F or V train at Second Avenue and Houston Street two stops uptown to West 4th Street.

❾ Washington Square Park

Welcome to the center of Greenwich Village. This neighborhood's bohemian tradition is best represented by this park and the characters in it. On the north end of the park, you'll see a row of elegant late-19th-century town houses and Washington Square Arch, patterned after the Arc de Triomphe in Paris. See p. 277.

❿ Union Square Park

About 10 blocks north of Washington Square Park, you'll find this small but welcome bit of park. And if it is a Monday, Wednesday, Friday, or Saturday, you'll be in for a treat because the city's best greenmarket, the **Union Square Greenmarket** 𝕉𝕉, will be buzzing with activity. See p. 276.

🍵 PETE'S TAVERN

A few blocks east of Union Square Park is Pete's Tavern, the city's oldest continually operating establishment. Look familiar? You may have seen it in an episode of *Seinfeld, Sex and the City,* or *Law & Order* or else on the big screen. Stop in for a pint to quench your thirst after that full day of walking. 129 E. 18th St. (at Irving Place). ℂ **212/473-7676.** www.petestavern.com. Subway: L, N, R, 4, 5, 6, to 14th St./Union Sq. See p. 374.

3 The Best of NYC in 3 Days

You've seen a sizable chunk of the best of Manhattan, but there's still plenty left to fill up a day. We haven't even gotten to some of the city's great museums or that urban oasis called Central Park. We'll do all that and maybe even escape to the wilds of the Bronx before the day is done. If the weather's nice, plan on a picnic in Central Park. *Start: B or C to 72nd Street.*

➊ The Dakota

We'll start our day in front of this 1884-built apartment building. This was standing when the only thing around it was greenery. The building has a dubious past: It was here where John Lennon lived (and where Yoko Ono still lives) and where he was shot and killed. Across the street in Central Park is **Strawberry Fields** *✿*, named in honor of the former Beatle; fans gather here every year on the anniversary of his death, December 8. See p. 260.

➋ American Museum of Natural History *✿✿✿*

Don't try to cover too much ground at this 4-square-block museum; you'll be here all day. Pick a few of the highlights, like the Fossils Halls where the dinosaurs reside, the Hall of Biodiversity, and the Culture Halls. On the 81st Street side of the building, you'll find the **Rose Center for Earth and Space,** where you can marvel at the beauty of the cosmos in the grand Hayden Planetarium. See p. 235.

➌ Central Park *✿✿✿*

From the Museum of Natural History, cross the street to Central Park and enter at 81st Street. Follow the path east, and just south of the Delacorte Theater, you'll see Belvedere Castle. Climb to the top and soak in the view of the park. To the north, you'll see the Great Lawn, sight of so many concerts, and beyond that the Jacqueline Kennedy Onassis Reservoir. To the south you'll see the lake with its rowboats (rent one if you have time) and the skyline of Manhattan. See p. 268.

➍ A PICNIC IN THE PARK

If you didn't pack a picnic lunch, stop in the Columbus Bakery (at 83rd St. and Columbus Ave.), just north of the Museum of Natural History, and get your lunch to go. Head to the park and grab a bench, or if the weather is nice, spread out a blanket and take in the sunshine.

➎ Metropolitan Museum of Art *✿✿✿*

Continuing east across Central Park, you'll hit Fifth Avenue and the Met. As with the Museum of Natural History, there is no way you can see all the Met has to offer in one visit, but stop by the Temple of Dendur, a gift from the Egyptian government, and the museum's collection of European paintings—including 37 Monets. There are various free (after the admission charge) museum highlight tours. They last an hour and will give you a pretty good overview of this great museum. See p. 239.

➏ Solomon R. Guggenheim Museum *✿*

Continuing on our mini-tour of Museum Mile, that stretch of artistic real estate that runs on upper Fifth Avenue, is the Guggenheim. You'll know it when you see it; there's nothing else like this Frank Lloyd Wright–designed museum, and now you have the chance to walk the spiraling rotunda. But get off the rotunda and take a look at some of the permanent collection that includes works by Picasso, Chagall, and Klee. Or wander into the

The Best of NYC in 3 Days

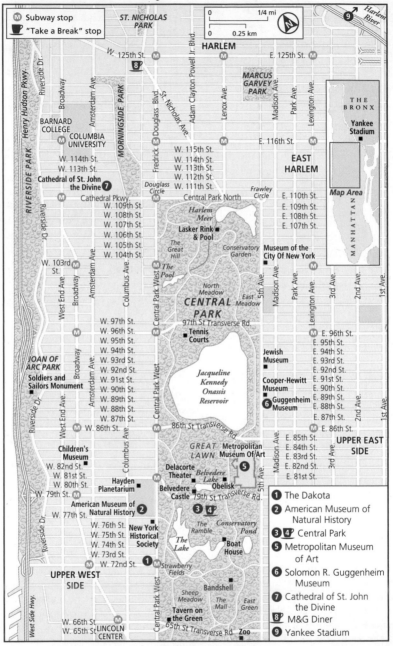

Subway stop

"Take a Break" stop

ST. NICHOLAS PARK

HARLEM

W. 125th St.

E. 125th St.

MARCUS GARVEY PARK

THE BRONX

Yankee Stadium

BARNARD COLLEGE

COLUMBIA UNIVERSITY

Riverside Dr.
Henry Hudson Pkwy.
RIVERSIDE PARK
Broadway
Amsterdam Ave.
MORNINGSIDE PARK
Fredrick Douglass Blvd
St. Nicholas Ave.
Adam Clayton Powell Jr. Blvd.
Lenox Ave.
Madison Ave.
Park Ave.
Lexington Ave.

E. 116th St.

EAST HARLEM

W. 114th St.
W. 113th St.

Cathedral of St. John the Divine

W. 115th St.
W. 114th St.
W. 113th St.
W. 112th St.
W. 111th St.

Douglass Circle

Map Area

MANHATTAN

Cathedral Pkwy.
W. 109th St.
W. 108th St.
W. 107th St.
W. 106th St.
W. 105th St.
W. 104th St.

Central Park North

Frawley Circle

E. 110th St.
E. 109th St.
E. 108th St.
E. 107th St.

Harlem Meer

Lasker Rink & Pool

The Great Hill

Conservatory Garden

Museum of the City Of New York

W. 103rd St.

The Pool

North Meadow

East Meadow

CENTRAL PARK

97th St Transverse Rd.

Tennis Courts

JOAN OF ARC PARK

Soldiers and Sailors Monument

W. 97th St.
W. 96th St.
W. 95th St.
W. 94th St.
W. 93rd St.
W. 92nd St.
W. 91st St.
W. 90th St.
W. 89th St.
W. 88th St.
W. 87th St.

E. 96th St.
E. 95th St.
E. 94th St.
E. 93rd St.
E. 92nd St.
E. 91st St.
E. 90th St.
E. 89th St.
E. 88th St.
E. 87th St.

Jacqueline Kennedy Onassis Reservoir

Jewish Museum

Cooper-Hewitt Museum

Guggenheim Museum

West End Ave.
Broadway
Amsterdam Ave.
Columbus Ave.
Central Park West
Madison Ave.
Park Ave.
Lexington Ave.
3rd Ave.
2nd Ave.
1st Ave.

W. 86th St.

86th St Transverse Rd.

E. 86th St.

E. 85th St.
E. 84th St.
E. 83rd St.
E. 82nd St.
E. 81st St.

UPPER EAST SIDE

Children's Museum

W. 82nd St.
W. 81st St.
W. 80th St.
W. 79th St.

Hayden Planetarium

American Museum of Natural History

GREAT LAWN

Metropolitan Museum Of Art

Delacorte Theater

Belvedere Lake

Belvedere Castle

Obelisk

79th St Transverse Rd.

W. 77th St.
W. 76th St.
W. 75th St.
W. 74th St.
W. 73rd St.
W. 72nd St.

New York Historical Society

The Ramble

Conservatory Pond

The Lake

Boat House

Strawberry Fields

UPPER WEST SIDE

Sheep Meadow

Bandshell

The Mall

East Green

W. 66th St.
W. 65th St.

LINCOLN CENTER

Tavern on the Green

65th St Transverse Rd.

Zoo

Riverside Dr.
West End Ave.
West Side Hwy.
Central Park West

❶ The Dakota
❷ American Museum of Natural History
❸ ❹ Central Park
❺ Metropolitan Museum of Art
❻ Solomon R. Guggenheim Museum
❼ Cathedral of St. John the Divine
❽ M&G Diner
❾ Yankee Stadium

0   1/4 mi
0   0.25 km

Harlem River

new Kandinsky Gallery for a dose of the master's eye-opening works. See p. 243.

Take the M96 crosstown bus at Fifth Avenue and 97th Street West. Get off at Amsterdam Avenue and 96th Street and transfer to an uptown M11 or M7 bus. Get off at 110th Street.

❼ Cathedral of St. John the Divine ⑂

On the east side of Amsterdam, you will see the world's largest Gothic cathedral. Construction began in 1892 and is still not finished. You can explore the inside of the cathedral on your own or opt for a tour. If you're here at Easter or during the Feast of St. Francis in October, don't miss the blessing of animals—where the creature congregation has been known to include an elephant or camel. See p. 266.

Take the M11 or M7 uptown bus to 125th St.

> **❽ M&G DINER**
> This is the place for first-rate soul food. If you're hungry, order the pan-fried chicken.

If all just want a coffee, a slice of home-made carrot cake goes perfectly with it. 383 W. 125th St., at St. Nicholas Avenue. ✆ **212/864-7326.** See p. 221.

Take the B or D train at the 125th Street station uptown to the Bronx. Get off at 161st St./River Avenue for:

❾ Yankee Stadium ⑂⑂

You come out of the subway station and you hear the din of the loudspeaker—maybe it's the voice of longtime Yankee announcer Bob Sheppard announcing the starting lineup. You are at the Big Ballpark in the Bronx. You've got your tickets and if you arrive early enough, visit Monument Park in the outfield, open to the public when the gates open and up to 45 minutes prior to game time. The 2008 season will be Yankee Stadium's final one with a new stadium set to open nearby in 2009. See p. 247.

4 The Essential New York Eating Itinerary

New York has countless restaurants of quality and variety. If you want a sampling of true New York cuisine, follow the "required eating" itinerary below. Whether you jam the stops below into 1, 2 or 3 days, a gargantuan appetite is required. For full reviews of the places listed below, see Chapter 7, "Where to Dine."

❶ Bagels with Lox

Start your New York food tour at **Barney Greengrass, the Sturgeon King** (541 Amsterdam Avenue; ✆ **212/724-4707**) where they have been making that world famous combination, bagels and lox, since 1908. If there is anything more satisfying than a fresh, out-of-the-oven bagel with a schmear of cream cheese and a razor-thin slice of lox, I don't know what it is. This combination might be one of the most popular breakfast items in New York.

❷ Cuban/Chinese

There used to be dozens of Cuban/Chinese restaurants in Manhattan, most on the Upper West Side. The boom began in the late 1950's after the Cuban revolution and the beginning of the Castro regime. Chinese-Cubans emigrated to New York and opened up restaurants serving both Cantonese-style Chinese food and traditional Cuban food. A few are left and my favorite is **Flor de Mayo** (2651 Broadway; ✆ **212/663-5520**. Here I can order a big bowl of wonton soup followed by a huge plate of yellow rice and black beans.

Essential New York Eating

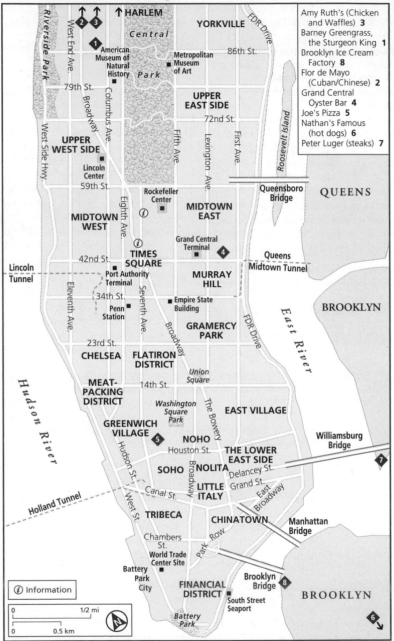

Riverside Park

West End Ave.

↑↑ ↑ HARLEM

2 **3**

Central

YORKVILLE

FDR Drive

1

American Museum of Natural History

86th St.

Metropolitan Museum of Art

Park

79th St.

Broadway

Columbus Ave.

UPPER EAST SIDE

72nd St.

Fifth Ave.

Lexington Ave.

First Ave.

Roosevelt Island

West Side Hwy.

UPPER WEST SIDE

Lincoln Center

59th St.

Eighth Ave.

Rockefeller Center

MIDTOWN EAST

Queensboro Bridge

QUEENS

MIDTOWN WEST

i

Grand Central Terminal

i

TIMES SQUARE

42nd St.

Eleventh Ave.

Port Authority Terminal

Seventh Ave.

MURRAY HILL

Queens Midtown Tunnel

4

Lincoln Tunnel

34th St.

Penn Station

Empire State Building

GRAMERCY PARK

East River

BROOKLYN

Broadway

FDR Drive

23rd St.

CHELSEA

FLATIRON DISTRICT

MEAT-PACKING DISTRICT

14th St.

Union Square

Hudson River

Washington Square Park

GREENWICH VILLAGE

5

NOHO

Houston St.

EAST VILLAGE

The Bowery

Williamsburg Bridge

7

SOHO

Hudson St.

West St.

Broadway

NOLITA

Delancey St.

THE LOWER EAST SIDE

Grand St.

East Broadway

Canal St.

LITTLE ITALY

TRIBECA

CHINATOWN

Manhattan Bridge

Chambers St.

Park Row

World Trade Center Site

Battery Park City

FINANCIAL DISTRICT

Brooklyn Bridge

8

BROOKLYN

South Street Seaport

Holland Tunnel

i Information

0   1/2 mi

0   0.5 km

Battery Park

6

❸ Chicken and Waffles

You're out late, maybe listening to jazz at one of Harlem's many clubs, it's getting near dawn, and you can't decide whether you want dinner or breakfast. You can't resist the fried chicken, but waffles sound good, too. So you try a little of both— maple syrup melding with the hot sauce; sweet with savory. The birthplace of this dish is said to be Wells Chicken and Waffles in Harlem in 1938. Wells is long gone, but chicken and waffles live on. For the best rendition, go to **Amy Ruth's** (113 W. 116th St.; ℂ **212/280-8779**) for chicken and waffles, as well as grits and fish cakes—another outstanding combo.

❹ The New York Oyster

There was a time when New York was more the Big Oyster than the Big Apple. The local harbor beds overflowed with oysters and the mollusk helped feed the city. You can recall those glory days at the **Grand Central Oyster Bar** in Grand Central Station (ℂ **212/490-6650**) where, since 1913, oysters have been the specialty. Order them on the half shell from Long Island, Washington State, Maine, Virginia, or Canada, with the Metro North commuter trains rumbling in the background. It's a true New York eating experience if there ever was one.

❺ A Slice of Pizza

Toss on some dried red pepper or granulated garlic, and eat it standing up to capture the grease before it stains your clothes. That's the way we've been eating pizza in New York for years. The classic New York slice, however, has been on the decline ever since an influx of chain pizzerias have corrupted the pizza landscape. For the best "slice" head to **Joe's**

Pizza (7 Carmine St.; ℂ **212/255-3946**) in the Village, open until the wee hours, satisfying your late night cravings.

❻ The Hot Dog

This might be an obvious choice, but I don't think so. You can find carts selling cheap hot dogs throughout the city. You might be tempted to try one just to say you did. And I think you should; it definitely is a New York experience. But even better, take the train out to Coney Island and sample a **Nathan's Famous** dog right on the boardwalk (1310 Surf Ave. ℂ **718/946-2202**). Maybe it's the salty sea air. Maybe it's the crisp skin of the hot dog, or the way it's perfectly fried. Whatever it is, you won't forget your Nathan's hot dog on Coney Island.

❼ The New York Strip

Some of New York's oldest restaurants are steakhouses, and for good reason. They keep it simple. Some might have sawdust on the floors, others clay pipes on the ceiling, or photos of celebrities on the walls, but that is about as fancy as they get. What they do is serve quality, properly-aged meat cooked to perfection and presented in a no-nonsense, no frills manner. And no one does that better than **Peter Luger** in Williamsburg, Brooklyn (178 Broadway; ℂ **718/387-7400**).

❽ Ice Cream with a View

If you've been able to sample the above essential New York eating experiences over 1, 2 or 3 days, finish your tour off at the **Brooklyn Ice Cream Factory** (1 Water Street; ℂ **718/246-3963**) where the homemade ice cream is absolutely delicious and the view at river's edge of Manhattan, just below the Brooklyn Bridge, is equally stunning.

5

Getting to Know New York City

This chapter gives you an insider's take on Manhattan's most distinctive neighborhoods and streets, tells you how to get around town, and serves as a handy reference to everything from personal safety to libraries and liquor.

1 Orientation

VISITOR INFORMATION

INFORMATION OFFICES

- The **Times Square Information Center,** 1560 Broadway, between 46th and 47th streets (where Broadway meets Seventh Ave.), on the east side of the street (© 212/869-1890; www.timessquarenyc.org), is the city's top info stop. This pleasant, attractive center features a helpful info desk offering loads of citywide information. There's also a tour desk selling tickets for Gray Line bus tours and Circle Line boat tours; you can also get public transit maps, and staff is there to answer all of your questions on the transit system; and there's a Broadway Ticket Center providing show information and selling full-price show tickets; there are also ATMs and currency exchange machines; and computer terminals with free Internet access courtesy of Yahoo! It's open daily from 8am to 8pm.

- The New York Convention and Visitors Bureau runs the **NYCVB Visitor Information Center** at 810 Seventh Ave., between 52nd and 53rd streets. In addition to information on citywide attractions and a multilingual counselor on hand to answer questions, the center has interactive terminals that provide free touch-screen access to visitor information via Citysearch (**www.citysearch.com**), a guide to events, dining, and nightlife, and you can also buy advance tickets to major attractions, which can save you from standing in long ticket lines (you can also buy a CityPass; see the box on p. 236). There's also an ATM, a gift shop, and a bank of phones that connect you directly with American Express card member services. The center is open Monday through Friday from 8:30am to 6pm, Saturday and Sunday from 9am to 5pm. For over-the-phone assistance, call © 212/484-1222, or check online at **www.nycvisit.com**.

PUBLICATIONS

For comprehensive listings of films, concerts, performances, sporting events, museum and gallery exhibits, street fairs, and special events, the following are your best bets:

- The *New York Times* (**www.nytimes.com** or www.nytoday.com) features terrific arts and entertainment coverage, particularly in the two-part Friday "Weekend" section and the Sunday "Arts & Leisure" section. Both days boast full guides to the latest happenings in Broadway and Off-Broadway theater, classical music, dance, pop and jazz, film, and the art world. Friday is particularly good for cabaret, family fun, and general-interest recreational and sightseeing events.

- **Time Out New York** (**www.timeoutny.com**) is my favorite weekly magazine. Dedicated to weekly goings-on, it's attractive, well organized, and easy to use. *TONY* features excellent coverage in categories from live music, theater, and clubs (gay and straight) to museum shows, dance events, literary readings, and kids' stuff. The regular "Check Out" section, will fill you in on upcoming sample and closeout sales, crafts and antiques shows, and other shopping-related scoops. A new issue hits newsstands every Thursday.
- The free weekly **Village Voice** (**www.villagevoice.com**), the city's legendary alterna-paper, is available late Tuesday downtown and early Wednesday in the rest of the city. From music to clubs, the arts and entertainment coverage couldn't be more extensive, and just about every live-music venue advertises its shows here.

Other useful weekly rags include the glossy **New York** magazine (**www.nymag. com**), which offers valuable restaurant reviews and whose listings section is a selective guide to city arts and entertainment; and the **New Yorker** (**www.newyorker.com**), which features an artsy "Goings On About Town" section at the front of the magazine. *Paper* (**www.papermag.com**) is a glossy monthly mag that serves as good prep for those of you who want to experience the hipper side of the city.

CITY LAYOUT

Open the sheet map that comes with this book and you'll see that the city is comprised of five boroughs: **Manhattan,** where most of the visitor action is; the **Bronx,** the only borough connected to the mainland United States; **Queens,** where Kennedy and LaGuardia airports are and which borders the Atlantic Ocean and occupies part of Long Island; **Brooklyn,** south of Queens, which is also on Long Island and is famed for its attitude, accent, and Atlantic-front Coney Island; and **Staten Island,** bordering Upper New York Bay on one side and the Atlantic Ocean on the other.

When most visitors envision New York, they think of Manhattan, the long finger-shaped island pointing southwest off the mainland—surrounded by the Harlem River to the north, the Hudson River to the west, the East River (really an estuary) to the east, and the fabulous expanse of Upper New York Bay to the south. Despite the fact that it's the city's smallest borough (14 miles long, 2¼ miles wide, 22 sq. miles), Manhattan contains the city's most famous attractions, buildings, and cultural institutions. For that reason, almost all of the accommodations and restaurants suggested in this book are in Manhattan.

In most of Manhattan, finding your way around is a snap because of the logical, well-executed grid system by which the streets are numbered. If you can discern uptown and downtown, and East Side and West Side, you can find your way around pretty easily. In real terms, **uptown** means north of where you happen to be, and **downtown** means south, although sometimes these labels have vague psychographic meanings (generally speaking, "uptown" chic vs. "downtown" bohemianism).

Avenues run north-south (uptown and downtown). Most are numbered. **Fifth Avenue** divides the East Side from the West Side of town and serves as the eastern border of Central Park north of 59th Street. **First Avenue** is all the way east and **Twelfth Avenue** is all the way west. The three most important unnumbered avenues on the East Side you should know are between Third and Fifth avenues: **Madison** (east of Fifth), **Park** (east of Madison), and **Lexington** (east of Park, just west of Third).

(Tips **Getting Oriented**

I've indicated the cross streets for every destination in this book, but be sure to ask for the cross street (or avenue) if you're calling for an address.

When you give a taxi driver an address, always specify the cross streets. New Yorkers, even most cab drivers, probably wouldn't know where to find 994 Second Ave., but they do know where to find 51st (street) and Second (avenue). If you're heading to the restaurant Aquavit, for example, tell them that it's on 55th Street between Madison and Park avenues. The exact number (in this case, no. 65) is given only for further precision.

If you have only the numbered address on an avenue and need to figure out the cross street, use the **Manhattan Address Locator** on p. 86.

Important unnumbered avenues on the West Side are **Avenue of the Americas,** which all New Yorkers call Sixth Avenue; **Central Park West,** which is what Eighth Avenue north of 59th Street is called as it borders Central Park on the west (hence the name); **Columbus Avenue,** which is what Ninth Avenue is called north of 59th Street; and **Amsterdam Avenue,** or Tenth Avenue north of 59th.

Broadway is the exception to the rule—it's the only major avenue that doesn't run uptown-downtown. It cuts a diagonal path across the island, from the northwest tip down to the southeast corner. As it crosses most major avenues, it creates **squares** (Times Sq., Herald Sq., Madison Sq., and Union Sq., for example).

Streets run east-west (crosstown) and are numbered consecutively as they proceed uptown from Houston (pronounced *House*-ton) Street. So to go uptown, simply walk north of, or to a higher-numbered street than, where you are. Downtown is south of (or a lower-numbered street than) your current location.

As I've already mentioned, Fifth Avenue is the dividing line between the **East Side** and **West Side** of town (except below Washington Sq., where Broadway serves that function). On the East Side of Fifth Avenue, streets are numbered with the distinction "East"; on the West Side of that avenue they are numbered "West." East 51st Street, for example, begins at Fifth Avenue and runs east to the East River, while West 51st Street begins at Fifth Avenue and runs west to the Hudson River.

If you're looking for a particular address, remember that even-numbered street addresses are on the south side of streets and odd-numbered addresses are on the north. Street addresses increase by about 50 per block starting at Fifth Avenue. For example, nos. 1 to 50 East are just about between Fifth and Madison avenues, while nos. 1 to 50 West are just about between Fifth and Sixth avenues. Traffic generally runs east on even-numbered streets and west on odd-numbered streets, with a few exceptions, such as the major east–west thoroughfares—**14th, 23rd, 34th, 42nd, 57th, 72nd, 79th, 86th,** and so on—which have two-way traffic. Therefore, 28 W. 23rd St. is a short walk west of Fifth Avenue; 325 E. 35th St. would be a few blocks east of Fifth.

Avenue addresses are irregular. For example, 994 Second Ave. is at East 51st Street, but so is 320 Park Ave. Thus, it's important to know a building's cross street to find it easily. If you don't have the cross street and you want to figure out the exact location using just the address, use the **Manhattan Address Locator,** later in this chapter.

Unfortunately, the rules don't apply to neighborhoods in lower Manhattan, south of 14th Street—such as Wall Street, Chinatown, SoHo, TriBeCa, and the Village— since they sprang up before engineers devised this brilliant grid scheme. A good map is essential when exploring these areas.

STREET MAPS   You'll find a useful pullout map of Manhattan at the back of this book. There's also a decent one available for free as part of the **Official NYC Visitor Kit** if you write ahead for information (see "Visitor Information," in chapter 3); you can also pick it up for free at the visitor centers listed above.

Even with all these freebies at hand, I suggest investing in a map with more features if you really want to zip around the city like a pro. **Hagstrom** maps are my favorites because they feature block-by-block street numbering—so instead of trying to guess the cross street for 125 Prince St., you can see right on your map that it's Greene Street. Hagstrom and other visitor-friendly maps are available at just about any good bookstore, including the Barnes & Noble and Borders branches around town; see chapter 9 for locations. You might also want to look for *The New York Map Guide: The Essential Guide to Manhattan* (Penguin), by Michael Middleditch, a 64-page book that maps the entire city, including attractions, restaurants, and nightlife spots.

Because there are always disruptions or changes in service, don't rely on any subway map that hasn't been printed by the Metropolitan Transit Authority; you can find out more on this in "Getting Around," later in this chapter.

MANHATTAN'S NEIGHBORHOODS IN BRIEF

Because they grew up over the course of hundreds of years, Manhattan neighborhoods have multiple, splintered personalities and fluid boundaries. Still, it's relatively easy to agree upon what they stand for in general terms—so if you stop a New Yorker on the street and ask him or her to point you to, say, the Upper West Side or the Flatiron District, they'll know where you want to go. From south to north, here is how I've defined Manhattan's neighborhoods throughout this book.

Downtown

Lower Manhattan: South Street Seaport & the Financial District   At one time, this was New York—period. Established by the Dutch in 1625 (hence the city's original name, Nieuw Amsterdam), New York's first settlements sprang up here, on the southern tip of Manhattan island; everything uptown was farm country and wilderness. While all that's changed, this is still the best place in the city to search for the past.

Lower Manhattan constitutes everything south of Chambers Street. **Battery Park,** the point of departure for the Statue of Liberty, Ellis Island, and Staten Island, is on the far southern tip of the island. The **South Street Seaport,** now touristy but still a reminder of times when shipping was the lifeblood of the city, lies a bit north on the east side; it's just south of the Brooklyn Bridge, which stands proudly as the ultimate engineering achievement of New York's 19th-century industrial age.

The rest of the area is considered the **Financial District,** but may be more famous now as **Ground Zero.** Until September 11, 2001, the Financial District was anchored by the **World Trade Center,** with the World Financial Center complex and residential Battery Park City to the west, and **Wall Street** running crosstown a little south and to the east. Construction has begun slowly on the new complex, but it will be years before its completion.

City Hall remains the northern border of the district, abutting Chambers Street (look for City Hall Park on the map). Most of the streets around here are narrow concrete canyons, with Broadway serving as the main uptown-downtown artery.

Just about all of the major subway lines congregate here before they either end or head to Brooklyn. See "Getting Around," later in this chapter, for information on where to gather the latest subway information.

TriBeCa Bordered by the Hudson River to the west, the area north of Chambers Street, west of Broadway, and south of Canal Street is the *Tri*angle *Be*low *Ca*nal Street, or TriBeCa. Since the 1980s, as SoHo became saturated with chic, the spillover has been transforming TriBeCa into one of the city's hippest residential neighborhoods, where celebrities and families coexist in cast-iron warehouses converted into expensive apartments. Artists' lofts and galleries as well as hip antiques and design shops pepper the area, as do some of the city's best restaurants.

Robert De Niro gave the neighborhood a tremendous boost when he established the Tribeca Film Center, and Miramax headquarters gave the area further capitalist-chic cachet. Still, historic streets like White (especially the Federal-style building at no. 2) and Harrison (the complete stretch west from Greenwich St.) evoke a bygone, more human-scale New York, as do a few holdout businesses and old-world pubs.

The main uptown-downtown drag is **West Broadway** (2 blocks west of Broadway). Consider the Franklin Street subway station on the 1 line to be your gateway to the action.

Chinatown New York City's most famous ethnic enclave is bursting past its traditional boundaries and has encroached on Little Italy. The former marshlands northeast of City Hall and below Canal Street, from Broadway to the Bowery, are where Chinese immigrants arriving from San Francisco were forced to live in the 1870s. This booming neighborhood is now a conglomeration of Asian populations. It offers tasty cheap eats in cuisines from Szechuan to Hunan to Cantonese to Vietnamese to Thai. Exotic shops offer strange foods, herbs, and souvenirs; bargains on clothing and leather are plentiful. It's a blast to walk down Canal Street, peering into the myriad electronics and luggage stores and watching crabs escape from their baskets at the fish markets.

The Canal Street (J, M, Z, N, R, 6, Q, W) station will get you to the heart of the action. The streets are crowded during the day and empty out after around 9pm; they remain quite safe, but the neighborhood is more enjoyable during the bustle.

Little Italy Little Italy, traditionally the area east of Broadway between Houston and north of Canal streets, is a shrinking community, due to the encroachment of thriving Chinatown. It's now limited mainly to **Mulberry Street,** where you'll find most restaurants and just a few offshoots. With rents going up in the increasingly

Downtown Revival

Lower Manhattan has rebounded and reinvented itself since the terrorist attacks of September 11, 2001. Read all about it at the website for the **Alliance for Downtown New York (www.downtownny.com)**, updated daily; check it for information on new developments and exciting downtown events.

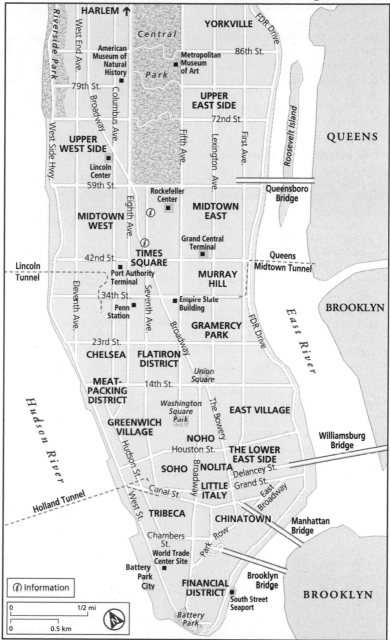

Manhattan Neighborhoods

HARLEM ↑

YORKVILLE

FDR Drive

Central

American
Museum of
Natural
History

Metropolitan
Museum
of Art

86th St.

Park

UPPER
EAST SIDE

79th St.

72nd St.

UPPER
WEST SIDE

Lincoln
Center

QUEENS

Riverside Park

West End Ave.

Broadway

Columbus Ave.

West Side Hwy.

Fifth Ave.

Lexington Ave.

First Ave.

Roosevelt Island

59th St.

Rockefeller
Center

Queensboro
Bridge

MIDTOWN
WEST

Eighth Ave.

ⓘ

MIDTOWN
EAST

Lincoln
Tunnel

42nd St.

ⓘ TIMES
SQUARE

Grand Central
Terminal

Queens
Midtown Tunnel

Port Authority
Terminal

MURRAY
HILL

34th St.

Penn
Station

Empire State
Building

Eleventh Ave.

Seventh Ave.

Broadway

GRAMERCY
PARK

FDR Drive

East River

BROOKLYN

23rd St.

CHELSEA

FLATIRON
DISTRICT

*Union
Square*

MEAT-
PACKING
DISTRICT

14th St.

Hudson River

*Washington
Square
Park*

The Bowery

EAST VILLAGE

GREENWICH
VILLAGE

NOHO

Houston St.

Williamsburg
Bridge

SOHO

NOLITA

THE LOWER
EAST SIDE

Delancey St.

Broadway

Hudson St.

LITTLE
ITALY

Grand St.

East
Broadway

Holland Tunnel

Canal St.

West St.

TRIBECA

CHINATOWN

Manhattan
Bridge

Park Row

Chambers
St.

World Trade
Center Site

Battery
Park
City

Brooklyn
Bridge

ⓘ Information

FINANCIAL
DISTRICT

South Street
Seaport

BROOKLYN

0   1/2 mi

0   0.5 km

*Battery
Park*

trendy Lower East Side, the chic spots are moving in, further intruding upon the old-world landscape. The best way to reach Little Italy is to walk east from the Spring Street station (on the no. 6 line) to Mulberry Street; turn south for Little Italy (you can't miss the year-round red, green, and white street decorations).

The Lower East Side The Lower East Side boasts the best of both old and new New York: Witness the stretch of Houston between Forsyth and Allen streets, where Yonah Shimmel's Knish Shop sits shoulder-to-shoulder with the Sunshine Theater, an arthouse cinema—and both are thriving, thank you very much. Some say that the Lower East Side has come full circle: Hipster 20-somethings with Ivy League educations and well-honed senses of entitlement have been drawn back to the neighborhood their immigrant grandparents worked their fingers to the bone to escape.

Of all the successive waves of immigrants and refugees who passed through this densely populated tenement neighborhood from the mid–19th century to the 1920s, Eastern European Jews left the most lasting impression. The Jewish communities, which popped up between Houston and Canal streets east of the Bowery, are now just part of history. The neighborhood has experienced quite a renaissance over the last few years and makes a fascinating stop for both nostalgists and nightlife hounds. Still, the blocks well south of Houston can be grungy in spots, so walk them with confidence and care after dark.

There are some remnants of what was once the largest Jewish population in America along **Orchard Street,** where you'll find great bargain-hunting in its many old-world fabric and clothing stores still thriving between the club-clothes boutiques and trendy lounges. Keep in mind that the old-world shops close early on Friday afternoon and all day on Saturday (the Jewish Sabbath). The exponentially expanding trendy set can be found in the blocks between Allen and Clinton streets south of Houston and north of Delancey, with more new shops, bars, and restaurants popping up in the blocks to the east every day.

This area is not well served by the subway system (one cause for its years of decline), so your best bet is to take the F train to Second Avenue (you can get off closer to First) and walk east on Houston; when you see Katz's Deli, you'll know you've arrived. You can also reach the neighborhood from the Delancey Street station on the F line, and the Essex Street station on the J, M, and Z lines.

SoHo & Nolita No relation to the London neighborhood of the same name, **SoHo** got its moniker as an abbreviation of "*So*uth of *Ho*uston Street." This fashionable neighborhood extends down to Canal Street, between Sixth Avenue to the west and Lafayette Street (1 block east of Broadway) to the east. It's easily accessible by subway: Take the N or R to the Prince Street station; the C, E, or 6 to Spring Street; or the F, B, D or V train to the Broadway-Lafayette stop.

An industrial zone during the 19th century, SoHo retains the impressive cast-iron architecture of the era, and in many places, cobblestone peeks out from beneath the street's asphalt. In the early 1960s, cutting-edge artists began occupying the drab and deteriorating buildings, soon turning it into the trendiest neighborhood in the city. SoHo is now a prime example of urban gentrification and a major New York attraction thanks to its impeccably restored buildings, fashionable

Visiting the Lower East Side

The **Lower East Side Business Improvement District** operates a neighborhood visitor center at 261 Broome St., between Orchard and Allen streets (✆ **866/ 224-0206** or 212/226-9010), that's open Monday through Saturday from 10am to 4pm (sometimes until 5pm). Stop in for an Orchard Street Bargain District shopping and dining guide (which they can also send you in advance), plus other information on this historic yet freshly hip 'hood. You can also find shopping, dining, and nightlife directories online at **www.lowereastsideny.com**.

restaurants, and stylish boutiques. On weekends the cobbled streets and narrow sidewalks are packed with shoppers, with the prime action between Broadway and Sullivan Street north of Grand Street.

Some critics claim that SoHo is a victim of its own popularity—witness the recent departure of art galleries and independent boutiques that fled to TriBeCa and Chelsea as well as the influx of mall-style stores such as J. Crew, Victoria's Secret, and Smith & Hawken. However, SoHo is still one of the best shopping neighborhoods in the city, and few are more fun to browse. High-end street peddlers set up along the boutique-lined sidewalks, hawking silver jewelry, coffee-table books, and their own art. At night the neighborhood is transformed into a terrific (albeit pricey) dining and barhopping neighborhood.

In recent years SoHo has been crawling its way east, taking over Mott and Mulberry streets—and Elizabeth Street in particular—north of Kenmare Street, an area now known as **Nolita** for its *No*rth of *Li*ttle *Ita*ly location. Nolita is becoming well known for its hot shopping prospects, which include a number of pricey antiques and home-design stores. Taking the no. 6 train to Spring Street will get you closest by subway, but it's just a short walk east from SoHo proper.

The East Village & NoHo The **East Village,** which extends between 14th

Street and Houston Street, from Broadway east to First Avenue and beyond to Alphabet City—Avenues A, B, C, and D—is where the city's real bohemia has gone. Once, flower children tripped along St. Marks Place and listened to music at the Fillmore East; now the East Village is a fascinating mix of affordable ethnic and trendy restaurants, upstart clothing designers and kitschy boutiques, punk-rock clubs (yep, still), and folk cafes. Several Off- and Off-Off-Broadway theaters also call this place home.

The gentrification that has swept the city has made a huge impact on the East Village, but there's still a seedy element that some won't find appealing—and some will. Now yuppies and other ladder-climbing types make their homes alongside old-world Russian immigrants, who have lived in the neighborhood forever, and the cross-dressers and squatters who settled here in between. The neighborhood still embraces ethnic diversity, with strong elements of its Ukrainian and Irish heritages, while more recent immigrants have taken over 6th Street between First and Second avenues, turning it into a Little India.

The East Village isn't very accessible by subway; unless you're traveling along 14th Street (the L line will drop you off at Third and First aves.), your best bet is to take the 4, 5, 6, N, Q, R, or W to 14th Street/Union Square; the N or R to 8th Street; or the 6 to Astor Place and walk east.

Until the 1990's, **Alphabet City** resisted gentrification and remained a haven of drug dealers and other unsavory types—no more. Bolstered by a major real-estate boom, this way-east area of the East Village has blossomed. French bistros and smart shops have popped up on every corner. Nevertheless, the neighborhood can be deserted late at night, since it's generally the province of locals. It's far off the subway lines, so know where you're going if you venture out here.

The southwestern section of the East Village, around Broadway and Lafayette between Bleecker and 4th streets, is called **NoHo** (for *No*rth of *Ho*uston), and has a completely different character. As you might have guessed from its name, this area has developed much more like its neighbor to the south, SoHo. Here you'll find a crop of trendy lounges, stylish restaurants, cutting-edge designers, and upscale antiques shops. NoHo is fun to browse; the Bleecker Street stop on the no. 6 line will land you in the heart of it, and the Broadway-Lafayette stop on the B, D, F, and V lines will drop you at its southern edge.

Greenwich Village Tree-lined streets crisscross and wind, following ancient streams and cow paths. Each block reveals yet another row of Greek Revival town houses, a well-preserved Federal-style house, or a peaceful courtyard or square. This is "the Village," from Broadway west to the Hudson River, bordered by Houston Street to the south and 14th Street to the north. It defies Manhattan's orderly grid system with streets that predate it, virtually every one chockablock with activity, and unless you live here, it may be impossible to master the lay of the land—so be sure to take a map along as you explore.

The Seventh Avenue line (1, 2, 3) is the area's main subway artery, while the West 4th Street station (where the A, C, and E lines meet the B, D, F, and V lines) serves as its central hub.

Nineteenth-century artists such as Mark Twain, Edgar Allan Poe, Henry James, and Winslow Homer first gave the Village its reputation for embracing the unconventional. Groundbreaking artists such as Edward Hopper and Jackson Pollock were drawn in, as were writers such as Eugene O'Neill, E. E. Cummings, and Dylan Thomas. Radical thinkers from John Reed to Upton Sinclair basked in the neighborhood's liberal ethos, and beatniks Allen Ginsberg, Jack Kerouac, and William Burroughs dug the free-swinging atmosphere.

Now, like so many neighborhoods, gentrification and escalating real-estate values conspire to push out the artistic element, but culture and counterculture still rub shoulders in cafes, internationally renowned jazz clubs, neighborhood bars, Off- and Off-Off-Broadway theaters, and an endless variety of tiny shops and restaurants.

The Village is probably the most chameleon-like of Manhattan's neighborhoods. Some of the highest-priced real estate in the city runs along lower Fifth Avenue, which dead-ends at **Washington Square Park.** Serpentine **Bleecker Street** stretches through most of the neighborhood and is emblematic of the area's historical bent. The tolerant anything-goes attitude in the Village has fostered a large gay community, still in evidence around **Christopher Street** and Sheridan Square (including the landmarked Stonewall Bar). The streets west of Seventh Avenue, an area known as the **West Village,** boast a more relaxed vibe and some of the city's most

---

Value **Free New York City Tours**

If you'd like to tour a specific neighborhood with an expert guide, call **Big Apple Greeter** (© 212/669-8159; www.bigapplegreeter.org) at least 3–4 weeks ahead of your arrival. To expedite your reservation, go to the website and fill out the form in advance. This nonprofit organization has specially trained volunteers who take visitors around town for a free 2- to 4-hour visit of a particular neighborhood. And they say New York isn't friendly!

---

charming and historic brownstones. Three colleges—New York University, Parsons School of Design, and the New School for Social Research—keep the area thinking young.

Streets are often crowded with weekend warriors and teenagers, especially on Bleecker, West 4th, 8th, and surrounding streets, and have been known to become increasingly sketchy west of Seventh Avenue in the very late hours, especially on weekends. Keep an eye on your wallet when navigating the weekend throngs. Washington Square Park was cleaned up a couple of years back, but it's still best to stay out of the area after dark.

Midtown

Chelsea & the Meat-Packing District
Chelsea has come on strong in recent years as a hip address, especially for the gay community. A low-rise composite of town houses, tenements, lofts, and factories, the neighborhood comprises roughly the area west of Sixth Avenue from 14th to 30th streets. (Sixth Ave. itself below 23rd St. is actually considered part of the Flatiron District; see below.) Its main arteries are Seventh and Eighth avenues, and it's primarily served by the C or E and 1 subway lines.

The **Chelsea Piers** sports complex to the far west and a host of shops (both unique boutiques and big names such as Williams-Sonoma), well-priced bistros, and thriving bars along the main drags have contributed to the area's rebirth.

Even the Hotel Chelsea—the neighborhood's most famous architectural and literary landmark, where Thomas Wolfe and Arthur Miller wrote, Bob Dylan composed "Sad-Eyed Lady of the Low Land," Viva and Edie Sedgwick of Andy Warhol fame lived, and Sid Vicious killed Nancy Spungeon—has undergone a renovation.

One of the most influential trends in Chelsea has been the establishment of far **West Chelsea** (from Ninth Ave. west) and the adjacent **Meat-Packing District** (south of West Chelsea, roughly from 17th St. to Little W. 12th St.) as the style-setting neighborhoods for the 21st century. What SoHo was in the 1960s, this industrial west world (dubbed "the Lower West Side" by *New York* magazine) is today. New restaurants, cutting-edge shopping, and superhot restaurants pop up daily in the Meat-Packing District, while the area from West 22nd to West 29th streets between Tenth and Eleventh avenues is home to numerous dance clubs and the cutting edge of today's New York art scene. The power of art can also be found at the Joyce Theater, New York's principal modern dance venue. This area is still in transition, however, and not for everyone. With galleries and bars in converted warehouses and former meat lockers, browsing can be frustrating, and the sometimes-desolate streets a tad intimidating. Your best bet is to have a specific destination (and an exact address) in mind, be it a restaurant, gallery, boutique, or nightclub, before you come.

The Flatiron District, Union Square & Gramercy Park These adjoining and at places overlapping neighborhoods are some of the city's most appealing. Their streets have been rediscovered by New Yorkers and visitors alike, largely thanks to the boom-to-bust dotcom revolution of the late 1990s; the Flatiron District served as its geographical heart and earned the nickname "Silicon Alley" in the process. These neighborhoods boast great shopping and dining opportunities and a central-to-everything location that's hard to beat. A number of impressive new hotels have been added to the mix over the last few years. The commercial spaces are often large, loft-like expanses with witty designs and graceful columns.

The **Flatiron District** lies south of 23rd Street to 14th Street, between Broadway and Sixth Avenue, and centers around the historic Flatiron Building on 23rd (so named for its triangular shape) and Park Avenue South, which has become a sophisticated new Restaurant Row. Below 23rd Street along Sixth Avenue (once known as the Ladies' Mile shopping district), mass-market discounters such as Filene's Basement, Bed Bath & Beyond, and others have moved in. The shopping gets classier on Fifth Avenue, where you'll find a mix of national names and hip boutiques. Lined with Oriental-carpet dealers and high-end fixture stores, Broadway is becoming the city's home-furnishings alley; its crowning jewel is the justifiably famous ABC Carpet & Home, with eight floors of gorgeous textiles, housewares, and gifts on one side of Broadway, and an equally dazzling display of floor coverings on the other.

Union Square is the hub of the entire area; the N, Q, R, 4, 5, 6, and L trains stop here, making it easy to reach from most other city neighborhoods. Long in the shadows of the more bustling (Times and Herald) and high-toned (Washington) city squares, Union Square has experienced a major renaissance. Local businesses joined forces with the city to rid the park of drug dealers a few years back, and now it's a delightful place to spend an afternoon. Union Square is best known as the setting for New York's premier greenmarket every Monday, Wednesday, Friday, and Saturday from 8am to 6pm. In-line skaters take over the market space in the after-work hours. A number of hip restaurants rim the square, as do superstores such as the city's best Barnes & Noble superstore and a Virgin Megastore.

From about 16th to 23rd streets, east from Park Avenue South to about Second Avenue, is the leafy, largely residential district known as **Gramercy Park.** The pity of the Gramercy Park district is that so few can enjoy the park: Built by Samuel Ruggles in the 1830s to attract buyers to the area, it is the only private park in the city and is locked to all but those who live on its perimeter (the rule is that your windows have to overlook the park in order for you to have a key). At the southern endpoint of Lexington Avenue (at 21st St.), it is one of the most peaceful spots in the city. If you know someone who has a magic key, go there.

At the northern edge of the area, fronting the Flatiron Building on 23rd Street and Fifth Avenue, is another of Manhattan's lovely little parks, **Madison Square.** Across from its northeastern corner once stood Stanford White's original Madison Square Garden (in whose roof garden White was murdered in 1906 by possibly deranged, but definitely jealous, millionaire Harry K. Thaw). It's now majestically presided over by the massive New York Life Insurance Building, the masterful New York State Supreme Court, and the Metropolitan Life Insurance Company, whose tower in 1909 was the tallest building in the world at 700 feet.

Times Square & Midtown West
Midtown West, the vast area from 34th to 59th streets west of Fifth Avenue to the Hudson River, encompasses several famous names: Madison Square Garden, the Garment District, Rockefeller Center, the Theater District, and Times Square. This is New York's tourism central, where you'll find the bright lights and bustle that draw people from all over. As such, this is the city's biggest hotel neighborhood, with options running the gamut from cheap to chic.

The 1, 2, 3 subway line serves the massive neon-lit station at the heart of Times Square, at 42nd Street between Broadway and Seventh Avenue, while the F, V, B, D line runs up Sixth Avenue to Rockefeller Center. The N, R line cuts diagonally across the neighborhood, following the path of Broadway before heading up Seventh Avenue at 42nd Street. The A, C, E line serves the West Side, running along Eighth Avenue.

If you know New York but haven't been here in a few years, you'll be quite surprised by the "new" **Times Square.** Longtime New Yorkers like to *kvetch*

nostalgic about the glory days of the old peep-show-and-porn-shop Times Square that this cleaned-up, Disneyfied version supplanted. And there really is not much here to offer the native New Yorker. The revival, however, has been nothing short of an outstanding success for tourism. Grand old theaters have come back to life as Broadway and children's playhouses, and scores of new family-friendly restaurants and shops have opened. Plenty of businesses have moved in— MTV studios overlook Times Square at 1515 Broadway, and *Good Morning America* has its own street-facing studio at Broadway and 44th Street. The neon lights have never been brighter, and Middle America has never been more welcome. Expect dense crowds, though; it's often tough to make your way along the sidewalks.

Most of the great Broadway theaters light up the streets off Times Square, in the West 40s just east and west of Broadway. At the heart of the **Theater District,** where Broadway meets Seventh Avenue, is the TKTS booth, where crowds line up daily to buy discount tickets for that day's shows.

To the west of the Theater District, in the 40s and 50s between Eighth and Tenth avenues, is **Hell's Kitchen,** an area that is much nicer than its ghoulish name and one of my favorites in the city. The neighborhood resisted gentrification until the mid-1990s but has grown into a charming, less touristy adjunct to the neighboring Theater District. Ninth Avenue, in particular, has blossomed into one of the city's

---

Impressions

I'm opposed to the redevelopment. I think there should be one neighborhood in New York where tourists are afraid to walk.

— Fran Leibowitz on the "new" Times Square

Manhattan Address Locator

To locate avenue addresses, cancel the last figure, divide by 2, and add (or subtract) the key number below. The answer is the nearest numbered cross street, approximately.

Avenue A:	add 3	11th Avenue:	add 15
Avenue B:	add 3	Amsterdam Avenue:	add 59
Avenue C:	add 3	Columbus Avenue:	add 59
First Avenue:	add 3		or 60
Second Avenue:	add 3	Lexington Avenue:	add 22
Third Avenue:	add 10	Madison Avenue:	add 27
Sixth Avenue:	subtract 12	Park Avenue:	add 34
Eighth Avenue:	add 9	Park Avenue South:	add 8
Ninth Avenue:	add 13	West End Avenue:	add 59
Tenth Avenue:	add 14	York Avenue:	add 4

Note special instructions for finding address locations on the following:

Fifth Avenue

63 to 108:	add 11	776 to 1286: cancel last figure
109 to 200:	add 13	of house number and subtract 18
201 to 400:	add 16	(do not divide house number by 2)
401 to 600:	add 18	1310 to 1494: cancel last figure
601 to 775:	add 20	of house number. For 1310, sub-
		tract 20, and for every additional
		20 street numbers, increase deduc-
		tion by 1

Seventh Avenue

1 to 1800:	add 12	above 1800: add 20

Broadway

Anything from 1 to 754 is south of 8th Street, and hence a named street.

756 to 846:	subtract 29	847 to 953: subtract 25
above 953:	subtract 31	

Central Park West

Cancel last figure and add 60

Riverside Drive

Cancel last figure and

Up to 567:	add 72	568 and up: add 78

finest dining avenues; just stroll along and you'll have a world of dining to choose from, ranging from American diner to sexy Mediterranean to traditional Thai. Stylish boutiques and bars have also popped up in this area in the last several years. Realtors have tried to rename the area Clinton, but locals have held fast to the Hell's Kitchen moniker with delight. In the last couple of years, it's become one of Manhattan's more popular gay neighborhoods, as rents in first the West Village, then Chelsea, have caused a northward migration.

Unlike Times Square, gorgeous **Rockefeller Center** has needed no renovation. Situated between 46th and 50th streets from Sixth Avenue east to Fifth, this Art Deco complex contains some of the city's great architectural gems, which house hundreds of offices, a number of NBC studios (including *Saturday Night Live, Late Night with Conan O'Brien,* and the famous glass-walled *Today* show studio at 48th St.), and some pleasing upscale boutiques (attention, shoppers: Saks Fifth Avenue is just on the other side of Fifth). If you can negotiate the crowds, holiday time is a great time to be here, as ice-skaters take over the central plaza and the huge Christmas tree twinkles against the night sky.

Along Seventh Avenue south of 42nd Street is the **Garment District,** of little interest to tourists except for its sample sales, where some great new fashions are sold off cheap to serious bargain hunters willing to scour the racks. That part of town plays host to many small theater companies if you're venturing into the Off-Off-Broadway scene. Other than that, it's a pretty commercial area. Between Seventh and Eighth avenues and 31st and 33rd streets, **Penn Station** sits beneath unsightly behemoth **Madison Square Garden,** where the Rangers, Liberty, and the Knicks play. Taking up all of 34th Street between Sixth and Seventh avenues is **Macy's,** the world's largest department store; exit Macy's at the southeast corner and you'll find more famous-label shopping around **Herald Square.** The blocks around 32nd Street just west of Fifth Avenue have developed into a thriving Koreatown, with midprice hotels and bright, bustling Asian restaurants offering

some of the best-value stays and eats in Midtown.

Midtown West is also home to some of the city's most revered museums and cultural institutions, including **Carnegie Hall, the Museum of Modern Art, and Radio City Music Hall,** to name just a few.

Midtown East & Murray Hill Midtown East, the area including Fifth Avenue and everything east from 34th to 59th streets, is the more upscale side of the Midtown map. This side of town is short of subway trains, served primarily by the Lexington Avenue 4, 5, 6 line.

Midtown East is where you'll find the city's finest collection of grand hotels, mostly along Lexington Avenue and near the park at the top of Fifth. The stretch of **Fifth Avenue** from Saks at 49th Street extending to the 24-hour Apple Store and F.A.O. Schwarz at 59th St. is home to the city's most high-profile haute shopping, including Tiffany & Co. and Bergdorf Goodman, but more mid-price names such as Banana Republic and Liz Claiborne have moved their stores in over the last few years. The stretch of 57th Street between Fifth and Lexington avenues is also known for high-fashion boutiques (Chanel, Hermès) and high-ticket galleries, but change is underway since names such as Levi's and Niketown squeezed in. You'll find plenty of spillover along **Madison Avenue,** a great strip for shoe shopping in particular.

Magnificent architectural highlights include the recently repolished **Chrysler Building,** with its stylized gargoyles glaring down on passersby; the Beaux Arts tour de force that is **Grand Central Terminal; St. Patrick's Cathedral;** and the glorious **Empire State Building.**

Far east, swank Sutton and Beekman places are enclaves of beautiful town houses, luxury living, and pocket parks that look out over the East River. Along this river is the **United Nations,** which isn't officially in New York City, or even the United States, but on a parcel of international land belonging to member nations.

Claiming the territory east from Madison Avenue, **Murray Hill** begins somewhere north of 23rd Street (the line between it and Gramercy Park is fuzzy), and is most clearly recognizable north of 30th Street to 42nd Street. This brownstone-lined quarter is largely a quiet residential neighborhood, most notable for its handful of good budget and mid-price hotels. The stretch of Lexington Avenue in the high 20s is known as Curry Hill and has usurped the East Village's Little India as the destination for inexpensive, high-quality Indian and Pakistani food.

Uptown

Upper West Side North of 59th Street and encompassing everything west of Central Park, the Upper West Side contains **Lincoln Center,** arguably the world's premier performing-arts venue; the new (in 2004) **Time Warner Center** with its upscale shops such as **Hugo Boss, A/X Armani,** and **Sephora; Jazz at Lincoln Center;** the **Mandarin Oriental Hotel;** the gargantuan **Whole Foods Market,** and possibly the most expensive food court in the world, with restaurants such as **Per Se** and **Masa.** The Upper West Side is also the home of the **American Museum of Natural History,** whose renovated Dinosaur Halls and magnificent Rose Center for Earth and Space garner rave reviews. You'll also find a growing number of midprice hotels whose larger-than-Midtown rooms and nice residential location make them some of the best values—and some of my favorite places to stay—in the entire city.

Unlike the more stratified Upper East Side, the Upper West Side is home to an egalitarian mix of middle-class yuppiedom, laid-back wealth (lots of celebs and media types call the grand apartments along Central Park West home), and ethnic families here from before gentrification.

The neighborhood runs all the way up to Harlem, around 125th Street, and encompasses **Morningside Heights,** where you'll find **Columbia University** and the perennial construction project known as the **Cathedral of St. John the Divine.**

But prime Upper West Side—the part you're most likely to explore—is the area running from Columbus Circle at 59th Street into the 80s, between the park and Broadway. North of 59th Street is where Eighth Avenue becomes Central Park West, the eastern border of the neighborhood (and the western border of Central Park); Ninth Avenue becomes Columbus Avenue, lined with attractive boutiques and cafes; and Tenth Avenue becomes Amsterdam Avenue, less charming than Columbus to the east and less trafficked than bustling Broadway (whose highlights are the gourmet megamarts Zabar's and Fairway) to the west; still, Amsterdam has blossomed into quite a happening restaurant and bar strip over the last couple of years. You'll find Lincoln Center in the mid-60s, where Broadway crosscuts Amsterdam.

Two major subway lines service the area: the 1, 2, 3 line runs up Broadway, while the B and C trains run up Central Park West, stopping at the Dakota apartments (where John Lennon was shot and Yoko Ono still lives) at 72nd Street, and at the Museum of Natural History at 81st Street.

Upper East Side North of 59th Street and east of Central Park is some of the city's most expensive residential real estate. This is New York at its most gentrified: Walk along Fifth and Park avenues, especially between 60th and 80th streets, and you're sure to encounter some of the wizened WASPs and Chanel-suited socialites that make up the most rarefied of the city's population. Madison Avenue from 60th Street well into the 80s is the moneyed crowd's main shopping strip, recently vaunting ahead of Hong Kong's Causeway Bay to become the most expensive retail real estate *in the world*—so bring your platinum card. You can also use it to stay at one of the neighborhood's luxurious hotels, such as the Carlyle or the Plaza Athénée, or to dine at four-star wonders such as Café Boulud and Daniel.

The main attraction of this neighborhood is **Museum Mile,** the stretch of Fifth Avenue fronting Central Park that's home to no fewer than 10 terrific cultural institutions, including Frank Lloyd Wright's **Guggenheim,** and anchored by the mind-boggling **Metropolitan Museum of Art.** But the elegant rows of landmark town houses are worth a look alone: East 70th Street, from Madison east to Lexington, is one of the world's most charming residential streets. If you want to see where real people live, move east to Third Avenue and beyond; that's where affordable restaurants and active street life start popping up.

A second subway line is in the works, but it's still no more than an architect's blueprint. For now, the Upper East Side is served solely by the crowded Lexington Avenue line (4, 5, 6 trains), so wear your walking shoes (or bring taxi fare) if you're heading up here to explore.

Harlem Harlem has benefited from a dramatic image makeover in the last few years, and with new restaurants, clubs, and stores is slowly becoming a neighborhood in demand.

Harlem is actually several areas. **Harlem proper** stretches from river to river, beginning at 125th Street on the West Side, 96th Street on the East Side, and 110th Street north of Central Park. East of Fifth Avenue, **Spanish Harlem (El Barrio)** runs between East 100th and East 125th streets. Harlem proper, in particular, is benefiting greatly from the revitalization that has swept so much of the city, with national-brand retailers moving in, restaurants and hip nightspots opening everywhere, and visitors arriving to tour historic sites related to the golden age of African-American culture, when great bands such as the Count Basie and Duke Ellington orchestras played the Cotton Club and Sugar Cane Club, and literary giants such as Langston Hughes and James Baldwin soaked up the scene.

Some houses date from a time when the area was something of a country retreat, and represent some of the best brownstone mansions in the city. On **Sugar Hill** (from 143rd to 155th sts., between St. Nicholas and Edgecombe aves.) and **Striver's Row** (W. 139th St. between Adam Clayton Powell Jr. and Frederick Douglass boulevards) are a significant number of fine town houses. For cultural visits, there's the Morris-Jumel Mansion, the Schomburg Center, the Studio Museum, and the Apollo Theater.

You'll find 125th a fun place to shop with its mix of national chains like Old Navy standing side-by-side with emporiums of hip-hop fashion.

By all means, come see Harlem—it's one of the city's most vital, historic neighborhoods, and no other feels quite so energized right now. Your best bet for seeing all the sights is to take a guided tour (see "Organized Sightseeing Tours," p. 278); if you head up on your own, come in daylight. Don't wander thoughtlessly, especially at night. If you head up after dark to a restaurant or nightspot, be clear and confident about where you're going and stay alert.

Washington Heights & Inwood At the northern tip of Manhattan, Washington Heights (the area from 155th St. to Dyckman St., with adjacent Inwood running to the tip) is home to a large segment of Manhattan's Latino community, plus an increasing number of yuppies who don't mind trading a half-hour subway commute to Midtown for lower rents. **Fort Tryon Park** and **the Cloisters** are the two big reasons for visitors to come up this way. The Cloisters houses the Metropolitan Museum of Art's stunning medieval collection, in a building perched atop a hill, with excellent views across the Hudson to the Palisades. Committed off-the-beaten-path sightseers might also want to visit the **Dyckman Farmhouse,** a historic jewel built in 1783 and the only remaining Dutch Colonial structure in Manhattan.

The Boroughs

Manhattan is just one of the five boroughs that make up the very Big Apple. The others are Brooklyn, the Bronx, Queens, and Staten Island.

Brooklyn Brooklynites are quick to tell you that their borough is the fourth-largest city in the United States. That's because this borough is about pride and attitude. And though it has been over 45 years since the team left, don't even talk about the Dodgers.

Brooklyn is also about neighborhoods and diversity; the borough is a pleasure to explore. Some highlights include New York's first historic district, **Brooklyn Heights,** with its elegant brownstones; the Promenade, with its spectacular view of Manhattan; and the romantic River Cafe. To get to Brooklyn Heights, take the A, C, F to Jay Street; the 2, 3, 4, 5 to Clark Street;

or the M (during rush hours), N, R to Court Street.

One of Brooklyn's most rapidly changing neighborhoods is **DUMBO** (Down Under the Manhattan Bridge Overpass). What was once a scattering of warehouses is now a thriving artist's colony, with those warehouses now converted into expensive lofts, and not so easy for artists to afford. The main drag is **Washington Street,** and businesses are beginning to populate the area. It's here where you'll find **Jacques Torres Chocolate,** the **Brooklyn Ice Cream Factory,** and **Grimaldi's Pizza.** The best way to get to DUMBO is the F train to York Street or the A or C to High Street.

Brooklyn's now, way past hip neighborhood (though the very hippest say it's "over") is **Williamsburg.** In the early 1990s, artists began to flee Manhattan's high rents to live here among the Hispanic and Hasidic communities already there. Now, though, the pioneers have seen their once independent and inexpensive enclave being transformed into Brooklyn's version of SoHo. There are a number of funky, youth-oriented boutiques along the neighborhood's main drag, **Bedford Avenue,** but Williamsburg is also the home of that venerable red-meat institution, **Peter Luger.** The best train to take to get to Williamsburg from Manhattan is the L to Bedford Avenue.

Other emerging neighborhoods are **Carroll Gardens, Cobble Hill,** and **Boerum Hill. Smith Street** cuts through all three and has become a booming restaurant destination. To get to Smith Street, the best train is the F, with stops at either Carroll Street or Bergen Street.

Downtown Brooklyn off Flatbush Avenue is probably best known for **BAM,** the **Brooklyn Academy of Music.** You'll also find a number of department stores and one of the borough's most beloved landmarks, **Junior's,** the diner noted for its cheesecakes. Many trains converge in downtown Brooklyn at the Pacific Street/ Atlantic Avenue station, including the 2, 3, 4, 5, B, D, M, N, Q, and R.

Park Slope is probably the heart of Brooklyn; it is here and in nearby Prospect Heights where you find the **Brooklyn Museum,** the **Brooklyn Botanical Gardens,** and **Prospect Park.** The 2, 3, 4 trains to Grand Army Plaza will land you close to all of the above.

In its heyday during the early 20th century, **Coney Island** was to New York what South Beach is to Miami. This was where everyone flocked to escape the heat and grime of a New York summer day. A few remnants of Coney Island's past remain, such as the long-defunct parachute ride. But during the summer you can still ride on one of the best roller coasters anywhere, the famous **Cyclone** (though the summer of 2007 will be the last one for the Cyclone's home, Astroland). Coney Island is also the home of the **New York Aquarium** and the minor-league baseball team the Cyclones. To get to Coney Island, take the F or Q to West 8th Street, Brooklyn.

The Bronx Perhaps the most famous destination in the Bronx, and next to Rome's Colosseum maybe one of the most celebrated sports arenas in the world, is **Yankee Stadium,** with 2008 to be that marvelous monument's last season. Even if you are a Yankee hater, you will be awed by the stadium The 4, B, or D trains all stop there.

The Bronx is also the home of the United States' largest metropolitan animal park, the **Bronx Zoo,** and the **New York Botanical Gardens.** Both are wonders worthy of an excursion. To get to the Bronx Zoo, you can take the 2 train to Pelham Parkway and walk to the Bronxdale entrance of the zoo. To get to the Botanical Gardens, you can take Metro-North from Grand Central Station to the Botanical Gardens station.

While visiting either the Bronx Zoo or the Botanical Gardens, stop at the Little Italy of the Bronx, **Arthur Avenue,** for a mouthwatering walk past meat markets, delis, vegetable stands, fish markets, cafes, and restaurants. To get to Arthur Avenue, take the 4, B, or D train to Fordham Road and transfer to the no. 12 bus east, or the no. 2 or 5 train to Pelham Parkway and the no. 12 bus west.

Queens Queens is the largest borough in New York and it's also the city's most ethnically diverse. There are more languages spoken in this 109 square miles than anywhere else on the planet. All that ethnicity translates into an adventurous eater's paradise. I've dined on Thai, Peruvian, Indian, Guyanese, Greek, Colombian, and Brazilian here, and I've barely scratched the surface. But there's more to Queens than just food.

Astoria, with its large Greek community, is also the home of the **American Museum of the Moving Image,** dedicated to the movies—film, video, and digital. To get there, take the R to Steinway Street or the N/W to 36th Avenue.

With former warehouses and factories being converted to expensive condos, **Long Island City,** directly across the river from Manhattan's Upper East Side, is becoming Queens' version of DUMBO. It is also where you will find a number of museums including the **Noguchi Museum, Socrates Park,** and the **P.S. 1 Contemporary Art Center.** The best train to take to get to Long Island City is the no. 7. The no. 7 train is also known as the International Express, running through one

Tips NYC Experiences to Avoid

New York has so much going for it, the good overwhelms the bad. But there is bad, and I'm not talking about the obvious. I'm talking about experiences that might be perceived as good, but take my word for it: They are not. So, despite what you have heard, the following are a few experiences you can avoid:

New Year's Eve in Times Square: You see it on television every year, and now you're here. This is your chance to be one of the thousands of revelers packed together in the frigid cold to watch the ball drop. *Don't do it!* Despite the happy faces you see on TV, the whole thing is a miserable experience and not worth the forced elation of blowing on a noisemaker at midnight with half a million others. You won't find many New Yorkers here; we know better.

Three-Card Monte: When you see a crowd gathered around a cardboard box with one man flipping cards, madly enticing innocent rubes into his game, while another guy scans the crowd for undercover cops, keep on walking. Don't stop and listen to the dealer's spiel or think you can be the one to beat him at his game. You can't. Buy a lottery ticket instead; your odds are much better.

Horse-Drawn Carriage Rides: Pity those poor beasts of burden. They get dragged out in the heat (though not extreme heat) and cold (though not extreme cold) with a buggy attached just to give passengers the feel of an old-world, romantic buggy ride through Central Park. But the horses look so forlorn, as if it's the last thing they want to do. And they don't even get a cut of the generous take: $40 for a 20-minute ride, $60 for 45 minutes, excluding tip. If you want a slow, leisurely ride through Central Park, minus the ripe and frequent smell of horse poop, consider an alternative called **Manhattan Rickshaw Company** (© **212/604-4729;** www.manhattanrickshaw. com). The beast of burden has two legs, and pedals you and a companion in the back of a pedicab, where the rate is negotiable but is usually about $1 per minute with a $10 minimum.

ethnic community after another; get off at just about any spot and you'll see signs in an assortment of languages. The no. 7 train will also take you to Flushing, where you'll find **Shea Stadium,** home of the Mets; the Louis Armstrong Stadium and the Arthur Ashe Stadium at **Flushing Meadow Park,** where the **U.S. Open** is held each September; and the **Queens Museum of Art** on the grounds of the 1964 World's Fair.

Staten Island Staten Island is the most remote of the boroughs and most enjoyably reached by ferry. There is a suburban feel to the borough, making it a haven for commuters. The free **Staten Island Ferry** gets you to the borough. If you decide to spend time in Staten Island, take in a **Staten Island Yankees** minor-league baseball game. The stadium is within walking distance of the ferry and has lovely views of downtown Manhattan.

Chain Restaurants: Oh yes; they're here, probably to stay—and most likely with more to come. I'm referring to those restaurants with familiar names like Olive Garden, Applebee's, Red Lobster, and Domino's. When you begin to feel the pangs of hunger, ask yourself: Did I come to New York to eat what I can eat in every city or town in this country? Or did I come here to experience what makes New York so unique? Well, that includes the amazing variety of unchained restaurants, from the coffee shops and diners to the bargain-priced ethnic cuisine and higher-end dining experiences. So bypass the old standards, and try something different and exciting. You won't regret it.

The Feast of San Gennaro: At one time this was a genuine Italian feast (see the films *Godfather II* and *Mean Streets* for the Feast in the good old days). Its decline has pretty much coincided with the decline of Little Italy, a neighborhood that is just a shell of what it once was. Now the Feast, held annually for 2 weeks in September, is just an overblown and overcrowded street fair with bad food, cheap red wine, and games of chance you have no chance of winning.

Driving in the City: You have been warned already about driving in the city, but some people are stubborn and just can't give up the so-called freedom of maneuvering a car in heavy traffic, battling yellow cabs, and searching fruitlessly for a legal parking spot. With subways, buses, and your feet, New York has the best and fastest public transportation. A car is a luxury you want no part of.

Waiting on Lines for Breakfast: (And please note, New Yorkers wait *on* line, not *in* line). Sometimes New Yorkers can be masochistic—and silly. They hear about a restaurant that serves a great breakfast, and they begin lining up on weekend mornings to eat. Sometimes they wait for over an hour, standing outside, winter or summer, to order pancakes, omelets, or whatever else the breakfast menu offers. They do this even though many coffee shops and diners are serving patrons the same foods at much less cost and without more than a minute's wait. Now what would you do?

2 Getting Around

Frankly, Manhattan's transportation systems are a marvel. It's simply miraculous that so many people can gather on this little island and move around it. For the most part, you can get where you're going pretty quickly and easily using some combination of subways, buses, and cabs; this section will tell you how to do just that.

But between traffic gridlock and subway delays, sometimes you just can't get there from here—unless you walk. Walking can sometimes be the fastest way to navigate the island. During rush hours, you'll easily beat car traffic while on foot, as taxis and buses stop and groan at gridlocked corners (don't even *try* going crosstown in a cab or bus in Midtown at midday). You'll also see a whole lot more by walking than you will if you ride beneath the street in the subway or fly by in a cab. So pack your most comfortable shoes and hit the pavement—it's the best, cheapest, and most appealing way to experience the city.

BY SUBWAY

Run by the **Metropolitan Transit Authority (MTA),** the much-maligned subway system is actually the fastest way to travel around New York, especially during rush hours. Some 3.5 million people a day seem to agree with me, as it's their primary mode of transportation. The subway is quick, inexpensive, relatively safe, and pretty efficient, as well as being a genuine New York experience.

The subway runs 24 hours a day, 7 days a week. The rush-hour crushes are roughly from 8 to 9:30am and from 5 to 6:30pm on weekdays; the rest of the time the trains are much more manageable.

PAYING YOUR WAY

The subway fare is $2 (half-price for seniors and those with disabilities), and children under 44 inches tall ride free (up to three per adult).

Tokens are no longer available. People now pay fares with the **MetroCard,** a magnetically encoded card that debits the fare when swiped through the turnstile (or the fare box on any city bus). Once you're in the system, you can transfer freely to any subway line that you can reach without exiting your station. MetroCards also allow you **free transfers** between the bus and subway within a 2-hour period.

MetroCards can be purchased from staffed token booths, where you can only pay with cash; at the ATM-style vending machines now located in just about every subway station in the city, which accept cash, credit cards, and debit cards; from a Metro-Card merchant, such as most Rite Aid drugstores or Hudson News at Penn Station and Grand Central Terminal; or at the MTA information desk at the Times Square Information Center, 1560 Broadway, between 46th and 47th streets.

MetroCards come in a few different configurations:

Tips Sidewalks of New York

What's the primary means New Yorkers use for getting around town? The subway? Buses? Taxis? Nope. Walking. They stride across wide, crowded pavements without any regard for traffic lights, weaving through crowds at high speeds, dodging taxis and buses whose drivers are forced to interrupt the normal flow of traffic to avoid flattening them. **Never take your walking cues from the locals.** Wait for walk signals and always use crosswalks—don't cross in the middle of the block. Do otherwise and you could quickly end up as a flattened statistic (or at least get a ticket for jaywalking).

Always pay attention to the traffic flow. Walk as though you're driving, staying to the right. Pay attention to what's happening in the street, even if you have the right of way. At intersections, keep an eye out for drivers who don't yield, turn without looking, or think a yellow traffic light means "Hurry up!" as you cross. Unfortunately, most bicyclists seem to think that the traffic laws don't apply to them; they'll often blithely fly through red lights and dash the wrong way on one-way streets, so be on your guard.

For more important safety tips, see "Playing It Safe," later in this chapter.

Subway Stops for New York's Top Attractions

ATTRACTIONS	SUBWAY STOPS
MUSEUMS	
American Museum of Natural History	B, C to 81st Street
The Cloisters	A to 190th Street
Ellis Island	4, 5 to Bowling Green or N, R to Whitehall Street
Guggenheim Museum	4, 5, 6 to 86th Street
Intrepid Sea-Air-Space Museum	A, C, E to 42nd Street–Port Authority
Metropolitan Museum of Art	4, 5, 6 to 86th Street
Museum of Modern Art	E, V to Fifth Avenue
HISTORIC BUILDINGS AND ARCHITECTURE	
Brooklyn Bridge	4, 5, 6 to Brooklyn Bridge–City Hall
Chrysler Building	4, 5, 6, 7, S to Grand Central–42nd Street
Empire State Building	B, D, F, V, N, R, Q, W to 34th Street–Herald Square
Grand Central Terminal	4, 5, 6, 7, S to Grand Central–42nd Street
Rockefeller Center	B, D, F, V to 47–50th streets–Rockefeller Center
Staten Island Ferry	1 to South Ferry (first five cars)
United Nations	4, 5, 6, 7, S to Grand Central–42nd Street
Yankee Stadium	4, B, D to 161st River Avenue–Yankee Stadium
NEIGHBORHOODS	
Chinatown	6, J, M, Z, N, R, Q, W to Canal Street
Greenwich Village	A, C, E, B, D, F, V to West 4th Street
Times Square	1, 2, 3, 7, N, R, W, S to 42nd Street–Times Square
Wall Street	4, 5 to Wall Street or N, R to Rector Street
CHURCHES	
Cathedral of St. John the Divine	1 to Cathedral Parkway (110th St.)
St. Patrick's Cathedral	B, D, F, V to 47–50th streets–Rockefeller Center or E, V to Fifth Avenue–53rd Street

Subway Service Interruption Notes

The subway map featured on the inside back cover of this book was as accurate as possible at press time, but service is always subject to change, so your best bet is to contact the **Metropolitan Transit Authority (MTA)** for the latest details; call © **718/330-1234** or visit **www.mta.nyc.ny.us**, where you'll find system updates that are thorough, timely, and clear. Also read any posters that are taped up on the platform or notices written on the token booth's whiteboard. Once in town, you can stop at the MTA desk at the **Times Square Information Center,** 1560 Broadway, between 46th and 47th streets (where Broadway meets Seventh Ave.) to pick up the latest subway map. (You can also ask for one at any token booth, but they might not always be stocked.)

Pay-Per-Ride MetroCards can be used for up to four people by swiping up to four times (bring the whole family). You can put any amount from $4 (two rides) to $80 on your card. Every time you put $10 or $20 on your Pay-Per-Ride MetroCard, it's automatically credited 20%—that's one free ride for every $10, or five trips. You can buy Pay-Per-Ride MetroCards at any subway station; an increasing number of stations now have automated MetroCard vending machines, which allow you to buy Metro-Cards using your major credit card. MetroCards are also available from shops and newsstands around town in $10 and $20 values. You can refill your card at any time until the expiration date on the card, usually about a year from the date of purchase, at any subway station.

Unlimited-Ride MetroCards, which can't be used for more than one person at a time or more frequently than 18-minute intervals, are available in four values: the **daily Fun Pass,** which allows you a day's worth of unlimited subway and bus rides for $7; the **7-Day MetroCard,** for $24; and the **30-Day MetroCard,** for $76. Seven- and 30-day Unlimited-Ride MetroCards can be purchased at any subway station or from a MetroCard merchant. Fun Passes, however, cannot be purchased at token booths—you can only buy them at a MetroCard vending machine; from a MetroCard merchant; or at the MTA information desk at the Times Square Information Center. Unlimited-Ride MetroCards go into effect not at the time you buy them but the first time you use them—so if you buy a card on Monday and don't begin to use it until Wednesday, Wednesday is when the clock starts ticking on your MetroCard. A Fun Pass is good from the first time you use it until 3am the next day, while 7- and 30-day MetroCards run out at midnight on the last day. These MetroCards cannot be refilled; throw them out once they've been used up and buy a new one.

Tips for using your MetroCard: The MetroCard swiping mechanisms at turnstiles are the source of much grousing among subway riders. If you swipe too fast or too slow, the turnstile will ask you to swipe again. If this happens, *do not move to a different turnstile,* or you may end up paying twice. If you've tried repeatedly and really can't make your MetroCard work, tell the token booth clerk; chances are good, though, that you'll get the movement down after a couple of uses.

If you're not sure how much money you have left on your MetroCard, or what day it expires, use the station's MetroCard Reader, usually located near the station entrance or the token booth (on buses, the fare box will also provide you with this information).

To locate the nearest MetroCard merchant, or for any other MetroCard questions, call © **800/METROCARD** or 212/METROCARD (212/638-7622) Monday through

Friday between 7am and 11pm, Saturday and Sunday from 9am to 5pm. Or go online to **www.mta.nyc.ny.us/metrocard**, which can give you a full rundown of MetroCard merchants in the tri-state area.

USING THE SYSTEM

As you can see from the full-color subway map on the inside back cover of this book, the subway system basically mimics the lay of the land aboveground, with most lines in Manhattan running north and south, like the avenues, and a few lines east and west, like the streets.

To go up and down the east side of Manhattan (and to the Bronx and Brooklyn), take the 4, 5, or 6 train.

To travel up and down the west side (and also to the Bronx and Brooklyn), take the 1, 2, or 3 line; the A, C, E, or F line; or the B or D line.

The N, R, Q, and W lines first cut diagonally across town from east to west and then snake under Seventh Avenue before shooting out to Queens.

The crosstown S line, the Shuttle, runs back and forth between Times Square and Grand Central Terminal. Farther downtown, across 14th Street, the L line works its own crosstown magic.

Lines have assigned colors on subway maps and trains—red for the 1, 2, 3 line; green for the 4, 5, 6 trains; and so on—but nobody ever refers to them by color. Always refer to them by number or letter when asking questions. Within Manhattan, the distinction between different numbered trains that share the same line is usually that some are express and others are local. **Express trains** often skip about three stops for each one that they make; express stops are indicated on subway maps with a white (rather than solid) circle. Local stops are usually about 9 blocks apart.

Directions are almost always indicated using "Uptown" (northbound) and "Downtown" (southbound), so be sure to know what direction you want to head in. The

---

Tips For More Bus & Subway Information

For additional transit information, call the Metropolitan Transit Authority's **MTA/New York City Transit's Travel Information Center** at 𝄐 **718/330-1234.** Extensive automated information is available at this number 24 hours a day, and travel agents are on hand to answer your questions and provide directions daily from 6am to 9pm. For online information that's always up-to-the-minute current, visit **www.mta.nyc.ny.us.**

To request system maps, call the Customer Service Line at 𝄐 **718/330-3322** (although realize that recent service changes may not yet be reflected on printed maps). Riders with disabilities should direct inquiries to 𝄐 **718/596-8585;** hearing-impaired riders can call 𝄐 **718/596-8273.** For MetroCard information, call 𝄐 **212/638-7622** weekdays from 7am to 11pm, weekends 9am to 5pm, or go online to **www.mta.nyc.ny.us/metrocard.**

You can get bus and subway maps and additional transit information at most information centers (see "Visitor Information" in "Orientation," earlier in this chapter). A particularly helpful MTA transit information desk is located at the **Times Square Information Center,** 1560 Broadway, between 46th and 47th streets, where you can also buy MetroCards. Maps are sometimes available in subway stations (ask at the token booth), but rarely on buses.

outsides of some subway entrances are marked UPTOWN ONLY or DOWNTOWN ONLY; read carefully, as it's easy to head in the wrong direction. Once you're on the platform, check the signs overhead to make sure that the train you're waiting for will be traveling in the right direction. If you do make a mistake, it's a good idea to wait for an express station, such as 14th Street or 42nd Street, so you can get off and change to the other direction without paying again.

The days of graffiti-covered cars are gone, but the stations—and an increasing number of trains—are not nearly as clean as they could be. Trains are air-conditioned (move to the next car if yours isn't), though during the dog days of summer the platforms can be sweltering. In theory, all subway cars have PA systems to allow you to hear the conductor's announcements, but they don't always work well. It's a good idea to move to a car with a working PA system in case sudden service changes are announced that you'll want to know about.

For **subway safety tips,** see "For More Bus & Subway Information," below.

BY BUS

Less expensive than taxis and more pleasant than subways (they provide a mobile sightseeing window on Manhattan), MTA buses are a good transportation option. Their big drawback: They can get stuck in traffic, sometimes making it quicker to walk. They also stop every couple of blocks, rather than the 8 or 9 blocks that local subways traverse between stops. So for long distances, the subway is your best bet; but for short distances or traveling crosstown, try the bus.

PAYING YOUR WAY

Like the subway fare, **bus fare** is $2, half-price for seniors and riders with disabilities, and free for children under 44 inches (up to three per adult). The fare is payable with a **MetroCard** or **exact change.** Bus drivers don't make change, and fare boxes don't accept dollar bills or pennies. You can't purchase MetroCards on the bus, so you'll have to have them before you board; for details on where to get them, see "Paying Your Way" under "By Subway," above.

If you pay with a MetroCard, you can transfer to another bus or to the subway for free within 2 hours. If you pay cash, you must request a **free transfer** slip that allows you to change to an intersecting bus route only (transfer points are listed on the transfer paper) within 1 hour of issue. Transfer slips cannot be used to enter the subway.

USING THE SYSTEM

You can't flag a city bus down—you have to meet it at a bus stop. **Bus stops** are located every 2 or 3 blocks on the right-side corner of the street (facing the direction

---

(*Tips*) Take a Free Ride

The Alliance for Downtown New York's **Downtown Connection** offers a free bus service that provides easy access to Downtown destinations, including Battery Park City, the World Financial Center, and South Street Seaport. The buses, which run daily, every 10 to 15 minutes, from 10am to 7:30pm, make dozens of stops along a 5-mile route from Chambers Street on the West Side to Beekman Street on the East Side. For schedules and more information, call the Downtown Alliance at (*C*) **212/566-6700** or visit www.downtownny.com.

> **Tips** **Taxi-Hailing Tips**
>
> When you're waiting on the street for an available taxi, look at the **medallion light** on the top of the coming cabs. If the light is out, the taxi is in use. When the center part (the number) is lit, the taxi is available—this is when you raise your hand to flag the cab. If all the lights are on, the driver is off-duty. A taxi can't take more than four people, so expect to split up if your group is larger.

of traffic flow). They're marked by a curb painted yellow and a blue-and-white sign with a bus emblem and the route number or numbers. Guide-a-Ride boxes at most stops display a route map and a hysterically optimistic schedule.

Almost every major avenue has its own **bus route.** They run either north or south: downtown on Fifth, uptown on Madison, downtown on Lexington, uptown on Third, and so on. There are **crosstown buses** at strategic locations all around town: 8th Street (eastbound); 9th (westbound); 14th, 23rd, 34th, and 42nd (east- and westbound); 49th (eastbound); 50th (westbound); 57th (east- and westbound); 65th (eastbound across the West Side, through the park, and then north on Madison, continuing east on 68th to York Ave.); 67th (westbound on the East Side to Fifth Ave. and then south on Fifth, continuing west on 66th St. through the park and across the West Side to West End Ave.); and 79th, 86th, 96th, 116th, and 125th (east- and westbound). Some bus routes, however, are erratic: The M104, for example, starts at the East River, then turns at Eighth Avenue and goes up Broadway. The buses of the Fifth Avenue line go up Madison or Sixth and follow various routes around the city.

Most routes operate 24 hours a day, but service is infrequent at night. Some say that New York buses have a herding instinct: They arrive only in groups. During rush hour, main routes have "limited" buses, identifiable by the red card in the front window; they stop only at major cross streets.

To make sure that the bus you're boarding goes where you're going, check the map on the sign that's at every bus stop, get your hands on a route map (see "For More Bus & Subway Information," above), or **just ask.** The drivers are helpful, as long as you don't hold up the line too long.

While traveling, look out the window not only to take in the sights but also to keep track of cross streets so you know when to get off. Signal for a stop by pressing the tape strip above and beside the windows and along the metal straps, about 2 blocks before you want to stop. Exit through the pneumatic back doors (not the front door) by pushing on the yellow tape strip; the doors open automatically (pushing on the handles is useless unless you're as buff as Hercules). Most city buses are equipped with wheelchair lifts, making buses the preferable mode of public transportation for wheelchair-bound travelers; for more on this topic, see "Specialized Travel Resources," on p. 50. Buses also "kneel," lowering down to the curb to make boarding easier.

BY TAXI

If you don't want to deal with public transportation, finding an address that might be a few blocks from the subway station, or sharing your ride with 3.5 million other people, then take a taxi. The biggest advantages are, of course, that cabs can be hailed on any street (provided you find an empty one—often simple, yet at other times nearly impossible) and will take you right to your destination. I find they're best used at night when there's little traffic to keep them from speeding you to your destination and when the subway may seem a little daunting. In Midtown at midday, you can usually walk to where you're going more quickly.

Official New York City taxis, licensed by the Taxi and Limousine Commission (TLC), are yellow, with the rates printed on the door and a light with a medallion number on the roof. You can hail a taxi on any street. *Never* accept a ride from any other car except an official city yellow cab (private livery cars are not allowed to pick up fares on the street).

The base fare on entering the cab is $2.50. The cost is 40¢ for every ⅕ mile or 40¢ per 60 seconds in stopped or slow-moving traffic (or for waiting time). There's no extra charge for each passenger or for luggage. However, you must pay bridge or tunnel tolls (sometimes the driver will front the toll and add it to your bill at the end; most times, however, you pay the driver before the toll). You'll also pay a $1 surcharge between 4 and 8pm and a 50¢ surcharge after 8pm and before 6am. A 15% to 20% tip is customary. (At press time the cab drivers were lobbying the city for a fare hike due to increased fuel costs).

Forget about hopping into the back seat and having some cigar-chomping, all-knowing driver slowly turn and ask nonchalantly, "Where to, Mac?" Nowadays most taxi drivers speak only an approximation of English and drive in engagingly exotic ways. Always wear your seat belt—taxis are required to provide them.

The TLC has posted a **Taxi Rider's Bill of Rights** sticker in every cab. Drivers are required by law to take you anywhere in the five boroughs, to Nassau or Westchester counties, or to Newark Airport. They are supposed to know how to get you to any address in Manhattan and all major points in the outer boroughs. They are also required to provide air-conditioning and turn off the radio on demand, and they cannot smoke while you're in the cab. They are required to be polite.

You are allowed to dictate the route that is taken. It's a good idea to look at a map before you get in a taxi. Taxi drivers have been known to jack up the fare on visitors who don't know better by taking a circuitous route between points A and B. Know enough about where you're going to know that something's wrong if you hop in a cab at Sixth Avenue and 57th Street to go to the Empire State Building (Fifth Ave. and 34th St.), say, and you suddenly find yourself on Ninth Avenue.

On the other hand, listen to drivers who propose an alternate route. These guys spend 8 or 10 hours a day on these streets, and they know where the worst traffic is, or where Con Ed has dug up an intersection that should be avoided. A knowledgeable driver will know how to get you to your destination quickly and efficiently.

Another important tip: **Always make sure the meter is turned on at the start of the ride.** You'll see the red LED readout register the initial $2.50 and start calculating the fare as you go. I've witnessed unscrupulous drivers buzzing unsuspecting visitors around the city with the meter off, and then overcharging them at drop-off time.

Always ask for the receipt—it comes in handy if you need to make a complaint or have left something in a cab. In fact, it's a good idea to make a mental note of the driver's four-digit medallion number (usually posted on the divider between the front and back seats) just in case you need it later. You probably won't, but it's a good idea to play it safe.

A taxi driver is obligated to take you to your desired destination. If a taxi driver is on duty but refuses to take you to your desired destination, write down the driver's name and medallion number and file a complaint with the Taxi and Limousine Commission.

For all driver complaints, including the one above, and to report lost property, call
© **311** or 212-NEWYORK (outside the metro area). For details on getting to and
from the local airports by taxi, see "By Plane" under "Getting There," in chapter 3.
For further taxi information—including a complete rundown of your rights as a taxi
rider—point your Web browser to **www.ci.nyc.ny.us/taxi.**

BY CAR

Forget driving yourself around the city. It's not worth the headache. Traffic is horren-
dous, and you don't know the rules of the road (written or unwritten) or the arcane
alternate-side-of-the-street parking regulations (in fact, precious few New Yorkers do).
You don't want to find out the monstrous price of parking violations or live the
Kafkaesque nightmare of liberating a vehicle from the tow pound. Not to mention the
security risks.

If you do arrive in New York City by car, park it in a garage (expect to pay at least
$25–$45 per day) and leave it there for the duration of your stay. If you drive a rental
car in, return it as soon as you arrive and rent another on the day you leave. Just about
all of the major car-rental companies, including **National** (© **800/227-7368;** www.
nationalcar.com), **Hertz** (© **800/654-3131;** www.hertz.com), and **Avis** (© **800/230-
4898;** www.avis.com), have multiple Manhattan locations.

TRAVELING FROM THE CITY TO THE SUBURBS

The **PATH** (© **800/234-7284;** www.panynj.gov/path) system connects cities in New
Jersey, including Hoboken and Newark, to Manhattan by subway-style trains. Stops
in Manhattan are at the World Trade Center, Christopher and 9th streets, and along
Sixth Avenue at 14th, 23rd, and 33rd streets. The fare is $1.50 one way.

New Jersey Transit (© **800/772-2222;** www.njtransit.com) operates commuter
trains from Penn Station, and buses from the Port Authority at Eighth Avenue and
42nd Street, to points throughout New Jersey.

The **Long Island Rail Road** (© **718/217-LIRR;** www.mta.nyc.ny.us/lirr) runs
from Penn Station, at Seventh Avenue between 31st and 33rd streets, to Queens
(ocean beaches, Shea Stadium, Belmont Park) and points beyond on Long Island, to
even better beaches and summer hot spots like Fire Island and the Hamptons.

Metro-North Railroad (© **800/METRO-INFO** or 212/532-4900; www.mta.nyc.
ny.us/mnr) departs from Grand Central Terminal, at 42nd Street and Lexington
Avenue, for areas north of the city, including Westchester County, the lovely Hudson
Valley, and Connecticut.

3 Playing It Safe

Sure, there's crime in New York City, but millions of people spend their lives here without being robbed or assaulted. In fact, New York is safer than any other big American
city and is listed by the FBI as somewhere around 150th in the nation for total crimes.
While that's quite encouraging for all of us, it's still important to take precautions. Visitors especially should remain vigilant, as swindlers and criminals are expert at spotting
newcomers who appear disoriented or vulnerable.

Men should carry their wallets in their front pockets and women should keep hold
of their purse straps. Cross camera and purse straps over one shoulder, across your
front, and under the other arm. Never hang a purse on the back of a chair or on a
hook in a bathroom stall; keep it in your lap or between your feet, with one foot

Impressions

I like it here in New York. I like the idea of having to keep eyes in the back of your head all the time.

—John Cale

through a strap and up against the purse itself. Avoid carrying large amounts of cash. You might carry your money in several pockets so that if one is picked, the others might escape. Skip the flashy jewelry and keep valuables out of sight when you're on the street.

Panhandlers are seldom dangerous and can be ignored (more aggressive pleas can firmly be answered, "Not today"). If a stranger walks up to you on the street with a long sob story ("I live in the suburbs and was just attacked and don't have the money to get home" or whatever), it's most likely a scam, so don't feel any moral compulsion to help. You have every right to walk away and not feel bad. Be wary of an individual who "accidentally" falls in front of you or causes some other commotion, because he or she may be working with someone else who will take your wallet when you try to help. And remember: You *will* lose if you place a bet on a sidewalk game of chance.

Certain areas should be approached with care late at night. I don't recommend going to the Lower East Side, Alphabet City in the far East Village, or the Meat-Packing District unless you know where you're going. Don't be afraid to go, but head straight for your destination and don't wander onto deserted side streets. The areas above 96th Street aren't the best, either (although they're improving almost by the day). Times Square has been cleaned up, and there'll be crowds around until midnight, when theater- and moviegoers leave the area. Still, stick to the main streets, such as Broadway or Ninth Avenue, Midtown West's newest restaurant row. The areas south of Times Square are best avoided after dark, as they're largely abandoned once the business day ends. Take a cab or bus when visiting the Jacob Javits Center on 34th Street and the Hudson River. Don't go wandering the parks after dark, unless you're going to a performance; if that's the case, stick with the crowd.

If you plan on visiting the outer boroughs, go during the daylight hours. If the subway doesn't go directly to your destination, your best bet is to take a taxi. Don't wander the side streets; many areas in the outer boroughs are absolutely safe, but neighborhoods change quickly, and it's easy to get lost.

All this having been said, don't panic. New York has experienced a dramatic drop in crime and is generally safe these days, especially in the neighborhoods that visitors are prone to frequent. There's a good police presence on the street, so don't be afraid to stop an officer, or even a friendly looking New Yorker (trust me—you can tell), if you need help getting your bearings.

SUBWAY SAFETY TIPS   In general, the subways are safe, especially in Manhattan. There are panhandlers and questionable characters like anywhere else in the city, but subway crime has gone down to 1960s levels. Still, stay alert and trust your instincts. Always keep a hand on your personal belongings.

When using the subway, **don't wait for trains near the edge of the platform** or on extreme ends of a station. During nonrush hours, wait for the train in view of the token-booth clerk or under the yellow DURING OFF HOURS TRAINS STOP HERE signs, and ride in the train operator's or conductor's car (usually in the center of the train;

you'll see his or her head stick out of the window when the doors open). Choose crowded cars over empty ones—there's safety in numbers.

Avoid subways late at night, and splurge on a cab after about 10 or 11pm—it's money well spent to avoid a long wait on a deserted platform. Or take the bus.

FAST FACTS: New York City

American Express Travel-service offices are at many Manhattan locations, including 295 Park Avenue South at 23rd Street (© 212/691-9797); at the New York Marriott Marquis, 1535 Broadway, in the eighth-floor lobby (© 212/575-6580); on the mezzanine level at Macy's Herald Square, 34th Street and Broadway (© 212/695-8075); and 374 Park Ave., at 53rd Street (© 212/421-8240). Call © 800/AXP-TRIP or go online to www.americanexpress.com for other city locations or general information.

Area Codes There are four area codes in the city: two in Manhattan, the original **212** and the new **646,** and two in the outer boroughs, the original **718** and the new **347.** Also common is the **917** area code, which is assigned to cellphones, pagers, and the like. All calls between these area codes are local calls, but you'll have to dial 1 + the area code + the seven digits for all calls, even ones made within your area code.

Business Hours In general, **retail stores** are open Monday through Saturday from 10am to 6 or 7pm, Thursday from 10am to 8:30 or 9pm, and Sunday from noon to 5pm (see chapter 9). **Banks** tend to be open Monday through Friday from 9am to 3pm and sometimes Saturday mornings.

Currency The most common bills are the $1 (a "buck"), $5, $10, and $20 denominations. There are also $2 bills (seldom encountered), $50 bills, and $100 bills (the last two are usually not welcome as payment for small purchases).

Coins come in seven denominations: 1¢ (1 cent, or a penny); 5¢ (5 cents, or a nickel); 10¢ (10 cents, or a dime); 25¢ (25 cents, or a quarter); 50¢ (50 cents, or a half dollar); and various (not often seen) dollar coins.

Customs **What You Can Bring Into the U.S.** Every visitor more than 21 years of age may bring in, free of duty, the following: (1) 1 liter of wine or hard liquor; (2) 200 cigarettes, 100 cigars (but not from Cuba), or 3 pounds of smoking tobacco; and (3) $100 worth of gifts. These exemptions are offered to travelers who spend at least 72 hours in the United States and who have not claimed them within the preceding 6 months. It is forbidden to bring in foodstuffs (particularly fruit, cooked meats, and canned goods) and plants (vegetables, seeds, tropical plants, and the like). Foreign tourists may carry in or out up to $10,000 in U.S. or foreign currency with no formalities; larger sums must be declared to U.S. Customs on entering or leaving, which includes filing form CM 4790. For details regarding U.S. Customs and Border Protection, consult your nearest U.S. embassy or consulate, or **U.S. Customs** (© 202/927-1770; www.customs.ustreas.gov).

What You Can Take Home from New York City:

Canadian Citizens: For a clear summary of Canadian rules, write for the booklet *I Declare,* issued by the **Canada Border Services Agency** (© 800/461-9999 in Canada, or 204/983-3500; www.cbsa-asfc.gc.ca).

U.K. Citizens: For information, contact **HM Customs & Excise** at ✆ **0845/010-9000** (from outside the U.K., 020/8929-0152), or consult their website at **www.hmce.gov.uk.**

Australian Citizens: A helpful brochure available from Australian consulates or Customs offices is *Know Before You Go.* For more information, call the **Australian Customs Service** at ✆ **1300/363-263,** or log on to **www.customs.gov.au.**

Doctors For medical emergencies requiring immediate attention, head to the nearest emergency room (see "Hospitals," below). For less urgent health problems, New York has several walk-in medical centers, such as **DOCS at New York Healthcare,** 55 E. 34th St., between Park and Madison avenues (✆ **212/252-6001**), for nonemergency illnesses. The clinic, affiliated with Beth Israel Medical Center, is open Monday through Friday from 8am to 7pm, Saturday from 9am to 1pm, and Sunday from 9am to 1pm. The **NYU Downtown Hospital** offers physician referrals at ✆ **212/312-5000.**

Electricity Like Canada, the United States uses 110 to 120 volts AC (60 cycles), compared to 220 to 240 volts AC (50 cycles) in most of Europe, Australia, and New Zealand. Downward converters that change 220–240 volts to 110–120 volts are difficult to find in the United States, so bring one with you.

Embassies & Consulates All embassies are in Washington, D.C. Some consulates are in New York and most nations have a mission to the United Nations. If your country isn't listed, call for directory information in Washington, D.C. (✆ **202/555-1212**) or log on to **www.embassy.org/embassies.**

The embassy of **Australia** is at 1601 Massachusetts Ave. NW, Washington, DC 20036 (✆ **202/797-3000;** www.austemb.org). There is a consulate in New York City.

The embassy of **Canada** is at 501 Pennsylvania Ave. NW, Washington, DC 20001 (✆ **202/682-1740;** www.canadianembassy.org). There is a consulate in New York City.

The embassy of **Ireland** is at 2234 Massachusetts Ave. NW, Washington, DC 20008 (✆ **202/462-3939;** www.irelandemb.org). Consulates are in Boston, Chicago, New York, and San Francisco. See website for complete listing.

The embassy of the **United Kingdom** is at 3100 Massachusetts Ave. NW, Washington, DC 20008 (✆ **202/588-7800;** www.britainusa.com). There is a consulate in New York City.

Emergencies Dial ✆ **911** for fire, police, and ambulance. The **Poison Control Center** can be reached at ✆ **800/222-1222** toll-free from any phone.

Holidays Banks, government offices, post offices, and many stores, restaurants, and museums are closed on the following legal national holidays: January 1 (New Year's Day), the third Monday in January (Martin Luther King, Jr., Day), the third Monday in February (Presidents' Day), the last Monday in May (Memorial Day), July 4 (Independence Day), the first Monday in September (Labor Day), the second Monday in October (Columbus Day), November 11 (Veterans' Day/Armistice Day), the fourth Thursday in November (Thanksgiving Day), and December 25 (Christmas). The Tuesday after the first Monday in November is Election Day, a federal government holiday in presidential-election years (held every 4 years, and next in 2008).

For more information on holidays see "New York City Calendar of Events," in chapter 3.

Hospitals The following hospitals have 24-hour emergency rooms. Don't forget your insurance card.

Downtown: New York University Downtown Hospital, 170 William St., between Beekman and Spruce streets (✆ 212/312-5063 or 212/312-5000); **St. Vincent's Hospital and Medical Center,** 153 W. 11th St., at Seventh Avenue (✆ 212/604-7000); and **Beth Israel Medical Center,** First Avenue and 16th Street (✆ 212/420-2000).

Midtown: Bellevue Hospital Center, 462 First Ave., at 27th Street (✆ 212/562-4141; **New York University Medical Center,** 550 First Ave., at 33rd Street (✆ 212/263-7300); and **St. Luke's/Roosevelt Hospital,** 425 W. 59th St., between Ninth and Tenth avenues (✆ 212/523-4000).

Upper West Side: St. Luke's Hospital Center, 1111 Amsterdam Avenue at 114th Street (✆ 212/523-4000); and **Columbia Presbyterian Medical Center,** 622 W. 168th St., between Broadway and Fort Washington Avenue (✆ 212/305-2500).

Upper East Side: New York Presbyterian Hospital, 525 E. 68th St., at York Avenue (✆ 212/472-5454); **Lenox Hill Hospital,** 100 E. 77th St., between Park and Lexington avenues (✆ 212/434-2000); and **Mount Sinai Medical Center,** 1190 Fifth Avenue at 100th Street (✆ 212/241-6500).

Hot Lines **Department of Consumer Affairs** ✆ 212/487-4444; and **taxi complaints** at ✆ 212/NYC-TAXI. If you suspect your car may have been towed, call the **Department of Transportation TOWAWAY Help Line** at ✆ 311. You can also call 311 for any non-emergency city matters or questions.

Internet Centers See the box "Where to Check Your E-Mail in the City That Never Sleeps," on p. 56.

Libraries The **New York Public Library** is on Fifth Avenue at 42nd Street (✆ **212/930-0830**). This Beaux Arts beauty houses more than 38 million volumes, and the beautiful reading rooms have been restored to their former glory. More efficient and modern, if less charming, is the mid-Manhattan branch at 455 Fifth Ave., at 40th Street, across the street from the main library (✆ **212/340-0833**). There are other branches in almost every neighborhood; you can find a list online at **www.nypl.org**.

Liquor Laws The minimum legal age to purchase and consume alcoholic beverages in New York is 21. Liquor and wine are sold only in licensed stores, which are open 6 days a week, with most choosing to close on Sunday. Liquor stores are closed on holidays and election days while the polls are open. Beer can be purchased in grocery stores and delis 24 hours a day, except Sunday before noon. Last call in bars is at 4am, although many close earlier.

Lost & Found Be sure to tell all of your credit card companies the minute you discover your wallet has been lost or stolen and file a report at the nearest police precinct. Your credit card company or insurer may require a police report number or record of the loss. Most credit card companies have an emergency toll-free number to call if your card is lost or stolen; they may be able to wire you a cash advance immediately or deliver an emergency credit card in a day or two. Visa's U.S. emergency number is © 800/847-2911 or 410/581-9994. American Express cardholders and traveler's check holders should call © 800/221-7282. MasterCard holders should call © 800/307-7309 or 636/722-7111. For other credit cards, call the toll-free number directory at © 800/555-1212.

Mail At press time, domestic postage rates were 26¢ for a postcard and 41¢ for a letter. For international mail, a first-class letter of up to 1 ounce costs 84¢ (63¢ to Canada and Mexico); a first-class postcard costs 75¢ (55¢ to Canada and Mexico); and a preprinted postal aerogramme costs 75¢. For more information go to **www.usps.com** and click on "Calculate Postage."

Always include zip codes when mailing items in the U.S. If you don't know your zip code, visit www.usps.com/zip4.

Newspapers & Magazines There are three major daily newspapers: the *New York Times,* the *Daily News,* and the *New York Post.*

If you want to find your hometown paper, visit **Universal News & Magazines,** at 234 W. 42nd St., between Seventh and Eighth avenues (© 212/221-1809), and 977 Eighth Ave., between 57th and 58th streets (© 212/459-0932); or **Hotalings News Agency,** 624 W. 52nd St., between Eleventh and Twelfth avenues (© 212/974-9419). Other good bets include the **Hudson** newsdealers, located in Grand Central Terminal, at 42nd Street and Lexington Avenue, and Penn Station, at 34th Street and Seventh Avenue.

Passports For Residents of Australia: You can pick up an application from your local post office or any branch of Passports Australia, but you must schedule an interview at the passport office to present your application materials. Call the **Australian Passport Information Service** at © 13-12-32, or visit the government website at www.passports.gov.au.

For Residents of Canada: Passport applications are available at travel agencies throughout Canada or from the central **Passport Office,** Department of Foreign Affairs and International Trade, Ottawa, ON K1A 0G3 (© 800/567-6868; www.ppt.gc.ca). *Note:* Canadian children who travel must have their own passport. However, if you hold a valid Canadian passport issued before December 11, 2001, that bears the name of your child, the passport remains valid for you and your child until it expires.

For Residents of Ireland: You can apply for a 10-year passport at the **Passport Office,** Setanta Centre, Molesworth Street, Dublin 2 (© 01/671-1633; www. irlgov.ie/iveagh). Those under age 18 and over 65 must apply for a 3-year passport. You can also apply at 1A South Mall, Cork (© 021/272-525) or at most main post offices.

For Residents of the United Kingdom: To pick up an application for a standard 10-year passport (5-yr. passport for children under 16), visit your nearest passport office, major post office, or travel agency or contact the **United Kingdom Passport Service** at © 0870/521-0410 or search its website at www.ukpa. gov.uk.

Pharmacies **Duane Reade** (www.duanereade.com) has 24-hour pharmacies in Midtown at 224 W. 57th St., at Broadway (© 212/541-9708); on the Upper West Side at 2465 Broadway, at 91st Street (© 212/663-1580); and on the Upper East Side at 1279 Third Ave., at 74th Street (© 212/744-2668).

Police Dial (℮) **911** in an emergency; otherwise, call (℮) **646/610-5000** or 718/610-5000 (NYPD headquarters) for the number of the nearest precinct.

Restrooms Public restrooms are available at the visitor centers in Midtown (1560 Broadway, between 46th and 47th sts.; and 810 Seventh Ave., between 52nd and 53rd sts.). Grand Central Terminal, at 42nd Street between Park and Lexington avenues, also has clean restrooms. Your best bet on the street is Starbucks or another city java chain—you can't walk more than a few blocks without seeing one. The big chain bookstores are good for this, too. You can also head to hotel lobbies (especially the big Midtown ones) and department stores like Macy's and Bloomingdale's. On the Lower East Side, stop into the Lower East Side BID Visitor Center, 261 Broome St., between Orchard and Allen streets (open every day, 10am–4pm, sometimes later).

Smoking Smoking is prohibited on all public transportation, in the lobbies of hotels and office buildings, in taxis, bars, restaurants, and in most shops.

Taxes Sales tax is 8.625% on meals, most goods, and some services, but it is not charged on clothing and footwear items under $110. **Hotel tax** is 13.25% plus $2 per room per night (including sales tax). **Parking garage tax** is 18.25%.

Time For the correct local time, dial (℮) **212/976-1616.** New York City is on Eastern Time (GMT -5 hours).

Tipping Tips are a very important part of certain workers' income, and gratuities are the standard way of showing appreciation for services provided. (Tipping is certainly not compulsory if the service is poor!) In hotels, tip **bellhops** at least $1 per bag ($2–$3 if you have a lot of luggage) and tip the **chamber staff** $1 to $2 per day (more if you've left a disaster area for him or her to clean up). Tip the **doorman** or **concierge** only if he or she has provided you with some specific service (for example, calling a cab for you or obtaining difficult-to-get theater tickets). In restaurants, bars, and nightclubs, tip **service staff** 15% to 20% of the check, tip **bartenders** 10% to 15%, tip **checkroom attendants** $1 per garment, and tip **valet-parking attendants** $1 per vehicle.

As for other service personnel, tip **cab drivers** 15% of the fare; tip **skycaps** at airports at least $1 per bag ($2–$3 if you have a lot of luggage); and tip **hairdressers** and **barbers** 15% to 20%.

Transit Information For information on getting to and from the airport, see "Getting There" in chapter 3, or call **Air-Ride** at (℮) **800/247-7433.** For information on subways and buses, call the **MTA** at (℮) **718/330-1234,** or see "Getting Around," earlier in this chapter.

Traveler's Assistance Travelers Aid (**www.travelersaid.org**) helps distressed travelers with all kinds of problems, including accidents, sickness, and lost or stolen luggage. There is an office on the first floor of Terminal 6 (JetBlue terminal) at JFK Airport ((℮) **718/656-4870**), and one in Newark Airport's Terminal B ((℮) **973/623-5052**).

Visas For information about U.S. Visas go to **http://travel.state.gov** and click on "Visas." Or go to one of the following websites:

Australian citizens can obtain up-to-date visa information from the **U.S. Embassy Canberra,** Moonah Place, Yarralumla, ACT 2600 ((℮) **02/6214-5600**) or by checking the U.S. Diplomatic Mission's website at **http://usembassy-australia. state.gov/consular**.

British subjects can obtain up-to-date visa information by calling the **U.S. Embassy Visa Information Line (© 0891/200-290)** or by visiting the "Visas to the U.S." section of the American Embassy London's website at **www.usembassy. org.uk**.

Irish citizens can obtain up-to-date visa information through the **Embassy of the USA Dublin,** 42 Elgin Rd., Dublin 4, Ireland (© **353/1-668-8777**; or by checking the "Consular Services" section of the website at **http://dublin.usembassy. gov**.

Citizens of **New Zealand** can obtain up-to-date visa information by contacting the **U.S. Embassy New Zealand,** 29 Fitzherbert Terrace, Thorndon, Wellington (© **644/472-2068**), or get the information directly from the website at **http://wellington.usembassy.gov**.

Weather For the current temperature and next day's forecast, look in the upper-right corner of the front page of the *New York Times* or call © **212/976-1212.** If you want to know how to pack before you arrive, point your browser to **www.cnn.com/weather** or **www.weather.com**.

Where to Stay

It's official: Hotel rates in New York are the most expensive in the United States. In 2006, the average price of a hotel room was close to $270 per night. But it seems that the outrageous hotel rates have not deterred visitors: More than 44 million came to the city that year. So get over any notions that you might find rates comparable to those back home. That said, there are bargains out there at every price level; but a bargain in New York might be a king's ransom in St. Louis.

If you want to spend less than $125 a night, you're probably going to have to put up with some inconveniences, such as sharing a hall bathroom with your fellow travelers. (Europeans seem to have an easier time with this than Americans.) If you want a room with standard amenities—such as a private bathroom or a real closet (rather than just a bar screwed to the wall)—plan on spending at least $150 a night. If you do better than that, you've made a good deal.

New York hotel rooms give everybody a new perspective on "small." Space is the city's biggest asset, and getting some costs. If you're on a tight budget, don't be surprised if your room isn't much bigger than the bed that's in it and your bathroom has a sink so small you'll have difficulty spitting out your toothpaste without spilling it. Even expensive rooms can be on the small side, lack closet space, or have smallish bathrooms.

PRICE CATEGORIES & RACK RATES The **rates** quoted in the listings below are "rack rates"—the maximum rates that a hotel charges for rooms. I've used these rack rates to divide the hotels into four price categories, ranging from "Very Expensive" to "Inexpensive," for easy reference. But rack rates are only guidelines, and there are often ways around them; see "Tips for Saving on Your Hotel Room," below.

The hotels listed below have provided us with their best rate estimates for 2007, and all quoted rates were correct at press time. Be aware, however, that **rates can change at any time.** Rates are always subject to availability, seasonal fluctuations, and plain-old rate hikes. It's smart to expect price shifts in both directions in late 2007 and 2008 as hoteliers adjust to new demand patterns.

PET POLICIES I've indicated in the listings below those hotels that accept pets. However, understand that these policies may have limitations, such as weight and breed restrictions; may require a deposit and/or a signed waiver against damages; and may be revoked at any time. Always inquire when booking if you're bringing Fluffy or Spike—*never* just show up with a pet in tow.

TIPS FOR SAVING ON YOUR HOTEL ROOM

In the listings below, I've tried to give you an idea of the kind of deals that may be available at particular hotels: which ones have the best discounted packages, which ones offer AAA and other discounts, which ones allow kids to stay with Mom and Dad for free, and so on. But there's no way of knowing what the offers will be when you're booking, so also consider these general tips:

- **Ask about special rates or other discounts.** Always ask whether a room less expensive than the first one quoted is available, or whether any special rates apply to you. You may qualify for corporate, student, military, senior, or other discounts. Mention membership in AAA, AARP, frequent-flier programs, or trade unions, which may entitle you to special deals. Find out the policy on children—do kids stay free or is there a special rate?

- **Choose your season carefully.** Room rates can vary dramatically—by hundreds of dollars in some cases—depending on what time of year you visit. Winter, from January through March, is best for bargains, with summer (especially July–Aug) second best. Fall is the busiest and most expensive season after Christmas, but November tends to be quiet and rather affordable, as long as you're not booking a parade-route hotel on Thanksgiving weekend. All bets are off at Christmastime—expect to pay top dollar for everything. For more on this subject, see "Money Matters" in "When to Go," in chapter 3.

- **Go uptown or downtown.** The advantages of a Midtown location are highly overrated, especially when saving money is your object. The subway can whisk you anywhere you want to go in minutes; even if you stay on the Upper West Side, you can be at the ferry launch for the Statue of Liberty in about a half-hour. You'll get the best value for your money by staying outside the Theater District, in the residential neighborhoods where real New Yorkers live, such as Greenwich Village, Chelsea, Murray Hill, or the Upper West Side. These are the neighborhoods where real New Yorkers hang out, too, so you won't want for good eats, nightlife, or Big Apple bustle.

- **Visit over a weekend.** If your trip includes a weekend, you might be able to save big. Business hotels tend to empty out, and rooms that go for $300 or more Monday through Thursday can drop dramatically, as low as $150 or less, once the execs have headed home. These deals are prevalent in the Financial District, but they're often available in tourist-friendly Midtown, too. Check the hotel's website for weekend specials. Or just ask when you call.

- **Shop online.** Hotels often offer "Internet only" deals that can save you 10% to 20% or more over what you'd pay if you booked over the telephone. Also, hotels often advertise all of their available deals on their websites, so you don't have to rely on a reservation agent to fill you in. What's more, some of the discount reservations agencies (see below) have sites that allow you to book online. And consider joining the **Playbill Online Theater Club (www.playbillclub.com),** a free service that offers some excellent members-only rates at select city hotels, in addition to discounts on theater tickets. American Automobile Association members can often score the best discounts by booking at **www.aaa.com**. Travel search sites such as **Orbitz** (www.orbitz.com), **Microsoft Expedia** (www.expedia.com), **Priceline** (www.priceline.com), and **Travelocity** (www.travelocity.com) offer other discount options. Shop around. And if you have special needs—a quiet room, a room with a view—call the hotel directly and make your needs known after you've booked online.

- **Dial direct.** When booking a room in a chain hotel, you'll often get a better deal by calling the hotel's reservation desk rather than the chain's main number.

- **Make deals with the budget chains.** With a few exceptions, I have not listed budget chains in this chapter. In my opinion, they tend to lack the character and local feel that most independently run hotels have. And it's that feel, I believe, that is so much a part of the travel experience. Still, when you're looking for a deal, they can be a good option. Most hotels—particularly chains like Comfort Inn and Best Western—are market-sensitive. Because they hate to see rooms sit empty, they'll often negotiate good rates at the last minute and in slow seasons.

  You can also pull out all the stops for discounts at a budget chain, from auto-club membership to senior status. You might be able to take advantage of corporate rates or discounted weekend stays. Most chain hotels let the kids stay with parents for free. Ask for every kind of discount; if you find that you get an unhelpful reservation agent, call back. Of course, there's no guarantee.

  Two chains with franchises in Manhattan include **Best Western** (© 800/780-7234; www.bestwestern.com), though their rack rates for New York hotels are higher than you'd expect, and **Howard Johnson** (© 800/446-4656; www.hojo.com). There's a Best Western at South Street Seaport and at two Midtown locations, and a Howard Johnson on the Lower East Side. Check their websites for all the details.

  At these and other franchised hotels—such as the ones run by **Apple Core Hotels** (www.applecorehotels.com), a management company that handles the **Comfort Inn Midtown,** the **Ramada Inn Eastside,** Manhattan's first **Red Roof** (p. 138), the **Super 8 Hotel Times Square,** and **La Quinta,** 7 W. 32nd St. (© 212/736-1600)—doubles can go for as little as $109. Check with the franchiser if you're not quoted a good advance-booking rate or through the management company's online reservations system; their global 800 and online reservations systems will often garner you a better rate, which might include a promotion—or, at minimum, an "Internet User's Rate" that's 10% lower than the standard.

  A good source for deals is **Choice Hotels** (© 877/424-6423; www.hotel choice.com), which oversees Comfort Inn, Quality Hotel, and Clarion Hotel chains, all of which have Manhattan branches.

  Another hotel to try is the **Hilton Garden Inn,** 790 Eighth Ave., at 48th Street (© 212/581-7000; www.hilton.com).

- **Investigate reservations services.** These outfits usually work as consolidators, buying up or reserving rooms in bulk, and then dealing them out to customers at a profit. You can get 10% to 50% off; but remember, these discounts apply to rack rates—inflated prices that people rarely end up paying. You may get a decent rate, but always call the hotel directly to see if you can do better.

  Quikbook (© 800/789-9887 or 212/779-7666; www.quikbook.com) is the best of the bunch. You might also try the **Hotel Reservations Network,** also known as HotelDiscount!com (© 800/715-7666; www.hoteldiscount.com).

Tips **More Advice on Accommodations**

For an easy-to-scan introduction to the best of what the city has to offer, check out the Best Hotel categories in chapter 1. For extra help in choosing a location, take a look at "Manhattan's Neighborhoods in Brief," in chapter 5.

Remember: All hotel rooms are subject to a **13.25% tax** plus $2 per night.

Note: Never just rely on a reservations service or an online-booking site. Do a little homework; compare the rack rates to the discounted rates being offered to see what kind of deal they're actually offering. If you're being offered a stay in a hotel I haven't recommended, do more research on it, especially if it isn't a reliable chain name like Holiday Inn or Hyatt. It's not a deal if you end up at a dump.

- **Avoid excess charges and hidden costs.** When you book a room, ask whether the hotel charges for parking. Use your own cellphone, pay phones, or prepaid phone cards instead of dialing direct from hotel phones, which usually have exorbitant rates. And don't be tempted by minibar offerings: Most hotels charge through the nose for water, soda, and snacks. Finally, ask about local taxes and service charges, which can increase the cost of a room by 15% or more. If a hotel insists upon tacking on an "energy surcharge" that wasn't mentioned at check-in, you can often make a case for getting it removed.

- **Buy a money-saving package deal.** A travel package that combines your airfare and your hotel stay for one price may just be the best bargain of all. In some cases, you'll get airfare, accommodations, transportation to and from the airport, plus extras—maybe an afternoon sightseeing tour, or restaurant and shopping discount coupons—for less than the hotel alone would have cost had you booked it yourself. For more on this, see "Packages for the Independent Traveler," in chapter 3.

- **Rely on a qualified professional.** Certain hotels give travel agents discounts in exchange for steering business their way, so if you're shy about bargaining, an agent may be better equipped to negotiate discounts for you.

- **Consider B&B accommodations or an apartment.** If Big Apple hotels seem too expensive, or you'd just like something a little more like home, consider renting a room in a genuine New York apartment—or even an entire apartment. These accommodations can range from spartan to splendid, from a hosted bedroom in a private home to an unhosted, fully equipped apartment with multiple bedrooms. No matter what, you can pretty much guarantee that you'll get more for your money than if you book into a regular hotel. However, you need to be rather independent-minded to enjoy this option. For more, see the sidebar "Plenty of Room at the Inn" on p. 120.

  The place to start with is **Manhattan Getaways** (© 212/956-2010; www. manhattangetaways.com). Judith Glynn maintains a beautifully kept and managed network of bed-and-breakfast rooms (from $110 nightly) and unhosted apartments (from $150) around the city. There's a 3-night minimum stay, and credit cards are accepted. Another decent bet is **A Hospitality Company** (© 800/ 987-1235 or 212/813-2244; www.metro-home.com), which owns and manages 300 apartments around Manhattan starting at $139 a night, or $850 weekly for a basic studio. These are rather sparsely furnished apartments, and the company offers little in the way of service (it took me 5 days to get my TV fixed when I was displaced from my home by renovation), but the apartments are clean and do the trick. There's no minimum stay, and credit cards are accepted. Cleaning services are available for longer stays.

  Additional agencies that can book you into a B&B room or a private apartment, with prices starting at $90 nightly, include **As You Like It** (© 800/277-0413 or 212/695-3404; www.furnapts.com); **Abode Apartment Rentals** (© 800/ 835-8880 or 212/472-2000; www.abodenyc.com); **City Sonnet** (© 212/614-3034; www.citysonnet.com); **Manhattan Lodgings** (© 212/677-7616;

www.manhattanlodgings.com); and **New York Habitat** (© **212/255-8018;** www. nyhabitat.com). Be sure to get all details in writing and an exact total up front to avoid disappointments.

1 South Street Seaport & the Financial District

To locate the hotels in this section, see the map on p. 115.

VERY EXPENSIVE

Ritz-Carlton New York, Battery Park ⭐⭐⭐   Perfect on almost every level, the only drawback to this Ritz-Carlton is its far downtown location. But that location, on the extreme southern tip of Manhattan, is also one of its strengths. Where else can you get, in most rooms anyway, magnificent views of New York Harbor from your bedroom—complete with telescope for close-ups of Lady Liberty? Where else can you have a cocktail in your hotel bar and watch the sun set over the harbor? And where else can you go for a morning jog around the Manhattan waterfront? This modern, Art Deco–influenced high-rise differs from the English-countryside look of most Ritz-Carlton properties, including its sister hotel on Central Park (p. 127), but that's where the differences end. You'll find the full slate of comforts and services typical of Ritz-Carlton here, from Frette-dressed feather beds to the chain's signature Bath Butler, who will draw a scented bath for you in your own deep soaking tub. Standard rooms are all very large and have huge bathrooms, while suites are bigger than most New York apartments. If you don't mind the location and the commute to Midtown and beyond, you won't find a more luxurious choice than this.

2 West St., New York, NY 10004. © **800/241-3333** or 212/344-0800. Fax 212/344-3801. www.ritzcarlton.com. 298 units. $350–$545 double; from $750 suite. Extra person 12 and over $30 (starting from $100 on club level). Check website for promotional weekend packages. AE, DC, DISC, MC, V. Valet parking $60. Subway: 4, 5 to Bowling Green. **Amenities:** Restaurant; lobby lounge (w/outdoor seating) for afternoon tea and cocktails; 14th-floor cocktail bar w/light dining and outdoor seating; state-of-the-art health club w/views; spa treatments; 24-hr. concierge; well-equipped business center w/24-hr. secretarial services; 24-hr. room service; laundry service; dry cleaning; Ritz-Carlton Club Level w/5 food presentations daily; technology butler and bath butler services. *In room:* A/C, TV w/pay movies and video games, dataport, minibar, fridge, hair dryer, safe, CD player, DVD w/surround sound in suites and Club rooms, wireless and high-speed Internet connectivity.

EXPENSIVE/MODERATE

Exchange Hotel ⭐   This cozy hotel is a solid, mid-priced choice if you are looking for a downtown location. A short walk from Wall Street, the South Street Seaport, Brooklyn Bridge, and Chinatown, the Exchange Hotel features personalized service and a few perks like free wireless Internet and a complimentary continental breakfast. Recently renovated in a sleek, contemporary style, standard and deluxe guest rooms are on the small size, but are outfitted nicely with plasma televisions, mini-refrigerators and microwaves. The suites are roomy with a separate living room, black leather furniture and a full-sized kitchen. Bathrooms are tight in both the guest rooms and suites and include those sadly very fashionable marble bowl sinks that look good, but don't leave much space of any of your toiletries. That minor complaint aside, the Exchange is a welcome addition to an area much too lacking in lodging.

129 Front St. (btwn Wall and Pine sts.) New York, N.Y. 10005. © **212/742-0003.** Fax 212/742-0124. www.exchange hotel.com. 53 units. AE, DC, MC, V. Rates: $299–$469. Parking $25. Subway: 2, 3 to Wall St. **Amenities:** Lounge; free complimentary continental breakfast; access to nearby fitness club; laundry/valet service. *In room:* A/C, TV, full-sized kitchens in suites, iron/ironing board, safe, free wireless Internet, microwave, mini-fridge, VCR.

Wall Street District Hotel by Holiday Inn ☆   This is one of lower Manhattan's most technologically advanced hotels. The comfortable queen-bedded rooms are stocked with everything an executive might need, including an 8-foot L-shaped work-station with desk-level inputs, dual-line portable phones, and the kind of office sup-plies you never bring but always need, such as paper clips and tape. About half the rooms have PCs with Microsoft Word and Office applications and a CD drive. The top floor is dedicated to SMART rooms, which feature Toshiba Satellite laptop com-puters (with carrying case), fax/printer/copiers, and other upgraded amenities, plus buffet breakfast. Room decor is chain standard, but fresh and comfortable; an easy chair and ottoman expand seating options. Management is always staying on the cut-ting edge with such techno-toys as a "Pocket Concierge" plug-in in the lobby that allows you to download local information to your PDA; an ATM-style machine for one-touch credit card check-in (similar to a self-serve gas pump); and cellular connec-tion services that allow you to forward your room calls to your cell phone. The staff prides itself on meeting the needs of its bullish guests, so expect to be well cared for.

15 Gold St. (at Platt St.), New York, NY 10038. ℂ 800/HOLIDAY, 212/232-7800, or 212/232-7700. Fax 212/425-0330. www.holidayinnwsd.com or www.holiday-inn.com. 138 units. $249–$400 double; from $389 suite. Check for discounts galore (AAA, AARP, corporate, government, military), plus deeply discounted weekend rates and other spe-cials. AE, DC, DISC, MC, V. Parking $30. Subway: 2, 3, 4, 5, A, C, J, M, Z to Fulton St./Broadway–Nassau St. **Ameni-ties:** Restaurant; bar; exercise room and access to nearby health club; concierge; self-service business center; 24-hr. room service; delivery from 24-hr. deli; laundry service; dry cleaning; executive-level rooms; CD library. In room: A/C, TV w/pay movies/Internet access/Nintendo, standard dataport, minibar, coffeemaker, hair dryer, iron, safe, CD player, high-speed Internet connectivity.

The Wall Street Inn ☆ *(Finds)*   This intimate hotel (along with **The Exchange,** p. 113) is one of the preferred choices for those working on the Street. It's also a good choice for visitors who don't want to work. This intimate, seven-story hotel is ideal for those who want a lower Manhattan location without corporate blandness. The lovely early American interiors boast a pleasing freshness. The hotel is warm, comforting, and serene, and the friendly, professional staff offers the kind of personalized service you won't get from a chain. Rooms aren't huge, but the bedding is top-quality and all the conveniences are at hand. Rooms ending in "01" are smallest; seventh-floor rooms are best: the bathrooms have extra counter space and whirlpool tubs.

9 S. William St. (at Broad St.), New York, NY 10004. ℂ 212/747-1500. Fax 212/747-1900. www.thewallstreetinn. com. 46 units. $279–$450 double. Rates include continental breakfast. Ask about corporate, group, and/or deeply dis-counted weekend rates (as low as $209 at press time). AE, DC, DISC, MC, V. Parking $36 nearby. Subway: 2, 3 to Wall St.; 4, 5 to Bowling Green. **Amenities:** Well-outfitted exercise room w/sauna and steam; concierge; business center; babysitting arranged; laundry service; dry cleaning; common guest kitchen w/microwave; video library. In room: A/C, TV/VCR, fax, fridge, hair dryer, iron, safe, high-speed Internet.

2 TriBeCa & Lower East Side

To locate the hotels in this section, see the map on p. 115.

VERY EXPENSIVE

Tribeca Grand Hotel ☆   This sister to the **Soho Grand** (p. 118) is set on a trian-gular plot just south of SoHo; its decidedly retro brick-and-cast-iron exterior blends perfectly with the surrounding neighborhood.

Set along open atrium-facing corridors, the streamlined guest rooms boast generous built-in work space (with a Herman Miller Aeron chair) and state-of-the-art technol-ogy. But because the rooms face the atrium, noise levels can be a problem, so each

Downtown Accommodations

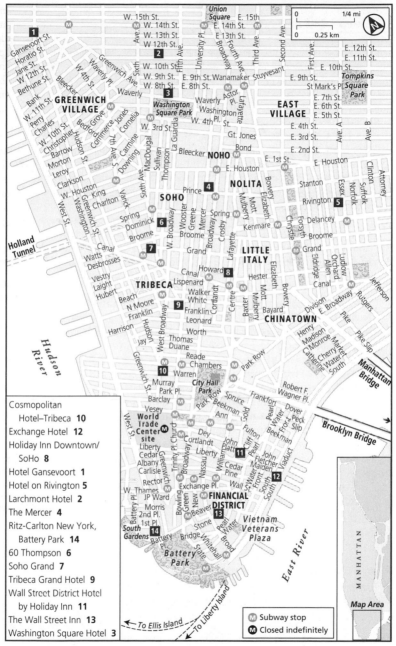

Cosmopolitan
  Hotel–Tribeca **10**
Exchange Hotel **12**
Holiday Inn Downtown/
  SoHo **8**
Hotel Gansevoort **1**
Hotel on Rivington **5**
Larchmont Hotel **2**
The Mercer **4**
Ritz-Carlton New York,
  Battery Park **14**
60 Thompson **6**
Soho Grand **7**
Tribeca Grand Hotel **9**
Wall Street District Hotel
  by Holiday Inn **11**
The Wall Street Inn **13**
Washington Square Hotel **3**

M Subway stop
M Closed indefinitely

Sleep Tight and . . .

My job as author of this book has many perks. One is to lie on 300-count Frette sheets, sample room service from three-star restaurants, and soak in Jacuzzi tubs in luxury hotels so I can accurately report to you whether that particular hotel is worthy of its astronomical rate. But the job comes with some risks and I encountered a grisly example recently. I had inspected a popular moderate hotel for possible inclusion into this book and was staying at the hotel to see if it lived up to the superficial tour I had previously taken. You learn much more by actually staying a night at a hotel than you do from a tour, and I had problems with the amenities in the room; no chair for example, a very small desk that was shared with a television, and inefficient use of space in the bathroom. Upon checkout, I decided I could not recommend the hotel to my readers.

The next day, after showering, as if exacting revenge on me for my decision and/or reinforcing it, I noticed red, itchy, weltlike blotches on my back and side. And the revelation hit me. I had been bitten by the new scourge of New York: bedbugs. I had read the articles saying that they were making a comeback and were on their way to replacing cockroaches as the number one pest, but I never thought I would become a victim.

Bedbugs apparently travel well and because of this the hotel industry is particularly vulnerable. They hide in mattresses and are nocturnal, biting while the victim is asleep. They are also very difficult to totally exterminate and require repeat visits from an exterminator; a hotelier's nightmare if there ever was one. The good news is that a bedbug bite does not transmit disease and is more an itchy nuisance than a health hazard.

Bedbugs do not discriminate as to class of hotel; they enjoy lounging in the beds of the best hotels as much as we do. If you are concerned, before you get into bed, check the mattress and the seams in and around the bed frame. You might see their droppings which are tiny blood-tinged specks. I know, that's why you came to New York; to search for bedbug droppings.

No hotel would ever broadcast that they have had a bedbug problem, but you might want to check a few travel message boards or websites including the one at www.frommers.com or at www.tripadvisor.com or www.hotelchatter.com to see if anyone has posted a message about bedbugs where you plan to stay. Otherwise, good night and sleep tight.

---

room is equipped with a noise-dulling device. The rooms, however, take a back seat to what's below: a dramatic eight-story atrium lobby, with its soaring proportions consumed by the popular **Church Lounge,** an upscale lounge and restaurant.

2 Sixth Ave. (at White & Church sts.), New York, NY 10013. ℂ **877/519-6600** or 212/519-6600. Fax 212/519-6700. www.tribecagrand.com. 203 units. From $350 double; from $699 suite. Promotional and Internet-only rates as low as $259 at press time; ask about corporate rates and value-added packages. AE, DC, DISC, MC, V. Parking $45. Subway: 1 to Franklin St.; A, C, E to Canal St. Pets accepted. **Amenities:** Restaurant; lounge; fitness center; well-connected 24-hr. concierge; business center w/complete workstations; 24-hr. room service; same-day laundry and dry cleaning; CD

libraries; coffee, tea, and cocoa bar on each floor; screening room. *In room:* A/C, TV/VCR w/Internet access, fax/printer/copier, standard dataport, minibar, hair dryer, safe, CD player, high-speed Internet connectivity, iPods.

EXPENSIVE

The Hotel on Rivington ★★   The contrast of a gleaming 21-story glass-tower luxury hotel in the midst of 19th- and early-20th-century Lower East Side low-rise tenement buildings is striking, but an accurate representation of what that neighborhood has become. From the floor-to-ceiling windows of your room, surrounded by modern amenities such as flat-panel televisions, Japanese soaking tubs in the bathrooms, and Tempur-Pedic mattresses on the beds, not only do you have incredible and totally unobstructed city views, but you can look down and spot ancient Lower East Side landmarks like the sign for the Schapiro Kosher wine factory, or the still-very-active Economy Candy store, est. 1937, or the shops of Orchard Street. You may not be close to the center of Manhattan if you stay at the Hotel on Rivington, but you will be in a dually historic and trendy location, where old-world customs and institutions coexist peacefully with the new and the supercool. The Hotel on Rivington is most definitely new and supercool but the comforts the hotel offers are timeless. Along with the aforementioned views, three-quarters of the rooms have private terraces, the option of in-room spa services, heated, tiled floors in the large bathrooms where you can enjoy your view of the city as you bathe—which also means someone with binoculars might just have a view of you as well. Room service is provided by the hotel's ultratrendy restaurant **THOR** (p. 168).

107 Rivington St. (between Ludlow & Essex sts.), New York, NY 10002. © **212/475-2600.** Fax 212/475-5959. www.hotelonrivington.com. 110 units. From $325 double. AE, DC, MC, V. Parking $50. Subway: F to Delancey St. **Amenities:** Restaurant; fitness center; in-room spa services available; concierge; 24-hr. room service; laundry service; dry cleaning. *In room:* A/C, TV, dataport, fridge, hair dryer, CD players and JBL On Stage iPod speaker system available, wireless high-speed Internet.

INEXPENSIVE

Cosmopolitan Hotel–Tribeca ★ *Value*   Behind a plain-vanilla TriBeCa awning is one of the best hotel deals in Manhattan for budget travelers who prefer a private bathroom. Everything is strictly budget but nice: The modern IKEA-ish furniture includes a work desk and an armoire (a few rooms have a dresser and hanging rack instead); for a few extra bucks, you can have a love seat, too. Beds are comfy, and sheets and towels are of good quality. Rooms are small but make the most of the limited space, and the whole place is pristine. The two-level minilofts have lots of character, but expect to duck on the second level. Management does a great job of keeping everything fresh. The TriBeCa location is safe, superhip, and subway-convenient. Services are kept at a bare minimum to keep costs down, so you must be a low-maintenance guest to be happy here.

95 W. Broadway (at Chambers St.), New York, NY 10007. © **888/895-9400** or 212/566-1900. Fax 212/566-6909. www.cosmohotel.com. 105 units. $175–$189 double. AE, DC, MC, V. Subway: 1, 2, 3 to Chambers St. *In room:* A/C, TV, dataport, ceiling fan.

3 SoHo

To locate the hotels in this section, see the map on p. 115.

VERY EXPENSIVE

The Mercer ★★★   The best of the downtown, celebrity-crawling, hip and trendy hotels, the Mercer is a place where even those who represent the antithesis of hip (and

I'm speaking personally) can feel at home. Though SoHo can be a bit over the top with its high-end boutiques, cutting-edge restaurants, and a constant parade of too serious fashionistas on the streets, it is still an exciting place. And the corner of Mercer and Prince streets, the location of the hotel, is probably the epicenter of SoHo. Still, once inside there is a pronounced calm—from the postmodern library lounge and the relaxed Mizrahi-clad staff, to the huge soundproof loft-like guest rooms; the hotel is a perfect complement to the scene outside your big window. The Mercer is one of the few New York hotels with ceiling fans, and even if you don't need them, they look nice whirring above your extremely comfortable bed. The tile-and-marble bathrooms have a steel cart for storage, and an oversize shower stall or oversize two-person tub (state your preference when booking). Just off the lobby is the **Kitchen** restaurant, one of Jean-Georges Vongerichten's earlier endeavors that is still going strong.

147 Mercer St. (at Prince St.), New York, NY 10012. ℂ **888/918-6060** or 212/966-6060. Fax 212/965-3838. www. mercerhotel.com. 75 units. $440–$480 double; $550–$680 studio; from $1,250 suite. AE, DC, DISC, MC, V. Parking $35 nearby. Subway: N, R to Prince St. **Amenities:** Restaurant; lounge; food and drink service in lobby; free access to nearby Crunch fitness center; 24-hr. concierge; secretarial services; 24-hr. room service; laundry service; dry cleaning; video, DVD, and CD libraries. In room: A/C, TV/DVD, dataport, minibar, safe, CD player, ceiling fan, wireless Internet access.

60 Thompson 𝒢   Some hotels have more comfortable rooms, others have better service, but few can match the all-around hipness of SoHo's 60 Thompson. A magnet for downtown celebs, 60 Thompson provides some excellent people-watching opportunities in the **Thom Bar** and the gorgeous rooftop bar, **A60.** The chic, soft-toned accommodations, designed by the same designer who did Giorgio Armani's Central Park West apartment, are spacious but spare, while bathrooms are enormous and luxuriously coated in Italian marble. The hotel has 11 suites including the magnificent Thompson Loft, a duplex penthouse suite with amazing views, four-poster bed, and a fireplace that is a favorite of visiting rock groups. Room service is available from the fabulous **Kittichai** (p. 171).

The Thompson is a smoker-friendly hotel, so ask for a non-smoking room or bring your ionizer if the smell of stale cigarette smoke bothers you.

60 Thompson St. (btwn Broome and Spring sts.), New York, NY 10012. ℂ **877/431-0400** or 212/431-0400. Fax 212/ 431-0200. www.thompsonhotels.com. 100 units. From $539 double; from $750 suite. AE, DISC, MC, V. Valet parking $43. Subway: C, E to Spring St. **Amenities:** Restaurant; 2 bars; access to nearby health club; concierge; 24-hr. room service (limited menu 1–7am); nonsmoking rooms. In room: A/C, TV, minibar, hair dryer, iron, safe, DVD/CD player, high-speed Internet.

Soho Grand   When the Soho Grand opened in 1996 as the first major hotel in SoHo, it became one of the trendiest hotels in New York. But after a decade and the opening of so many other hotels that followed in that chic tradition, the Soho Grand still retains its cool. The **Grand Bar,** one level above the street and just a few feet from the check-in desk, with its sofas and comfy chairs, was one of the first "lounge bars" in New York and has remained a hot spot. Guest rooms, however, have not quite kept up with the times and could use a makeover; bathrooms are a good size but spare.

Make sure you ask for a non-smoking room; the hotel attracts a hip, European crowd that enjoys a nicotine fix and the cigarette stench can linger well after the guests have departed. But you choose the Soho Grand more for the name and all that it implies rather than for comfort and service.

310 W. Broadway (at Grand St.), New York, NY 10013. ℂ **800/965-3000** or 212/965-3000. Fax 212/965-3244 (reservations) or 212/965-3200 (guests). www.sohogrand.com. 363 units. From $354 double; from $5,000 loft suites.

I don't speak sign language.

A hotel can close for all kinds of reasons.
Our Guarantee ensures that if your hotel's undergoing construction, we'll let you know in advance. In fact, we cover your entire travel experience. See www.travelocity.com/guarantee for details.

You'll never roam alone.

Corporate, promotional, and Internet-only rates as low as $259; your travel agent may be able to do even better. AE, DC, DISC, MC, V. Parking $45. Subway: A, C, E, N, R, 1 to Canal St. Pets accepted. **Amenities:** Restaurant; bar and lounge; fitness center; concierge; 24-hr. room service; laundry service; dry cleaning; nonsmoking rooms; butler's pantry w/complimentary coffee, tea, and hot chocolate on every floor. *In room:* A/C, TV/VCR, dataport, minibar, hair dryer, safe, CD player, iPods.

MODERATE

Holiday Inn Downtown/SoHo   This Holiday Inn is actually on the northern edge of Chinatown, but its just-off-SoHo location is perfect for hipsters who want access to the chic scene without its high price tag. It's everything you'd expect from this good-value chain: clean, well outfitted, reliable, and comfortable. The guest rooms are standard but have everything you need. Doubles are a good-value bet for small families or sharing friends. You'll find Asian touches throughout the hotel—a nod to the brink-of-Chinatown location—and a well-respected Asian restaurant. Rack rates are high, but it's easy to snag a discount or score a room on the low end with advance booking.

138 Lafayette St. (at Howard St., 1 block north of Canal St.), New York, NY 10013. ✆ **800/HOLIDAY** or 212/966-8898. Fax 212/966-3933. www.holidayinn-nyc.com. 227 units. From $279 double; from $389 executive suite. Extra person $20. Children 18 and under stay free in parent's room. Check for AAA, AARP, government, corporate, and other discounts. AE, DC, DISC, MC, V. Parking $44. Subway: 6, J, M, N, R, Q, W to Canal St. **Amenities:** Restaurant; bar; access to nearby health club; concierge; fax and copy service; room service (6:30am–11pm); laundry service; dry cleaning. *In room:* A/C, TV w/pay movies, fax (in most junior suites), dataport, coffeemaker, hair dryer, iron, CD player.

4 Greenwich Village & the Meat-Packing District

To locate the hotels in this section, see the map on p. 115.

EXPENSIVE

Hotel Gansevoort 🏨🏨   This sleek, 14-floor zinc-colored tower, with its open, sprawling clubby lobby, the popular Jeffrey Chodorow–owned, Jeffrey Beers–designed restaurant **Ono,** and the indoor/outdoor rooftop bar and pool (with music piped underwater), is the symbolic anchor of the white hot Meat Packing district. Despite its potentially excessive trendiness, the Gansevoort offers excellent, personable service. As well, rooms are a good size with comfortable furnishings in soft tones and high-tech amenities like plasma televisions and wireless Internet. Suites have a living room and separate bedroom and some have small balconies and bay windows. Corner suites offer adjoining guest rooms for families or larger parties. The generous-size bathrooms are done up in ceramic, stainless steel, and marble and are impeccably appointed. In all the guest rooms and throughout the hotel, original art by New York artists is on display. The **G Spa,** a 5,000-square-foot spa and fitness center and the indoor/outdoor O Bar are destinations unto themselves.

By the time you read this, the Meat-Packing District might be on the outs, but you can be sure the Hotel Gansevoort is here to stay.

18 Ninth Ave. (at 13th St.), New York, NY 10014. ✆ **877/426-7386** or 212/206-6700. Fax 212/255-5858. www.hotel gansevoort.com. 187 units. From $450 double; from $795 suite. Parking $40. Subway: A, C, E to 14th St. Pet-friendly floors. **Amenities:** Restaurant; rooftop bar and lounge; indoor/outdoor pool; spa and fitness center; concierge; business center; 24-hr. room service; laundry service; dry cleaning; rooftop garden. *In room:* A/C, TV, dataport, minibar, hair dryer, iron, safe, dual-line telephones, voice mail, wireless and high-speed Internet.

INEXPENSIVE

Larchmont Hotel 🏨🏨 *Value*   On a beautiful tree-lined block in a residential part of Greenwich Village, this is a wonderful European-style hotel. If you're willing to share a bathroom, it's hard to do better for the money. The entire place has an air of warmth

Plenty of Room at the Inn

When you think of accommodations in New York, you usually think big—tall, sturdy, monoliths with hundreds of rooms. You don't think of quaint antiques-laden guesthouses or inns where a home-cooked breakfast is served. But New York is a diverse city and that diversity can be found in its accommodations, too. So if you want an alternative to the quintessential huge New York hotel and would prefer a taste of urban hominess where you might actually meet your innkeeper, here are a few options.

On the steep end of the economic scale, but worth the price if authentic 19th-century Victorian romance is what you are seeking, is the fabulous **Inn at Irving Place** 𝒜𝒜. Housed in a 170-year-old townhouse, rates range from $325 to $495 and the rooms are named after late-19th- or early-20th-century New Yorkers, many inspired by the works of Edith Wharton and Henry James. Complimentary breakfast is served in Lady Mendl's parlor, where, if the weather is nippy, you'll find a comforting fire roaring. See p. 126 for a detailed review.

Breakfast prepared by culinary students of the New School is one of the highlights of the **Inn on 23rd Street** 𝒜𝒜𝒜. Each of the inn's 14 rooms, which range from $219 to $359, were distinctly decorated by the personable owners, Annette and Barry Fisherman, with items they've collected from their travels over the years. See p. 122 for a detailed review.

The first home of the Gay Men's Health Crisis, an 1850 brownstone in the heart of Chelsea, is now the charming **Colonial House Inn,** 318 W. 22nd St., between Eighth and Ninth avenues (© **800/689-3779** or 212/243-9669; www.colonialhouseinn.com). This 20-room four-story walk-up caters to a largely gay and lesbian clientele, but everybody is welcome, and straight couples are a common sight. Some rooms have shared bathrooms; deluxe rooms have private bathrooms and some have working fireplaces. There's a roof deck with a clothing-optional area. Breakfast is included in the rates, which range from $85 to $150 for a shared bathroom or $135 to $150 for a deluxe room.

On the increasingly popular yet still residential Upper West Side is the aptly named **Country Inn the City** 𝒜, 270 W. 77th St., between Broadway

and sophistication; the butter-yellow lobby even *smells* good. Each bright guest room is tastefully done in rattan and outfitted with a writing desk, a mini-library of books, an alarm clock, a wash basin, and a few extras that you normally have to pay a lot more for, such as cotton bathrobes, slippers, and ceiling fans. Every floor has two shared bathrooms (with hair dryers) and a small, simple kitchen. The management is constantly renovating, so everything feels clean and fresh. What's more, those looking for a hip downtown base couldn't be better situated, since some of the city's best shopping, dining, and sightseeing—plus your choice of subway lines—are just a walk away. This hotel has a devoted following that recommends it to all their friends, so book *well* in advance (the management suggests 6–7 weeks' lead time).

and West End Avenue (© **212/580-4183**; www.countryinnthecity.com). This 1891 town house has only four rooms, but all are spacious, quaintly decorated, and equipped with full kitchens. Rates range from $150 to $300 and include breakfast items stocked in your refrigerator. But you're on your own in many respects; there is no resident innkeeper and a maid services your room only every few days. Still, if you are the independent sort, the inn's charm makes it an excellent choice.

If you want the genuine New York brownstone experience, go to Harlem. Okay so the name is not inviting, but the **Harlem Flophouse**, 242 W. 123rd St, between Adam Clayton Powell and Frederick Douglass Blvds. (© **212/ 662-0678**; www.harlemflophouse.com) is anything but a flophouse. Owner Renee Calvo has restored the historic row house to Harlem Renaissance splendor when the "flophouse" was frequented by top musicians and artists of that era. If you visit in the summer, you just might get invited to one of Calvo's impromptu barbecues. Rates ($100–$125) includes free Wi-Fi, for $15 extra you get a full breakfast.

Like Harlem, Brooklyn also boasts a number of historic districts with restored brownstones, some of which have been converted to inns. One of the most interesting is **Akwaaba Mansion**, 347 MacDonough St. (© **718/ 455-5958**; www.akwaaba.com), a meticulously restored 1860s Italianate villa in Bedford-Stuyvesant, outfitted with Afrocentric elegance. Four suites are available in the 18-room home, each with private bathroom with either a claw-foot or a Jacuzzi tub ($150–$165 double)—including a hearty, Southern-style breakfast.

The historic neighborhood of Park Slope is the heart of brownstone Brooklyn and home to **Bed & Breakfast on the Park,** 113 Prospect Park West (© **718/499-6115**; www.bbnyc.com). In an 1895 Victorian town house across the street from Prospect Park, this inn has two beautifully outfitted units (from $300). A sumptuous breakfast is served in the formal dining room. Six more rooms with private bathrooms are available for guests who are willing to splurge.

27 W. 11th St. (btwn Fifth and Sixth aves.), New York, NY 10011. © **212/989-9333**. Fax 212/989-9496. www.larch monthotel.com. 62 units, all with shared bathroom. $80–$115 single; $109–$135 double. Rates include continental breakfast. Children under 13 stay free in parent's room. AE, MC, V. Parking $25 nearby. Subway: A, B, C, D, E, F, V to W. 4th St. (use 8th St. exit); F to 14th St. **Amenities:** Tour desk; room service (10am–6pm); common kitchenette. *In room:* A/C, TV, hair dryer, safe, ceiling fan

Washington Square Hotel   Popular with a young international crowd, this affordable hotel sits behind a pretty facade facing Washington Square Park (historically Henry James territory, now the midst of New York University) in the heart of Greenwich Village. The lobby is a pleasant place for tea in the afternoon and cocktails in the evening. The rooms are tiny but pleasant. Each comes with a firm bed, a private bathroom, and a small closet with a pint-size safe. It's worth paying a few extra dollars for a south-facing room on a high floor, since the others can be a bit dark. Bathrooms were also renovated, with the addition of granite counters. On-site is a good restaurant and lounge, **North Square Lounge,** which even draws locals with its stylish design, well-priced cocktails and international bistro fare, and Sunday jazz brunch.

103 Waverly Place (btwn Fifth and Sixth aves.), New York, NY 10011. ℂ 800/222-0418 or 212/777-9515. Fax 212/979-8373. www.wshotel.com. 160 units. $156–$175 single; $185–$210 double; $225–$260 quad. Rates include continental breakfast. Inquire about special rates and jazz packages. AE, MC, V. Parking $30 nearby. Subway: A, B, C, D, E, F, V to W. 4th St. (use 3rd St. exit). **Amenities:** Restaurant and lounge; exercise room; laundry service; dry cleaning. *In room:* A/C, TV, dataport, hair dryer, iron, safe, high-speed Internet access.

5 Chelsea

To locate the hotels in this section, see the map on p. 124.

MODERATE

Inn on 23rd Street 🟊🟊🟊 *Finds*   Behind an unassuming entrance in the middle of bustling 23rd Street is one of New York's true lodging treasures: a real urban bed-and-breakfast with as personal a touch as you will find anywhere. All 14 guest rooms are spacious. Each has a king or queen bed outfitted with a supremely comfy pillow-top mattress and top-quality linens, satellite TV, a large private bathroom with thick Turkish towels, and a roomy closet. Rooms have themes based on how they are designed; there's the Rosewood Room, with '60s built-ins; the elegantly Asian Bamboo Room; and Ken's Cabin, a large, lodgelike room with cushy, well-worn leather furnishings and wonderful Americana relics. I stayed in the Victorian suite where the decor curiously included framed Victorian-era dental tools. The inn features a lovely library where the complimentary breakfast is served and where there is also an honor bar where you can make yourself a drink for cheaper than you would pay in any hotel in the city. Other perks include free high-speed Internet access in the rooms, Wi-Fi in the library, and wine and cheese served on Friday and Saturday. The only drawback is that the inn is so comfortable and accommodating you might be tempted to lounge around all day instead of getting out there and seeing the town.

131 W. 23rd St. (btwn Sixth and Seventh aves.), New York, NY 10011. ℂ 877/387-2323 or 212/463-0330. Fax 212/463-0302. www.innon23rd.com. 14 units. $219–$259 double; $359 suite. Rates include continental breakfast. Extra person $25. Children under 12 stay free in parent's room. AE, DC, DISC, MC, V. Parking $20 nearby. Subway: F, 1 to 23rd St. **Amenities:** Fax and copy service; cozy library w/stereo and VCR. *In room:* A/C, TV, dataport, hair dryer, iron, high-speed Internet access.

INEXPENSIVE

Also consider the intimate **Colonial House Inn** (ℂ **800/689-3779** or 212/243-9669). For more information, see the sidebar "Plenty of Room at the Inn," above.

Chelsea Lodge 🟊🟊 *Value*   In a lovely brownstone on a landmark block in the heart of Chelsea, this small hotel is utterly charming and a terrific value—arguably the best in the city for budget-minded travelers. Impeccable renovations have restored original woodwork to mint condition. The beds are the finest and best outfitted I've seen in this price category.

The only place with a similar grown-up sensibility for the same money is Greenwich Village's **Larchmont Hotel** (p. 119), but there, all bathroom facilities are shared; at Chelsea Lodge, each room has its own sink and in-room shower stall, so you only have to share a cute toilet room with your neighbors. I won't kid you—rooms are petite, the open closets are small, and beds are full-size (queens wouldn't cut it). But considering the stylishness, the amenities, and the great neighborhood, you'd be hard-pressed to do better for the money. Best for couples rather than shares. *Tip:* Try to book no. 2A, which is bigger than most, or one of the first-floor rooms, whose high ceilings make them feel more spacious.

318 W. 20th St. (btwn Eighth and Ninth aves.), New York, NY 10011. © 800/373-1116 or 212/243-4499. Fax 212/243-7852. www.chelsealodge.com. 26 units, all with semiprivate bathroom. $109 single; $119 double. AE, DC, DISC, MC, V. Parking about $27 nearby. Subway: 1 to 18th St.; C, E to 23rd St. *In room:* A/C, TV, ceiling fan, wireless Internet.

6 Union Square, the Flatiron District & Gramercy Park

To find the hotels described in this section, see p. 124.

VERY EXPENSIVE

Gramercy Park Hotel ✸✸✸   Shuttered for 2 years, this 1925-built legend bordering charming Gramercy Park has been redone stunningly by famed hotelier Ian Schrager. Schrager, who pioneered the "boutique hotel" concept in the 1990's with the Royalton, Morgan's, and Paramount, has shifted gears and said goodbye to that sleek, chic look to create a hotel so quirky in style it's impossible to define. Start with the lobby, with its eclectic mix of art: there are Julian Schnabel-designed lamps (Schnabel was a main contributor to the design concept of the hotel and his pieces abound), two 10-foot Italian fireplaces, red velvet curtains, Moroccan tiles, bronze tables, and a magnificent Venetian glass chandelier. What once was a 500-plus room hotel now features only 185 rooms so, where the former version had tiny rooms, now there is space. But the space and design differ dramatically room to room—this is as far removed from a cookie-cutter hotel that you will find. More than half of the rooms are suites, some with views overlooking Gramercy Park, and all have mahogany English drinking cabinets where the mini-bar and DVD player is hidden, some variation of the overstuffed lounge chair, and a portrait of Schnabel's friend, the late Andy Warhol. Beds are velvet-upholstered, tables feature leather tops, and photos by world famous photo-journalists adorn the walls. Bathrooms are large and feature wood-paneled walls. If you choose to leave your room, the hotel's magnificent **Rose Bar** is where you should venture first, but make sure you are on the "list." At press time, the hotel's restaurant had not yet opened.

2 Lexington Ave (at 21st St), New York, N.Y. 10010. © 212/920-3300. Fax 212/673-5890. www.gramercyparkhotel.com. 185 units. From $525 double; from $675 suite. AE, DC, DISC, MC, V. Parking $55. Subway: 6 to 23rd St. **Amenities:** Restaurant; 2 bars, fitness center and spa, 24-hour room service, laundry service; dry cleaning; 24-hour concierge. *In room:* A/C, TV w/DVD/CD, dataport, minibar, hair dryer, safe, iPod and docking station, wireless and high speed Interent.

EXPENSIVE

Carlton Hotel on Madison Avenue ✸✸   This 1904 Beaux Arts hotel, formerly known as the Seville Hotel, was getting worn around the edges when it was rescued by architect David Rockwell and refurbished magnificently in 2005. The highlight of that $60-million renovation is the grand, sweeping lobby complete with a marble curving staircase and a cathedral-like high ceiling. While **The Roger** (p. 145) a few blocks up, also recently renovated, went for a cool, sleek, modern-tropical look, the Hotel Carlton has tried to recapture the majestic glory of the past blended with New Age nods like contemporary furnishings in the lobby along with a bubbling, two-story waterfall. Rooms are a generous size and retain that Beaux Arts motif with the

Midtown, Chelsea & Gramercy Park Accommodations

continues on opposite page

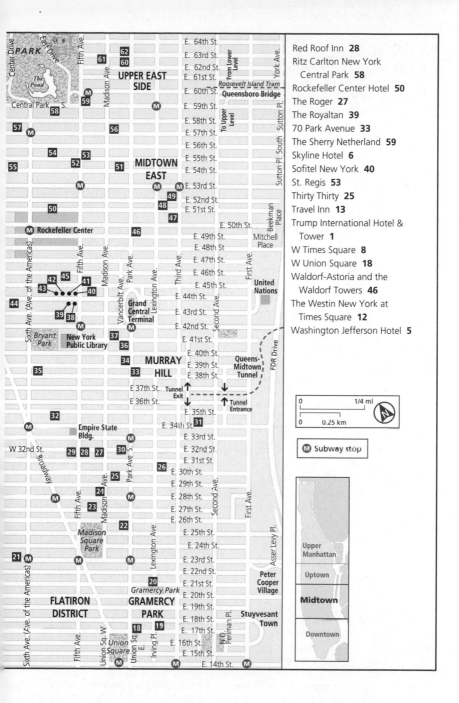

E. 64th St.
E. 63rd St.
E. 62nd St.
E. 61st St.
E. 60th St.
E. 59th St.
E. 58th St.
E. 57th St.
E. 56th St.
E. 55th St.
E. 54th St.
E. 53rd St.
E. 52nd St.
E. 51st St.
E. 50th St.
E. 49th St.
E. 48th St
E. 47th St.
E. 46th St.
E. 45th St.
E. 44th St.
E. 43rd St.
E. 42nd St.
E. 41st St.
E. 40th St.
E. 39th St.
E. 38th St.
E 37th St.
E 36th St.
E. 35th St.
E. 34th St.
E. 33rd St.
E. 32nd St.
E. 31st St.
E. 30th St.
E. 29th St.
E. 28th St.
E. 27th St.
E. 26th St.
E. 25th St.
E. 24th St.
E. 23rd St.
E. 22nd St.
E. 21st St.
E. 20th St.
E. 19th St.
E. 18th St.
E. 17th St.
E. 16th St.
E. 15th St.
E. 14th St.

East River Drive
Fifth Ave.
Madison Ave.
UPPER EAST SIDE
Roosevelt Island Tram
Queensboro Bridge
York Ave.
Sutton Pl.
Sutton Pl. South
From Lower Level
To Upper Level
MIDTOWN EAST
Beekman Place
Rockefeller Center
Mitchell Place
United Nations
Grand Central Terminal
First Ave.
Second Ave.
Third Ave.
Lexington Ave.
Park Ave.
Vanderbilt Ave.
Sixth Ave. (Ave. of the Americas)
Fifth Ave.
Bryant Park
New York Public Library
MURRAY HILL
Queens-Midtown Tunnel
FDR Drive
Tunnel Exit
Tunnel Entrance
Empire State Bldg.
W 32nd St.
Broadway
Madison Square Park
Gramercy Park
FLATIRON DISTRICT
GRAMERCY PARK
Lexington Ave.
Park Ave. S.
Union Sq. W.
Union Sq. E.
Irving Pl.
Union Square
N.D. Perlman Pl.
Asser Levy Pl.
Peter Cooper Village
Stuyvesant Town
Center Drive
PARK
The Pond
Central Park S.

Red Roof Inn **28**
Ritz Carlton New York Central Park **58**
Rockefeller Center Hotel **50**
The Roger **27**
The Royaltan **39**
70 Park Avenue **33**
The Sherry Netherland **59**
Skyline Hotel **6**
Sofitel New York **40**
St. Regis **53**
Thirty Thirty **25**
Travel Inn **13**
Trump International Hotel & Tower **1**
W Times Square **8**
W Union Square **18**
Waldorf-Astoria and the Waldorf Towers **46**
The Westin New York at Times Square **12**
Washington Jefferson Hotel **5**

0   1/4 mi
0   0.25 km

Ⓜ **Subway stop**

Upper Manhattan
Uptown
Midtown
Downtown

addition of modern amenities like wireless Internet and iPod clock radios. The marble bathrooms offer plenty of counter space; some rooms have bathtubs while others just have showers. Off the lobby is the acclaimed bi-level restaurant **Country** (p. 201) where above the upstairs dining room, a stained-glass skylight dome that had been boarded up since World War II has been meticulously restored.

88 Madison Ave. (btwn 28th and 29th sts.), New York, NY 10016. ✆ **212/532-4100**. Fax 212/889-8683. www.carlton hotelny.com. 316 units. $329 standard; from $450 suite. AE, DC, DISC, MC, V. Valet parking $40. Subway: 6 to 28th St./Lexington Ave. **Amenities:** Restaurant; concierge; business center; limited room service; laundry service; dry cleaning. *In room:* A/C, TV, iron/ironing board, safe, iPod clock radio, wireless Internet.

Hotel Giraffe 🦒🦒   In the increasingly fashionable Madison Park area, this hotel is a real charmer with a calm, intimate feel to it. Guest rooms are stylish, evoking an urban European character, with high ceilings, velveteen upholstered chairs, and original black-and-white photographs from the 1920s and 1930s. All the rooms are a good size with high ceilings, while deluxe rooms and suites feature French doors that lead to small balconies with large windows and remote-controlled blackout shades. Bathrooms are spacious with plenty of marble counter space and glass-paneled doors, and all rooms have generous marble-topped desks with free high-speed Internet access. But what really separates this hotel from so many others are its services: A continental breakfast is included in the rate and served in the hotel's elegant lobby, where coffee, cookies, and tea are available all afternoon, and wine, cheese, and piano music are offered each evening. There is also a lovely rooftop garden—the perfect place for a glass of wine or morning coffee during warm weather.

365 Park Ave. South (at 26th St.), New York, NY 10016. ✆ **877/296-0009** or 212/685-7700. Fax 212/685-7771. www.hotelgiraffe.com. 73 units. $325–$425 double; from $425 1- or 2-bedroom suite; from $2,500 penthouse suite. Rates include continental breakfast and evening wine and cheese accompanied by piano music. Check website or ask about reduced rates (as low as $299 at press time). AE, DC, MC, V. Parking $28. Subway: 6 to 28th St. **Amenities:** Restaurant; 2 bars; complimentary access to nearby gym; concierge; business services; limited room service; laundry service; dry cleaning; rooftop garden; video and CD libraries. *In room:* A/C, TV/VCR, dataport, minibar, hair dryer, iron, safe, CD player, high-speed wireless Internet.

Inn at Irving Place 🦒🦒   If it weren't for the street noise outside—or the high-speed wireless Internet in your room—upon entering the inn you would think you were transported to the 19th-century New York of *The Age of Innocence.* This 170-year-old town house offers antique charm more easily found in the Berkshires than in the heart of what used to be Silicon Alley. All rooms are spacious, with period antique furniture and art, nonworking fireplaces, and big bathrooms with pedestal sinks and brass fixtures, while the junior suites feature small but luxurious sitting areas. The rooms are named for famous 19th-century New Yorkers such as Edith Wharton, O. Henry, and Washington Irving. The Madame Olenska (bonus points if you know who she was) junior suite features a king bed and a window nook overlooking Irving Place where you can curl up with a glass of sherry or a cup of tea. Breakfast in bed, tea served in your room, or in-room massages can all be easily arranged by the inn's helpful staff. And if the sweetness of a bygone era begins to wear on you, venture downstairs for a blast of reality at **Cibar,** a popular martini bar that features a DJ nightly.

56 Irving Place (btwn 17th and 18th sts.), New York, NY 10003. ✆ **800/685-1447** or 212/533-4600. Fax 212/533-4611. www.innatirving.com. 12 units. From $415 superior suite; from $585 junior suite. Extra person $25. Rates include continental breakfast. 2-night minimum on weekends. AE, DC, MC, V. Parking $25–$30 nearby. Subway: N, R, 4, 5, 6 to 14th St./Union Sq. No children under 12. **Amenities:** 2 restaurants; lounge; access to nearby health club; concierge; 24-hr. room service; in-room massage; laundry service; dry cleaning; video and CD libraries. *In room:* A/C, TV/VCR, dataport, minibar, hair dryer, CD player, laptops and fax machines on request.

W Union Square ⋆ Überarchitect David Rockwell transformed the magnificent 1911 Guardian Life building overlooking leafy Union Square into a new gem, successfully fusing original Beaux Arts detailing with bold, clean-lined modernism and a relaxing, grown-up air. Rooms boast distinctive touches, such as luminous mother-of-pearl counters in the bathrooms. Star chef Todd English's Mediterranean-accented **Olives** restaurant gets raves, and nightclub impresario Rande Gerber's dark and sultry **Underbar** is just downstairs.

201 Park Ave. South (at 17th St.), New York, NY 10003. (⌀ **212/253-9119.** Fax 212/253-9229. www.starwood.com. $349–$550 double. Check website for specials. AE, DC, DISC, MC, V. Subway: N, R, W, 4, 5, 6 to Union Sq. **Amenities:** Restaurant; bar; fitness center; concierge; 24-hr. room service; laundry service; valet services; video library. *In room:* A/C, TV/DVD, dataport, fridge, Internet access.

INEXPENSIVE

Gershwin Hotel ⋆ *(Kids* Nestled between Le Trapeze (a swingers club) and the Museum of Sex, and with its own glowing protruding horns as your landmark, the proximity to erotica is really just a coincidence. This creative-minded, Warholesque hotel caters to up-and-coming artistic types—and well-established names with an eye for good value—with its bold modern art collection and wild style. The lobby was recently renovated, and along with a new bar, **Gallery at the Gershwin,** much of the original art remains. The standard rooms are clean and bright, with Picasso-style wall murals and Philippe Starck–ish takes on motel furnishings. Superior rooms are best, as they're newly renovated, and well worth the extra $10; all have either a queen bed, two twins, or two doubles, plus a newish private bathroom with cute, colorful tile. If you're bringing the brood, two-room suites, or Family Rooms, are a good option. For the *very* low budget traveler, the Gershwin also offers hostel-style accommodations at $33 a night in multi-bed rooms.

The hotel is more service-oriented than you usually see at this price level, and the staff is professional. At press time, a restaurant was in the works for late 2007.

7 E. 27th St. (btwn Fifth and Madison aves.), New York, NY 10016. (⌀ **212/545-8000.** Fax 212/684-5546. www. gershwinhotel.com. 150 units. $109–$300 double; $230–$300 family room. Extra person $20. Check website for discounts or other value-added packages. For hostel rooms, use this website: www.gershwinhostel.com. AE, MC, V. Parking $25 3 blocks away. Subway: N, R, 6 to 28th St. **Amenities:** Bar; tour desk; babysitting; laundry service; dry cleaning; Internet access. *In room:* A/C, TV, dataport, hair dryer, iron, wireless Internet

7 Times Square & Midtown West

To find the hotels described in this section, see p. 124.

VERY EXPENSIVE

Ritz-Carlton New York, Central Park ⋆⋆⋆ *(Kids* There's a lot to like about this hotel—from its enviable location overlooking Central Park to the impeccable and personable service—but what I like best is that this undoubtedly luxury hotel manages to maintain a homey elegance and does not intimidate you with an overabundance of style.

Rooms are spacious and decorated in traditional, English country style. Suites are larger than most New York apartments. Rooms facing Central Park come with telescopes, and all have flat-screen TVs with DVD players; the hotel even has a library of Academy Award–winning films available. The marble bathrooms are also oversize and feature a choice of bathrobes, terry or linen, and extravagant Frederic Fekkai bath amenities. For families who can afford the steep prices, the hotel is extremely kid-friendly. Suites have sofa beds, and cribs and rollaway beds can be brought in. Children are given in-room cookies and milk. You can even bring your dog (under 60 lb.); if it rains, the pooch gets to wear a Burberry trench coat. Now *that's* homey elegance. While the kids and dogs are entertained, the older folks can be pampered with facials or massages at the Switzerland-based La Prairie spa or dine at the hotel's restaurant, **BLT Market.**

50 Central Park South (at Sixth Ave.), New York, NY 10019. ✆ **212/308-9100.** Fax 212/207-8831. www.ritzcarlton. com. 260 units. $650–$1,295; from $995 for a suite. Package and weekend rates available. AE, DC, DISC, MC, V. Parking $50. Subway: N, R, W to 5th Ave and F to 57th St. Pets under 60 lb. accepted. **Amenities:** Restaurant; bar; lobby lounge for tea and cocktails; fitness center; La Prairie spa and facial center; concierge; complimentary Bentley limousine service; business center; 24-hr. room service; babysitting; overnight laundry; dry cleaning; technology butler and bath butler services. *In room:* A/C, TV/DVD, dataport, minibar, hair dryer, iron, safe, high-speed Internet connectivity, telescopes in rooms w/park view.

EXPENSIVE

Affinia Manhattan ✿ You'll never forget you are in New York when you stay at the Affinia Manhattan. From the large lobby—sort of a miniversion of the Waldorf= Astoria's, where a Grand Central Station–like information booth in its center features a series of televisions with video images of New York landmarks—to check-in, where you are offered a complimentary glass of "Snapple Apple" juice, to the King Kong doll you'll find on the bed in your room, it's all Big Apple here. Furthering the New York theme, "New York Experience" kits are available, free of charge, including a walking-tour kit, sports' fanatic kit (the hotel is 2 blocks from Madison Square Garden), and a fashionista kit, which, among other things, features a guide to local boutiques and a monthly schedule of sample sales. Though the New York theme is fun, all you really need to do is look out your window, where you just might see the Empire State Building, and you'll know very well what city you are in. Like other Affinia properties (see **The Benjamin** on p. 140, and the **Affinia Dumont** on p. 140), all rooms are suites with full kitchens. The room decor here is old-school—no edgy furniture or amenities, but there is plenty of space. Bathrooms are small by comparison but include New York details like black-and-white tiled floors.

371 Seventh Ave. (at 31st St.), New York, NY 10001. ✆ **212/563-1800.** Fax 212/643-8028. www.affinia.com. 526 units (all suites). Rates from $339. Check website for specials and Internet rates, which were as low as $199 at press time. AE, DC, MC, V. Parking $40. Subway: 1, 2, 3 to 34th St. **Amenities:** Restaurant; bar; fitness center; concierge; business center; room service; laundry service; dry cleaning. *In room:* A/C, TV, kitchen, hair dryer, iron/ironing board, safe, high-speed Internet, 2-line cordless phone.

The Algonquin ✿✿ Is this a literary clubhouse or a hotel? The atmosphere in this 1902 landmark building is so steeped in writers' lore that you'll feel guilty turning on the television instead of reading the latest issue of the *New Yorker* that's provided in the guest rooms. Or maybe the television will be a welcome respite from the barrage of witticisms and prose displayed throughout the hotel. Rooms can be extremely cramped, but they are equipped with possibly the most comfortable, inviting beds in the city as well as 21st-century technology like high-speed Internet and flat-screen televisions. If you have a tendency toward claustrophobia, head to the plush lobby, where you can sit in cushy chairs, sip exquisite (and expensive) cocktails, have a snack, or just read or play on your laptop (the lobby is Wi-Fi-equipped). For a special splurge, stay in one of the roomy one-bedroom suites, where all that is missing to get you going on that novel you've been toying with is a manual Smith Corona typewriter.

Meals are served in the recently renovated and celebrated **Round Table Room,** while the fabulous **Oak Room** (p. 370) is one of the city's top cabaret rooms, featuring such esteemed talents as Andrea Marcovicci and Julie Wilson. The publike **Blue Bar** is home to a rotating collection of Hirschfeld drawings that's well worth a browse.

59 W. 44th St. (btwn Fifth and Sixth aves.), New York, NY 10036. © **888/304-2047** or 212/840-6800. Fax 212/944-1419. www.algonquinhotel.com. 174 units. $249–$699 double; from $349 suite. Check website or inquire about discounted rates or special package deals. AE, DC, DISC, MC, V. Parking $28 across the street. Subway: B, D, F, V to 42nd St. **Amenities:** 2 restaurants; lounge; bar; exercise room; concierge; limited room service; laundry service; dry cleaning. *In room:* A/C, TV w/pay movies, dataport, hair dryer, iron, safe, high-speed Internet.

The Blakely New York 🎕🎕 *(Finds* The Blakely has a clubby yet modern feel to it and is an excellent small-Midtown-hotel option. The rooms are all generously sized: None are smaller than 300 square feet and, if it matters to you, some have views of the City Center dome across the street. The dark cherrywood furniture helps perpetuate the clubhouse aura that is contrasted, happily, by modern amenities such as flatscreen TVs and wireless Internet in all the rooms. Marble bathrooms are well sized and appointed; bathroom suites have separate tubs and showers. The lobby, though redesigned after the renovation, remains small and can get hectic at times, but the staff is helpful and efficient. Off the lobby is the Italian restaurant **Abboccato** (p. 190), from the owners of Oceana and Molyvos.

136 W. 55th St. (btwn Sixth and Seventh aves.), New York, NY 10019. © **212/245-1800.** Fax 212/582-8332. www.blakelynewyork.com. 120 units. $260–$365 double; $585–$695 suite. Check the website for packages and seasonal specials. AE, DISC, MC, V. Parking $33. Subway: N, R to 57th St. **Amenities:** Restaurant; complimentary access to nearby health club; concierge; limited room service. *In room:* A/C, TV, minibar, fridge, coffeemaker, iron/ironing board, safe, CD/DVD player, microwave, wireless Internet.

Doubletree Guest Suites Times Square 🎕 *(Kids* For many, the location of this 43-story Doubletree, in the heart of darkness known as Times Square, where the streets are constantly gridlocked, the neon burns holes into your eye sockets, the noise level is ear-splitting, and where, lucky you, there is an Olive Garden across the street and a McDonald's next door, might offer a more Vegas-like experience than a true New York one. But at times we all must make sacrifices for our children, and this Doubletree, location and all, is perfect for the kids. From the fresh-baked chocolate-chip cookies served upon arrival, the spacious, affordable suites big enough for two 5-year-olds to play hide-and-seek (as mine did), and the all-day children's room-service menu to the proximity to the gargantuan Toys "R" Us, the TKTS Booth, and other kid-friendly Times Square offerings, this Doubletree is hard to beat for families. Bathrooms have two entrances so the kids don't have to traipse through the parent's rooms, and every suite has two televisions with PlayStation so while Nickelodeon is on one, CNN can be tuned in on the other.

1568 Broadway (at 47th St. & Seventh Ave.), New York, NY 10036. © **800/222-TREE** or 212/719-1600. Fax 212/921-5212. www.doubletree.com. 460 units. From $349 suite. Extra person $20. Children under 18 stay free in parent's suite. Ask about senior, corporate, and AAA discounts and special promotions. AE, DC, DISC, MC, V. Parking $35. Subway: N, R to 49th St. **Amenities:** Restaurant; lounge; fitness center; concierge; limited room service; babysitting; laundry service; dry cleaning. *In room:* A/C, 2 TVs w/pay movies and video games, dataport, minibar, fridge, wet bar w/coffeemaker, hair dryer, iron, safe, high-speed Internet connectivity, microwave.

Hotel Mela The first new NYC hotel to open in 2007, Hotel Mela adds to the hotel-heavy presence on West 44th St. Compared to the Millenium Broadway across the street, the 230-room Hotel Mela seems miniscule. Advertised as a "luxury boutique" property, the hotel was converted from an office building and that sleek, contemporary spirit, despite a few antique touches in design, prevails. The hotel has a more corporate feel to it, but with a central location; close to Times Square, Rockefeller Center, Bryant

Park and the rest of midtown makes it an ideal spot for the leisure traveler as well. Rooms, though a bit on the small side, are well equipped with comfortable beds, kings or queens, Egyptian combed cotton linen sheets, 310-count duvet covers, LCD TVs, and free wireless Internet. The bathrooms make the most of space with plenty of shelf room. The Asian-inspired hotel's restaurant, **Saju,** offers 24-hour room service. Service is personable making the Hotel Mela a good, solid addition to those who seek something a bit more intimate in hectic Times Square.

120 W. 44th St. (btwn Broadway and 6th Ave.), New York, NY 10036. © **877/452-6352.** Fax 212/704-9680. www. hotelmela.com. 230 units. Doubles from $439 (check the Internet for specials as low as $259 at press time). AE, DC, DISC, MC, V. Parking $45. Subway: B, D, F, V to 42nd St. **Amenities:** Restaurant; bar; fitness center; concierge; 24-hour room service; same day dry cleaning and laundry. *In room:* A/C, TV, minibar, hair dryer, safe, CD, wireless Internet access.

Le Parker Meridien 🐾🐾 *Kids*   Not many hotels in New York can rival the attributes of this hotel: Its location on 57th Street, not too far from Times Square and a close walk from Central Park and Fifth Avenue shopping, is practically perfect; the 17,000-square-foot fitness center, called Gravity, features state-of-the-art equipment, basketball and racquetball courts, a spa, and a rooftop pool; three excellent restaurants, including **Norma's** (p. 195), where breakfast is an art, and the aptly named **Burger Joint,** rated by many as the best hamburger in the city; a gorgeous, bustling lobby that also serves as a public space; and elevators with televisions that continuously show *Tom and Jerry* and *Rocky and Bullwinkle,* and Charlie Chaplin shorts that are a wonder for the kids. The spacious hotel rooms, though a bit on the Ikea side, have a fun feel to them, with hidden drawers and swirling television platforms, inventively exploiting an economical use of space. Rooms have wood platform beds with feather beds, built-ins that include large work desks, stylish Aeron chairs, free high-speed Internet, and 32-inch flat-screen televisions with VCR, CD and DVD players. The slate-and-limestone bathrooms are large but unfortunately come with shower only. A stay at Le Parker Meridien is a New York experience in itself.

118 W. 57th St. (btwn Sixth and Seventh aves.), New York, NY 10019. © **800/543-4300** or 212/245-5000. Fax 212/307-1776. www.parkermeridien.com. 731 units. $600–$800 double; from $780 suite. Extra person $30. Excellent packages and weekend rates often available (as low as $225 at press time). AE, DC, DISC, MC, V. Parking $45. Subway: F, N, Q, R to 57th St. Pets accepted. **Amenities:** 3 restaurants; rooftop pool; fantastic fitness center and spa; concierge (2 w/Clefs d'Or distinction); weekday morning courtesy car to Wall St.; full-service business center; 24-hr. room service; laundry service; dry cleaning. *In room:* A/C, 32-in. TV w/DVD/CD player, dataport, minibar, hair dryer, iron, safe, high-speed Internet access, nightly complimentary shoeshine.

The London NYC 🐾   Its curiously un-New York name aside, The London, formerly the RHIGA Royal Hotel, after a major renovation, is the quintessential New York midtown hotel. A property now of LXR Luxury Resorts, The London NYC features a sleek, airy look. The lobby is high-ceilinged and bright with white marble attended by black-coated, derby-wearing porters. Off the lobby is the blue-gray leather-wrapped **London Bar** while through a set of closed doors is the hotel's restaurant, **Gordon Ramsay at The London,** helmed by famed chef, Gordon Ramsay. The rooms, excuse me, the *flats* (this is The London) are spacious with big windows providing spectacular views of the neighborhood—the hotel with 54 floors is one of the New York's tallest. If you suffer from vertigo, the shades are operated electronically as is the mood lighting . . . if you are in the mood. With flat screen LCD televisions, iHome iPod docking stations wireless Internet (inexplicably for a daily charge), and the addition of oak parquet floors give the hotel's cool feel more of a rustic homey touch. The white-tiled bathrooms have been designed by the bath purveyor Water-works and feature their amenities. The hotel's suites include two televisions, a separate parlor area, some with French doors, and baths with two showerheads. Located in a prime midtown neighborhood close to MoMA, City Center, and Rockefeller Center, The London, though a bit corporate-cold, is a welcome change from the worn RHIGA Royal.

151 W. 54th St. (btwn Sixth and Seventh aves.) New York, N.Y. 10019. ℂ ℂ **866/690-2029** or 212/307-5000. Fax 212/468-8747. www.thelondonnyc.com. 562 units. $499–$1,199 double, AE, DC, MC, V. Parking $55. Subway: B, D, E to Seventh Ave. **Amenities:** Restaurant; bar; fitness center; concierge; 24-hour business center; 24-hour room service; laundry service; dry cleaning. *In room:* A/C, TV, minibar, hair dryer, safe, iPod home docking stations, wireless Internet access.

The Michelangelo ⟨★★⟩ *(Finds)*

Owned by the Italian-based Starhotel, this is the group's only U.S. property and it offers a welcome dose of Italian hospitality in the heart of New York. From the moment you enter the spacious lobby, which is adorned with Italian marble, you feel as if you have departed from the rapid-fire sight-and-sound assault of nearby Times Square. Off the lobby is a lounge where coffee and cappuccino are served all day and a complimentary Italian breakfast of pastries and fruit is offered each morning. The rooms come in various sizes and are decorated in three styles: Art Deco, country French, and neoclassical. I prefer the country French, but whatever the style, the rooms are all of a good size and include marble foyers, Italian fabrics, king beds, and two television sets (one in the bathroom). The bathrooms are well maintained and feature deep whirlpool bathtubs. Service is helpful and friendly, creating a relaxed, casual atmosphere that's rare in many New York hotels.

152 W. 51st St. (btwn Sixth and Seventh aves.), New York, NY 10019. ℂ **800/237-0990** or 212/765-0505. Fax 212/581-7618. www.michelangelohotel.com. 178 units. From $345 double; from $625 suite. Rates include Italian breakfast. Visit website for (sometimes substantial) discounts. AE, DC, DISC, MC, V. Parking available 2 blocks away: $29 per day self-park, $40 per day valet. Subway: N, R to 49th St. **Amenities:** Restaurant; lounge; fitness center; concierge; complimentary morning limo service to Wall St.; 24-hr. room service; laundry service; dry cleaning. *In room:* A/C, TV, fax, minibar, hair dryer, iron, safe, high-speed Internet.

The Muse ⟨★⟩

The beauty of The Muse is that it is a Times Square hotel that feels like it's miles away; an inspired oasis in the midst of the Vegas-like hokeyness, bustle, and noise that is now Times Square. In the intimate, mahogany-paneled lobby, you will be personally checked in by a concierge and brought to your room by a bellman, who will familiarize you with the amenities. But while he's doing that, you might be marveling at the classical contemporary decor and not really paying attention. All the rooms are good-size with feather beds and custom linens. The bathrooms are sumptuous and well outfitted. Service is solid and anticipatory; you even get your own personalized business cards. My only complaint, and it's not one that is unusual in New York, was the cacophony of garbage trucks working on 46th Street before sunrise. Try to secure a back room if street noise is an issue.

130 W. 46th St. (btwn Sixth and Seventh aves.), New York, NY 10036. ℂ **877/692-6873** or 212/485-2400. Fax 212/485-2789. www.themusehotel.com. 200 units. $199–$399 double; from $399 suite. AE, DC, DISC, MC, V. Parking $43. Subway: B, D, F, V to 42nd St. Pets accepted. **Amenities:** Restaurant; good fitness room; concierge; business services; limited room service; in-room massage; laundry service; dry cleaning. *In room:* A/C, TV w/pay movies, dataport, coffeemaker, hair dryer, iron, safe, CD player, high-speed Internet connectivity.

The Shoreham ⟨★⟩

No, it's not on the luxury level of the Peninsula or the St. Regis down the block. But after a multimillion-dollar renovation in 2005 that spruced up the rooms with organic, citrus tones, modernized the lobby, and added amenities like champagne or sparkling water upon check-in and a 24-hour self-service coffee bar, and at just about half the price, the Shoreham is a more than worthy, less expensive alternative to those other hotels down the block. Rooms vary in size and amenities and though all have been upgraded or totally renovated, better to spring for a deluxe or a suite where you will get a bigger bathroom, some with five-head rain showers and Jacuzzis and all with flat-panel high-definition televisions. The hotel offers the little extras that give you value, such as complimentary shoeshine, *New York Times,* two bottles of Voss water, wireless Internet, and for fashionistas, a complimentary daily copy of *Women's Wear Daily.* At press time, a fitness center was under construction to be completed by the time you read this.

33 W. 55th St. (btwn Fifth and Sixth aves.), New York, NY 10019. © **800/553-3347** or 212/247-6700. Fax 212/765-9741. www.shorehamhotel.com. 174 units. $309–$609 double. Check website for Internet rates and other special deals. AE, MC, V. Parking nearby $45 with in/out privileges. Subway: B, D, E to Seventh Ave. **Amenities:** Restaurant; bar; 24-hr. cappuccino and coffee; fitness club; 24-hr. room service; room spa service; laundry service; dry cleaning; complimentary shoeshine. *In room:* A/C, TV, minifridge, hair dryer, iron/ironing board, safe, VCR/DVD/CD player, wireless Internet.

Sofitel New York 🏵🏵🏵 *Finds*   There are many fine hotels on the centrally located block of 44th Street between Fifth and Sixth avenues (see the sidebar "Hotel Row," on p. 134), but the best in this writer's estimation is the soaring Sofitel. Upon entering the hotel and the warm, inviting lobby with check-in tucked off to the side, you wouldn't think you were entering a hotel that is this young, which is one of the reasons why the hotel is so special. The designers have successfully melded modern, new-world amenities with European old-world elegance. The rooms are spacious and ultra-comfortable, adorned with art from New York and Paris. The lighting is soft and romantic, the walls and windows soundproof. Suites are extra-special, equipped with king beds, two televisions, and pocket doors separating the bedroom from a sitting room. Bathrooms in all rooms are magnificent, with separate showers and soaking tubs. Owned by the Accor Hotels & Resorts company of France, Sofitel reflects its heritage with a greeting of *bonjour* or *bonsoir* at reception; a unique gift shop with hard-to-find French products, including perfumes and cosmetics; and a stylish French restaurant called **Gaby** that bakes delicious croissants for breakfast.

45 W. 44th St. (btwn Fifth and Sixth aves.), New York, NY 10036. © **212/354-8844.** Fax 212/354-2480 www.sofitel.com. 398 units. $299–$599 double; from $439 suite. 1 child stays free in parent's room. AE, DC, MC, V. Parking $45. Subway: B, D, F, V to 42nd St. Pets accepted. **Amenities:** Restaurant; bar; exercise room; concierge; 24-hr. room service; laundry service; dry cleaning. *In room:* A/C, TV w/pay movies and Internet access, dataport, minibar, hair dryer, iron, safe, CD player, high-speed Internet connectivity.

The Westin New York at Times Square 🏵   This happy, welcome paradox is a high-tech, high-style high-rise with a warm yet quirky personality. The warmth comes from the inside, from the extra-attentive staff, but the quirkiness is outside, realized in its odd, wavy exterior. The 10-color, mostly copper and blue, glass edifice looks more like a transplant from Miami Beach than something familiar to the New York City terrain. No wonder—the hotel was designed by the Miami-based architectural firm Arquitectonica. And if that isn't enough to distinguish itself, the hotel also boasts a beam of light that rises through an atrium, then up to the top of the 45-story tower and into the already well-illuminated sky of Times Square.

Though style is big here, there's plenty of substance, too. The rooms are spacious, with the Club Rooms and Suites being the biggest. All feature the same amenities, including Westin's Heavenly Bed—a custom Simmons Beautyrest pillow-top mattress set dressed in layer upon layer of fluffy down and crisp white linen—and the signature Heavenly Bath, featuring the luxurious two-head shower. The hotel is located on busy Eighth Avenue, taking up the block between 42nd and 43rd streets; rooms facing 42nd Street and Eighth can be loud. The hotel also features a state-of-the-art fitness center and spa, but surprisingly, there is a fee for guests to use the facility.

270 W. 43rd St. (at Eighth Ave.), New York, NY 10036. ⓒ 800/WESTIN-1, 888/627-7149, or 212/201-2700. Fax 212/201-2701. www.westinnewyork.com. 863 units. $249–$599 double; $469–$2,000 suite. AE, DC, DISC, MC, V. Parking $27, $48 valet parking. Subway: A, C, or E to 42nd St. **Amenities:** Restaurant; bar; 2,500-sq.-ft. fitness center and spa ($10 per day, $30 per week); concierge and theater desk; business center; 24-hr. room service; laundry service; dry cleaning; currency exchange; internal access to E Walk, a 200,000-sq.-ft. entertainment-and-retail complex featuring a 13-movie theater. *In room:* A/C, TV w/pay movies, dataport, minibar, hair dryer, safe, high-speed Internet.

W Times Square ⊛   Who said Times Square hotels can't be hip? The W Hotel group, a subsidiary of Starwood Hotels & Resorts, bucked that trend by bringing a distinct downtown feel to the heart of Times Square. Take the elevator to the seventh floor to the ultra-modern, loungelike lobby to check-in, where the only way to distinguish hotel employees from guests is the tiny "W" pin they wear. Otherwise, everyone is dressed in the dark tones of Kenneth Cole–designed "urban" attire. The lobby bar always seems to be busy—or maybe that's just the lounge music that plays continuously throughout all the hotel's public spaces. Most rooms boast magnificent views of the neon spectacle of Times Square, but all that neon means a bright room; thankfully, the shades do a good job of blocking out most of that light at night and the double-paned windows keep the rooms surprisingly quiet. Standard rooms are compact but roomy enough, with a big Plexiglas desk, mirrors everywhere (is that good or bad?), a 27-inch TV, and the Westin (sister company of Starwood) Heavenly Bed. Bathrooms in the standard rooms are small and a bit clumsy, featuring a semi-open shower stall and a huge sink that takes up what little counter space there is. Suites are similarly designed and will get you an extra bathroom and a flat-screen television. The hotel's restaurant, **Blue Fin,** is highly rated for seafood, and **The Whiskey,** run by nightclub impresario Rande Gerber, is a popular destination for drinks.

1567 Broadway (at 47th St.), New York, NY 10036. ⓒ 888/625-5144 or 212/930-7400. Fax 212/930-7500. www.whotels.com. 507 units. From $259 double; from $599 suite. AE, DC, DISC, MC, V. Parking $52. Subway: N, R to 49th St. Pets up to 40 lb. accepted. **Amenities:** Restaurant; 2 bars; fitness center and spa; concierge; 24-hr. room service; laundry service; dry cleaning. *In room:* A/C, TV w/DVD/CD, minibar, hair dryer, iron, safe, high-speed Internet.

MODERATE

Casablanca Hotel ⊛⊛ *(Value)*   Try to picture the exotic, romantic setting of the movie *Casablanca*—ceiling fans, mosaic tiles, and North African–themed art—and then try to picture that setting in the heart of neon-blinding, cacophonous Times Square. The combination seems unlikely, but really, who wouldn't want a desert oasis in the middle of all that mayhem? And that's what the Casablanca Hotel really is: a calming refuge where you can escape from the noise and crowds. Where, in **Rick's Café,** the Casablanca's homey guest lounge, you can sit by a fire, read a paper, check your e-mail, watch television on the gargantuan-size screen, or sip a cappuccino from the serve-yourself cappuccino/espresso machine. Or, if the days or nights are balmy, you can lounge on the rooftop deck or second-floor courtyard. Or you can just retreat to your room. They might not be the biggest around, but they are well outfitted with the aforementioned ceiling fans, bathrobes, free bottles of water, complimentary high-speed Internet access, and beautifully tiled bathrooms where, if you wish, you can open the window and let sounds outside remind you where you really are. The

Hotel Row

There are hundreds of hotels in Manhattan, but most are spread out over a good chunk of real estate. There is, however, 1 block—West 44th Street, between Fifth and Sixth avenues—where the hotels stand practically side by side.

The block has a sophisticated, urbane, and literary feel to it, probably stemming from the presence of the 1902-built **Algonquin** 🎬🎬 (59 W. 44th St.; p. 128), where the *New Yorker* was born, where Lerner and Loewe wrote *My Fair Lady,* and—most famously—where some of the biggest names in 1920s literati, among them Dorothy Parker, met to trade boozy quips at the celebrated Algonquin Round Table.

Next to the Algonquin, at 55 W. 44th St., sits the 65-room Jeffrey Bilhuber–designed **City Club** (📞 **212/921-5500**; www.cityclubhotel.com). The structure started out in 1904 as a gentlemen's club and saw many incarnations over the last century, but its latest life, as the ultrafashionable City Club, casts aside the usual style of the New York "boutique" property—cramped and minimalist decor that make a virtue of discomfort. City Club's modernist elements are tempered with traditional touches such as Queen Anne chairs, natural Frette linens, vintage books, chocolate marble, and Hermès bath products you'd be afraid to steal. This haven for mavens of fashion also is the home of one of Daniel Boulud's restaurant's, **db Bistro Moderne** (p. 191).

For many years there was a barbershop adjacent to the lobby of the **Iroquois Hotel**, 49 W. 44th St. (📞 **212/840-3080**; www.iroquoisny.com), called the Dumont Barbershop and Shoeshine. The shop's principal barber, Louis Fontana, used to notice a young man hanging out on the stoop of the hotel, which, at the time, was a men's residence. When Louie (as he was known by

Casablanca is an HK Hotels property (The Library, Gansevoort, Elysée, and Giraffe), and like those hotels, service is top-notch. Because of its location, moderate prices, and size (only 48 rooms), the Casablanca is in high demand, so book early.

147 W. 43rd St. (just east of Broadway), New York, NY 10036. 📞 **888/922-7225** or 212/869-1212. Fax 212/391-7585. www.casablancahotel.com. 48 units. $249–$299 double; from $399 suite. Rates include continental breakfast, all-day cappuccino, and weekday wine and cheese. Check website for Internet rates and other special deals. AE, DC, MC, V. Parking $25 next door. Subway: N, R, 1, 2, 3 to 42nd St./Times Sq. **Amenities:** Cyber lounge; free access to New York Sports Club; concierge; business center; limited room service; laundry service; dry cleaning; video library. *In room:* A/C, TV/VCR, dataport, minibar, hair dryer, CD player, ceiling fan.

Hotel 41 🎬 *Finds*   Like the **Casablanca Hotel** (p. 133) a few blocks up, Hotel 41 offers a stylish, comfortable, and moderate alternative to the many gleaming, glittering and more pricey hotels that tower over Times Square. Just seven floors high, the Hotel 41 features minimalist modern decor in the guest rooms. Rooms, for these prices, are of decent size, but what sets the hotel apart are the freebies: high-speed Internet, complimentary continental breakfast, free espresso or cappuccino all day, in-room DVD players with the hotel's DVD library available for viewing, plush his regulars) asked the kid why he was hanging around the barbershop, the kid stuttered that he needed a haircut but couldn't afford one; he was an actor looking for work. "Kid, what's your name?" the legend goes. The kid answered, "James Dean." Big-hearted Louis gave him a haircut for free that day. That's a true story and part of the legend of the Iroquois Hotel. The 114-room hotel, after a full renovation some years ago, is now a member of the Small Luxury Hotels of the World and features a suite named after its former most famous resident.

Just next to the Iroquois, at 45 W. 44th St., is the **Sofitel New York** (p. 132); from the appearance of the lobby and entrance, you might think you have entered a hotel built in the same era as the others. But take a look from across the street at the glittering curved tower that was built less than 6 years ago. Despite its newness, the hotel blends in perfectly on historic Hotel Row.

Closer to Fifth Avenue and on the south side of the block at 12 W. 44th St. is **The Mansfield** (© 800/255-5167 or 212/944-6050), which was built as a bachelor's residence in 1905 and, in keeping with the block's literary and artistic tradition, was once the home of poet W.B. Yeats's father. The hotel was completely renovated in 2007 restoring it to its former grandeur. Finally, and closer to Sixth Avenue, at 44 W. 44th St., is the Philippe Starck–designed **Royalton** (© 800/697-1791 or 212/869-4400; www.morgans hotelgroup.com. Though it is also set in an early-20th-century building, the feel is late 1990s, with that minimalist Starck style. The solitary homage to the past is the presence of working fireplaces in 40 of the hotel's 169 rooms. In keeping with the block's artistic tradition, the Royalton is a favorite of music, fashion, and film types.

bathrobes in the rooms, double-paned windows (a necessity in Times Sq.), refrigerators in all rooms, and luxurious amenities like Aveda bath products. If you plan to stay for more than a few days, try for one of the junior suites or, for a splurge, Penthouse no. 2, which features a large outdoor deck. Service is boutique-friendly, and off the lobby is **Bar 2156** a lively bar/restaurant (where breakfast is served) that draws a local after-work crowd. Next to the Nederlander Theater, where the hit musical *Rent* has been playing for years, you really couldn't ask for a better Times Square location.

206 W. 41st St. (btwn Seventh and Eighth aves.), New York, NY 10036. © 212/703-8600. Fax 212/302-0895. www. hotel41nyc.com. 47 units. $289–$469 double; $609–$999 suite. Check the website for Internet specials. AE, DC, DISC, MC, V. Parking $30. Subway: 1, 2, 3, 7, A, C, E, N, Q, R, S, W to Times Sq. Pets accepted **Amenities:** Restaurant; bar; access to nearby fitness center; limited room service; continental breakfast; coffee all day. *In room:* A/C, TV/DVD, fridge, hair dryer, safe, free high-speed Internet.

Hotel Metro (Kids)   The Metro is the choice in Midtown for those who don't want to sacrifice either style or comfort for affordability. This Art Deco–style jewel has larger rooms than you'd expect for the price. They're outfitted with smart retro furnishings, playful fabrics, fluffy pillows, smallish but beautifully appointed marble bathrooms, and alarm clocks. Only about half the bathrooms have tubs, but the others have shower stalls big enough for two (junior suites have whirlpool tubs). The family room is an ingenious invention: a two-room suite that has a second bedroom in lieu of a sitting area; families on tighter budgets can opt for a roomy double/double. The neo-Deco design gives the place an air of New York glamour that I've not otherwise seen in this price range. A great collection of black-and-white photos, from Man Ray classics to Garbo and Dietrich portraits, adds to the vibe. The comfy, fire-lit library/lounge area off the lobby, where complimentary buffet breakfast is laid out and the coffeepot's on all day, is a popular hangout. Service is attentive, and rooftop terrace boasts a breathtaking view of the Empire State Building and makes a great place to order up room service from the stylish—and good—**Metro Grill.**

45 W. 35th St. (btwn Fifth and Sixth aves.), New York, NY 10001. (©) 800/356-3870 or 212/947-2500. Fax 212/279-1310. www.hotelmetronyc.com. 179 units. $210–$365 double; $245–$420 triple or quad; $255–$425 family room; $275–$475 suite. Extra person $25. 1 child under 13 stays free in parent's room. Rates include continental breakfast. Check with airlines and other package operators for great-value package deals. AE, DC, MC, V. Parking $20 nearby. Subway: B, D, F, V, N, R to 34th St. **Amenities:** Restaurant; alfresco rooftop bar in summer; good fitness room; salon; limited room service; laundry service; dry cleaning. *In room:* A/C, TV, dataport, fridge, hair dryer, iron, high-speed Internet.

Hotel QT ⟨⟨ *Value* Owned by Andre Balazs, of **The Mercer** (p. 117), Hotel QT offers much of The Mercer's style without the hefty rates. From its enviable Midtown location, to many extras like a swimming pool in the lobby, steam room and sauna, free high-speed Internet, complimentary continental breakfast, and good-size rooms including a number with bunk beds, Hotel QT, which opened in 2005, is now one of the best moderate options in the Times Square area. Upon entering, you check in at a kiosk/front desk where you pick up periodicals or essentials to stock your minibar. Making your way to the elevators, you might see guests swimming in the lobby pool or having a drink at the pool's swim-up bar, an unusual site in the Big Apple. The rooms are sparse in tone, but the queen- and king-size platform beds are plush and dressed with Egyptian cotton sheets. The biggest drawback is the bathrooms: There are no doors on the bathrooms—sliding doors conceal the shower (none of the rooms have tubs) and the toilet. But for prices this low along with the extras offered, who are we to quibble?

125 W. 45th St. (btwn Sixth Ave. and Broadway), New York, NY 10036. (©) 212/354-2323. Fax 212/302-8585. www.hotelqt.com. 140 units. $199–$350 double. AE, DC, MC, V. Parking nearby $25. Subway: B, D, F, V to 47th–50th St./Rockefeller Center. **Amenities:** Bar; swimming pool; gym; sauna; steam room; complimentary continental breakfast. *In room:* A/C, TV, minifridge, hair dryer, iron/ironing board, safe, CD player, DVD player, free high-speed and wireless Internet, free local calls, 2-line speakerphones.

Novotel New York ⟨ *Kids* Run expertly by the French company Accor (**Sofitel,** p. 132), this towering hotel on the northern fringe of Times Square, with its bilingual staff and a selection of international newspapers, attracts an international crowd. But domestic visitors shouldn't neglect what is a good moderate option in one of the busiest parts of the city. The vast, sunny lobby on the seventh floor, with open views of Times Square, is the hotel's pride and joy; it is also the location of the underrated **Café Nicole,** where a breakfast buffet is offered. Guest rooms, though pleasant and of a decent size, are more motel-like in decor. Rooms were recently renovated and many have spectacular views of Times Square and/or the Hudson River. All are soundproof. A family-friendly hotel, kids under 16 can stay free in their parent's room and eat free at Café Nicole (with some restrictions).

226 W. 52nd St. (at Broadway), New York, NY 10019. ☎ **212/315-0100.** Fax 212/765-5369 www.novotel.com. 480 units. From $209 double. 2 children under 16 eat for free and stay free in parent's room. AE, DC, DISC, MC, V. Parking $30. Subway: B, D, E to Seventh Ave. Pets accepted. **Amenities:** Restaurant; bar; fitness room; concierge; limited room service; dry cleaning. *In room:* A/C, TV, minibar, hair dryer, high-speed and wireless Internet.

Washington Jefferson Hotel ℛ   This is one of the few affordable hotels in the heart of my favorite Manhattan neighborhood for dining, Hell's Kitchen. The lobby has a warm and welcoming ambience, with a friendly, snappily attired staff and more than a dash of designer style. Snazzy blue-carpeted halls lead to rooms that are *small*—don't say I didn't warn you—but attractively outfitted in a palette of soft grays. Nice touches include platform beds with generous cushioned headboards and fluffy goose-down comforters. The gorgeous limestone-and-slate bathrooms are stylish and relatively spacious, although some have showers only. Score one of the 18 king rooms if you can; they're roomy and boast a pullout love seat as well as a Jacuzzi tub in the bathroom. The Japanese restaurant in the hotel is just a sample of some of the different ethnic cuisines you will find in the neighborhood.

318 W. 51st St. (btwn Eighth and Ninth aves.), New York, NY 10019. ☎ **212/246-7550.** Fax 212/246-7622. www.wjhotel.com. 135 units. $179–$349 double. Ask about special deals. AE, DC, DISC, MC, V. Parking $35 nearby. Subway: C, E to 50th St. **Amenities:** Restaurant; exercise room; limited room service. *In room:* A/C, TV w/pay movies/video games/Internet access, dataport, hair dryer, iron, safe.

INEXPENSIVE

Americana Inn ℛ *(Value*   The least expensive hotel from the Empire Hotel Group—the people behind the Lucerne, and the Newton among other top-notch properties—is a star in the budget-basic category. Linoleum floors give the rooms a somewhat unfortunate institutional quality, but the hotel is professionally run and immaculately kept. Rooms are mostly spacious, with good-size closets, private sinks, and an alarm built into the TV; the beds are the most comfortable I've found at this price. Most rooms come with a double bed or two twins; a few can accommodate three guests in two twin beds and a pullout sofa or in three twins. One hall bathroom accommodates every three rooms or so; all are spacious and spotless. Every floor has a common kitchenette with microwave, stove, and fridge (BYO cooking utensils, or go plastic). The five-story building has an elevator, and four rooms are accessible for travelers with disabilities. The Garment District location is convenient for Midtown sightseeing and shopping; ask for a back-facing room away from the street noise.

69 W. 38th St. (at Sixth Ave.), New York, NY 10018. ☎ **888/HOTEL-58** or 212/840-6700. Fax 212/840-1830. www.newyorkhotel.com. 50 units, all with shared bathroom. $110–$150 double. Extra person $20 Check website for specials (winter rates as low as $60 double). AE, MC, V. Parking $30 nearby. Subway: B, D, F, V to 34th St. **Amenities:** Common kitchen. *In room:* A/C, TV, hair dryer (ask reception).

Broadway Inn ℛ *(Finds*   More like a San Francisco B&B than a Theater District hotel, this lovely, welcoming inn is a charmer. The second-floor lobby sets the homey, easygoing tone with stocked bookcases, cushy seating, and cafe tables where breakfast is served. The rooms are basic but comfy, outfitted in an appealing neo-Deco style with firm beds, good-quality linens and textiles, and nice bathrooms (about half have showers only). The whole place is impeccably kept. Two rooms have king beds and whirlpool tubs, but the standard doubles are just fine for two if you're looking to save some dough. If there are more than two of you, or you're staying a while, the suites—with pullout sofa, microwave, mini-fridge, and lots of closet space—are a great deal. The location can be noisy, but double-paned windows keep the rooms surprisingly peaceful; still, ask for a back-facing one if you're extra-sensitive.

The inn's biggest asset is its terrific staff, who go above and beyond the call to make guests happy; they'll even give you a hot-line number upon check-in so you can call for directions, advice, and other assistance while you're on the town. Service doesn't get any better in this price range. This corner of the Theater District makes a great home base, especially for theatergoers. The inn has inspired a loyal following, so reserve early. However, there's no elevator in the four-story building, so overpackers and travelers with limited mobility should book elsewhere.

264 W. 46th St. (at Eighth Ave.), New York, NY 10036. 🕿 800/826-6300 or 212/997-9200. Fax 212/768-2807. www. broadwayinn.com. 41 units. $159–$199 single; $169–$299 double; $325–$450 suite. Extra person $10. Children under 12 stay free in parent's room. Rates include continental breakfast. Check website for specials. AE, DC, DISC, MC, V. Parking $25 3 blocks away. Subway: A, C, E to 42nd St. **Amenities:** 2 neighboring restaurants where inn guests have special discounts; concierge; fax and copy service. *In room:* A/C, TV, dataport, fridge, hair dryer, iron, wireless Internet

La Quinta Inn Manhattan *Value* The first and only La Quinta Inn in Manhattan is another excellent Midtown budget choice. Housed in a 1904 Beaux Arts structure on the block known as Little Korea, La Quinta Inn offers standard motel amenities along with motel-like prices. Like the other Apple Core properties, including the Red Roof Inn across the street, service is friendly and a continental breakfast adds to the value. The rooms are basic in motel-room decor and size, but there's nothing wrong with that, especially at these prices. Bathrooms are small but clean and well equipped. There's even a cozy rooftop bar that offers indoor and outdoor seating in the shadow of the majestic Empire State Building. And if you like Korean barbecue and dumplings, you won't have to travel far; the block is packed with some good Korean restaurants.

17 W. 32nd St. (btwn Fifth and Sixth aves.), New York, NY 10001. 🕿 800/567-7720 or 212/790-2710. www.apple corehotels.com. 181 units. $89–$329 double (usually less than $189). Rates include continental breakfast. Children under 13 stay free in parent's room. AE, DC, DISC, MC, V. Parking $26. Subway: B, D, F, N, R, V to 34th St. **Amenities:** Breakfast room; bar; exercise room; concierge; business center; laundry service; dry cleaning. *In room:* A/C, TV w/pay movies and video games, dataport, coffeemaker, iron, wireless Internet.

Red Roof Inn 🎯 *Value* Manhattan's first and only Red Roof Inn offers relief from Midtown's high-priced hotel scene. The hotel occupies a former office building that was gutted and laid out fresh, allowing for more spacious rooms and bathrooms than you'll usually find in this price category. The lobby feels smart, and elevators are quiet and efficient. In-room amenities—including coffeemakers and TVs with on-screen Web access—are better than most competitors', and furnishings are new and comfortable. Wi-Fi wireless Internet is available throughout the property. The location—on a bustling block lined with nice hotels and affordable Korean restaurants, just a stone's throw from the Empire State Building and Herald Square—is excellent.

Be sure to compare the rates offered by Apple Core Hotel's reservation line (the management company) and those quoted on Red Roof's national reservation line and website, as they can vary significantly. Complimentary continental breakfast adds to the good value.

6 W. 32nd St. (btwn Broadway and Fifth Ave.), New York, NY 10001. 🕿 800/567-7720, 800/RED-ROOF, or 212/643-7100. Fax 212/643-7101. www.applecorehotels.com or www.redroof.com. 171 units. $89–$329 double (usually less than $189). Rates include continental breakfast. Children under 13 stay free in parent's room. AE, DC, DISC, MC, V. Parking $26. Subway: B, D, F, N, R, V to 34th St. **Amenities:** Breakfast room; wine-and-beer lounge; exercise room; concierge; laundry service; dry cleaning. *In room:* A/C, TV w/pay movies and Internet access, dataport, fridge, coffeemaker, hair dryer, iron, video games, wireless Internet.

Family-Friendly Hotels

Lugging the kids to New York City can be a daunting experience. Finding a hotel that makes that experience, whether it is in the accommodations or in the amenities, a bit less daunting can be a huge help. Here are some of the city's best accommodations for families:

Doubletree Guest Suites Times Square (Times Sq.; p. 129)   An entire floor of childproof suites, plus a Kids Club for ages 3 to 12.

Gershwin Hotel (Flatiron District; p. 127)   High space-to-dollar ratio with the Family Room, a two-room suite.

Hotel Beacon (Upper West Side; p. 149)   In-room kitchenette, on-site laundromat, and spacious rooms in a kid-friendly neighborhood—what more do you want?

Hotel Metro (Midtown West; p. 135)   The sitting rooms of the hotel's Family Room suites are smartly converted into second bedrooms.

Le Parker Meridien (Midtown West; p. 130)   Cartoons playing in the elevators, a great swimming pool, a kid-friendly burger joint in the lobby, and spacious rooms and suites.

The Lowell (Upper East Side; p. 154)   Total *luxe*, but with the feel of a residential dwelling. Most units are equipped with a kitchenette or full kitchen.

Novotel New York (Midtown West; p. 136)   Kids under 16 stay free in their parent's room and eat free at the hotel's beautiful Café Nicole.

The Regency (Midtown East; p. 145)   A big welcome by longtime kids' concierge Kaptain Kidz, with goodies for the children upon arrival.

Ritz-Carlton New York, Central Park (Midtown West; p. 127)   You'll pay dearly for it, but kids love the in-room cookies and milk.

Skyline Hotel and **Travel Inn** (Midtown West; p. 139)   Inexpensive ($10) parking at the Skyline and free at Travel Inn, oversize rooms, and swimming pools (a rarity in affordable hotels).

Skyline Hotel *Kids* *Value*   This fairly-recently renovated motor hotel offers predictable comforts and some uncommon extras—inexpensive storage parking ($10 per day) and a lovely indoor pool—that make it a good value. A pleasant lobby leads to motel-standard rooms that are bigger than most in this price range. There are two room categories: standard, with two twin beds, and deluxe, with either a king bed with sofa or a queen bed. The deluxe with king and sofa is best for families. They boast decent-size closets, small work desks (in most), and double-paned windows that open to let fresh air in and shut out a surprising amount of street noise when closed. Some rooms have brand-new bathrooms, but the older ones are still fine. Everything is well kept. Another plus for the family is the pool, which has a tiled deck and plush deck chairs, but it's only open limited hours, so call ahead if it matters.

725 Tenth Ave. (at 49th St.), New York, NY 10019. © **800/433-1982** or 212/586-3400. Fax 212/582-4604. www. skylinehotelny.com. 230 units. $209–$389 standard; $219–$409 deluxe. Extra person $20. Children 14 and under stay

free in parent's room. Check website or inquire about special rates (as low as $99 at press time). AE, DC, DISC, MC, V. Parking $10 (charge for in/out privileges). Subway: A, C, E to 50th St. Pets accepted with $200 deposit. **Amenities:** Restaurant; bar w/extensive beer list; indoor pool; big-screen TV; Internet access in lobby. *In room:* A/C, TV w/pay movies/video games/high-speed Internet, dataport, hair dryer, iron, safe.

Travel Inn *Kids* *Value*   Extras such as a huge outdoor pool and sun deck, a sunny and up-to-date fitness room, and *free* parking (with in and out privileges!) make the Travel Inn another terrific deal, similar to the one offered by the **Skyline Hotel** (see above). Like the Skyline, the Travel Inn may not be loaded with personality, but it does offer the clean, bright regularity of a good chain hotel—an attractive trait in a city where "quirky" is the catchword at most affordable hotels. Rooms are oversize and comfortably furnished, with extra-firm beds and work desks; even the smallest double is sizable and has a roomy bathroom, and double/doubles make great affordable shares for families. A total renovation over the last couple years has made everything feel like new, even the tiled bathrooms. Though a bit off the track, Off-Broadway theaters and affordable restaurants are at hand, and it's a 10-minute walk to the Theater District.

515 W. 42nd St. (just west of Tenth Ave.), New York, NY 10036. ℂ **888/HOTEL58**, 800/869-4630, or 212/695-7171. Fax 212/268-3542. www.newyorkhotel.com. 160 units. $105–$250 double. Extra person $10. Children under 16 stay free in parent's room. AAA discounts available; check website for special Internet deals. AE, DC, DISC, MC, V. Free self-parking. Subway: A, C, E to 42nd St./Port Authority. **Amenities:** Coffee shop; terrific outdoor pool w/deck chairs and lifeguard in season; fitness center; Gray Line tour desk; 24-hr. room service. *In room:* A/C, TV, dataport, hair dryer, iron, Internet access

8 Midtown East & Murray Hill

To find the hotels described in this section, see p. 124.

VERY EXPENSIVE

Affinia Dumont *舛舛*   The Affinia Dumont is the perfect choice for fitness-focused guests: Instead of those basic New York City guide magazines stocked in the rooms, you get a choice of *Sports Illustrated, Shape,* or *Men's Fitness.* Plus, when you book a room, you can request a complimentary "Fit Kit" that will be prepared based on your needs for an in-room workout. But you might want to venture out and to the hotel's terrific fitness spa, complete with the most advanced weights, cardio equipment, and massage and skin treatments. But even if you don't want to break a sweat, the hotel features amenities that make it an attractive option. The spacious suites range from studios to two-bedrooms, and all include full kitchens, at least one 27-inch TV, a large desk with an ergonomic chair, the "Affinia Bed," with a custom-designed mattress and four-selection "pillow menu," and a minibar stocked with unusual options, such as health elixirs with names like Depth Recharger or Virtual Buddha. The hotel is a bit away from the center of Midtown, but still within easy walking distance of Herald Square shopping, the Empire State Building, Madison Square Garden, and Grand Central Station.

150 E. 34th St. (btwn Third and Lexington aves.), New York, NY 10016. ℂ **212/481-7600**. Fax 212/889-8856. www.affinia.com. 241 units. From $350 studio suite; from $450 1-bedroom suite; from $650 2-bedroom suite. AE, DC, MC, V. Valet parking $42. Subway: 6 to 33rd St. **Amenities:** Restaurant; health club and spa; fitness concierge; concierge; limited room service; coin-operated laundry; grocery-shopping service. *In room:* A/C, TV/VCR, dataport, full kitchen, minibar, hair dryer, iron, safe (laptop size), Fit Kit, high-speed Internet.

The Benjamin *舛舛舛*   From the retro sign and clock on Lexington Avenue to the high-ceilinged marble lobby, when you enter The Benjamin, it's as if you've suddenly stepped into the jazz era of 1920s New York. But once you get to your spacious room and notice the high-tech amenities, such as Bose Wave radios, Internet browsers and video games for the TVs, high-speed Internet access, fax machines, ergonomic chairs and moveable workstations, you will know you are most definitely in the 21st century. Many of the amenities are geared toward business travelers, but why should they be the only ones to experience all this comfort and luxury? All rooms are airy, but the deluxe studios and one-bedroom suites are extra large. There are even a few one-bedroom suites with terraces. How many hotels can claim a "sleep concierge" or *guarantee* a good night's sleep? And don't forget the pillow menu featuring 11 options, including buckwheat and Swedish Memory, in which foam designed by NASA reacts to your body temperature. I chose the standard down pillow and did not have to exercise the guarantee. If you are a light sleeper, however, book a room off Lexington Avenue, which can get busy most weeknights and mornings. Bathrooms feature Frette robes, TV speakers, and water pressure from the shower head strong enough to make you think you've just experienced a deep-tissue massage. The hotel also features a good fitness center and the Woodstock Spa and Wellness Center.

125 E. 50th St. (at Lexington Ave.), New York, NY 10022. © **888/4-BENJAMIN,** 212/320-8002, or 212/715-2500. Fax 212/715-2525. www.thebenjamin.com. 209 units. From $459 superior double; from $499 deluxe studio; from $559 suite. Call or check website for special weekend-stay offers. AE, DC, DISC, MC, V. Parking $45. Subway: 6 to 51st St.; E, F to Lexington Ave. Pets accepted. **Amenities:** Restaurant; cocktail lounge; state-of-the-art exercise room; full-service spa; concierge; sleep concierge; business services; 24-hr. room service; dry cleaning; valet service. *In room:* A/C, TV w/pay movies/video games/Internet access, fax/copier/printer, dataport, kitchenette, minibar, coffeemaker, laptop-size safe, china, high-speed Internet connection, microwave.

Four Seasons Hotel New York 𝒜𝒜   Designed by überarchitect I. M. Pei, this modernist tower of honey-hued limestone rises 52 stories, making it the city's tallest hotel and providing hundreds of rooms with a view. As soon as you enter the soaring lobby, with its marble floors and backlit onyx ceiling, you'll know this place is special. From the stellar service—only surpassed by the Ritz-Carlton hotels and Trump International—to the fantastic facilities, including a luxurious spa, this is a stunner.

The completely soundproof guest rooms are among the city's largest, averaging 600 square feet (183 sq. meters). Each is beautifully furnished in an understated but plush contemporary style and has an entrance foyer, a sitting area, an oversize oval desk with two leather chairs, custom built-ins, coffered ceilings, and massive windows (50% of which boast Central Park views). About two dozen of the priciest rooms also have terraces. The mammoth Florentine marble bathrooms have soaking tubs that fill in 60 seconds, and separate showers with pressure controls. Other special touches include goose-down pillows, Frette-made beds, oversize bath towels, and cushy robes, plus multidisk CD players in the suites. But at these prices, why charge extra for Internet access? In 2006, the hotel got another upgrade, if that is possible, when the acclaimed French chef, Joel Robuchon opened **L'Atelier de Joel Robuchon** in the hotel.

57 E. 57th St. (btwn Park and Madison aves.), New York, NY 10022. © **800/819-5053,** 800/487-3769, or 212/758-5700. Fax 212/758-5711. www.fourseasons.com. 368 units. $625–$925 double; from $1,550 suite. Extra rollaway bed $50. Weekend rates from $595. Also check for value-added packages and other deals. AE, DC, DISC, MC, V. Parking $60. Subway: N, R, 4, 5, 6 to 60th St. **Amenities:** Restaurant; bar w/evening entertainment; lobby lounge for afternoon tea and light fare; 5,000-sq.-ft. spa and fitness center w/whirlpool, steam, and sauna; children's program; concierge; business center w/secretarial services; 24-hr. room service; in-room massage; babysitting; laundry service w/1-hr. pressing; dry cleaning. *In room:* A/C, TV w/pay movies, dataport, minibar, hair dryer, safe, high-speed Internet connectivity.

The Peninsula-New York 𝒜𝒜𝒜   The paparazzi were waiting outside as I lugged my overnight bag into the hotel lobby and for a moment they contemplated an explosion of flashbulbs. It didn't take them long, however, to realize I was no celeb—just a fortunate soul spending a night at the marvelous Peninsula Hotel. Housed in a beauty of a landmark Beaux Arts building, the Peninsula is the perfect combination of old-world charm and modern, state-of-the-art technology. Rooms are huge with plenty of closet and storage space, but best of all is the bedside control panel that allows you to regulate lighting, television, stereo, air-conditioning, and signal the DO NOT DISTURB sign on your door. Even though you really don't have to leave the comfort of your bed, eventually you will need to go to the bathroom, and when you do, you'll not be disappointed. The huge marble bathrooms all have spacious soaking tubs with yet another control panel at your fingertips including the controls for, in most rooms, a television so you can watch while taking your bubble bath (now that's happy excess). The Peninsula also features one of the best and biggest New York hotel health clubs and spas, the rooftop **Pen-Top Bar,** and a faultless concierge desk. All this wonderfulness, however, doesn't come cheap, but if a splurge is what you want, you won't do much better than the Peninsula.

700 Fifth Ave. (at 55th St.), New York, NY 10019. © 800/262-9467 or 212/956-2888. Fax 212/903-3949. www. peninsula.com. 239 units. $650–$850 double; from $1,110 suite. Extra person $50. Children under 12 stay free in parent's room. Winter weekend package rates from $585 at press time. AE, DC, DISC, MC, V. Valet parking $55. Subway: E, V to Fifth Ave. Pets accepted. **Amenities:** Restaurant; rooftop bar; library-style lounge for afternoon tea and cocktails; tri-level rooftop health club and spa w/treatment rooms, heated pool, exercise classes, whirlpool, sauna, and sun deck; 24-hr. concierge; business center; 24-hr. room service; in-room massage; babysitting; laundry service; dry cleaning. *In room:* A/C, TV w/pay movies, fax, minibar, hair dryer, laptop-size safe, complimentary "water bar" w/5 choices of bottled water, T1 Internet connectivity, wireless Internet.

St. Regis ✿✿✿   When John Jacob Astor built the St. Regis in 1904, he set out to create a hotel that would reflect the elegance and luxury he was used to in hotels in Europe. Over a hundred years later, the St. Regis, now a New York landmark, still reflects that European splendor. Located on Fifth Avenue and close to Rockefeller Center, St. Patrick's Cathedral, and Saks, this Beaux Arts classic is a marvel; antique furniture, crystal chandeliers, silk wall coverings, and marble floors adorn both the public spaces and the high-ceilinged, airy guest rooms. The suites are particularly ornate, some with French doors, four-poster beds, and decorative fireplaces. The marble bathrooms are spacious and feature separate showers and tubs. In a nod to the future, plasma televisions were recently added in all the rooms, along with LCD screens in the bathrooms. Service is efficiently white-gloved and every guest is assigned a personal, tuxedoed butler, on call 24 hours to answer any reasonable requests. The hotel has a large fitness center and a spa that is the first in New York to offer the skin-care line from the renowned Carita Spa of Paris. **Afternoon tea** is served daily in the Astor Court.

Even if the St. Regis is beyond your budget, take a walk through the sumptuous lobby and have a drink in the hotel bar, the world-renowned **King Cole Bar** (see "Checking into Hotel Bars," in chapter 10), birthplace of the Bloody Mary and home to the famous *Old King Cole* mural by Maxfield Parrish.

2 E. 55th St. (at Fifth Ave.), New York, NY 10022. © 212/753-4500. Fax 212/787-3447. www.stregis.com. 256 units. $695–$995 double; from $1,150 suite. Check Internet for specials as low as $400 at press time. AE, DC, DISC, MC, V. Parking $55. Subway: E, V to Fifth Ave. **Amenities:** Restaurant; historic bar; tea lounge; fitness center and spa; concierge; 24-hr. room service; babysitting; laundry service; 24-hr. butler service; valet service. *In room:* A/C, TV, minibar, hair dryer, safe, DVD/CD player, high-speed Internet connectivity.

The Sherry-Netherland ✿✿✿   One of New York's classic grand dame hotels, this 1927-built beauty, from the marble-and-bronze lobby and the Italian

Renaissance–painted paneled elevators, the Sherry is pure old-school luxury. Though it's a big building, only 77 rooms are used for the hotel; the rest are private residential co-ops. Guest rooms vary in decor, but each is grandly proportioned with high ceilings, big bathrooms, and walk-in closets. The rooms are spacious and every one features high-quality furnishings and art. About half are suites with kitchenettes that have a cook-top or microwave, often both. Bathrooms are huge and impeccably designed and outfitted. And with an enviable location at Fifth and 58th opposite Central Park and adjacent to the Plaza Hotel, most of the rooms have glorious views. Other perks include a welcoming box of Godiva chocolates, and complimentary soft drinks, water, and mineral water. And though the hotel is from a different, more refined era, it's not stuffy—the hotel's white-gloved elevator operator and I had a refreshing discussion about the Yankees' prospects for the upcoming season.

781 Fifth Ave. (at 59th St.), New York, NY 10022. (© 877/743-7710 or 212/355-2800. Fax 212/319-4306. www.sherry netherland.com. 77 units. $499–$1,250 double; from $785 1- or 2-bedroom suite. Children stay free in parent's room. AE, DC, DISC, MC, V. Parking $55. Subway: N, R to Fifth Ave. Pets accepted. **Amenities:** Fitness room; concierge; business center; salon; limited room service; in-room massage; babysitting; laundry service; dry cleaning; video library. *In room:* A/C, TV/VCR, fax, fridge w/free soft drinks, free high-speed Internet.

EXPENSIVE

Also consider another all-suite hotel from the Affinia group, this one called **Affinia 50**, 155 E. 50th St., between Third and Lexington avenues (© **212/751-5710;** www. affinia.com).

Dylan Hotel   In the landmarked 1903-built Chemist's Club building, the Dylan is a combination of Beaux Arts opulence and modern, sleek Jeffrey Beers-designed interiors. That combination is evident in the lobby with muted colors and glass paneling centered around a magnificent, gilded age, marble staircase. The rooms also reflect that mix with impressive 11-foot ceilings along with high tech amenities like iHome clock radios. The Carrara marble bathrooms with Italian-porcelain-bowl style sinks look nice, but I find them cumbersome and lacking in shelf space. If you can, check out the Alchemy Suite, the former Chemist Club's mock laboratory with a vaulted ceiling, stained glass windows, and stone doorways; it's most definitely a one-of-a-kind room. The **Benjamin Steakhouse** (see p. 185) is the hotel's restaurant and features a ten-foot working fireplace. And, it's a block from Grand Central Station and Bryant Park. Though the rates are comparable, The Dylan doesn't offer the services of the **Library Hotel** (across the street) but if you can't get a room there, it's a perfectly acceptable local alternative.

52 E. 41st St, New York, N.Y. 10017 (btwn Park and Madison aves.); (© **212/338-0500.** Fax 212/338-0369. www. dylanhotel.com. 107 units. Doubles from $429; suites from $899. Check website for specials. AE, DC, DISC, MC, V. Parking $45. Subway: 4, 5, 6, 7, S to Grand Central Station-42nd St. **Amenities:** Restaurant; fitness center; 24-hour concierge; 24-hour business center; limited room service (breakfast, dinner until 11pm); laundry service; dry cleaning. *In room:* A/C, TV, dataport, minibar, iron/ironing board, safe, high speed and wireless Internet (complimentary).

Hotel Elysée *஺஺*   This romantic gem of a hotel in the heart of Midtown might be easy to miss: It's dwarfed by modern glass towers on either side of it. But that it is so inconspicuous is part of the Elysée's immense romantic appeal. Built in 1926, the hotel has a storied past as the preferred address for artists and writers including Tennessee Williams, Jimmy Breslin, Maria Callas and Vladimir Horowitz (who donated a Steinway, which still resides in the Piano Suite), John Barrymore, Marlon Brando, and Ava Gardner, who once had a tryst here with football legend Paul Hornung. The hotel still retains that sexy, discreet feel and now is run expertly by HK Hotels (The Giraffe, The Gansevoort, and The Library). Rooms were recently renovated and have many quirky features; some have fireplaces, others have kitchens or solariums, and all are decorated in country-French furnishings. Good-size bathrooms are done up in Italian marble and are well outfitted. Off the gorgeous black and white marble-floored lobby is the legendary **Monkey Bar** and the restaurant, formerly a steakhouse, at press time was closed for renovations to convert the space into a new Asian concept helmed by chef Patricia Yeo (**Sapa,** see p. 187). On the second floor is the Club Room, where a free continental breakfast is offered daily along with complimentary wine and cheese weekday evenings.

60 E. 54th St. (btwn Park and Madison aves.), New York, NY 10022. ℂ **800/535-9733** or 212/753-1066. Fax 212/ 980-9278. www.elyseehotel.com. 101 units. From $295 double; from $425 suite. Check the website for seasonal specials. Rates include continental breakfast and weekday evening wine and cheese. AE, DC, DISC, MC, V. Parking $30. Subway: E, V to Fifth Ave. **Amenities:** Restaurant; bar; free access to nearby gym; concierge; limited room service; laundry service; dry cleaning. *In room:* A/C, TV/VCR, dataport, minibar, hair dryer, iron, safe, wireless Internet.

The Kitano New York 𝞓𝞓𝞓 *Finds*   Owned by the Kitano Group of Japan, this elegant Murray Hill gem offers a unique mix of East and West sensibilities. The marble and mahogany lobby, with its Y-shaped staircase and Botero bronze *Dog,* is one of the most attractive in New York. The hotel was first opened in 1973; in the mid-1990s, along with acquiring an 1896 landmark town house next door, the Kitano was fully renovated. If you're a lucky (and wealthy) individual, you'll get the opportunity to stay in one of three one-bedroom town-house suites, each with sunken living room, bay windows, and original, eclectic art. Or, if your sensibilities are Eastern-oriented, the hotel offers a Tatami suite, with tatami mats, rice paper screens, and a Japanese Tea Ceremony room. Most rooms are not quite that luxurious or unique, but all include tasteful mahogany furniture, soundproof windows, and, for a real taste of Japan, green tea upon arrival; marble bathrooms are large and have heated towel racks and removable shower heads. The sky-lit **Garden Café** in the town house offers contemporary American cuisine, while **Hakubai** serves traditional multi-course kaiseki cuisine. There's also an interesting gift shop in the lobby specializing in unique Japanese items. But best of all is the mezzanine-level bar where Wednesday through Saturday evenings it turns into the acclaimed **Jazz at the Kitano.**

66 Park Ave. (at 38th St.), New York, NY 10016. ℂ **212/885-7000.** Fax 212/885-7100. www.kitano.com. 149 units. $480–$605 double; from $715 suite. Check website for specials, as low as $239 at press time. AE, DC, DISC, MC, V. Parking $40. Subway: 4, 5, 6, 7, S to Grand Central. **Amenities:** 2 restaurants; bar w/live jazz; access to a nearby health club; concierge; complimentary limo service to Wall St. on weekdays; limited room service; laundry service; dry cleaning. *In room:* A/C, TV, fax, dataport, hair dryer, iron, complimentary tea, high-speed Internet.

The Library Hotel 𝞓𝞓 *Finds*   New York is not Las Vegas, so I'm usually wary of the hotel as high concept, but in this case the concept works: a hotel 1 block from the New York Public Library, each of whose 10 guest-room floors is dedicated to 1 of the 10 major categories of the Dewey Decimal System. When I visited the hotel, I was appropriately booked into a "Geography and Travel" room. There I was greeted with books such as *Barcelona,* by Robert Hughes, and *Bella Tuscany,* by Frances Mayes. The most disappointing thing about all those books is that I was only staying 1 night and didn't have the chance to read any of them. Still, there was something about having them by my bed; perhaps their soothing aura comforted me. Overall, the hotel has a pleasing, informal feel. Guest rooms, which come in three categories—petite (really small), deluxe, and junior suites—feature mahogany built-ins, generous desks, and immaculate marble bathrooms; all are extremely comfortable. The Library's public spaces—a reading room where weekday wine and cheese and a complimentary daily breakfast are served, a writer's den with a fireplace and flat-screen television, and a rooftop terrace—all help make The Library a welcome refuge in the heart of the city.

299 Madison Ave. (at 41st St.), New York, NY 10017. © 877/793-7323 or 212/983-4500. Fax 212/499-9099. www. libraryhotel.com. 60 units. $345–$435 double; $525 Love Room or junior suite; $960 2-room family suite. Rates include continental breakfast buffet, all-day snacks, and weekday wine and cheese. Inquire about corporate, promotional, and weekend rates (as low as $329 at press time). AE, DC, MC, V. Parking $30 nearby. Subway: 4, 5, 6, 7, S to 42nd St./Grand Central. **Amenities:** Restaurant; free access to nearby health club; business center; 24-hr. room service; laundry service; dry cleaning; video library of American Film Institute's Top 100 films. *In room:* A/C, TV/VCR, dataport, minibar, hair dryer, iron, laptop-size safe, CD player, high-speed Internet connectivity.

The Regency ★★ *Kids*

Mirroring the elegance of Park Avenue and with its enviable location close to Central Park, Bloomingdale's, and the white-gloved shops of Madison Avenue, The Regency has long been a haven for celebrities and those who aspire to celebrity status. On one of my visits to the hotel, I saw New York Yankee outfielder Hideki Matsui amble through the glittering, marble-laden lobby. But even if you aren't on the cover of a magazine, a stay at The Regency might make you feel like a star. The guest rooms are all huge, featuring a king bed or two doubles, a large marble writing desk with an ergonomic chair, and a small eating table. The bathrooms, though not enormous, are equipped with terry-cloth robes and a small television. Suites are typically grandiose, ranging from the 450-square-foot Executive, with two bathrooms and French doors, to the Grand Suite, with two bedrooms and two marble bathrooms. Despite its elegance, The Regency is a surprisingly good choice for kids. Children under 18 stay free when sharing a room with their parents; rollaway beds are an additional $25 for the stay. Even pets get the special treatment, with the hotel providing services such as place mats with food and water bowls and a room-service menu for pets. Complimentary homemade hot chocolate is served in the lobby in the winter months, replaced by lemonade in the summer. The hotel's restaurant, 540 Park Avenue, is one of the great power-breakfast spots in the city, while **Feinstein's at The Regency** (p. 369) is considered the standard when it comes to cabaret.

540 Park Ave. (at 61st St.), New York, NY 10021. © 212/759-4100. Fax 212/826-5674. www.loewshotels.com. 351 units. $419–$699 double; from $539 suite. Children under 18 stay free in parent's room; additional $25 for rollaway bed. AE, DC, MC, V. Parking $49. Subway: 4, 5, 6, N, R to 59th St. Pets accepted. **Amenities:** 2 restaurants; cabaret; fitness center; children's program; concierge; 24-hr. room service; laundry service; dry cleaning. *In room:* A/C, TV w/VCR, dataport, minibar, hair dryer, iron, safe, CD player, high-speed Internet.

The Roger ★★

The hotel's namesake, Roger Williams, in time abandoned his puritanical roots to become a secular leader. This Murray Hill hotel, formerly known as the Roger Williams, shed its traditional, slightly worn veneer and was reborn in 2005 with a glitzy, colorful new look and style—not to mention a hip name. This Roger wears its new look well. Starting from the welcoming lobby with its odd assortment of mod yet comfortable seating and where small jazz combos entertain 3 nights a week, to the many different varieties of rooms—some small, some generous, some with huge landscaped terraces, others with views of the nearby Empire State building and all with impressive amenities such as colorful quilts, flat-panel televisions, complimentary high-speed and wireless Internet, and good-size marble bathrooms—the Roger is now one of the top choices in what is a quiet yet convenient Midtown location. A floating granite staircase leads from the lobby to a mezzanine lounge, where you can have breakfast in the morning and drink cocktails by candlelight at night.

131 Madison Ave. (at E. 31st St.), New York, NY 10016. 📞 **888/448-7788** or 212/448-7000. Fax 212/448-7007. www.hotelrogerwilliams.com. 200 units. $250–$300 double. AE, DC, DISC, MC, V. Subway: 6 to 28th St./Lexington Ave. **Amenities:** Lounge; fitness center; concierge; laundry service; dry cleaning; complimentary Wi-Fi; conference suite. *In room:* A/C, flat-screen TV, minibar, iron/ironing board, safe, high speed/wireless Internet.

70 Park Avenue 🛏 Formerly the Doral Park Avenue, this Murray Hill property underwent a complete renovation when the San Francisco-based Kimpton Hotels took it over. Part of the renovation included design by Jeffrey Bilhuber who, with his warm earth tones, has created a homey, residential feel. Albeit this is one home that is absolutely state-of-the-art, with 42-inch flat-screen televisions, MAINstage Music & Theater Sound System, and wireless Internet. And in keeping with Kimpton's New Age trademark, the hotel encourages environmental awareness (including guest recycling and water-saving programs) and guests get a yoga channel on their TVs.

The lobby is a beauty with a long wooden table that serves as the concierge station and a 14-foot limestone and sandstone fireplace. Guest rooms, though not overly large, are efficiently constructed with an economical use of space: Note the minibar tucked into a dresser and the mahogany armoire that serves as the closet. In the room where I stayed, there were five huge mirrors, which could be a good thing or a bad thing depending on your self-esteem. Bathrooms in standard rooms are a bit tight but well outfitted, while a number of guest rooms offer two-person whirlpool spa tubs. On premises is the gorgeous **Silverleaf Tavern.**

70 Park Ave. (btwn 37th and 38th sts.), New York, NY 10016. 📞 **877/707-2752** or 212/973-2400. Fax 212/973-2401. www.70parkave.com. 205 units. $325–$525 double; from $1,000 suites. AE, DC, DISC, MC, V. Valet parking $42. Subway: 4, 5, 6, 7, S to Grand Central. Pets accepted. **Amenities:** Restaurant; bar; complimentary wine reception, access to nearby fitness center; concierge; 24-hr. room service; laundry service. *In room:* A/C, TV, dataport, minibar, hair dryer, iron, safe, cordless telephone, DVD/CD player, high-speed Internet; voice mail.

Waldorf=Astoria and the Waldorf Towers 🛏🛏🛏 If you are looking for the epitome of old-school elegance, you can't do better than the Waldorf=Astoria. This massive 1-square-block Art Deco masterpiece is not only a hotel icon, it's a genuine New York City landmark. Here you'll find a lobby so big and grand, it's reminiscent of Grand Central Station, including having its own signature clock. With over 1,000 rooms, the pace can be hectic, and at times the lines for checking in might remind you of the post office. Thankfully, service here is much more efficient than the post office and it won't be long before you're in your room. And what rooms they are; no two the same, yet all are airy, with high ceilings, traditional decor, comfortable linens and beds, and spacious marble bathrooms, along with fax machines and high-speed Internet access. If you crave more luxury, book a room on the **Astoria** level, which features huge suites, deluxe bathroom amenities, access to the clubby Astoria Lounge for breakfast or afternoon hors d'oeuvres, and free entry to the hotel's fitness club (other guests pay a fee); for even more opulence, try a suite in the **Waldorf Towers,** where most rooms are bigger than most New York City apartments.

One of three bars in the hotel, **Sir Harry's Bar,** off the lobby, is the main gathering spot for a pre- or post-dinner cocktail, but even better is the **Bull and Bear,** with its round mahogany bar, classic cocktail creations, and celebrated steaks (see "The Prime Cut," in chapter 7). **Oscars,** which also has a bar, offers breakfast, lunch, and dinner, **Peacock Alley,** off the main lobby is also open for breakfast, lunch and dinner, and **Inagiku** serves innovative Japanese cuisine.

301 Park Ave. (btwn 49th and 50th sts.), New York, NY 10022. 📞 **800/WALDORF**, 800/774-1500, or 212/355-3000. Fax 212/872-7272 (Astoria) or 212/872-4799 (Towers). www.waldorfastoria.com or www.waldorf-towers.com. 1,245

units (180 in the Towers). Waldorf=Astoria $229–$485 double; from $349 suite. Waldorf Towers $329–$739 double; from $515 suite. Extra person $35. Children under 18 stay free in parent's room. Corporate, senior, seasonal, and weekend discounts may be available (as low as $189 at press time), as well as attractive package deals. AE, DC, DISC, MC, V. Parking $55. Subway: 6 to 51st St. **Amenities:** 4 restaurants; 4 bars; 3,000-sq.-ft. fitness center and excellent spa; concierge and theater desk; expansive 24-hr. business center; salon; 24-hr. room service; laundry service; dry cleaning; executive-level rooms. Tower rooms include butler service, Clefs d'Or concierge. *In room:* A/C, TV w/pay movies, dataport, minibar, coffeemaker, hair dryer, iron, high-speed Internet connectivity (in executive-level rooms and suites). Waldorf Towers suites include kitchenette or wet bar w/fridge, safe.

MODERATE

Doubletree Metropolitan Hotel ℛ *Value*   It might be the middle of January and the wind chills are below zero, but one look at the exterior of the Metropolitan and a walk inside the retro-cool lobby and you'll think you are in Miami Beach around 1961. That's because the hotel was designed in 1961 by the renowned architect Morris Lapidus, the man responsible for Miami's legendary Fontainebleau and Eden Roc hotels. But in 1961, were you given fresh-baked chocolate-chip cookies upon check-in? Most recently a Loews Hotel, in 2004 the Doubletree brand (cookies and all) took over the hotel and poured $35 million into renovations updating the Art Deco feel throughout the hotel. The lobby is now stocked with mod furniture on which guests can lounge and surf the Internet on their laptops (the public spaces have wireless capability). Guest rooms are on the smallish side and even with the renovations (including LCD televisions) still have a cookie-cutter, motel feel to them, but the beds are, like other Doubletree properties, extremely comfortable, guaranteeing the "Sweet Dreams by Doubletree Sleep Experience." The renovations and the exemplary Doubletree service are a huge improvement on what the hotel once offered and now it's a good mid-price option in the middle of Manhattan.

569 Lexington Ave. (at 51st St.), New York, NY 10022. © 212/752-7000. Fax 212/758-6311. www.dtnewyork.com. 755 units. Rates $250–$350 single; $300–$450 double. Check website for specials as low as $199. AE, DC, MC, V. Parking $30 nearby. Subway: 6 to 51st St.; E, V to Lexington Ave. **Amenities:** Restaurant; bar; fitness center; concierge; business center; limited room service; barbershop; nail salon. *In room:* A/C, TV, hair dryer, iron, safe, high-speed Internet, 2-line telephone.

INEXPENSIVE

Hotel Grand Union *Value*   This centrally located hotel is big with budget-minded international travelers. A pleasant white-on-white lobby leads to clean and spacious rooms with nice extras that are uncommon in this price category, such as hair dryers and free HBO. Fluorescent overhead lighting, unattractive colonial-style furniture, and an utter lack of natural light dampen the mood—but considering the roominess, low rates, and central-to-everything location, the Grand Union is a good deal. Room no. 309, a nicely configured quad with two twins and a queen in a separate alcove, is great for families. Most bathrooms have been outfitted in granite or tile; ask for a newly renovated one. The staff is helpful, and there's a pleasant sitting room off the lobby and an adjacent coffee shop for morning coffee or a quick burger.

34 E. 32nd St. (btwn Madison and Park aves.), New York, NY 10016. © 212/683-5890. Fax 212/689-7397. www. hotelgrandunion.com. 95 units. $145–$170 single or double; $175–$195 twin or triple; $195–$220 quad. Call or check website for special rates (as low as $90 at press time). AE, DC, DISC, MC, V. Parking $22 nearby. Subway: 6 to 33rd St. **Amenities:** Coffee shop; tour desk; fax service; Wi-Fi. *In room:* A/C, TV, dataport, fridge, hair dryer.

Hotel Thirty Thirty ℛ *Value*   Thirty Thirty is just right for bargain-hunting travelers looking for a splash of style with an affordable price tag. The design-conscious tone is set in the loftlike industrial-modern lobby. Rooms are mostly on the smallish side but do the trick for those who intend to spend their days out on the town rather than holed up here. They're done in a natural palette with a creative edge—purplish carpet, khaki bedspread, woven wallpaper—that comes together more attractively than you might expect. Configurations are split between twin/twins (great for friends), queens, and queen/queens (great for triples, budget-minded quads, or shares that want more spreading-out room). Nice features include cushioned headboards, firm mattresses, two-line phones, nice built-in wardrobes, and spacious, nicely tiled bathrooms. A few larger units have kitchenettes, great if you're staying in town for a while, as you'll appreciate the extra room and the fridge. No room service, but delivery is available from nearby restaurants.

30 E. 30th St. (btwn Madison and Park aves.), New York, NY 10016. ℂ 800/497-6028 or 212/689-1900. Fax 212/ 689-0023. www.thirtythirty-nyc.com. 243 units. $169–$225 double; $189–$249 double with kitchenette; $245–$325 quad. Call for last-minute deals, or check website for special promotions (as low as $99 at press time). AE, DC, DISC, MC, V. Parking $30 1 block away. Subway: 6 to 28th St. Pets accepted with advance approval. **Amenities:** Restaurant; concierge; laundry service; dry cleaning. *In room:* A/C, TV, dataport, hair dryer, Internet access.

Murray Hill Inn   In a renovated five-story walk-up in a pleasant and quiet residential neighborhood, the Murray Hill Inn is shoestring basic—but there's no arguing with its cleanliness, which is key when judging accommodations in this price range. Rooms are tiny and outfitted with not much more than either one or two beds with motel-standard bedspread and furnishings, a wall rack, a phone, and a small TV; most rooms with shared bathroom also have private sinks (request one when booking). These Euro-style rooms share the in-hall bathrooms that are new and spotless. Some of the doubles have an alcove that can accommodate a third traveler on a cot if you're on an extra-tight budget. Rooms with private bathrooms are definitely the nicest; they're spacious, with new bathrooms and dataports on the telephones. Most also have pullout sofas that can accommodate an extra traveler or two. Don't expect much in terms of facilities beyond a pleasant (if tiny) lobby, plus a plain downstairs sitting area with a vending machine, an ATM, and a luggage-storage area. Services are kept to a bare minimum to keep costs down, but the staff is personable.

143 E. 30th St. (btwn Lexington and Third aves.), New York, NY 10016. ℂ 888/996-6376 or 212/683-6900. Fax 212/545-0103. www.murrayhillinn.com. 45 units, 3 with shared bathroom. $99 double with shared bathroom; $129–$159 double with private bathroom; $95–$169 private deluxe. Extra person $15. Children under 12 stay free in parent's room. AE, MC, V. Parking about $25 nearby. Subway: 6 to 28th St. *In room:* A/C, TV, wireless Internet.

9 Upper West Side

To find the hotels described in this section, see p. 150.

VERY EXPENSIVE

Trump International Hotel & Tower 𝒶𝒶𝒶   From the outside, it's the prototypical, not very attractive Trump creation—a tall, dark monolith, hovering over Columbus Circle and lower Central Park. But go inside and spend a night or two at the Trump International, experience services such as your own Trump Attaché, a personal concierge who will provide comprehensive services (your wish is their command); take advantage of such first-class facilities as the 6,000-square-foot health club with lap pool and a full-service spa; or order room service from the hotel's signature restaurant, the four-star **Jean-Georges.** Not only will you dispel any prejudices you might have had toward The Donald, you might even begin to comprehend why someone would be willing to sell their soul for the chance to become the master builder's apprentice.

Guest rooms are surprisingly understated, with high ceilings and floor-to-ceiling windows, some with incredible views of Central Park and all with telescopes for taking in the view, and marble bathrooms with Jacuzzi tubs. But if that's not enough—it certainly was for me—you also get two complimentary bottles of Trump water, complete with a picture of The Donald on each one. For a hotel this well run, you can forgive the man for his excesses.

1 Central Park West (at 60th St.), New York, NY 10023. ℭ 212/299-1000. Fax 212/299-1150. www.trumpintl.com. 167 units. From $765 double; from $1,200 1- or 2-bedroom suite. Children stay free in parent's room. Check website for special rates and package deals; also try booking through www.travelweb.com for discounted rates. AE, DC, DISC, MC, V. Parking $48. Subway: A, B, C, D, 1 to 59th St./Columbus Circle. **Amenities:** Restaurant; spa and health club w/steam, sauna, and pool; Clefs d'Or concierge; staffed business center w/secretarial services; 24-hr. room service; in-room massage; babysitting; laundry service; dry cleaning; butler (personal attaché); CD library. *In room:* A/C, TV/VCR w/pay movies and video games, fax/copier/printer, dataport, minibar, coffeemaker, hair dryer, iron, laptop-size safe, DVD/CD player, high-speed Internet connectivity.

MODERATE

In addition to the hotels below, also consider the romantic **Country Inn the City** ⭒, 270 W. 77th St., between Broadway and West End Avenue (ℭ **212/580-4183;** www.countryinnthecity.com), comprised of four self-contained units in a charming 1891 town house (see "Plenty of Room at the Inn," on p. 120).

Excelsior Hotel   The elegant Excelsior almost gives the Lucerne (see below) a run for its money. Everything is fresh throughout, from the richly wood-paneled lobby to the comfy guest rooms to the small but state-of-the-art exercise room. The chic residential location is across from the Museum of Natural History and steps from Central Park. However, the staff doesn't quite live up to the Lucerne's impeccable example. Freshly done in an attractive traditional style, the guest rooms boast high-quality furnishings, commodious closets, two-line phones, thick terry bathrobes, a work desk, free bottled water, and full-length dressing mirrors (a nice touch). The pretty new bathrooms are most impressive. The two-bedded rooms are large enough to accommodate budget-minded families (a few even have two queens), and suites feature pullout sofas and pants presses. The sunny museum-facing rooms are only worth the extra dough if a park view is really important to you, as all rooms are relatively bright and quiet. Housekeeping is impeccable throughout the hotel. On the second floor is a gorgeous library-style lounge with working fireplace, books, games, gorgeous leather seating, writing desks, and a large flat-screen TV with DVD player. All in all, this is a good mid-price choice.

45 W. 81st St. (btwn Columbus Ave. and Central Park West), New York, NY 10024. ℭ 212/362-9200. Fax 212/580-3972. www.excelsiorhotelny.com. 198 units. $199–$399 double; $299–$499 1-bedroom suite; $499–$899 2-bedroom suite. Extra person $20. Children 12 and under stay free in parent's room. Inquire about seasonal rates and specials (winter rates can go as low as $199 double). AE, DC, DISC, MC, V. Parking $27 nearby. Subway: B, C to 81st St./Museum of Natural History. **Amenities:** Breakfast room w/2 open-air decks and daily breakfast buffet; exercise room; concierge; laundry service; dry cleaning. *In room:* A/C, TV w/pay movies/video games/Internet access, fax/copier, dataport, hair dryer, iron, safe, wireless Internet

Hotel Beacon ⭒⭒ (Kids) (Value)   Okay, so you're not in Times Square or in trendy SoHo, but when you're at the Hotel Beacon, you're on the Upper West Side, and for families, you won't find a better location—or value. Close to Central Park and Riverside Park, the Museum of Natural History and Lincoln Center, and major subway lines, it's not like the Beacon is in a desolate spot. Rooms here are generously sized and feature a kitchenette, a roomy closet, and a new marble bathroom. Virtually all standard rooms feature two double beds, and they're plenty big enough to sleep a family on a

Uptown Accommodations

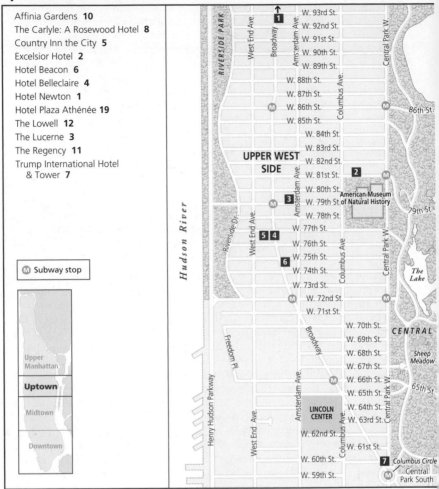

Affinia Gardens **10**
The Carlyle: A Rosewood Hotel **8**
Country Inn the City **5**
Excelsior Hotel **2**
Hotel Beacon **6**
Hotel Belleclaire **4**
Hotel Newton **1**
Hotel Plaza Athénée **19**
The Lowell **12**
The Lucerne **3**
The Regency **11**
Trump International Hotel
& Tower **7**

Ⓜ Subway stop

Upper Manhattan
Uptown
Midtown
Downtown

UPPER WEST SIDE

American Museum of Natural History

CENTRAL

The Lake

Sheep Meadow

LINCOLN CENTER

Columbus Circle
Central Park South

budget. The large one- and two-bedroom suites are some of the best bargains in the city; each has two closets and a pullout sofa in the well-furnished living room. The two-bedrooms have a second bathroom, making them well outfitted enough to house a small army—including my own. And the view from our room and many in the hotel is a true New York vista: the magnificent, turn-of-the-20th-century Ansonia building, ballet dancers limbering up at a dance studio, and fresh fruit and vegetables being replenished at Fairway market across the street. There's no room service, but a wealth of good budget dining options that deliver, along with excellent markets like the aforementioned Fairway, make the Beacon even more of a home away from home.

2130 Broadway (at 75th St.), New York, NY 10023. Ⓒ **800/572-4969** or 212/787-1100. Fax 212/724-0839. www. beaconhotel.com. 236 units. $210–$225 single or double; from $270 1- or 2-bedroom suite. Extra person $15.

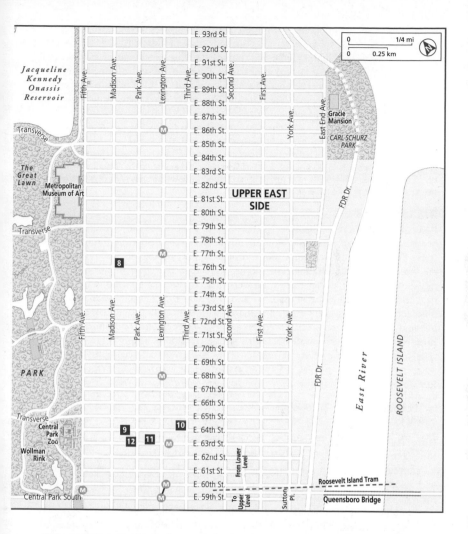

Children under 17 stay free in parent's room. Check website for special deals (doubles from $145; 1-bedroom suites as low as $195 at press time). AE, DC, DISC, MC, V. Parking $41 1 block away. Subway: 1, 2, 3 to 72nd St. **Amenities:** Coffee shop adjacent; access to health club in the building; concierge; laundry service; dry cleaning; coin-op laundry; fax and copy service; Internet center. *In room:* A/C, TV w/pay movies, kitchenette, hair dryer, iron, laptop-size safe.

The Lucerne *★★* *(Finds)*   This magnificent 1903 landmark building has had many incarnations over the years, including one as a dormitory for Columbia University students. But most recently it has been transformed into a luxury boutique hotel, and that transformation has been a triumph on many levels. As a longtime resident of the Upper West Side, I can easily say the Lucerne best captures the feel of that special neighborhood. Service is impeccable, especially for a moderately priced hotel and everything is fresh and immaculate. The rooms are all comfortable and big enough for kings, queens, or two doubles, with attractive bathrooms complete with travertine counters. Some of the rooms have views not only of the Hudson River but of one of my favorite pubs, the Dublin House (see chapter 10). The suites here are extra-special and include a kitchenette, a stocked mini-fridge, a microwave, and a sitting room with a sofa and extra television. The highly rated **Nice Matin** (p. 212) offers room service for breakfast, lunch, and dinner. But if you don't want to dine there, you can sample some of the neighborhood food at nearby Zabar's or H&H Bagels.

201 W. 79th St. (at Amsterdam Ave.), New York, NY 10024. (C) **800/492-8122** or 212/875-1000. Fax 212/579-2408. www.thelucernehotel.com. 216 units. $230–$360 double or queen; $180–$330 king or junior suite; $220–$410 1-bedroom suite. Extra person $20. Children under 16 stay free in parent's room. AAA discounts offered; check website for special Internet deals. AE, DC, DISC, MC, V. Parking $29 nearby. Subway: 1 to 79th St. **Amenities:** Restaurant; fitness center; business center; limited room service; laundry service; dry cleaning. *In room:* A/C, TV w/Nintendo and Internet access, dataport, coffeemaker, hair dryer, iron.

INEXPENSIVE

Hotel Belleclaire ✿   This Beaux Arts hotel, which underwent a facelift in 2004, boasts a great Upper West Side location and renovated, stylish guest rooms that are larger than most. The accommodations, though simple, do the job, and the management seems intent on pleasing. The rooms have small, freshly tiled bathrooms with tub/shower combos (six have roll-in showers to accommodate travelers with disabilities). Beds have cushioned headboards and there are nice fabric-covered cubes for modular seating; closets are small. The shared-bathroom units are the same but have in-room sinks and share hall bathrooms at a ratio of three to one. The family suite features two attached, semiprivate bedrooms with a bathroom, a minifridge, and a big walk-in closet. This is a decent choice in a first-class residential neighborhood.

250 W. 77th St. (at Broadway), New York, NY 10024. (C) **877/HOTEL-BC** (468-3522) or 212/362-7700. Fax 212/362-1004. www.hotelbelleclaire.com. 189 units, 39 with shared bathroom. $139 double with shared bathroom; $189 double with private bathroom; $299 family suite. Ask about AAA, group, and other discounts. AE, DC, DISC, MC, V. Parking $25 nearby. Subway: 1 to 79th St. **Amenities:** Access to nearby health club; tour desk; laundry service; dry cleaning; fax. *In room:* A/C, TV w/pay movies and games, dataport, fridge, hair dryer, iron, wireless Internet.

Hotel Newton ✿ *Value*   On the northern extreme of the Upper West Side, the Newton doesn't scream "budget" at every turn. As you enter the pretty lobby, you're greeted by a uniformed staff that's attentive and professional. The rooms are generally large, with good, firm beds, a work desk, and a sizable new bathroom, plus roomy closets in most (a few of the cheapest have wall racks only). Some are big enough to accommodate families, with two doubles or two queen beds. The suites feature two queen beds in the bedroom, a sofa in the sitting room, plus niceties such as a microwave, mini-fridge, and iron, making them well worth the few extra dollars. The bigger rooms and suites have been upgraded with cherrywood furnishings, but even the older laminated furniture is much nicer than I usually see in this price range. The AAA-approved hotel is impeccably kept. The 96th Street express subway stop is just a block away, and the Key West Diner next door is a favorite for huge, cheap breakfasts.

2528 Broadway (btwn 94th and 95th sts.), New York, NY 10025. (C) **888/HOTEL58** or 212/678-6500. Fax 212/678-6758. www.newyorkhotel.com. 110 units. $95–$175 double or junior suite. Extra person $25. Children under 15 stay free in parent's room. AAA, corporate, senior, and group rates available; check website for special Internet deals. AE, DC, DISC, MC, V. Parking $27 nearby. Subway: 1, 2, 3 to 96th St. **Amenities:** 24-hr. room service. *In room:* A/C, TV, hair dryer, wireless Internet.

10 Upper East Side

To find the hotels described in this section, see p. 150.

VERY EXPENSIVE

The Carlyle: A Rosewood Hotel ☆☆☆   This 34-story grande dame towers over Madison Avenue majestically, perfectly epitomizing the old-world, moneyed neighborhood where it stands. Service is white-glove (literally) and doormen actually wear bowler hats; many celebrities and dignitaries, some with faces obscured by silk scarves, sip tea in the hotel's cozy Gallery. Guest rooms range from singles to seven-room suites, some with terraces and full dining rooms. All have marble bathrooms with whirlpool tubs and all the amenities you'd expect from a hotel of this caliber. The English manor–style decor is luxurious but not excessive, creating the comfortably elegant ambience of an Upper East Side apartment. Many apartments have breathtaking views of either downtown or the West Side and Central Park.

The lobby was renovated recently: The marble floors and columns, the original clock, and the Piranesi prints and murals were restored, and new features such as Baccarat light fixtures, a new reception desk, and expanded concierge space were added. The hotel's **Carlyle Restaurant** features excellent French fare, while the supper club **Cafe Carlyle** (p. 369) is the place for first-rate cabaret. Charming **Bemelmans Bar,** named after illustrator Ludwig Bemelmans, who created the Madeline books and painted the mural here (see "Checking into Hotel Bars," in chapter 10), is a great spot for cocktails; there's live jazz Monday through Saturday evenings.

35 E. 76th St. (at Madison Ave.), New York, NY 10021. ✆ **800/227-5737** or 212/744-1600. Fax 212/717-4682. www. thecarlyle.com. 180 units. $650–$950 double; from $950 1- or 2-bedroom suite. AE, DC, DISC, MC, V. Parking $48. Subway: 6 to 77th St. Pets accepted under 25 lbs. **Amenities:** 3 restaurants (including one of the city's best cabaret rooms); tearoom; bar; high-tech fitness room w/sauna, Jacuzzi, and spa services; concierge; 24-hr. room service; laundry service; dry cleaning; video library. *In room:* A/C, TV/VCR, fax/copier/printer, dataport, pantry kitchenette or full kitchen w/minibar, hair dryer, safe, CD player, high speed Internet

Hotel Plaza Athénée ☆☆☆   This hideaway in New York's most elegant neighborhood (the stretch of Madison Ave. in the 60s) is a mirror image of that elevated social strata; it's elegant, luxurious, and oozing with sophistication. With antique furniture, hand-painted murals, and the Italian-marble floor that adorns the exquisite lobby, the Plaza Athénée has a European feel. And in that tradition, service here is as good as it gets, with personalized check-in and attentive staff at every turn. The rooms come in a variety of shapes and sizes, and are all high-ceilinged and spacious; entrance foyers give them a residential feel. They are designed in rich fabrics and warm colors that help set a tone that makes you want to lounge in your room longer than you should. The suites have so much closet space, it made this New Yorker, used to miniscule apartment closets, envious. Many of the suites have chaises, which you don't often see in New York hotels, and a few have terraces large enough to dine on. The Portuguese-marble bathrooms are outfitted with thick robes made exclusively for the hotel; put one on and you might never want to take it off. The lush, leather-floored lounge is called **Bar Seine** and is a welcome spot for a pre-dinner cocktail. The restaurant, **Arabelle,** receives high praise for its weekend brunch.

37 E. 64th St. (btwn Madison and Park aves.), New York, NY 10021. ✆ **800/447-8800** or 212/734-9100. Fax 212/ 772-0958. www.plaza-athenee.com. 149 units. $555–$825 double; from $1,200 suite. Check for packages and seasonal specials (as low as $495 at press time). AE, DC, DISC, MC, V. Parking $53. Subway: F to Lexington Ave. **Amenities:** Restaurant; bar; fitness center; Clefs d'Or concierge; business center; 24-hr. room service; laundry service; dry cleaning. *In room:* A/C, TV, fax, dataport, minibar, hair dryer, safe, high-speed Internet connectivity.

The Lowell ℛℛℛ *(Kids* The Lowell's style of luxury is best described as elegant, sophisticated 20th-century opulence. It has the feel of a residential dwelling; the lobby is small and clubby with first-rate European, old-world service. The rooms are the real treasures; each different from the other and all a good size. About two-thirds are suites with kitchenettes or full kitchens; some have private terraces and most have working fireplaces. In the rooms you'll also find nice big, cushy armchairs, lots of leather, interesting artwork, and porcelain figurines scattered about. Bathrooms are Italian marble and outfitted with Bulgari amenities. The **Pembroke Room** offers breakfast, including a hearty English breakfast and afternoon tea, while the **Post House** is best known for their steaks. On a quiet, tree-lined street 1 block from Central Park and right in the middle of Madison Avenue shopping, the Lowell's location is ideal for those who want (and can afford) an urban retreat away from the Midtown madness.

28 E. 63rd St. (btwn Madison and Park aves.), New York, NY 10021. © **212/838-1400.** Fax 212/319-4230. www. lowellhotel.com. 70 units. From $635 doubles; from $935 suites. Ask about packages and weekend and seasonal rates. AE, DC, DISC, MC, V. Parking $49. Subway: F to Lexington Ave. Pets under 15 lb. accepted. **Amenities:** 2 restaurants; tearoom; well-outfitted fitness room; 24-hr. concierge; limousine service; secretarial services; 24-hr. room service; babysitting; laundry service; dry cleaning; video library. *In room:* A/C, TV/VCR/DVD, fax/copier/dataport, minibar, hair dryer, CD player, wireless Internet.

EXPENSIVE

Affinia Gardens ℛ *(Finds* One of the newest members of the Affinia hospitality group (**The Benjamin,** p. 140, **Dumont,** p. 140, **Affinia Manhattan,** p. 128), this Upper East Side property has a residential feel that is true to the neighborhood. Affinia has transformed the hotel into an oasis of tranquility. While the Dumont stresses fitness and the Affinia Manhattan emphasizes the New York experience, Affinia Gardens' theme is serenity. Off the lobby is the lounge, appropriately called "Serenity," a 24-hour quiet zone where you can sit in comfort, sip tea, and unwind. If you choose to relax in your room, you won't be disappointed. You can order, free of charge, a "tranquility kit" that includes meditation CDs and books, massage tools, chair massager, and floor pillows. Or you can just lay back on the very comfortable Affinia bed and snooze to the calming natural sound of the ocean, brook, wind, or forest that come with the clock radio/CD player. This is an all-suite hotel and rooms range from junior suites to two-bedrooms; all are generously sized and come with full kitchens. Bathrooms, proportionally, are on the smallish side but well outfitted. Though it's in a good, highly desirable New York neighborhood, the hotel is a bit out of the way from the center of things. But that can be a plus if tranquility is truly what you seek.

215 E. 64th St. (btwn Second and Third aves.), New York, NY 10021. © **866/AFFINIA** or 212/355-1230. Fax 212/758-7858. www.affinia.com. 136 units. Rates from $399, all suites. Check website for specials and Internet rates. Valet parking $32. AE, DC, DISC, MC, V. Subway: 6 to 68th St.–Lexington Ave. Fitness club; small business center; limited room service; coin-operated laundry. *In room:* A/C, TV/DVD, dataport, kitchen, iron, safe, CD player/clock radio, high-speed Internet.

7

Where to Dine

Attention, foodies: Welcome to your mecca. Without a doubt, New York is the best restaurant town in the country, and one of the finest in the world. Other cities might have particular specialties, but no other culinary capital spans the globe as successfully as the Big Apple.

New Yorkers can be fickle: One moment a restaurant is hot, the next it's passé. So restaurants close with a frequency we wish applied to the arrival of subway trains. Always call ahead.

But there's one thing we all have to face sooner or later: Eating in New York isn't cheap. The primary cause? The high cost of real estate, which is reflected in what you're charged. Wherever you're from, particularly if you hail from the reasonably priced American heartland, New York's restaurants will seem *expensive*. Yet good value abounds, especially if you're willing to try ethnic cuisine (including types you may not have had before), and venture beyond tourist zones into neighborhoods like Chinatown, the East Village, Harlem, and even the Upper West Side. Still, I've included inexpensive restaurants in every neighborhood, including some of the city's best-kept secrets, so you'll know where to get good value for your money no matter where you are in Manhattan.

RESERVATIONS

Reservations are always a good idea in New York, and a virtual necessity if your party is bigger than two. Do yourself a favor and call ahead as a rule of thumb so you won't be disappointed. If you're booking dinner on a weekend night, it's a good idea to call a few days in advance if you can.

Call *far* ahead for any special meal you don't want to miss—a month in advance is a good idea. Most top places start taking reservations exactly 30 days in advance, so if you want to eat at a hot restaurant at a popular hour—Saturday at 8pm, say, at Chanterelle—be sure to mark your calendar and start dialing 30 days prior at 9am. If you're booking a holiday dinner, call even earlier.

But if you didn't call well ahead and your heart's set on dinner at BLT Steak or Buddakan, don't despair. Often, early or late hours—between 5:30 and 6:30pm or after 9pm—are available, especially on weeknights. And try calling the day before or first thing in the morning, when you may be able to take advantage of a last-minute cancellation. Or go for lunch, which is usually much easier to book without lots of advance notice. If you're staying at a hotel with a concierge, don't be afraid to use them—they can often get you into hot spots that you couldn't get into on your own.

But what if they don't *take* reservations? Lots of restaurants, especially at the affordable end of the price continuum, don't take reservations at all. One of the ways they keep prices down is by packing people in as quickly as possible. Thus, the best cheap and mid-price restaurants often have a wait. Again, your best bet is to go early. Often you can get in more quickly on a weeknight. Or just go, knowing that you're

---

Tips Make Reservations in Advance

OpenTable (www.opentable.com) allows you to book a reservation—and get an instant confirmation—over the Web at about 150 restaurants throughout Manhattan. You'll also find that an increasing number of restaurants offer online reservations through their own websites.

---

going to have to wait if you head to a popular spot; hunker down with a cocktail at the bar and enjoy the festivities around you.

SMOKING POLICY

You cannot light up in any restaurant in the city. Some restaurants entice smokers with back gardens or patios where smoking is permitted, but otherwise, you'll have to step out to the sidewalk (or "Bloomberg Lounge") for a cigarette. Some restaurants provide benches, chairs and ashtrays, but it gets mighty cold out there in the winter.

TIPPING

Tipping is easy in New York. The way to do it: Double the 8.375% sales tax and _voilà_, happy waitstaff. In fancier venues, another 5% is appropriate for the captain. If the wine steward helps, hand him or her 10% of the bottle's price.

Leave $1 per item, no matter how small, for the checkroom attendant.

MORE SOURCES FOR SERIOUS FOODIES

Of course, New York has far more fabulous dining than I have room to discuss here—although the listings below are enough to keep you fat and happy for a year, much less the length of a vacation. But if you'd like a wider selection, a few good sources are available online or from your local bookstore.

Your best online sources are the online arm of the weekly _New York_ magazine (**www. nymag.com**), which also features a daily food blog; **New York Today** (**www.nytoday. com),** the _New York Times_'s arts and lifestyle site, where you can access a database of the paper's stellar restaurant reviews; and the _Village Voice_ (**www.villagevoice.com**), especially for the cheap-eats reviews by Robert Sietsema. For a good online source with reader's reviews and menus, try **www.menupages.com**, which has over 6,000 menus online.

Without a doubt, the best online source for the serious foodie is **www.chowhound. com**, a national website with message boards in local areas, including New York, where you can make an inquiry about a certain restaurant, type of food, location, and so on, and within a few hours, you might have five or more informative responses.

The _Zagat Survey,_ which has made a name for itself rating restaurants based on extensive diner surveys, maintains a searchable database of city restaurants at **www. zagat.com**, so if you're willing to do your research before you leave home (or if you're toting a laptop), there's no need to acquire a hard copy of the no-frills guide. They do, however, charge a fee to access the online information. At press time, a year's subscription of Zagat online was $19.95 and a 30-day subscription was $4.95.

The slick weekly _Time Out New York_ has an "Eat Out" section that always includes listings for _TONY_'s 100 Favorite Restaurants in every issue, as well as coverage of new openings and dining trends. Weekly _New York_ magazine also maintains extensive restaurant listings in its listings section at the back of the magazine.

1 Restaurants by Cuisine

AMERICAN

See also "Contemporary American," below.

Artie's New York Delicatessen (Upper West Side, $, p. 199)

Big Nick's Burger and Pizza Joint 🎔 (Upper West Side, $, p. 213)

Brgr 🎔 (Chelsea, $, p. 202)

Bubby's Pie Company 🎔 (TriBeCa and Brooklyn, $$, p. 164 and 221)

Burger Joint 🎔🎔 (Midtown West, $, p. 202)

City Bakery 🎔 (Flatiron District, $, p. 188)

Clinton St. Baking Company 🎔 (Lower East Side, $, p. 170)

Cookshop 🎔🎔 (Chelsea, $$$, p. 182)

Country 🎔🎔 (Midtown East, $$$, p. 201)

Good Enough to Eat 🎔 (Upper West Side, $, p. 214)

The Grocery (Brooklyn, $$, p. 222)

Norma's 🎔🎔 (Midtown West, $$, p. 195)

New York Burger Co. (Flatiron District $, p. 202)

The Odeon 🎔 (TriBeCa, $$, p. 166)

P.J. Clarke's 🎔 (Midtown East, Financial District, $$, p. 202)

Rare Bar & Grill 🎔 (Greenwich Village, Midtown East, $$, p. 202)

Serendipity 3 🎔 (Upper East Side, $, p. 217)

Shake Shack (Flatiron District, $, p. 202)

Tavern on the Green (Upper West Side, $$$, p. 210)

Telepan 🎔🎔 (Upper West Side, $$$, p. 211)

Walker's (TriBeCa, $, p. 371)

ASIAN FUSION/PAN-ASIAN/PACIFIC RIM

Buddakan 🎔 (Chelsea, $$$, p. 179)

Cendrillon 🎔🎔 (SoHo, $$, p. 171)

Nyonya 🎔 (Chinatown, $, p. 167)

BARBECUE/SOUTHERN

Blue Smoke (Flatiron District, $$, p. 193)

Daisy May's BBQ (Midtown West, $$, p. 193)

Dinosaur Bar-B-Que 🎔 (Harlem, $, p. 218)

Rack & Soul (Upper West Side, $$, p. 193)

RUB 🎔🎔 (Chelsea, $$, p. 183 and 193)

Virgil's Real BBQ 🎔🎔 (Times Square, $$, p. 195)

BRAZILIAN

Porcao 🎔 (Flatiron District, $$$, p. 187)

BREAKFAST & BRUNCH

Absolute Bagels (Upper West Side, $, p. 189)

Artie's New York Delicatessen (Upper West Side, $, p. 199)

Barney Greengrass, the Sturgeon King (Upper West Side, $, p. 199)

Big Wong King 🎔 (Chinatown, $, p. 166)

Bubby's Pie Company 🎔 (TriBeCa and Brooklyn, $$, p. 164 and 221)

Café Luluc (Brooklyn, $$, p. 222)

Clinton St. Baking Company 🎔 (Lower East Side, $, p. 170)

Ess-A-Bagel (Midtown East, $, p. 189)

Good Enough to Eat 🎔 (Upper West Side, $, p. 214)

Katz's Delicatessen 🎔🎔 (Lower East Side, $, p. 170)

Metro Marche 🎔 (Times Square, $$, p. 194)

Murray's Bagels (Greenwich Village, $, p. 189)

Norma's 🎔🎔 (Midtown West, $$, p. 195)

Sylvia's (Harlem, $, p. 221)

Veselka 🎔 (East Village, $, p. 176)

Key to Abbreviations: $$$$ = Very Expensive $$$ = Expensive $$ = Moderate $ = Inexpensive

CHINESE

Big Wong King 𝆄 (Chinatown, $, p. 166)

Little Pepper (Queens, $, p. 224)

New York Noodletown 𝆄𝆄 (Chinatown, $, p. 166)

Wo Hop (Chinatown, $, p. 174)

CONTEMPORARY AMERICAN

Country 𝆄𝆄 (Midtown East, $$$, p. 201)

Ouest 𝆄𝆄𝆄 (Upper West Side, $$$, p. 211)

The River Café (Brooklyn, $$$$, p. 220)

THOR 𝆄 (Lower East Side, $$$, p. 168)

Water's Edge 𝆄𝆄 (Queens, $$$, p. 223)

CONTINENTAL

Tavern on the Green (Upper West Side, $$$, p. 210)

FILIPINO

Cendrillon 𝆄𝆄 (SoHo, $$, p. 171)

Ihawan (Queens, $, p. 224)

FRENCH

Brasserie Aix 𝆄𝆄 (Upper West Side, $$$, p. 210)

Café Boulud 𝆄 (Upper East Side, $$$, p. 216)

Café Gray 𝆄𝆄 (Upper West Side, $$$$, p. 208)

Café des Artistes 𝆄 (Upper West Side, $$$$, p. 205)

Capsouto Frères 𝆄 (TriBeCa, $$$, p. 161)

Chanterelle 𝆄𝆄𝆄 (TriBeCa, $$$$, p. 161)

Country 𝆄𝆄 (Midtown East, $$$, p. 201)

Daniel (Upper East Side, $$$$, p. 209)

db Bistro Moderne 𝆄 (Midtown West, $$$, p. 191)

Jean-Georges 𝆄𝆄𝆄 (Upper West Side, $$$$, p. 209)

Landmarc 𝆄𝆄 (TriBeCa, $$$, p. 162)

Le Bernardin (Midtown West, $$$$, p. 209)

Marseille 𝆄 (Midtown West, $$, p. 194)

Mas 𝆄𝆄 (Greenwich Village, $$$, p. 176)

Metro Marche 𝆄 (Times Square, $$, p. 194)

Nice Matin 𝆄 (Upper West Side, $$, p. 212)

Paradou 𝆄 (Meat-Packing District, $$$, p. 178)

Sapa 𝆄𝆄 (Flatiron District, $$$, p. 187)

GOURMET SANDWICHES/ DELI/TAKEOUT

Absolute Bagels (Upper West Side, $, p. 189)

Artie's New York Delicatessen (Upper West Side, $, p. 199)

Barney Greengrass, the Sturgeon King (Upper West Side, $, p. 199)

Carnegie Deli (Midtown West, $, p. 199)

Eisenberg's Coffee Shop (Flatiron District, $, p. 175)

Ess-A-Bagel (Midtown East, $, p. 189)

Gray's Papaya (Upper West Side and Greenwich Village, $, p. 213)

H&H Bagels (Upper West Side and Midtown West, $, p. 189)

Junior's (Brooklyn, Midtown East, $, p. 222)

Kalustyan's 𝆄 (Midtown East, $, p. 205)

Katz's Delicatessen 𝆄𝆄 (Lower East Side, $, p. 170)

Kossar's Bialys (Lower East Side, $, p. 189)

Murray's Bagels (Greenwich Village, $, p. 189)

Nathan's Famous (Brooklyn, $, p. 222)

Stage Deli (Midtown West, $, p. 199)

Shorty's 𝆄 (Midtown West, $, p. 165)

GREEK

Anthos ⟨⟨ (Midtown West, $$$$, p. 189)

Kefi ⟨⟨⟨ (Upper West Side, $$, p. 212)

Molyvos ⟨⟨ (Midtown West, $$$, p. 192)

Parea ⟨ (Flatiron District, $$$, p. 187)

Thalassa ⟨ (TriBeCa, $$$, p. 162)

Uncle Nick's (Midtown West, $, p. 198)

INDIAN

Bombay Talkie ⟨ (Chelsea, $$, p. 183)

Brick Lane Curry House ⟨ (East Village, $$, p. 173)

Dévi ⟨⟨ (Flatiron District, $$$, p. 186)

Tamarind ⟨⟨ (Flatiron District, $$$, p. 188)

ITALIAN

Abboccato ⟨⟨ (Midtown West, $$$, p. 190)

A Voce ⟨⟨ (Flatiron District, $$$, p. 185)

Barbetta ⟨⟨ (Midtown West, $$$, p. 191)

Barbuto ⟨ (Greenwich Village, $$, p. 179)

Becco ⟨ (Midtown West, $$, p. 194)

Bread ⟨ (Nolita/SoHo, $, p. 173)

Bread Tribeca ⟨ (TriBeCa, $$, p. 164)

Carmine's ⟨ (Upper West Side and Times Square, $$, p. 212 and 194)

Celeste ⟨⟨ (Upper West Side, $, p. 214)

'Cesca ⟨⟨ (Upper West Side, $$$, p. 210)

Dani ⟨ (SoHo, $$$, p. 170)

Dominick's (Bronx, $$, p. 218)

Ferdinando's Focacceria ⟨ (Brooklyn, $, p. 223)

Fiamma Osteria ⟨⟨ (SoHo, $$$, p. 171)

Frankie and Johnnie's Pine Restaurant (Bronx, $$, p. 218)

'inoteca ⟨⟨ (Lower East Side, $$, p. 168)

La Lunetta (Brooklyn, $$, p. 222)

Landmarc ⟨⟨ (TriBeCa, $$$, p. 162)

Lupa ⟨⟨ (SoHo, $$, p. 172)

Maremma ⟨⟨ (Greenwich Village, $$, p. 179)

Mario's Restaurant (Bronx, $$, p. 218)

Nick's Family-Style Restaurant and Pizzeria ⟨ (Upper East Side, $, p. 217)

Paola's ⟨ (Upper East Side, $$$, p. 216)

JAPANESE

Le Miu ⟨⟨ (East Village, $$$, p. 173)

Masa (Upper West Side, $$$$, p. 205)

Sapporo ⟨ (Midtown West, $, p. 198)

JEWISH DELI

Artie's New York Delicatessen (Upper West Side, $, p. 199)

Barney Greengrass, the Sturgeon King (Upper West Side, $, p. 199)

Carnegie Deli (Midtown West, $, p. 199)

Junior's (Brooklyn, Midtown East, $, p. 222)

Katz's Delicatessen ⟨⟨ (Lower East Side, $, p. 170)

Mo Pitkin's House of Satisfaction ⟨ (East Village, $$, p. 175)

Stage Deli (Midtown West, $, p. 199)

KOREAN

Mandoo Bar ⟨ (Midtown West and Greenwich Village, $, p. 198)

LATIN AMERICAN/SPANISH/ SOUTH AMERICAN

El Faro ⟨ (Greenwich Village, $$, p. 205)

Flor de Mayo (Upper West Side, $, p. 214)

MEDITERRANEAN

A.O.C. Bedford ✹✹ (Greenwich Village, $$$, p. 176)

Landmarc ✹✹ (TriBeCa, $$$, p. 162)

Savann ✹ (Upper West Side, $$, p. 213)

MEXICAN/TEX-MEX/ SOUTHWESTERN

Noche Mexicana ✹ (Upper West Side, $, p. 215)

Pampano ✹✹ (Midtown East, $$$, p. 201)

MIDDLE EASTERN

Afghan Kebab House (Midtown West, $, p. 197)

Kalustyan's ✹ (Midtown East, $, p. 205)

Zaytoons (Brooklyn, $$, p. 222)

PIZZA

Big Nick's Burger and Pizza Joint ✹ (Upper West Side, $, p. 213)

DiFara Pizza ✹ (Brooklyn, $, p. 196)

Grimaldi's Pizzeria (Brooklyn, $, p. 196)

Joe's Pizza (Greenwich Village, $, p. 179)

John's Pizzeria (Times Square, Greenwich Village, and Upper East Side, $, p. 196)

Lombardi's (Little Italy, $, p. 197)

Pala ✹ (Lower East Side, $$, p. 168)

Patsy's Pizzeria ✹✹ (Harlem, $, p. 197)

Totonno's Pizzeria Napolitano (Upper East Side and Brooklyn, $, p. 197)

PORTUGUESE

Pao! ✹ (SoHo, $$, p. 172)

SCANDINAVIAN

Aquavit ✹✹✹ (Midtown East, $$$, p. 200)

SEAFOOD

BLT Fish ✹✹ (Flatiron District, $$$, p. 186)

Le Bernardin (Midtown West, $$$$, p. 209)

The Neptune Room ✹ (Upper West Side, $$$, p. 210)

New York Noodletown ✹✹ (Chinatown, $, p. 166)

Oceana ✹✹✹ (Midtown East, $$$, p. 201)

Oyster Bar & Restaurant ✹ (Midtown East, $$, p. 205)

Vincent's Clam Bar (Little Italy, $$, p. 166)

SOUL FOOD

Amy Ruth's (Harlem, $, p. 220)

Charles' Southern Style Kitchen ✹ (Harlem, $, p. 220)

Copeland's (Harlem, $$, p. 220)

M&G Diner (Harlem, $, p. 221)

Miss Mamie's Spoonbread Too (Harlem, $$, p. 221)

Rack & Soul (Upper West Side, $$, p. 193)

Sylvia's (Harlem, $, p. 221)

SPANISH

El Faro ✹ (Greenwich Village, $$, p. 175)

La Nacional ✹✹ (Chelsea, $$, p. 183)

STEAK

Ben Benson's Steakhouse (Midtown West, $$$$, p. 185)

Benjamin Steakhouse ✹ (Midtown East, $$$$, p. 189)

BLT Steak ✹✹✹ (Midtown East, $$$, p. 200)

Bull and Bear (Midtown East, $$$, p. 184)

Frankie & Johnnie's ✹✹ (Midtown West, $$$, p. 191)

Harry's Steak and Café ✹✹ (Financial District, $$$, p. 162)

Jackson Avenue Steakhouse ✹ (Queens, $$$, p. 223)

Kobe Club ✹ (Midtown West, $$$$, p. 190)

Keens Steakhouse ✹✹✹ (Midtown West, $$$, p. 192)

Michael Jordan's—The Steak
House 𝒢𝒢 (Midtown East, $$$,
p. 184)

Peter Luger Steakhouse 𝒢𝒢
(Brooklyn, $$$, p. 220)

Porter House New York 𝒢𝒢 (Upper
West Side, $$$$, p. 208)

Quality Meats 𝒢 (Midtown West,
$$$$, p. 185)

Strip House 𝒢𝒢 (Greenwich Village,
$$$, p. 178)

Uncle Jack's Steakhouse 𝒢 (Midtown
West, $$$$, p. 185)

SWISS

Trestle on Tenth 𝒢 (Chelsea, $$$,
p. 182)

THAI

Arunee Thai (Queens, $, p. 224)

Kittichai 𝒢 (SoHo, $$$, p. 171)

Wondee Siam 𝒢 (Midtown West, $,
p. 199)

UKRAINIAN

Veselka 𝒢 (East Village, $, p. 176)

VIETNAMESE

Pho Viet Huong 𝒢 (Chinatown, $,
p. 167)

Sapa 𝒢𝒢 (Flatiron District, $$$,
p. 187)

---

2 Financial District, South Street Seaport & TriBeCa

To find the restaurants reviewed below, see the map on p. 163.

VERY EXPENSIVE

Chanterelle 𝒢𝒢𝒢 CONTEMPORARY FRENCH   One of New York's best "special occasion" restaurants mainly because, well, they treat you so special here. The dining room is a charmer with daily floral displays and an interesting modern-art collection. Tables are far enough apart to give diners plenty of intimacy, something rare in many New York restaurants these days. Your server will work with you on your choices, pairing items that go best together. The French-themed menu is seasonal and changes every few weeks, but one signature dish appears on almost every menu: a marvelous grilled seafood sausage. Cheese lovers should opt for a cheese course—the presentation and selection can't be beat. The wine list is superlative but expensive. Still, you don't come to Chanterelle on the cheap—you come to celebrate.

2 Harrison St. (at Hudson St.). © **212/966-6960.** www.chanterellenyc.com. Reservations recommended well in advance. Fixed-price lunch $42; a la carte lunch $22–$30; 3-course fixed-price dinner $95; tasting menu $125. AE, DISC, MC, V. Mon–Wed 5:30–10:30pm; Mon–Sat noon–2:30pm; Thurs–Sat 5:30–11pm; Sun 5–10pm. Subway: 1 to Franklin St.

EXPENSIVE

Capsouto Frères 𝒢 FRENCH   In 1980, before the triangle below Canal Street was given the acronym TriBeCa, and before the neighborhood became rife with celebrities and hip restaurants, Capsouto Frères opened. And through TriBeCa's amazing growth and its devastation after 9/11 and subsequent rebirth, Capsouto Frères has not only survived—a feat unto itself—but it has thrived with a loyal following. What accounts for the restaurant's longevity during all that tumult? Is it the simple, home-style French cuisine served here: the famous soufflés; the spicy *saucisson;* the always reliable sole meunière, steak frites, or cassoulet; the warm, wood-floored, high-ceilinged always-festive dining room; the gregarious and engaging hosts; the *freres* Jacques, Sammy, and Albert? Or is it a combination of all of the above? Whatever it is, it works.

Sturdy and reliable Capsouto Frères offers a literal taste of what it was like before Robert De Niro "discovered" TriBeCa.

451 Washington St. (at Watts St.). © 212/966-4900. www.capsoutofreres.com. Reservations recommended. Lunch prix fixe $24, main courses $12–$24; dinner prix fixe $35, main courses $16–$29. AE, DC MC, V. Tues–Fri noon–3:30pm; Sun–Thurs 6–10pm; Fri–Sat 6–11pm; brunch Sat–Sun noon–3:30pm. Subway: 1, A, C, E to Canal St.

Harry's Steaks & Café 𝒦𝒦 *(Finds* STEAKHOUSE   Harry's is a crowd pleaser. It's a steakhouse, with all the accoutrements of your traditional red meat joint; dry-aged beef with hearty sides; it's a café, with a bountiful original menu, but equally dense selection, and it's a lively, Wall Street-area bar with a well stocked spirits and wine selection. When you enter, you'll see the bar and you'll hear the traders celebrating their day's winnings, adjacent to the bar is the large café featuring leather banquettes. Down a few steps from the Café is the steakhouse, carved out of an old stone wine cellar. But it really doesn't matter where you eat, the kitchen is the same and you can order from either menu. When I visited, I chose to mix and match from both menus. I started with a superb Greek salad topped with white anchovies from the Café menu followed by the grilled triple cut pork chops served on a delicious bed of sauerkraut, accompanied by a Mason jar of fresh apple sauce with a chili pepper embedded in it. The side of escarole with white beans and prosciutto was almost a meal unto itself. The dry-aged rib steak is as good as you'll find anywhere west of Peter Luger's, but it was the crackling pork shank, from the Café menu, a gargantuan shank on the bone, its skin fried to a crackling that stole the show. Just looking at it could send one's cholesterol soaring, but experiencing it is worth the health risk.

1 Hanover Square (at Pearl St.) © 212/785-9200. www.harrysnyc.com. Reservations recommended. Main courses: $13–$43. AE, DC, DISC, MC, V. Café open 7 days; 11:30am–midnight; Steakhouse Mon–Fri 11am–11pm. Subway: 2, 3 to Wall St.

Landmarc 𝒦𝒦 *(Finds* MEDITERRANEAN/FRENCH/ITALIAN   This cozy, intimate TriBeCa restaurant is too good to be considered just a neighborhood joint. Chef/owner Marc Murphy has put his own distinctive spin on this Italian/French rendition of a bistro. You'll find excellent smoked mozzarella and ricotta fritters alongside escargots bordelaise. It will be up to you to decide whether you imagine yourself in a Tuscan trattoria or a Provençal bistro. Or you can mix and match cuisines. Try the pasta of the day accompanied by mussels with a choice of sauce—Provençal, Dijonnaise, or the comforting blend of shallots, parsley, and white wine. Steaks and chops are cooked over an open fire and the steaks are offered with a variety of sauces; I had the hangar with a shallot bordelaise that complemented the meat perfectly. What keeps the neighbors pouring in, along with the excellent food, are the remarkably affordable wines sold, not by the glass, but by the bottle or half bottle. Desserts are simple, small, and priced that way, with none more than $3. For a special treat or if you've brought the kids, ask for the cotton candy. Now you won't find *that* in a Tuscan trattoria. Landmarc recently added an uptown location, at the Time Warner Center (10 Columbus Circle. © 212/823-6123).

179 W. Broadway (btwn Leonard and Worth sts.). © 212/343-3883. www.landmarc-restaurant.com. Reservations recommended. Main courses $15–$34. AE, DC, DISC, MC, V. Mon–Fri noon–2am; Sat, Sun 9am–2pm and 5:30pm–2am. Subway: 1 to Franklin St.

Thalassa 𝒦 GREEK   Greek food is best when prepared simply with the freshest ingredients, especially fish, and Thalassa does a remarkable job of living up to that standard. The variety of seafood is staggering: When I visited, the options included

Where to Dine in the Financial District, TriBeCa, Chinatown & Little Italy

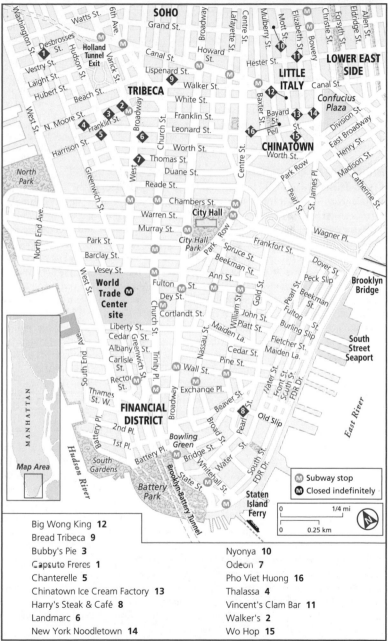

Big Wong King **12**
Bread Tribeca **9**
Bubby's Pie **3**
Capsuto Freres **1**
Chanterelle **5**
Chinatown Ice Cream Factory **13**
Harry's Steak & Café **8**
Landmarc **6**
New York Noodletown **14**

Nyonya **10**
Odeon **7**
Pho Viet Huong **16**
Thalassa **4**
Vincent's Clam Bar **11**
Walker's **2**
Wo Hop **15**

fresh langoustines from Scotland, pound-and-a-half shrimp from Mexico, and a number of oyster selections. For starters, the kataifi-pastry-wrapped diver scallops with sheep's milk butter was a revelation, while the octopus, simply grilled with a red-wine vinaigrette, was as good as I've had west of Astoria. The main courses won't disappoint either; the pan-roasted Dover sole was delicately prepared and perfectly seasoned with a touch of olive oil and lemon, while the sea bream with slices of diver scallops on top was exceptional. The knowledgeable sommelier can help you select a Greek wine, of which there are many, from the restaurant's cellar, where a number of unusual and good Greek cheeses are also stored. The restaurant is large; tables are spaced well enough apart for intimacy and service is attentive and pleasant.

179 Franklin St. (btwn Greenwich and Hudson sts.). ℂ 212/941-7661. www.thalassanyc.com. Reservations recommended. Prix-fixe lunch $24; main courses dinner $28–$42. AE, DC, DISC, MC, V. Mon–Fri noon–3pm and 6–11pm; Fri–Sat 5:30pm–midnight; Sun 5–10pm. Subway: 1 to Franklin St.

MODERATE

Bread Tribeca 𝄢 NORTHERN ITALIAN   Bread Tribeca is one of the few restaurants in New York to feature the cuisine of Italy's Liguria region. What is Ligurian cuisine? Seafood is a big part of it, and Bread Tribeca does a good job with its *fritto misto,* a mixture of fried fish (such as calamari, cod, and mussels) and vegetables; and its *zuppa de pesce,* assorted seafood in a saffron-tomato sauce. Homemade pastas are another trademark of Ligurian food, and at Bread Tribeca you'll find *pansotti,* ravioli-like dumplings served with a walnut sauce; and fresh *taglierini,* a spaghetti-like pasta that's slightly overwhelmed by the dense combination of haricots verts, potatoes, and a surprisingly subtle pesto. A wood-burning oven turns out excellent thin-crust pizzas and roasted meats and, like its sister restaurant (see **Bread,** p. 173), the breads are superb, including a remarkable combination of sardine, tomato, and peperoncini slathered on a baguette. Most of the tables are communal, so if the restaurant is crowded, don't expect intimacy; and the 50-inch television that runs movies (when I was there last, *Chocolat*) is often a distraction, not a complement, to the food. On weekends a deejay spins calming, low-key music to accompany the rustic food.

301 Church St. (at Walker St.). ℂ **212/334-0200.** www.breadtribeca.com. Reservations recommended. Main courses $9–$27 lunch; $14–$27 dinner. AE, DC, DISC, MC, V. Sun–Thurs 11:30am–11pm; Fri–Sat 11:30am–midnight. Subway: A, C, E to Canal St.

Bubby's Pie Company 𝄢 AMERICAN   You might have to wait on line to eat at Bubby's. You might get squeezed in at a table perilously close to another couple. And you might have to talk quite loudly to maintain a conversation with your dining companion. But your level of discomfort will subside as soon as you begin to consume Bubby's comfort food. Whether it is the slow-cooked pulled barbecue pork, the magnificent, lighter-than-air meatloaf, or the buttermilk-fried half chicken, coupled with sides like collard greens, sautéed spinach, macaroni and cheese, or baked beans, Bubby's dishes define comfort. Take Bubby's advice and save room for the desserts, especially the homemade pies; one taste of the chocolate peanut-butter pie immediately brought on happy childhood flashbacks. Breakfast is big here and lasts well into the middle of the day. On weekends, though, here in trendy TriBeCa, the wait for brunch can be lengthy. Celebrities need comfort, too, and you might spot one or two at Bubby's seeking anonymity and down-home chow. Bubby's also has a branch across the river in the DUMBO neighborhood of Brooklyn *Kids.*

120 Hudson St. (at N. Moore St.). ℂ **212/219-0666.** www.bubbys.com. Reservations recommended for dinner (not accepted for brunch). Main courses $10–$15 breakfast, brunch, and lunch; $10–$21 dinner. DC, DISC, MC, V.

Food in a N.Y. Minute

I do my best in this chapter to not mention the fast-food-chain options in the city. There was a time, though it's hard to believe, that McDonald's and Domino's pizza (oops I mentioned their names) were not to be found in New York. They are here now and, sadly, they are here to stay. But you needn't resort to the same options you can find in any town when you need a quick food fix. Here are a few original options you should consider before parting the golden arches.

New York is a hot dog town. You can buy them from street vendors all over the city and doing so is something everyone should experience. But once might be enough. If you want an original New York dog, **Nathan's Famous,** established in 1916, is the best example. There are Nathan's Famous hot dogs all over the city now, but though the hot dogs are the same, they just don't taste as good as the ones served in its original location on the **Coney Island boardwalk** in Brooklyn, 1310 Surf Ave., at Stillwell Avenue (© **718/946-2202**). If a 145-pound Japanese man can eat 53½ hot dogs in 12 minutes, you can certainly handle at least two—including an order of their fantastic crinkle-cut fries.

For the cheapest quick meal, nothing can match **Gray's Papaya.** This 24-hour hot-dog stand is a New York institution. Hot dogs go for 75¢, and the "Recession Special," two hot dogs and a drink, overly sweetened papaya, piña colada, or orange juice, is a whopping $3.50. The hot dogs are delicious, though for your own good, don't be tempted to eat more than two despite the low prices. There are three Gray's Papaya around the city, but the best is the original at the corner of 72nd Street and Broadway, at 2090 Broadway (© **212/799-0243**).

Like the hot dog, pizza is also a New York staple. I discuss the best pizza in New York in the box "Pizza, New York–Style" (p. 196), but most of the places mentioned in that box require sitting down and ordering a whole pie. For the quick slice, my personal favorite is **Joe's Pizza,** 7 Carmine St., at Bleecker Street (© **212/255-3946**). Joe's offers the epitome of what a slice is supposed to taste like: thin-crusted with the proper balance of sauce, which actually has flavor, and cheese that doesn't taste like something you could bounce off a wall. And because Joe's is so popular, the pizza turns over quickly, almost always guaranteeing a fresh slice. Be prepared to wait in line during busy evening hours and then take your slice outside and eat it like a real New Yorker—standing up.

In Philadelphia, arguments rage over who makes the best cheesesteak. But we are in New York, and of the few Philly-style-cheesesteak establishments, my pick is **Shorty's,** formerly known as Tony Luke's ★, 576 Ninth Ave., between 41st and 42nd streets (© **212/967-3055**). On the edge of the Theater District, in the shadow of the Port Authority Bus Terminal, Shorty's location is about as gritty as it gets. But that just adds to the appeal of Shorty's gargantuan sandwiches. The cheesesteak with your choice of cheese juices—Provolone, American, or Whiz (go for the Whiz, of course)—drenching the fresh Italian roll is hard to resist, but if you can, order the roast pork Italian: roast pork with peppers, onions, and broccoli rabe. Try squeezing into your seat at the theater after one of *those!*

Mon–Thurs 8am–11pm; Fri 8am–midnight; Sat 9am–4:30pm and 6pm–midnight; Sun 9am–10pm. Subway: 1 to Franklin St. Bubby's Brooklyn: 1 Main St. (at Water St.). ℂ **718/222-0666**. Subway: A, C to High St.; F to York St.

The Odeon ⍟ AMERICAN BRASSERIE   For over 2 decades The Odeon has been a symbol of the TriBeCa sensibility; in fact, the restaurant can claim credit for the neighborhood's cachet—it was the first to lure artists, actors, writers, and models to the area below Canal Street before it was given its moniker. Why did they come? They came to drink, schmooze, and enjoy the hearty no-frills brasserie grub like the country frisée salad with bacon, Roquefort cheese, and pear vinaigrette and the truffled poached egg, *moules frites* (mussels with fries), and sautéed cod. Though the restaurant is not quite the celebrity magnet it was in its heyday of the 1980s, the food, drink, and that inviting, open, Art Deco-ish room has withstood the test of time and has surpassed trendy to claim well-deserved New York establishment status.

145 W. Broadway (at Thomas St.). ℂ **212/233-0507**. Reservations recommended. Main courses $13–$35 at lunch; $19–$35 at dinner (most less than $21); fixed-price lunch $27. AE, DC, DISC, MC, V. Mon–Fri noon–11pm; Sat 11:30am–midnight; Sun 11:30am–11pm. Subway: 1, 2, 3 to Chambers St.

INEXPENSIVE

For an inexpensive alternative in TriBeCa, consider the pub **Walker's** (see chapter 10), 16 N. Moore St., at Varick Street (ℂ **212/941-0142**), where you can get a good burger and fries for less than $10.

3 Chinatown

To find the restaurants reviewed below, see the map on p. 163.

INEXPENSIVE

Also consider two restaurants that have stood the test of time, **Wo Hop,** 17 Mott St., between Worth and Mosco streets (ℂ **212/267-2536**), and **Vincent's Clam Bar,** 119 Mott St., at Hester Street (ℂ **212/226-8133;** www.originalvincents.com). For more on both, see the box "Old Friends" on p. 174.

Big Wong King ⍟ CHINESE/CANTONESE   A couple of years ago, Big Wong was called New Big Wong. This year they want to be called Big Wong King. No matter. They will always be Big Wong and that's a good thing. Why mess with success? For over 30 years, Big Wong has been an institution for workers from the nearby courthouses and Chinese families who come to feast on congee (rice porridge) and fried crullers for breakfast (see "Breakfast, Not Brunch," on p. 215). They also come for the superb roasted meats, the pork and duck seen hanging in the window, the comforting noodle soups, and the terrific barbecued ribs. This is simple, down-home Cantonese food—lo mein, chow fun, bok choy in oyster sauce—cooked lovingly, and so cheap. If you don't mind sharing a table, Big Wong is a must at any time of day.

67 Mott St. (btwn Canal and Bayard sts.). ℂ **212/964-0540**. Appetizers $1.50–$5; congee $1.50–$6; soups $3–$5; Cantonese noodles $5.25–$11. No credit cards. Daily 7am–10pm. Subway: N, R.

New York Noodletown ⍟⍟ CHINESE/SEAFOOD   So what if the restaurant has all the ambience of a school cafeteria? I'm wary of an overadorned dining room in Chinatown; the simpler the better. New York Noodletown is simple, but the food is the real thing. Seafood-based noodle soups are spectacular, as is the platter of chopped roast pork. Those two items alone would make me happy. But I'm greedy and wouldn't leave

---

Tips A Chinatown Sweet Treat

When in Chinatown, after sitting down at a dim sum banquet or a noodle joint, skip the feeble dessert offerings and head to one of my favorite ice cream shops in the city, the **Chinatown Ice Cream Factory** ⟲, 65 Bayard St., between Mott and Elizabeth streets (ℂ **212/608-4170**). The ice cream here features Asian flavors like almond cookie, litchi, and an incredible green tea.

---

the restaurant without one of its perfectly prepared shrimp dishes, especially the salt-baked shrimp. If your hotel room has a fridge, take the leftovers home—they'll make a great snack the next day. New York Noodletown keeps very long hours, which makes it one of the best late-night bets in the neighborhood, too.

28½ Bowery (at Bayard St.). ℂ 212/349-0923. Reservations accepted. Main courses $4–$15. No credit cards. Daily 9am–3am. Subway: N, R, 6 to Canal St.

Nyonya ⟲ *Finds* ASIAN/MALAYSIAN   You won't find many Malaysian restaurants in New York, but one of the few, and one of the best, is Chinatown's Nyonya. This spacious, bustling restaurant designed like a South Asian tiki hut offers efficient, friendly service, but it's the huge portions of exotic, spicy food that are the real treat. Coconut milk, curry, and chili-pepper-laden dishes are staples of Malaysian cuisine and the norm at Nyonya. The Malaysian national dish, *roti canai* (an Indian pancake with a curry-chicken dipping sauce), is outstanding. The noodle soups are meals in themselves; *prawn mee* (egg noodles, shredded pork, large shrimp in a spicy shrimp broth) is sinus-clearing, while the curry spareribs are spectacular. Even the drinks and desserts are exotic, including *sooi pooi* drink (sour plum) and *pulut hitam* (creamy black glutinous rice with coconut milk). But vegetarians beware: There's not much on the menu for you here; most dishes are prepared in either a meat or fish broth.

194 Grand St. (btwn Mulberry and Mott sts.). ℂ 212/334-3669. Appetizers $2.25–$8; noodle soups $4.25–$6; main dishes $5.25–$16. No credit cards. Sun–Thurs 11am–11:30pm; Fri–Sat 11am–midnight. Subway: 6 to Spring St.

Pho Viet Huong ⟲ *Value* VIETNAMESE   Chinatown has its own enclave of Vietnamese restaurants, and the best is Pho Viet Huong. The menu is vast and needs intense perusing, but your waiter will help you pare it down. The Vietnamese know soup, and *pho*, a beef-based soup served with many ingredients, is the most famous, but the hot and sour *canh* soup, with either shrimp or fish, is the real deal. The small version is more than enough for two to share while the large is more than enough for a family. The odd pairing of barbecued beef wrapped in grape leaves is another of the restaurant's specialties and should not be missed, while the *bun,* various meats and vegetables served over rice vermicelli, are simple, hearty, and inexpensive. You'll even find Vietnamese sandwiches here: French bread filled with ham, chicken, eggs, lamb, and even pâté. For the daring, there are the frogs' legs, but don't expect what you're used to at your friendly neighborhood French restaurant—these require patience and fortitude. All of the above is best washed down with an icy cold Saigon beer.

73 Mulberry St. (btwn Bayard and Canal sts.). ℂ 212/233-8988. Appetizers $3–$8.50; soups $6–$7; main courses $10–$25. AE, MC, V. Sun–Thurs 10am–10pm; Fri–Sat 10am–11pm. Subway: 6, N, R, Q to Canal St.

4 Lower East Side

EXPENSIVE

THOR *꘠* *(Finds* CONTEMPORARY AMERICAN   Enter through the eggshell entrance to the Hotel on Rivington, turn right before the elevators, and you are in THOR (not the Greek god, but the acronym for The Hotel on Rivington). As you enter you'll notice the expansive lounge area and that, if it's past 9pm, most of the couches and plush chairs will be occupied and it will be noisy. Move toward the dining room and observe the high glass ceiling and how effective it is in transforming the bar noise into a cacophonous din. Now that you've accepted that THOR will not be the place for intimate conversation, concentrate on the innovative seasonal menu. Since your waiter probably won't be able to hear you, point to the squid with black pasta, tarragon, and fava beans or the gnocchi with wild mushrooms and prosciutto from the "Warm Plates in the Middle" section of the menu, followed by either delicately steamed red snapper with clams, olives, and artichokes in a potato broth or the sublimely tender, roasted veal loin with pumpkin, carrots, apples, and red-wine onions. There will be no need for talk once your food comes—just eat, enjoy, and take in the noise. But leave room for THOR's exceptional dessert, which celebrates THOR's neighborhood, the Lower East Side Breakfast: espresso ice cream with a cigarette cookie served in a coffee mug.

107 Rivington St. (btwn Ludlow & Essex). (℗ **212/796-8040.** www.hotelonrivington.com. Reservations recommended. Small plates $9–$17; entrees $25–$28. AE, DC, DISC, MC, V. Daily 7–11am; lunch Mon–Fri noon–3pm; brunch Sat–Sun 11am–3pm; dinner Sun–Wed 6pm–midnight, Thurs–Sat 6pm–1am. Subway: F to Delancey St.

MODERATE

'inoteca *꘠꘠* *(Finds* ITALIAN SMALL PLATES   The Lower East Side was once the home to many Kosher wine factories, but you'll find only Italian wines at cozy 'inoteca. The list is over 250 bottles long, but even better are the exquisitely prepared small plates that complement the wines. Though the Italian-language menu is a challenge, servers are helpful in translating. The panini stand out in their freshness and their delicacy, with the *coppa* (a spicy cured ham) with hot peppers and *rucola* (arugula) being the standout. The *tramezzini,* a crustless sandwich, is nothing like the crustless sandwiches served at high tea. Here, among other things, you can have yours stuffed with tuna and chick peas or with *pollo alla diavola,* spicy shredded pieces of dark-meat chicken. The "Fritto" section includes a wonderful mozzarella *in corroza,* breaded mozzarella stuffed with a juicy anchovy sauce and lightly fried. Whatever you order, don't rush; 'inoteca is a place to go slow, to savor both wine and food.

98 Rivington St. (at Ludlow St.). (℗ **212/614-0473.** www.inotecanyc.com. Reservations accepted for parties of 6 or more. Panini $8–$17; *piatti* (small plates) $8–$11. AE, MC, V. Daily noon–3am. Brunch Sat–Sun 10am–4pm. Subway: F, J, M, Z to Delancey St.

Pala *꘠* PIZZA   Don't go to Pala expecting your typical New York City pizza. The owners studied how pizza was made in Italy and have done their best to try to replicate it. Apparently, traditional New York City pizza can be tough to digest (the only pizza I have trouble digesting is bad pizza—or eating too much of it), so Pala has concocted a special pizza-making process, including a slow-rising dough that they claim makes their pies easier on the belly. I can attest that consuming practically a whole *zucca* pie (oblong-shaped and topped with sautéed pumpkin, pancetta, and smoked *scamorza* cheese) along with a few slices of a *bufala cruda* (buffalo mozzarella, cherry-tomato

Where to Dine in SoHo, Nolita, the East Village & on the Lower East Side

Bread **12**
Brick Lane Curry House **3**
Cendrillon **14**
Clinton St. Baking Co. **8**
Fiamma Osteria **16**
inoteca **9**
Katz's Delicatessen **7**
Kittichai **15**
Kossar's Bialys **11**

Le Miu **2**
Lombardi's Pizza **13**
Lupa **5**
Mo Pitkin's House of Satisfaction **4**
Pala **6**
Pao! **17**
THOR **10**
Veselka **1**

sauce, and fresh basil) did no damage to my stomach except for possibly expanding it. I'm sure the glass of sparkling, chilled Lambrusco, a nice complement to the pizza, aided in my digestion, but I must give credit to Pala's scientific approach. There's nothing scientific about the non-pizza items like the addictive *fiori di zucca* (fried zucchini blossoms stuffed with buffalo mozzarella and anchovies) or the tender, marinated fresh artichokes with lemon, oil, and Parmesan cheese shavings. Pala, which opened in early 2006, is loud and lively with long wooden, picniclike tables—a welcome addition to the Lower East Side culinary scene.

198 Allen St. (btwn Stanton and Houston sts.). ② 212/614-7252. www.pala-ny.com. Pizza $12–$22. AE. Tues–Thurs 4pm–midnight; Fri 4pm–1am; Sat noon–1am; Sun noon–midnight. Subway: F, V to Second Ave.

INEXPENSIVE

Clinton St. Baking Company 🌟 *Finds* AMERICAN   Though they are open all day, breakfast and desserts are the best offerings here. The blueberry pancakes with maple butter and the buttermilk-biscuit egg sandwich are worth braving the morning lines for, while the desserts, all homemade and topped with a scoop or two of ice cream from the Brooklyn Ice Cream Factory, are good any time of day.

4 Clinton St. (at Houston St.). ② 646/602-6263. Main courses $8–$14. No credit cards. Mon–Fri 8am–11pm (closed 4–6pm); Sat 10am–11pm; Sun 10am–4pm. Subway: F or V to Second Ave.

Katz's Delicatessen 🌟🌟 *Value* JEWISH DELI   Arguably the city's best Jewish deli. The motto is "There's Nothing More New York Than Katz's," and it's spot-on. Founded in 1888, this cavernous, brightly lit place is suitably Noo Yawk, with dill pickles, Dr. Brown's cream soda, and old-world attitude to spare. Take the ticket they give you when you come in and either head for the cafeteria-style line, or seat yourself in the "waiter service" area. But one word of caution: Katz's has become a serious tourist destination so if you see a big tour bus parked in front, you might be in for a long wait. (And remember to tip your carver, who gives you a plate with a sample of the succulent pastrami or corned beef as he prepares your sandwich!)

205 E. Houston St. (at Ludlow St.). ② 212/254-2246. Reservations not accepted. Sandwiches $3–$10; other main courses $5–$18. AE, DC, DISC, MC, V. ($20 minimum). Sun–Tues 8am–10pm; Wed 8am–11pm; Thurs 8am–midnight; Fri–Sat 8am–3am. Subway: F to Second Ave.

5 SoHo & Nolita

To locate the restaurants reviewed below, see the map on p. 169.

EXPENSIVE

Dani 🌟 ITALIAN   You would think in a city with countless residents of Sicilian ancestry that there would be more authentic Sicilian restaurants. Sadly, that is not the case in Manhattan, but the good news is that Dani is one of the few and does an exemplary job with that very special cuisine. Located in SoHo, the dining room is open, high-ceilinged and airy. But that open space tends to project sound and when the not-so-appropriate rock soundtrack is blaring, conversation can be difficult. You don't need to talk, however, to enjoy what you are eating and chef Don "Dani" Pintabona will see that you do starting with the Sicilian fish sampler: fluke, citrus sardine, and pickled Spanish mackerel that will make you long for a long weekend in Palermo. Of the pastas, it's hard to resist that Sicilian specialty, *chitarra con sarde,* homemade pasta with sardines, fennel, and currants, but if you do, the second best option would be the *bucatini con moscardino,* bucatini with baby octopus, chilies, and cherry tomatoes. Of the "secondi," the grilled swordfish with capers, pine nuts, and raisins is about as good a representation of Sicilian cuisine as you will find. Of the desserts, the grapefruit and campari granita makes the most fitting finish.

333 Hudson St (at Charlton St.) © 212/633-9333; www.danirestaurant.com. Reservations recommended. Main courses: $18–$23; Family style $55 per person, 7-course tasting menu $75. AE, DC, DISC, MC, V. Hours: Mon–Fri noon–3pm; Mon–Thurs 5:30–10:30pm; Fri–Sat 5:30–11pm. Subway: C, E to Spring St.

Fiamma Osteria 🍴🍴 MODERN ITALIAN   From Stephen Hanson (Blue Water Grill, Ruby Foo's, Dos Caminos), the Steven Spielberg of restaurateurs, comes his art-house effort, and this one wins all the awards. A Hanson trademark, the restaurant is beautifully designed, depicting a modern northern-Italian style with mirrors, lustrous red walls, leather chairs, and a glass elevator that can deposit you on any of the four floors. But the decor here is surpassed by the sumptuous, modern Italian food. Start with an antipasti of grilled octopus in an olive vinaigrette sprinkled with ceci beans (chickpeas) and cooled by chopped mint leaves, and then move on to a pasta or two: The *agnolini* (braised oxtail and beef shank ravioli) and the buffalo milk ricotta *tortelli* are both outstanding. We often tend to neglect Italian main courses in favor of pastas, but doing that here would be a mistake. The *orata* (grilled *daurade* with cranberry beans in a Manila clam broth), the pan-roasted cod with shrimp and broccolini, and the *nodino* (seared veal chop with sage and sweet-and-sour cipollini onions) are too good to pass up. Fiamma is blessed to have the services of pastry chef extraordinaire Elizabeth Katz; her dessert creations are second to none. Her *torta,* a dark-chocolate praline cake layered with hazelnut brittle and gianduja gelato, is an absolute master-piece. Dinner is a scene, so don't expect intimacy, but lunch, with a similar menu, is a much more relaxed option.

206 Spring St. (btwn Sixth Ave. and Sullivan St.). © 212/653-0100. Reservations recommended. Pasta $22–$26; main courses $29–$44. AE, DISC, MC, V. Mon–Fri noon–2:30pm; Sun–Thurs5:30–11pm; Fri–Sat 5:30pm–midnight. Subway: C, E to Spring St.

Kittichai 🍴 THAI   The hotel **60 Thompson** (p. 118) and its public spaces are a magnet for people of the beautiful kind, and Kittichai, the restaurant that shares the hotel's address, more than reinforces that reputation. From the Thai-silk-and-wood-covered walls to the model-like servers to the luminous reflecting pool where candles float peacefully in the restaurant's center, everything is pristine at Kittichai. But don't let all that style intimidate you from trying the restaurant's inventive and flavorful food. Kittichai offers Thai tapas and, of these, the fish cakes and the sesame-spiced chicken lollipops stand out. And even a vegetarian might be tempted by the chocolate back-ribs appetizer. For the entrees, I was extremely content with the hearty short ribs in green curry while the clay-pot prawns with vermicelli and prosciutto (that Thai sta-ple) was like nothing I'd ever had in any other Thai restaurant. Despite the peaceful aura created by the design, Kittichai can reach high decibel levels, so be prepared.

60 Thompson St. (btwn Broome and Spring sts.). © 212/219-2000. www.kittichairestaurant.com. Reservations rec-ommended. Appetizers $7–$19; main courses $19–$36. Sun–Wed 5:30–11pm; Thurs–Sat 5:30pm–midnight. Subway C, E to Spring St.

MODERATE

Cendrillon 🍴🍴 *Finds* FILIPINO/ASIAN   In SoHo, whether dining, drinking, or shopping, you must be on guard for excessive pretense. But there is nothing preten-tious about Cendrillon. This is authentic yet innovative Filipino food in a comfort-able setting with exposed brick, a skylight in the main dining room, and cozy booths up front. How authentic? Try a shot of *lambagong*, also known as coconut grappa. It's a potent alcoholic drink distilled from the coconut flower sap and blended with sugarcane sap, and as far as I know, Cendrillon is the only restaurant in New York to serve this Filipino specialty. The drink will ignite your appetite for the flavors to follow, like the amazing squash soup with crab dumplings or the fresh *lumpia* with tamarind and peanut sauce (Asian vegetables wrapped in a purple-yam–and-rice wrapper). Cendrillon's chicken adobo (chicken braised in a marinade of vinegar, soy, chiles, and garlic) renders the bird as tender and tasty as you could ever imagine, while Romy's (the chef/owner) spareribs, marinated in rice wine and garlic, rubbed with spices, and cooked in a Chinese smokehouse, are as good as any ribs I've had cooked in a Texas smokehouse. You'll be tempted by just about everything on this menu, but save room for the exotic desserts like the Buko pie, made with coconut and topped with vanilla-bean ice cream, or the *halo halo*, a parfait stuffed with ice creams and sorbets with flavors like avocado, jackfruit, and purple yam.

45 Mercer St. (btwn Broome and Grand sts.). © 212/343-9012. www.cendrillon.com. Main courses $15–$24. AE, DISC, MC, V. Sun 11am–10pm; Tues–Sat 11am–10:30pm. Subway: N/R to Prince St.; 6 to Spring St.; 1/9 to Canal St.; A, C, E to Canal St.

Lupa *★★* *Value* ROMAN ITALIAN Since it first opened in late 1999, this Roman-style *osteria h*as remained a hot ticket. For one, it's blessed with an impeccable pedigree: One of its owners is Mario Batali, the Food TV "Iron Chef" who has built a mini-empire in the Manhattan restaurant world. Second, it offers high-quality food at good value—you can eat well here and not have to max out your credit card. And finally, the food is consistently tasty—but don't expect big portions. That's part of the secret to the good value, but don't worry—you won't starve. The menu is thoughtful and creative, focusing on lusty Roman fare like ricotta gnocchi with sausage and fennel, or pork saltimbocca. Wines, too, have been thoughtfully chosen, and you can order a bottle from the extensive list or sample one of several varieties that come in a carafe. Here, perhaps more than at any other Batali enterprise, the service hits just the right notes: Servers are both warm and supremely knowledgeable. Make a reservation, or go early to snag one of the tables set aside for walk-ins.

170 Thompson St. (btwn Houston and Bleecker sts.). © 212/982-5089. www.luparestaurant.com. Reservations recommended. *Primi* $9–$16; *secondi* $16–$20. AE, MC, V. Daily noon–midnight. Subway: B, D, F, Q, A, C, E to W. 4th St.

Pao! *★* PORTUGUESE New York has multiple restaurants of almost every ethnicity, yet there is a surprising scarcity of Portuguese eateries. Of the few, this cozy, comfortable charmer is the best. Pao!, which translates to bread, keeps it simple, and the results are pure and authentic. Start with *caldo verde*, traditional Portuguese soup, made with kale, potatoes, and wonderfully smoky *linguica* (Portuguese sausage). The baked-octopus salad, tender and soaked in a garlic/cilantro vinaigrette, rivals any I've had in numerous Greek restaurants, while the cod cakes, another Portuguese standard, are light and not too salty. The combination of pork and seafood might seem odd, but it's common in Portugal; Pao!'s pairing of pork and clams is an acquired taste—one I've happily acquired. Salt cod is to Portugal what hamburgers are to the United States, and I'll take Pao!'s hearty *bacalhau a braz*—salt cod with egg, onion, and straw potatoes—over hamburger most any day. To complement the food, stick with a delicious Portuguese wine, from which there are many to choose. Desserts are egg-based and delicate; the soft pound cake with lemon egg custard filling is heavenly.

322 Spring St. (at Greenwich St.). © 212/334-5464. Reservations recommended. AE, DC, MC, V. Lunch $12–$14; dinner $17–$20. Mon–Fri noon–2:30pm; daily 6–11pm. Subway: C, E to Spring St.

INEXPENSIVE

Also consider **Lombardi's Pizza,** 32 Spring St., between Mott and Mulberry streets (© 212/941-7994; see "Pizza, New York–Style," p. 196).

Bread ⓕ ITALIAN   The older, smaller sibling of **Bread Tribeca** (p. 164) does bread like no other sandwich shop. The bread comes from Balthazar Bakery down the street, but it's what they do with it that makes this eatery so special. For example, they take a rustic ciabatta loaf, slather it with Sicilian sardines, Thai mayonnaise, tomato, and lettuce, and then turn it over to their panini press. The result is a gooey convergence of flavors that you will attempt to gobble down gracefully. It *will* fall apart, but that's okay; someone will be along shortly with more napkins. Besides the spectacular sardine sandwich, the Italian tuna with mesclun greens and tomatoes in a lemon dressing, and the fontina with grilled zucchini, eggplant, arugula, and tomato in a balsamic vinaigrette are also standouts. Really, there are no losers on the bread side of Bread's menu, which also includes salads, pastas, and "plates." The 32-seat restaurant is in chic Nolita, and if you are lucky, you might even be treated by the sight of a breathtakingly thin model doing her best to keep the contents of one of Bread's sandwiches from staining her designer duds.

20 Spring St. (btwn Mott & Elizabeth sts.). © 212/334-1015. Reservations not accepted. Breads $7–$9.50; plates $6–$16. AE, DC, DISC, MC, V. Daily 10:30am–midnight. Subway: 6 to Spring St.

6 The East Village & NoHo

To locate the restaurants reviewed below, see the map on p. 163.

EXPENSIVE

Le Miu ⓕⓕ *Finds* JAPANESE   What happens when four celebrated Japanese chefs from various notable restaurants (Nobu 57 and Megu to name two) come together to open their own joint? In some cases, the result could be chaos, but in the case of Le Miu, good things happened. The restaurant, a slim, austere space tucked away on a bustling East Village block, is a refuge for those seeking absolutely fresh, delicately prepared sushi standards along with some interesting innovations. The Le Miu tartar, tuna, yellowtail, and salmon tartar topped with caviar is a welcoming beginning followed by sardine with ginger ceviche. The Saikyo miso marinated black cod in a phyllo jacket and the king crab leg with a curry milk sauce are revelations that I will now have to happily schlep down to the East Village to continue to experience, especially since the prices, for sushi this good, are hard to beat. Le Miu also has an impressive hot- and cold-sake list—the perfect companion to the chef's creations.

107 Ave. A (btwn 6th and 7th sts.). © 212/473-3100. www.lemiusushi.com. Reservations recommended. Prix-fixe $55–$75; main courses $14–$28. AE, DC, MC, V. Tues–Sun 5:30pm–midnight. Subway: F, V to Second Ave.

MODERATE

Brick Lane Curry House ⓕ *Finds* INDIAN   The vibrancy of the traditional Indian restaurants, seemingly interconnected on the block of East 6th Street known as "Little India," has diminished over the years, but this relatively new addition has added some welcome vigor. The food is so good at Brick Lane that they don't even need the requisite sitar players to draw in customers. But beware: They don't compromise on their spice. In fact, they might just have the hottest dish to be found in the city. It's a curry called "*phaal*" that requires a verbal disclaimer by the customer to not hold the restaurant liable for any physical or emotional damage incurred from eating it. If you

Moments Old Friends

New York has many restaurants that are considered institutions; places that have been around forever and are known throughout the world. When you think of classic New York restaurants that have survived for decades, you might think of the **Carnegie Deli** (see the box "The New York Deli News," later in this chapter), the **Grand Central Oyster Bar** (p. 205), or **Peter Luger Steakhouse** (p. 220). But there are countless lesser-known restaurants that can also be considered New York institutions. You may not have heard of them, but those of us who live here know about them. The menus remain pretty much the same; not succumbing to the ever-changing food trends, the service is usually old-school; turnover is low and your waiter will probably recognize you from your last visit, which might have been a year or two earlier. At these places, it's not about the quality of the food, which will most likely not be four-star, it's more about the familiar. And there is always something comforting about the familiar.

I first experienced Chinatown's **Wo Hop,** 17 Mott St., between Worth and Mosco streets (*©* **212/267-2536**), established in 1938, when I was in college. Of course it had to be cheap, and you couldn't find a cheaper restaurant in New York. It was open 24 hours—I have fond memories of dining late at night and then ascending the stairs from the subterranean restaurant to witness a sunny dawn; portions were huge and the food was dense. Time has stood still at Wo Hop, and though the prices have gone up, it's still one of the cheapest eateries in the city, still open 24 hours, and still dishing out huge portions of dense food. Here you'll find those Chinese-American classics you might remember from your youth: egg drop soup, chow mein, egg foo young, subgum (bonus points to anyone who knows what "subgum" means) vegetables. And though most of the food here is heavily battered and swimming in corn-starch-thickened "brown" sauces, either oyster or black bean, there is no denying Wo Hop's comfort level.

At around the same time I discovered Wop Hop, I was introduced to **Vincent's Clam Bar,** 119 Mott St., at Hester Street (*©* **212/226-8133**; www. originalvincents.com), a few blocks up in Little Italy. At the time, there was still a remnant of what Little Italy used to be that is now gone. But Vincent's has been around since 1904, and though like the rest of Little Italy, there is

are able to finish it, the restaurant promises a bottle of beer on the house. But there is no need to blister your intestines: The other, less hazardous, curries will bring on a good enough sweat, including the excellent Madras and the tangy Goan. Brick Lane's signature *boti* rolls (chicken tikka served in fresh-baked bread) are special while the *rassam* soup of the day, a thin, clear soup that changes daily, will help clear your sinuses even before you touch a curry. There are also a number of vegan items.

306–308 E. 6th St. (btwn First and Second aves.). *©* 212/979-2900. www.bricklanecurryhouse.com. Reservations recommended. Appetizers $6–$10; curries $12–$19. AE, DC, DISC, MC, V. Sun–Thurs noon–11pm; Fri–Sat noon–1am. Subway: 6 to Astor Place.

a touristy, theme-restaurant atmosphere to it, where else can you actually still order that old Italian-American favorite, scungilli? Like the shrinking Italian presence in Little Italy, scungilli (sliced conch) has practically disappeared from the menus of Italian restaurants. Here they pile it so high on top of your linguine that if you are able to eat it all, you just might begin to understand why its demand has dwindled. Vincent's tomato sauce is unique and tastes exactly how I remember it from my first visit; rich and tomato-paste-thickened. It comes in three flavors, sweet, medium, and hot, but beware: The hot is fiery, and the best way to experience it is with a semi-stale biscuit and as an accompaniment to fried seafood.

I admit I'm a relative newcomer to **El Faro** ⟨R⟩, 823 Greenwich St., at Horatio Street (ⓒ **212/929-8210**; www.elfaronyc.com), the oldest Spanish restaurant in New York, which will celebrate its 80th birthday in 2007. But one visit and you will feel like you are a regular and longtime friend of the Lurgis family, who has owned the restaurant since 1959. Maybe you'll get to sit in what was writer James Baldwin's favorite corner table—the restaurant is mentioned in his biography—or one of the tables off the bar, possibly the one where a resident ghost is rumored to occasionally sit. The menu features dishes brought from Spain that are now familiar, such as *paella a la Valenciana,* shrimp *al ajillo,* and *mariscada* (mixed seafood) with green sauce. All this is complemented with El Faro's potent signature sangria, also known as "truth serum."

People ask me for recommendations for a "real deal" diner in New York. My answer is always: **Eisenberg's Coffee Shop,** 174 Fifth Ave., at 22nd Street (ⓒ **212/675-5096**). This old-world luncheonette has been dishing up the same eggs/bacon/burgers/sandwiches since 1929, at pretty much the same prices—adjusted slightly for inflation, of course. The waiters and cooks seemingly have been working at Eisenberg's since the Eisenhower era. More likely than not, you'll be greeted with a growled "Hiya, sweetheart," or a gravelly "What'll it be, love?" If a tuna sandwich were on a "Best of" list, Eisenberg's version would win. Feel a little run down? A bowl of Eisenberg's matzo-ball soup will perk you up. Or sit at the counter and order an egg cream with real, from-the-bottle, seltzer.

Mo Pitkin's House of Satisfaction ⟨R⟩ *Finds* JEWISH/LATINO   I've had Chino-Latino food, but the Judeo-Latino mix at Mo Pitkin's is a first for me—and possibly for New York. The legend (and I stress "legend") is that Mo was a Chino-Latino short-order cook as well as a porter at an East Broadway *mikvah,* thus his love for all things Jewish-Latino took hold. That love is seen on the playful menu where, though it may not sound like an appetizing combination, you can pair potato latkes with ceviche. Or better yet, start with matzo-ball soup followed by shrimp *al ajillo.* The best way to experience the Judeo-Latino mix at Mo's is the "Pickins" appetizer plate, where you can combine any six items including chorizo meatballs, chopped liver, deviled eggs, whitefish *escabeche,* beef brisket (fiery with horseradish), and sherry-marinated mushrooms served on a gorgeous platter with inscriptions in Hebrew. Just don't ask your waiter for translations. The "Cuban Reuben," corn beef and coleslaw paired with slices of roast pork, is a revelation. Of the entrees, the Hartman Family Brisket (Mo's is owned by Phil and Jesse Hartman) is tender and thick with gravy just like your Jewish grandmother would make—and in fact, the recipe is from the Hartman brothers' grandmother. The dining room features roomy leather banquettes while upstairs there is a performance space with live music and comedy acts that's become a happening venue (there's a cover charge for the performances).

34 Ave. A (btwn 2nd and 3rd sts.). (✆ 212/777-5660. www.mopitkins.com. Main courses $10–$22. AE, DISC, MC, V. Sun–Wed 5pm–midnight; Thurs–Sat 5pm–2am. Subway: F, V to Second Ave.

INEXPENSIVE

Veselka ✫ UKRAINIAN DINER   Whenever the craving hits for hearty eastern European fare at old-world prices, Veselka fits the bill with fluffy and light (if that's possible) pierogi (small doughy envelopes filled with potatoes, cheese, or sauerkraut), *kasha varnishkes* (cracked buckwheat and noodles with mushroom sauce), stuffed cabbage, grilled Polish kielbasa, freshly made potato pancakes, and classic soups, like a sublime borscht. Breakfast is special here (see "Breakfast, Not Brunch," p. 215). If all you want is a burger, don't worry—it's a classic, too.

Despite the authentic fare, the diner is comfortable, modern, and appealing, with an artsy slant and delicious house-made desserts. Veselka surpasses its status as a popular after-hours hangout with clubbers and other night owls to be a favorite at any hour.

144 Second Ave. (at 9th St.). (✆ 212/228-9682. Reservations not accepted. Main courses $5–$13. AE, DC, DISC, MC, V. Daily 24 hr. Subway: 6 to Astor Place.

7 Greenwich Village & the Meat-Packing District

EXPENSIVE

A.O.C. Bedford ✫✫ *Finds* MEDITERRANEAN   You'll find this brick-walled, cozy, romantic charmer tucked away on equally cozy and romantic Bedford Street in the West Village. Here the A.O.C. in the restaurant name stands for *appellation d'origine controlee*—the French designation for high-quality food products. But on the menu you'll not only find A.O.C. products from France, but D.O.C, the Italian designation, and D.O, the Spanish. If the appetizer of octopus "carpaccio" is on the menu, which changes seasonally, your octopus, pounded thin and tender, will be served with D.O. dry red pepper from Spain, and A.O.C *fleur de sel* from France or the Caesar salad will have D.O.C-grade Parmesan cheese from Italy. But you won't need all those designations to know that what you are eating is of high quality—just a few bites will suffice. The paella marinera, a constant on the menu, is prepared for two, stuffed with jumbo shrimp (heads on for more flavor), squid, scallops, mussels, and clams and cooked in Spanish Calasparra rice. Another standout is the duck, a crispy breast prepared best medium rare, and served with a Bosc pear. Finish with a selection of cheeses, A.O.C., D.O.C.-, and D.O.-quality only, of course. The restaurant has an impressive wine list and bottles are decanted at your table.

14 Bedford St. (btwn Sixth Ave. and Downing St.). (✆ 212/414-4764. www.aocbedford.com. Reservations recommended. Main courses $21–$32. AE, DC, MC, V. Sun–Thurs 5:30–11pm; Fri–Sat 5:30–11:30pm. Subway: 1 to Houston St.

Mas ✫✫ *Finds* FRENCH   I've never had the pleasure of dining in a French country farmhouse, but if the experience at Mas is anything like it, I know now what I've been

Where to Dine in Greenwich Village & the Meat-Packing District

A.O.C. Bedford **12**
Barbuto **3**
Dani **14**
El Faro **2**
Gray's Papaya **8**
Joe's Pizza **10**
John's Pizza **9**

Mandoo Bar **7**
Maremma **4**
Mas **13**
Murray's Bagels **5**
Paradou **1**
Rare Bar & Grill **11**
Strip House **6**

Ⓜ Subway stop

missing. This "farmhouse" is located in the West Village, and though there are nods to the rustic in the decor with wood beams and a bar of sandstone with stools made from tree trunks from one of the owner's farms in Massachusetts, there is also an atmosphere of sophistication. A glass-enclosed wine cellar is visible from the small dining room, the restaurant stays open late, and you'll find hipsters in jeans and T-shirts as well as folks in power suits. And it's that combination, along with the creative menu, that makes Mas so special. The dishes are innovative and the ingredients are fresh, many supplied by upstate New York farms. The tender, perfectly prepared braised pork belly, from Flying Pig Farm, is served with polenta and a stew of escargot and lima beans; the duck breast, from Stone Church Farm, melds magically with apple puree, sautéed Brussels sprouts, and chestnuts; and the trout Piscator, rainbow trout from the Neversink River, is stuffed with watercress and smoked trout and topped with a tangy apple-and-horseradish dressing. Service is low-key but attentive, and the seating, though somewhat cramped, is not enough to dim the romantic aura.

39 Downing St. (btwn Bedford and Varick sts.). (C) 212/255-1790. Reservations recommended. 4-course tasting menu $68; 6-course $95; main courses $32–$36. AE, DC, DISC, MC, V. Mon–Sat 6pm–4am (small-plate tasting menu after 11:30pm). Subway: 1 to Houston St.

Paradou (R) (Finds) FRENCH It's nice to find a restaurant in the overhyped hysteria of the Meat Packing District where you can actually have a conversation. Even better is that the food here, traditional Provencal cuisine, is as down to earth and genuine as the restaurant itself. Take your time with a glass of Chablis while grazing on the *assiette de la terre,* a French antipasto plate with artisanal hams, salami, pate, asparagus and haricort vert. The menu changes seasonally, but you'll always find the *zaatar* chicken "under brick" with truffled mashed potatoes, and for good reason. It's hard to order anything else, it's that good. The staff is helpful and the environment here is fun with regular events like "Dirty Bingo," live music, and frequent wine tastings. The restaurant also features a lovely garden, enclosed in the winter, for year round use.

8 Little W. 12th St (at Ninth Ave.) (C) 212/463-8345. www.paradounyc.com. Entrees: $19–$25. AE, MC, V. Mon–Wed 6pm–midnight; Thurs–Fri 6pm–1am; Sat noon–1am; Sun noon–10pm. Subway: A, C, E to 14th St.

Strip House (R)(R) STEAKS With a photo gallery of seminude burlesque performers decorating the red velvet walls, roomy burgundy banquettes, and a steady flow of lounge music, you may, as I once did, mistakenly refer to the Strip House as the Strip Club. But despite the faux-*Playboy* look, the only decadence here is in the titanic portions of perfectly charred and seasoned red meat, specifically, the strip steak. I had the strip on the bone that I still remember with fondness. The filet mignon is simply and impeccably prepared and the porterhouse for two, carved at your table, is in the Peter Luger league. The sides here are innovative variations on the standards: creamed spinach with black truffles, french fries with herbs and garlic, and, best of all, the crisp goose-fat potatoes. Is goose fat a good fat or a bad fat? Only your dietitian knows for sure, but if you have a dietitian, you're probably in the wrong restaurant. Desserts are monumental, especially the multilayered chocolate cake, so have your waiter bring extra forks for sharing. With the exception of those few banquettes, seating is tight, so don't expect intimacy—unless it is with your neighbor.

13 E. 12th St. (btwn University Place and Fifth Ave.). (C) 212/328-0000. www.striphouse.net Reservations recommended. Main courses $28–$51. AE, DC, DISC, MC, V. Sun–Thurs 5–11pm; Fri–Sat 5pm–midnight. Subway: L, N, R, Q, 4, 5, 6 to 14th St./Union Sq.

MODERATE

Barbuto COUNTRY ITALIAN   Star chef Jonathan Waxman returned to New York after 12 years away to helm the quietly elegant Washington Park (now defunct) but ended up cooking in an open kitchen in the looser, more casual environs of this West Village trattoria. The food is fresh and solid, and many of the best dishes are prepared in the blazing wood-fired oven. Start with salt cod cakes and baby greens; a good pasta choice is the Genovese-style penne *rigate* and pesto with haricots verts. The space has a sunny feel and gets cooking in the warm weather, when the garage-style doors are folded up and the alfresco space takes on a party atmosphere.

775 Washington St. (at W. 12th St.). ✆ **212/924-9700**. www.barbutonyc.com. Reservations recommended. Main courses $18–$25. AE, DC, MC, V. Mon–Wed noon–11pm; Fri–Sat noon–midnight; Sun noon–10pm. Subway: A, C, E to 14th St.

Maremma ITALIAN/WESTERN   Maremma's chef/owner, Cesare Casella, is the Sergio Leone of the New York restaurant scene. Leone was the director of many "spaghetti Westerns," and in 2005 Casella opened New York's first and only spaghetti Western restaurant. Maremma is the name of the rocky, rough coastal region of Tuscany where Italian cowboys roam the land and the menu is the unlikely mix of Tuscan and cowboy cuisine. Here you'll find small plates on the menu like Casella's spin on the traditional sloppy Joe he calls "sloppy Giuseppe," made with tender pieces of shredded beef over thick-crusted Tuscan bread, or the *bordatino di mare*, sticks of fried seafood with a crispy polenta crust served with spicy "Tuscan ketchup." The addition of chocolate to the wild-boar ragu that covers the fresh pappardelle is Casella's nod to the West, while a touch of bourbon Westernizes the tomato-and-*grana-padano* sauce served over artisanal pasta. The Tuscan fries, traditional fries but with herbs and garlic sprinkled on them, are an addictive revelation. Not only is Maremma the only Italian/Western restaurant in New York, it is also probably the only restaurant in New York that serves Rocky Mountain oysters (also known as bull's testicles). Are you cowboy enough to try them?

228 W. 10th St. (between Bleecker and Hudson sts.). ✆ **212/645-0200**. Reservations recommended. Small plates $9 $12; big plates $16–$28. AE, DC, DISC, MC, V. Mon–Wed 5:30–11pm; Thurs–Sat 5:30pm–midnight. Subway: 1 to Christopher St.

INEXPENSIVE

The downtown branch of **Gray's Papaya** is at 402 Sixth Ave., at 8th Street (✆ **212/260-3532**). The original **John's Pizzeria** is at 278 Bleecker St., near Seventh Avenue (✆ **212/243-1680;** see "Pizza, New York–Style," on p. 196). For one of the best slices of pizza, go to **Joe's Pizza,** 7 Carmine St., at Bleecker Street (✆ **212/255-3948**). Also, you'll find **Murray's Bagels** at 500 Sixth Ave., between 12th and 13th streets (✆ **212/462-2830;** see "The Hole Truth: N.Y.'s Best Bagels," on p. 189).

Also consider the new Greenwich Village outpost of the Korean dumpling house **Mandoo Bar,** 71 University Place (✆ **212/358-0400**).

8 Chelsea

To locate the restaurants in this section, see the map on p. 180.

EXPENSIVE

Buddakan ✿ ASIAN   Is Buddakan a bus depot disguised as a nightclub with a restaurant inside, or is it a restaurant with a night club persona housed inside a garishly

Where to Dine in Midtown, Chelsea, Flatiron District & Gramercy Park

Abboccato **58**
Afghan Kebab House **5**
Anthos **53**
Aquavit **56**
A Voce **40**
Barbetta **10**
Becco **9**
Benjamin Steakhouse **48**
Blue Smoke **41**
BLT Fish **28**
BLT Steak **58**
Bombay Talkie **24**
Brgr **20**
Buddakan **26**
Burger Joint **59**
Carmine's **15**
Carnegie Deli **2**
City Bakery **30**
Cookshop **25**
Country **43**
Daisy Mae's BBQ **11**
DB Bistro Moderne **50**
Devi **29**
Eisenberg's Coffee Shop **34**
Ess-A-Bagel **32, 52**
Frankie & Johnnie's **12, 46**
John's Pizza **14**
Junior's Cheescake **49**
Kalustyan's **42**
Keen's Steakhouse **45**
Kobe Club **60**
La Nacional **27**
Le Bernardin **6**
Mandoo Bar **44**
Marseille **13**
Metro Marche **17**
Michael Jordan's Steakhouse **49**
Mickey Mantle's **62**
Molyvos **1**
Murray's Bagels **22**
New York Burger Co. **35, 38**
Norma's **59**
Oceana **54**
Oyster Bar & Restaurant **49**
Pampano **51**

continues on opposite page

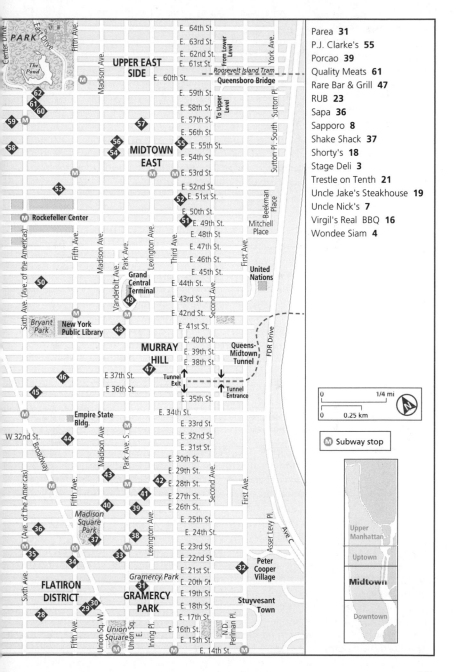

Parea **31**
P.J. Clarke's **55**
Porcao **39**
Quality Meats **61**
Rare Bar & Grill **47**
RUB **23**
Sapa **36**
Sapporo **8**
Shake Shack **37**
Shorty's **18**
Stage Deli **3**
Trestle on Tenth **21**
Uncle Jake's Steakhouse **19**
Uncle Nick's **7**
Virgil's Real BBQ **16**
Wondee Siam **4**

designed—Buddha icons along with Renaissance Bacchanal paintings—bus depot? My expectations were of a loud, dance club scene in a large, 16,000-square-feet bi-level space where the food would be showy, but flavorless. I was right about the loud, dance club scene, but I was wrong about the flavorless food. The "Brasserie" is the main dining room on the lower level and the steps can seem steep after a few too many cocktails in the upstairs lounge like the signature *Heat,* a combination of tequila, Cointreau, and chilled cucumbers. Though they were not steep enough to deter a man from being carried down in his wheelchair on the night I dined there. To fortify yourself after those cocktails don't hesitate to order some of Buddakan's superb appetizers like the edamame dumplings, the crab and corn fritters, and most notably, the crispy calamari salad. In fact, you can make your meal out of sharing appetizer—the extensive menu at Buddakan works best for large parties and has the now obligatory "communal" table. But if you order one entrée, make sure it's the sizzling short rib; tender and removed from the bone and sitting on top of a bed of mushroom chow fun.

75 Ninth Ave (at 16th St.). ℂ 212/989-6699. www.buddakannyc.com. Dim Sum–appetizers $9–$13; main courses $17–$35. AE, DC, MC, V. Hours: Sun–Wed 5:30pm–midnight; Thurs–Sat 5:30pm–1am. Subway: A, C, E to 14th St.

Cookshop ⓡⓡ AMERICAN   On far west Tenth Avenue, with a prime view of a parking garage across the street, Cookshop is brawny and boisterous with food to match. Seating can be tight and you would hear your neighbor's conversation if it weren't so loud in the restaurant. But never mind: enjoy the chef's creations. A pizza with shaved king oyster mushrooms and *stracchino* cheese or the grilled Montauk squid in a *salsa verde* make good starters to complement the restaurant's innovative cocktails. Or combine a few of the snacks like the addictive fried spiced hominy or the smoked pork tacos as starters for the table. Cookshop offers entree options in four categories: sauté, grill, wood oven, and rotisserie. The whole roasted porgy, head and all, cooked in the wood oven is moist and full of flavor, while the chili-braised beef short ribs served over cheddar grits from the sauté section are properly tender to the bone. Service is casually efficient and helpful. Maybe Cookshop's emergence to restaurant-barren Tenth Avenue will be the beginnings of a new eating mecca.

156 Tenth Ave. (at 20th St.). ℂ 212/924-4440. www.cookshopny.com. Reservations recommended. Main courses $21–$36. AE, DC, MC, V. Mon–Sat 5:30pm–midnight; Sun 11:30am–3pm and 5:30–10pm. Subway: C, E to 23rd St.

Trestle On Tenth ⓡ   MODERN SWISS/FRENCH   There was a bar/restaurant on the corner of 24th and Tenth Avenue that, for many years, I used to frequent where the pints were good and cheap and the burgers satisfying. It had a garden and fireplace to add to the homey ambiance and it was one of the few places to eat on what was once-desolate Tenth Avenue. That place is gone, but in its location is Trestle on Tenth where the ambiance is still homey, but now mimics the burgeoning development of the West Chelsea neighborhood. The fireplace is no longer in use, but the garden is and instead of burgers, chef/owner Ralf Kuettel has devised an innovative Alpine-based menu: Alpine meaning the food is drawn from influences of the northern regions of France and Kuettel's native Switzerland. Start with a selection of cured meats and aged Swiss cheeses to accompany a glass of wine or a pint of hearty beer. The salad of butter lettuce speckled with thick bits of smoked bacon in a buttermilk dressing is a good prelude to one of the restaurant's many robust entrée options like the unique lamb saddle layered on mustard greens with cippolini onions, the lamb bordered by a layer of fat purposely kept on to keep the meat tender and moist. For something less rich, opt for the seared wild sturgeon with baby bok choy and hen of the wood mushrooms. Trestle on Tenth is the perfect place to unwind and ponder the art you might have experienced at some of the neighborhood's numerous galleries.

242 Tenth Ave. (at 24th St.) ℂ 212/645-5659. www.trestleontenth.com. Main Courses; $18–$24. AE, DC, MC, V. Tue–Thurs noon–3pm and 5:30–10:30pm; Fri noon–3pm and 5:30–11pm; Sat 5:30–11pm; Sun 5:30–10pm. Subway: C, E to 23rd St.

MODERATE

Bombay Talkie 🏵 INDIAN   If it's in any way possible while dining in a stylish, modern restaurant in Chelsea, try to imagine you are on the streets of Bombay and you are hungry. There are inexpensive food options everywhere on those streets, and here at Bombay Talkie, with a Bollywood movie constantly playing behind the bar and a soundtrack on the speakers to match, some of those options are replicated for you in a much more comfortable environment. You can munch on a *dosa,* a thin, lightly fried bread stuffed with coconut and mustard-seed chicken or spiced potatoes. Or you might want to try the *Pau Bhaji,* grilled bread served with mixed, gingery vegetables. Whatever you choose, wash it down with one of the restaurant's innovative cocktails, like a passionfruit margarita or an Indian beer. The restaurant has two levels, a few booths on the lower level, and a long communal table, fun for large groups. Bombay Talkie is the perfect spot for a respite from Chelsea gallery-hopping.

189 Ninth Ave. (btwn 21st and 22nd sts.). ℂ 212/242-1900. www.bombaytalkie.com. Reservations recommended. Street bites $6–$9; main courses $11–$16. AE, MC, V. Sun–Thurs 5–10:30pm; Fri–Sat 5–11:30pm. Subway: C, E to 23rd St.

La Nacional 🏵🏵 *(Finds)* SPANISH/TAPAS   It's not easy finding the oldest Spanish restaurant in New York; in fact, the search for this unmarked restaurant on West 14th Street might get you a bit frustrated. Once you find it though, your perseverance will be rewarded. Founded in 1868 as a gathering spot for the Benevolent Spanish Society, La Nacional, a social club, is a hidden treat. At one time food was secondary to the company of Spanish expatriates who congregated here, filling the room with smoke and loud talk of Spanish politics and football. It was here where Gabriel Garcia Lorca spent countless hours documenting his New York City experience. The cigarette smoke has been replaced by the smoke of the grill, which turns out tasty tapas with sardines, octopus, and shrimp. There is a somewhat formal dining room in the front, while in the back, next to the open kitchen, there are a few tables and TVs usually tuned to soccer matches. Come and share a bottle of Spanish wine and make a meal out of the tapas—the *albondigas* (Spanish meatballs), *boquerones* (white anchovy filets), and aforementioned octopus are my favorites—or you can order the restaurant's excellent paella. Tapas range from $4 to $9 while no entree is more than $18. In a ballroom on the second level, the club sponsors flamenco performances and dance lessons.

239 W. 14th St. (btwn Seventh and Eighth aves.). ℂ 212/243-9308. Tapas $7–$9; main courses $16–$18. AE, DC, DISC, MC, V. Sun–Wed noon–10pm; Thurs–Sat noon–11pm. Subway: A, C, E, 1, 2, 3 to 14th St.

RUB 🏵🏵 BARBECUE   RUB is short for Righteous Urban Barbecue—a contradiction in terms if there ever was one. Since when was barbecue an urban thing—not to mention righteous? But I confess, the name is cool and after tasting some of the BBQ that comes out of the restaurant's custom-made, New York City Health Department–approved smoker, righteous is an apt description. Co-owned by Kansas City pit master Paul Kirk, who has won seven World Barbecue Championships and is a member of the Barbecue Hall of Fame, the arrival of RUB in New York in 2005 was eagerly anticipated

The Prime Cut: Steaks! Steaks! Steaks!

New York, some say, is the city that never sleeps. It's also, apparently, the city that can't get enough steak. The number of prime-cut palaces just continues to sprout like mushrooms. **Peter Luger Steakhouse** ✿✿ (p. 220) has been the steakhouse standard for years, but it gets a serious run for it's money from, stylishly ensconced in the TimeWarner Center, newcomer **Porter House New York** ✿✿ (p. 208) Beginning the steak as style trend a few years back was **BLT Steak** ✿✿✿ (p. 200), which proves there is substance with the style. Going overboard on the style side as well as pretty much everything else is **Kobe Club,** ✿ (p. 190) the nightclub posing as a steakhouse specializing in its namesake beef. Despite its bawdy name, **Strip House** ✿✿ (p. 178) steaks are no-nonsense. Wall Street traders and financial bigwigs often have carnivorous reputations and at **Harry's Steak and Café** ✿✿ (p. 162) they don't have to go far to satisfy their cravings. Some of the city's oldest restaurants are steakhouses and two of the oldest of those are **Frankie & Johnnie's** ✿✿ (p. 191) and **Keens Steakhouse** ✿✿✿ (p. 192) which was formerly known as a chophouse for their selection of chops like their acclaimed mutton chop. Here are some more meateries to try:

Don't expect an overpriced burger factory with waiters in Bulls jerseys and basketball-shaped plates from **Michael Jordan's—The Steak House** ✿✿, on the mezzanine level overlooking the main concourse at Grand Central Terminal (✆ **212/655-2300;** www.theglaziergroup.com). Bursting with Beaux Arts–meets–Art Deco grandeur, Michael Jordan's is wholly for grownups. And with a perfect view of the legendary sky ceiling, this is more than just the city's best-looking steakhouse—it's an incredible "only in New York" dining experience.

One of the best of the traditional old-world steakhouses is the clubby, fun **Bull and Bear,** in the Waldorf=Astoria, 301 Park Ave., between 49th and

by those barbecue fanatics who are aware that there is a Barbecue Hall of Fame. Could chef Kirk replicate what he achieved at competitions in his New York restaurant, where pollutant-inducing smokers are illegal? The answer is no. You will never get that true smoked taste without creating some serious smoke, but that doesn't mean what you do get at RUB is bad. On the contrary, the smoked turkey and barbecued chicken are the best I've had; moist inside with a distinctive smoked flavor, and the ribs, St. Louis–style, were delicate and crispy, yet tender and meaty. The "burnt ends," the fatty part of the brisket, however, were a bit tough. The best way to get a taste of all of RUB's barbecue is the humongous "Taste of the Baron," where a little of everything is piled high on a platter. The restaurant is cramped and loud and the prices urban (meaning high) but the food at RUB will provide all the comfort you need.

208 W. 23rd St. (btwn Seventh and Eighth aves.). ✆ **212/524-4300.** www.rubbbq.net. Sandwiches $9–$12; platters $15–$23; Taste of the Baron $46; AE, MC, V. Tues–Thurs noon–11pm; Fri–Sat noon–midnight. Subway: 1 to 23rd St.

50th streets (© **212/872-4900**), which serves the best New York strip I've had in the city.

There are better steaks to be had in New York, but there aren't many better steakhouses than **Ben Benson's Steakhouse,** 123 W. 52nd St., between Sixth and Seventh avenues (© **212/581-8888**; www.benbensons.com). Smack in the middle of Midtown, Ben Benson's is loud and large, and though it's definitely a man's world at Ben's, women are treated with "respect" here.

Like Ben Benson's, **Uncle Jack's Steakhouse** ⍟, 440 Ninth Ave., at 34th St. (© **212/244-0005**; www.unclejacks.com), is testosterone-fueled and the decor is plush and bawdy with huge banquettes. Portions are monstrous; the 48-ounce porterhouse, Uncle Jack's signature dish, is large enough for a big family.

Most entrees at these steakhouses tend to fall in the $22-to-$38 range. Always book ahead and inquire about dress codes, especially at the old-school spots.

There are steakhouses with claims to Peter Luger's all over the city, a few started by ex-Luger waiters. But the **Benjamin Steakhouse** ⍟, 52 E. 41st St, in the Dylan Hotel (© **212/297-9177**; www.benjaminsteakhouse.com), is the only one to feature an ex-chef, Chef Arturo, from Luger's. The result is not quite Luger's quality steaks, but with better service and in a dramatic room highlighted by a huge walk-in fireplace.

Like the Benjamin, **Quality Meats** ⍟ 57 W. 58th St., between Fifth and Sixth Aves. (© **212/371-7777**), is set in a stunning, bi-level space designed by the famous team of AvroKO (Sapa, p. 187). And the quality of the food matches the quality of the design with some non-traditional steakhouse menu items like pan-roasted lamb t-bones with figs and mint and a flatiron steak with blackberries.

9 Union Square, the Flatiron District & Gramercy Park

To locate the restaurants in this section, see the map on p. 180.

EXPENSIVE

A Voce ⍟⍟ MODERN ITALIAN   The kind of food that is served at A Voce; rustic Italian for the most part with exceptional nods to innovation, seems somewhat out of place in the loud, postmodern dining room in a sleek high rise just off Madison Park. The restaurant would, I believe, be better suited in the Art Deco New York Life building next door. But that is a minor gripe considering the extraordinary tastes created by chef, Andrew Carmellini, formerly of **Café Boulud** (p. 216). At A Voce you can start with something peasant-pleasing like Sardinian sheep's milk ricotta and slather it on thick, crusty grilled bread or you can sample the hip, wild *branzini* *tartara* (Mediterranean sea bass)—something no peasant would ever dare eat. The same can be said for the "secondi." Chef Carmellini offers "My Grandmother's meat ravioli" and though my grandmother never made meat ravioli—she thought meat ravioli was something you poured from a can—Carmellini's nonna's meat ravioli is so good it certainly was *not* from a can, or, continuing on that rustic theme, the "country-style Tuscan tripe," with barlotti beans, tomato, fried duck egg, and grilled ciabatta bread, which (minus the duck egg) would have made my normally dour Calabrese grandfather happy. A Voce offers daily specials called "del mercato" which usually features the chef's more unique creations like, on the day I visited a "rabbit terrina" with salt-cured *foie gras*. You won't go wrong whether you try the rustic or the modern. The chef's palate-cleansing citrus tiramisu is the perfect conclusion.

41 Madison Avenue (at 26th St.) ℰ 212/545-8555. www.avocerestaurant.com. AE, DC, MC, V. Main courses: $18–$39; Mon–Fri 11:45am–2:30pm; 5:30–11pm; Sat–Sun 5:30–11pm. Subway: N, R, W to 23rd St.

BLT Fish ℱℱ SEAFOOD   The seafood branch of the **BLT** (Bistro Laurent Tourondel, BLT Steak, see p. 200, BLT Prime, BLT Market) empire, is actually two restaurants with two distinct kitchens. The downstairs is a moderately priced faux-seafood shack with a raw bar, fried fare, and the much-in-demand (deservedly so) lobster roll. Upstairs (you can walk the steps or take a glass elevator) is the elegant (with prices to match) dining room. Here you can sit under a skylight or near the open kitchen and watch an army of servers move from the kitchen with huge platters where whole fish sit, dressed up beautifully and ready for consumption. One example is the crispy red snapper "Cantonese style" that is filleted tableside. Another is the sea-salt-crusted New Zealand pink snapper, for which you'll have to crack the hard salt shell to get to the tender, juicy flesh underneath. Of the "smaller" dishes, the Maine Day boat sea scallops stand out along with the Alaskan black cod in a honey reduction sauce. For starters, the spicy tuna tartare and the grilled sardines are not to be missed. But with fish this fresh, you really won't go wrong with anything on the menu here. Like BLT Steak and BLT Prime, don't expect quiet conversation.

21 W. 17th St. (btwn Fifth and Sixth aves.). ℰ 212/691-8888. www.bltfish.com. Reservations recommended. Prices $25–$35. BLT Fish Mon–Thurs 5:30–11pm; Fri–Sat 5:30–11:30pm. BLT Fish Shack Mon–Fri 11:45am–2:30pm; Mon–Thurs 5:30–11pm; Fri–Sat 5:30–11:30pm; Sun 5–10pm. Subway: 4, 5, 6, N, R, Q, W, L to 14th St/Union Sq.

Dévi ℱℱ INDIAN   With the number of Indian restaurants in New York City, you would think another one would be redundant. But few of them are like this restaurant. Dévi offers $60 tasting menus (vegetarian and non-vegetarian), and that's really the way to go. The menu features nine small courses that will let you sample much of what the restaurant has to offer. Some of the highlights include tender tandoori chicken stuffed with spicy herbs, halibut coated in a cilantro rub accompanied with mint coconut chutney and lemon rice, *zimikand koftas*, delicate yam koftas in a creamy tomato-onion sauce, and the addictive, crispy okra, the Indian equivalent of french fries. With the tasting menus, you get a choice of desserts; I strongly recommend the fabulous *falooda*, an Indian sundae that's a refreshing combination of noodles with honey-soaked basil seeds, mango, and strawberry sorbet in lemongrass-infused coconut milk. Seating is comfortable and service is knowledgeable, though servers regrettably don bright orange uniforms that look a bit too much like prison garb.

8 E. 18th St. (btwn Fifth Ave. and Broadway). ℰ 212/691-1300. www.devinyc.com. Reservations recommended. AE, DISC, MC, V. Main courses $15–$31; tasting menus $60. Mon–Sat noon–2:30pm; Mon–Sat 5:30–10:30pm; Sun 5–10pm Subway: N, R, W, Q, 4, 5, 6 to 14th St./Union Sq.

Parea ⚘ GREEK   With its sleek, communal tables, whitewashed walls, and thick, Greek columns in the handsome dining room, Parea is like the futuristic version of the old-fashioned *taverna*. But there is nothing old-fashioned about the menu which highlights a number of creative *mezedes*. Bring your family and friends and share small plates like zucchini *keftedes*, lightly fried zucchini stuffed with Greek cheese and served with a tangy lemon sauce, Greek sausage *kalamaki* accompanied with lemon yogurt and chilies, smoked trout *spinailo*, the Greek version of smoked sable, and crispy pork. The mezedes are the perfect companion to a glass of good Greek wine of which Parea has an impressive list or, even better, an innovative cocktail like the "Ginger Rickey" a concoction of ouzo, cognac, ginger syrup, and lemon-lime soda. If you want something more substantial, the entrees like black cod *ladolemono*, cod with cranberry beans in a lemony broth is special as is the hanger steak *skara*, a perfectly cooked hanger steak rubbed with oregano and chilies and served with Greek fries. Save room for the desserts, particularly Greek doughnuts with a sweet cream dipping sauce.

36 E. 20th St. (btwn Park Ave. South and Lexington ave.) ⓒ 212/777-8448. www.parea-ny.com. Reservations recommended. Mezedes $7; main courses $23–$29. AE, DC, DISC, MC, V. Mon–Thurs noon–2:30pm and 5:30–11pm; Fri noon–2:30pm and 5:30pm–midnight; Sat 5:30pm–midnight; Sun 5:30–10pm. Subway: 4, 5, 6, L, N, Q, R, N, W to 14th St-Union Square.

Porcao ⚘ BRAZILIAN   If you decide to dine at Porcao, make sure you not only bring a hefty appetite but also a serious craving for meat, red in particular. Porcao is a *rodizio*, a Rio-originated concept where waiters roam from table to table with skewers of hot, juice-dripping meat cooked *churrasco*-style, meaning cooked upright on a skewer over hot coals. There is no menu at Porcao: You pay one price for all you can eat including 10 kinds of meats, a rolling tray of salmon, sides liked fried yucca and fried banana, and a full salad bar. Turn your pig chip up to the green side and the waiters will arrive at your table, and then slice off a piece of meat that you will gracefully catch with the tongs provided. Before you have a chance to sample the meat, possibly the tender, juicy, *picanha*, the noble part of the sirloin, or the equally delicious *alcatra*, top sirloin, there will be another to serve you. To slow the process, turn your chip to red, and the waiters will halt until you are ready for more. The room is sprawling with high ceilings and if you get thirsty, your host, via his headphones, will summon a cart where caipirinhas, the lime-and-*cachaca* (sugar-cane liquor) Brazilian specialty drink, are made at your table. Desserts (and drinks) are not included in the all-you-can-eat price, but if there is any way, save some room for the fabulous coconut pudding. The bar here is a lively scene—off the bar there's also a Scotch club where regulars can store their own bottle(s).

360 Park Ave. South (at 26th St.). ⓒ 212/252-7080. www.porcaous.com. Rodizio $51; executive lunch $23. AE, DC, MC, V. Mon–Thurs noon–11pm; Fri–Sat 2pm–midnight; Sun 11am–10pm. Subway: 6 to 28th St.

Sapa ⚘⚘ FRENCH/VIETNAMESE   I am usually wary of "fusion" cuisine, but in Sapa's case, the combination of French and Vietnamese based on the two countries' respective histories is a natural one. It also helps that the food at Sapa is helmed by the talented Patricia Yeo. Begin your journey in the Mediterranean, with a spectacular salad of romaine hearts, endive, and Taleggio cheese with pear fritters in a pear vinaigrette. Move quickly to Vietnam and sample one or two rolls prepared at Sapa's "roll bar"; the spiced yellowfin tartare with avocado and green papaya sprouts was my favorite. When it comes to the main courses, there is a reason Yeo's ginger-crusted ahi tuna over braised oxtail is her signature dish; the unusual mix might seem too rich, but they mesh together perfectly. The restaurant is cavernous, with high ceilings and bright white walls, and service is extremely personable and knowledgeable. The dining experience at Sapa is exotic on every level—even the restroom area, with its candle-adorned bubbling pool, Chinese screens decorating the row of bathroom doors, and soft music, is worth the trip even if you don't have to go.

43 W. 24th St. (btwn Broadway and Sixth Ave.). ℂ 212/929-1800. www.sapanyc.com. Reservations recommended. Roll bar $8–$12; main courses $22–$32. AE, DISC, MC, V. Mon–Sat 11:30am–3:30pm; midday menu Mon–Sat 3:30–5:30pm; Mon–Fri 5:30–11:30pm; Sat 6pm–midnight; Sun 5:30–10:30pm; Sun brunch 10:30am–3:30pm. Subway: F, V to 23rd St.

Tamarind 🡒🡒 INDIAN One of the best Indian restaurants in Manhattan, Tamarind offers innovative and flavorful variations on the old standards. The room is sleek and bleached white, giving it a gallery-like feel; in the middle of the restaurant adjacent to the bar is a glassed-in cubicle where you can watch the chefs work the tandoor ovens. And just about anything that comes out of those ovens is spectacular. Start with the *bhel poori,* assorted crisps and noodles with sweet and sour chutneys, and one of the soups. I love the she-crab soup with nutmeg, ginger juice, and saffron. Try not to fill up on the tandoor-baked breads—the nan is hard to resist. You can't go wrong with any of the tandoor-baked entrees; the *jhinga angarey,* jumbo prawns marinated in yogurt and chiles, is my favorite. If you venture from the tandoor, try the lamb *pasanda,* apricot-filled grilled lamb in a cashew-and-saffron sauce or Tamarind swordfish marinated in tamarind chutney and fenugreek leaves. There are a number of vegetarian options; the Raji vegetarian *thali,* an assortment of tandoori salad, lentils, vegetables, chutneys, and relishes, is a treat. Desserts are special, too; try the *gujjia,* a samosa filled with semolina, raisins, cashews, and coconut. Service is efficient and friendly and the owners will most likely stop by your table and greet you like a regular.

41–43 E. 22nd St. (btwn Broadway and Park Ave.). ℂ 212/674-7400. Reservations recommended. Main courses $11–$30. AE, DC, MC, V. Daily 11:30am–3pm and 5:30–11:30pm. Subway: N, R, 6 to 23rd St.

INEXPENSIVE

Don't forget **Eisenberg's Coffee Shop,** 174 Fifth Ave., at 22nd Street (ℂ **212/675-5096**), for the New York diner experience. For more, see "Old Friends," on p. 174.

Also consider Danny Meyer's popular **Shake Shack** 🡒, in Madison Square Park (ℂ **212/889-6600**). For healthy burgers, try either outlet of the **New York Burger Co.,** 303 Park Ave. South, between 23rd and 24th streets (ℂ **212/254-2727**), and 678 Sixth Ave., between 21st and 22nd streets (ℂ **212/229-1404**). For a burger with boutique quality meat, try **Brgr,** 287 Seventh Ave, at 26th St (ℂ **212/488-7500**) For more on all three, see the sidebar "Where to Find Your (Burger) Bliss," on p. 202.

City Bakery 🡒 *(Kids* ORGANIC AMERICAN City Bakery offers comfort food that manages to be delicious, nutritious, *and* eco-friendly. Its salad bar is unlike any other in the city, where the integrity of the ingredients is as important as the taste. This is health food, all right—roasted beets with walnuts, glistening sautéed greens, lavender eggplant tossed in miso—but with heart and soul, offering such favorites as French toast with artisanal bacon, flavorful mac 'n cheese, tortilla pie, smoked salmon with all the trimmings on Sunday. The "bakery" refers to the plethora of sinful desserts; kids love the spinning wheel of chocolate and the homemade marshmallows. *One caveat:* It's a bit pricey for a salad bar, but oh, what good eats.

3 W. 18th St. (btwn Fifth and Sixth aves.). ℂ 212/366-1414. Salad bar $13 per lb.; soups $4–$7; sandwiches $5–$10. AE, MC, V. Mon–Fri 7:30am–7pm; Sat 7:30am–6:30pm; Sun 9am–6pm. Subway: N, R, Q, 4, 5, 6 to Union Sq.

The Hole Truth: N.Y.'s Best Bagels

Not many things are more New York than a bagel, and New Yorkers are loyal to their favorite bagel purveyors. In fact, discussions about who makes the best bagel can lead to heated arguments. Following are the top contenders:

Absolute Bagels, 2708 Broadway, between 107th and 108th streets (② 212/932-2052). A new player on the bagel scene, their egg bagels, hot out of the oven, melt in your mouth, and their whitefish salad is perfectly smoky though not overpowering.

Ess-A-Bagel, 359 First Ave., at 21st Street (② 212/260-2252; www.ess-a-bagel.com). When it comes to size, Ess-a-Bagel's are the best of the biggest; plump, chewy, and oh so satisfying. Also at 831 Third Ave., between 50th and 51st streets (② 212/980-1010).

H&H Bagels, 2239 Broadway, at 80th Street (② 212/595-8003; www.handh bagel.com). Long reputed as the best bagel in New York—which may have resulted in the arrogant price hike to $1 a bagel. Some complain they are a bit too sweet, but I disagree. The bagels here are always fresh and warm, the bagel aficionado's prerequisite. Also at 639 W. 46th St., at Twelfth Avenue (② 212/765-7200). Takeout only.

Kossar's Bialys, 367 Grand St, at Essex St. (② 877-4-BIALYS; www.kossars bialys.com). We know about their bialys, but don't forget about their bagels. Also hand rolled, the result is a slightly crunchy exterior with a tender, moist middle. Sure you came for the bialys, but you will leave with both.

Murray's Bagels, 500 Sixth Ave., between 12th and 13th streets (② 212/462-2830), and 242 Eighth Ave., at 23rd Street (② 646/638-1334). There's nothing like a soft, warm bagel to begin your day, and Murray's does them beautifully. Their smoked fish goes perfectly on their bagels.

10 Times Square & Midtown West

To locate the restaurants in this section, see the map on p. 180.

VERY EXPENSIVE

In addition to the choices below, consider the *New York Times,* four-star winner **Le Bernardin,** 155 W. 51st St., between Sixth and Seventh avenues (② 212/489-1515; www.le-bernardin.com). See the sidebar "Food Splurge" on p. 209.

Also consider the steakhouses in the box "The Prime Cut" on p. 184, **Uncle Jack's Steakhouse** ✦, 440 Ninth Ave., at 34th Street (② 212/244-0005; www.unclejacks. com), **Ben Benson's Steakhouse,** 123 W. 52nd St., between Sixth and Seventh avenues (② 212/581-8888; www.benbensons.com), **Benjamin Steakhouse,** 52 E. 41st St, in the Dylan Hotel (② 212/297-9177; www.benjaminsteakhouse.com), and **Quality Meats** ✦ 57 W. 58th St., between Fifth and Sixth aves. (② 212/371-7777).

Anthos ✦✦ INNOVATIVE GREEK   With a few tweaks, higher prices and even more intriguing pairings, Anthos is **Onera,** the former Upper West Side restaurant helmed by chef/owner Michael Psilakis (**Kefi,** see p. 212), transplanted to a new location across from legendary **21 Club** and in the heart of the power crowd of midtown. With hostess and co-owner Donatella Arpaia, of **David Burke & Donatella,** Psilakis has a grand, albeit slick stage in which to showcase his immense talents. The only nods here to Greek traditional cuisine are the grilled octopus, a Greek salad, and the side order of moussaka that comes with the perfectly prepared lamb chop, loin. Psilakis's signature Greek "crudo," or raw *mezes,* yellowtail, diver scallops, and tuna, that were so popular at Onera, thankfully are on Anthos's menu. The sardine escabeche, a row of properly briny, fresh from the sea, sardines each on a sliver of cucumber along with the potato and garlic *skorkalia* soup, not really a soup at all, and the above-mentioned octopus are more than enough to make your meal. But a meal of only the mezes and you would miss out on entrees like the whole simply grilled, bursting with meat, *loup de mer,* served boned but with the head included or the tantalizing crispy turbot with eggplant puree. Desserts are irresistible; don't miss the sesame ice cream encased in a halvah shell. Service is first rate and it better be considering the location and the price you are paying.

36 W. 52nd St. (btwn 5th and 6th aves) ⓒ 212/582-6900. Reservations recommended. Main course: $26–$45. AE, DC, DISC, MC, V. Mon–Fri noon–2:45pm; Mon–Thurs 5–10:30pm; Fri–Sat 5–11pm. Subway: B, D, F, V to 47 & 50, Rockefeller Center.

Kobe Club ⓖ STEAKHOUSE   There are many variations of the traditional steakhouse, but the Kobe Club takes the concept to the extreme. Glorying in excess, the Kobe Club is about fun—albeit wildly expensive fun. Here you are in what could be considered a combination night club/restaurant/theater. It's dark with a relentless disco beat blaring; thousands of glimmering samurai swords dangle from the ceiling; a blazing forest fire flickers on a video screen, and private, leather-seated booths and big communal tables are scattered throughout the room. The show begins with a cocktail; the signature Kobe Punch, a mix of Grey Goose vodka with a choice of fresh squeezed juice served in a glass, carafe or silver punch bowl ($150), is the best opening act accompanied by the tantalizing American "kobe" beef cheek ravioli in a truffle sauce. Bring a pocket flashlight and hope that the cocktail will help you get through the overly complicated "mix and match mains" section of the menu where you can pair American, Australian, and Japanese "kobe" beef from bulls descended from Japanese Wagyu cattle. And then pick two sauces, butters or toppings from the extensive list along with the complimentary "house" steak sauce, and three types of salts. Or, just take a deep breath and go for the "Samurai's Flight" a combination of the three countries' (Australia, Japan, America) "kobe" and a 6-ounce American prime filet, a "bargain" at $190 for two people. Finally, try to enjoy the rich beef by not thinking about the enormous tab that will soon materialize on your table.

68 W. 58th St (btwn 5th and 6th aves.) ⓒ 212/644-5623. www.chinagrillmanagement.com. AE, DC, MC, V. Main courses: $25–$39;. Wagyu beef $35–$150 Hours: Mon–Fri 11:30am–2:30pm; Mon–Wed 5:30–11pm; Thurs–Sat 5:30–11:30pm. Subway: N, Q, R, W to 57th St.

EXPENSIVE

Abboccato ⓖⓖ ITALIAN   The Italian entry from the Livanos family, owners of **Molyvos** (p. 192) and **Oceana** (p. 201) and no ordinary Italian this! The menu is ambitious and hearty, with offerings that include appetizers like the *affetati misti* (a platter of cured meats), *pesce crudo* (raw fish marinated in olive oil), and grilled tripe and unusual, rustic pastas such as spaghettini with razor clams and mullet roe, orecchiette with cuttlefish, plus staples like tagliatelle Bolognese and spaghetti carbonara. Rich meat mains include suckling pig cooked in milk and hazelnuts and the intense *vaniglia e cioccolato,* vanilla-scented veal cheeks and chocolate-and-spice-stewed wild boar. Service is good, but not up to Oceana's levels. The room is a throwback; its round yellow booths are reminiscent of 1960s New York Italian.

136 W. 55th St. (btwn Sixth and Seventh aves.). © 212/265-4000. www.abboccato.com. Reservations recommended. Pasta $23–$26; main courses $32–$42. AE, DC, MC, V. Daily 6:30–10:30am; Mon–Sat noon–3pm; Mon–Thurs 5:30–11:30pm; Fri 5:30–11pm; Sat 5–11pm; Sun 4–10pm. Subway: N, R, Q, W to 57th St.

Barbetta ✶✶ ITALIAN   The debate over what is New York's oldest restaurant rages on, and Barbetta (est. 1906) is in the thick of that debate. But there is no debate over Barbetta's sustained excellence during that period. The first, and still one of the few, New York restaurants to serve cuisine from Piemonte (the Piedmont), Italy's northwestern-most region, Barbetta's food, like the restaurant's sumptuous decor, is richly elegant. This is far from your typical red-sauce joint. At Barbetta, if you dine in the autumn or winter, you just might have the pleasure of white truffles, flown in from Piemonte, and shaved over your already decadent *gnochetti ai formaggi,* freshly made, delicate gnocchi in an unforgettable cheese sauce, or the stunning creation of an edible quail's nest filled with *fonduta* cheese and surrounded by three tiny, speckled quail's eggs. On the menu you can choose from one of the restaurant's 1906 creations like the *bolliti misti,* a Piemontesi specialty, a mix of boiled meats and broth served from an antique silver cart, but for a meal this unique, you must order 48 hours in advance. If you just can't go to an Italian restaurant without ordering something in tomato sauce, you won't go wrong with the 1906-creation *tajarin,* strands of homemade pasta in a simple but perfectly done tomato-basil sauce. Barbetta also features an impressive Italian wine list and, in the warmer months, one of the city's most romantic outdoor gardens. Though this is a Theater District restaurant and many come for the pre-theater prix-fixe, Barbetta is best experienced at a relaxed, leisurely pace.

321 W. 46th St. (btwn Eighth and Ninth aves.). © 212/246-9171. www.barbettarestaurant.com. Reservations recommended. Prix-fixe dinner $49; main courses lunch $22–$29, dinner $28–$36. AE, DC, MC, V. Mon–Sat noon–2pm and 5–11pm. Subway: C, E to 50th St.

db Bistro Moderne ✶ FRENCH BISTRO   Daniel Boulud of **Café Boulud** (p. 216) and **Daniel** (p. 209) fame opened db Bistro Moderne as a casual alternative to his other restaurants. Casual in this case means you get architect Jeffrey Beers to put a hip spin on the contemporary French bistro; the result immediately attracts a fashion-conscious crowd (meaning you can wear a T-shirt here—but make sure it's Armani). To round out the "casual" experience, add a hamburger. But this is not your typical $5.95 burger deluxe; no, Boulud's creation comes in at $29 and is made with minced sirloin, *foie gras,* preserved black truffle, and braised short ribs, served on a Parmesan onion roll. If any hamburger is worth $29—and this point is debatable—this one is. Despite the silly burger excess, the food is, like all Boulud's ventures, outstanding—especially those bistro favorites bouillabaisse, coq au vin, and frogs' legs.

55 W. 44th St. (btwn Fifth and Sixth aves.). © 212/391-2400. Reservations required. Lunch entrees $28–$32; pretheater 3-course prix fixe $45; dinner entrees $29–$36. AE, DC, MC, V. Mon–Sat noon–2:30pm; daily 5–11pm; Sun, Mon til 10pm. Subway: B, D, F, Q to 42nd St.

Frankie & Johnnie's ✶✶ STEAKHOUSE   When restaurants open other branches of their originals, red flags go up. Does that mean the restaurant has instantly become a chain and thus quality has eroded to chain-food status? In the case of Frankie & Johnnie's, the legendary Theater District former-speakeasy-turned-steakhouse, which opened another outlet in 2005 in the two-story townhouse owned once by actor John Barrymore, those fears were quickly allayed after one bite of their signature sirloin. It also helps that the dining room on the second floor of the town house is gorgeous, especially the Barrymore room, the actor's former study with stained-glass ceiling panels, dark wood walls, and a working fireplace. Not only are Frankie & Johnnie's steaks vastly underrated in the competitive world of New York steakhouses, but the other non-steak options are superb as well. The crabcake appetizer had an overwhelmingly high crab-to-cake ratio—and that's a good thing in my book—while the sides of hash browns were the best I've ever had. Pastas and seafood are abundant on the menu and I'm sure they are excellent, but what's the point? Service is steakhouse old-school, and if you are staying in Midtown, the restaurant provides complimentary stretch limo service to and from the restaurant.

32 W. 37th St. (btwn Fifth and Sixth aves.). (C) **212/997-8940.** www.frankieandjohnnies.com. Reservations recommended. Main courses $25–$36. Mon–Fri noon–2:30pm; Mon–Thurs 4–10:30pm; Fri–Sat 4–11pm. Subway: B, C, D, N, R, Q, W, V to 34th St./Herald Sq. Also at 269 W. 45th St. (at Eighth Ave.). (C) **212/997-9494.** Subway: 1, 2, 3, 7, A, C, E, N, R, Q, S, W to 42nd St.

Keens Steakhouse 🍴🍴🍴 STEAKHOUSE   Until the latter part of the 20th century, Keens, which was established in the same location in 1885, referred to itself as a "chop house." They are now officially known as a steakhouse, but I wish they had remained true to their roots and hadn't submitted to modern-day marketing and made that change. To their credit, they are a steakhouse in name only. They serve the basics of a steakhouse—the porterhouse for two, aged, T-Bone, and filet mignon with the requisite sides like creamed spinach and hash browns—but they still serve chops: lamb chops, prime rib, short ribs, and most notably, mutton chops. It is the mutton chop that has made Keens the true original that it is. The monstrous cut has two flaps of long, thick, rich, subtly gamy meat on either side of the bone that look kind of like mutton-chop sideburns. So which came first, the sideburns or the chop? Keens is no gussied-up remake of old New York: It's the real thing, from the thousands of ceramic pipes on the ceiling (regular diners were given their own personal pipes, including celebrities like Babe Ruth, George M. Cohan, and Albert Einstein) to the series of rooms on two floors with wood paneling, leather banquettes, fireplaces (in some), a clubby bar with a three-page menu of single malts, and even the framed playbill Lincoln was reading at the Ford Theater that infamous evening in 1865. You might have a better porterhouse at **Peter Luger Steakhouse** (p. 220), but you'll have more fun at Keens.

72 W. 36th St. (at Sixth Ave.). (C) **212/947-3636.** www.keens.com. Reservations recommended. Main courses $26–$45. AE, DC, DISC, MC, V. Mon–Fri 11:45am–10:30pm; Sat 5–10:30pm; Sun 5–9pm. Subway: B, D, F, N, R, W, Q, V to 34th St./Herald Sq.

Molyvos 🍴🍴 GREEK   When Molyvos opened in1997 it was heralded as a trailblazer of upscale and innovative Greek cuisine. Now, over ten years later, upscale and innovative Greek is the current "in vogue" cuisine in Manhattan. Molyvos's longterm success is based on its ability to please those who want simple, unpretentious traditional Greek food as well as exciting, original Greek accented creations. For those who like their Greek unadulterated, you won't go wrong with cold *mezedes,* such as the spreads *tzatziki, melitzanosalata,* and *taramosalata,* and hot *mezedes* like spinach pie or grilled octopus. For Greek food with an edge there is ouzo cured salmon on a chickpea fritter or the terrific seafood Cretan bread salad. Just a sampling of the *mezedes* alone should be enough for anyone's hearty appetite but with entrees as good as grilled

Urban BBQ: The Best 'cue in New York City

New York is known for many things, but barbecue is not one of them. That is, thankfully, slowly changing. That hankering for slow cooked, charred meat, so popular in the south and heartland, has made its way to the big city. And, really, what is more primal and satisfying than the sensation of tearing slow-smoked meat from bone, eating the meat with your fingers and then, of course, licking that sweet and savory sauce off your own natural utensils. New York is not Memphis or Kansas City in the barbecue universe, but every year new "joints" pop up and we no longer embarrass ourselves when it comes to the fine art of smoking meats.

My current favorite is **RUB** ☆☆ (p. 183) helmed by a Kansas City pitmaster named Paul Kirk. The smoked turkey and chicken were as close to perfection as I've found anywhere. Close to the West Side Highway, **Dinosaur Bar-B-Que** (p. 218), a Syracuse transplant bbq joint, is like a roadhouse in atmosphere and the pulled pork is as good as it gets north of 125th St. In the heart of tourist trap mecca, Times Square, lies a kitschy, theme barbecue joint, **Virgil's Real BBQ** ☆☆ (p. 195) that, especially for a theme restaurant, serves remarkably good 'cue.

French-trained and a former chef at Daniel, Adam Perry Lang, curiously, or maybe not so curiously, gave up the haute French cuisine to open his own joint called **Daisy May's BBQ,** 623 11th Ave., at 46th St. (© 212/977-1500; www.daisymaysbbq.com) with stellar results. Daisy May carts can be found in various locations around the city, but if you can't find a cart, squeeze into his cafeteria-style restaurant for Memphis-style dry-rub ribs and you'll think that you are a block from the Mississippi River, not the Hudson.

Restaurateur Danny Meyer has made his name with such celebrated restaurants as the Gramercy Tavern, Eleven Madison Park, and the Union Square Café. A St. Louis native, Meyer wanted to replicate the barbecue he remembered growing up so he opened **Blue Smoke,** 116 E. 27th St., between Lexington and Park aves. (© 212/447-7733; www.jazzstandard.net) as part of the jazz club, the **Jazz Standard** (see chapter 10). Blue Smoke offers the usual array of barbecue, made in Meyer's custom-built smoker, but with a few quirks like a fried bologna sandwich.

My favorite soul restaurant is **Charles' Southern-Style Kitchen** (see the box: "The Soul of Harlem" on p. 220) so when the Charles of Charles's Southern-Style Kitchen, Charles Gabriel opened a barbecue joint called **Rack & Soul,** 2818 Broadway, at 109th St (© 212/222-4800) in my neighborhood I was ecstatic. Though not as inexpensive as Gabriel's soul kitchen, Rack & Soul not only offers his trademark fried chicken, but also barbecued baby back ribs that are so good you might just have to pass on his chicken, or bite the bullet and go for a combo platter where you can get a taste of both.

garides, wild head-on prawns barbecued "soulvaki-style" and the *chios* pork and *gigante* bean stew, not ordering one would be a mistake. The knowledgeable sommelier will pair your choices with a comparable Greek wine, of which there are many. Or, skip the wine and sample one or two of the dozens of ouzos available, but don't skip the desserts. Sure you've had baklava before, but have you ever had chocolate baklava? Yes, it's as good as it sounds.

871 Seventh Ave. (btwn 55th and 56th sts.). 📞 212/582-7500. www.molyvos.com. Reservations recommended. Main courses $17–$29 at lunch (most less than $20); $20–$36 at dinner (most less than $25); fixed-price lunch $24; pre-theater 3-course dinner $36 (5:30–6:45pm). AE, DC, DISC, MC, V. Mon–Thurs noon–11:30pm; Fri–Sat noon–midnight; Sun noon–11pm. Subway: N, R to 57th St.; B, D, E to Seventh Ave.

MODERATE

The family-style Italian restaurant **Carmine's** has a Times Square branch at 200 W. 44th St., between Broadway and Eighth Avenue (📞 **212/221-3800**).

Becco 🍴 *Finds* ITALIAN   If you're a fan of *Lidia's Italian-American Kitchen* on PBS, you'll be happy to know you can sample Lidia Bastianich's simple, hearty Italian cooking here. Becco, on Restaurant Row, is designed to serve her meals "at a different price point" (read: cheaper) than her East Side restaurant, Felidia. The prices are not rock-bottom, but in terms of service, portions, and quality, you get tremendous bang for your buck at Becco (which means to "peck, nibble, or savor something in a discriminating way"). The main courses can head north of the $20 mark, but take a look at the prix-fixe menu ($17 at lunch, $22 at dinner), which includes either a Caesar salad or antipasto plate, followed by a "Symphony of Pasta," unlimited servings of the three fresh-made daily pastas. There's also an excellent selection of Italian wines at $25 a bottle. If you can't make up your mind about dessert, have them all: A tasting plate includes gelato, cheesecake, and whatever else the dessert chef has whipped up that day. Lidia herself does turn up at Becco and Felidia; you can even dine with her (see website for details).

355 W. 46th St. (btwn Eighth and Ninth aves.). 📞 212/397-7597. www.becconyc.com. Reservations recommended. Main courses lunch $13–$25, dinner $19–$35. AE, DC, DISC, MC, V. Mon noon–3pm and 5-10pm; Tue noon–3pm and 5pm–midnight; Wed 11:30am–2:30pm and 4pm–midnight; Thurs–Fri noon–3pm and 5pm– midnight; Sat 11:30am–2:30pm and 4pm–midnight; Sun noon–10pm. Subway: C, E to 50th St.

Marseille 🍴 FRENCH   Lively and casual with open, high ceilings and a tiled floor creating a Casablanca-like ambience, this restaurant, named after the infamous port city in France, features the food of that city, including its North African influences. That means you'll find entrees like Moroccan chicken, couscous, and tangine on the menu along with Provençal specialties like bouillabaisse, which comes in three varieties (chicken, vegetarian, and traditional, made with fish—stick with the traditional), short-rib daube, salad niçoise, and soup *au pistou.* You can make a meal of the *meze* (small plates), which feature a tangy grilled *merguez* sausage, anchovies and roasted peppers, *brandade* (whipped salt cod), tapenade, and broiled sardines wrapped in *lardo* (thick bacon). Located in the Film Center building on Ninth Avenue, this is a good pre-theater choice, but even better when the pre-theater rush is over.

630 Ninth Ave. (at 44th St.). 📞 212/333-2323. www.marseillenyc.com. Meze $4–$13; main courses $16–$28. AE, DC, MC, V. Mon–Fri noon–3pm; Sat–Sun 11am–4pm; Sun–Mon 5:15–11pm; Tues–Sat 5:15pm–midnight. Subway: A, C, E, 7 to 42nd St./Times Sq.

Metro Marche 🍴 FRENCH   Now, while scurrying through Port Authority, if you are hungry, or thirsty, you don't have to settle for soggy pizza or a trans-fat laden fast food hamburger. You can stop at Metro Marche, the ambitious (for Port Authority) new-in 2006 bistro located in that hub of transportation for an authentic Belgian draft beer with a pot of *moules frites*. Inside the lively restaurant you'll quickly forget you are in a bus depot, and not a particularly attractive one at that, and whether waiting for a bus or for a nearby Broadway show to start, this is as good a place as any to spend an hour or two. Most of the bistro standards are on the menu including a hearty onion soup overflowing with cheese, a rich pate, and a watercress and frisée salad, the strong Roquefort cheese softened by a subtle citrus vinaigrette. You can get a decent hamburger here or the popular steak *frites*, but it's hard to pass up the aforementioned *moules frites*, prepared *mariniere, dijonaise,* or *diablo* (red pepper) style. Save room for an aperitif; you'll need it once you leave Metro Marche for the harsh reality that lies outside its welcoming doors.

625 Eighth Ave (at 41st St.) © 212/239-1010. Main courses: $11–$20. AE, MC, V. Open daily for breakfast, lunch, and dinner 6:30am–11pm. Subway: A, C, E, 7 to 42nd St.

Norma's 🖈🖈 *Finds* CREATIVE AMERICAN BREAKFAST   Nowhere is breakfast treated with such reverence, and decadence, as at Norma's, a soaring, ultramodern ode to the ultimate comfort food. There's something for everyone on the huge menu. Classics come in styles both simple and haute: Blueberry pancakes come piled high with fresh Maine berries and Devonshire cream, while buttermilks are topped with fresh Georgia peaches and chopped walnuts. Even oatmeal is special: genuine Irish McCann's, dressed with sautéed green apples and red pears and brûléed for a flash of sugary sweetness. Don't pass on the apple-wood-smoked bacon, so good it's worth blowing any diet for. Norma's can even win over breakfast foes with creative sandwiches, a generous Cobb with seared ahi, and a terrific chicken potpie. Not cheap for breakfast, but definitely worth the splurge.

At Le Parker Meridien Hotel, 118 W. 57th St. (btwn Sixth and Seventh aves.). © 212/708-7460. www.normasnyc. com. Reservations accepted. Main courses $8–$23 (most $13–$18). AE, DC, DISC, MC, V. Mon–Fri 6:30am–3pm; Sat–Sun 7am–3pm. Subway: B, N, Q, R, W to 57th St.

Virgil's Real BBQ 🖈🖈 *Kids* BARBECUE/SOUTHERN   In the heart of the theme-restaurant wasteland known as Times Square is a theme restaurant that actually has good food. The "theme" is Southern barbecue and the restaurant, sprawling over two levels, is made to look and feel like a Southern roadhouse with good-ol'-boy decorations on the walls and blues on the soundtrack. Virgil's does an admirable job in re-creating that authentic flavor so hard to find north of the Mason-Dixon line. The spice-rubbed ribs are slow-cooked and meaty, but it's the Owensboro lamb (smoked slices of lamb) and the Texas beef brisket that are the standouts. Both are melt-in-your-mouth tender; the lamb is sprinkled with a flavorful mustard sauce, while the brisket is perfect with a few dabs of Virgil's homemade spicy barbecue sauce. For starters, the corn dogs with poblano mustard are something New Yorkers rarely have the pleasure of experiencing, while the BBQ nachos—tortilla chips slathered with melted cheese and barbecued pulled pork—are a meal in themselves. Desserts are what you would expect from a restaurant emulating a Southern theme: big and sweet. Try the homemade ice cream sandwich made with the cookie of the day. Virgil's is a great place to bring the kids; if they're noisy, no one will notice.

152 W. 44th St. (btwn Sixth and Seventh aves.). © 212/921-9494. www.virgilsbbq.com. Reservations recommended. Sandwiches $10–$13; main courses and barbecue platters $15–$24 (most less than $19). AE, DC, DISC, MC, V. Sun–Mon 11:30am–11pm; Tues–Sat 11:30am–midnight. Subway: 1, 2, 3, 7, N, R to 42nd St./Times Sq.

Pizza, New York–Style

Once the domain of countless first-rate pizzerias, Manhattan's pizza offerings have noticeably dropped in quality. The proliferation of Domino's Pizza, Pizza Hut, and other chains into the market have lowered pizza standards. Still, there is plenty of good pizza to be found. Don't be tempted by sad imitations; when it comes to pizza, search out the real deal. Here are some of the best:

DiFara Pizza ⚘, 1424 Avenue J, Brooklyn, at E. 15th St. (© **718/258-1367**). DiFara's is ballyhooed in all the local publications that claim it's the best pizza in the city. And though the exterior is nondescript, looking like your basic neighborhood pizzeria and the interior is cramped, and to be kind, somewhat unkempt with bits of congealed cheese, olive oil, sauce, and crust from possibly a generation of diners still on the tables, DiFara's lives up to its reputation thanks to the stubborn zeal of owner Dominic DeMarco, who, for over 40 years, makes every pizza himself. Stooped but determined, DeMarco, in his own deliberate way and using top ingredients, crafts each pizza finishing with hand grated parmesan cheese, a few dollops of extra-virgin olive oil, and then, using scissors, hand cutting fresh basil onto the pie. The result is a work of art, but one that might test your patience. Expect to wait an hour for a pie, maybe a bit less for a slice. But after one taste, you will know it was worth it.

Grimaldi's Pizzeria, 19 Old Fulton St., between Front and Water streets (© **718/858-4300**; www.grimaldis.com). If you need incentive to walk across the Brooklyn Bridge, Grimaldi's, in Brooklyn Heights, easily provides it. In fact, the pizza is so good, made in a coal oven with a rich flavorful sauce and homemade mozzarella, you might run across the bridge to get to it. *Be warned:* It can get very crowded at dinnertime.

John's Pizzeria, 278 Bleecker St., near Seventh Avenue South (© **212/ 243-1680**). Since it has expanded from this original location—there are now three in the city—the once-gleaming luster of John's has faded slightly, but the pizza is still a cut above the rest. Thin-crusted and out of a coal oven with the proper ratio of tomato sauce to cheese, John's pizza has a loyal following. Though the quality at all of the locations is good, the original

INEXPENSIVE

If you're looking for the quintessential New York deli, you have a choice between the **Stage Deli,** 834 Seventh Ave., between 53rd and 54th streets (© 212/245-7850), known for its jaw-distending celebrity-named sandwiches, and the **Carnegie Deli,** 854 Seventh Ave., at 55th Street (© 800/334-5606), the place to go for the best pastrami, corned beef, and cheesecake in town. For more, see the sidebar "The New York Deli News," on p. 199.

There is a nice outlet of **John's Pizzeria** in Times Square, 260 W. 44th St., between Broadway and Eighth Avenue (© 212/391-7560; subway: 1, 2, 3, 7, A, B, C, E, N, R, W, Q, S to 42nd St./Times Sq.; see the box "Pizza, New York–Style," above). Also

Bleecker Street location is the most old-world romantic and my favorite. Also at 260 W. 44th St., between Broadway and Eighth Avenue (ⓒ 212/391-7560), and 408 E. 64th St., between York and First avenues (ⓒ 212/935-2895).

Lombardi's, 32 Spring St., between Mulberry and Mott streets (ⓒ 212/941-7994; www.firstpizza.com). Claiming to be New York's first "licensed" pizzeria, Lombardi's opened in 1905 and still uses a generations-old Neapolitan family pizza recipe. The coal oven kicks out perfectly cooked pies, some topped with ingredients such as pancetta, homemade sausage, and even fresh-shucked clams. It's hard to go wrong here no matter what tops the pizza. A garden in the back makes it even more inviting during warm weather.

Patsy's Pizzeria 𝒢𝒢, 2287 First Ave., between 117th and 118th streets (ⓒ 212/534-9783). My favorite, and also the favorite of Frank Sinatra, who liked it so much he had pies packed and flown out to Las Vegas. The coal oven here has been burning since 1932, and though the neighborhood in east Harlem where it is located has had its ups and downs, the quality of pizza at Patsy's has never wavered. Try the marinara pizza, a pie with fresh marinara sauce but no cheese that's so good you won't miss the mozzarella. Unlike the other pizzerias mentioned here, you can order by the slice at Patsy's. Don't be fooled by imitators using Patsy's name; this is the original and the best.

Totonno's Pizzeria Napolitano, 1524 Neptune Ave., between West 15th and West 16th streets, Coney Island, Brooklyn (ⓒ 718/372-8606). This unassuming little pizzeria has been at the same spot since 1924 and it makes pizzas almost exactly as it did 80 years ago—thin crust, fresh sauce, and mozzarella, and that's about it. Don't even think about asking for an exotic topping on these pies (and why would you?). Enjoy it in all its simple unadorned glory. Totonno's second branch, on the Upper East Side, 1544 Second Ave., between 80th and 81st streets (ⓒ 212/327-2800), opened about 10 years ago—go ahead and order the exotic toppings there, but for the real deal, go to Coney Island.

consider the aptly named **Burger Joint** 𝒢𝒢, in the lobby of Le Parker Meridien Hotel, 118 W. 57th St. (ⓒ 212/708-7414), for cheap yet excellent no-frills burgers (see the box "Where to Find Your (Burger) Bliss," on p. 202).

For the New York version of the Philadelphia cheese steak, try **Tony Luke's** 𝒢, at 576 Ninth Ave., between 41st and 42nd streets (ⓒ 212/967-3055).

Afghan Kebab House 𝒱𝒶𝓁𝓊ℯ MIDDLE EASTERN   You'll find Afghan Kebab Houses all over the city. Are they related? Who knows, but I like this one best for its heaping plates of first-rate Middle Eastern fare. Kebabs are the first order of business: all are pleasing, but my favorite is the *sultani,* chunks of ground lamb marinated in aromatic spices and broiled over wood coals with green peppers and tomatoes. The *tikka kebab,* in lamb or beef, is impressive, as is the chicken korma, slow-cooked with onions, tomatoes, peppers, and fresh herbs. All plates come with amazingly aromatic brown Indian basmati rice and flat Afghan bread. The room is simple and well worn but evocative, with Oriental carpets serving as table runners. Service is attentive.

764 Ninth Ave. (btwn 51st and 52nd sts.). ℂ 212/307-1612 or 212/307-1629. Reservations accepted. Main courses $10–$16 (most under $12). AE, DC, DISC, MC, V. Daily 11am–11pm. Subway: C, E to 50th St.

Mandoo Bar ⍟ *(Finds* KOREAN   The heart of Manhattan's Koreatown is 32nd Street between Fifth and Sixth avenues—and the number of Korean restaurants on that 1 block is dizzying. You'll know you've found Mandoo Bar when you see the two women in the window rolling and stuffing fresh *mandoo* (Korean for dumpling). Because of the constant preparation, the dumplings, stuffed with a variety of ingredients, are incredibly fresh. There's the *mool mandoo* (basic white dumplings filled with pork and vegetables), the *kimchee mandoo* (steamed dumplings stuffed with potent kimchi [Korean spiced cabbage], tofu, pork, and vegetables), the green vegetable *mool mandoo* (boiled dumplings filled with mixed vegetables), and the *goon mandoo* (pan-fried dumplings filled with pork and vegetables). You really can't go wrong with any of these dumplings, so sample them all with a Combo Mandoo. Soups are also special here; try the beef noodle in a spicy, sinus-clearing broth. With seating that is nothing more than wooden benches, Mandoo Bar is better suited for quick eats rather than a lingering meal—a perfect lunch break from shopping in Herald Square or visiting the nearby Empire State Building.

2 W. 32nd St. (just west of Fifth Ave.). ℂ 212/279-3075. Reservations not accepted. Main courses $7–$17. AE, MC, V. Daily 11:30am–11pm. Subway: B, D, F, N, Q, R, V, W to 34th St./Herald Sq. Also at 71 University Place (btwn 10th and 11th sts.). ℂ 212/358-0400. Subway: N, R, W, Q, 4, 5, 6, L to 14th St./Union Sq.

Sapporo ⍟ *(Value* JAPANESE NOODLES   Peruse the community bulletin board as you enter Sapporo and you might find yourself a deal on an apartment—that is, if you can read Japanese. Thankfully, the menu is in English in this longtime Theater District Japanese noodle shop. If the mostly Japanese clientele doesn't convince you of Sapporo's authenticity, the din of satisfied diners slurping huge bowls of steaming ramen (noodle soup with meat and vegetables) will. And though the ramen is Sapporo's specialty, the *gyoza* (Japanese dumplings) and the *donburi* (pork or chicken over rice with soy-flavored sauce) are also terrific. Best of all, nothing on the menu is over $10 and that's not easy to find in the oft-overpriced Theater District.

152 W. 49th St. (btwn Sixth and Seventh aves.). ℂ 212/869-8972. Reservations not accepted. Main courses $6–$9. No credit cards. Mon–Sat 11am–11pm; Sun 11am–10pm. Subway: N, R to 49th St.

Uncle Nick's GREEK   For stupendous portions of surprisingly good traditional Greek food at ridiculous prices, come to Uncle Nick's. Turn off your cellphone upon entering, not because you might disturb your neighbors, but because there is no way you will be able to have a phone conversation in this loud restaurant. But how can you talk if your mouth is filled with one or more of Nick's Greek dips like *taramosalata* or *tzatziki,* or his perfectly tender, grilled baby octopus? If you haven't filled up on his appetizers, order one of Nick's grilled specialties: The grilled lamb kabob is an absolute winner and guaranteed for leftovers, while the gyro plate is a challenge for those with even the heartiest appetites. Seafood is also good, especially the swordfish kabobs. Desserts are standard; you won't have room for them anyway. Service is friendly to match the rollicking atmosphere here. Next door is the slightly more intimate Uncle Nick's Ouzeria, specializing in *mezedes,* Greek small dishes like tapas.

The New York Deli News

There's nothing more Noo Yawk than hunkering down over a mammoth pastrami on rye at an authentic Jewish deli, where anything you order comes with a bowl of lip-smacking sour dills and a side of attitude. Here are some of the best:

Artie's New York Delicatessen, 2290 Broadway, between 82nd and 83rd streets (© **212/579-5959;** www.arties.com). Compared to the legends below, Arties, which has been around since 1999, is the new kid on the deli block but can hold its own on the playground with the big boys, thank you very much (especially in the wiener department).

Barney Greengrass, the Sturgeon King, 541 Amsterdam Ave., between 86th and 87th streets on the Upper West Side (© **212/724-4707**). This unassuming, daytime-only deli has become legendary for its high-quality salmon (sable, gravlax, Nova Scotia, kippered, lox, pastrami—you choose), whitefish, and sturgeon (of course).

Carnegie Deli, 854 Seventh Ave., at 55th Street (© **800/334-5606** or 212/757-2245; www.carnegiedeli.com). It's worth subjecting yourself to surly service, tourist-targeted overpricing, and elbow-to-elbow seating for some of the best pastrami and corned beef in town. Even big eaters may be challenged by mammoth sandwiches with names like "Fifty Ways to Love Your Liver" (chopped liver, hard-boiled egg, lettuce, tomato, and onion).

Katz's Delicatessen 𝕽𝕽, the city's best deli, remains fabulously old-world despite its hipster-hot Lower East Side location at 205 E. Houston St., at Ludlow Street (© **212/254-2246**). For more on Katz's, see p. 170.

Stage Deli, 834 Seventh Ave., between 53rd and 54th streets (© **212/245-7850;** www.stagedeli.com). Noisy and crowded and packed with tourists, it's still as authentic as they come. The celebrity sandwiches, ostensibly created by the personalities themselves, are jaw-distending mountains of top-quality fixings: The Tom Hanks is roast beef, chopped liver, onion, and chicken fat, while the Dolly Parton is (drumroll, please) twin rolls of corned beef and pastrami.

---

747 Ninth Ave. (btwn 50th and 51st sts.). © 212/245-7992. Appetizers $8–$15; main courses $15–$25. Sun–Thurs noon–10:30pm; Fri–Sat noon–11:30pm. Subway: C or E to 50th St. Nick's Ouzeria next door at 749 Ninth Ave. © 212/397-2892.

Wondee Siam 𝕽 *Finds* THAI Hell's Kitchen offers countless ethnic culinary variations and one of the most prevalent is Thai—there are at least six Thai restaurants in a 5-block radius. My favorite among these is the tiny, zero-ambience Wondee Siam. I don't need colorful decorations or a fish tank to enjoy authentic, uncompromisingly spicy Thai food and that's what I get at Wondee Siam. Here you don't have to worry that your waiter will assume you want a milder form of Thai. If there is a little red asterisk next to your item, you can be sure it is appropriately spicy. The soups are terrific, especially the sinus-clearing *tom yum*. In fact, there is a whole section of yum (chiles) dishes on the menu; my favorite being the *larb gai*, minced ground chicken with ground toasted rice. The curries are first-rate as are the noodles, including the mild pad Thai. This is BYOB and you'll want to do so to complement the spicy food. If you want a bit more comfort, try Wondee Siam II 1 block up. But make sure you ask your waiter not to dumb down the spice and serve up the food authentic Thai-style.

792 Ninth Ave. (btwn 52nd and 53rd sts.). ℂ 212/459-9057. Reservations not accepted. Main courses $8.50–$18 (most under $10). No credit cards. Mon–Sat 11am–11pm; Sun 11am–10:30pm. Subway: C, E to 50th St. Wondee Siam II, 813 Ninth Ave. (btwn 53rd and 54th sts.). ℂ 917/286-1726.

11 Midtown East & Murray Hill

To locate the restaurants in this section, see the map on p. 180.

EXPENSIVE

Aquavit ✸✸✸ SCANDINAVIAN   I'll miss the waterfall and the intimate town-house setting that Aquavit vacated in 2005. Thankfully, however, the food and staff have had no trouble adjusting to the transition. Everything remains first-rate. The restaurant is now in the bottom of a glass tower on East 55th Street, and designed in sleek Scandinavian style with modernist furniture. In the front of the restaurant is an informal and less expensive cafe, while past a long bar is the dining room.

After the move, if anything, the food has improved. The smoked fish—all the fish—is prepared perfectly. I often daydream about the herring plate: four types of herring accompanied by a tiny glass of *aquavit*, distilled liquor not unlike vodka flavored with fruit and spices, and a frosty Carlsberg beer. The hot smoked Arctic char on the main a la carte menu, served with clams and bean puree in a mustard green broth, is also a winner. Most fixed-price menus offer a well-chosen beverage accompaniment option.

65 E. 55th St. (btwn Park and Madison aves.). ℂ 212/307-7311. www.aquavit.org. Reservations recommended. Cafe main courses $9–$32; 3-course fixed-price meal $24 at lunch, $35 at dinner; main dining room fixed-price meal $39 at lunch, $82 at dinner ($39 for vegetarians); 3-course pre-theater dinner (5:30–6:15pm) $55; tasting menus $58 at lunch, $115 at dinner ($90 for vegetarians); supplement for paired wines $30 at lunch, $80 at dinner. AE, DC, MC, V. Mon–Fri noon–2:30pm; Sun–Thurs 5:30–10:30pm; Fri–Sat 5:15–10:30pm. Subway: E, F to Fifth Ave.

BLT Steak ✸✸✸ STEAKHOUSE/BISTRO   Steakhouses are often stereotyped as bastions of male bonding; testosterone-fueled with red meat and hearty drinks. But BLT (Bistro Laurent Tourendel) Steak breaks that mold in a big way; on the night I visited, I noticed more women—slinky and model-like—chomping on thick cuts of beef than men. That doesn't mean men can't also enjoy the beef here; served in cast-iron pots and finished in steak butter with a choice of sauces—béarnaise, red wine, horseradish, and bleu cheese, to name a few. The signature is the porterhouse for two (a whopping $70), but I recommend the New York strip or the short ribs braised in red wine. Both dishes can be shared, which may be a good idea, especially after devouring the airy complimentary popovers and sampling an appetizer like the incredible tuna tartare or a side of onion rings, potato gratin, or creamy spinach. Even after sharing one of the meats, you might not have room for the chestnut-chocolate sundae or peanut-butter chocolate mousse, and that would be a shame. This is not a restaurant for intimate conversation; even the music was muffled by the din of the diners.

106 E. 57th St. (btwn Park and Lexington aves.). ℂ 212/752-7470. www.bltsteak.com. Reservations highly recommended. Main courses $24–$39. AE, DC, MC, V. Mon–Fri 11:45am–2:30pm; Mon–Thurs 5:30–11pm; Fri–Sat 5:30–11:30pm. Subway: 4, 5, 6, N, R, W to 59th St.

Country 💎💎 FRENCH/AMERICAN   Supervised by chef Geoffrey Zakarian, the chef of the popular and acclaimed Town restaurant, it's hard to believe that this stunningly elegant, urbane restaurant in the recently renovated Hotel Carlton could be the "Country" in Zakarian's Town/Country duo. There's really nothing country about the place. And that's not a knock. Gorgeously designed by architect David Rockwell, the restaurant's magnificent centerpiece is the restored 200-square-foot Tiffany skylight dome that was hidden over the years by a dropped ceiling. Zakarian's prix-fixe menu changes every other week and matches the decor's sophisticated style. When I visited for an early spring dinner, warm asparagus in a light lemon vinaigrette was an outstanding first-course option while the lamb cannelloni (tender pieces of shredded lamb in a wonton-thin dumpling) made the perfect second-course accompaniment. Of the third-course options, the striped bass with crushed herbs, potatoes, and clams was the standout. A selection of cheeses is offered as a dessert option and it's hard to resist. Downstairs are the more countrified, darker, wood-paneled booths of Café at Country.

90 Madison Ave. (at 29th St.). ⓒ 212/889-7100. Reservations required. Prix-fixe $105; 5-course tasting menu $110; 4-course tasting menu $105; 6-course $135. AE, DC, DISC, MC, V. Sun–Thurs 5:30–10pm; Fri–Sat 5:30–11pm. Café at Country main courses $15–$27. Mon–Sat 11:30am–3pm and 5:30–11pm; Sun 10:30am–3pm. Subway: N/R to 28th St.; 6 to 28th St.

Oceana 💎💎💎 SEAFOOD   When you enter Oceana, the nautical themes are obvious. But this is no seafood shack—it's more like a luxury ocean liner. Standouts include tartare of yellowfin tuna with daikon radish, black cardamom, and horseradish sorbet; striped bass wrapped in a ham croissant; and stuffed artichoke and Icelandic cod basted in butter and herbs. His dishes look so good on the plate you might not want to eat them, but that would be a big mistake. In this case the artwork is extremely edible. Oceana also features an excellent wine list and your waiter will help pair wines with your dishes if you desire. Though this is not your everyday restaurant—prices are too steep for that—the atmosphere is relaxed and the service is personable.

55 E. 54th St. (btwn Park and Madison aves.). ⓒ 212/759-5941. www.oceanarestaurant.com. Reservations recommended. 3-course prix fixe $48 lunch, $78 dinner. AE, DISC, MC, V. Mon–Fri noon–2:30pm and 5:30–10:30pm; Sat 5–10:30pm. Subway: E, F to Fifth Ave.

Pampano 💎💎 MEXICAN SEAFOOD   I'm usually wary of overly presented and overpriced Mexican food, much preferring the working-stiff stuff I can buy from the taco trucks in east Harlem. Pampano, however, does things with Mexican ingredients, especially seafood, that no taco truck I know has ever done before—and the lovely, lush townhouse location is so much more comfortable. You might want to venture from the fish on the menu, but I wouldn't recommend it. Start with the tasting of either three or four ceviches; they are all spectacular, especially the mahimahi bathed in lemon juice, cilantro, chiles, and avocado. For a rare and special treat, try a lobster taco—you won't find that at your local *taqueria.* Of the entrees, it would be difficult to order anything but the fantastic *pampano adobado,* sautéed pompano with creamy black rice, roasted garlic, and chile *guajillo* sauce, but you won't suffer too much if you settle for the memorable pan-fried baby red snapper in a *chile de arbol* sauce. Save room for chocolate flan for dessert and maybe a cleansing shot of one of the restaurant's many excellent tequilas. Pampano is a scene, but a festive one with a lively bar and a beautiful upstairs dining area.

209 E. 49th St. (at Third Ave.). ⓒ 212/751-4545. Reservations recommended. Main courses $23–$30. AE, DC, MC, V. Mon–Fri 11:30am–2:30pm; Mon–Wed 5–10pm; Thurs–Sat 5–10:30pm; Sun 5–9:30pm. Subway: E, V to Lexington Ave./53rd St.; 6 to 51st St.

Where to Find Your (Burger) Bliss in NYC

New York is hamburger happy. And that happiness has nothing to do with Mickey D's or BK. It's about real, solid, locally made burgers and there are plenty of places to find them without resorting to supersizing yourself. Here are some:

Brgr ⍟ 287 Seventh Ave. at 26th St (✆ **212/488-7500**). The newest addition to this rarefied list opened in late 2006 and features top quality meats and homemade toppings. The beef is natural angus from Montana Legend beef but just as good are the turkey burgers made from Plainville Farms all-natural turkeys. Some of the toppings include Roquefort cheese, sweet onion marmalade, and homemade burger sauce. Save room for a Brgr shake made with Ronnybrook farms milk and ice cream.

Burger Joint ⍟⍟ Located discreetly behind a curtain in the lobby of Le Parker Meridien Hotel, 118 W. 57th St. (✆ **212/708-7414**), this is like the burger joint you might remember in college—only the burgers are better. And for a place off the lobby of a fancy hotel, it's downright cheap.

New York Burger Co., 303 Park Ave. South, between 23rd & 24th streets (✆ **212/254-2727**), and 678 Sixth Ave., between 21st & 22nd streets (✆ **212/229-1404**). Here you won't feel guilty as you devour the burgers at this "healthy" fast-food alternative. The beef is all-natural, Coleman beef devoid of hormones or antibiotics and served on a fresh-baked brioche. What do they taste like? The burgers have plenty of flavor and come in a number of varieties.

P.J. Clarke's ⍟ 915 Third Ave., at 55th Street (✆ **212/317-1616**; www.pjclarkes.com). P.J. Clarke's has been a Midtown institution for over 50 years and its hamburger, like the restaurant's old wood walls, broken telephone booth, and hidden dining nook for two, has been blessedly preserved. Nothing more than a slab of chopped meat cooked to order, on a bun, and for the curious price of $8.10, the hamburger is a simple masterpiece. A new Clarke's opened in the Financial District downtown at 4 World Financial Center (✆ **212/285-1500**).

Rare Bar & Grill ⍟ 303 Lexington Ave., between 37th & 38th streets (✆ **212/481-1999**). You might pay a little more for your burger at Rare Bar & Grill—they range from $9–$20—but you are paying for 8 ounces of Grade A American chuck beef that is ground daily at the restaurant. Rare has a number of interesting varieties; my favorite is the M&M burger with caramelized shallots, cheddar cheese, and apple-smoked bacon flambéed in whiskey. Rare is so popular they recently opened another branch downtown, at 228 Bleecker St., between Carmine and Downing streets (✆ **212/691-7273**).

Shake Shack, in Madison Square Park (✆ **212/889-6600**). Open from the beginning of spring through most of November, Danny Meyer of Gramercy Tavern, The Modern, and Eleven Madison Park fame is behind this "shack" in the middle of Madison Square Park where adoring fans line up early and often for takeout burgers, hot dogs, and milkshakes. Try to come during off-hours, if possible, to avoid the lines; the burgers are good, but we're just talking hamburgers here—not worth waiting interminably for.

Kids Family-Friendly Restaurants

While it's always smart to call ahead to make sure a restaurant has kids' menus and highchairs, you can count on the following to be especially accommodating. What kid doesn't love pizza? See the sidebar "Pizza, New York–Style," on p. 196, for suggestions.

Here are some other options for the whole family:

Big Nick's Burger and Pizza Joint ☞ (p. 213) In the unlikely event that your kids can't find anything they like on the 27-page menu, they can just tune in to the nonstop *Three Stooges* marathon playing on the restaurant's TVs.

Bubby's Brooklyn ☞ (p. 221) Larger than the TriBeCa branch, this Bubby's has a tremendous view of Manhattan and is across the street from a playground.

Carmine's ☞ (p. 194 and 212) This rollicking family-style Italian restaurant was created with kids in mind. You won't have to worry about them making too much noise here.

City Bakery ☞ (p. 188) What child wouldn't be taken with the chocolate spinning wheel and homemade marshmallows? As a bonus, the organic fare is nutritious *and* delicious.

Dinosaur Bar-B-Que ☞ (p. 218) Loud and casual, kids come away with dinosaur tattoos to go with the barbecue-sauce stains that they will undoubtedly wear on their clothes.

Good Enough to Eat ☞ (p. 214) Comfort food for kids, like macaroni and cheese, pizza, and great desserts.

Mickey Mantle's (p. 382) As a player, the Mick had a reputation for being testy with autograph hounds and children, but he more than made up for it in retirement when he opened his extremely kid-friendly restaurant located just across the street from Central Park.

Nick's Family-Style Restaurant and Pizzeria ☞ (p. 217) With locations in both Queens and Manhattan, Nick's has been wowing families for over a decade with its praiseworthy pizza and Italian specialties.

Serendipity 3 (p. 217) Kids will love this whimsical restaurant and ice cream shop, which serves up a huge menu of American favorites, followed up by colossal ice cream treats.

Tavern on the Green (p. 210) Your kids will be wowed by the Central Park setting, and a children's menu makes them easy and affordable to feed. What's more, if the little ones get rambunctious, you just have to take them outdoors to blow off a little steam.

Virgil's Real BBQ ☞☞ (p. 195) This pleasing Times Square barbecue joint welcomes kids with open arms—and Junior will be more than happy, I'm sure, to be *expected* to eat with his hands.

Where the Editor Eats . . .

After a long day of shepherding Frommer's Travel Guides from manuscript to publication, this editor can use a good meal, a stiff drink, and a kind word. Here are some places where I can find them:

In the East Village, I've been going to **Christine's** (208 First Ave., between 12th & 13th sts.; ☎ **212/979-2810;** subway: L to First Ave.) for a couple of decades now, since I was a little typesetter correcting the spelling in gun and hairstyle magazines. The prices haven't gone up much, but it's a lot spiffier than it used to be. The waitresses are still the same bored, pretty eastern European women, the mushroom barley soup is still awesome, and you can still get a full dinner with entrees from kielbasa (like my Polish grandma used to make) to chicken livers with mushrooms to stuffed cabbage, all with two veggies for under $10, and pierogies of many varieties (a half-order of four will run you less than $5). And there's a garden in the back where you can eat in the warm weather. (They don't serve alcohol, but there are plenty of bars in the neighborhood).

Over in the West Village, I like to swing by **Cowgirl Hall of Fame** (519 Hudson St., at W. 10th St.; ☎ **212/633-1133;** subway: 1 to Christopher St.) for a blood orange margarita and not-too-expensive Tex-Mex-style snacks or dinners (from chicken-fried chicken and chicken-fried steak, to Frito pie, Whisky Pork Chops, a bunch of salads, and veggie options). It's a *very* mixed scene, with local families piling into the dining room with the kids, a gayish crowd at the bar, and people who just want to hang out in the almost-hidden rec-room-style lounge toward the back. The staff is friendly and sassy and part of the show.

Zuni (598 Ninth Ave., just below 43rd St.; ☎ **212/765-7626;** www.zuniny. com) is Off-Off-Broadway central; each evening waves of actors, directors, techies, and audiences flood the place from various theaters in the neighborhood. They make the bar a fun scene, with the booths in the back quiet enough to hear yourself talk, but with enough room to tablehop if you see friends. The menu is American/eclectic with a tilt toward Mexican (ask about the quesadilla of the day!). Also recommendable are the sandwiches (grilled salmon with wasabi aioli, an excellent burger) and solid entrees with daily specials and soups. The bar makes good, strong drinks. It's a bargain for the area, which means it'll cost more than a hole-in-the-wall, but a *lot* less than, say, Esca (which is directly across the street).

A little further uptown, **Druids** (736 Tenth Ave., between 50th and 51st sts.; ☎ **212/307-6410;** subway: A, C, E to 50th St.) calls itself a "Gourmet Irish Pub." Whatever. It's a really good restaurant (not cheap, but we consider it a good value "splurge") disguised as an Irish pub. The giveaways are the excellent menu that's not afraid of meat dishes (from duck breast to rack of lamb to venison), with a pasta of the day, a solid wine list, and an ambience that's sort of a combo of County Something-or-Other and Downtown, with original art on the walls and various vintage tchotchkes over the bar. There's also a back garden.

—Kathleen Warnock

MODERATE

Also consider **P.J. Clarke's** &, 915 Third Ave., at 55th Street (© **212/317-1616;** www.pjclarkes.com), for their old-world charm and legendary hamburger. For a more innovative, experimental hamburger, try **Rare Bar & Grill,** 303 Lexington Ave., between 37th and 38th streets (© **212/481-1999**). For more information on both, see the box "Where to Find Your (Burger) Bliss," on p. 202.

INEXPENSIVE

The lower concourse of **Grand Central Terminal** &&, 42nd Street at Park Avenue, has developed into a quick-bite bonanza that is an ideal choice for lunch—and the setting is an architecture-lover's delight. Head downstairs and choose from among the many outlets, offering everything from bratwurst to sushi. Standouts include **Junior's,** an offshoot of the Brooklyn stalwart, serving deli sandwiches, terrific steak burgers, and their world-famous cheesecake in their own waiter-serviced dining area.

For a glorious meal, dining under an impressive curved and tiled ceiling, try the New York landmark **Oyster Bar & Restaurant** & (© **212/490-6650;** www.oyster barny.com). Excellent soups and sandwiches (most for under $10) fall into the "inexpensive" category, but you will head on up into "moderate" and "expensive" for full meals of the fresh, well-prepared seafood. For a complete list of vendors, check out www.grandcentralterminal.com.

In addition to the listings below, there's also **Ess-A-Bagel** (see "The Hole Truth: N.Y.'s Best Bagels," p. 189) at 831 Third Ave., at 51st Street (© **212/980-1010**).

Kalustyan's & MIDDLE EASTERN/INTERNATIONAL DELI   The heady smell of spices and barrels full of nuts and other delicacies may have you lingering on the first floor, but before you start loading up with exotica, take the stairs up to the deli. A smiling little man in a white hat will likely be there to greet you. Magazine and newspaper articles plastered all over the place feature photographs of your new friend, the smiling little man with the white cap. Ask for the *mujadarra* (a traditional Arabian lentil-and-rice dish with caramelized onions, served as a salad or in pita bread), pay $4, and settle in at one of the little windowside tables.

123 Lexington Ave. (at 28th St.). © 212/685-3451. www.kalustyans.com. Soups, salads, sandwiches under $10. AE, MC, V. Mon–Sat 10am–8pm; Sun 11am–7pm. Subway: 6 to 28th St.

12 Upper West Side

To locate the restaurants in this section, see the map on p. 206.

VERY EXPENSIVE

Also consider the two four-star-rated restaurants on Columbus Circle: **Jean-Georges** &&&, in the Trump International Hotel & Tower, 1 Central Park West, at 60th Street/Columbus Circle (© **212/299-3900;** www.jean-georges.com), and **Masa,** in the Time Warner Center, 10 Columbus Circle (© **212/823-9800**). See the sidebar "Food Splurge" on p. 209.

Café des Artistes & FRENCH   One of the oldest restaurants in Manhattan, Café des Artistes was established in 1917 as a haven for artists, many whom lived in the surrounding area or upstairs at the Hotel des Artistes. One of those artists was Howard Chandler Christy, who painted the gorgeous "wood nymph" murals that still adorn the restaurant. Now, however, not many artists can afford the solid, country French food served at the Café. But this is a place to splurge—to soak in not only the history

Where to Dine Uptown

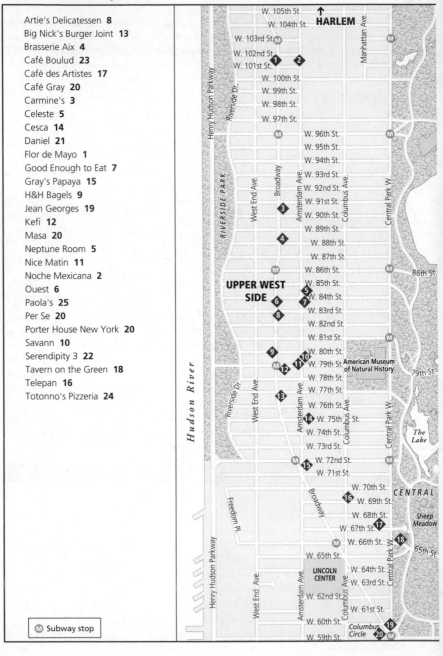

M Subway stop

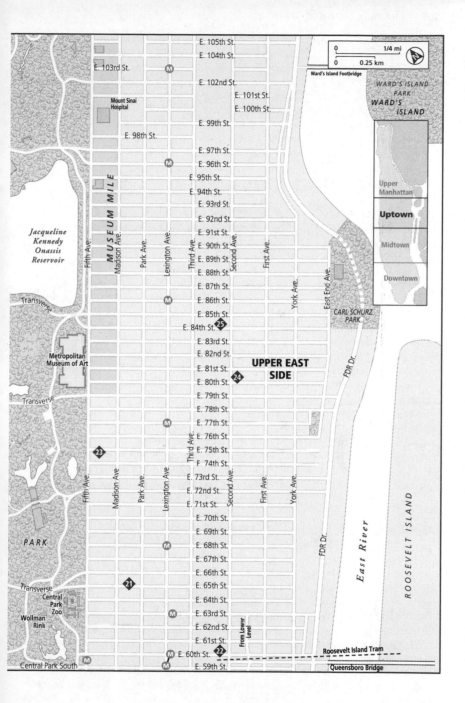

E. 105th St.
E. 104th St.
E. 103rd St.
E. 102nd St.
E. 101st St.
E. 100th St.
Mount Sinai Hospital
E. 99th St.
E. 98th St.
E. 97th St.
E. 96th St.
E. 95th St.
E. 94th St.
E. 93rd St.
E. 92nd St.
E. 91st St.
E. 90th St.
E. 89th St.
E. 88th St.
E. 87th St.
E. 86th St.
E. 85th St.
E. 84th St.
E. 83rd St.
E. 82nd St.
E. 81st St.
E. 80th St.
E. 79th St.
E. 78th St.
E. 77th St.
E. 76th St.
E. 75th St.
E. 74th St.
E. 73rd St.
E. 72nd St.
E. 71st St.
E. 70th St.
E. 69th St.
E. 68th St.
E. 67th St.
E. 66th St.
E. 65th St.
E. 64th St.
E. 63rd St.
E. 62nd St.
E. 61st St.
E. 60th St.
E. 59th St.

Jacqueline Kennedy Onassis Reservoir

Fifth Ave.
MUSEUM MILE
Madison Ave.
Park Ave.
Lexington Ave.
Third Ave.
Second Ave.
First Ave.
York Ave.
East End Ave.

Transverse
Metropolitan Museum of Art
Transverse

UPPER EAST SIDE

CARL SCHURZ PARK

FDR Dr.

PARK

Transverse
Central Park Zoo
Wollman Rink
Central Park South

Madison Ave.
Park Ave.
Lexington Ave.
Third Ave.
Second Ave.
First Ave.
York Ave.

From Lower Level

FDR Dr.

East River

ROOSEVELT ISLAND

Roosevelt Island Tram
Queensboro Bridge

Ward's Island Footbridge

WARD'S ISLAND PARK
WARD'S ISLAND

0   1/4 mi
0   0.25 km

Upper Manhattan
Uptown
Midtown
Downtown

but the romantic aura emanating from those murals. You won't find any fancy twists on French cooking here and I recommend sticking with the old favorites such as the starters—salmon five ways or snails (not escargots?)—or entrees such as Dover sole with brown butter sauce, roasted duck, or the challengingly hearty *pot-au-feu,* complete with marrow bone. For dessert, the chocolate bread pudding is a treat, while the hot-fudge Napoleon was truly, as described by my waiter, a "killer." The waiters here have been around the block a few times, so service is refreshingly old-school. The restaurant does a brisk, pre–Lincoln Center business, so if you want intimacy and romance, the main reason to come here, reserve before or after the crush.

1 W. 67th St. (at Central Park West). © 212/877-3500. www.cafenyc.com. Reservations strongly recommended. Jackets preferred for men. Main courses $18–$29 for lunch; $29–$49 for dinner. AE, DC, DISC, MC, V. Mon–Fri noon–3pm; brunch Sat 11am–3pm; Sun 10am–3pm; Mon–Sat 5–11:45pm; Sun 5:30–11pm. Subway: 1 to 66th St.

Café Gray ⓡⓡ FRENCH/ASIAN/EASTERN EUROPEAN   Gray Kunz, a four star winner from the *New York Times* when he was the head chef of the now departed Lespinasse, in 2004, opened his own place amongst the most prestigious (and expensive) food court in the world in the Time Warner Center. Café Gray sits on a corner of the third floor overlooking Central Park. The problem is, you cannot see much of Central Park from the restaurant's dining room. Instead, blocking the view is the live show of talented cooks preparing your meal in the expansive open kitchen. You just can't have it all here. But you won't care once those well-trained cooks plate your dishes and your server begins bringing them to you. And if one of those first plates holds the unparalleled starter of risotto with a mushroom fricassee, the mushroom gravy rich and melding mouth wateringly with the starch of the risotto, the lack of Central Park view will no longer be worthy of complaint. It seems that short ribs are on every menu of all the new trendy restaurants. That may be because they all are trying to equal Chef Kunz's remarkable braised short ribs he pairs with a delicate mound of soft grits in a *meux* mustard sauce. And though the menu changes seasonally, the short ribs will always be available. Desserts, as they seem to do at so many quality restaurants, sometimes exceed the main courses in grandeur and the chocolate pistachio soufflé is no exception. Service is impeccable and welcomingly casual, but with all the commotion in the kitchen do not expect a hushed environment.

Time Warner Center (at 59th St.), 3rd floor. © 212/823-6338. www.cafegray.com. Main courses: $28–$43. AE, DC, DISC, MC, V. Tue–Fri noon–2pm; Sun–Wed 5:30–10pm; Thurs–Sat 5:30–11pm. Subway: 1,A,B,C,D to 59th St, Columbus Circle.

Porter House New York ⓡⓡ STEAKHOUSE   Michael Lomonaco, the former chef of Windows on the World, the famed rooftop restaurant of the World Trade Center, experienced first hand the tragedy of September 11, 2001 when he lost not only his restaurant, but so many of his friends and employees. It's only fitting that he has rebounded with a new-in 2006 restaurant featuring windows not looking out on the world, but almost as good—looking out on Central Park. The space, located in the Time Warner Center on Columbus Circles, is designed by Jeffrey Beers (**Fiamma Osteria,** see p. 171), is sleek with large leather banquettes for groups along with smaller, white table- clothed tables by the floor-to-ceiling windows. But even if there was no view, this steakhouse satisfies the essentials of the best red meat emporiums, with a few inventive twists. I gambled by ordering the chili-rubbed rib eye—would chili obscure the natural flavor of the meat? My gamble paid off; the chili was subtle and actually brought out the cut's essence. If you want your steak straight ahead, the

Food Splurge: Places to Empty Your Wallet

New York can often be silly with excess, especially when it comes to food. This is, after all, the city where a restaurant offers a seasonal double-truffle burger for $99 and a breakfast joint recently pushed a caviar-stuffed frittata (that's an omelet with salty fish eggs) for $1,000. But in this city, there is never a shortage of people who are willing to fork it over just for the pleasure of eating in a restaurant with a bunch of stars from some prestigious reviewer. The waiting lists for reservations at these places are sometimes months long. We, of course, would never waste our hard-earned money on such a frivolous thing as perfectly prepared and presented food in a memorable environment where the customer is really treated like royalty. Or *would* we?

Well, you only live once. So if you are going to go for it, here are five of New York's most expensive and best restaurants:

Daniel, 60 E. 65th St., between Madison & Park avenues (✆ **212/288-0033**; www.danielnyc.com). Neo-Renaissance features—rich mahogany doors, elegant Corinthian columns, and a soaring terra-cotta-tiled ceiling—make an ideal setting for acclaimed chef Daniel Boulud's faultless classic-goes-country French cooking. His eight-course tasting menu goes for $175, while you can get away relatively "cheap" here with a three-course prix fixe for $96.

Jean-Georges ★★★, in the Trump International Hotel & Tower, 1 Central Park West, at 60th Street/Columbus Circle (✆ **212/299-3900**; www.jean-georges.com). Another *New York Times* four-star winner, the signature restaurant of Jean-Georges Vongerichten is the ultimate special-occasion restaurant. And it better be a special occasion if you are going to shell out around $100 for his tasting menu, not including wine.

Le Bernardin, 155 W. 51st St., between Sixth and Seventh avenues (✆ **212/554-1515**; www.le-bernardin.com). Always one of the top New York restaurants in the *Zagat* guide, Le Bernardin also garnered four stars from the *New York Times* in 2005. So I guess it must be good. One of these days, when I save up enough money to pay for the $150 tasting menu, I hope to find out.

Masa, 10 Columbus Circle (✆ **212/823-9800**). This sushi joint in the Time Warner Center became a major conversation piece when the *Times* gave it four stars in 2005. The conversation was not so much about the undoubtedly exquisite sushi prepared by genius chef/owner Masayoshi Takayama, but more about the price, starting at $300 and sometimes climbing to $500 per person for the chef's *omakase* (chef's choice) lunch or dinner.

dry-aged prime strip steak, cooked to perfection and bursting with flavor, won't let you down. Lomonaco tweaks some of the obligatory sides like adding pieces of thick smoky bacon to the creamed spinach and offering porcini mushrooms on a bed of polenta as an alternative to mashed potatoes. But it's the meat—and that you are eating it overlooking Central Park—that makes Porter House New York so special.

10 Columbus Circle (4th Floor) in the Time Warner Center (at 60th St.) ⓒ 212/823-9500. www.porterhouse newyork.com. Main courses: $24–$39. AE, DC, DISC, MC, V. Mon–Sat noon–4pm; Sun noon–3pm; Mon–Thurs 5–10:30pm; Fri–Sat 5–11pm. Subway: A,B,C,D,1 trains to 59th St-Columbus Circle.

EXPENSIVE

Also consider the legendary Central Park **Tavern on the Green,** Central Park West and West 67th Street (ⓒ **212/873-3200**). Here, food takes a back seat to dining in one of the city's prettiest settings. Views are wonderful; in good weather, try for a seat in the outdoor garden, with its whimsical topiary shrubs and Japanese lanterns. It's also a great place to visit during the holidays, and there's a menu just for kids.

Brasserie Aix 𝕬𝕬 MODERN FRENCH   This smartly designed, airy, and comfortable tri-level restaurant is helmed by chef Didier Virot, formerly the executive chef at Jean-Georges, and offers fresh twists on the traditional cuisine of Provence. Virot takes a classic dish like the vegetable soup *pistou* and adds fresh raw sardines—it not only works, it enhances the soup. Both the baked chicken with star anise, honey, mushrooms, and fingerling potatoes and the Atlantic char with a smoked-salmon sauce were done to perfection. The only mistake I encountered was the bland gnocchi with Jerusalem artichoke and black-truffle cream. Desserts are adventurous and may not be for everyone, but it's not often you have the chance to experience Provence salad, sugared green tomatoes, and celery topped with mint sorbet; or a licorice panna cotta. Despite the crowds, Aix's service is personable; waitresses in dowdy brown uniforms are cheerfully helpful, but the restaurant is loud, so don't expect intimacy.

2398 Broadway (at 88th St.). ⓒ 212/874-7400. www.aixnyc.com. Reservations highly recommended. Main courses $26–$39. AE, MC, V. Sun–Thurs 5:30–11pm; Fri–Sat 5:30pm-midnight. Subway: 1 to 86th St.

'Cesca 𝕬𝕬 ITALIAN COUNTRY   It's not easy to describe the Italian food served in 'Cesca; it's like nothing many New Yorkers have experienced. Where else have you had roasted sardines paired with a "soft" egg? With a roaring wood-burning oven as its centerpiece—which is used to roast everything from oysters to peppers—this is as rustic as it gets. Chef/restaurateur Tom Valenti even roasts mushrooms with a rich creamy cheese-filled polenta. It's like you're in an Italian farmhouse where you are served slow-cooked meats like pork shank, the fat cooked off and the meat falling from the bone, or a potato gnocchi with tender braised duck. The food is so intense here; a little goes a long way. But save room for the equally interesting desserts like honey goat-milk gelato or fresh figs with fig gelato. Service is friendly and informal and the restaurant is spacious and comfortable, with a large bar area with long tables where you snack on marinated olives, *fritto misto,* or spicy parmigiana fritters while sipping Italian wines from regions like Sicily, Puglia, or Trentino. This is one of the most popular restaurants on the Upper West Side, so call well ahead for reservations.

164 W. 75th St. (at Amsterdam Ave.). ⓒ 212/787-6300. Reservations strongly recommended. Main courses $17–$34. AE, DC, MC, V. Mon–Thurs 5–11pm; Fri–Sat 5–11:30pm; Sun noon–10pm. Subway: 1, 2, 3 to 72nd St.

The Neptune Room 𝕬 SEAFOOD   The Upper West Side is smoked-fish turf, but when The Neptune Room arrived in 2004, the neighborhood had its first seafood "shack." I use the word shack figuratively because the restaurant, with its aged yacht decor, is much more stylish than that. It's The Neptune Room's "Bait Bar" that gives it that seafood-shack feel. Raw fresh oysters from both coasts, littleneck clams, shrimp cocktail, ceviches, cured anchovies, grilled octopus, and spicy, quickly steamed calamari come served on small plates over crushed ice and are delicious. The shack theme quickly fades when you move to the main courses and ponder Mediterranean-based items like the wonderful cioppino (seafood stew), Parmesan-crusted skate, or the roasted whole-fish; the branzino (Mediterranean sea bass) I had was perfectly cooked and subtly seasoned in olive oil and herbs. In between shack mode and the Mediterranean seafood tour, cleanse your palate with one of the restaurant's excellent salads; the country salad made with frisée, apples, Gorgonzola, and candied almonds was a revelation. Service is knowledgeable and the wine list, all from the Mediterranean, is impressive.

511 Amsterdam Ave. (btwn 84th and 85th sts.). © 212/496-4100. www.neptuneroom.com. Reservations recommended. Bait Bar $7; main courses $19–$29. AE, MC, V. Sun–Mon 5:30–10pm; Tues–Thurs 5:30–11pm; Fri–Sat 5:30–11:30pm; Sat–Sun brunch 11:30am–3pm. Subway: 1 to 86th St.

Ouest 𝒢𝒢𝒢 CONTEMPORARY AMERICAN   When chef/restaurateur Tom Valenti opened Ouest in 2002, it signaled a renaissance in the Upper West Side dining scene. He followed the success of Ouest up with the superb 'Cesca (see above), but Ouest still remains the neighborhood's shining star. With red banquettes and an intimate balcony area, Ouest is both cozy and clubby. Service is personable but also professional—so good you'll need to keep reminding yourself that you are on the Upper West Side. But what really draws the crowds is Valenti's mastery in the kitchen, especially with meats like his signature braised lamb shank or his melt-in-your-mouth braised beef short ribs. The quality suffers not one iota when you switch to seafood. The sautéed skate is perfectly prepared with a simple sauce of parsley and olive oil, while the baby calamari in a spicy tomato sopressata sauce appetizer was so good I actually smiled as I ate it.

2315 Broadway (at 84th St.). © 212/580-8700. www.ouestny.com. Reservations required well in advance. Main courses $23–$36. AE, DC, DISC, MC, V. Mon–Thurs 5:30–11pm; Fri–Sat 5:30–11:30pm; Sun 11am–10pm. Subway: 1, 2 to 86th St.

Telepan 𝒢𝒢 AMERICAN   It's risky naming a restaurant after yourself, but also displays brash confidence in your abilities. Daniel Boulud has done it; Jean Georges Vongrichten has done it; David Bouley has done it . . . all with positive results. And in 2006, Bill Telepan did it, opening his own restaurant under his name and, like the aforementioned trio; Chef Telepan's risk has paid off. The venue for Telepan is an Upper West Side townhouse with a dining room painted in soothing lime green. The cool design compliments the menu which changes seasonally but always features farm fresh products. I had the good fortune to dine in the spring and was greeted with fresh ramps, fiddleheads, and young peas in many of the dishes I sampled. There was no fresh produce, however, in the foie gras donuts listed as a "share." The "donuts" are dusted with cocoa and cinnamon and might work as well with a cup of java as with a cocktail. Of the appetizers, the standout was the wild green frittata which did indeed come with in-season ramps. Telepan offers Mid Courses and of them, the pea pancakes with pea agnolotti looked and, more importantly, tasted greenmarket fresh. Save room for an entrée, specifically the haddock with a sweet lobster sauce. Whatever you choose to eat, you'll have no problem finding a complementary wine from the restaurant's long and impressive list. Telepan has become a pre-Lincoln Center favorite so if you want to avoid the crush, make a reservation for after curtain.

72 W. 69th St (at Columbus Ave.) © 212/580-4300; www.telepan-ny.com. Reservations recommended. Main courses: $29–$36; Four-course tasting menu $59; five-course tasting menu $69. AE, DC, MC, V. Lunch; Wed–Fri 11:30am–2:30pm; Dinner; Mon–Thurs 5–11pm; Fri–Sat 5–11:30pm; Sun 5–10:30pm; Brunch Sat–Sun 11am–2:30pm. Subway: B,C to 72 nd St.

MODERATE

Also consider **Rack & Soul,** 2818 Broadway, at 109th St (© **212/222-4800**) for the unbeatable combination of barbecued ribs and pan-fried southern style fried chicken.

Carmine's ☆ *Kids* FAMILY-STYLE SOUTHERN ITALIAN   Everything is B-I-G at this rollicking family-style mainstay with two locations, on the Upper West Side (the original) and in Times Square. In many cases big means bad, but not here. Carmine's, with a dining room vast enough to deserve its own zip code, and massive portions, turns out better pasta and entrees than most 20-table Italian restaurants. I've never had pasta here that wasn't al dente, and the marinara sauce is as good as any I've had in Manhattan. The salads are always fresh and the fried calamari perfectly tender. Rigatoni marinara, linguini with white-clam sauce, and ziti with broccoli are pasta standouts, while the best meat entrees include veal parmigiana, broiled porterhouse steak, shrimp scampi, and the remarkable chicken *scarpariello* (chicken pan-broiled with a lemon-rosemary sauce). The tiramisu is pie-size, thick, creamy, and bathed in Kahlúa and Marsala. Order half of what you think you'll need. Don't expect intimate conversation; in fact, it's downright loud. Unless you come early, expect to wait.

2450 Broadway (btwn 90th and 91st sts.). © **212/362-2200.** www.carminesnyc.com. Reservations recommended before 6pm; accepted only for 6 or more after 6pm. Family-style main courses $19–$65 (most $23 or less). AE, DC, DISC, MC, V. Sun–Thurs 11:30am–11pm; Fri–Sat 11:30am–midnight. Subway: 1, 2, 3 to 96th St. Also at 200 W. 44th St. (btwn Broadway and Eighth Ave.). © **212/221-3800.** Subway: A, C, E, N, R, S, 1, 2, 3, 7 to 42nd St./Times Sq.

Kefi ☆☆☆ *Finds* GREEK   In the previous edition of this book, I wrote that Onera, the former Greek restaurant in the same Upper West Side location as Kefi, was not your father's Greek restaurant. Onera, owned by chef Michael Psilakis has been transformed by Psilakis into Kefi and back to something much closer to your father's Greek. More accurately, Kefi is like your Greek mother's (if you had a Greek mother) kitchen and in fact, the restaurant was inspired by Psilakis's mother and her traditional recipes. So gone is the Offal Tasting menu of Onera and in are Greek standards like moussaka, spinach pie, Greek salad, and grilled fish. But oh what Psilakis does with the standards. The *mezes* (Greek appetizers) are good enough to make up a meal; it's hard to resist the selection of spreads accompanied by pita, the warm feta, tomatoes, capers and anchovies, and especially the sublime grilled octopus salad, as good as I've had anywhere. But something's gotta give if you want to save room for entrees like the flat noodles with braised rabbit, the grilled whole branzino with potatoes, olives, tomatoes and feta, or the slow cooked, comforting lamb shank on a bed of orzo. If it is humanly possible after indulging in all of the above, don't miss out on the desserts, most notably the walnut cake with maple walnut ice cream. Service is casual and the space is a bit cramped, but not enough to deter you from the many pleasures of Kefi.

222 W. 79th St. (btwn Broadway and Amsterdam Ave.) © **212/873-0200.** Reservations not taken. Main courses $10–$20. Cash only. Tue–Thurs 5–10:30pm; Fri–Sat 5–11pm; Sun 5–10pm. Subway: 1 to 79th St.

Nice Matin ☆ FRENCH PROVENÇAL   Named after Nice's major newspaper, appropriately you'll find Provençal classics like *pistou, pissaladiere,* and *velouté* of mussels on the menu. You'll also find innovations like the creamy, delicious fava-bean tortelloni, moist grilled sea bass with artichokes stewed in olive oil, and a rich daube of beef short ribs with chickpea fries. There are specials daily; and on Monday, normally not a great day to dine out, the *aioli monstre* is featured—salt cod, shrimp, meats, and vegetables accompanied by a tangy, fresh aioli. On any day you can order the five-napkin burger, also accompanied by that pleasingly persistent aioli. If cholesterol is no concern, opt for the decadently dense sweet-and-sour cream for dessert. Located in the Lucerne hotel, the restaurant, open for breakfast, lunch, and dinner, is loud and busy, so unless you can snare a comfortable booth, don't expect intimacy.

201 W. 79th St. (at Amsterdam Ave.). © 212/873-NICE. Reservations recommended. Main courses $9.25–$20 at lunch, $16–$25 at dinner. AE, DC, MC, V. Breakfast Mon–Fri 7–11:30am; Sat–Sun 7–11am. Lunch Mon–Sat 11:30am–3:30pm. Dinner Mon–Sat 5:30pm–midnight; Sun 5–11pm. Brunch Mon–Sat 7am–3:30pm; Sun 7am–2:30pm. Subway: 1 to 79th St.

Savann 𝒦 MEDITERRANEAN   The restaurant scene on Amsterdam Avenue in the low 80s is particularly volatile, but for over 9 years, Savann has survived on that difficult stretch of real estate thanks to consistently top-notch food, personable service, and a casual, low-key atmosphere. This is a neighborhood place with regulars who swear by the food. Some favorites include the home-cured gravlax, here served over a chickpea-scallion pancake in a flying-fish caviar and dill sauce; the grilled calamari; the Seafood Savann, a medley of seafood in a light tomato sauce served over linguine; the mixed seafood phyllo purse; and the perfectly cooked filet mignon. For dessert don't miss the *tarte tatine,* a homemade apple tart served with cinnamon ice cream and warm honey. In warm weather, the sidewalk cafe is a great place for people-watching.

414 Amsterdam Ave. (btwn 79th and 80th sts.). © 212/580-0202. www.savann.com. Reservations recommended. Main courses $12–$27 (most under $20). AE, MC, V. Mon–Fri noon–3:30pm; Sat–Sun 11am–3:30pm; daily 4–11pm. Subway: 1 to 79th St.

INEXPENSIVE

For breakfast or lunch, also consider **Artie's Delicatessen,** 2290 Broadway, between 82nd and 83rd streets (© 212/579-5959; www.arties.com), and **Barney Greengrass, the Sturgeon King,** 541 Amsterdam Ave., between 86th and 87th streets (© 212/724-4707), two of the best Jewish delis in town. See "The New York Deli News" sidebar on p. 199 for further details.

You'll find some of the best bagels in New York on the Upper West Side, including **H&H Bagels,** 2239 Broadway, at 80th Street (© 212/595-8003), and **Absolute Bagels,** 2788 Broadway, between 106th and 107th streets (© 212/932-2052). For more information, see the box "The Hole Truth: N.Y.'s Best Bagels," on p. 189.

For non-vegetarians and the non-health-minded, consider the cheapest, yet in some ways most comforting, indulgence: **Gray's Papaya,** 2090 Broadway, at 72nd Street (© 212/799-0243). This 24-hour hot-dog stand is a New York institution. See the box "Food in a N.Y. Minute" for more.

Big Nick's Burger and Pizza Joint 𝒦 *Kids* AMERICAN/PIZZA   A neighborhood landmark since 1962, Big Nick's has a menu that seems to have grown each year of its existence—it's now a whopping 27 pages long. Trying to decide if you want the Madrid burger, with olives, feta, and pimentos, with or without buffalo meat; a slice of Hawaiian pizza; or just an order of the spinach pie can be exhausting. If reading the menu is too much for you, peruse the numerous photos of celebrities who have supposedly chowed down at Big Nick's over the years, or just keep your eyes on the non-stop *Three Stooges* marathon playing on the restaurant's televisions. Whatever you do, you'll never forget your Big Nick's experience. With all those diversions, it's a great place to take the kids; they'll never be bored.

2175 Broadway (at 77th St.). © 212/362-9238. www.bignicksnyc.com. Reservations not accepted. Main courses $3.50–$19 (most less than $10). MC, V. Daily 24-hr. Subway: 1 to 79th St.

Celeste 🍴🍴 *(Finds)* ITALIAN   Tiny but charming Celeste features its own wood-burning pizza oven, which churns out thin-crusted, simple but delicious pizzas. But pizza is not the only attraction here; the *"fritti"* (fried) course is unique; the *fritto misto de pesce* (fried mixed seafood) is delectable, but the fried zucchini blossoms, usually available in the summer and fall, are amazing. The fresh pastas are better than the dried pasta; I never thought the fresh egg noodles with cabbage, shrimp, and sheep's cheese would work, but it was delicious. Not on the menu but usually available are plates of rare, artisanal Italian cheeses served with homemade jams. Though the main courses are also good, stick with the pizzas, antipasto, *frittis,* and pastas. For dessert, try the gelato; the pistachio was the best I've ever had in New York. The restaurant has been "discovered," so go early or go late or expect a wait.

502 Amsterdam Ave. (btwn 84th and 85th sts.). 📞 **212/874-4559.** Reservations not accepted. Pizza $10–$12; antipasto $7–$10; pasta $10; main courses $14–$16. No credit cards. Mon–Sat 5–11pm; Sun noon–10:30pm. Subway: 1 to 86th St.

Flor de Mayo *(Finds)* CUBAN/CHINESE   Cuban/Chinese cuisine is a New York phenomenon that started in the late 1950s when Cubans of Chinese heritage immigrated to New York after the revolution. Most of the immigrants took up residence on the Upper West Side, and Cuban/Chinese restaurants flourished. Many have disappeared, but the best one, Flor de Mayo, still remains and is so popular that a new branch opened further south on Amsterdam Avenue. The kitchen excels at both sides of the massive menu, but the best dish is the *la brasa* half-chicken lunch special—beautifully spiced and slow-roasted until it's fork tender and falling off the bone, served with a giant pile of fried rice, bounteous with roast pork, shrimp, and veggies. Offered Monday through Saturday until 4:30pm, the whole meal is just $6.95, and it's enough to fortify you for the day. Service and atmosphere are reminiscent of Chinatown: efficient and lightning-quick. My favorite combo: the hearty, noodles-, greens-, shrimp-, and pork-laden Chinese soup with yellow rice and black beans.

2651 Broadway (btwn 100th and 101st sts.). 📞 **212/663-5520** or 212/595-2525. Reservations not accepted. Main courses $4.50–$19 (most under $10); lunch specials $5–$7 (Mon–Sat to 4:30pm). AE, MC, V ($15 minimum). Daily noon–midnight. Subway: 1 to 103rd St. Also at 484 Amsterdam Ave. (btwn 83rd and 84th sts.). 📞 **212/787-3388.** Subway: 1 to 86th St.

Good Enough to Eat 🍴 *(Kids) (Finds)* AMERICAN HOME COOKING   For over 25 years the crowds have been lining up on weekends outside Good Enough to Eat to experience chef/owner Carrie Levin's incredible breakfasts (see "Breakfast, Not Brunch," p. 215). As a result, lunch and dinner have been somewhat overlooked. Too bad, because these meals can be just as great as the breakfasts. The restaurant's cow motif and farmhouse knickknacks imply hearty, home-cooked food, and that's what's done best here. Stick with the classics: meatloaf with gravy and mashed potatoes; turkey dinner with cranberry relish, gravy, and cornbread stuffing; macaroni and cheese; griddled corn bread; and the BBQ sandwich, roast chicken with barbecue sauce and homemade potato chips. And save room for the homemade desserts; though the selection is often overwhelming, I can never resist the coconut cake. This is food you loved as a kid, which is one reason why the kids will love it today. There are only 20 tables here, so expect a wait on weekends during the day or for dinner after six.

483 Amsterdam Ave. (btwn 83rd and 84th sts.). 📞 **212/496-0163.** www.goodenoughtoeat.com. Breakfast $5.25–$12; lunch $8.50–$15; dinner $8.50–$23 (most under $18). AE, MC, V. Breakfast Mon–Fri 8:30am–4pm, Sat–Sun 9am–4pm; lunch Mon noon–4pm, Tues–Fri 11:30am–4pm; dinner Mon–Thurs 5:30–10:30pm, Fri–Sat 5:30–11pm, Sun 5:30–10:30pm. Subway: 1 to 86th St.

Breakfast, Not Brunch!

Brunch has always been a pet peeve of mine. I mean, what is it really but a slightly fancier version of breakfast at inflated prices? And it's not even served until mid-morning—and only on weekends. I'll take breakfast any day over brunch—*especially* on weekends. Here are some of my favorite breakfast spots:

Big Wong King ⊛, 67 Mott St., between Canal and Bayard streets (© 212/964-0540). No eggs. No coffee. No pancakes. Can this be breakfast? You bet it is! Not much is more satisfying in the morning than a hot bowl of congee (rice porridge with either pork, beef, or shrimp) accompanied with a fried cruller and tea served in a glass. It might sound a little unusual, but you won't be alone; Big Wong is a favorite for breakfast among the residents of Chinatown. Opens daily at 8:30am. For more on Big Wong King, see p. 166.

Bubby's Pie Company ⊛, 120 Hudson St., at North Moore Street (© 212/219-0666; www.bubbys.com). I don't usually order grits north of the Mason-Dixon line, but I make an exception at Bubby's. They are the perfect complement to Bubby's Breakfast: two eggs, toast, bacon, and a cup of joe. Open at 8am Monday through Friday and 9am Saturday and Sunday. For more on Bubby's, see p. 164.

Clinton St. Baking Company ⊛, 4 Clinton St., at Houston Street (© 646/602-6263). The lines are long on weekend mornings, but you can get breakfast all day here. Meaning you can eat their unbelievable pancakes at four in the afternoon—if that's breakfast time for you.

Good Enough to Eat ⊛, 483 Amsterdam Ave., between 83rd and 84th streets (© 212/496-0163). The wait for breakfast at this Upper West Side institution on the weekends is ridiculous, so try to go during the week when you can gorge on pumpkin French toast; a "Wall Street" omelet, with honey-mustard-glazed ham with Vermont cheddar; or "Peter Paul" pancakes, filled with Belgian chocolate chips, coconut, and topped with coconut. I'm getting hungry writing this. Opens at 8am Monday through Friday and 9am Saturday and Sunday. See p. 214.

Norma's ⊛⊛, at Le Parker Meridien Hotel, 118 W. 57th St., between Sixth and Seventh avenues (© 212/708-7460). An ode to the ultimate comfort food. It's pricey, but worth it for classics done with style and creativity. See p. 195.

Veselka ⊛, 144 Second Ave., at 9th Street (© 212/228-9682). The Greek diner might be extinct in Manhattan, but this Ukrainian diner lives on. And we are all grateful because New York just would not be the same without Veselka's buckwheat pancakes and cheese blintzes. Open 24 hours. See p. 176.

Noche Mexicana ⊛ *Finds* MEXICAN   This Mexican restaurant serves some of the best tamales in New York. Wrapped in cornhusks, as a good tamale should be, they come in two varieties: in a red mole sauce with shredded chicken or in a green tomatillo sauce with shredded pork. There are three tamales in each order, which costs only $5, making it a cheap and almost perfect lunch. The burritos are authentic and meals unto themselves. The *tinga* burrito, shredded chicken in a tomato-and-onion chipotle sauce, is my favorite. Each is stuffed with rice, beans, and guacamole. Don't get fancy here; stick with the tamales, burritos, and soft tacos, the best being the taco *al pastor,* a taco stuffed with pork marinated with pineapple and onions.

852 Amsterdam Ave. (btwn 101st and 102nd sts.). (℃ 212/662-6900 or 212/662-7400. Burritos $6.50–$8.50; tacos $2; tamales $6; Mexican dishes $9.50–$11. AE, DISC, MC, V. Sun–Thurs 10am–11pm; Fri–Sat 10am–midnight. Subway: 1 to 103rd St.

13 Upper East Side

To locate the restaurants in this section, see the map on p. 206.

VERY EXPENSIVE

Also consider elegant **Daniel,** 60 E. 65th St., between Madison and Park avenues (℃ 212/288-0033; www.danielnyc.com). See the sidebar "Food Splurge," on p. 209.

EXPENSIVE

Café Boulud ♠ *Value* FRENCH   Dying to try the stellar cuisine of Daniel Boulud, New York's best French chef, but can't quite afford **Daniel?** Then head to Café Boulud, Boulud's more casual playground for new ideas and culinary cross-pollinations. Daniel's high style has been pleasingly laid back and toned down here. With the food, Boulud has gone eclectic, offering four menus: *La Tradition,* featuring Boulud's signature French-country classics; *Le Potager,* a vegetarian menu; *La Saison,* seasonal dishes; and *Le Voyage,* a monthly globe-hopping menu highlighting Tuscany, Thailand, or somewhere in between. The experimental nature of the wide-ranging menu makes choosing a thrill, and even the most inventive dishes tend to dazzle the palate. But in true Boulud tradition, La Tradition and La Saison are where the kitchen really excels. The poached Dover sole with baby leeks and sauce vin blanc is truly memorable. All in all, a first-rate dining experience at more palatable prices than cuisine this memorable usually costs. Don't be in a rush, though, especially at lunch.

20 E. 76th St. (btwn Madison and Fifth aves.). (℃ 212/772-2600. www.danielnyc.com. Reservations recommended. Main courses $25–$40 at lunch, $26–$43 at dinner; 2- or 3-course prix-fixe lunch $30–$38. AE, DC, DISC, MC, V. Daily 5:45–11pm; Tues–Sat noon–2:30pm (no lunch Sat July–Aug). Subway: 6 to 77th St.

Paola's ♠ ITALIAN   There is no shortage of Italian restaurants on the Upper East Side, but strength is not always in numbers and many are mediocre at best. There is nothing, however, mediocre about Paola's, and having survived and thrived in the neighborhood for over 10 years is testament to the restaurant's quality and charms. The charm begins with Paola herself, almost always present and always the gracious host. The two dining rooms are comforting and inviting; the larger centered around a wood-burning oven used to cook many of the restaurant's meat dishes, the other the smaller, but cozy, wine room. Most appealing of all is the menu. Hope that Paola has found baby artichokes the day you visit because you will want to begin with the *carciofi alla Giudea,* artichokes prepared in the style of the Roman Jews—cooked twice and addictively crispy. The pastas are usually homemade; the pappardelle with a duck-meat ragu is a standout, while the hand-rolled *trofie* served with pesto is a Paola's specialty. The *stinco d'agnello,* slow-roasted lamb shank with sage and parmesan polenta, is a hearty main course something roasted in the wood burning oven, as are the naturally raised, corn-fed poussins, served with potato gratin and sautéed greens. Fig ice cream topped with port-soaked figs is the decadent way to finish your meal.

245 E. 84th St. (btwn Second and Third aves.). ℂ **212/794-1890.** www.paolasrestaurant.com. Reservations recommended. Pasta $14–$17; main courses $22–$30. AE, MC, V. Sun–Fri 1–4pm; Sun–Wed 5–10pm; Thurs–Sat 5–11pm. Subway: 4, 5, 6 to 86th St.

INEXPENSIVE

For better-than-average pizza, head to **Totonno's Pizzeria Napolitano,** 1544 Second Ave., between 80th and 81st streets (ℂ **212/327-2800**), the Manhattan branch of the famous Totonno's in Coney Island (see the box "Pizza, New York–Style," on p. 196).

Nick's Family-Style Restaurant and Pizzeria 🎇 *Kids* ITALIAN Since 1994, Nick Angelis has wowed them in Forest Hills, Queens, with his pizza. In 2003 he took his act to Manhattan, where the pizza is garnering equally high praise. The pizza here is thin-crusted, with the proper proportions of creamy, homemade mozzarella and fresh tomato sauce. But this is much more than a pizzeria: Try the light, lemony baked clams or "Josephine's" perfectly breaded eggplant parmigiana. If you dare combine pizza with a calzone, this is the place; Nick's calzone, stuffed with ricotta and mozzarella cheese, is spectacular. The orecchiette with broccoli rabe and sausage is the pasta winner, while the filet of sole oreganato Livornese with mussels is the standout main course. Save room for an extra-large cannoli for dessert; the shell is perfectly flaky and the filling ultra-creamy. Full orders are enough to feed two or three and are a great bargain for a group, but half-orders are also available. The room is comfortable and far from fancy. Go early or be prepared to wait.

1814 Second Ave. (at 94th St.). ℂ **212/987-5700.** Pizza $12–$14; macaroni half-orders $6–$12, full orders $12–$24; entree half-orders $8.50–$12, full orders $17–$24. AE, DC, DISC, MC, V. Sun–Thurs 11:30am–11pm; Fri–Sat 11:30am–11:30pm. Subway: 6 to 96th St.

Serendipity 3 🎇 *Kids* AMERICAN You'd never guess that this whimsical place was once a top stop on Andy Warhol's itinerary. Wonders never cease—and neither does the confection at this delightful restaurant and sweets shop. Tucked into a cozy brownstone a few steps from Bloomingdale's, happy people gather here at marble-topped ice-cream–parlor tables for burgers and foot-long hot dogs, country meatloaf with mashed potatoes and gravy, and salads and sandwiches with cute names like "The Catcher in the Rye" (their own twist on the BLT, with chicken and Russian dressing—on rye, of course). The food isn't great, but the main courses aren't the point—they're just an excuse to get to the desserts. The restaurant's signature is frozen hot chocolate, a slushy version of everybody's cold-weather favorite, but other crowd-pleasers include dark double devil mousse, celestial carrot cake, lemon icebox pie, and anything with hot fudge. So cast that willpower aside and come on in—Serendipity is an irony-free charmer to be appreciated by adults and kids alike.

225 E. 60th St. (btwn Second and Third aves.). ℂ 212/838-3531. www.serendipity3.com. Reservations accepted for lunch and dinner (not dessert only). Main courses $7.50–$20; sweets and sundaes $6–$20 (most under $10). AE, DC, DISC, MC, V. Sun–Thurs 11:30am–midnight; Fri 11:30am–1am; Sat 11:30am–2am. Subway: N, R to Lexington Ave.; 4, 5, 6 to 59th St.

14 Harlem

To locate these restaurants, see the map on p. 219.

INEXPENSIVE

Also consider **Patsy's Pizzeria** &&& (see "Pizza, New York–Style," on p. 196), and see the sidebar "The Soul of Harlem," on p. 220, for great soul-food restaurants.

Dinosaur Bar-B-Que & (Kids) BARBECUE   It's one thing for a genuine Southern barbecue joint to infiltrate Manhattan, but it's quite another when the barbecue inter-loper is from up north. Now *that's* chutzpah! The popular Syracuse-based barbecue chain that built its reputation with bikers entered the New York City market in 2005 with a roadhouse-like restaurant on the outskirts of west Harlem. What can Syracuse know about barbecue, you ask? Well, they know pulled pork, which is slow-cooked till it's tender. And they know Texas brisket for the same reasons. The ribs I sampled didn't fare as well, but two out of three ain't bad—especially for a Yankee. Sides are standard: coleslaw, macaroni salad, collard greens, and standout barbecue beans. The restaurant is loud, but if you're lucky, you might be able to catch some of the good blues playing over the din. There's a lively bar and service is as down-home as an upstate restaurant can be. Though its location is seemingly remote—close to the West Side Highway—it's only a 3-block walk from the no. 1 train.

646 W. 131st St. (at Twelfth Ave.). ✆ 212/694-1777. www.dinosaurbarbque.com/nyc/nyc.htm. Main courses $13–$22. AE, MC, V. Tues–Thurs 11:30am–11pm; Fri–Sat 11:30am–midnight; Sun noon–10pm. Subway: 1 to 125th St.

15 The Outer Boroughs

THE BRONX

If you are looking for old-fashioned, Italian-American food—the kind you used to get before waiters began asking if you want your water tap or sparkling—look no further than the Bronx. The best concentration of Italian-American "red sauce" restaurants can be found in the Little Italy of the Bronx, on and around **Arthur Avenue.** One of my favorites is **Mario's Restaurant,** 2342 Arthur Ave., between Crescent Avenue and East 187th Street (✆ 718/584-1188), where the Neapolitan pizza is magnificent and the ziti with broccoli unforgettable. Reservations are accepted, as are American Express, Discover, Diners Club, MasterCard, and Visa. Wonderful **Dominick's,** on the same block at 2335 Arthur Ave. (✆ 718/733-2807), is the inspiration behind family-style re-creations like Carmine's. There's no menu here, but trust your waiter to ramble off what is on the day's menu, which almost always includes tender calamari marinara and luscious veal Francese. There's always a crowd so go early or expect to wait for a communal table. Reservations are not accepted and please, cash only.

To get to Arthur Avenue, take the no. 4 or D train to Fordham Road and then the no. 12 bus East; the no. 2 or 5 train to Pelham Parkway, and the no. 12 bus West; or the Metro-North Harlem line to Fordham Road, and the shuttle bus to Belmont and the Bronx Zoo.

A few miles east of Arthur Avenue you'll find another classic Italian "red sauce" restaurant. This one, **Frankie and Johnnie's Pine Restaurant,** 1913 Bronxdale Ave., between Matthews and Muliner avenues (✆ 718/792-5956), has been around so long, I remember watching the Times Square ball drop on a black-and-white televi-sion in the dining room while devouring a bowl of *zuppa di pesce* one lonely New Year's Eve many years ago. I remember that New Year's, though lonely, very fondly

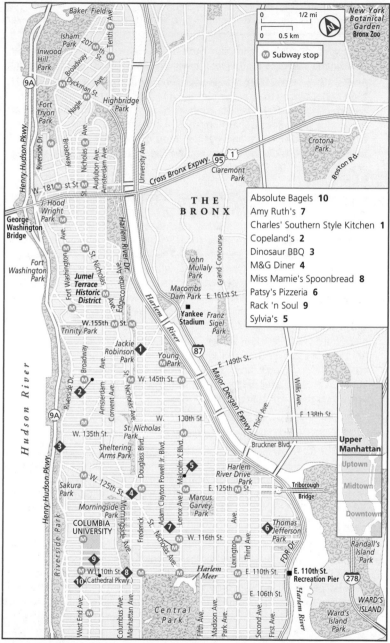

Absolute Bagels **10**
Amy Ruth's **7**
Charles' Southern Style Kitchen **1**
Copeland's **2**
Dinosaur BBQ **3**
M&G Diner **4**
Miss Mamie's Spoonbread **8**
Patsy's Pizzeria **6**
Rack 'n Soul **9**
Sylvia's **5**

The Soul of Harlem

There is much soul in Manhattan, but Harlem seems to possess the mother lode when it comes to food. Here is one man's primer to Harlem's soul food:

Amy Ruth's, 113 W. 116th St., between Lenox and Seventh avenues (© 212/ 280-8779). Claiming to be authentic soul, Amy Ruth's has become a mecca for Harlem celebs, with the kitschy gimmick of naming platters after some of them, such as the Rev. Al Sharpton (chicken and waffles) and the Rev. Calvin O. Butts III (chicken wings and waffles). Most of the celebrities gained their fame in Harlem, as did the chicken and waffles, or fried whiting and waffles, or steak and waffles. You can't go wrong with anything here as long as waffles are included.

Charles' Southern Style Kitchen ⚝, 2837 Eighth Ave., between 151st and 152nd streets (© 877/813-2920 or 212/926-4313). Nothing fancy about this place, just a brightly lit, 25-seater on a not-very-attractive block in upper Harlem. But you don't come here for fancy, you come for soul food at its simplest and freshest. And come hungry. The $13 all-you-can-eat buffet features crunchy, moist, pan-fried chicken; ribs in a tangy sauce, with meat falling off the bone; smoky stewed oxtails in a thick brown onion gravy; macaroni and cheese; collard greens with bits of smoked turkey; black-eyed peas; and corn bread, warm and not overly sweet. Hours can be erratic, so call ahead before you make the trek.

Copeland's, 547 W. 145th St., between Broadway and Amsterdam Avenue (© 212/234-2357). With food almost as good as Charles' but in a much more elegant setting (you'll find tables adorned with china and white table-cloths), Copeland's has been dishing out excellent soul food for 40 years. Fried chicken is their trademark, but I favor the braised short ribs. The jazz buffet on Tuesday, Wednesday, and Thursday nights is a double treat.

---

mainly because of that *zuppa di pesce*. Now the Pine, as it's known, has become popular as a hangout for New York Yankees who crave pasta after their games at Yankee Stadium. As a result, you'll find plenty of baseball memorabilia on the walls. Reservations are not accepted, and cash only. Take the no. 2 or 5 train to Bronx Park East.

BROOKLYN
VERY EXPENSIVE

At the foot of the Brooklyn Bridge, with spectacular views of the New York skyline, **The River Café,** 1 Water St. (© 718/522-5200), could possibly be the most romantic special-occasion restaurant in New York. Service is good, prices are steep, and the contemporary Continental cuisine is more than adequate, but nothing can top that view.

EXPENSIVE

Peter Luger Steakhouse ⚝⚝ STEAKS   If you love steak, then book a table here and hop a cab to Williamsburg. Expect loads of attitude and nothing in the way of decor or atmosphere (beer hall is the theme)—but this 114-year-old institution is

M&G Diner, 383 W. 125th St., at St. Nicholas Avenue (✆ **212/864-7326**). All the soul-food joints I've listed here serve top-notch fried chicken, but the best I've had is the perfectly pan-fried, supermoist bird at the M&G. This small, no-frills diner, open 8am–11:30pm, is a treat any time of day. Start your day with a breakfast of eggs with salmon croquettes or eggs with grits or finish it with the chicken, chitterlings, or meatloaf. All the sides are freshly made, and the desserts, especially the sweet-potato pie, are phenomenal. There's also a great jukebox loaded with soul to complement the food.

Miss Mamie's Spoonbread Too, 366 W. 110th St., between Columbus and Manhattan avenues (✆ **212/865-6744**). Entering this strawberry-curtained charmer is like stepping into South Carolina. But you are in Harlem, or at least the southern fringe of Harlem, and you won't be paying South Carolina soul prices, or Harlem soul prices, either. Still, despite the prices, Miss Mamie's is the real deal, especially their barbecued ribs, falling off the bone in a sweet peppery sauce, and the smothered chicken, fried and then covered with thick pan gravy.

Sylvia's, 328 Lenox Ave., between 126th and 127th streets (✆ **212/996-0660;** www.sylviassoulfood.com). Sylvia is the self-proclaimed queen of not only Harlem soul food but all soul food. In reality, Sylvia is queen of self-promotion. Sylvia's now has become a franchise, with canned food products, beauty and hair products, and fragrances and colognes. With all that attention to merchandising, the food at her original Harlem restaurant has suffered and now has regressed into a tourist trap. If you plan to go, however, make it on Sunday for the gospel brunch, which is an absolute joy.

porterhouse heaven. The first-rate cuts—the only ones they serve—are dry-aged on the premises and come off the grill dripping with fat and butter, crusty on the outside and tender pink within. It's the best steak in the five boroughs. Nonbelievers can order sole or lamb chops, but don't bother if you're not coming for the cow. The $5.95 Peter Luger burger is a little-known treasure. As sides go, the German fried potatoes are crisp and delicious, and the creamed spinach is everything it should be. Bring wads of cash because this place is expensive but doesn't take credit cards (other than their own house account). And call far, far in advance, especially during the holiday seasons.

178 Broadway (at Driggs Ave.), Williamsburg, Brooklyn. ✆ 718/387-7400. www.peterluger.com. Reservations essential; call a month in advance for weekend bookings. Main courses $5–$20 at lunch; $20–$32 at dinner. No credit cards (Peter Luger accounts only). Mon–Thurs 11:45am–9:45pm; Fri–Sat 11:45am–10:45pm; Sun 12:45–9:45pm. Subway: J, M, Z to Marcy Ave. (Or take a cab.)

MODERATE

Consider the DUMBO outpost of the comforting, comfort-food Bubby's (p. 164), **Bubby's Brooklyn,** 1 Main St., at Water Street (✆ **718/222-0666**).

Restaurants Grow in Brooklyn

It might seem like a stretch to leave Manhattan to experience fine, innovative dining. But a trend is developing in Brooklyn; top chefs are staking out claims all over the increasingly gentrified borough. There is one street in particular that has become a mecca for exciting restaurants. That street is Smith and it runs through the neighborhoods of Boerum Hill, Cobble Hill, and Carroll Gardens.

The Smith Street awakening began in 2005 when **The Grocery**, 288 Smith St. (© **718/596-3335**), cracked into the top food category with a rating of 26, if that means anything. But the awakening was only for those not familiar with The Grocery, because those in the neighborhood would often line up for a taste of the market fresh dishes prepared by chef/owners Charles Kiely and Sharon Pachter.

There are a number of Italian restaurants on Smith Street but one I particularly like is at 116 Smith Street, **La Lunetta** (© **718/488-6269**), specializing in small plates and interesting pastas like penne with homemade ricotta and lamb.

Representing a Gallic slant is **Café Luluc,** 214 Smith St. (© **718/625-3815**) with its high tin-ceilings and open, airy space giving it a bistro feel. But the bistro specialties aside, Café Luluc is open every day for breakfast, lunch, and dinner and is most popular for its eggs.

It's worth traveling to Smith Street to **Zaytoons**, 283 Smith St. (© **718/ 875-1880**; www.zaytoonsrestaurant.com) for Middle Eastern food as good, or arguably better, than you will find on the other side of the East River.

You can reach most of these restaurants fairly easily if you take the F train to Carroll St., which has an exit right onto Smith St.

INEXPENSIVE

The fabulous **Grimaldi's Pizza** is at 19 Old Fulton St., between Front and Water streets (© **718/858-4300**); and out in Coney Island, the 1924-established and little-changed **Totonno's** is at 1524 Neptune Ave., between West 15th and West 16th streets (© **718/ 372-8606**). See "Pizza, New York–Style," on p. 196, for more information.

Also in Coney Island is the famous **Nathan's Famous,** 1310 Surf Ave., at Stillwell Avenue (© **718/946-2202**), for hot dogs by the beach. See how many you can eat.

If you are traveling to BAM to see a show, you'll be tempted to have either your pre- or post-theater meal at **Junior's,** 386 Flatbush Ave., at DeKalb Avenue (© **718/852-5257**). Everyone knows about Junior's world-famous cheesecake, the epitome of New York cheesecake, but don't miss the opportunity to experience the authentic Brooklyn atmosphere here, complete with old-school waiters you'll not soon forget. Don't expect anything fancy, but do expect great cheesecake.

The best ice cream in New York can be found right over the Brooklyn Bridge at the **Brooklyn Ice Cream Factory,** Fulton Ferry Landing Pier, Brooklyn (© **718/246-3963**). Everything is freshly made, including the hot fudge for your sundae.

Ferdinando's Focacceria ⊕ ITALIAN/SICILIAN   You might think that focaccia, that wonderful Italian bread coated with olive oil, herbs, and tomato sauce, is a recent culinary innovation. Think again. They've been making focaccia at Ferdinando's since 1904. But the focaccia they make at this Sicilian restaurant, in the increasingly trendy neighborhood of Carroll Gardens, is nothing like the focaccia you've tasted. Here the specialty focaccia is *panelle,* a deep-fried pancake made of chickpea flour. You can have your panelle plain or you can have it topped with ricotta and grated cheese. The restaurant also features Sicilian specials like marinated octopus, stuffed calamari, tripe in tomato sauce, and a magnificent *caponatina* (eggplant salad).

151 Union St. (btwn Columbia and Hicks sts.), Cobble Hill. ℂ **718/855-1545.** Panelle $4; main courses $15–$22. No credit cards. Mon–Thurs 11am–7pm; Fri–Sat 11am–10pm Subway: F, G to Carroll St.

QUEENS
EXPENSIVE
Water's Edge ⊕⊕ CONTEMPORARY AMERICAN   When it comes to dining with the best views of the Manhattan skyline, many consider The River Café tops. But the view from Water's Edge, where the lights of the Citicorp, Chrysler, United Nations, and Empire State buildings flicker right across the river, gives The River Café a run for its money. Throw in free ferry service from Manhattan (a 10-min. ride) to the restaurant, the possibility of watching a family of swans frolicking in the river as you dine, and the succulent seasonal cuisine by chef Ari Nieminen, and the Water's Edge experience becomes memorable. It's rare when views this good are matched by magnificent food, but Nieminen is up to the task. In the spirit of autumn, the season I visited the restaurant, the hearty, tender pomegranate-marinated venison stew came served inside a mini-pumpkin served with figs, cranberries, and chestnuts, while the decadently rich seared duck *foie gras* was accompanied by delicious black-mission-fig chutney. For a real splurge, Water's Edge offers tasting menus and wine pairings with the course. But this is Queens and the splurge won't hit you quite as hard in the wallet as it would if you went to that other restaurant on the river in Brooklyn.

East River & 44th Dr., Long Island City, Queens. ℂ **718/482-0033.** www.watersedgenyc.com. Main courses $26–$36; 4-course tasting menu $75. AE, DC, DISC, MC, V. Mon–Fri noon–3pm and 5:30–11pm; Sat 5:30–11pm; closed Sun. Subway: E, V to 23rd St./Ely Ave.

MODERATE/EXPENSIVE
Jackson Avenue Steakhouse ⊕ *Finds* STEAKS   This is an old-style steakhouse with prices more manageable than the Manhattan superstars (and Brooklyn's Peter Luger), and it's one stop on the no. 7 train into Queens. On a recent occasion, two of us had drinks, appetizers, filet mignon with portobello mushroom in Madeira wine reduction, coffee, and dessert for around $150. The ambience is casual; the waitstaff will remember you after one visit as well as your drink of choice. The rooms are handsome and wood-paneled, with a fireplace in the back room and stained glass in some of the windows. The meats (steaks, chops, rack of lamb) range from $28 on up to $85 for the chateaubriand (for two). There are also seafood and chicken entrees. There's an affordable sandwich and pasta menu (until 5pm, or after if they know you) that runs from around $9 for burgers to $15-ish for the higher-end pastas. You can also make a good-value meal from the appetizers, salads and soups. Executive chef Francisco "Paco" Gonzalez often kibitzes at the bar, where a local crowd gathers.

12–23 Jackson Ave., Long Island City, Queens. ℂ **718/784-1412.** www.jacksonsteakhouse.com. Main courses $15–$35; appetizers $5–$13. AE, DC, DISC, MC, V. Mon–Thurs 11:30am–10pm; Fri 11:30am–11pm; Sat 5–11pm; Sun 3–10pm. Subway: 7 to Vernon/Jackson.

INEXPENSIVE

The no. 7 train is sometimes known as the International Express (see chapter 8). Take it out of Manhattan and through the borough of Queens and you will pass one ethnic neighborhood after another. You could write a book on all the different restaurants located around the no. 7 train in Queens. Here are a few of my favorites:

Get off at the 69th Street stop in Woodside, walk 1 block north, and you might begin to detect the aroma of barbecued meats. That smell is coming from **Ihawan,** 40–06 70th St. (© **718/205-1480**), which claims to be home of the best barbecue in town. But unless you've been to the Philippines, Ihawan's country of origin, this is barbecue unlike any you've tasted before. Here you can sample barbecued pork on bamboo skewers, grilled marinated pork chops, and the local favorite, grilled marinated pork belly. The menu here also includes other Filipino specialties such as *dinuguan,* pork stewed in pork-blood gravy, and *lapu-lapu,* a whitefish, served in tamarind soup.

If you get off the train at the 82nd Street/Jackson Heights stop, a few steps from the elevated tracks, you'll find **Arunee Thai,** 37–68 79th St., off Roosevelt Avenue (© **718/205-5559**). Here, the Thai food is so authentic (and the clientele mostly Thai) that the menus are written in Thai and English. Everything is delicious, and the spice level is not toned down for delicate palates. The fish, served whole on the bone, with chili, garlic, and hot-and-sour sauce, will either take the chill off a cold winter's day or, if it's summer, the chiles will cool down your overheated body and soul.

Exit the last stop of the no. 7 train, Flushing-Main Street and you might think you're in downtown Beijing. Where you are is Flushing's Chinatown, bigger than Manhattan's and crammed with tea houses, noodle shops, banquet halls, bakeries and Asian supermarkets. The food choices are staggering and you won't go wrong at just about any of the countless restaurants. My favorite is a bare bones Szechuan restaurant called **Little Pepper,** 133-43 Roosevelt Avenue (© **718/739-7788**), where the food is as authentic as it gets, which means spicy. There are exotic items on the menu like bull frog, rabbit, eel, and a variety of offal, but if that is too challenging, you can't go wrong with the basics like the double-cooked pork or the family-style soups.

8

Exploring New York City

If this is your first trip to New York, face the facts: It will be impossible to take in the entire city—this time. Because New York is almost unfathomably big and constantly changing, you could live your whole life here and still make fascinating daily discoveries—we New Yorkers do. This chapter is designed to give you an overview of what's available in this multi-faceted place so you can narrow your choices to an itinerary that's digestible for the amount of time you'll be here—be it a day, a week, or something in between.

So don't try to tame New York—you can't. Decide on a few must-see attractions, and then let the city take you on its own ride. See chapter 4 ("Suggested New York City Itineraries") for my suggestions on what to see and how to cram it all in 1, 2, or 3 days. But inevitably, as you make your way around the city, you'll be blown off course by unplanned diversions that are just as much fun as what you meant to see.

After all, the true New York is in the details. As you dash from sight to sight, take time to admire a cornice on a prewar building, linger over a cup of coffee at a sidewalk cafe, or just idle away a few minutes on a bench watching New Yorkers parade through their daily lives.

1 Sights & Attractions by Neighborhood

MANHATTAN

CHELSEA

EAST VILLAGE & NOHO

THE FLATIRON DISTRICT/ UNION SQUARE

GREENWICH VILLAGE

HARLEM

LOWER EAST SIDE

Downtown Attractions

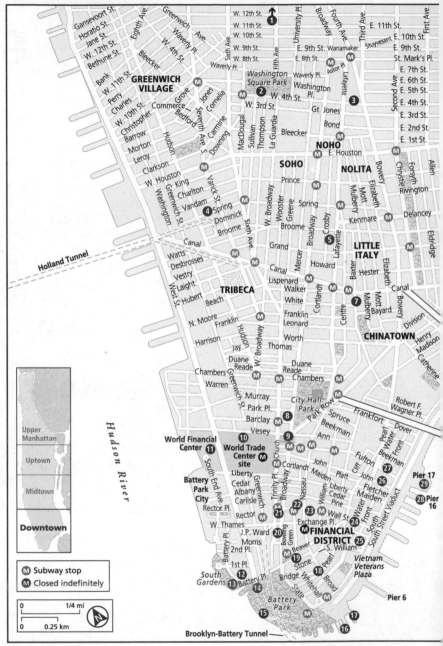

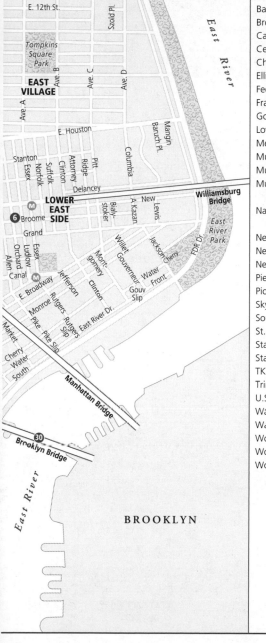

Midtown Attractions

Uptown Attractions

Ⓜ Subway stop

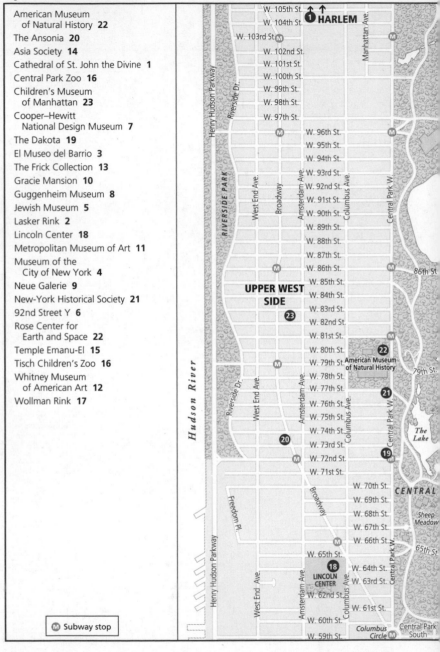

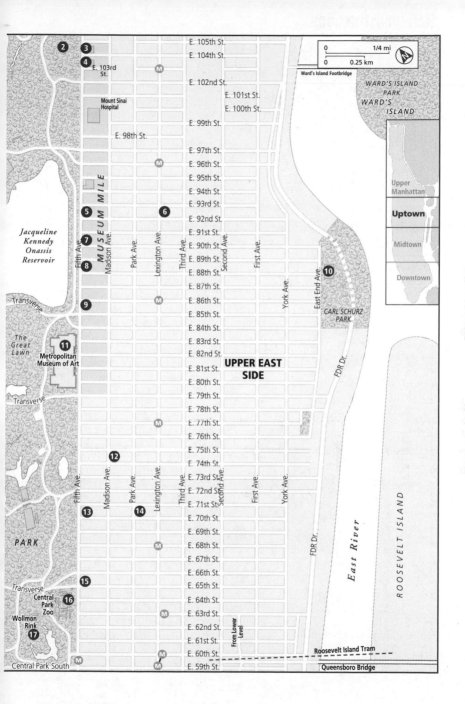

E. 105th St.
E. 104th St.
E. 103rd St.
E. 102nd St.
E. 101st St.
E. 100th St.
E. 99th St.
E. 98th St.
E. 97th St.
E. 96th St.
E. 95th St.
E. 94th St.
E. 93rd St.
E. 92nd St.
E. 91st St.
E. 90th St.
E. 89th St.
E. 88th St.
E. 87th St.
E. 86th St.
E. 85th St.
E. 84th St.
E. 83rd St.
E. 82nd St.
E. 81st St.
E. 80th St.
E. 79th St.
E. 78th St.
E. 77th St.
E. 76th St.
E. 75th St.
E. 74th St.
E. 73rd St.
E. 72nd St.
E. 71st St.
E. 70th St.
E. 69th St.
E. 68th St.
E. 67th St.
E. 66th St.
E. 65th St.
E. 64th St.
E. 63rd St.
E. 62nd St.
E. 61st St.
E. 60th St.
E. 59th St.

Mount Sinai Hospital

Jacqueline Kennedy Onassis Reservoir

MUSEUM MILE

Fifth Ave.
Madison Ave.
Park Ave.
Lexington Ave.
Third Ave.
Second Ave.
First Ave.
York Ave.
East End Ave.
FDR Dr.

Transverse

The Great Lawn

Metropolitan Museum of Art

UPPER EAST SIDE

Transverse

CARL SCHURZ PARK

East River

ROOSEVELT ISLAND

PARK

Transverse

Central Park Zoo

Wollman Rink

Central Park South

From Lower Level

Roosevelt Island Tram

Queensboro Bridge

Ward's Island Footbridge

WARD'S ISLAND PARK
WARD'S ISLAND

0   1/4 mi
0   0.25 km

Upper Manhattan

Uptown

Midtown

Downtown

Harlem Attractions

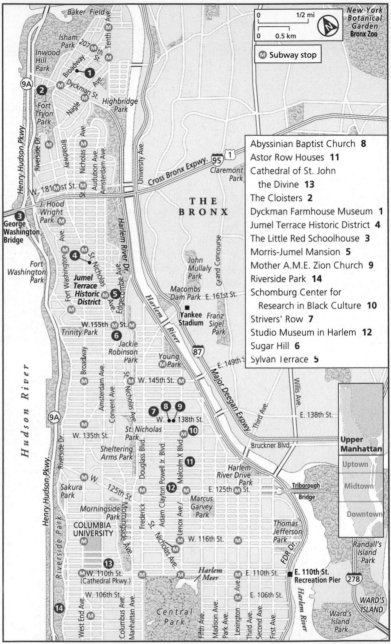

Abyssinian Baptist Church **8**
Astor Row Houses **11**
Cathedral of St. John
  the Divine **13**
The Cloisters **2**
Dyckman Farmhouse Museum **1**
Jumel Terrace Historic District **4**
The Little Red Schoolhouse **3**
Morris-Jumel Mansion **5**
Mother A.M.E. Zion Church **9**
Riverside Park **14**
Schomburg Center for
  Research in Black Culture **10**
Strivers' Row **7**
Studio Museum in Harlem **12**
Sugar Hill **6**
Sylvan Terrace **5**

Ⓜ Subway stop

Tips Subway Access Alert

On almost every weekend, and throughout the year, changes in normal subway service tend to occur. I *strongly* recommend you check with the **Metropolitan Transit Authority** at (C) **718/330-1234** or **www.mta.nyc.ny.us** before you plan your travel routes; your hotel concierge or any token-booth clerk should also be able to assist you.

2 The Top Attractions

In addition to the choices below, don't forget **Central Park** 🐌🐌🐌, the great green swath that is, just by virtue of its existence, New York City's greatest marvel. Central Park is so big and multifaceted that it earns its own section, starting on p. 268.

American Museum of Natural History 🐌🐌🐌 *Kids*   This is one of the hottest museum tickets in town, thanks to the **Rose Center for Earth and Space** 🐌, whose four-story-tall planetarium sphere hosts the show, *Cosmic Collisions,* narrated by Robert Redford, about the violent beginnings of the universe. Prepare to be blown away by this astounding, literally earth-shaking short film.

Buy your tickets in advance for the Space Show in order to guarantee admission (they're available online); I also recommend buying tickets in advance for a specific IMAX film or special exhibition, such as the Butterfly Conservatory (see below), especially during peak seasons (summer, autumn, holiday time) and for weekend visits; otherwise, you might miss out.

Other must-sees include the Big Bang Theater, which re-creates the theoretical birth of the universe; the main Hall of the Universe, with its very own 16-ton meteorite; and the terrific Hall of Planet Earth, which focuses on the geologic processes of our home planet (great volcano display!). All in all, you'll need a minimum of 2 hours to fully explore the Rose Center. *Tip:* Friday night is a great time to plan your visit, as the center isn't overcrowded, live jazz and food fill the Hall of the Universe, and, bathed in blue light, the sphere looks magical.

The rest of the 4-square-block museum is nothing to sneeze at, either. Founded in 1869, it houses the world's greatest natural-science collection in a group of buildings made of towers and turrets, pink granite, and red brick. The diversity of the holdings is astounding: some 36 million specimens, ranging from microscopic organisms to the world's largest cut gem, the Brazilian Princess Topaz (21,005 carats). Rose Center aside, it would take you all day to see the entire museum, and then you *still* wouldn't get to everything. If you don't have a lot of time, you can see the best of the best on free **highlights tours** offered daily every hour at 15 minutes after the hour from 10:15am to 3:15pm. Free daily **spotlight tours,** thematic tours that change monthly, are also offered; stop by an information desk for the day's schedule. **Audio Expeditions,** high-tech audio tours that allow you to access narration in the order you choose, are also available to help you make sense of it all.

If you only see one exhibit, see the **dinosaurs** 🐌, which take up the fourth floor.

The **Hall of Biodiversity** is an impressive multimedia exhibit, but its doom-and-gloom story about the future of rainforests and other natural habitats might be too much for the little ones. Kids 5 and up should head to the **Discovery Room,** with lots of hands-on exhibits and experiments. (*Parents, be prepared:* There seems to be a gift shop overflowing with stuffed animals at every turn.) The **Hall of Human Origins** in the newly opened Anne and Bernard Spitzer Hall traces the evolution of man and even offers children's workshops where kids can compare skull casts of early humans.

⟨Value⟩ A Money & Time-Saving Tip

CityPass may be New York's best sightseeing deal. Pay one price ($53, or $44 for kids 12-17) for admission to six major attractions: The American Museum of Natural History (admission only; does not include Space Show), the Guggenheim Museum, the Empire State Building, the Museum of Modern Art, and a 2-hour Circle Line harbor cruise. Individual tickets would cost more than twice as much.

More important, CityPass is not a coupon book. It contains actual tickets, so you can bypass lengthy lines. This can save you hours, since sights such as the Empire State Building often have ticket lines of an hour or more.

CityPass is good for 9 days from the first time you use it. It's sold at all participating attractions and online at **http://citypass.com**. To avoid online service and shipping fees, you may buy the pass at your first attraction (start at an attraction that's likely to have the shortest admission line, such as the Guggenheim, or arrive before opening to avoid a wait at such spots as the Empire State Building). However, if you begin your sightseeing on a weekend or during holidays, when lines are longest, online purchase may be worthwhile.

For more information, call CityPass at ℰ **208/787-4300** (note, however, that CityPass is not sold over the phone).

The museum excels at **special exhibitions,** so check to see what will be on while you're in town in case any advance planning is required. The magical **Butterfly Conservatory** 𐩒, a walk-in enclosure housing nearly 500 free-flying tropical butterflies, has developed into a can't-miss fixture from October through May; check to see if it's in the house while you're in town.

Central Park West (btwn 77th and 81st sts.). ℰ **212/769-5100** for information, or 212/769-5200 for tickets (tickets can also be ordered online). www.amnh.org. Suggested admission $14 adults, $11 seniors and students, $8 children 2–12; Space Show and museum admission $22 adults, $17 seniors and students, $13 children under 12. Additional charges for IMAX movies and some special exhibitions. Daily 10am–5:45pm; Rose Center open 1st Fri of every month until 8:45pm. Subway: B, C to 81st St.; 1 to 79th St.

Brooklyn Bridge 𐩒𐩒 ⟨Moments⟩   Its Gothic-inspired stone pylons and intricate steel-cable webs have moved poets like Walt Whitman and Hart Crane to sing the praises of this great span, the first to cross the East River and connect Manhattan to Brooklyn. Begun in 1867 and ultimately completed in 1883, the Brooklyn Bridge is now the city's best-known symbol of the age of growth that seized the city during the late 19th century. Walk across the bridge and imagine the awe that New Yorkers of that age felt at seeing two boroughs joined by this span. It's still astounding.

Walking the bridge: Walking the Brooklyn Bridge is one of my all-time favorite New York activities, although there's no doubt that the Lower Manhattan views from the bridge now have a painful resonance as well as a joyous spirit. A wide wood-plank pedestrian walkway is elevated above the traffic, making it a relatively peaceful, and popular, walk. It's a great vantage point from which to contemplate the New York skyline and the East River.

There's a sidewalk entrance on Park Row, just across from City Hall Park (take the 4, 5, or 6 train to Brooklyn Bridge/City Hall). But why do this walk *away* from Manhattan, toward the far less impressive Brooklyn skyline? Instead, for Manhattan skyline views, take an A or C train to High Street, one stop into Brooklyn. From there, you'll be on the bridge in no time: Come above ground, then walk through the little park to Cadman Plaza East and head downslope (left) to the stairwell that will take you up to the footpath. (Following Prospect Place under the bridge, turning right onto Cadman Plaza East, will also take you directly to the stairwell.) It's a 20- to 40-minute stroll over the bridge to Manhattan, depending on your pace, the amount of foot traffic, and the number of stops you make to behold the spectacular views (there are benches along the way). The footpath will deposit you right at City Hall Park.

Tasty tips: The perfect complement to your stroll over the Brooklyn Bridge is a stop for pizza at **Grimaldi's** (see p. 196), followed by homemade ice cream at the **Brooklyn Ice Cream Factory** (© **718/246-3963**), at the Fulton Ferry Fire Boat House on the river and in the shadow of the bridge. The pizza and ice cream will fortify you for your stroll into Manhattan.

Subway: A, C to High St.; 4, 5, 6 to Brooklyn Bridge–City Hall.

Ellis Island 𝒢𝒢 One of New York's most moving sights, the restored Ellis Island opened in 1990, slightly north of Liberty Island. Roughly 40% of Americans (myself included) can trace their heritage back to an ancestor who came through here. For the 62 years when it was America's main entry point for immigrants (1892–1954), Ellis Island processed some 12 million people. The greeting was often brusque—especially in the early years of the century (until 1924), when as many as 12,000 came through in a single day. The statistics can be overwhelming, but the **Immigration Museum** skillfully relates the story of Ellis Island and immigration in America by placing the emphasis on personal experience.

It's difficult to leave the museum unmoved. Today you enter the Main Building's baggage room, just as the immigrants did, and then climb the stairs to the **Registry Room,** with its dramatic vaulted tiled ceiling, where millions waited anxiously for medical and legal processing. A step-by-step account of the immigrants' voyage is detailed in the exhibit, with haunting photos and touching oral histories. What might be the most poignant exhibit is **Treasures from Home,** 1,000 objects and photos donated by descendants of immigrants, including family heirlooms, religious articles, and rare clothing and jewelry. Outside, the

Impressions

If you're bored in New York, it's your own fault.

—Myrna Loy

American Immigrant Wall of Honor commemorates the names of more than 500,000 immigrants and their families, from Myles Standish and George Washington's great-grandfather to the forefathers of John F. Kennedy, Jay Leno, and Barbra Streisand. You can even research your own family's history at the interactive **American Family Immigration History Center.** You might also make time to see the award-winning short film *Island of Hope, Island of Tears,* which plays on a continuous loop in two theaters. Short live theatrical performances depicting the immigrant experience are also often part of the day's events.

Touring tip: Ferries run daily to Ellis Island and Liberty Island from Battery Park and Liberty State Park at frequent intervals; see Statue of Liberty listing (p. 244) for details.

In New York Harbor. © **212/363-3200** (general info), or 212/269-5755 (ticket/ferry info). www.nps.gov/elis, www.ellisisland.org, or www.statuereservations.com. Free admission (ferry ticket charge). Daily 9:30am–5:15pm (last ferry departs around 3:30pm). For subway and ferry details, see the Statue of Liberty listing on p. 244 (ferry trip includes stops at both sights).

Empire State Building ✦✦✦   It took 60,000 tons of steel, 10 million bricks, 2.5 million feet of electrical wire, 120 miles of pipe, and 7 million man-hours to build. King Kong climbed it in 1933—and again in 2005. A plane slammed into it in 1945.

Impressions

It's the nearest thing to heaven we have in New York.

—Deborah Kerr to Cary Grant in *An Affair to Remember,* on the Empire State Building

---

The World Trade Center superseded it in 1970 as the island's tallest building. And in 1997, a gunman ascended it to stage a deadly shooting. On that horrific day of September 11, 2001, it once again regained its status as New York City's tallest building, after 31 years of taking second place. And through it all, the Empire State Building has remained one of the city's favorite landmarks and its signature high-rise. Completed in 1931, the limestone-and-stainless-steel streamline Deco dazzler climbs 102 stories (1,454 ft.) and now harbors the offices of fashion firms, and, in its upper reaches, a jumble of high-tech broadcast equipment.

Always a conversation piece, the Empire State Building glows every night, bathed in colored floodlights to commemorate events of significance—red, white, and blue for Independence Day; green for St. Patrick's Day; red, black, and green for Martin Luther King Day; blue and white for Hanukkah; even lavender and white for Gay Pride Day (you can find a complete lighting schedule online). The familiar silver spire can be seen from all over the city.

The best views, and what keeps the nearly three million visitors coming every year, are the ones from the 86th- and 102nd-floor **observatories.** The lower one is best—you can walk out on a windy deck and look through coin-operated viewers (bring quarters!) over what, on a clear day, can be as much as an 80-mile visible radius. The citywide panorama is magnificent. One surprise is the flurry of rooftop activity, an aspect of city life that thrives unnoticed from our everyday sidewalk vantage point. The higher observation deck is glass-enclosed and cramped.

Light fog can create an admirably moody effect, but it goes without saying that a clear day is best. Dusk brings the most remarkable views and the biggest crowds. Consider going in the morning, when the light is still low on the horizon, keeping glare to a minimum. Starry nights are pure magic.

In your haste to go up, don't rush through the three-story-high marble **lobby** without pausing to admire its features, which include a wonderful Streamline mural.

350 Fifth Ave. (at 34th St.). ✆ **212/736-3100.** www.esbnyc.com. Observatory admission $18 adults, $16 seniors and children 12–17, $12 children 6–11, free for children under 6. Daily open 8am–2am, last elevator at 1:15am. Subway: B, D, F, N, R, Q, V, W to 34th St.; 6 to 33rd St.

Grand Central Terminal ✦✦   Even if you're not catching one of the subway lines or Metro-North commuter trains that rumble through Grand Central Terminal, come for a visit; it's one of the most magnificent public places in the country. And even if you arrive and leave by subway, be sure to exit the station, walking a couple of blocks south, to about 40th Street, before you turn around to admire Jules-Alexis Coutan's neoclassical sculpture *Transportation* hovering over the south entrance, with a majestic Mercury, the Roman god of commerce and travel, as its central figure.

The greatest visual impact comes when you enter the vast majestic **main concourse.** The high windows allow sunlight to penetrate the space, glinting off the half-acre Tennessee marble floor. The brass clock over the central kiosk gleams, as do the

---

Tips **Empire State Building Ticket Buying**

Lines can be horrible at the concourse-level ticket booth, so be prepared to wait—or consider purchasing **advance tickets** online using a credit card at **www.esbnyc.com.** You'll pay slightly more—tickets were priced $2 higher on the website at press time—but it's well worth it, especially if you're visiting during busy seasons, when the line can be shockingly long. You're not required to choose a time or date for your tickets in advance; they can be used on any regular open day. However, order them well before you leave home, because only regular mail is free. Expect them to take 7 to 10 days to reach you (longer if you live outside of the U.S.). Overnight delivery adds $15 to your total order. With tickets in hand, you're allowed to proceed directly to the second floor—past everyone who didn't plan as well as you did!

Now you can call in advance to get an estimate of your wait in line along with the visibility from the observatory. Dial ℂ **877/692-8439** for the service.

Remember: Advance purchase of a CityPass (see the box on p. 236) will get you admission to the Empire State Building plus five other attractions.

---

gold- and nickel-plated chandeliers piercing the side archways. The masterful **sky ceiling,** a brilliant greenish blue, depicts the constellations of the winter sky above New York. They're lit with 59 stars, surrounded by dazzling 24-carat gold and emitting light fed through fiber-optic cables, their intensities roughly replicating the magnitude of the actual stars as seen from Earth. Look carefully and you'll see a patch near one corner left unrestored as a reminder of the neglect once visited on this splendid overhead masterpiece. On the east end of the main concourse is a grand **marble staircase.**

This dramatic Beaux Arts splendor serves as a hub of social activity as well. Excellent-quality retail shops and restaurants have taken over the mezzanine and lower levels. The highlights of the west mezzanine are **Michael Jordan's–The Steak House,** a gorgeous Art Deco space that allows you to dine within view of the sky ceiling (see "The Prime Cut: Steaks! Steaks! Steaks!" on p. 184) as well as the gorgeously restored **Campbell Apartment** (p. 382), which serves cocktails. Off the main concourse at street level, there's a nice mix of specialty shops and national retailers, as well as the truly grand **Grand Central Market** (p. 205) for gourmet foods. The **New York Transit Museum Store** (p. 331), in the shuttle passage, houses city transit-related exhibitions and a terrific gift shop that's worth a look for transit buffs. The **lower dining concourse** ⋒ houses a stellar food court and the famous **Oyster Bar & Restaurant** (see chapter 7 for details on both).

The **Municipal Art Society** (ℂ **212/935-3960;** www.mas.org) offers a walking tour of Grand Central Terminal on Wednesday at 12:30pm, which meets at the information booth on the Grand Concourse (for a $10 "suggested donation").

42nd St. at Park Ave. ℂ **212/340-2210** (events hot line). www.grandcentralterminal.com. Subway: S, 4, 5, 6, or 7 to 42nd St./Grand Central.

Metropolitan Museum of Art ⋒⋒⋒   Home of blockbuster after blockbuster, the Metropolitan Museum of Art attracts some five million people a year, more than any other spot in New York City. And it's no wonder—this place is magnificent. At 1.6 million square feet, this is the largest museum in the Western Hemisphere. Nearly all

Moments **Evenings at the Met**

On **Friday and Saturday evenings,** the Met remains open late not only for art viewing but also for cocktails in the Great Hall Balcony Bar (5–8pm) and classical music from a string ensemble. A slate of after-hours programs (gallery talks, walking tours, family programs) changes by the week; call for the current schedule. The restaurant stays open until 10pm (last reservation at 8:30pm), and dinner is usually accompanied by piano music.

the world's cultures are on display through the ages—from Egyptian mummies to ancient Greek statuary to Islamic carvings to Renaissance paintings to Native American masks to 20th-century decorative arts—and masterpieces are the rule. You could go once a week for a lifetime and still find something new on each visit.

So unless you plan on spending your entire vacation in the museum (some people do), you cannot see the entire collection. My recommendation is to give it a good day—or better yet, 2 half days so you don't burn out. One good way to get an overview is to take advantage of the little-known **Museum Highlights Tour,** offered every day at various times throughout the day (usually between 10:15am and 3:15pm; tours also offered in Spanish, Italian, German, and Korean). Even some New Yorkers who've spent many hours in the museum could profit from this once-over. Visit the museum's website for a schedule of this and subject-specific walking tours (Old Masters Paintings, American Period Rooms, Arts of China, Islamic Art, and so on); you can also get a schedule of the day's tours at the Visitor Services desk when you arrive. A daily schedule of **Gallery Talks** is available as well.

The least overwhelming way to see the Met on your own is to pick up a map at the round desk in the entry hall and choose to concentrate on what you like, whether it's 17th-century paintings, American furniture, or the art of the South Pacific. Highlights include the American Wing's **Garden Court,** with its 19th-century sculpture; the terrific ground-level **Costume Hall;** and the **Frank Lloyd Wright room.** The beautifully renovated **Roman and Greek galleries** are overwhelming, but in a marvelous way, as are the collections of **Byzantine Art** and later **Chinese art.** The highlight of the astounding **Egyptian collection** is the **Temple of Dendur,** in a dramatic, purpose-built glass-walled gallery with Central Park views. The **Greek Galleries,** which at last fully realize McKim, Mead & White's grand neoclassical plans of 1917, and the **Ancient Near East Galleries,** are particularly of note. But it all depends on what your interests are. **Special exhibitions** can range from "Orazio and Artemisia Gentileschi: Father and Daughter Painters in Baroque Italy" to "Earthly Bodies: Irving Penn's Nudes, 1949–50."

The big news this season at the Met is that after 50 years of being used as a dining area, the **Greek and Roman galleries** reopened in the spring of 2007 after a $220 million renovation redesigned and expanded the galleries to 57,000 square feet. The galleries now exhibit ancient artifacts that had been in storage including 30,000 of the square footage devoted to Roman collections.

The Met now opens on "holiday Mondays." On those Mondays, such as Memorial Day or Labor Day, the museum is open from 9:30am to 5:15pm.

To purchase tickets for concerts and lectures, call © **212/570-3949** (Mon–Sat 9:30am–5pm). The museum contains several dining facilities, including a **full-service**

restaurant serving Continental cuisine (© **212/570-3964** for reservations). The roof garden is worth visiting if you're here from spring to autumn, offering peaceful views over Central Park and the city.

The Met's medieval collections are housed in upper Manhattan at **The Cloisters** 😺😺; see the full listing on p. 249.

Fifth Ave. at 82nd St. © **212/535-7710.** www.metmuseum.org. Admission (includes same-day entrance to the Cloisters) $15 adults, $10 seniors and students, free for children under 12 when accompanied by an adult. Sun, holiday Mon (Memorial Day, Labor Day, etc.), and Tues–Thurs 9:30am–5:15pm; Fri–Sat 9:30am–8:45pm. Strollers are permitted in most areas—inquire at Information Desks for gallery limitations. Oversized and jogging strollers are prohibited. Subway: 4, 5, 6 to 86th St.

Museum of Modern Art 😺😺   The newer, larger MoMA, after a 2-year renovation, is almost twice the space of the original. The renovation, designed by Yoshio Taniguchi, highlights space and light, with open rooms, high ceilings, and gardens— a beautiful work of architecture and a perfect complement to the art within. This is where you'll find van Gogh's *Starry Night*, Cezanne's *Bather*, Picasso's *Les Demoiselles d'Avignon*, and the great sculpture by Rodin, *Monument to Balzac*. Whenever I visit, I like to browse the fun "Architecture and Design" department, with examples of design for appliances, furniture, and even sports cars. MoMA also features edgy new exhibits and a celebrated film series that attracts serious cinephiles. But the heart of the museum remains the **Abby Aldrich Rockefeller Sculpture Garden,** which has been enlarged; the museum's new design affords additional views of this lovely space from other parts of the museum. MoMA is one of the most expensive museums in New York, but does have a "free" day: on Fridays from 4-8pm.

11 W. 53rd St. (btwn Fifth and Sixth aves.). © **212/708-9400.** www.moma.org. Admission $20 adults, $16 seniors, $12 students, children under 16 free accompanied by an adult. Sat–Mon and Wed–Thurs 10:30am–5:30pm; Fri 10:30am–8pm. Subway: E, V to Fifth Ave.; B, D, E to Seventh Ave.

Rockefeller Center 😺😺   A Streamline Moderne masterpiece, Rockefeller Center is one of New York's central gathering spots for visitors and New Yorkers alike. A prime example of the city's skyscraper spirit and historic sense of optimism, it was erected mainly in the 1930s, when the city was deep in the Depression as well as its most passionate Art Deco phase. Designated a National Historic Landmark in 1988, it's now the world's largest privately owned business-and-entertainment center, with 18 buildings on 21 acres.

For a dramatic approach to the entire complex, start at Fifth Avenue between 49th and 50th streets. The builders purposely created the gentle slope of the Promenade, known here as the **Channel Gardens** because it's flanked to the south by La Maison Française and to the north by the British Building (the Channel, get it?). You'll also find a number of attractive shops along here, including a big branch of the **Metropolitan Museum of Art Store,** a good stop for elegant gifts. The Promenade leads to the **Lower Plaza,** home to the famous ice-skating rink in winter (see next paragraph) and alfresco dining in summer in the shadow of Paul Manship's freshly gilded bronze statue *Prometheus.* All around, the flags of the United Nations' member countries flap in the breeze. Just behind *Prometheus,* in December and early January, towers the city's official and majestic Christmas tree.

The **Rink at Rockefeller Center** 😺 (© **212/332-7654;** www.rockefellercenter. com) is tiny but positively romantic, especially during the holidays, when the giant Christmas tree's multicolored lights twinkle from above. The rink is open from mid-October to mid-March, and you'll skate under the magnificent tree for the month of

Heading for the Top of the Rock

Giving the Empire State Building some friendly competition when it comes to spectacular views, is the observation deck of 30 Rockefeller Plaza known as the **Top of the Rock** 𝕲𝕲. The deck, which comprises floors 67 to 70, which had been closed since 1986, reopened in late 2005. The stately deck was constructed in 1933 to resemble the grandeur of a luxury ocean liner, and unlike the Empire State Building, the observation deck here is more spacious and the views, though not quite as high, just as stunning. You might have just as much fun getting up there as you will on the deck itself; the sky-shuttle elevators with glass ceilings project images from the 1930s through the present day as it zooms its way up. Reserved-time tickets help minimize the lines and are available online at **www.topoftherocknyc.com**. The observation deck is open daily from 8:30am to midnight; admission rates are $18 for adults, $16 for seniors, $11 for ages 6 to 11, and free for children under 6. For more information, call ℭ **877/NYC-ROCK** (877/692-7625) or 212/698-2000 or visit www.topoftherocknyc.com.

December. The focal point of this "city within a city" is the building at 30 Rockefeller Plaza 𝕲, a 70-story showpiece towering over the plaza. It's still one of the city's most impressive buildings; walk through for a look at the granite-and-marble lobby, lined with monumental sepia-toned murals by José Maria Sert. You can pick up a walking-tour brochure on the center's art and architecture at the main information desk in this building. On the 65th floor, the legendary **Rainbow Room** is once again open to the public on a limited basis (see p. 382).

NBC television maintains studios throughout the complex. *Saturday Night Live* and *Late Night with Conan O'Brien* originate at 30 Rock (see "Talk of the Town: TV Tapings," on p. 284, for tips on getting tickets). NBC's *Today* show is broadcast live on weekdays from 7 to 10am from the glass-enclosed studio on the southwest corner of 49th Street and Rockefeller Plaza; come early if you want a visible spot, and bring your HI MOM! sign.

The 70-minute **NBC Studio Tour** (ℭ **212/664-3700;** www.shopnbc.com) will take you behind the scenes at the Peacock network. The tour changes daily but might include the *Today* show, *NBC Nightly News, Dateline NBC*, and/or *Saturday Night Live* sets. Who knows? You may even run into Brian Williams or Meredith Viera in the hall. Tours run every 15–30 minutes Monday through Saturday from 8:30am to 5:30pm, Sunday from 9:30am to 4:30pm (later on certain summer days); of course, you'll have a better chance of encountering some real live action on a weekday. Tickets are $19 for adults, $16 for seniors and children 6 to 12. You can reserve your tickets for either tour in advance (reservations are recommended) or buy them right up to tour time at the **NBC Experience** store, on Rockefeller Plaza at 49th Street. They also offer a 75-minute **Rockefeller Center Tour** hourly every day between 10am and 4pm. Tickets are $12 for adults, $10 for seniors and children 6 to 12; two-tour combination packages are available for $23.

Other notable buildings throughout the complex include the **International Building,** on Fifth Avenue between 50th and 51st streets, worth a look for its Atlas statue out front; and the **McGraw-Hill Building,** on Sixth Avenue between 48th and 49th streets, with its 50-foot sun triangle on the plaza.

The restored **Radio City Music Hall** ⟨⟩, 1260 Sixth Ave., at 50th Street (℃ **212/ 247-4777;** www.radiocity.com), is perhaps the most impressive architectural feat of the complex. Designed by Donald Deskey and opened in 1932, it's one of the largest indoor theaters, with 6,200 seats. But its true grandeur derives from its magnificent Art Deco appointments. The crowning touch is the stage's great proscenium arch, which from the distant seats evokes a faraway sun setting on the horizon of the sea. The men's and women's lounges are also splendid. The theater hosts the annual **Christmas Spectacular,** starring the Rockettes. The illuminating 1-hour **Stage Door Tour** is offered Monday through Saturday from 10am to 5pm, Sunday from 11am to 5pm; tickets are $17 for adults, $10 for children under 12.

Btwn 48th and 50th sts., from Fifth to Sixth aves. ℃ **212/485-7200.** www.radiocity.com. Subway: B, D, F, V to 47th–50th sts./Rockefeller Center.

Solomon R. Guggenheim Museum ⟨⟩   It's been called a bun, a snail, a concrete tornado, and even a giant wedding cake; bring your kids, and they'll probably see it as New York's coolest opportunity for skateboarding. Whatever description you choose to apply, Frank Lloyd Wright's only New York building, completed in 1959, is best summed up as a brilliant work of architecture—so consistently brilliant that it competes with the art for your attention. If you're looking for the city's best modern art, head to MoMA or the Whitney first; come to the Guggenheim to see the house. Though you might not see much except scaffolding; the exterior of the museum is being restored with a completion date scheduled for late 2007.

But the restoration has no effect on what's inside and it's easy to see the bulk of what's on display in 2 to 4 hours. The museum's spiraling rotunda circles over a slowly inclined ramp that leads you past changing exhibits that, in the past, have ranged from "Matthew Barney: The Cremaster Cycle" to "Norman Rockwell: Pictures for the American People," said to be the most comprehensive exhibit ever of the beloved painter's works. Usually the progression is counterintuitive: from the first floor up, rather than from the sixth floor down. If you're not sure, ask a guard before you begin. Permanent exhibits of 19th- and 20th-century art, including strong holdings of

---

Moments **Roosevelt Island Tram**

Want to take in a little-known but spectacular view of the New York skyline? Take them for a ride on the Roosevelt Island Tram (℃ **212/832-4543,** ext. 1; www.rioc.com.) This is the tram you have probably seen in countless movies, most recently *Spider-Man.* The tram originates at 59th Street and Second Avenue, costs $2 each way ($2 round-trip for seniors), and takes 4 minutes to traverse the East River to Roosevelt Island, where there are a series of apartment complexes and parks. During those 4 minutes you will be treated to a gorgeous view down the East River and the East Side skyline, with views of the United Nations and four bridges: the Queensboro, Williamsburg, Manhattan, and Brooklyn. On a clear day you might even spot Lady Liberty. And don't worry, despite what you've seen in the movies, the tram is safe, and your friendly neighborhood Spider-Man has everything under control. The tram operates daily from 6am until 2:30am and until 3:30am on weekends.

Kandinsky, Klee, Picasso, and French Impressionists, occupy a stark annex called the **Tower Galleries,** an addition (accessible at every level) that some critics have claimed made the entire structure look like a toilet bowl backed by a water tank (judge for yourself—I think there may be something to that view).

The Guggenheim runs some special programs, including free docent tours daily, a limited schedule of lectures, free family films, avant-garde screenings for grown-ups, curator-led guided gallery tours on select Friday afternoons, and the **World Beat Jazz Series,** which resounds through the rotunda on Friday and Saturday from 5 to 8pm.

1071 Fifth Ave. (at 89th St.). © 212/423-3500. www.guggenheim.org. Admission $18 adults, $15 seniors and students, free for children under 12, pay-what-you-wish Fri 6–8pm. Sat–Wed 10am–5:45pm; Fri 10am–7:45pm. Subway: 4, 5, 6 to 86th St.

Staten Island Ferry 🐸 *(Value)*   In 2006 the Staten Island Ferry celebrated its 100th anniversary. Over the years it has been one of New York's best bargains—sometimes costing a nickel and most of the time, like now, costing nothing at all. It's New York's best freebie—especially if you just want to glimpse the Statue of Liberty and not climb her steps. You get an hour-long excursion (round-trip) into the world's biggest harbor. This is not strictly a sightseeing ride but commuter transportation to and from Staten Island. As a result, during business hours, you'll share the boat with working stiffs reading papers and drinking coffee inside, blissfully unaware of the sights outside.

You, however, should go on deck and enjoy the harbor traffic. The old orange-and-green boats usually have open decks along the sides or at the bow and stern; try to catch one of these if you can, since the newer white boats don't have decks. Grab a seat on the right side of the boat for the best view. On the way out of Manhattan, you'll pass the Statue of Liberty (the boat comes closest to Lady Liberty on the way to Staten Island), Ellis Island, and from the left side of the boat, Governor's Island; you'll see the Verrazano Narrows Bridge spanning from Brooklyn to Staten Island in the distance.

When the boat arrives at St. George, Staten Island, if you are required to disembark, follow the boat-loading sign on your right as you get off; you'll circle around to the next loading dock, where there's usually another boat waiting to depart for Manhattan. The skyline views are simply awesome on the return trip. Well worth the time spent.

Departs from the Whitehall Ferry Terminal at the southern tip of Manhattan. © 718/727-2508. www.ci.nyc.ny.us/ html/dot. Free admission. 24 hr.; every 20–30 min. weekdays, less frequently during off-peak and weekend hours. Subway: R, W to Whitehall St.; 4, 5 to Bowling Green; 1 to South Ferry (ride in one of the 1st 5 cars).

Statue of Liberty 🐸🐸🐸 *(Kids)*   For the millions who came by ship to America in the last century—either as privileged tourists or needy, hopeful immigrants—Lady Liberty, standing in the Upper Bay, was their first glimpse of America. No monument so embodies the nation's, and the world's, notion of political freedom and economic potential. Even if you don't make it out to Liberty Island, you can get a spine-tingling glimpse from Battery Park, from the New Jersey side of the bay, or during a ride on the Staten Island Ferry (see above). It's always reassuring to see her torch lighting the way.

Proposed by French statesman Edouard de Laboulaye as a gift from France to the United States, commemorating the two nations' friendship and joint notions of liberty, the statue was designed by sculptor Frédéric-Auguste Bartholdi with the engineering help of Alexandre-Gustave Eiffel (who was responsible for the famed Paris tower) and unveiled on October 28, 1886. *Touring tips:* Ferries leave daily every half-hour to 45 minutes from 9am to about 3:30pm, with more frequent ferries in the morning and extended hours in summer. Try to go early on a weekday to avoid the crowds that swarm in the afternoon, on weekends, and on holidays.

A stop at **Ellis Island** 🏛🏛 (p. 237) is included in the fare, but if you catch the last ferry, you can only visit the statue or Ellis Island, not both.

You can buy ferry tickets **in advance** via **www.statuereservations.com**, which will allow you to board without standing in the sometimes-long ticket line; however, there is an additional service charge of $1.75 per ticket. Even if you've already purchased tickets, arrive as much as 30 minutes before your desired ferry time to allow for increased security procedures prior to boarding. The ferry ride takes about 20 minutes.

Once on Liberty Island, you'll start to get an idea of the statue's immensity: She weighs 225 tons and measures 152 feet from foot to flame. Her nose alone is 4½ feet long, and her index finger is 8 feet long.

After September 11, 2001, access to the base of the statue was prohibited, but in the summer of 2004, access, albeit still somewhat limited (you can't climb to the statue's crown), was once again allowed. Now you can explore the Statue of Liberty Museum, peer into the inner structure through a glass ceiling near the base of the statue, and enjoy views from the observation deck on top of a 16-story pedestal.

Hornblower Yachts (the same company that runs the Alcatraz ferry in San Francisco), will take over the ferries and tours to the Statue of Liberty in late 2007, replacing the Circle Line (which held the franchise for many years). If you're going to be visiting Lady Liberty toward the end of the year, go to **www.statuecruises.com** for more information. Before then, you can still get information and book tickets at **www. circlelinedowntown.com**.

On Liberty Island in New York Harbor. 📞 **212/363-3200** (general info), or 212/269-5755 (ticket/ferry info). www. nps.gov/stli or www.circlelinedowntown.com. Free admission; ferry ticket to Statue of Liberty and Ellis Island $12 adults, $9.50 seniors, $4.50 children 3–17. Daily 9am–3:30pm (last ferry departs around 3:30pm); extended hours in summer. Subway: 4, 5 to Bowling Green; 1 to South Ferry. Walk south through Battery Park to Castle Clinton, the fort housing the ferry ticket booth.

Times Square *(Overrated)*

There's no doubting that Times Square has evolved into something much different than it was well over a decade ago, when it had a deservedly sleazy reputation. There is much debate among New Yorkers about which incarnation was better. For the natives, Times Square is a place we go out of our way to avoid. The crowds, even by New York standards, are stifling; the restaurants, mostly national chains, aren't very good; the shops, also mostly national chains, are unimaginative; and the attractions, like **Madame Tussaud's New York** wax museum, are kitschy. I suppose it's a little too Vegas for us. Still, you've come all this way; you've got to at least take a peek, if only for the amazing neon spectacle of it.

Most of the Broadway theaters are around Times Square, so plan your visit before or after the show you're going to see. For your pre-theater meal, walk 2 blocks west to Ninth Avenue where you'll find a number of relatively inexpensive, good restaurants. If you are with the kids, the Ferris wheel in the **Toys "R" Us** store makes a visit to Times Square worthwhile.

Subway: 1, 2, 3, 7, S, N, Q, R, W to Times Sq.; A, C, E to 42nd St.–Port Authority.

Wall Street & the New York Stock Exchange

Wall Street—it's an iconic name, and the world's prime hub for bulls and bears everywhere. This narrow 18th-century lane (you'll be surprised at how little it is) is appropriately monumental, lined with neoclassical towers that reach as far skyward as the dreams and greed of investors who built it into the world's most famous financial market.

At the heart of the action is the **New York Stock Exchange (NYSE),** the world's largest securities trader, where billions change hands. The NYSE came into being in

World Trade Center Site (Ground Zero)

Do you call a place where over 3,000 people lost their lives an "attraction"? Or do you now call it a shrine? This is the quandary of the World Trade Center site. What had been a big hole for 5 years is a little more than that; construction began in early 2006 on the proposed "Freedom Tower" to be built at the site. But even though work is ongoing, there is still political bickering on what will rise from that hole. The new design retains essential elements of the original—soaring 1,776 feet into the sky, its illuminated mast evoking the Statue of Liberty's torch. From the square base, the Tower will taper into eight tall isosceles triangles, forming an octagon at its center. An observation deck will be located 1,362 feet above ground. Of course, all this could change by the time this book comes out.

For now, you can see the site through a viewing wall on the Church Street side of the site; on that "Wall of Heroes" are the names of those who lost their lives that day along with the history of the site, including photos of the construction of the World Trade Center in the late 1960s and how, after it opened in 1972, it changed the New York skyline and downtown. A walk along the Wall of Heroes remains a painfully moving experience.

The site is bounded by Church, Barclay, Liberty, and West streets. Call ⓒ 212/484-1222 or go to www.nycvisit.com or www.southstseaport.org for viewing information; go to www.downtownny.com for lower-Manhattan area information and rebuilding updates. The Tribute Center gives guided tours of the site. Call ⓒ 212/422-3520 or visit www.tributewtc.org for more information. Tours are given Mon–Fri at 11am, 1pm and 3pm; Sat and Sun at noon, 1, 2, and 3pm. The fee is $10 for adults; under 12 free.

1792, when merchants met daily under a nearby buttonwood tree to try to pass off to each other the U.S. bonds that had been sold to fund the Revolutionary War. By 1903, they were trading stocks of publicly held companies in this Corinthian-columned Beaux Arts "temple" designed by George Post. About 3,000 companies are now listed on the exchange, trading nearly 314 billion shares valued at about $16 trillion. Unfortunately, the NYSE is no longer open to the public for tours.

20 Broad St. (between Wall St. and Exchange Place). ⓒ 212/656-3000. www.nyse.com. Subway: J, M, Z to Broad St.; 2, 3, 4, 5 to Wall St.

Whitney Museum of American Art 𝔊𝔊   What is arguably the finest collection of 20th-century American art in the world belongs to the Whitney thanks to the efforts of Gertrude Vanderbilt Whitney. A sculptor herself, Whitney organized exhibitions by American artists shunned by traditional academies, assembled a sizable personal collection, and founded the museum in 1930 in Greenwich Village.

Today's museum is an imposing presence on Madison Avenue—an inverted three-tiered pyramid of concrete and gray granite with seven seemingly random windows designed by Marcel Breuer, a leader of the Bauhaus movement. The permanent collection consists of an intelligent selection of major works by Edward Hopper, George Bellows, Georgia O'Keeffe, Roy Lichtenstein, Jasper Johns, and other significant artists. A second-floor space is devoted exclusively to works from its permanent collection from 1900 to 1950, while the rest is dedicated to rotating exhibits.

Shows are usually well-curated and more edgy than what you'd see at MoMA or the Guggenheim (though not as left-of-mainstream as what you'll find at the New Museum). Topics range from topical surveys, such as "American Art in the Age of Technology" and "The Warhol Look: Glamour Style Fashion" to in-depth retrospectives of famous or lesser-known movements (such as Fluxus, the movement that spawned Yoko Ono, among others) and artists (Mark Rothko, Keith Haring, Duane Hanson, Bob Thompson). Free **gallery tours** are offered daily, and music, screenings, and lectures fill the calendar. The Whitney is also notable for having the best museum restaurant in town: **Sarabeth's at the Whitney,** worth a visit in its own right. For details on the **Whitney Museum of American Art at Altria,** the petite Midtown annex, see p. 260.

945 Madison Ave. (at 75th St.). © 877/WHITNEY or 212/570-3676. www.whitney.org. Admission $15 adults, $10 seniors and students, free for children under 12, pay-what-you-wish Fri 6–9pm. Wed–Thurs and Sat–Sun 11am–6pm; Fri 1–9pm. Subway: 6 to 77th St.

Yankee Stadium 𝄞𝄞 Next to the Colosseum in Rome, there aren't many more famous sports arenas in the world than the House That Ruth Built. The Yankees play from April until October (and, since they seem to be in the playoffs most years, mostly through Oct). Depending on who's in town, tickets, which range in price from $12 to $115, can be tough to score. But if you plan in advance, and even if you don't, you should be able to purchase a seat by going through a broker or scalping (be careful of forgeries) the day of a game. If you are not visiting during the baseball season, tours of the stadium, including Monument Park, are held year-round. For more information, see the section "Spectator Sports," later in this chapter. This is your last chance to get to what's left of the 1923-built Yankee Stadium. A new stadium is in the works and scheduled to open in the same area for the 2009 season.

161st St. and River Ave., the Bronx. © 718/293-6000. www.yankees.com. Tickets $12–$115. Subway: 4, B, D to 161st St.

3 More Manhattan Museums

For the **Brooklyn Museum of Art** 𝄞𝄞, the **New York Transit Museum,** the **American Museum of the Moving Image** 𝄞, the **Queens Museum of Art,** the **Isamu Noguchi Garden Museum** 𝄞, the **P.S. 1 Contemporary Art Center,** and the **Louis Armstrong House Museum** 𝄞, see "Highlights of the Outer Boroughs," later in this chapter.

If you're traveling with the kids, also consider the museums listed under "Especially for Kids," on p. 287, which include the **Children's Museum of Manhattan** 𝄞, the **Sony Wonder Technology Lab,** and the **New York Hall of Science** 𝄞.

If you're interested in historic-house museums, see the box called "In Search of Historic Homes," on p. 263.

Also, don't forget to see what's on at the monumental **New York Public Library** 𝄞𝄞, which regularly holds excellent exhibitions. See p. 262.

American Folk Art Museum 𝄞𝄞 This gorgeous, ultramodern boutique museum is not only a stunning structure, but it also heralds American folk art's entry into the top echelon of museum-worthy art.

The modified open-plan interior features an extraordinary collection of traditional works from the 18th century to the self-taught artists and craftspeople of the present, reflecting the breadth and vitality of the American folk-art tradition. A splendid variety of quilts, in particular, makes the textiles collection the museum's most popular. The book-and-gift shop is outstanding, filled with one-of-a-kind objects.

Tips Be an Early Bird

New York is the city that never sleeps, and you shouldn't either—at least not too much. Get an early start on your day. Check opening times for museums and attractions and be there as soon as they open to avoid the crowds. It's no fun waiting on lines or peering over throngs of people to view exhibits. So remember the early bird gets the worm, and the uncrowded attraction!

---

45 W. 53rd St. (btwn Fifth and Sixth aves.). © 212/265-1040. www.folkartmuseum.org. Admission $9 adults, $7 seniors and students, free for children under 12, free to all Fri 5:30–8pm. Tues–Thurs and Sat–Sun 10:30am–5:30pm; Fri 10:30am–7:30pm. Subway: E, V to Fifth Ave.

Asia Society   The Asia Society was founded in 1956 by John D. Rockefeller III with the goal of increasing understanding between Americans and Asians through art exhibits, lectures, films, performances, and international conferences. The society is a leader in presenting contemporary Asian and Asian-American art. After a $30-million renovation that doubled the exhibition space, the society's headquarters is bigger, smarter, and better than ever. Never has so much of the core collection, which comprises Rockefeller's Pan-Asian acquisitions dating from 2000 B.C. to the 19th century, been on display before. Well-curated temporary exhibits run the gamut from "The New Way of Tea," exploring Japan's elaborate tea ceremony, to "Through Afghan Eyes: A Culture in Conflict, 1987–1995," a study in photographs and video. Additionally, the mammoth calendar of events ranges from film screenings to arts lectures to discussion panels featuring experts in Pan-Asian and global politics, business, and more; call or check the website for a current schedule.

725 Park Ave. (at 70th St.). © 212/288-6400. www.asiasociety.org. Gallery admission $10 adults, $7 seniors, $5 students with ID, free for children under 16, free to all Fri 6–9pm. Tues–Sun 11am–6pm (Fri to 9pm; except July 4–Labor Day). Subway: 6 to 68th St./Hunter College.

Center for Jewish History *(Finds)*   This 125,000-square-foot complex is the largest repository of Jewish history, art, and literature in the Diaspora. It unites five of America's leading institutions of Jewish scholarship: the **American Jewish Historical Society** (www.ajhs.org), the national archives of the Jewish people in the Americas; the **Leo Baeck Institute** (www.lbi.org), documenting the robust history of German-speaking Jewry from the 17th century until annihilation under the Nazis; the **Yeshiva University Museum** (www.yumuseum.org), with general-interest exhibits, plus a renowned collection of Judaica objects confiscated by the Nazis; the **YIVO Institute for Jewish Research** (www.yivoinstitute.org), focusing on exhibits exploring the diversity of the Jewish experience; and the **American Sephardi Federation** (www.asfonline.org), representing the spiritual, cultural, and social traditions of the American Sephardic communities (Jews from southern Europe, North Africa, and the Middle East). Together, this union represents about 100 million archival documents, 500,000 books, and thousands of objects of art and ephemera, ranging from Thomas Jefferson's letter denouncing anti-Semitism to memorabilia of famous Jewish athletes.

The main gallery space is the Yeshiva Museum, which comprises four galleries, an outdoor sculpture garden, and a children's workshop; a range of exhibits also showcase various holdings belonging to the other institutions as well. A central feature is the **Reading Room,** home to open stacks accessible by serious researchers and lay historians alike, as well as the **Center Genealogy Institute,** which offers assistance in family-history research. Another huge component of the center is its 250-seat state-of-the-art auditorium, home to a packed schedule of lectures, music, and film presentations. If you get hungry, a kosher cafe is on-site.

15 W. 16th St. (btwn Fifth and Sixth aves.). © 212/294-8301. www.cjh.org. Admission to Yeshiva University Museum $8 adults, $6 seniors and students; free admission to all other facilities. Yeshiva University Museum Sun and Tues–Thurs 11am–5pm. Reading Room and Genealogy Institute Mon–Thurs 9:30am–5pm; Fri by appt. All other exhibition galleries Mon–Thurs 9am–5pm; Fri 9am–4pm., Sun 11am–4pm. Subway: L, N, R, 4, 5, 6 to 14th St./Union Sq.; F, V to 14th St.

The Cloisters 𝄐𝄐 If it weren't for this branch of the Metropolitan Museum of Art, many New Yorkers would never get to this northernmost point in Manhattan. This remote yet lovely spot is devoted to the art and architecture of medieval Europe. Atop a cliff overlooking the Hudson River, you'll find a 12th-century chapter house, parts of five cloisters from medieval monasteries, a Romanesque chapel, and a 12th-century Spanish apse brought intact from Europe. Surrounded by peaceful gardens, this is the one place on the island that can approximate the kind of solitude suitable to such a collection. Inside you'll find extraordinary works that include the Unicorn tapestries, sculpture, illuminated manuscripts, stained glass, ivory, and precious metal work.

Despite its remoteness, the Cloisters are quite popular, especially in fine weather, so try to schedule your visit during the week rather than on a crowded weekend afternoon. A free guided **Highlights Tour** is offered Tuesday through Friday at 3pm and Sunday at noon; gallery talks are also a regular feature. Additionally, **Garden Tours** are offered Tuesday through Sunday at 1pm in May, June, September, and October; lectures and other special programming are always on Sunday from noon to 2pm; and medieval music concerts are regularly held in the stunning 12th-century Spanish chapel. For an extra-special experience, you may want to plan your visit around one.

At the north end of Fort Tryon Park. © 212/923-3700. www.metmuseum.org. Suggested admission (includes same-day entrance to the Metropolitan Museum of Art) $20 adults, $15 seniors, $10 students, free for children under 12. Nov–Feb Tues–Sun 9:30am–4:45pm; Mar–Oct Tues–Sun 9:30am–5:15pm. Subway: A to 190th St., then a 10-min. walk north along Margaret Corbin Dr., or pick up the M4 bus at the station (1 stop to Cloisters). Bus: M4 Madison Ave. (Fort Tryon Park–The Cloisters).

Cooper-Hewitt National Design Museum 𝄐 Part of the Smithsonian Institution, the Cooper-Hewitt is housed in the Carnegie Mansion, built by steel magnate Andrew Carnegie in 1901 and renovated to the tune of $20 million in 1996. Some 11,000 square feet of gallery space is devoted to changing exhibits that are invariably well conceived, engaging, and educational. Shows are both historic and contemporary in nature, and topics range from "The Work of Charles and Ray Eames: A Legacy of Invention" to "Russell Wright: Creating American Lifestyle" to "The Architecture of Reassurance: Designing the Disney Theme Parks." Many installations are drawn from the museum's own vast collection of industrial design, drawings, textiles, wall coverings, books, and prints.

On your way in, note the fabulous Art Nouveau–style copper-and-glass canopy above the entrance. And be sure to visit the garden, ringed with Central Park benches from various eras.

2 E. 91st St. (at Fifth Ave.). © 212/849-8400. www.cooperhewitt.org. Admission $12 adults, $9 seniors and students, free for children under 12, free to all Fri 5–9pm. Mon–Thurs 10am–5pm; Fri 10am–9pm; Sat 10am–6pm; Sun noon–6pm. Subway: 4, 5, 6 to 86th St.

Dahesh Museum of Art If you consider yourself a classicist, this small museum is for you. It's dedicated to 19th- and early-20th-century European academic art, a continuation of Renaissance, baroque, and rococo traditions that were overshadowed by the arrival of Impressionism on the art scene. (If you're not familiar with this academic school, expect lots of painstaking renditions of historical subjects and pastoral life.) Artists represented include Jean-Léon Gérôme, Lord Leighton, and Edwin Long, whose *Love's Labour Lost* is a cornerstone of the permanent collection.

580 Madison Ave. (btwn 56th and 57th sts.). ℂ 212/759-0606. www.daheshmuseum.org. Admission $10 adults, $8 seniors, $6 students, free for children under 12 and to all 1st Thurs of the month 6–9pm. Tues–Sun 11am–6pm; 1st Thurs of the month until 9pm. Subway: F, N, R, Q, W to 57th St.; 4, 5, 6 to 59th St.

El Museo del Barrio   What started in 1969 with a small display in a classroom in East Harlem is today the only museum in America dedicated to Puerto Rican, Caribbean, and Latin American art. The northernmost Museum Mile institution has a permanent exhibit ranging from pre-Columbian artifacts to photographic art and video. The display of *santos de palo* (wood-carved religious figurines) is noteworthy, as is "Taíno, Ancient Voyagers of the Caribbean," dedicated to the highly developed cultures that Columbus encountered when he landed in the "New World." The well-curated exhibitions tend to focus on 20th-century artists and contemporary subjects.

1230 Fifth Ave. (at 104th St.). ℂ 212/831-7272. www.elmuseo.org. Suggested admission $6 adults, $4 seniors (free on Thurs) and students, free for children under 12. Wed–Sun 11am–5pm. Subway: 6 to 103rd St.

The Frick Collection 𝕲𝕲   Henry Clay Frick could afford to be an avid collector of European art after amassing a fortune as a pioneer in the coke and steel industries at the turn of the 20th century. To house his treasures and himself, he hired architects Carrère & Hastings to build this 18th-century French-style mansion (1914), one of the most beautiful remaining on Fifth Avenue.

Most appealing about the Frick is its intimate size and setting. This is a living testament to New York's vanished Gilded Age—the interior still feels like a private home (albeit a really, really rich guy's home) graced with beautiful paintings, rather than a museum. Come here to see the classics by some of the world's most famous painters: Titian, Bellini, Rembrandt, Turner, Vermeer, El Greco, and Goya, to name only a few. A highlight of the collection is the **Fragonard Room,** graced with the sensual rococo series "The Progress of Love." The portrait of Montesquieu by Whistler is also stunning. Included in the price of admission, the AcousticGuide audio tour is particularly useful because it allows you to follow your own path rather than a proscribed route. A free 22-minute video presentation is screened in the Music Room every half-hour from 10am to 4:30pm (from 1:30 on Sun); starting with this helps to set the tone for what you'll see.

In addition, free **chamber music concerts** are held twice a month, generally every other Sunday at 5pm in fall and winter and select Thursdays at 5:45pm in warm weather, and once-a-month **lectures** are offered select Wednesdays at 5:30pm; call or visit the website for the current schedule and ticket information.

1 E. 70th St. (at Fifth Ave.). ℂ 212/288-0700. www.frick.org. Admission $15 adults, $10 seniors, $5 students. Children under 10 not admitted; children under 16 must be accompanied by an adult. Tues–Sat 10am–6pm; Sun 11am–5pm. Closed all major holidays. Subway: 6 to 68th St./Hunter College.

International Center of Photography 𝕲 *(Finds*   The ICP is one of the world's premier educators, collectors, and exhibitors of photographic art. The state-of-the-art gallery space is ideal for viewing rotating exhibitions of the museum's 50,000-plus prints as well as visiting shows. The emphasis is on contemporary photographic works, but historically important photographers aren't ignored. This is a "must see" on any photography buff's list.

1133 Sixth Ave. (at 43rd St.). ℂ 212/857-0000. www.icp.org. Admission $12 adults, $8 seniors and students, under 12 free. Tues–Thurs and Sat–Sun 10am–6pm; Fri 10am–8pm. Subway: B, D, F, V to 42nd St.

Tips   *Intrepid* in Drydock

The much-loved U.S.S. *Intrepid* battleship/museum is sitting in drydock in Bayonne, New Jersey at the moment, and you won't be able to see it this time out. After getting stuck in the Hudson, the *Intrepid* was towed away from its home on the West Side piers for a much-needed refurbishment. It is scheduled to return to the pier at W. 46th St. sometime in 2008. For information and updates, call © 212/245-0072 or visit www.intrepidmuseum.org.

The Jewish Museum   Housed in a Gothic-style mansion renovated in 1993 by AIA Gold Medal winner Kevin Roche, this wonderful museum now has the world-class space it deserves to showcase its remarkable collections, which chronicle 4,000 years of Jewish history. The two-floor permanent exhibit, "Culture and Continuity: The Jewish Journey," tells the story of the Jewish experience from ancient times through today, and is the museum's centerpiece. Artifacts include daily objects that might have served the authors of the books of Genesis, Psalms, and Job, and a great assemblage of intricate torahs. A wonderful collection of classic TV and radio programs is available for viewing through the **Goodkind Resource Center** (as any fan of television's golden age knows, its finest comic moments were Jewish comedy). The scope of the exhibit is phenomenal, and its story an enlightening—and intense—one. A random-access audio guide is geared to families (free with admission). In addition to the in-house shop, don't miss the Jewish Museum Design Shop, housed in the adjacent brownstone.

1109 Fifth Ave. (at 92nd St.). © 212/423-3200. www.thejewishmuseum.org. Admission $12 adults, $10 seniors and students, free for children under 12, pay-what-you-wish on Saturdays. Check website for special online admission discounts ($2 off at press time). Sat–Wed 11am–5:45pm; Thurs 11am–8pm; Fri 11am–3pm. Subway: 4, 5 to 86th St.; 6 to 96th St.

Lower East Side Tenement Museum   *Kids*   This museum is the first-ever National Trust for Historic Preservation site that was not the home of someone rich or famous. It's something quite different: a five-story tenement that 10,000 people from 25 countries called home between 1863 and 1935—people who had come to the United States looking for the American dream and made 97 Orchard St. their first stop. The tenement museum tells the story of the great immigration boom of the late 19th and early 20th centuries, when the Lower East Side was considered the "Gateway to America." A visit here makes a good follow-up to an Ellis Island trip—what happened to all the people who passed through that famous way station?

The only way to see the museum is by guided tour. Two primary tenement tours, held on all open days and lasting an hour, offer a satisfying exploration of the museum: **Piecing It Together: Immigrants in the Garment Industry,** which focuses on the restored apartment and the lives of its turn-of-the-20th-century tenants, an immigrant Jewish family named Levine from Poland; and **Getting By: Weathering the Great Depressions of 1873 and 1929,** featuring the homes of the German-Jewish Gumpertz family and the Sicilian-Catholic Baldizzi family, respectively. A knowledgeable guide leads you into each dingy urban time capsule, where several apartments have been restored to their lived-in condition, and recounts the real-life stories of the families who occupied them in fascinating detail. You can pair them for an in-depth look at the museum, since the apartments and stories are so different; however, one tour serves as an excellent introduction if you don't want to invest an entire afternoon here.

These tours are not really for kids, however, who won't enjoy the serious tone and "don't touch" policy. Much better for them is the 45-minute, weekends-only **Confino Family Apartment** tour, a living-history program geared to families, which allows kids to converse with an interpreter who plays teenage immigrant Victoria Confino (ca. 1916); kids can also handle whatever they like and try on period clothes.

The hour-long **Streets Where We Lived** neighborhood heritage walking tour is also offered on weekends from April through December. Small permanent and rotating exhibits, including photos, videos, and a model tenement, are housed in the visitor center and exhibition space in the tenement building at 97 Orchard St. Special tours and programs are sometimes on the schedule.

Tours are limited in number and sell out quickly, so it pays to buy tickets in advance, which you can do online or over the phone by calling Ticketweb at ✆ **800/965-4827.**

108 Orchard St. (btwn Delancey and Broome sts.). ✆ 212/982-8420. www.tenement.org. Tenement and walking tours $15 adults, $11 seniors and students; Confino Apt. $14 adults, $10 seniors and students. Tenement tours depart Tues–Fri every 40 min. 1–4pm; Sat–Sun every half-hour 11am–4:45pm. Confino Apt. tour Sat–Sun hourly noon–3pm. Walking tour Apr–Dec Sat–Sun 1 and 3pm. Subway: F to Delancey St.; J, M, Z to Essex St.

Morgan Library 𝄞𝄞 *(Finds*   This New York treasure, boasting one of the world's most important collections of original manuscripts, rare books and bindings, master drawings, and personal writings has reopened after 2 years of extensive renovations. Those renovations include a welcoming entrance on Madison Avenue; new and renovated galleries, so that more of the library's holdings can be exhibited; a modern auditorium; and a new Reading Room with greater capacity and electronic resources and expanded space for collections storage. Some of the Library's recent exhibitions include one on the life of **Bob Dylan** through music, letters, and memorabilia and an exhibit on illustrator, **Saul Steinberg.** You can lunch in the intimate **Morgan Dining Room** as if you were dining in JP's own quarters.

225 Madison Ave. (between 36th and 37th sts). ✆ 212/590-0300. www.themorgan.org. $12 adults, $8 seniors and students, under 12 free. Tues–Thurs 10:30am–5pm, Fri 10:30am–9pm, Sat 10am–6pm, Sun 11am–6pm. Subway: 4, 5, 6 to 33rd St.

Museum of Arts and Design 𝄞 *(Finds*   Formerly called the American Craft Museum, this small but aesthetically pleasing museum is the nation's top showcase for contemporary crafts. The collection focuses on objects that are prime examples of form and function, ranging from jewelry to baskets to vessels to furniture. You'll see a strong emphasis on material as well as craft, whether it be fiber, ceramics, or metal. Special exhibitions can range from Expressionist clay sculpture to fine bookbinding, and can celebrate movements or single artisans. Stop into the gorgeous **shop** even if you don't make it into the museum. In 2008, the museum will move to the quirky and controversial building designed by modernist architect Edward Durrell Stone in 1963 at 2 Columbus Circle.

40 W. 53rd St. (btwn Fifth and Sixth aves.). ✆ 212/956-3535. www.americancraftmuseum.org. Admission $9 adults, $7 students and seniors, free for children under 12, pay-what-you-wish Thurs 6–8pm. Fri–Wed 10am–6pm; Thurs 10am–8pm. Subway: E, V to Fifth Ave.

Museum of Chinese in the Americas   Located in the heart of Chinatown, on the second floor of a century-old school building, this museum is dedicated to "reclaiming, preserving, and interpreting the history and culture of Chinese and their descendants in the Western Hemisphere." Past exhibitions include "Have You Eaten Yet? The

Chinese Restaurant in America" and ongoing is "Many True Stories: Life in China-town on and after September 11" which chronicles how that tragedy affected the structure of the neighborhood.

70 Mulberry St. (at Bayard St.) ℂ 212/619-4785. www.moca-nyc.org. Admission: $2 adults, $1 senior, Free on Fri-days and for children under 12. Open Tue–Sun noon–6pm. Subway: 6, N, R, Q, W, J, M, Z to Canal St.

Museum of Jewish Heritage—A Living Memorial to the Holocaust ℛ In

the south end of Battery Park City, the Museum of Jewish Heritage occupies a strik-ingly spare six-sided building designed by award-winning architect Kevin Roche, with a six-tier roof alluding to the Star of David and the six million murdered in the Holo-caust. The permanent exhibits—"Jewish Life a Century Ago, The War Against the Jews," and "Jewish Renewal"—recount the daily prewar lives, the unforgettable hor-ror that destroyed them, and the tenacious renewal experienced by European and immigrant Jews in the years from the late 19th century to the present. The museum's power derives from the way it tells that story: through the objects, photographs, docu-ments, and, most poignantly, through the videotaped testimonies of Holocaust vic-tims, survivors, and their families, all chronicled by Steven Spielberg's Survivors of the Shoah Visual History Foundation. Thursday evening is dedicated to panel discussions, performances, and music, while Sunday is dedicated to family programs and work-shops; a film series is also a regular part of the calendar

While advance tickets are not usually necessary, you may want to purchase them to guarantee admission; call ℂ **212/945-0039.** Audio tours narrated by Meryl Streep and Itzhak Perlman are available at the museum for an additional $5.

36 Battery Place (at 1st Place), Battery Park City. ℂ 212/968-1800. www.mjhnyc.org. Admission $10 adults, $7 sen-iors, $5 students, free for children under 12 and for everyone Wed 4–8pm. Check website for $2-off admission coupon. (available at press time). Sun–Tues and Thurs 10am–5:45pm; Wed 10am–8pm; Fri and eves of Jewish holidays 10am–3pm. Subway: 4, 5 to Bowling Green.

Museum of Sex (Finds How many cities can claim their own Museum of Sex? Not

many in the U.S., that's for sure! This one, despite its provocative title, offers a stud-ied, historical look at the history of sex in our culture. In 2007, the exhibit "Kink: The Geography of the Erotic Imagination" and "Action: Sex and the Moving Image" were featured. Don't miss a trip through the gift shop—definitely not your typical museum shop. How about a $1,375 snakeskin souvenir to show your friends back home? *Note:* Many of the displays are very graphic, so the museum may not be for everyone.

233 Fifth Ave. (at 27th St.). ℂ 212/689/6337. www.museumofsex.com. Admission adults $15 plus tax; students and seniors $14 plus tax. No one under 18 admitted. Sun–Fri 11am–6:30pm; Sat 11am–8pm. Last ticket sold 45 min. before museum closing. Subway: N, R, 6 to 28th St.

Museum of Television & Radio If you can resist the allure of this museum, I'd

wager you've spent the last 70 years in a bubble. You can watch and hear all the great personalities of TV and radio—from Uncle Miltie to Johnny Carson to Jerry Sein-feld—at a private console (available for 2 hrs.). You can also conduct computer searches to pick out the great moments of history, viewing almost anything that made its way onto the airwaves, from the Beatles' first appearance on *The Ed Sullivan Show* to the crumbling of the Berlin Wall (the collection consists of 75,000 programs and commercials). Selected programs are also presented in two theaters and two screening rooms, which can range from "Barbra Streisand: The Television Performances" to lit-tle-seen Monty Python episodes.

Art for Art's Sake: The Gallery Scene

Manhattan has more than 500 private art galleries, selling everything from old masters to tomorrow's news. Galleries are free to the public, generally Tuesday through Saturday from 10am to 6pm. Saturday afternoon gallery hopping, in particular, is a favorite pastime—nobody will expect you to buy, so don't worry.

The best way to winnow down your choices is by perusing the "Art Guide" in the Friday weekend section of the *New York Times,* or in the back of the Sunday "Arts & Leisure" section; the listings section at the back of the weekly *New York* magazine, which I find to be particularly descriptive and user-friendly; the Art section in the weekly *Time Out New York;* or the *New Yorker*'s weekly "Goings on About Town" section. You can also find the latest exhibition listings online at **www.nymetro.com**, whose "Arts" page gives you full access to *New York* magazine's listings, **www.artnet.com**, and **www.galleryguide.org**. An excellent source—more for practicals on the galleries and the artists and genres they represent rather than current shows—is **www.artincontext.org**. The *Gallery Guide* is available at most galleries around town.

I suggest picking a gallery or a show in a neighborhood that seems to suit your taste, and just start browsing from there. Be aware that my list below doesn't even begin to scratch the surface. There are many, many more galleries in each neighborhood, as well as smaller concentrations of galleries in areas like the East Village, TriBeCa, and Brooklyn (check the Art in Context site).

Keep in mind that uptown galleries tend to be more traditional and exclusive-feeling, downtown galleries more high-ticket contemporary, and far-west Chelsea galleries the most cutting-edge. Museum-quality works dominate uptown, while raw talent and emerging artists are most common in west Chelsea. But there are constant surprises in all neighborhoods.

UPTOWN   Uptown galleries are clustered in and around the glamorous crossroads of Fifth Avenue and 57th Street as well as on and off stylish Madison Avenue in the 60s, 70s, and 80s. Unlike their upstart Chelsea and SoHo counterparts, these blue-chip galleries maintain a quiet white-glove demeanor. They include art-world powerhouses **Gagosian Gallery,** 980 Madison Ave. (© 212/744-2313; www.gagosian.com), and **PaceWildenstein,** 32 E. 57th St. (© 212/421-3292; www.pacewildenstein.com), whose focus is on classic modernism, representing such artists as Jim Dine, Barbara Hepworth, and Claes Oldenburg; **Richard Gray Gallery,** 1018 Madison Ave., fourth floor (© 212/472-8787; www.richardgraygallery.com), featuring American and European contemporary works, with artists ranging from Joan Miró to David Hockney; the **Margo Feiden Galleries,** 699 Madison Ave. (© 212/677-5330; www.alhirschfeld.com), the sole authorized representative of the works of the late master ink caricaturist Al Hirschfeld; the **Mary Boone Gallery,** 745 Fifth Ave. (© 212/752-2929; www.maryboonegallery.com), known for success with such artists as Ross Bleckner and Nancy Ellison; and **Wildenstein & Co, Inc.,** the classical big brother of **PaceWildenstein,** 19 E. 64th St. (© 212/879-0500; www.wildenstein.com), both specializing in big-ticket works: old masters, Impressionism, and Renaissance paintings and drawings.

CHELSEA   The area in the West 20s between Tenth and Eleventh avenues is home to the avant-garde of today's New York art scene, with West 26th serving as the unofficial "gallery row." Most galleries are not in storefronts but in the large spaces of multistory former garages and warehouses. Galleries worth seeking out include **Paula Cooper,** 534 W. 21st St. (© 212/255-1105), a heavyweight in the modern-art world, specializing in conceptual and minimal art; one of Chelsea's biggest galleries, the **Matthew Marks Gallery,** 523 W. 24th St. (© 212/243-0200); the **George Billis Gallery,** 511 W. 25th St., 9F (© 212/645-2621; www.georgebillis.com), which shows works by talented emerging artists; **Barbara Gladstone Gallery,** 515 W. 24th St. (© 212/206-9300; www.gladstonegallery.com); uptown powerhouse **Gagosian Gallery,** 555 W. 24th St. (© 212/741-1111; www.gagosian.com), which shows such major modern artists as Richard Serra and Julian Schnabel; **Kinz Tillou Feigen** 535 W. 20th St. (© 212/929-0500; www.ktfgallery.com), the modern counterpart to the uptown Old Masters gallery; **Cheim & Read,** 547 W. 25th St. (© 212/242-7727; www.cheimread.com), which often shows works by such high-profile pop artists as Diane Arbus and Robert Mapplethorpe; **Alexander and Bonin,** 132 Tenth Ave. (© 212/367-7474; www.alexanderandbonin.com), which mounts excellent solo exhibitions; **James Cohan Gallery,** 533 W. 26th St. (© 212/714-9500; www.jamescohan.com), particularly strong in modern photography; and **Lehmann Maupin,** 540 W. 26th St. (© 212/255-2923; www.lehmann maupin.com), whose roster runs the gamut from young unknowns to contemporary masters like Ross Bleckner. For a comprehensive listing of the Chelsea galleries, check the website www.westchelseaarts.com.

DOWNTOWN   SoHo remains colorful, if less edgy than it used to be, with the action centered around West Broadway and encroaching onto the edge of Chinatown. **Peter Blum Gallery,** 99 Wooster St. (© 212/343-0441), which showcased the divine Kim Sooja, a Korean artist who uses traditional Korean bedcovers to comment on the promise of wedded bliss; **O. K. Harris,** 383 W. Broadway (© 212/431-3600; www.okharris.com), which shows a fascinating variety of contemporary painting, sculpture, and photography; and **Louis K. Meisel,** 141 Prince St. (© 212/677-1340; www.meiselgallery.com), specializing in photo-realism and American pinup art (yep, Petty and Vargas girls). In TriBeCa, try **Cheryl Hazan Arts Gallery,** 35 N. Moore St. (© 212/343-8964; www.cherylhazan.com), or **DFN Gallery,** 210 11th Ave. 6th Fl. (© 212/334-3400; www.dfngallery.com), which focus on fresh, distinctive contemporary art.

25 W. 52nd St. (btwn Fifth and Sixth aves.). © 212/621-6600. www.mtr.org. Admission $10 adults, $8 seniors and students, $5 children under 14. Tues–Sun noon–6pm (Thurs until 8pm) Subway: B, D, F, V to 47–50th sts./Rockefeller Center; E, V to 53rd St.

Museum of the City of New York   A wide variety of objects—costumes, photographs, prints, maps, dioramas, and memorabilia—trace the history of New York City from its beginnings as a humble Dutch colony in the 16th century to its present-day prominence. Two outstanding permanent exhibits are the re-creation of John D. Rockefeller's master bedroom and dressing room, and the space devoted to "Broadway!," a history of New York theater. Kids will love "New York Toy Stories," a permanent exhibit showcasing toys and dolls owned and adored by centuries of New York children. The permanent "Painting the Town: Cityscapes of New York" explores the changing cityscape from 1809 to 1997, and carries new profundity in the wake of the September 11, 2001, terrorist attacks In the summer of 2007, MCNY featured the fun exhibit, The Glory Days: New York Baseball, 1947-1957."

1220 Fifth Ave. (at 103rd St.). © 212/534-1672. www.mcny.org. Suggested admission $9 adults, $5 seniors, students, and children, $20 families. Tues–Sun 10am–5pm. Admission free Sun 10am–noon. Subway: 6 to 103rd St.

National Museum of the American Indian, George Gustav Heye Center   This impressive collection represents the Smithsonian Institution. The collection spans more than 10,000 years of native heritage, gathered a century ago mainly by New York banking millionaire George Gustav Heye. About 70% of the collection is dedicated to the natives of North America and Hawaii; the rest represents the cultures of Mexico and Central and South America. There's a wealth of material here, but it's not as well organized as it could be. The museum also hosts temporary themed exhibitions and interpretive programs, plus free storytelling, music, and dance presentations.

The museum is housed in the beautiful 1907 Beaux Arts **U.S. Customs House** &, designed by Cass Gilbert and a National Historic Landmark that's worth a look in its own right.

1 Bowling Green (btwn State and Whitehall sts.). © 212/514-3700. www.nmai.si.edu. Free admission. Daily 10am–5pm (Thurs until 8pm). Subway: 4, 5 to Bowling Green; R, W to Whitehall, 1 to South Ferry.

Neue Galerie New York *Finds*   This museum is dedicated to German and Austrian art and design, with a particular focus on the early 20th century. Displayed on two floors, the collection features painting, works on paper, decorative arts, and other media from such artists as Klimt, Kokoschka, Kandinsky, Klee, and leaders of the Wiener Werkstätte decorative arts and Bauhaus applied arts movements, such as Adolf Loos and Mies van der Rohe, respectively. The gallery made headlines in 2006 when it acquired Klimt's *Portrait of Adele Bloch-Bauer I*—dubbed the Golden Adele—for a record-setting $135 million. The museum floated the idea of adding a high premium (up to $50) to view its new masterpiece, but the outcry caused the management to reconsider. You can see "The Golden Adele" for the $15 admission fee without extra charge. Once occupied by Mrs. Cornelius Vanderbilt III, the impeccably restored, landmark-designated 1914 Carrère & Hastings building (they built the New York Public Library as well) is worth a look itself. **Cafe Sabarsky** is modeled on a Viennese cafe, so museum-goers in need of a snack break can expect a fine Linzer torte.

1048 Fifth Ave. (at 86th St.). © 212/628-6200. www.neuegalerie.org. Admission $15 adults, $10 seniors and students, under 12 not admitted, under 16 must be accompanied by an adult. Fri 11am–9pm; Thur, Sat, Sun, Mon. 11am–6pm. Subway: 4, 5, 6 to 86th St.

New Museum of Contemporary Art (Ⓚ   This contemporary-arts museum has moved closer to the mainstream in recent years, but it's only a safety margin in from the edge as far as most of us are concerned. Expect adventurous and well-curated exhibitions. Previous schedules have included *Portrait of the Lost Boys,* New Zealander Jacqueline Fraser's moving narrative made of sumptuous fabric and fragile wire sculptures that examines the high incidence of suicide among teenage boys in New Zealand, and "John Waters: Change of Life," photographs by the filmmaker who brought us *Pink Flamingos* and *Hairspray.* In late 2007, the museum will move to a new 60,000-square-foot, $35-million home on the Bowery at Prince Street. It will be the first new art museum ever constructed from the ground up below 14th Street.

556 W. 22nd St. (at Eleventh Ave.). Ⓒ 212/219-1222. www.newmuseum.org. Admission $6 adults, $3 seniors and students, free to visitors 18 and under, $3 Thurs after 6pm. Tues–Wed and Fri–Sat noon–6pm; Thurs noon–8pm (Zenith Media Lounge to 6:30pm). Subway: C, E to 23rd St.

New York City Fire Museum (Ⓚ (Ⓚids   Housed in a three-story 1904 firehouse, the former quarters of FDNY Engine Co. 30, this museum offers one of the country's most extensive collections of fire-service memorabilia from the 18th century to the present. It is also the best place to pay tribute to the 343 heroic firefighters who lost their lives blocks away in the World Trade Center disaster. Expect ongoing changing exhibits relating to the September 11, 2001, terrorist attack. Other displays range from vintage fire marks to fire trucks (including the last-known example of a 1921 pumper) to the gear and tools of modern firefighters. Also look for leather hoses, fireboats, and Currier & Ives prints, plus a new exhibit on fire safety and burn prevention especially geared toward families. Best of all, real firefighters are almost always on hand to share stories and fire-safety information with kids. The retail store sells authorized FDNY logo wear and souvenirs. Call ahead for details on scheduling a guided tour.

278 Spring St. (btwn Varick and Hudson sts.). Ⓒ 212/691-1303. www.nycfiremuseum.org. Suggested admission $5 adults, $2 seniors and students, $1 children under 12. Tues–Sat 10am–5pm; Sun 10am–4pm. Subway: C, E to Spring St.1 to Houston St.

New York City Police Museum   Located in the first precinct station house, built in 1901, the museum exhibits police equipment from throughout the years such as pistols, uniforms, and vehicles along with really fun stuff like master burglar Willie Sutton's lock picks and a machine gun used by Al Capone. At press time, a permanent exhibit chronicling the role the NYPD played in the response to the September 11 terrorist attacks was under construction.

100 Old Slip (btwn Water–South sts.). Ⓒ 212/480-3100. www.nycpolicemuseum.org. Admission: $5 adults, $3 seniors, $2 children 6-18, free for under 6. Mon–Sat 10am–5pm. Subway: 2, 3 to Wall St.

New-York Historical Society (Ⓚ   Launched in 1804, the New-York Historical Society is a major repository of American history, culture, and art, with a special focus on New York and its broader cultural significance. The grand neoclassical edifice near the Museum of Natural History has finally emerged from the renovation tent. Now open on the fourth floor is the **Henry Luce III Center for the Study of American Culture,** a state-of-the-art study facility and gallery of fine and decorative arts, which displays more than 40,000 objects amassed over 200 years—including paintings, sculpture, Tiffany lamps, textiles, furniture, even carriages—that had previously been in storage for decades. Also look for paintings from Hudson River School artists Thomas Cole, Asher Durand, and Frederic

Church, including Cole's five-part masterpiece "The Course of Empire." Of particular interest to scholars and ephemera buffs are the extensive Library Collections, which include books, manuscripts, maps, newspapers, photographs, and more documents chronicling the American experience. (An appointment may be necessary to view some or all of the Library Collections, so call ahead.) The 2006 exhibit "Slavery in New York" was so popular it has now become permanent and the companion exhibit, "New York Divided: Slavery and the Civil War" was through September 2007.

An extensive, top-quality calendar of programs runs the gamut from story hours to Irving Berlin music nights to lectures by such luminaries as Ric Burns to expert-led walks through Manhattan neighborhoods; call or check the website for the schedule.

170 Central Park West (at 77th St.). ✆ 212/873-3400. www.nyhistory.org. Admission $10 adults, $7 seniors and educators, $6 students, free for children 12 and under. Free on Fridays from 6 to 8pm Tues–Sun 10am–6pm. (Fri until 8pm). Subway: B, C to 81st St.; 1 to 79th St.

Scandinavia House: The Nordic Center in America *(Finds)*   Dedicated to both the shared and unique cultures of Denmark, Finland, Iceland, Norway, and Sweden, Scandinavia House features two floors of galleries and an outdoor sculpture terrace displaying rotating art and design exhibits that can range from "Scandia: Important Early Maps of the Northern Regions" to "Strictly Swedish: An Exhibition of Contemporary Design." The rest of the space, including the 168-seat Victor Borge Hall, is dedicated to a full calendar of lectures, films, music and drama performances, and scholarly presentations, all of a Nordic ilk. The exquisite modern building—designed to showcase Scandinavian materials and aesthetics—is worth a look in itself, especially if you're a modern-architecture buff. Guided tours are offered Tuesday and Thursday at 2pm and last a half-hour; they're free, but reservations are recommended.

The shop is a riot of fine Scandinavian design, and the excellent **AQ Café**—an offshoot of the terrific Midtown restaurant **Aquavit** (p. 200)—serves up Swedish meatballs and other Scandinavian delicacies.

58 Park Ave. (btwn 37th and 38th sts.). ✆ 212/879-9779. www.scandinaviahouse.org. Suggested admission to 3rd- and 4th-floor galleries $3, $2 seniors and students; free admission to other spaces. Exhibitions Tues–Sat noon–6pm; cafe Mon–Sat 10am–5pm; store Mon–Sat noon–6pm. Subway: 6 to 33rd St.; 4, 5, 6, 7, S to 42nd St./Grand Central.

Schomburg Center for Research in Black Culture   Arturo Alfonso Schomburg, a black Puerto Rican, set himself to accumulating materials about blacks in America, and his massive collection—one of the largest collections of African-American materials in the world—is housed and preserved at this research branch of the New York Public Library. The Exhibition Hall, the Latimer/Edison Gallery, and the Reading Room host changing exhibits related to black culture, such as "Lest We Forget: The Triumph over Slavery" and "Masterpieces of African Motherhood." A rich calendar of talks and performing-arts events is also part of the program. Make an appointment for a guided tour so you can see the 1930s murals by Harlem Renaissance artist Aaron Douglas; it'll be worth your while. Academics and others interested in a more complete look at the center's holdings can preview what's available online. Call to inquire about current exhibitions and information on tours and public programs.

515 Malcolm X Blvd. (Lenox Ave., btwn 135th and 136th sts.). ✆ 212/491-2200. www.nypl.org. Free admission. Gallery Tues–Sat 10am–6pm; Sun 1–5pm. Subway: 2, 3 to 135th St.

Skyscraper Museum   Wowed by the sheer verticality in this town? Awed by the architectural marvel that is the high-rise? You're not alone. If you'd like to learn more about the technology, culture, and muscle behind it all, seek out this formerly itinerant museum, which moved into its first permanent home in 2004 in the 38-story Skidmore, Owings & Merrill tower that also houses the Ritz-Carlton New York, Battery Park. The new space comprises two galleries, one housing a permanent exhibition dedicated to the evolution of Manhattan's commercial skyline, the other for changing shows. In 2007 the museum featured "Giants: The Twin Towers and the Twentieth Century," about the building of the World Trade Center (and not the destruction of) including video documentaries and memorabilia.

39 Battery Place (Little West St. and 1st Place). ⓒ 212/968-1961. www.skyscraper.org. Admission: $5 adults, $2.50 seniors and students. Wed–Sun noon–6pm. Subway: 4, 5 to Bowling Green.

South Street Seaport & Museum *(Kids*   Dating back to the 17th century, this landmark historic district on the East River encompasses 11 square blocks of historic buildings, a maritime museum, several piers, shops, and restaurants.

You can explore most of the Seaport on your own. It's a beautiful but somewhat odd place. The mainly 18th- and 19th-century buildings lining the cobbled streets and alleyways are impeccably restored but nevertheless have a theme-park air about them, no doubt due to the mall-familiar shops housed within. The Seaport's biggest tourist attraction is Pier 17, a historic barge converted into a mall, complete with food court and cheap-jewelry kiosks.

Despite its rampant commercialism, the Seaport is well worth a look. There's a good amount of history to be discovered here, most of it around the **South Street Seaport Museum,** a fitting tribute to the sea commerce that once thrived here. On weekends the museum dedicates Saturday and Sunday afternoons to family fun with music, art, and other activities for children 4 and older.

In addition to the galleries—which house paintings and prints, ship models, scrimshaw, and nautical designs, as well as frequently changing exhibitions—there are a number of historic ships berthed at the pier to explore, including the 1911 four-masted *Peking* and the 1893 Gloucester fishing schooner *Lettie G. Howard.* A few of the boats are living museums and restoration works in progress; the 1885 cargo schooner ***Pioneer*** (ⓒ **212/748-8786**) offers 2-hour public sails daily from early May through September. Tickets for the early and late voyages (1pm and 9:30pm) are $25 for adults, $20 for students/seniors and children 12 and under. Add $5 to the prices for the 4pm and 7pm departures. If you'd rather keep those sea legs on dry land, the museum offers a number of guided walking tours; call or check **www.southstseaport. org** for details.

Even **Pier 17** has its merits. Head up to the third-level deck overlooking the East River, where the long wooden chairs will have you thinking about what it was like to cross the Atlantic on the *Normandie.* From this level you can see south to the Statue of Liberty, north to the Gothic majesty of the Brooklyn Bridge, and Brooklyn Heights on the opposite shore.

At the gateway to the Seaport, at Fulton and Water streets, is the ***Titanic* Memorial Lighthouse,** a monument to those who lost their lives when the ocean liner sank on April 15, 1912. It was erected overlooking the East River in 1913 and moved to this spot in 1968, just after the historic district was so designated.

A variety of events take place year-round, ranging from street performers to concerts to fireworks. Check the website or dial ⓒ **212/SEA-PORT.**

At Water and South sts.; museum visitor center is at 12 Fulton St. ⓒ 212/748-8600 or 212/SEA-PORT. www.southst seaport.org. Museum admission $8 adults, $6 students and seniors, $4 children 5–12, free for children under 5.

Museum Apr–Oct Tues–Sun 10am–6pm, Thurs 10am–8pm; Nov–Mar Fri–Mon 10am–5pm. Subway: 2, 3, 4, 5 to Fulton St. (walk east, or downslope, on Fulton St. to Water St.).

Studio Museum in Harlem   This small but lovely museum is devoted to presenting 19th- and 20th-century African-American art as well as 20th-century African and Caribbean art and traditional African art and artifacts. Rotating exhibitions are a big part of the museum's focus, such as "Smithsonian African-American Photography: The First 100 Years, 1842–1942"; the silk-screens and lithographs of Jacob Lawrence; and an annual exhibition of works by emerging artists as part of its Artists-in-Residence program. In 2007, the museum featured "Africa Comics," the first exhibition of African comic art in the U.S. There's also a small sculpture garden, a good gift shop, and a full calendar of special events.

144 W. 125th St. (btwn Lenox Ave. and Adam Clayton Powell Blvd.). © 212/864-4500. www.studiomuseum.org. Admission $7 adults, $3 seniors and students, free for children under 12, free to all 1st Sat of the month. Wed–Fri noon–6pm; Sat–Sun 10am–6pm. Subway: 2, 3 to 125th St.

Whitney Museum of American Art at Altria   This Midtown branch of the **Whitney Museum of American Art** 🅐🅐 (p. 246) features an airy sculpture court and a petite gallery that hosts changing exhibits, usually the works of living contemporary artists. Well worth peeking into if you happen to be in the neighborhood. Free gallery talks are offered Wednesday and Friday at 1pm.

120 Park Ave. (at 42nd St., opposite Grand Central Terminal). © 800/WHITNEY. www.whitney.org. Free admission. Gallery Mon–Wed and Fri 11am–6pm; Thurs 11am–7:30pm. Sculpture Court Mon–Sat 7:30am–9:30pm; Sun 11am–7pm. Subway: S, 4, 5, 6, 7 to 42nd St./Grand Central.

4 Skyscrapers & Other Architectural Highlights

For details on the **Empire State Building** 🅐🅐🅐, see p. 238; for **Grand Central Terminal** 🅐🅐, p. 238; for **Rockefeller Center** 🅐🅐, p. 241; for the **U.S. Customs House,** p. 264; and for the **Brooklyn Bridge** 🅐🅐, p. 236. You might also wish to check out "Places of Worship," later in this chapter, for treasures like St. Patrick's Cathedral, Temple Emanu-El, and the **Cathedral of St. John the Divine** 🅐. See also chapter 2, "A Traveler's Guide to New York's Architecture," for a look at the city's evolving architecture.

In addition to checking out the landmarks below, architecture buffs may also want to seek out these notable buildings: The **Lever House,** built in 1952 at 390 Park Ave., between 53rd and 54th streets, and the neighboring **Seagram Building** (1958), at 375 Park Ave., are the city's best examples of the form-follows-function, glass-and-steel International style, with the latter designed by master architect Mies van der Rohe. Also in Midtown East is the **Sony Building,** at 550 Madison Ave., designed in 1984 by Philip Johnson, with a pretty rose-granite facade and a playful Chippendale-style top that puts it a cut above the rest on the block.

The Upper West Side is home to two of the city's prime examples of residential architecture. On Broadway, between 73rd and 74th streets, is the **Ansonia,** looking for all the world like a flamboyant architectural wedding cake. This splendid Beaux Arts building has been home to the likes of Stravinsky, Toscanini, and Caruso, thanks to its virtually soundproof apartments. (It was also the spot where members of the Chicago White Sox plotted to throw the 1919 World Series, a year before Babe Ruth moved in after donning the New York Yankees' pinstripes.) Even more notable is the **Dakota,** at 72nd Street and Central Park West. Legend has it that the angular 1884 apartment house—accented with gables, dormers, and oriel windows that give it a

Harlem's Architectural Treasures

Originally conceived as a bucolic suburbia for 19th-century Manhattan's moneyed set, Harlem has always had more than its share of historic treasures. To find them, pay a call on the **Astor Row Houses,** 130th Street between Fifth and Lenox avenues, a fabulous series of 28 redbrick townhouses built in the early 1880s by the Astor family and graced with wooden porches, generous yards, and ornamental ironwork.

Equally impressive is **Strivers' Row,** West 139th Street between Adam Clayton Powell, Jr., and Frederick Douglass boulevards, where hardly a brick has changed among the gorgeous McKim, Mead & White neo-Italian Renaissance town houses since they were built in 1890. Once the original white owners had moved out, these lovely houses attracted the cream of Harlem, "strivers" like Eubie Blake and W. C. Handy.

Handsome brownstones, limestone townhouses, and row houses are atop **Sugar Hill,** 145th to 155th streets, between St. Nicholas and Edgecombe avenues, named for the "sweet life" enjoyed by its residents. In the early 20th century, such prominent blacks as W. E. B. DuBois, Thurgood Marshall, and Roy Wilkins lived in the now-landmark building at 409 Edgecombe Ave.

And if you're venturing this far uptown, don't miss the **Jumel Terrace Historic District,** west of St. Nicholas Avenue between 160th and 162nd streets. Of particular note is **Sylvan Terrace,** which feels more like an upstate Hudson River town than a part of Harlem—well worth seeking out for architecture lovers. A walk along it will lead you directly to the grand **Morris-Jumel Mansion** ⍟, which is open to the public for tours (see "In Search of Historic Homes," below).

brooding appeal—earned its name when its developer, Edward S. Clark, was teased by friends that he was building so far north of the city that he might as well be building in the Dakotas. The building's most famous resident, John Lennon, was gunned down outside the 72nd Street entrance on December 8, 1980; Yoko Ono still lives inside.

Chrysler Building ⍟⍟   Built as Chrysler Corporation headquarters in 1930 (they moved out decades ago), this is perhaps the 20th century's most romantic architectural achievement, especially at night when the lights in its triangular openings play off its steely crown. As you admire its facade, be sure to note the gargoyles reaching out from the upper floors, looking for all the world like streamline-Gothic hood ornaments.

There's a fascinating tale behind this building. While it was under construction, its architect, William Van Alen, hid his final plans for the spire that now tops it. Working at a furious pace in the last days of construction, the workers assembled in secrecy the elegant pointy top—and then they raised it right through what people had assumed was going to be the roof, and for a brief moment it was the world's tallest building (a distinction stolen by the Empire State Building a few months later). Its exterior chrome sculptures are magnificent and spooky. The observation deck closed long ago, but you can visit its lavish ground-floor interior, which is Art Deco to the max. The ceiling mural depicting airplanes and other marvels of the first decades of the 20th century evince the bright promise of technology. The elevators are works of art, masterfully covered in exotic woods (especially note the lotus-shaped marquetry on the doors).

405 Lexington Ave. (at 42nd St.). Subway: S, 4, 5, 6, 7 to 42nd St./Grand Central.

Flatiron Building   This triangular masterpiece was one of the first skyscrapers. Its wedge shape is the only way the building could fill the triangular property created by the intersection of Fifth Avenue and Broadway, and that happy coincidence created one of the city's most distinctive buildings. Built in 1902 and fronted with limestone and terra cotta (not iron), the Flatiron measures only 6 feet across at its narrow end. So called for its resemblance to the laundry appliance, it was originally named the Fuller Building, then later "Burnham's Folly" because folks were certain that architect Daniel Burnham's 21-story structure would fall down. It didn't. There's no observation deck, and the building mainly houses publishing offices, but there are a few shops on the ground floor. The building's existence has served to name the neighborhood around it—the Flatiron District, home to a bevy of smart restaurants and shops.

175 Fifth Ave. (at 23rd St.). Subway: R to 23rd St.

New York Public Library ⟡⟡   The New York Public Library, adjacent to **Bryant Park** ⟡ (p. 275) and designed by Carrère & Hastings (1911), is one of the country's finest examples of Beaux Arts architecture, a majestic structure of white Vermont marble with Corinthian columns and allegorical statues. Before climbing the broad flight of steps to the Fifth Avenue entrance, note the famous lion sculptures—*Fortitude* on the right, and *Patience* on the left—so dubbed by whip-smart former mayor Fiorello La Guardia. At Christmastime they don natty wreaths to keep warm.

This library is actually the **Humanities and Social Sciences Library,** only one of the research libraries in the New York Public Library system. The interior is one of the finest in the city and features **Astor Hall,** with high arched marble ceilings and grand staircases. Thanks to restoration and modernization, the stupendous **Main Reading Rooms** have been returned to their stately glory and moved into the computer age (goodbye, card catalogs!). After a $5-million restoration, what was once known only as Room 117, a Beaux Arts masterpiece with incredible views of Fifth Avenue and 42nd Street is now known as the Lionel Pincus and Princess Firyal Map Division. Here you will find possibly the finest and most extensive collection of maps in the world.

Even if you don't stop in to peruse the periodicals, you may want to check out one of the excellent rotating **exhibitions.** Call or check the website to see what's on while you're in town. There's also a full calendar of **lecture programs,** with past speakers ranging from Tom Stoppard to Cokie Roberts; popular speakers often sell out, so it's a good idea to purchase tickets in advance.

Fifth Ave. at 42nd St. ⓒ 212/930-0830 (exhibits and events) or 212/661-7220 (library hours). www.nypl.org. Free admission to all exhibitions. Tues–Wed 11am–7:30pm; Thurs–Sat 10am–6pm; Sun 1–5pm. Subway: B, D, F, V to 42nd St.; S, 4, 5, 6, 7 to Grand Central/42nd St.

United Nations   In the midst of New York City is this working monument to world peace. The U.N. headquarters occupies 18 acres of international territory—neither the city nor the United States has jurisdiction here—along the East River from 42nd to 48th streets. Designed by an international team of architects (led by American Wallace

In Search of Historic Homes

The **Historic House Trust of New York City** preserves 19 houses, located in city parks in all five boroughs. Those particularly worth seeking out include the **Morris-Jumel Mansion** in Harlem at 65 Jumel Terrace, at 160th Street, east of St. Nicholas Avenue (℃ **212/923-8008;** www.morrisjumel.org; Wed–Sun 10am–4pm), a grand colonial mansion built in the Palladian style (ca. 1765) and now Manhattan's oldest surviving residential house.

Built around 1764, the **Dyckman Farmhouse Museum,** farther uptown at 4881 Broadway, at 204th Street (℃ **212/304-9422;** www.historichousetrust. org; Wed–Sat 11am–4pm; Sun noon–4pm), is the only Dutch colonial farmhouse remaining in Manhattan, stoically and stylishly surviving the urban development that grew up around it.

The **Edgar Allan Poe Cottage,** 2460 Grand Concourse, at East Kingsbridge Road in the Bronx (℃ **718/881-8900;** www.bronxhistoricalsociety.org; Sat 10am–4pm, Sun 1–5pm), was the last home (1846–49) of the brilliant but troubled poet and author, who moved his wife here because he thought the "country air" would be good for her tuberculosis. The house is outfitted as a memorial to the writer, with period furnishings and exhibits on his life and times.

The **Merchant's House Museum,** 29 E. 4th St., between Lafayette Street and Bowery in NoHo (℃ **212/777-1089;** www.merchantshouse.org; Thurs–Mon noon–5pm), is a rare jewel: a perfectly preserved 19th-century home, complete with intact interiors, whose last resident is said to be the inspiration for Catherine Sloper in Henry James's *Washington Square.*

Each of the 15 other houses also has a fascinating story to tell. A brochure listing the locations and touring details of all 19 of the historic homes is available by calling ℃ **212/360-8282.** You'll also find information online at www.historichousetrust.org. Admission to each house is generally no more than $5 ($8 at Merchant's House).

K. Harrison and including Le Corbusier) and finished in 1952, the complex along the East River weds the 39-story glass slab Secretariat with the free-form General Assembly on beautifully landscaped grounds donated by John D. Rockefeller, Jr. One hundred eighty nations use the facilities to arbitrate worldwide disputes.

Guided tours leave every half-hour or so and last 45 minutes to an hour. Your guide will take you to the General Assembly Hall and the Security Council Chamber and introduce the history and activities of the United Nations and its related organizations. Along the tour you'll see donated objects and artwork, including charred artifacts that survived the atomic bombs at Hiroshima and Nagasaki, stained-glass windows by Chagall, a replica of the first *Sputnik,* and a colorful mosaic called *The Golden Rule,* based on a Norman Rockwell drawing, which was a gift from the United States in 1985.

If you take the time to wander the beautifully landscaped **grounds,** you'll be rewarded with lovely views and some surprises. The mammoth monument *Good*

Historic Downtown Structures

New York is neither Rome nor Athens, yet the city can boast a few old structures, at least New World old. To find a good sampling of "ancient" New York, head downtown, where it all began.

You might want to first stop at the southern tip of the island at Battery Park where an old fort called **Castle Clinton National Monument** (② 212/344-7220; www.nps.gov/cacl) still stands. The fort, or what remains of it, was built between 1808 and 1811 to defend New York Harbor against the British. In the mid–19th century the fort was the city's first immigration center. A small museum was added to the monument in 1986, with exhibits that follow the evolution of the fort.

Not far from Castle Clinton, at 1 Bowling Green, is the relatively modern 1907-built **U.S. Customs House** ⊛, which houses the National Museum of the American Indian, George Gustav Heye Center (p. 256). Designed by Cass Gilbert and now a National Historic Landmark, the granite structure features giant statues carved by Daniel Chester French (of Lincoln Memorial fame) lining the front that personify Asia (pondering philosophically), America (bright-eyed and bushy-tailed), Europe (decadent and whose time has passed), and Africa (sleeping). Inside, the airy oval rotunda designed by Spanish engineer Raphael Guastavino was frescoed by Reginald Marsh to glorify the shipping industry (and, by extension, the Customs office once housed here).

One of Wall Street's most recognizable sights is the imposing, majestic **Federal Hall National Memorial,** 26 Wall St. (② 212/825-6888; www.nps.gov/feha). Built in 1842, the memorial, with the 1883-built statue of George Washington on the steps directly across from the New York Stock Exchange, was erected on the site of New York's first City Hall. Inside it's now a museum, with exhibits that elucidate the events surrounding the memorial and other aspects of American history. The infrastructure of the memorial suffered from the massive shock of the nearby attack on the World Trade Center; as a result, the memorial is undergoing a $16-million rehabilitation. Call to see if the museum's reopened in time for your visit.

George Washington was a visible presence in 18th-century New York and he worshiped at the still-standing **St. Paul's Chapel,** built in 1766 and part of the Trinity Church (p. 267) at 74 Trinity Place (② 212/233-4164). The chapel now serves as a memorial to the victims of 9/11.

So now we know where Washington worshiped, but where did he eat? At **Fraunces Tavern,** the same place where he bade farewell to his officers at the end of the American Revolution. This 1907-built tavern is an exact replica of the original 1717 tavern. It's now a museum, at 54 Pearl St., near Broad Street (② 212/425-1778; www.frauncestavernmuseum.org), and an actual restaurant.

Defeats Evil, donated by the Soviet Union in 1990, fashioned a contemporary St. George slaying a dragon from parts of a Russian ballistic missile and an American Pershing missile.

For an unusual treat, try a multiethnic meal while visiting the U.N. at the **Delegates' Dining Room** (© **212/963-7625**).

At First Ave. and 46th St. © **212/963-8687.** www.un.org/tours. Guided tours $12 adults, $9 seniors, $8.50 high school and college students, $6.50 children 5–14. Children under 5 not permitted. Daily tours every half-hour 9:30am–4:45pm; Sat, Sun 10am to 4:30pm Jan–Feb; limited schedule may be in effect during the general debate (late Sept to mid-Oct). Subway: S, 4, 5, 6, 7 to 42nd St./Grand Central.

Woolworth Building ⊛   This soaring "Cathedral of Commerce" cost Frank W. Woolworth $14 million worth of nickels and dimes in 1913. Designed by Cass Gilbert, it was the world's tallest edifice until 1930, when it was surpassed by the Chrysler Building. At its opening, Pres. Woodrow Wilson pressed a button from the White House that illuminated the building's 80,000 electric light bulbs. The neo-Gothic architecture is rife with spires, gargoyles, flying buttresses, vaulted ceilings, 16th-century-style stone-as-lace traceries, castle-like turrets, and a churchlike interior. Housing financial institutions and high-tech companies, the grand tower is still dedicated to the almighty dollar.

Step into the lofty marble entrance arcade to view the gleaming mosaic Byzantine-style ceiling and gold-leafed neo-Gothic cornices. The corbels (carved figures under the crossbeams) in the lobby include whimsical portraits of the building's engineer Gunvald Aus measuring a girder (above the staircase to the left of the main door), Gilbert holding a model of the building, and Woolworth counting coins (both above the left-hand corridor of elevators). Stand near the security guard's podium and crane your neck for a glimpse at Paul Jennewein's murals *Commerce* and *Labor,* half hidden up on the mezzanine. Cross Broadway for the best overview of the exterior.

233 Broadway (at Park Place, near City Hall Park). Subway: 2, 3 to Park Place; R to City Hall.

5 Places of Worship

New York has an incredible range of renowned religious institutions, notable for their history, architecture, and/or inspirational music. I've listed two of Harlem's premier gospel institutions below; if you would rather go to one of these gospel services in the company of a knowledgeable guide, see "Organized Sightseeing Tours," on p. 278 of this chapter. Additionally, if you would like to hear the rousing gospel of the four-time Grammy Award–winning **Brooklyn Tabernacle Choir** ⊛, see p. 294.

If you do plan to attend a gospel service, be prepared to stay for the entire 1½- to 2-hour service. It is impolite to exit early. (Services are extremely popular, so you'll find it just plain difficult to leave before the end anyway.)

Abyssinian Baptist Church ⊛   The most famous of Harlem's more than 400 houses of worship is this Baptist church, founded downtown in 1808 by African-American and Ethiopian merchants. It was moved uptown to Harlem back in the 1920s by Adam Clayton Powell, Sr., who built it into the largest Protestant congregation—white or black—in America. His son, Adam Clayton Powell, Jr. (for whom the adjoining boulevard was named), carried on his tradition, and also became the first-ever black U.S. congressman. Abyssinian is now the domain of the fiery, activist-minded Rev. Calvin O. Butts, whom the chamber of commerce has declared a "living

treasure." The Sunday morning services—at 9 and 11am—offer a wonderful opportunity to experience the Harlem gospel tradition.

132 Odell Clark Place (W. 138th St., btwn Adam Clayton Powell Blvd. and Lenox Ave.). © **212/862-7474.**
www.abyssinian.org. Subway: 2, 3, B, C to 135th St.

Cathedral of St. John the Divine *✦*   The world's largest Gothic cathedral, St.
John the Divine has been a work in progress since 1892. Its sheer size is amazing
enough—a nave that stretches two football fields and a seating capacity of 5,000—but
keep in mind that there is no steel structural support. The church is being built using
traditional Gothic engineering—blocks of granite and limestone are carved out by
master masons and their apprentices—which may explain why construction is still
ongoing, more than 100 years after it began, with no end in sight. In fact, a December 2001 fire destroyed the north transept, which housed the gift shop. But this
phoenix rose from the ashes quickly; the cathedral was reopened to visitors within a
month, even though the scent of charred wood was still in the air and restoration will
not be complete for months to come. That's precisely what makes this place so wonderful: Finishing isn't necessarily the point.

Though it's the seat of the Episcopal Diocese of New York, St. John's embraces an
interfaith tradition. Internationalism is a theme found throughout the cathedral's
iconography. Each chapel is dedicated to a different national, ethnic, or social group.
The genocide memorial in the Missionary chapel—dedicated to the victims of the
Ottoman Empire in Armenia (1915–23), of the Holocaust (1939–45), and in Bosnia-
Herzegovina since 1992—moved me to tears, as did the FDNY memorial in the
Labor chapel. Although it was originally conceived to honor 12 firefighters killed in
1966, hundreds of personal notecards and trinkets of remembrance have evolved it
into a moving tribute to the 343 firefighting heroes killed on September 11, 2001.

You can explore the cathedral on your own, or on the **Public Tour,** offered 6 days
a week; also inquire about the periodic (usually twice monthly) **Vertical Tour,** which
takes you on a hike up the 11-flight circular staircase to the top, for spectacular views.
At press time, these were still suspended due to the fire. Check the website for updates.
St. John the Divine is also known for presenting outstanding workshops, musical
events, and important speakers. The free **New Year's Eve concert** draws thousands of
New Yorkers; so, too, does its annual **Feast of St. Francis** (Blessing of the Animals),
held in early October (see the "New York City Calendar of Events," in chapter 3). Call
for event information and tickets. To hear the incredible pipe organ in action, attend
the weekly **Choral Evensong and Organ Meditation** service, which highlights one
of the nation's most treasured pipe organs, Sunday at 6pm.

1047 Amsterdam Ave. (at 112th St.). © **212/316-7490,** 212/932-7347 for tour information and reservations,
212/662-2133 for event information and tickets. www.stjohndivine.org. Suggested admission $2; tour $5. Mon–Sat
7am–6pm; Sun 7am–7pm. Tours offered Tues–Sat 11am; Sun 1pm. Worship services Mon–Sat 8 and 8:30am (morning prayer and holy Eucharist), 12:15pm, and 5:30pm (1st Thurs service 7:15am); Sun 8, 9, and 11am and 6pm; AIDS
memorial service 4th Sat of the month at 12:15pm. Subway: B, C, 1 to Cathedral Pkwy.

The Church of the Transfiguration *Finds*   When you come upon this oddly beautiful historic structure amidst modern high-rise condos in the burgeoning Madison
Square neighborhood, you will once again be awed at the diversity of New York. Also
known as The Little Church Around the Corner, this Episcopalian house of worship
with its twists and turns has been compared to a "holy cucumber vine." Built in 1849,
the church was granted United States landmark status in 1973. Its history includes
sheltering escaped slaves during the Civil War draft riots, being one of the first

churches to hand out food for the poor at the start of the Depression, and, most significantly, for its close relationship to the theater. In 1923 the Episcopal Actor's Guild was formed at the church and some of the noted actors involved include Basil Rathbone, Mary Pickford, Tallulah Bankhead, with Charlton Heston, Barnard Hughes, and, most recently Sam Waterston serving as presidents.

1 E. 29th St. (btwn Fifth and Madison aves.). ✆ 212/684-6770. www.littlechurch.org. Subway: 6 to 28th St.

Mother A.M.E. Zion Church
Another of Harlem's great gospel churches is this African Methodist Episcopal house of worship, the first black church to be founded in New York State. Established on John Street in Lower Manhattan in 1796, Mother A.M.E. was known as the "Freedom Church" for the central role it played in the Underground Railroad. Among the escaped slaves the church hid was Frederick Douglass; other famous congregants have included Sojourner Truth and Paul Robeson. Mother A.M.E. relocated to Harlem in 1914 and moved into this grand edifice in 1925. Rousing Sunday services are at 11am.

140–7 W. 137th St. (btwn Adam Clayton Powell Blvd. and Lenox Ave.). ✆ 212/234-1544. Subway: 2, 3, B, C to 135th St.

St. Patrick's Cathedral
This incredible Gothic white-marble-and-stone structure is the largest Roman Catholic cathedral in the United States, as well as the seat of the Archdiocese of New York. Designed by James Renwick, begun in 1859, and consecrated in 1879, St. Patrick's wasn't completed until 1906. Strangely, Irish Catholics picked one of the city's WASPiest neighborhoods for St. Patrick's. After the death of the beloved John Cardinal O'Connor in 2000, Pope John Paul II installed Bishop Edward Egan, whom he elevated to cardinal in 2001. The vast cathedral seats a congregation of 2,200; if you don't want to come for Mass, you can pop in between services to get a look at the impressive interior. The St. Michael and St. Louis altar came from Tiffany & Co. (also located here on Fifth Ave.), while the St. Elizabeth altar—honoring Mother Elizabeth Ann Seton, the first American-born saint—was designed by Paolo Medici of Rome.

Fifth Ave. (btwn 50th and 51st sts.). ✆ 212/753-2261. www.ny-archdiocese.org. Free admission. Sun–Fri 7am–8:30pm; Sat 8am–8:30pm. Mass Mon–Fri 7, 7:30, and 8am, noon, and 12:30, 1, and 5:30pm; Sat 8am, noon, and 12:30 and 5:30pm; Sun 7, 8, 9, and 10:15am (Cardinal's mass), noon, and 1 and 5:30pm; holy days 7, 7:30, 8, 8:30, and 11:30am, noon, and 12:30, 1, and 5:30pm. Subway: B, D, F, V to 47–50th sts./Rockefeller Center.

Temple Emanu-El
Many of New York's most prominent and wealthy families are members of this Reform congregation—the first to be established in New York City—housed in the city's most famous synagogue. The largest house of Jewish worship in the world is a majestic blend of Moorish and Romanesque styles, symbolizing the mingling of Eastern and Western cultures. The temple houses a small but remarkable collection of Judaica in the Herbert & Eileen Bernard Museum, including a collection of Hanukkah lamps with examples ranging from the 14th to the 20th centuries. Three galleries also tell the story of the congregation Emanu-El from 1845 to the present. Tours are given after morning services Saturday at noon. Inquire for a schedule of lectures, films, music, symposiums, and other events.

1 E. 65th St. (at Fifth Ave.). ✆ 212/744-1400. www.emanuelnyc.org. Free admission. Daily 10am–5pm. Services Sun–Thurs 5:30pm; Fri 5:15pm; Sat 10:30am. Subway: N, R to Fifth Ave.; 6 to 68th St.

Trinity Church
Serving God and mammon, this Wall Street house of worship—with neo-Gothic flying buttresses, beautiful stained-glass windows, and vaulted ceilings—

was designed by Richard Upjohn and consecrated in 1846. At that time, its 280-foot spire dominated the skyline. Its main doors, embellished with biblical scenes, were inspired in part by Ghiberti's famed doors on Florence's Baptistery. The historic Episcopal church stood strong while office towers crumbled around it on September 11, 2001; however, an electronic organ has temporarily replaced the historic pipe organ, which was severely damaged by dust and debris. The gates to the historic church currently serve as an impromptu memorial to the victims of 9/11, with countless tokens of remembrance left by both locals and visitors alike.

The church runs a brief tour daily at 2pm (a second Sun tour follows the 11:15am Eucharist); groups of five or more should call 𝄞 212/602-0872 to reserve. There's a small museum at the end of the left aisle displaying documents (including the 1697 church charter from King William III), photographs, replicas of the Hamilton-Burr duel pistols, and other items. Surrounding the church is a churchyard whose monuments read like an American history book: a tribute to martyrs of the American Revolution, Alexander Hamilton, Robert Fulton, and many more. Lined with benches, this makes a wonderful picnic spot on warm days.

Also part of Trinity Church is **St. Paul's Chapel,** at Broadway and Fulton Street, New York's only surviving pre-Revolutionary church, and a transition shelter for homeless men until it was transformed into a relief center after September 11, 2001; it returned to its former duties in mid-2002. Built by Thomas McBean, with a templelike portico and fluted Ionic columns supporting a massive pediment, the chapel resembles London's St. Martin-in-the-Fields. In the small graveyard, 18th- and early-19th-century notables rest in peace and modern businesspeople sit for lunch.

Trinity holds its renowned **Noonday Concert series** of chamber music and orchestral concerts Monday and Thursday at 1pm; call 𝄞 212/602-0747 or visit the website for the schedule and to see if concert programming has resumed at St. Paul's.

At Broadway and Wall St. 𝄞 212/602-0800 or 212/602-0872 for concert information. www.trinitywallstreet.org. Free admission and free tours; $2 suggested donation for noonday concerts. Museum Mon–Fri 9–11:45am; Sun–Fri 1–3:45pm; Sat 10am–3:45pm. Services Mon–Fri 8:15am, 12:05, and 5:15pm (additional Healing Service Thurs at 12:30pm); Sun 9 and 11:15am (also 8am Eucharist service at St. Paul's Chapel, btwn Vesey and Fulton sts.). Subway: 4, 5 to Wall St.

6 Central Park & Other Places to Play

Without the miracle of civic planning that is **Central Park** 𝖆𝖆𝖆, Manhattan would be a virtual unbroken block of buildings. Instead, smack in the middle of Gotham, an 843-acre natural retreat provides a daily escape valve and tranquilizer for millions of New Yorkers. (For a lovely color map of the park and its major attractions, you can turn to the insert at the front of this book.)

While you're in the city, be sure to take advantage of the park's many charms—not the least of which is its sublime layout. Frederick Law Olmsted and Calvert Vaux won a competition with a plan that marries flowing paths with sinewy bridges, integrating them into the natural rolling landscape with its rocky outcroppings, man-made lakes, and wooded pockets. Construction concluded in 1870 and designers predicted the hustle and bustle to come, and tactfully hid traffic from the eyes and ears of park-goers by building roads that are largely hidden from the bucolic view.

On just about any day, Central Park is crowded with New Yorkers and visitors alike. On nice days, especially weekend days, it's the city's party central. Families come to play in the snow or the sun, depending on the season; in-line skaters come to fly through the crisp air and twirl in front of the band shell; couples come to stroll or paddle the lake; dog owners come to hike and throw Frisbees to Bowser; and just about everybody comes to sunbathe at the first sign of summer. On beautiful days the crowds are part of the appeal—folks come here to peel off their urban armor and relax, and the common goal puts a general feeling of camaraderie in the air. On these days the people-watching is more compelling than anywhere else in the city. But even on the most crowded days, there's always somewhere to get away from it all, if you just want a little peace and quiet and a moment to commune with nature.

ORIENTATION & GETTING THERE   Look at your map of the city—that great green swath in the center of Manhattan is Central Park.

It runs from 59th Street (also known as Central Park South) at the south end to 110th Street at the north end, and from Fifth Avenue on the east side to Central Park West (the equivalent of Eighth Ave.) on the west side. A 6-mile rolling road, **Central Park Drive,** circles the park, and has a lane set aside for bikers, joggers, and in-line skaters. A number of **transverse (crosstown) roads** cross the park at major points—at 65th, 79th, 86th, and 97th streets—but they're built down a level, largely out of view, to minimize intrusion on the bucolic nature of the park.

A number of subway stops and lines serve the park, and which one you take depends on where you want to go. To reach the southernmost entrance on the west side, take an A, B, C, D, 1 to 59th Street/Columbus Circle. To reach the southeast corner entrance, take the N, R to Fifth Avenue; from this stop, it's an easy walk into the park to the Information Center in the **Dairy** (✆ 212/794-6564; daily 11am–5pm, to 4pm in winter), midpark at about 65th Street. Here you can ask questions, pick up park information, and purchase a good park map.

If your time for exploring is limited, I suggest entering the park at 72nd or 79th Street for maximum exposure (subway: B, C to 72nd St. or 81st St./Museum of Natural History). From here, you can pick up park information at the visitor center at **Belvedere Castle** (✆ 212/772-0210; Tues–Sun 10am–5pm, to 4pm in winter), midpark at 79th Street. There's also a visitor center at the **Charles A. Dana Discovery Center** (✆ 212/860-1370; daily 10am–5pm, to 4pm in winter), at the northeast corner of the park at Harlem Meer, at 110th Street between Fifth and Lenox avenues (subway: 2, 3 to Central Park North/110th St.). The Dana Center is also an environmental education center hosting workshops, exhibits, music, and park tours, and lends fishing poles for fishing in Harlem Meer (park policy is catch-and-release).

Food carts and vendors are set up at all of the park's main gathering points, so finding a bite to eat is never a problem. You'll also find a fixed food counter at the **Conservatory,** on the east side of the park north of the 72nd Street entrance, and both casual snacks and more sophisticated New American dining at **The Boat House,** on the lake near 72nd Street and Park Drive North (✆ 212/517-2233).

GUIDED WALKS   The **Central Park Conservancy** offers a slate of free walking tours of the park; call ✆ 212/360-2726 or check **www.centralparknyc.org** for the current schedule (click on the "Walking Tours" button on the left). The Dana Center hosts ranger-guided tours on occasion (call ✆ 212/860-1370, or 311 for a schedule). Also consider a private walking tour; many of the companies listed in "Organized Sightseeing Tours," later in this chapter, offer guided tours of the park.

FOR FURTHER INFORMATION   Call the main number at ✆ 212/310-6600 for recorded information, or 212/628-1036 to speak to a person. Call ✆ 888/NY-PARKS for events information. The park also has two comprehensive websites that are worth checking out: the city parks department's site at **www.centralpark.org**, and the Central Park Conservancy's site at **www.centralparknyc.org**, both of which feature excellent maps and a far more complete rundown of park attractions and activities than I have room to include here. If you have an **emergency** in the park, dial ℭ **311,** which will link you to the park rangers.

SAFETY TIP   Even though the park has the lowest crime rate of any of the city's precincts, keep your wits about you, especially in the more remote northern end. It's a good idea to avoid the park entirely after dark, unless you're heading to one of the restaurants for dinner or to a **SummerStage** or **Shakespeare in the Park** event (see "Park It! Shakespeare, Music & Other Free Fun," p. 360), when you should stick with the crowds. For more safety tips, see "Playing It Safe," in chapter 5.

EXPLORING THE PARK
The best way to see Central Park is to wander along the park's 58 miles of winding pedestrian paths, keeping in mind the following highlights.

Before starting your stroll, stop by the **Information Center** in the Dairy (ℭ **212/ 794-6564;** Tues to Sun, 10am to 5pm.), midpark in a 19th-century-style building overlooking Wollman Rink at about 65th Street, to get a good park map and other information on sights and events, and to peruse the kid-friendly exhibit on the park's history and design.

The southern part of Central Park is more formally designed and heavily visited than the relatively rugged and remote northern end. Not far from the Dairy is the **Carousel,** with 58 hand-carved horses (ℭ 212/879-0244; everyday, weather permitting, Apr–Nov 10am–6pm, to 4:30pm in winter; rides are $1.50); the zoo (see below); and the Wollman Rink for roller- or ice-skating (see "Activities," below).

The **Mall,** a long formal walkway lined with elms shading benches and sculptures of sometimes forgotten writers, leads to the focal point of Central Park, **Bethesda Fountain** ℛ (along the 72nd St. transverse road). **Bethesda Terrace** and its grandly sculpted entryway border a large **lake** where dogs fetch sticks, rowboaters glide by, and dedicated early-morning anglers try their luck at catching carp, perch, catfish, and bass. You can rent a rowboat at or take a gondola ride from **Loeb Boathouse,** on the eastern end of the lake (see "Activities," below). Boats of another kind are at **Conservatory Water** (on the east side at 73rd St.), a stone-walled pond flanked by statues of both **Hans Christian Andersen** and **Alice in Wonderland.** On Saturday at 10am, die-hard yachtsmen race remote-controlled sailboats in fierce competitions that follow Olympic regulations. (Sorry, model boats aren't for rent.)

If the action there is too intense, **Sheep Meadow** on the southwestern side of the park is a designated quiet zone, where Frisbee throwing and kite flying are as energetic as things get. Another respite is **Strawberry Fields** ℛ, at 72nd Street on the west side. This memorial to John Lennon, who was murdered across the street at the Dakota apartment building (72nd St. and Central Park West, northwest corner), is a gorgeous garden centered around an Italian mosaic bearing the title of the lead Beatle's most famous solo song, and his lifelong message: IMAGINE. In keeping with its goal of promoting world peace, the garden has 161 varieties of plants, donated by each of the 161 nations in existence when it was designed in 1985. This is a wonderful place for peaceful contemplation.

Bow Bridge, a graceful lacework of cast iron designed by Calvert Vaux, crosses over the lake and leads to the most bucolic area of Central Park, the **Ramble.** This dense 38-acre woodland with spiraling paths, rocky outcroppings, and a stream is the best spot for bird-watching and feeling as if you've discovered an unimaginably leafy forest right in the middle of the city.

North of the Ramble, **Belvedere Castle** is home to the **Henry Luce Nature Observatory** (© 212/772-0210) Tues to Sun, 10am to 5pm, worth a visit if you're with children. From the castle, set on Vista Rock (the park's highest point at 135 ft.), you can look down on the **Great Lawn,** where softball players and sun worshipers compete for coveted greenery, and the **Delacorte Theater,** home to Shakespeare in the Park (see chapter 10). The small **Shakespeare Garden** south of the theater is scruffy, but it does have plants, herbs, trees, and other greenery mentioned by the Bard. Behind the Belvedere Castle is the **Swedish Cottage Marionette Theatre** (© 212/988-9093), hosting marionette plays for children throughout the year; call to see what's on.

Continue north along the east side of the Great Lawn, parallel to East Drive. Near the glass-enclosed back of the **Metropolitan Museum of Art** (p. 239) is **Cleopatra's Needle,** a 69-foot obelisk originally erected in Heliopolis around 1475 B.C. It was given to the city by the khedive of Egypt in 1880. (The khedive bestowed to the city of London a similar obelisk, which sits on the embankment of the Thames.)

North of the 86th Street Transverse Road is the **Jacqueline Kennedy Onassis Reservoir,** renamed for the beloved first lady, who lived nearby and often enjoyed a run along the 1½-mile jogging track that circles the reservoir.

North of the reservoir is my favorite part of the park. It's much less traversed and in some areas absolutely tranquil. The **North Meadow** (at 96th St.) features 12 baseball and softball fields. Sadly, the North Meadow is circled by a not-very-attractive fence, and 6 months of the year that fence is locked and the meadow closed. An unfortunate recent trend in Central Park has been the proliferation of fences. They have become so prevalent that at times you get the feeling you are not really in a park but a museum.

North of the North Meadow at the northeast end of the park is the **Conservatory Garden** (at 105th St. and Fifth Ave.), Central Park's only formal garden, with a magnificent display of flowers and trees reflected in calm pools of water. (The gates to the garden once fronted the Fifth Ave. mansion of Cornelius Vanderbilt II.) **The Lasker Rink and Pool** (© 212/534-7639) is the only swimming pool in Central Park, and in the winter it's converted to a skating rink that offers a less hectic alternative to Wollman Rink (see "Activities," below). **Harlem Meer** and its boathouse were recently renovated and look beautiful. The boathouse now berths the **Charles A. Dana Discovery Center,** near 110th Street between Fifth and Lenox avenues (© 212/ 860-1370) open Tues–Sun, 10am to 5pm, where children learn about the environment and borrow fishing poles for catch-and-release at no charge. **The Pool** (at W. 100th St.), possibly the most idyllic spot in all of Central Park, was recently renovated and features willows, grassy banks, and a pond populated by some very well-fed ducks. You might even spot an egret and a hawk or two.

GOING TO THE ZOO

Central Park Zoo/Tisch Children's Zoo (Kids)   Here is a pleasant refuge within a refuge where lithe sea lions frolic in the central pool area with beguiling style, gigantic but graceful polar bears glide back and forth across a watery pool that has glass walls through which you can observe very large paws doing very smooth strokes, monkeys seem to regard those on the other side of the fence with knowing disdain, and in the hot and humid Tropic Zone, large colorful birds swoop around in freedom, sometimes landing next to nonplused visitors.

Because of its small size, the zoo is at its best with its displays of smaller animals. The indoor multilevel Tropic Zone is a real highlight, its steamy rainforest home to everything from black-and-white colobus monkeys to Emerald tree boa constrictors to a leaf-cutter ant farm; look for the new dart-poison-frog exhibit, which is very cool. So is the large penguin enclosure in the Polar Circle, which is better than the one at San Diego's SeaWorld. In the Temperate Territory, look for the Asian red pandas (cousins to the big black-and-white ones), which look like the world's most beautiful raccoons. Despite their pool and piles of ice, however, the polar bears still look sad.

The entire zoo is good for short attention spans; you can cover the whole thing in 1½ to 3 hours, depending on the size of the crowds and how long you like to linger. It's also very kid-friendly, with lots of well-written and -illustrated placards that older kids can understand. For the littlest ones, there's the $6-million **Tisch Children's Zoo** *&*. With goats, llamas, potbellied pigs, and more, this petting zoo and playground is a real blast for the 5-and-under set.

830 Fifth Ave. (at 64th St., just inside Central Park). ℭ 212/439-6500. www.wcs.org/zoos. Admission $8 adults, $4 seniors, $3 children 3–12, free for children under 3. Summer hours (Apr–Oct) weekdays 10am–5pm, weekends 10am–5:30pm; winter hours (Nov–Mar) daily 10am–4:30pm. Last entrance 30 min. before closing. Subway: N, R to Fifth Ave.

ACTIVITIES

The 6-mile rolling road circling the park, **Central Park Drive,** has a lane set aside for bikers, joggers, and in-line skaters. The best time to use it is when the park is closed to traffic: Monday to Friday 10am to 3pm (except Thanksgiving to New Year's) and 7 to 10pm. It's also closed from 7pm Friday to 6am Monday, but when the weather is nice, the crowds can be hellish.

BIKING   Off-road mountain biking isn't permitted; stay on Central Park Drive or your bike may be confiscated by park police.

You can rent 3- and 10-speed bikes as well as tandems in Central Park at the **Loeb Boathouse,** midpark near 72nd Street and Park Drive North, just in from Fifth Avenue (ℭ **212/517-2233** or 212/517-3623), for $9 to $15 an hour, with a complete selection of kids' bikes, cruisers, tandems, and the like ($200 deposit required); at **Metro Bicycles,** 1311 Lexington Ave., at 88th Street (ℭ **212/427-4450**), for about $7 an hour, or $35 a day; and at **Toga Bike Shop,** 110 West End Ave., at 64th Street (ℭ **212/799-9625;** www.togabikes.com), for $30 a day. No matter where you rent, be prepared to leave a credit card deposit.

BOATING   From March through November, gondola rides and rowboat rentals are available at the **Loeb Boathouse,** midpark near 74th Street and Park Drive North, just in from Fifth Avenue (ℭ **212/517-2233** or 212/517-3623). Rowboats cost $12 cash for the first hour, $2.50 for every 15 minutes thereafter, and a $20 deposit is required; reservations are accepted. (Note that rates were not set for the summer season at press time, so these may change.)

HORSE-DRAWN CARRIAGE RIDES   At the entrance to the park at 59th Street and Central Park South, you'll see a line of **horse-drawn carriages** waiting to take passengers on a ride through the park or along certain of the city's streets. Horses belong on city streets as much as chamber pots belong in our homes. You won't need me to tell you how forlorn most of these horses look; if you insist, a ride is about $50 for two for a half-hour, but I suggest skipping it.

ICE-SKATING   Central Park's **Wollman Rink** ⑰, on the east side of the park between 62nd and 63rd streets (✆ **212/439-6900;** www.wollmanskatingrink.com) is the city's best outdoor skating spot, more spacious than the tiny rink at Rockefeller Center. It's open for skating from mid-October to mid-April, depending on the weather. Rates are $9.50 for adults ($12 on weekends), $4.75 for seniors and kids under 12 ($8.25 on weekends), and skate rental is $5; lockers are available (locks are $3.75). **Lasker Rink** ✆ **212/534-7639,** on the east side around 106th Street, is a less expensive alternative to the more crowded Wollman Rink. Open November through March. Rates are $4.50 for adults, $2.25 for kids under 12, and skate rental is $4.75.

IN-LINE SKATING   Central Park is the city's most popular place for blading. See the beginning of this section for details on Central Park Drive, the main drag for skaters. On weekends, head to West Drive at 67th Street, behind Tavern on the Green, where you'll find trick skaters weaving through a New York Roller Skating Association (NYRSA) slalom course, or to the Mall in front of the band shell (above Bethesda Fountain) for twirling to tunes. In summer **Wollman Rink** ⑰ converts to a hotshot roller rink, with half-pipes and lessons available (see "Ice-Skating," above).

   You can rent skates for $20 a day from **Blades Board and Skate,** 156 W. 72nd St., between Broadway and Columbus Avenue (✆ **212/787-3911;** www.blades.com). Wollman Rink (see above) also rents in-line skates for park use at similar rates.

PLAYGROUNDS   Nineteen Adventure Playgrounds are scattered throughout the park, perfect for jumping, sliding, tottering, swinging, and digging. At Central Park West and 81st Street is the **Diana Ross Playground** ⑰, voted the city's best by *New York* magazine. Also on the west side is the **Spector Playground,** at 85th Street and Central Park West, and, a little farther north, the **Wild West Playground,** at 93rd Street. On the east side is the **Rustic Playground,** at 67th Street and Fifth Avenue, a delightfully landscaped space rife with islands, bridges, and big slides; and the **Pat Hoffman Friedman Playground,** right behind the Metropolitan Museum of Art at East 79th Street, is geared toward older toddlers.

RUNNING   Marathoners and wannabes regularly run in Central Park along the 6-mile **Central Park Drive,** which circles the park (please run toward traffic to avoid being mowed down by wayward cyclists and in-line skaters). The **New York Road Runners** (✆ **212/860-4455;** www.nyrr.org), organizers of the New York City Marathon, schedules group runs 7 days a week at 6am and 6pm, leaving from the entrance to the park at 90th Street and Fifth Avenue. (For the NYRRC's list of the suggested running routes, see the box titled "Running the City," below.)

SWIMMING   The only pool in Central Park, **Lasker Pool** (on the east side at around 106th St.; ✆ **212/534-7639**), is open July 1 through Labor Day weekend. Rates are $4 for adults, $2 for kids under 12. Bring a towel.

OTHER PARKS

For parks in Brooklyn and Queens, see "Highlights of the Outer Boroughs," later in this chapter. For more information on these and other city parks, go online to **www.nycgovparks.org**.

Battery Park ⑰⑰   As you traverse Manhattan's concrete canyons, it's sometimes easy to forget that you're actually on an island. But here, at Manhattan's southernmost tip, you get the very real sense that just out past Liberty, Ellis, and Staten islands is the vast Atlantic Ocean.

<hr>

(*Tips* **Running the City**

Here are the **New York Road Runners'** top picks for routes in Manhattan:

- **Jacqueline Kennedy Onassis Reservoir:** Possibly the most famous running route in the world; presidential candidates have run this 1½-mile route as well as the famous former first lady for whom it is now named.
- **The Loop in Central Park:** I used to run past Madonna and her bodyguards when she was a frequenter of the 6-mile loop. Now I see Howard Stern jogging, no bodyguards in sight, but usually with a female companion or two.
- **East River:** Entering on 63rd Street and York Avenue and running up to 125th Street and back is a 6-mile jog where you will pass Gracie Mansion, high-rises overlooking the river, and fishermen testing the river waters.
- **Hudson River South:** Enter at Chelsea Piers at West 23rd Street and continue down to Battery Park City and back for this approximately 5-mile run. In the warm months it's a carnival downtown, with in-line skaters, kayakers, musicians, and cyclists crowding the slim downtown park.
- **Hudson River North:** This approximately 6-mile run starts at Riverbank State Park at 145th Street on the Hudson River and continues through lovely Riverside Park, passing the 79th Street Boat Basin, and ending at the *Intrepid* Sea-Air-Space Museum.

<hr>

The 21-acre park is named for the cannons built to defend residents after the American Revolution. **Castle Clinton National Monument** (the place to purchase tickets for the Statue of Liberty and Ellis Island ferry; see listings earlier in this chapter) was built as a fort before the War of 1812, though it was never used as such.

Battery Park is a park of monuments and memorials, many paying tribute to tragedy and death. Here you will find the **East Coast Memorial,** dedicated to 4,601 serviceman who died in Atlantic coastal waters during World War II; the **New York Korean War Veterans Memorial;** the American **Merchant Mariner's Memorial,** dedicated to Merchant Mariner's lost at sea; the *Salvation Army Memorial;* the Hope Garden dedicated to those who live with HIV or have died from AIDS; the **Irish Hunger Memorial,** a tribute to those who died during the potato famine in Ireland; and the 22-ton **bronze sphere** by Fritz Koenig that was recovered from the rubble of the World Trade Center, where it stood on the plaza between the two Twin Towers as a symbol of global peace, also stands here—severely damaged but still whole. Mingling throughout these memorials you will find the requisite T-shirt vendors, hot-dog carts and Wall Streeters eating deli sandwiches on the many park benches. Pull up your own bench for a good view out across the harbor.

From State St. to New York Harbor. www.thebattery.org. Subway: R, W to Whitehall St.; 1 to South Ferry; 4, 5 to Bowling Green.

Riverside Park *(ids) (finds)*   I spent much of my time in my early years in New York in Riverside Park (*©* **212/408-0264;** www.nycgovparks.org) staring at the New Jersey skyline, jogging along the wind-swept Hudson river, playing hoops at the courts on 77th Street (when I still could jump), taking strolls along the promenade on hot summer nights, and watching the comings or goings of the unusual community that lives in the boats at the 79th Street Boat Basin. This underrated beauty designed by Frederick Law Olmsted, the same man who designed Central Park, stretches 4 miles from 72nd Street to 158th Street. The serpentine route along the Hudson River offers a variety of lovely river vistas, 14 playgrounds, two tennis courts, softball and soccer fields, a skate park, beach volleyball, the aforementioned Boat Basin, two cafes—the **Boat Basin Café** at 79th Street (© **212/496-5542**) and **Hurley's Hudson Beach Café** at 105th Street (© **917/370-3448**), open April through September only—and monuments such as the Eleanor Roosevelt statue at 72nd Street, the Soldiers and Sailors Monument at 90th Street, and Grant's Tomb at 122nd Street (© **212/666-1640**) Open daily 9am to 5pm. But here's the best part: On a hot summer day, when Central Park is teeming with joggers, sunbathers, and in-line skaters, Riverside Park, just a few blocks from Central Park's western fringe, is comparatively serene. The Riverside Park Fund (© **212/870-3070;** www.riversideparkfund.org) has an excellent website with a comprehensive list of events and gives a history with illustrations of the parkland. They also sell a map of the park for $2 (see website).

Bryant Park ⊛   Another success story in the push for urban redevelopment, Bryant Park is the latest incarnation of a 4-acre site that was, at various times in its history, a graveyard and a reservoir. Named for poet and *New York Evening Post* editor William Cullen Bryant (look for his statue on the east end), the park actually rests atop the New York Public Library's many miles of underground stacks. Another statue is also notable: a squat and evocative stone portrait of Gertrude Stein, one of the few outdoor sculptures of women in the city.

This simple green swath, just east of Times Square, is welcome relief from Midtown's concrete, taxi-choked jungle, and good weather attracts brown-baggers from

---

Finds   Frozen in Time: Governor's Island

Stand at the edge of Battery Park and look southwest about 800 yards into New York Harbor and you will see an island. No, it's not Staten Island, but **Governor's Island** and one of the first settlements of the Dutch West India Company in 1624. Later it was used as a military fort during the pre- and post-Revolutionary War period and most recently was the site of the 1988 summit between Ronald Reagan and USSR President Mikhail Gorbachev. In 2003 Governor's Island was transferred to the state and city of New York and, with the exception of 22 acres designated as a National Monument, the remaining 150 acres belong to the city and state and are open to the public from June through August. The island is a place frozen in time—kind of a ghost town where you'll find abandoned mansions, forts, bus stops (but no buses) and parade grounds. The views of downtown Manhattan are spectacular and the lack of cars and traffic make it a serene antidote to the bustle of the Financial District. Plans are in the works to convert 40 acres into public parkland and a waterfront esplanade but, in typically slow New York fashion when it comes to developing public spaces, no definitive design plans have yet been unveiled or approved. In the meantime, enjoy it as is. Ferries are free, but have a limited 250-passenger capacity. © **212/440-2202;** www.govisland.com. Subway: 1 to South Ferry, R/W to Whitehall St.

neighboring office buildings. Just behind the library is **Bryant Park Grill** (✆ 212/ 840-6500), a gorgeous, airy bistro with spectacular views but merely decent New American food. Still, brunch is a good bet, and the grill's two summer alfresco restaurants—**The Terrace,** on the Grill's roof, and the casual **Cafe,** with small tables beneath a canopy of trees—are extremely pleasant on a nice day.

Le Carrousel complements the park's French classical style. It's not as big as the Central Park Carousel but utterly charming nonetheless, with 14 different animals that revolve to the sounds of French cabaret music. Le Carrousel is open all year, weather permitting, 11am to 7pm, and costs $1.75 to ride.

A new addition to Bryant Park in 2005 was a welcome one—another skating rink, this one known as The Pond. Skating on The Pond is free but, unfortunately, the rink is only open from the middle of October until the middle of January, though, at press time, there were rumors that The Pond's season might be extended in 2007–08

Additionally, the park plays host to New York's **Seventh on Sixth** fashion shows, set up in billowy white tents (open to the trade only) in the spring and fall.

Behind the New York Public Library, at Sixth Ave. btwn 40th and 42nd sts. Subway: B, D, F, Q to 42nd St.; 7 to Fifth Ave.

Union Square Park   Here's a delightful place to spend an afternoon. Reclaimed from drug dealers and abject ruin in the late 1980s, Union Square Park is now one of the city's best assets and home of the New York's most famous **greenmarket** (see box below). The seemingly endless subway work should no longer be disturbing the peace by the time you're here. This patch of green remains, with or without the construction, the focal point of the newly fashionable Flatiron and Gramercy Park neighborhoods. Don't miss the grand equestrian statue of George Washington at the south end or the bronze statue (by Bartholdi, the sculptor of the Statue of Liberty) of the Marquis de Lafayette at the eastern end, gracefully glancing toward France. A **cafe** is open at the north end of the park in warm weather.

From 14th to 17th sts., btwn Park Ave. South and Broadway. Subway: 4, 5, 6, L, N, or R to 14th St./Union Sq.

Tips **The Greening of New York**

Whenever I travel to a city anywhere around the world, I make it a priority to visit that city's greenmarket, or farmers market. I've been to some great ones, and I might be a bit prejudiced, but I haven't been to many better than the **Union Square Greenmarket** ✮✮ in New York City. New York has greenmarkets throughout the city on different days of the week, but the biggest and best is at Union Square every Monday, Wednesday, Friday, and Saturday. You'll find pickings from upstate and New Jersey farms, fresh fish from Long Island, homemade cheese and other dairy products, baked goods, plants, and organic herbs and spices. It's a true New York scene with everyone from models to celebrated chefs poring over the bounty. The Union Square Greenmarket is open year-round but is at its peak August through October when the local harvest—tomatoes, corn, greens, grapes, peppers, and apples—flourishes. If you are lucky enough to be in the city during this period, don't miss the bonanza, and pick up some apples or grapes for your travels around the city—but check it out no matter what the season. For more information and locations and schedules, see the Council on the Environment of New York City website at www.cenyc.org or call ✆ 212/788-7900.

Moments **The Little Red Lighthouse (and the Great Gray Bridge . . .)**

Also known as **Jeffrey's Hook Lighthouse,** this little red lighthouse located under the George Washington Bridge in Fort Washington Park on the Hudson River was the inspiration for the 1942-children's book classic, *The Little Red Lighthouse and The Great Gray Bridge,* by Hildegarde Swift and Lynd Ward. Built in New Jersey in 1880 and reconstructed and moved to its current spot in 1921, it was operational until 1947. The lighthouse was to be removed in 1951, but because of its popularity there was a public outcry and it was saved. It's now a New York City landmark and on the list of National Register of Historic Place. It's a fun place for the kids to explore and scenic picnic spot in nice weather. It's open to the public with guided tours by the New York City Urban Rangers (© **212/304-2365**) from Spring through Fall.

Washington Square Park You'll be hard-pressed to find much "park" in this mainly concrete square—a burial ground in the late 18th century—but it's undeniably the focal point of Greenwich Village. Chess players, skateboarders, street musicians, New York University students, gay and straight couples, the occasional film crew, and not a few homeless people compete for attention throughout the day and most of the night. (If anyone issues a friendly challenge to play you in the ancient and complex Chinese game of Go, don't take them up on it—you'll lose money.)

In the 1830s, elegant Greek Revival town houses on **Washington Square North,** known as "The Row" (note especially nos. 21–26), attracted the elite. Stanford White designed Washington Arch (1891–92) to commemorate the centenary of George Washington's inauguration as first president. The arch was refurbished in 2004 and now features exterior lighting.

At the southern end of Fifth Ave. (where it intersects Waverly Place btwn MacDougal and Wooster sts.). Subway: A, C, E, F, V to W. 4th St. (use 3rd St. exit).

CHELSEA PIERS

One of the city's biggest—and most successful—private urban-development projects is the 30-acre **Chelsea Piers Sports & Entertainment Complex** (© **212/336-6666; www.chelseapiers.com**). Jutting out into the Hudson River on four huge piers between 17th and 23rd streets, it's a terrific multifunctional recreational facility.

The **Sports Center** (© **212/336-6000**), a three-football-fields-long megafacility, does health clubs one better. It offers not only the usual cardiovascular training, weights, and aerobics but also a four-lane quarter-mile indoor running track, a boxing ring, basketball courts, a sand volleyball court, a gorgeous 25-yard indoor pool with a whirlpool and sun deck, the world's most challenging rock-climbing wall plus a bouldering wall, and the **Spa at Chelsea Piers,** which offers massage, reflexology, facials, and the like. Day passes to the Sports Center are $50 for nonmembers; spa treatments are extra, of course.

The **Golf Club** (© **212/336-6400**) has 52 all-weather fully automated hitting stalls on four levels and a 200-yard, net-enclosed, artificial-turf fairway jutting out over the water, making it the best place in the city to hit a few. Prices start at $20 for 80 balls (118 balls during off-peak hours), and club rentals are available.

The **Sky Rink** (℃ **212/336-6100**) has twin around-the-clock indoor rinks for recreational skating and pickup hockey games with Hudson River views. General skating is $12 for adults, $9 for seniors and kids 12 and under; skate rental is $6.50 Due to organized skating activities, general skating is limited, so call ahead to find out schedules of availability.

The **Field House** (℃ **212/336-6500**) is mainly for team sports, but young rock climbers will enjoy the 30-foot indoor **climbing wall,** designed for kids as well as grown-ups. Open climbs are $18, with climbs limited to 2½ hours on weekdays, they start taking same-day climb reservations at 9am, and weekends can book up quickly. Children's lessons are available. **Batting cages** are $2 per 10 pitches.

Feeling like a little 10-pin tonight? State-of-the-art **AMF Chelsea Piers Lanes** (℃ **212/835-BOWL;** www.amf.com offers 40 lanes of fun. Games are $8.75 per person, and shoe rental is $5.

Beyond its athletics, the complex is a destination in and of itself. The 1¼-mile esplanade has benches and picnic tables with terrific river views; they serve as the perfect vantage point for watching the *QEII* head out to sea, or the navy and Coast Guard ships sailing in for Fleet Week each May.

Getting there: Chelsea Piers is accessible by taxi and the M23 or M14 crosstown buses. The nearest subway is the C and E at 23rd Street and Eighth Avenue, then pick up the M23 or walk 4 long blocks west. Another option is to take the A, C, E to 14th Street or the L train to Eighth Avenue, walk to the river, then follow the walking/riding/running path along the river north.

7 Organized Sightseeing Tours

Reservations are required for some of the tours listed below, but even if they're not, it's always best to call ahead to confirm prices, times, and meeting places.

HARBOR CRUISES

If you'd like to sail the New York Harbor aboard the 1885 cargo schooner *Pioneer,* see the listing for South Street Seaport & Museum on p. 259.

Note that some of the lines below may have limited schedules in winter, especially for evening cruises. Call ahead or check online for current offerings.

Bateaux New York   The most elegant and romantic of New York's evening dinner cruises. Cruises are aboard the *Celestial,* designed to accommodate 300 guests with two suites, one dance floor, two outdoor strolling decks, a state-of-the-art sound system, and windows galore. Dinner is a three-course sit-down affair, with jackets and ties suggested for men, evening dresses for women. The food isn't what you'd get at Jean-Georges, but Bateaux (sister to egalitarian Spirit Cruises; see below) offers a very nice supper-club-style night on the town, and the views are fabulous. A live quartet entertains with jazz standards and pop vocal tunes.

Departs from Pier 62, Chelsea Piers, W. 23rd St. and Twelfth Ave. ℃ 212/727-7735. www.bateauxnewyork.com. 2-hr. lunch cruises $46; 3-hr. dinner cruises $88–$117. Subway: C, E to 23rd St.

Circle Line Sightseeing Cruises *☆☆*   A New York institution, the Circle Line is famous for its 3-hour tour around the entire 35 miles of Manhattan. This **Full Island** cruise passes by the Statue of Liberty, Ellis Island, the Brooklyn Bridge, the United Nations, Yankee Stadium, the George Washington Bridge, and more, including Manhattan's wild northern tip. The panorama is riveting, and the commentary isn't bad.

The Attack of the Double-Decker Buses

They are everywhere. There is no escape. They clog up the already over-crowded streets, spewing exhaust, their red or blue exteriors splashed with a garish display of self-promotion and advertising, loudspeakers blaring as the people huddled on the upper deck (swathed in plastic panchos when it rains) look down at the natives on the streets. I'm talking about double-decker buses. They run in the morning, they run at night, they run all day long. Can you tell I'm not a fan? I think New York is best appreciated on foot, or on public buses and subways. Sure these double-decker buses have guides but take the facts they dish out with a grain of salt; they aren't always accurate. If you insist, the top bus tour is **Gray Line New York Tours.** Tours depart from various locations. ℭ **800/669-0051** or 212/445-0848; www.graylinenewyork.com. Hop-on, hop off bus tours from $39 adults, $29 children 5–11.

The big boats are basic but fine, with lots of deck room for everybody to enjoy the view. Snacks, soft drinks, coffee, and beer are available onboard for purchase.

If 3 hours is more than you or the kids can handle, go for either the 2-hour **Semi-Circle** or the **Sunset/Harbor Lights** cruise, both of which show you the highlights of the skyline. There's also a 1-hour **Seaport Liberty** version that sticks close to the south end of the island. But of all the tours, the kids might like **The Beast** best, a thrill-a-minute speedboat ride offered in summer only.

In addition, a number of adults-only **Live Music and DJ Cruises** sail regularly from the seaport from May through September ($20–$40 per person). Depending on the night of the week, you can groove to the sounds of jazz, Latin, gospel, dance tunes, or blues as you sail along viewing the skyline.

Departing from Pier 83, at W. 42nd St. and Twelfth Ave. Also departing from Pier 16 at South St. Seaport, 207 Front St. ℭ **212/563-3200.** www.circleline42.com and www.seaportmusiccruises.com. Sightseeing cruises $12–$29 adults, $16–$24 seniors, $13–$16 children 12 and under. Subway to Pier 83: A, C, E to 42nd St. Subway to Pier 16: J, M, Z, 2, 3, 4, 5 to Fulton St.

New York Waterway ⓇⓇ   New York Waterway, the nation's largest privately held ferry service and cruise operator, like Circle Line, also does the 35-mile trip around Manhattan, but does it in 2 hours, taking in all the same sights. They also offer a staggering amount of different sightseeing options, including a very good 90-minute New York Harbor Cruise, a Romantic Twilight Cruise, a Friday Dance Party Cruise, and Baseball Cruises to Yankee games.

Departing from 38th St. Ferry Terminal, at W. 38th St. and Twelfth Ave. ℭ **800/533-3779.** www.nywaterway.com. Sightseeing cruises $22 adults, $18 seniors, $12 children. Free bus transportation from 57th, 49th, 42nd, and 34th sts. to 38th St. Terminal; you can flag down any of the big red buses labeled NY WATERWAY or wait at any of the bus stops along those streets.

Spirit Cruises   Spirit Cruises' modern ships are floating cabarets that combine sightseeing in New York Harbor with freshly prepared meals, musical revues, and dancing to live bands. The atmosphere is festive, fun, and relaxed. The buffet meals are nothing special, but they're fine.

Departing from Pier 61 at Chelsea Piers, W. 23rd St. and Twelfth Ave. ℭ **866/211-3806.** www.spiritcruises.com. 2-hr. lunch cruises $36–$48; 3-hr. dinner cruises $65–$125. Inquire about children's rates. Subway: C, E to 23rd St.

Transportation Alternatives

You really don't want to burden that nag with a carriage ride through Central Park in the middle of the summer, do you? Better you should hire a real beast of burden—a driver of a pedicab who probably really needs the money. Pedicabs are becoming very common sights on the streets of New York. The drivers are friendly, informative, and don't litter the streets. **Manhattan Pedicab, Inc.** (© 212/586-9486; www.ajnfineart.com/mpedicab.html), one of the two primary pedicab companies, charges $35 for a half-hour, $65 for a full hour, and $10 for an impromptu street pickup. Tours are also available, including Upper East and Upper West Side Bar and Restaurant Tours, and a Central Park–Rockefeller Center Tour. Another option is the **Manhattan Rickshaw Company** (© 212/604-4729; www.manhattanrickshaw.com), where fares range from $8 to $15 for a pickup to $50 for an hour-long ride.

AIR TOURS

Liberty Helicopters   How about a bird's-eye view of Manhattan? These flight-seeing trips offer a quick thrill—literally. Five-minute tours from Midtown take in the Midtown skyscrapers and Central Park, while longer tours last 10 or 15 minutes and take in a wider view that includes lower Manhattan and the Statue of Liberty. If you opt for the longest tour, you'll fly far enough uptown to take in the George Washington Bridge and Yankee Stadium. Flights leave every 15 minutes daily from 9am to 9pm, but note that at least a 24-hour advance reservation is required.

Departing 1 block north of VIP Heliport, W. 30th St. and Twelfth Ave. © 212/967-6464. www.libertyhelicopters.com. Pilot-narrated tours $69–$186. Subway: A, C, E to 34th St.

SPECIALTY TOURS

In addition to the options below, for those interested in touring lower Manhattan, the Downtown Alliance (© 212/606-4064; www.downtownny.com) offers two free walking tours: a **Historic Downtown Tour** every Tuesday at noon and **a Wall Street Walking Tour** every Thursday and Saturday at noon. Both tours are 90 minutes long and are free. Also, both the Municipal Art Society (see below) and the Grand Central Partnership offer free walking tours of **Grand Central Terminal** ⊛⊛ Wednesday at 12:30pm and Friday at 12:30pm, respectively (though there is a "suggested donation" for those tours); see p. 238.

The Alliance for Downtown New York, the Business Improvement District in charge of lower Manhattan, offers a free 90-minute **Wall Street Walking Tour** ⊛ every Thursday and Saturday at noon, rain or shine. This guided tour explores the vivid history and amazing architecture of the nation's first capital and the world center of finance. Stops include the New York Stock Exchange, Trinity Church, Federal Hall National Monument, and many other sites of historic and cultural importance. Tours meet on the steps of Cass Gilbert's gorgeous **U.S. Customs House** ⊛ (p. 264), at 1 Bowling Green (subway: 4, 5 to Bowling Green). Reservations are not required (unless you're a group), but you can call © 212/606-4064 or visit **www.downtownny.com/discover/?sid=48** to confirm the schedule.

CULTURAL ORGANIZATIONS

The **Municipal Art Society** ⊛ (© 212/439-1049 or 212/935-3960; www.mas.org) offers excellent historical and architectural walking tours aimed at intelligent, individualistic travelers. Each is led by a highly qualified guide who offers insights into the significance of buildings, neighborhoods, and history. Topics range from the urban history of Greenwich Village to "Williamsburg: Beyond the Bridge," to an examination of the "new" Times Square. Weekday walking tours are $12; weekend tours are $15. Reservations may be required depending on the tour, so it's best to call ahead. The full schedule is available online.

The **92nd Street Y** ✵ (✆ **212/415-5500;** www.92ndsty.org) offers a wonderful variety of walking and bus tours, many featuring funky themes or behind-the-scenes visits. Subjects can range from "Diplomat for a Day at the U.N." to "Secrets of the Chelsea Hotel," or from "Artists of the Meat-Packing District" to "Jewish Harlem." Prices range from $25 to $60 (sometimes more for bus tours), but many include ferry rides, afternoon tea, dinner, or whatever suits the program. Guides are well-chosen experts on their subjects, ranging from respected historians to an East Village poet, mystic, and art critic (for "Allen Ginsberg's New York" and "East Village Night Spots"), and many routes travel into the outer boroughs; some day trips even reach beyond the city. Advance registration is required for all walking and bus tours. Schedules are planned a few months in advance, so check the website for tours that might interest you.

INDEPENDENT OPERATORS

NYC Discovery Tours (✆ **212/465-3331**) offers more than 70 tours of the Big Apple divided into five categories: neighborhood (including "Central Park" and "Brooklyn Bridge and Heights"), theme (such as "Gotham City Ghost Tour" and "Art History NYC"), biography ("John Lennon's New York"), tavern/food tasting, and American history and literature ("The Charles Dickens Tours"). Tours are about 2 hours long and cost $13 per person ($20 for food tasting tours).

All tours from **Joyce Gold History Tours of New York** ✵✵ (✆ **212/242-5762;** www.nyctours.com) are offered by Joyce Gold herself, an instructor of Manhattan history at New York University and the New School for Social Research, who has been conducting history walks around New York since 1975. Her tours can really cut to the core of this town; Joyce is full of fascinating stories about Manhattan and its people. Tours are arranged around themes like "The Colonial Settlers of Wall Street," "The Genius and Elegance of Gramercy Park," "Downtown Graveyards," "The Old Jewish Lower East Side," "Historic Harlem," and "TriBeCa: The Creative Explosion." Tours are offered most weekends March to December and last from 2 to 3 hours, and the

---

Tips **Take the M5: A City Bus That Hits the Highlights**

If your feet are worn out from walking, but you still want to see some sights, I suggest hopping on the M5 bus. Its route runs from Washington Heights down to Greenwich Village. If you board uptown, around 125th St and Riverside Drive and take it downtown, you'll pass landmarks such as Grant's Tomb, Riverside Church, Lincoln Center, Columbus Circle, St. Patrick's Cathedral, Rockefeller Center, the New York Public Library, Empire State Building, Flatiron building, and Washington Square. And all you need is $2 from your Metrocard (or exact coin change) and your trusty *Frommer's New York City* guide book with your maps in hand. The bus will move slowly enough where you will be able to consult your book and find the corresponding landmarks.

price is $15 per person; reservations are not required. Private tours can be arranged year-round, either for individuals or groups.

Myra Alperson, founder and lead tour guide for **NoshWalks** (© 212/222-2243; www.noshwalks.com), knows food in New York City and knows where to find it. For the past 6 years, Alperson has been leading adventurous, hungry walkers to some of the city's most delicious neighborhoods. From the Uzbek, Tadjik, and Russian markets of Rego Park, Queens, to the Dominican coffee shops of Washington Heights in upper Manhattan, Alperson has left no ethnic neighborhood unexplored. Tours are conducted on Saturday and Sunday, leaving around 11:30am and 2:30pm. The preferred means of transportation is subway and the tours generally last around 3 hours and cost about $33 (Bronx Bites tours higher; check website for updated prices), not including the food you will undoubtedly buy on the tour. Space is limited, so book well in advance.

On Location Tours (© 212/209-3370; www.sceneontv.com) offers narrated minibus tours through TV history on their Manhattan TV Tour; tickets are $34 for adults. Or, if you want to see Carrie Bradshaw's Big Apple, cut right to the chase and take the company's 3½-hour *Sex and the City* Tour, which includes over 40 show-related sights; tickets are $38. Most tours are on Saturday and depart from the Times Square Visitors Center (see "Orientation," in chapter 5), tours at 11am and 3pm. There's also a 4 -hour *Sopranos* Tour that will take you over to New Jersey for an afternoon of sights that range from Satriale's Pork Store to the Bada-Bing! club; this tour leaves from Bryant Park on Saturday and Sunday at 2pm and costs $42. Reservations are strongly suggested for all tours, as most sell out in advance; it also makes sense to confirm days and times and check for any additional offerings.

Harlem Spirituals (© 800/660-2166 or 212/391-0900; www.harlemspirituals.com) specializes in gospel and jazz tours of Harlem that can be combined with a traditional soul-food meal. A variety of options are available, including a tour of Harlem sights with gospel service, and a soul-food lunch or brunch as an optional add-on. The Harlem jazz tour includes a neighborhood tour, dinner at a family-style soul-food restaurant, and a visit to a local jazz club; there's also an Apollo Theater variation on this tour. Bronx and Brooklyn tours are also an option for those who want a taste of the outer boroughs. Prices start at $49, $39 for children, for a Harlem Gospel tour, and go up from there based on length and inclusions (tours that include food and entertainment are pay-one-price). All tours leave from Harlem Spirituals' Midtown office (690 Eighth Ave., between 43rd and 44th sts.), and transportation is included.

Active visitors with an adventurous spirit can hook up with **Bike the Big Apple** (© 201/837-1133; www.bikethebigapple.com). Tours by Bike offers guided half-day, full-day, and customized tours through a variety of city neighborhoods, including the fascinating but little-explored upper Manhattan and Harlem; an ethnic tour that takes you over the legendary Brooklyn Bridge, through Chinatown and Little Italy, and to Ground Zero; and around Flushing, Queens, where you'll feel like you're biking around Hong Kong. You don't have to be an Ironman candidate to participate; tours are designed for the average rider, with an emphasis on safety and fun; shorter rides are available, but the rides generally last around 5 hours. Tours are offered year-round; prices run $65–$75 and include all gear, including the bike.

Inside CNN   Take the 45-minute guided tour of CNN studios in the Time Warner Center, 10 Columbus Circle (© 866/4CNNYC; www.cnn.com/insidecnn), and learn a little about the newsgathering process. The tour includes views of three of

Offbeat New York Tours

So maybe you've taken a harbor cruise or the bus tour, but you don't feel you got a taste of the gritty, quirky, neurotic elements that make New York unique. You want to see those sights that even many native New Yorkers have never seen. Here are a few alternatives to the conventional tours that might satisfy that need:

Soundwalk (www.soundwalk.com): This innovative company behind the audio self-guided-tour CDs debuted in 2003, with audio tours offering insider's peeks at Chinatown, the Lower East Side, Times Square, DUMBO, and the Meat-Packing District. All of these are great fun and will take you places no tour bus will, but my favorite is the three-CD set **"Bronx Soundwalk."** The CD set includes *Baseball,* a tour of Yankee Stadium and environs, narrated by longtime employee Tony Morante; *Graffiti,* a tour of Hunts Point and the trail of some of the legendary graffiti artists, narrated by BG183 (aka Sotero Ortiz), founding member of the TATS Cru and Mural Kings of the Bronx; and *Hip Hop,* a Bronx River tour narrated by hip-hop DJ the Original Jazzy Jay, which takes you to the birthplace of hip-hop and the haunts of rap pioneers like Afrika Bambataa and Cool Herc. These tours are *very* authentic; on the Bronx tour you'll even visit the G&R Pastry Shop where Mr. Steinbrenner, we learn, is a big fan of the shop's cheese Danish. CDs range from $13 to $25; all you need is a portable CD player, map, MetroCard, walking shoes, and an adventurous spirit. You can purchase CDs on the website or at retailers listed on the site.

Wildman Steve Brill ☆ (www.wildmanstevebrill.com): If you ever get stranded in Central Park, a tour with Wildman Steve Brill might help you survive. I've seen him in the park, raggedy beard, shorts, hiking boots, and pith helmet, leading groups of eager-eyed followers while instructing them on what flora and fauna they can forage—breaking off a stick of some edible tree and gnawing on it as an example. Brill's Central Park tours occur twice monthly and are not only hilarious, they actually are educational. If you're lucky, maybe he'll regale you with his tale of his arrest by a park ranger for eating a dandelion. Reservations must be made in advance; call © **914/835-2153.** Suggested donation is $12.

Hidden Jazz Haunts (www.bigapplejazz.com): This tour, hosted by New York jazz expert Gordon Polatnick, is the real deal for jazz buffs. Polatnick's tours are small (2–10 people) and are tailor-made to the jazz interests of his clients. If you're into bebop, he'll show you Minton's Playhouse, the still-standing but now defunct jazz club that was the supposed birthplace of bop. From there he'll take you to other active Harlem clubs that he feels embody that Minton's bebop spirit. If you're into the 1960s bohemian Village scene, he'll take you to clubs that represent that Golden era of Village jazz clubs. Big Apple Jazz has a store and performance space at 2236 Seventh Ave, between 131st and 132nd Streets. The tour fee is $75 per hour, with a 4 hour minimum for most tours, plus cost of entrance fees, drinks, et cetera. They described the tours as "customizable." For reservations, call © **212/283-JAZZ.**

CNN's working studios, demonstrations, and hands-on use of television technology. The tour costs $15 for adults, $14 for seniors, $11 for children 4 to 18, and are free for children 3 and under.

8 Talk of the Town: TV Tapings

The trick to getting tickets for TV tapings in this city is to be from out of town. You visitors have a much better chance than we New Yorkers; producers are gun-shy about filling their audiences with obnoxious locals and see everybody who's not from New York as being from the heartland—and therefore their target TV audience.

If you're set on getting tickets to a show, request them as early as possible—6 months ahead isn't too early, and earlier is better for the most popular shows. Most shows have "ticket request" areas on their websites, which will ask you the number of tickets you want, your preferred dates of attendance (be as flexible as you can), and your address *and* phone number. Tickets are always free. Even if you send in your request early, don't be surprised if tickets don't arrive at your house until shortly before the tape date.

If you come to town without any tickets, all is not lost. Because they know that every ticket holder won't make it, many studios give out a limited number of standby tickets on the day of taping. If you can just get up a little early and don't mind standing in line for a couple (or a few) hours, you have a good chance of getting one (note that the Letterman show no longer has standby lines, you have to call). Now, the bad news: Only one standby ticket per person is allowed, so *everybody* who wants to get in has to get up at the crack of dawn and stand in line. And even if you get your hands on a standby ticket, it doesn't guarantee admission; they usually only start seating standbys after the regular ticket holders are in. Still, chances are good.

For additional information on getting tickets to tapings, call the NYCVB at © **212/ 484-1222.** And remember—you don't need a ticket to be on the *Today* show.

If you do attend a taping, be sure to bring a sweater, even in summer. As anybody who watches Letterman knows, it's *cold* in those studios. And bring ID, as proof of age may be required.

The Colbert Report Jon Stewart's star reporter Steve Colbert, of *The Daily Show,* became so popular he was given his own show on Comedy Central. Now he is giving Stewart a run for his money in the ratings. As of press time, tickets to *The Colbert Report* were only available on a standby basis. Arrive at the studio no later than 5pm: 513 W. 54th St., between Tenth and Eleventh avenues. Check the website, **www.comedy central.com/shows/the_colbert_report**, for ticket information.

The Daily Show with Jon Stewart Comedy Central's irreverent, often hilarious mock newscast tapes Monday through Thursday at 5:45pm, at 513 W. 54th St. *The Daily Show* no longer takes phone requests. For tickets, send an e-mail with your full name and daytime phone number to **requesttickets@thedailyshow.com**. Last-minute ticket requests *only* are allowed by telephone on the Friday prior to the desired show.

Late Night with Conan O'Brien Conan's taking over the Tonight show in a couple of years, so if you want to see him on "Late Night," better do it soon. Tapings are Tuesday through Friday at 5:30pm (plan on arriving by 4:45pm if you have tickets), and you must be 16 or older to attend. You can reserve up to four tickets in advance by calling © **212/664-3056.** Standby tickets are distributed on the day of taping at 9am outside 30 Rockefeller Plaza, on the 49th Street side of the building (under the NBC Studios awning), on a first-come, first-served basis (read: come early if you actually want to get one).

The Late Show with David Letterman Here's the most in-demand TV ticket in town. Submit ticket requests online at **www.cbs.com/latenight**; or stop by the Ed Sullivan Theater from Monday to Friday from 9:30am to 12:30pm or Saturday and Sunday from 10:00am to 6:00pm to submit an in-person request. Tapings are Monday through Thursday at 5:30pm (arrive by 4:15pm), with a second taping Thursday at 8pm (arrive by 6:45pm). You must be 18 or older to attend. On tape days, there are no standby lines anymore; call ℂ **212/247-6497** at 11am for up to two standby tickets; start dialing early, because the machine will kick in as soon as all standbys are gone. If you do get through, you may have to answer a question about the show to score tickets.

Live! with Regis and Kelly Tapings with Regis Philbin and Kelly Ripa are Monday through Friday at 9am at the ABC Studios at 7 Lincoln Sq. (Columbus Ave. and W. 67th St.) on the Upper West Side. You must be 10 or older to attend (under 18s must be accompanied by a parent). Send your postcard (four tickets max) at least a *full year* in advance to *Live!* Tickets, Ansonia Station, P.O. Box 230777, New York, NY 10023-0777 (ℂ **212/456-3054**). Standby tickets are sometimes available. Arrive at the studio no later than 7am and request a standby number; standby tickets are handed out on a first-come, first-served basis, so earlier is better.

Rachael Ray Show You can apply to be featured on the show (if you fit one of the topics they are doing a segment on, like "Do you have a crush on a reality TV star?" or "Kids not turning out the way you expected?") or request tickets on the website (**www.rachaelrayshow.com**). Demand for the tickets is high, and you may be in for a long wait (over a year!). When it's in production, the show tapes twice a day on Tuesdays, Wednesdays and Thursdays at Ray's studio at 222 East 44th Street (between 2nd and 3rd aves.). You must be over 16 years old to attend a taping, and bring a valid photo ID. There's a rather detailed dress code (no capris! No sequins!). You can also stop by on the day of taping to see if standby tickets are available.

Saturday Night Live *SNL* tapings are Saturday at 11:30pm (arrival time 10pm); there's also a full dress rehearsal at 8pm (arrival time 7pm). You must be 16 or older to attend. Here's the catch: Written requests are taken only in August and the odds are always long. However, you can try for standby tickets on the day of the taping, which are distributed at 7am outside 30 Rockefeller Plaza, on the 49th Street side of the building (under the NBC Studios awning), on a first-come, first-served basis; only one ticket per person will be issued. If you want to try your luck with advance tickets, call ℂ **212/664-3056** *as far in advance of your arrival in New York as possible* to determine the current ticket-request procedure.

The *Today* Show Anybody can be on TV with Matt and cuddly weatherman Al Roker and Meredith Vieira. All you have to do is show up outside *Today's* glass-walled studio at Rockefeller Center, on the southwest corner of 49th Street and Rockefeller Plaza, with your HI, MOM! sign. Tapings are Monday through Friday from 7 to 10am, but come at the crack of dawn if your heart's set on being in front. Who knows? If it's a nice day, you may even get to chat with Meredith, Matt, or Al in a segment. Come extra early to attend a Friday Summer Concert Series show.

Total Request Live The countdown show that made Carson Daly a household name is broadcast live from MTV's second-floor glass-walled studio at 1515 Broadway,

---

Tips Who Wants to Be on a Game Show?

The syndicated daily version of *Who Wants to Be a Millionaire*, hosted by Mered-ith Vieira, goes through a lot of contestants and is always on the lookout for smart cookies to sit in the Hot Seat. Check the website (**http://millionairetv.com**) to see if auditions are being held while you're in town (auditions are usually held Aug–Dec). You can sign up over the 'net to attend a taping/take the test on a spe-cific date, and will receive an e-mail confirmation. When the show is taping, you'll be expected to attend as an audience member for a couple of episodes in addition to taking the test (all the better to practice your skills on "Ask the Audi-ence"). On your audition date, report to the ABC studios at 30 W. 67th St. (off Central Park West). Bring ID! You'll take a multiple-choice test and if you score in the top 10% or so, you'll have a brief interview with show staff. If you're selected for the contestant pool, you'll get a postcard telling you that you're in con-tention for a spot. If you're selected to go into the Hot Seat, you'll have to plan another trip to New York City, so remember where you put this book!

---

at 44th Street in Times Square, weekdays at 3:30pm. Crowds start gathering below at all hours, depending on the drawing power of the day's guest. Audience tickets can some-times be reserved in advance by calling the *TRL* **Ticket Reservation Hot Line** at ✆ **212/398-8549** or send your reservation requests to **trlcasting@mtvstaff.com**; you must be between 16 and 24 to attend. If you're not able to score reservations, arrive by 2pm (preferably earlier) if you want a prayer of making it into the in-studio audience; a producer usually roams the crowd asking music trivia questions like "What's Lindsay Lohan's middle name?" (Morgan!) and "Who's the lead singer of Death Cab for Cutie (Ben Gibbard!)?", giving away standby tickets for correct answers. And don't forget to make your DAMIEN FAHEY RULES signs large enough to be captured on camera. You may also be able to watch or participate in other MTV tapings; stop by the MTV Store on the corner of 44th and Broadway, where flyers for tapings and events are some-times stacked next to the register.

The View   ABC's hugely popular girl-power gabfest tapes live Monday through Fri-day at 11am (ticket holders must arrive by 9:30am). Requests, which should be made 12 to 16 weeks in advance, can be submitted online (**www.abc.go.com/theview**) or via postcard to Tickets, *The View*, 320 W. 66th St., New York, NY 10023. Since exact-date requests are not usually accommodated, try standby: Arrive at the studio before 10am and put your name on the standby list; earlier is better, since tickets are handed out on a first-come, first-served basis. You must be 18 or older to attend.

Who Wants to Be a Millionaire   The trivia show is filmed at ABC's Upper West Side studios from late summer through the end of the year. To request tickets to be an audience member, you can send a postcard to *Who Wants to Be a Millionaire*, Colum-bia University Station, P.O. Box 250225, New York, NY 10025. Ticket requests are limited to four, and you must be 18 or older to attend. You can also request tickets online at http://millionairetv.com or call ✆ **212/479-7755**.

9 Especially for Kids

Some of New York's sights and attractions are designed specifically with kids in mind, and I've listed those below. But many I've discussed in the rest of this chapter are terrific for kids as well as adults; so I've included cross-references to the best of them.

Probably the best place of all to entertain the kids is in **Central Park** 𝕱𝕱𝕱, which has kid-friendly diversions galore (see the section beginning on p. 268). For kid-friendly theatrical performances, see the "Kids Take the Stage: Family-Friendly Theater" box, on p. 348.

For general tips and additional resources, see "For Families" under "Specialized Travel Resources" in chapter 3.

MUSEUMS

In addition to the museums specifically for kids detailed below, consider the following, discussed elsewhere in this chapter: The **American Museum of Natural History** 𝕱𝕱𝕱 (p. 235), whose dinosaur displays are guaranteed to wow both you and the kids; the **New York City Fire Museum** 𝕱 (p. 257), in a real firehouse; the **American Museum of the Moving Image** 𝕱 (p. 298), where you and the kids can learn how movies are actually made (and play vintage video games); the **Lower East Side Tenement Museum** 𝕱 (p. 251), whose weekend living-history program intrigues school-age kids; the **New York Transit Museum** (p. 296), where kids can explore vintage subway cars and other hands-on exhibits; and the **South Street Seaport & Museum** (p. 259), which little ones will love for its theme-park-like atmosphere and old boats bobbing in the harbor.

Children's Museum of the Arts *(Kids)*   Interactive workshop programs for children ages 1 to 12 and their families are the attraction here. Kids dabble in puppet making and computer drawing or join in singalongs and live performances. Also look for rotating exhibitions of the museum's permanent collection featuring WPA work. Call or check the website for the current exhibition and activities schedule.

182 Lafayette St. (btwn Broome and Grand sts.). (✆ **212/941-9198** or 212/274-0986. www.cmany.org. Admission $8 for everyone 65 and under, pay-what-you-wish Thurs 4–6pm. Wed–Sun noon–5pm (Thurs to 6pm). Subway: 6 to Spring St.

Children's Museum of Manhattan 𝕱 *(Kids)*   Here's a great place to take the kids when they're tired of being told not to touch. Designed for ages 2 to 12, this museum is strictly hands-on. Interactive exhibits and activity centers encourage self-discovery—and a recent expansion means that there's even more to keep the kids busy and learning. The Time Warner Media Center takes children through the world of animation and helps them produce their own videos. The Body Odyssey is a zany, scientific journey through the human body. This isn't just a museum for the 5-and-up set—there are exhibits designed for babies and toddlers, too. The schedule also includes art classes and storytellers, and a full slate of entertainment on weekends.

212 W. 83rd St. (btwn Broadway and Amsterdam Ave.). (✆ **212/721-1234**. www.cmom.org. Admission $9 children and adults, $6 seniors. School season Wed–Sun and school holidays 10am–5pm; summer Tues–Sun 10am–5pm. Subway: 1 to 86th St.

New York Hall of Science 𝕱 *(Kids)*   Children of all ages will love this huge hands-on museum, which bills itself as "New York's Only Science Playground." This place is amazing for school-age kids. Exhibits let them be engulfed by a giant soap bubble (shades of Veruca Salt, Mom and Dad?), float on air in an antigravity mirror, compose music by dancing in front of light beams, and explore the more-than-miniature world of microbes. There are even video machines that kids can use to retrieve astronomical images, including pictures taken by the *Galileo* in orbit around Jupiter. There's a Preschool Discovery Place for the really little ones. But probably best of all is the summertime Outdoor Science Playground for kids 6 and older—ostensibly lessons in physics, but really just a great excuse to laugh, jump, and play on jungle gyms, slides, seesaws, spinners, and more.

The museum is located in **Flushing Meadows–Corona Park,** where kids can enjoy even more fun beyond the Hall of Science. Not only are there more than 1,200 acres of park and playgrounds, but there's also a zoo, a carousel, an indoor ice-skating rink, an outdoor pool, and bike and boat rentals. Kids and grown-ups alike will love getting an up-close look at the Unisphere steel globe, which was not really destroyed in *Men in Black.* The park is also home to the **Queens Museum of Art** (p. 301) as well as Shea Stadium and the U.S. Open Tennis Center.

47–01 111th St., in Flushing Meadows–Corona Park, Queens. (C) 718/699-0005. www.nyscience.org. Admission $11 adults, $8 seniors and children 2–17, free on Fri 2–5pm Sept–June 30. Additional $3 for Science Playground. Mon–Thurs 9:30am–2pm; Fri 9:30am–5pm; Sat–Sun 10am–6pm. (Mon–Fri 9:30am–5pm July–Aug). Subway: 7 to 111th St.

Sony Wonder Technology Lab *(Kids)*   Not as much of an infomercial as you'd expect. Both kids and adults love this four-level high-tech science-and-technology center, which explores communications and information technology. You can experiment with robotics, explore the human body through medical imaging, edit a music video, mix a hit song, design a video game, and save the day at an environmental command center. The lab also features the first high-definition interactive theater in the United States. Admission is absolutely free; this place is extremely popular, however, so it's wise to make reservations in advance. Reservations can be made up to 3 months in advance by calling (C) 212/833-5414 Monday through Friday between 9am and 2pm. Otherwise, you may not get in, or you may get tickets that require you to return at a different time.

Sony Plaza, 550 Madison Ave. (at 56th St.). (C) 212/833-8100, or 212/833-5414 for reservations. www.sonywonder techlab.com. Free admission. Sun noon–5pm; Tues–Sat 10am–5pm; last entrance 30 min. before closing. Subway: E, V or N, R to Fifth Ave.; 4, 5, 6 to 59th St.

OTHER KID-FRIENDLY DIVERSIONS

SHOPPING   Everybody loves to shop in New York—even kids. Don't forget to take them to **Books of Wonder; **that temple of sneakerdom, **Niketown;** the **NBA Store; Dylan's Candy Bar,** for a real Willy Wonka experience; and **Toys "R" Us** in Times Square, with its very own indoor Ferris wheel. See chapter 9 for details.

SKY-HIGH VIEWS   Kids of all ages can't help but turn dizzy with delight at views from atop the **Empire State Building**(*Kids*) (p. 238). The Empire State Building also has the **New York Skyride** ((C) 212/279-9777; www.skyride.com), which is a short motion-flight-simulation sightseeing tour of New York, in case the real one isn't enough for your kids. Open daily 10am to 10pm; tickets are $26 for adults, $19 for seniors and kids 12 to 17, $18 for kids 6 to 11 and seniors; combination Empire State observation deck/New York Skyride tickets are available at a discount.

SPECIAL EVENTS   Children's eyes grow wide at the yearlong march of **parades** (especially Macy's Thanksgiving Day Parade), **circuses** (Big Apple, and Ringling Bros. and Barnum & Bailey), and **holiday shows** (the Rockettes' Christmas and Easter performances). See the "New York City Calendar of Events," in chapter 3, for details.

ZOOS & AQUARIUMS   Bigger kids will love the legendary **Bronx Zoo** (see below), while the **Central Park Zoo** 🐾, with its Tisch Children's Zoo (p. 271), is particularly suitable for younger kids. At the **New York Aquarium** at Coney Island (p. 296), kids can touch starfish and sea urchins and watch bottle-nosed dolphins and California sea lions stunt-swim in the outdoor aqua theater. Brooklyn's **Prospect Park** 🐾🐾 (p. 296) also boasts a wonderful little zoo.

10 Highlights of the Outer Boroughs
IN THE BRONX

In addition to the options below, literary buffs might also want to visit the **Edgar Allan Poe Cottage,** the final home for the brilliant but troubled author of *The Raven, The Tell-Tale Heart,* and other masterworks. See the sidebar "In Search of Historic Homes," on p. 263.

Bronx Zoo Wildlife Conservation Park 🐾🐾🐾 *Kids*   Founded in 1899, the Bronx Zoo is the largest metropolitan animal park in the United States, with more than 4,000 animals living on 265 acres, and one of the city's best attractions.

One of the most impressive exhibits is the **Wild Asia Complex.** This zoo-within-a-zoo comprises the **Wild Asia Plaza** education center; **Jungle World,** an indoor re-creation of Asian forests, with birds, lizards, gibbons, and leopards; and the **Bengali Express Monorail** (open May–Oct), which takes you on a narrated ride high above free-roaming Siberian tigers, Asian elephants, Indian rhinoceroses, and other nonnative New Yorkers (keep your eyes peeled—the animals aren't as interested in seeing you). The **Himalayan Highlands** is home to 17 extremely rare snow leopards, as well as red pandas and white-naped cranes. The 6½-acre **Congo Gorilla Forest** is home to Western lowland gorillas, okapi, red river hogs, and other African rainforest animals.

The **Children's Zoo** (open Apr–Oct) allows young humans to learn about their wildlife counterparts. Kids can compare their leaps to those of a bullfrog, slide into a turtle shell, climb into a heron's nest, see with the eyes of an owl, and hear with the ears of a fox. There's also a petting zoo. Camel rides are another part of the summertime picture, as is the **Butterfly Zone** and the **Skyfari** aerial tram (each an extra $3 charge).

If the natural settings and breeding programs aren't enough to keep zoo residents entertained, they can always choose to ogle the two million annual visitors. But there are ways to beat the crowds. Try to visit on a weekday or on a nice winter's day. In summer, come early in the day, before the heat of the day sends the animals back into their enclosures. Expect to spend an entire day here—you'll need it.

Getting there: Liberty Lines' BxM11 express bus, which makes stops on Madison Avenue, will take you directly to the zoo; call 📞 **718/652-8400.** By subway, take the no. 2 train to Pelham Parkway and then walk west to the Bronxdale entrance.

Fordham Rd. and Bronx River Pkwy., the Bronx. 📞 **718/367-1010.** www.bronxzoo.com. Admission $14 adults, $12 seniors, and $10 for children 2–12; discounted admission Nov–Mar; free Wed year-round. There may be nominal additional charges for some exhibits. Nov–Mar daily 10am–4:30pm (extended hours for Holiday Lights late Nov to early Jan), Apr–Oct Mon–Fri 10am–5pm, Sat–Sun 10am–5:30pm. Transportation: See "Getting there," above.

New York Botanical Garden 🐾   A National Historic Landmark, the 250-acre New York Botanical Garden was founded in 1891 and today is one of America's foremost public gardens. The setting is spectacular—a natural terrain of rock outcroppings, a river with cascading waterfalls, hills, ponds, and wetlands.

Value A Trolley in the Bronx

Proving that the Bronx is not the bad-boy borough it has often been portrayed as in movies, the Bronx Tourism Council (© **718/590-3518;** www.Ilovethebronx.com) sponsors free tours in a quaint trolley-replica bus. The **Bronx Trolley** operates on weekends and holidays from April through October and nighttime during the Christmas holiday season and makes stops at **Arthur Avenue** (p. 91), the **Bronx Zoo** (p. 289), and the **New York Botanical Garden** (p. 289), On the weekends, the trolley departs at 9:30am from the NYC Visitors Information Center at Seventh Avenue & 53rd Street in Manhattan and makes hop on/hop off stops throughout the day. On the first Wednesday of every month, the trolley is transformed into the **Bronx Cultural Trolley** and is sponsored by the Bronx Council of the Arts (© **718/931-9500** www.bronxarts.org). The trolley takes you on a cultural tour of the lower Grand Concourse area of the South Bronx.

Highlights of the Botanical Garden include the 27 **specialty gardens,** an exceptional **orchid collection,** and 40 acres of **uncut forest,** as close as New York gets to its virgin state before the arrival of Europeans. The **Enid A. Haupt Conservatory,** a stunning series of Victorian glass pavilions that recall London's former Crystal Palace, shelters a rich collection of tropical, subtropical, and desert plants as well as seasonal flower shows. There's also a **Children's Adventure Garden.** Natural exhibits are augmented by year-round educational programs, musical events, bird-watching excursions, lectures, special family programs, and many more activities. Best of all is the annual **Holiday Train Show** (late Nov to early Jan; call for exact dates), where railway trains and trolleys wind their way through more than 100 replicas of historic New York buildings and attractions—such as the Statue of Liberty, the Metropolitan Museum of Art, and the Garden's own Enid A. Haupt Conservatory—all made from plant parts and other natural materials. There are so many ways to see the garden—tram, golf cart, walking tours—that it's best to call or check the website for more information.

Getting there: Take Metro-North (© **800/METRO-INFO** or 212/532-4900; www. mta.nyc.ny.us/mnr) from Grand Central Terminal to the New York Botanical Garden station; the ride takes about 20 minutes. By subway, take the D or 4 train to Bedford Park, then take bus Bx26 or walk southeast on Bedford Park Boulevard for 8 long blocks.

200th St. and Kazimiroff Blvd., the Bronx. © **718/817-8700.** www.nybg.org. Admission $3 adults, $2 seniors and students, $1 children 2–12. Extra charges for Everett Children's Adventure Garden, Enid A. Haupt Conservatory, T. H. Everett Rock Garden, Native Plant Garden, and narrated tram tour; entire Garden Passport package $13 adults, $11 seniors and students, $5 children 2–12. Apr–Oct Tues–Sun and Mon holidays 10am–6pm; Nov–Mar Tues–Sun and Mon holidays 10am–5pm. Transportation: See "Getting there," above.

Wave Hill (Kids (Finds   Formerly a private estate with panoramic views of the Hudson River and the Palisades, Wave Hill has, at various times in its history, been home to a British U.N. ambassador as well as Mark Twain and Theodore Roosevelt. Set in a stunningly bucolic neighborhood that doesn't look anything like you'd expect from the Bronx, its 28 gorgeous acres were bequeathed to the city of New York for use as a public garden that is now one of the most beautiful spots in the city. It's a wonderful place to commune with nature, both along wooded paths and in beautifully manicured herb and flower gardens, where all of the plants are clearly labeled by careful horticulturists. Benches are positioned throughout the property for quiet contemplation and spectacular views. It's a great spot

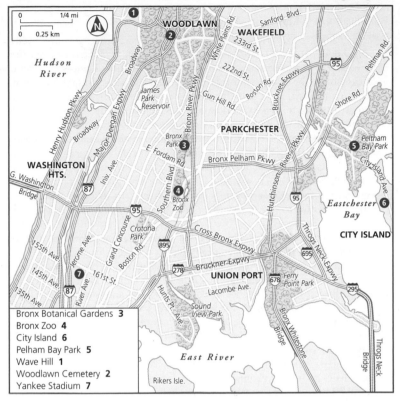

Bronx Botanical Gardens **3**
Bronx Zoo **4**
City Island **6**
Pelham Bay Park **5**
Wave Hill **1**
Woodlawn Cemetery **2**
Yankee Stadium **7**

for taking in the Hudson River vibe without having to rent a car and travel to Westchester to visit the Rockefeller estate; in 2004 a 28-acre public garden and cultural center opened, making it even more attractive and accessible. Programs range from horticulture and environmental education, landscape history, and forestry to dance performances and concerts.

Getting there: Take the no. 1 subway to 231st Street, then take the Bx7 or Bx10 bus to the 252nd Street stop; or take the A train to 207th Street and pick up the Bx7 to 252nd Street. From the 252nd Street stop, walk west across the parkway bridge and turn left; at 249th Street, turn right. Metro North trains (© **212/532-4900**) go from Grand Central to the Riverdale station; from there, it's a 5-block walk to Wave Hill.

675 W. 249th St. (at Independence Ave.), the Bronx. © **718/549-3200**. www.wavehill.org. Admission $4 adults, $2 seniors and students; free admission in winter and Sat mornings and Tues in summer. Tues–Sun 9am–4:30pm; extended hours in summer (check ahead). Transportation: See "Getting there," above.

SEEING THE BRONX WITH A NATIVE

If you join up with **Bronx Tours** (© **646/685-7725**; www.bronxtours.net), Bronx native Maurice Valentine, aka Mo, will personally escort you around a Bronx you never knew existed. The Bronx that Mo will show you is a culturally rich, proud borough and far more than just the home of a great zoo and baseball stadium. His tours last about 3 hours and cost $40.

Mo's Bronx Hit List

Below are some of Mo's personal favorite spots to visit in the Bronx and some of the ones he includes in his tours.

1. **The Point Community Development Corporation** (940 Garrison Ave.; ℂ **718/ 542-4139;** www.thepoint.org; subway: 6 train to Hunts Point Ave.). The Point Community Development Corporation, or just "The Point" as the locals know it, is a community space to keep the young people of the neighborhood out of trouble. It has grown from its humble beginnings in the early 1990s into a cultural mecca. At The Point you can check out photographic exhibitions of works produced by talented young people under the tutelage of the International Center of Photography (ICP); the Edge Theater, where there's a menu of movies, plays, musical performances, and other art-related activities; performances and tutelage by the Rock Steady Crew, whose break-dance style grew out of the late-1970s movement; and graffiti art by none other than Tats Cru, whose work has been featured in movies, commercials and on the streets of NYC. At The Point you'll also find Angel Rodriguez, one of NYC's most important Puerto Ricans, with over 40 years' experience in performing salsa and mambo music, not to mention his legendary conga sessions, which you can catch at the Edge Theater.

2. **Pelham Bay Park.** Most tourists think the largest park in New York City is Central Park. Surprise! The Bronx's own Pelham Bay Park is. In the northeast corner of the Bronx, Pelham Bay Park was created in 1888 and covers over 2,700 acres. It is also the playground for residents of nearby Co-op City, the biggest private-housing development on the East Coast. The park boasts an equestrian center where you can take lessons or go on guided horseback tours, lagoons where you can canoe, and extensive trails along which you can bike or hike. You are also only a short bus ride away from the Bronx's only beach, Orchard Beach, which was created by New York City's infamous commissioner of parks, Robert Moses, in the early 20th century. Subway: 6 to Pelham Bay Park.

3. **City Island** (www.cityisland.com). Take the no. 6 train to its last stop, Pelham Bay Park. Then transfer to City Bus Bx29 towards hidden-treasure City Island. During colonial times City Island was known as Minneford Island, which reflected the area's connection to its traditional owners, the Sinawoy Minneford tribe. Today City Island is connected to the mainland by a 600-foot-long bridge that literally takes you from parkland to fishing village. The island itself is a little over a mile long and a quarter of a mile wide and houses native Bronxites, whose heritage on the island can be traced back more than 150 years. On City Island, marinas dot the tiny coast. The marinas played an important part in the war effort during World Wars I and II, playing host to the construction of minesweepers and costal patrol craft. In more recent times, however, City Island has been involved in the construction of yachts that have won several America Cup titles. City Island offers an abundance of top-quality seafood restaurants, including the late great Salsa musician Tito Puente's own spot.

4. **The Bronx Museum of the Arts** (1040 Grand Concourse, at 165th St.; ℂ **718/ 681-6000;** www.bronxmuseum.org; subway: B, D to 167th St.–Grand Concourse). The Bronx Museum of the Arts was founded in 1971 and specializes in contemporary art produced by talented New Yorkers of Latin, Asian, and African-American descent. The museum displays a number of works inspired by the Bronx itself with over 700 pieces in the permanent collection. The artwork was made

public in 1986, and exhibitions over the years have included "One Planet Under a Groove Hip-Hop, Contemporary Art" (2001), and "Urban Mythologies: The Bronx Represented Since the 1960s" (1999). For those travelers on a budget, admission to the museum won't set you back much at $5 for adults and $3 for children. The museum is a 15-minute walk from Yankee Stadium and a good complement to a day watching the Yankees play there.

5. **Woodlawn Cemetery** (Webster Ave. and 233rd St.; ✆ 718/920-0500; www.the woodlawncemetery.org; subway: 4 to Woodlawn Station). Woodlawn Cemetery is no ordinary cemetery. It was created in 1863 and is best known for its ornate and imaginative mausoleums and monuments. The grounds stretch over 400 acres and house the country's first community mausoleum, which opened in 1967. Woodlawn Cemetery is one of the city's most famous, and you'll find a number of notable people laid to rest here including salsa superstar Celia Cruz, jazz geniuses Miles Davis and Duke Ellington, former mayor of New York City Fiorello La Guardia, Joseph Pulitzer, songwriter George M. Cohan, and theater impresario Oscar Hammerstein. Weekend guided tours are available.

IN BROOKLYN

For details on walking the **Brooklyn Bridge** ⭐⭐, see p. 236.

It's easy to link visits to the Brooklyn Botanic Garden, the Brooklyn Museum of Art, and Prospect Park, since they're all an easy walk from one another, just off **Grand Army Plaza.** Designed by Frederick Law Olmsted and Calvert Vaux as a suitably grand entrance to their Prospect Park, it boasts a grand Civil War memorial arch designed by John H. Duncan (1892–1901) and the main **Brooklyn Public Library,** an Art Deco masterpiece completed in 1941 (the garden and museum are just on the other side of the library, down Eastern Pkwy.). The entire area is a half-hour subway ride from midtown Manhattan.

Brooklyn Botanic Garden ⭐   Down the street from the Brooklyn Museum of Art (see below) is the most popular botanic garden in the city. This peaceful 52-acre sanctuary is at its most spectacular in May when the thousands of deep pink blossoms of cherry trees are abloom. Well worth seeing is the spectacular **Cranford Rose Garden,** one of the largest and finest in the country; the **Shakespeare Garden,** an English garden featuring plants mentioned in his writings; a **Children's Garden;** the **Osborne Garden,** a 3-acre formal garden; the **Fragrance Garden,** designed for the blind but

---

(Moments An Arts Party Grows in Brooklyn

First Saturday is the Brooklyn Museum of Art's ambitious and popular program that takes place on, you guessed it, the first Saturday of each month. It runs from 5 to 11pm and includes free admission and a slate of live music, films, dancing, curator talks, and other entertainment that can get pretty esoteric— think karaoke, lesbian poetry, silent film, experimental jazz, and disco. On a recent Saturday, events included a traditional Irish dance performance, a panel discussion on contemporary black photographers, a screening of *Hair,* and a dance party featuring a funk-and-soul DJ from Brooklyn Underground. As "only in New York" events go, First Saturday is a good one—you can always count on a full slate of cool.

appreciated by all noses; and the extraordinary **Japanese Hill-and-Pond Garden.** The renowned **C. V. Starr Bonsai Museum** is home to the world's oldest and largest collection of bonsai, while the impressive $2.5-million Steinhardt Conservatory holds the garden's extensive indoor plant collection.

900 Washington Ave. (at Eastern Pkwy.), Brooklyn. ℭ 718/623-7200. www.bbg.org. Admission $5 adults, $3 seniors and students, free for children under 16, free to all Tues and Sat 10am–noon year-round, plus Wed–Fri from mid-Nov through Feb. Apr–Sept Tues–Fri 8am–6pm, Sat–Sun 10am–6pm; Oct–Mar Tues–Fri 8am–4:30pm, Sat–Sun 10am–4:30pm. Subway: Q to Prospect Park; 2, 3 to Eastern Pkwy./Brooklyn Museum.

Brooklyn Museum of Art 🕂🕂   One of the nation's premier art institutions, the Brooklyn Museum of Art rocketed into public consciousness in 1999 with the controversial "Sensation: Young British Artists from the Saatchi Collection," which drew international media attention and record crowds who came to see just what an artist— and a few conservative politicians—could make out of a little elephant dung.

Indeed, the museum is known for its consistently remarkable temporary exhibitions as well as its excellent permanent collection. The museum's grand Beaux Arts building, designed by McKim, Mead & White (1897), befits its outstanding holdings, most notably the Egyptian, Classical, and Ancient Middle Eastern collection of sculpture, wall reliefs, and mummies. The decorative-arts collection includes 28 American period rooms from 1675 to 1928 (the extravagant Moorish-style smoking room from John D. Rockefeller's 54th St. mansion is my favorite). Other highlights are the African and Asian arts galleries, dozens of works by Rodin, a good costumes and textiles collection, and a diverse collection of both American and European painting and sculpture that includes works by Homer, O'Keeffe, Monet, Cézanne, and Degas.

Spring 2007 brought the opening of the **Elizabeth A. Sackler Center for Feminist Art,** which will feature permanent and rotating exhibitions of art made by women. One of the prizes of the collection is Judy Chicago's famous "The Dinner Party."

200 Eastern Pkwy. (at Washington Ave.), Brooklyn. ℭ 718/638-5000. www.brooklynmuseum.org. Suggested admission $8 adults, $4 seniors and students, free for children under 12, free to all 1st Sat of the month 11am–11pm. Wed–Fri 10am–5pm; 1st Sat of the month 11am–11pm, each Sat thereafter 11am–6pm; Sun 11am–6pm. Subway: 2, 3 to Eastern Pkwy./Brooklyn Museum.

Brooklyn Tabernacle 🕂   Under the direction of passionate orator Pastor Jim Cymbala and his choral-director wife, Carol, this nondenominational Christian revival church has grown into one of the largest—with a congregation of nearly 10,000 from all walks of city life—and most renowned inner-city churches in the nation. Folks come from all over the world to see the 275-voice, four-time Grammy Award–winning **Brooklyn Tabernacle Choir,** one of the nation's most celebrated gospel choirs.

Brooklyn Tabernacle relocated from Flatbush Avenue to 392 Fulton St., on Fulton Mall in the heart of downtown Brooklyn, in mid-2002. The gloriously renovated 1918 building is the fourth-largest theatrical space in the five boroughs, and seats nearly 4,000 for each service. Still, come early for a prime seat, especially when the choir sings (at the noon and 4pm Sun services).

17 Smith St. (btwn Fulton and Livingston sts.), downtown Brooklyn. ℭ 718/290-2000. www.brooklyntabernacle.org. Services Sun 9am, noon, and 3:30pm; Tues 7pm. Subway: A, C, F to Jay St./Borough Hall; 2, 3 to Hoyt St.; 4, 5 to Borough Hall; M, R to Lawrence St.

Coney Island 🕂🕂 *Moments*   Sure, Coney Island is just a shell of what it was in its heyday in the early 20th century. But it's that shell and what remains that make it such an intriguing attraction. The almost mythical Parachute Jump, recently refurbished, though

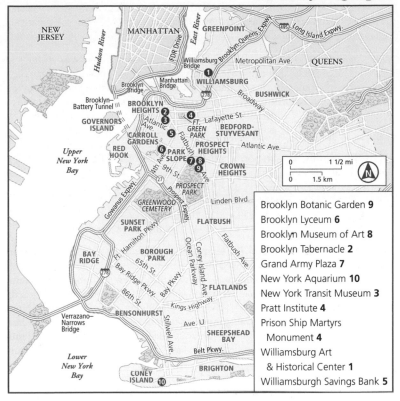

NEW JERSEY

MANHATTAN

GREENPOINT

Long Island Expwy.

Hudson River

FDR Drive

East River

Brooklyn-Queens Expwy.

Williamsburg Bridge

Metropolitan Ave.

QUEENS

❶

WILLIAMSBURG

Brooklyn Bridge

Manhattan Bridge

BUSHWICK

Broadway

Brooklyn–Battery Tunnel

BROOKLYN HEIGHTS ❷

❸

FT. Lafayette St.

GOVERNORS ISLAND

Atlantic Ave.

❹ GREEN PARK

BEDFORD-STUYVESANT

CARROLL GARDENS

Flatbush Ave.

❺

Atlantic Ave.

Upper New York Bay

RED HOOK

❻ PARK SLOPE

PROSPECT HEIGHTS

4th Ave.

❼❽

❾

CROWN HEIGHTS

9th St.

Gowanus Expwy.

27

PROSPECT PARK

Prospect Expwy.

0   1 1/2 mi

0   1.5 km

N

GREENWOOD CEMETERY

Linden Blvd.

SUNSET PARK

Ft. Hamilton Pkwy.

FLATBUSH

BAY RIDGE

278

BOROUGH PARK

65th St.

Bay Ridge Pkwy.

Bay Pkwy.

Ocean Parkway

Coney Island Ave.

Flatbush Ave.

FLATLANDS

86th St.

Kings Highway

Verrazano–Narrows Bridge

BENSONHURST

Ave. U

Stillwell Ave.

SHEEPSHEAD BAY

Belt Pkwy.

Lower New York Bay

CONEY ISLAND ❿

BRIGHTON

Brooklyn Botanic Garden **9**
Brooklyn Lyceum **6**
Brooklyn Museum of Art **8**
Brooklyn Tabernacle **2**
Grand Army Plaza **7**
New York Aquarium **10**
New York Transit Museum **3**
Pratt Institute **4**
Prison Ship Martyrs
  Monument **4**
Williamsburg Art
  & Historical Center **1**
Williamsburgh Savings Bank **5**

long inoperable, stands as a monument to Coney Island. But this is not a dead amusement park; **Astroland,** home of the famed **Cyclone** roller coaster, has some great rides for children and adults; though 2007 will be its last season. The new owners will keep the Cyclone, however, and the **Wonder Wheel,** next door at Deno's, will still be in operation. The best amusement of all, however, is the people-watching. Maybe because it is at the extreme edge of New York City, but Coney Island attracts more than its share of the odd, freaky, and funky. It's here where **Nathan's Famous Hot Dogs** holds its annual hot-dog-eating contest on July 4 at noon; where the wholly entertaining **Mermaid Parade** spoofs the old bathing-beauty parades (late June); and where members of the **Polar Bear Swim Club** show their masochistic gusto by taking a plunge into the icy ocean on January 1. The best time to visit is between Memorial Day and mid-September, when the rides and amusement park are open. Bring your bathing suit and test the waters.

If you are here in the summer, or even if you are not, I recommend a visit to Coney Island just to see it and you can always visit the nearby **Coney Island Museum,** 1208 Surf Ave. (© **718/372-5159;** www.coneyisland.com). Open Saturdays and Sundays year round, here you will find relics from Coney Island's heyday as the premier amusement park in the world. Check out an original "steeplechase horse," vintage bumper cars, or fun-house distortion mirrors. And for a mere 99¢, even if all you want to do is use the clean bathroom, the museum is a bargain.

Subway: D, F, N, Q to Coney Island–Stillwell Ave., Brooklyn.

New York Aquarium *Kids*   Because of the long subway ride (about an hour from midtown Manhattan) and its proximity to Coney Island, it's best to combine the two attractions, preferably in the summer. This surprisingly good aquarium is home to hundreds of sea creatures. Taking center stage are Atlantic bottle-nosed dolphins and California sea lions that perform daily during summer at the **Aquatheater.** Also basking in the spotlight are gangly Pacific octopuses, sharks, and a brand-new sea-horse exhibit. Black-footed penguins, California sea otters, and a variety of seals live at the **Sea Cliffs exhibit,** a re-creation of a Pacific coastal habitat. But my absolute favorites are the beautiful white Beluga whales, which exude buckets of aquatic charm. Children love the hands-on exhibits at **Discovery Cove.** There's an indoor oceanview cafeteria and an outdoor snack bar, plus picnic tables.

502 Surf Ave. (at W. 8th St.), Coney Island, Brooklyn. ℂ 718/265-3400. www.nyaquarium.com. Admission $12 adults, $8 seniors and children 2–12, Daily 10am–5:30pm. Subway: D, F, N, Q to Coney Island–Stillwell Ave., Brooklyn.

New York Transit Museum *Kids*   Housed in a real (decommissioned) subway station, this recently renovated underground museum is a wonderful place to spend an hour or so. The museum is small but very well done, with good multimedia exhibits exploring the history of the subway from the first shovelful of dirt scooped up at groundbreaking (Mar 24, 1900) to the present. Kids and parents alike will enjoy the interactive elements and the vintage subway cars, old wooden turnstiles, and beautiful station mosaics of yesteryear. A new exhibit dedicated to surface transportation is called "On the Streets: New York's Trolleys and Buses." All in all, a minor but remarkable tribute to an important development in the city's history.

The even smaller **Gallery Annex & Store at Grand Central Station** also houses rotating exhibitions and a terrific transit-themed gift shop (see "Museum Stores," in chapter 9). A second museum store, along with a travel-information kiosk, is at the **Times Square Information Center;** see chapter 5.

Boerum Place and Schermerhorn St., Brooklyn. ℂ 718/694-1600. http://mta.info/mta/museum/index.html. Admission $5 adults, $3 seniors and children 3–17, free for seniors Wed noon–4pm. Tues–Fri 10am–4pm; Sat–Sun noon–5pm. Subway: A, C, to Hoyt St.; F to Jay St.; M, R to Court St.; 2, 3, 4, 5 to Borough Hall. Gallery Annex: In Grand Central Terminal (on the main level, in the shuttle passage next to the Station Masters' office), 42nd St. and Lexington Ave. ℂ 212/878-0106. Subway: 4, 5, 6, 7, S to 42nd St./Grand Central.

Prospect Park *Kids*   Designed by Frederick Law Olmsted and Calvert Vaux after their great success with Central Park, this 562 acres of woodland, meadows, bluffs, and ponds is considered by many to be their masterpiece and the *pièce de résistance* of Brooklyn.

The best approach is from Grand Army Plaza, presided over by the monumental **Soldiers' and Sailors' Memorial Arch** (1892) honoring Union veterans. For the best view of the lush landscape, follow the path to Meadowport Arch, and proceed through to the Long Meadow, following the path that loops around it (it's about an hour's walk). Other park highlights include the 1857 Italianate mansion **Litchfield Villa** on Prospect Park West; the **Friends' Cemetery** Quaker burial ground (where Montgomery Clift is eternally prone—sorry, it's fenced off to browsers); the wonderful 1906 Beaux Arts **boathouse;** the 1912 **carousel,** with white wooden horses salvaged from a famous Coney Island merry-go-round (open Apr–Oct; rides 50¢); and **Lefferts**

Homestead Children's Historic House Museum (© 718/789-2822), a 1783 Dutch farmhouse with a museum of period furniture and exhibits geared toward kids (open Apr–Nov Thurs–Sun noon–5pm; Dec–March open Sat and Sun, noon to 4pm.) There's a map at the park entrance that you can use to get your bearings.

On the east side is the **Prospect Park Zoo** (© 718/399-7339), a modern children's zoo where kids can walk among wallabies, explore a prairie-dog town, and more. Admission is $6 for adults, $2.25 for seniors, $2 for children 3 to 12. From April through October, it's open Monday through Friday from 10am to 5pm (to 5:30pm weekends and holidays); November through March, open daily from 10am to 4:30pm.

At Grand Army Plaza, bounded by Prospect Park West, Parkside Ave., and Flatbush Ave., Brooklyn. © 718/965-8951 or 718/965-8999 for events information. www.prospectpark.org. Subway: 2, 3 to Grand Army Plaza (walk down Plaza St. West 3 blocks to Prospect Park West and the entrance) or Eastern Pkwy./Brooklyn Museum.

BROOKLYN HEIGHTS HISTORIC DISTRICT

Just across the Brooklyn Bridge is **Brooklyn Heights** ✿, a peaceful neighborhood of tree-lined streets, more than 600 historic houses built before 1860, landmark churches, and restaurants. Even with its magnificent promenade providing sweeping views of lower Manhattan's ragged skyline, it feels more like its own village than part of the larger urban expanse.

This is where Walt Whitman lived and wrote *Leaves of Grass,* one of the great accomplishments in American literature. And in the 19th century, fiery abolitionist Henry Ward Beecher railed against slavery at **Plymouth Church of the Pilgrims** on Orange Street between Henry and Hicks streets (his sister wrote *Uncle Tom's Cabin*). If you walk down **Willow Street** between Clark and Pierrepont, you'll see three houses (nos. 108–112) in the Queen Anne style that was fashionable in the late 19th century, as well as an attractive trio of Federal-style houses (nos. 155–159) built before 1829. Also visit lively **Montague Street,** the main drag of Brooklyn Heights and full of cafes and shops. On Water Street, under the Brooklyn Bridge, is the **River Café** (© 718/ 522-5200; www.rivercafe.com), where a drink or dinner at twilight, as the lights of Manhattan begin to flicker on, will offer an unforgettable view.

GETTING THERE   Bounded by the East River, Fulton Street, Court Street, and Atlantic Avenue, the Brooklyn Heights Historic District is one of the most outstanding and easily accessible NYC sights beyond Manhattan. The neighborhood is reachable via a number of subway trains: the A, C, F to Jay St.; the 2, 3, 4, 5 to Clark Street or Borough Hall; or the R to Court Street.

It's easy to link a walk around Brooklyn Heights and along its promenade with a walk over the **Brooklyn Bridge** ✿✿ (p. 236), a tour that makes for a lovely afternoon on a nice day. Take a no. 2 or 3 train to **Clark Street** (the first stop in Brooklyn). Turn right out of the station and walk toward the water, where you'll see the start of the **Brooklyn Promenade.** Stroll along the promenade admiring both the stellar views of lower Manhattan to the left and the gorgeous brownstones to the right, or park yourself on a bench for a while to contemplate the scene.

The promenade ends at Columbia Heights and Orange Street. To head to the bridge from here, turn left and walk toward the Watchtower Building. Before heading downslope, turn right immediately after the playground onto Middagh Street. After 4 or 5 blocks, you'll reach a busy thoroughfare, Cadman Plaza West. Cross the street and follow the walkway through little **Cadman Plaza Park;** veer left at the fork in the walkway. At Cadman Plaza East, turn left (downslope) toward the underpass, where you'll find the stairwell up to the Brooklyn Bridge footpath on your left.

BROOKLYN TOURS

When you're heading for Brooklyn, look up **New York Like a Native Tours** (© 718/ 393-7537; www.nylikeanative.com). There are New York natives and there are Brooklyn natives—please don't confuse the two. Norman Oder is the latter and proud of it. His tours cover the borough, the fourth-largest city in America, as extensively as anyone, from his "Brooklyn 101," which takes visitors to the heart of Brooklyn, Grand Army Plaza, Prospect Park, Park Slope, and Brooklyn Heights, to the more neighborhood-specific tours like that of the Polish-populated Greenpoint and the Orthodox and Hasidic Jewish Borough Park. Tours run from 2 to 3 hours and prices range from $15 to $18, not including food.

How to See Brooklyn Like a Native

Here are five Brooklyn sights that, according to Norman Oder of the above-mentioned New York Like a Native tours, are often missed by guidebooks but much appreciated by Brooklyn natives.

1. **Williamsburg Art & Historical Center.** Located in the stately, 1867-built Kings County Savings Bank, this is the largest gallery space in what once was gallery-heavy Williamsburg. The shows here are funky and diverse. Not far from Peter Luger Steakhouse (p. 220), browsing the museum is a good way to work off one of Luger's porterhouses.

2. **Williamsburgh Savings Bank.** Built in 1929 on the edge of the up-and-coming Fort Greene neighborhood, at 512 feet, is Brooklyn's tallest building. Brooklynites have checked the time on the tower's clock for years. It is currently being transformed into luxury condos.

3. **Prison Ship Martyrs Monument.** In Fort Greene Park (www.fortgreenepark.org) this oft-overlooked monument, designed by the legendary architectural firm of McKim, Meade & White, was dedicated by President Taft in 1908 and commemorates the sacrifices of more than 11,000 patriots during the Revolutionary War. (Open for outside views during daylight hours.) Subway: R, Q, B to DeKalb Avenue or 2, 3, 4, 5 to Nevins Street.

4. **Pratt Institute** (www.pratt.edu). Before Brooklyn native Pete Hamill went on to a celebrated writing career, he studied art here. The campus has a terrific sculpture garden and a wide array of works, surrounded by buildings both modern and classic. Subway: G to Clinton-Washington.

5. **Brooklyn Lyceum** (227 Fourth Ave.; © 866/GOWANUS; www.brooklynlyceum. com). On the edge of the very residential neighborhood known as Park Slope, this quirky and cavernous performance space for music, theater, and more was once a public bathhouse. Subway: R to Union St.

IN QUEENS

For details on the **New York Hall of Science** and **Flushing Meadows–Corona Park** (also home to the Queens Museum of Art; see below), see p. 288.

American Museum of the Moving Image (Kids)   Head here if you truly love movies. Unlike Manhattan's Museum of Television & Radio (p. 253), which is more of a library, this is a thought-provoking museum examining how moving images—film, video, and digital—are made, marketed, and shown; it encourages you to consider their impact on society as well. It's housed in part of the Kaufman Astoria Studios, which once were host to W.C. Fields and the Marx Brothers, and more

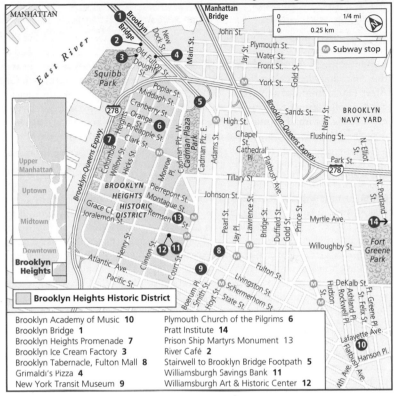

recently have been used by Martin Scorsese (*The Age of Innocence*), Woody Allen (*Radio Days*), Bill Cosby (his *Cosby* TV series), and *Sesame Street.*

The museum's core exhibit, **Behind the Screen,** is a thoroughly engaging two-floor installation that takes you step-by-step through the process of making, marketing, and exhibiting moving images. There are more than 1,000 artifacts on hand, from technological gadgetry to costumes, and interactive exhibits where you can try your own hand at sound-effects editing or create your own animated shorts, among other simulations. Special-effects benchmarks—from the mechanical mouth of *Jaws* to the blending of past and present in *Forrest Gump*—are explored and explained. And in a nod to Hollywood nostalgia, memorabilia that wasn't swept up by the Planet Hollywood chain is displayed, including a Hopalong Cassidy lunch box, an E.T. doll, celebrity coloring books, and Dean Martin and Jerry Lewis hand puppets. Also on display are sets from *Seinfeld.* Even better are the daily hands-on demonstrations, where you can watch film editors, animators, and the like at work.

"Insiders' Hour" tours are offered Saturday and Sunday at 2pm. Additionally, the museum hosts free **film and video screenings,** often accompanied by artist appearances, lectures, or discussions. Seminars often feature film and TV pros discussing their craft; past guests have included Spike Lee, Terry Gilliam, Chuck Jones, and Atom Egoyan, so it's worth checking if someone's on while you're in town.

35th Ave. at 36th St., Astoria, Queens. ℂ **718/784-0077.** www.movingimage.us. Admission $10 adults, $7.50 seniors and college students, $5 children 5–18, free for children under 5. Wed–Thurs 11am–5pm; Fri 11am–8pm; Sat–Sun 11am–6:30pm; Free 4–8pm every Friday (evening screenings Sat–Sun 6:30pm). Subway: R to Steinway St.; N to Broadway.

Isamu Noguchi Garden Museum *Ⓡ* *Finds*   No place in the city is more Zen than this marvelous indoor/outdoor garden museum showcasing the work of Japanese American sculptor Isamu Noguchi (1904–88). The museum showcases the beautifully curated collection of the artist's masterworks in stone, metal, wood, and clay; you'll even see theater sets, furniture, and models for gardens and playgrounds that Noguchi designed. A new gallery highlights the artist's work in interior design.

9–01 33rd Rd. (at Vernon Blvd.), Long Island City, Queens. ℂ **718/545-8842.** www.noguchi.org. Suggested admission $10 adults, $5 seniors and students. Wed–Fri 10am–5pm; Sat–Sun 11am–6pm. Subway: N to Broadway. Walk west on Broadway toward Manhattan until Broadway ends at Vernon Blvd.; turn left on Vernon and go 2 blocks.

Louis Armstrong House Museum *Ⓡ* *Finds*   What is it about celebrities' homes that we find so fascinating? Is it that we get to see how they lived away from the glare of the cameras; how they functioned on a daily basis just like the rest of us? Armstrong was an international celebrity and could have lived anywhere, yet this unassuming, bi-level house in the working-class neighborhood of Corona, Queens, was the great Satchmo's home from 1943 until his death in 1971. It was bought and designed by his fourth wife, Lucille, who lived in it until her death in 1983. No one has lived in the house since, and in 2003 the house, a National Historic Landmark and a New York City landmark, opened its doors to the public as a museum. The 40-minute tour takes you through the small, impeccably preserved home and explains the significance of each room to both Louis and Lucille. My favorite is Armstrong's den, where he kept his reel-to-reel tape recordings, cataloging everything he taped—music, conversations, and compositions, some of which are displayed on his desk. The house also includes a small exhibit with some of his memorabilia, including two of his trumpets, and a

---

Moments **The International Express**

The no. 7 train, which originates in Manhattan at Times Square, makes three stops in that borough, and then snakes, mostly above ground, through the heart of ethnic Queens, is also popularly known as the International Express. Built by immigrants in the early 1900s, the no. 7 IRT (Interborough Rapid Transit) brought those same immigrants to homes on the outer fringes of New York City. That tradition has continued as immigrants from around the world have settled close by the no. 7's elevated tracks. Get off in Sunnyside and notice Romanian grocery stores and restaurants; a few stops further in Jackson Heights you'll see Indians in saris and Sikhs in turbans; go all the way to Flushing and you'll think you are in Chinatown. You are—Flushing's Chinatown, as big or bigger than Manhattan's. In 1999 the Queens Council on the Arts nominated the International Express for designation as a National Millennium Trail and that resulted in its selection as representative of the American immigrant experience by the White House Millennium Council, the United States Department of Transportation, and the Rails-to-Trails Conservancy. For more about the International Express and for tours, visit the **Queens Council on the Arts** website at www.queenscouncilarts.org (ℂ **718/647-3377**).

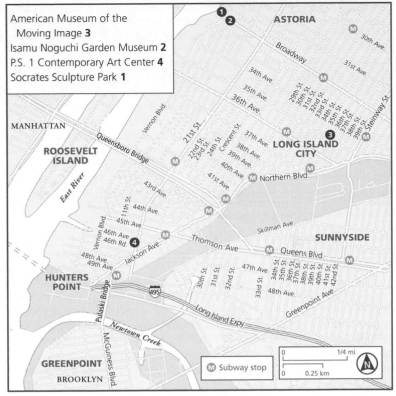

American Museum of the
   Moving Image **3**
Isamu Noguchi Garden Museum **2**
P.S. 1 Contemporary Art Center **4**
Socrates Sculpture Park **1**

gift shop, where many of his CDs are for sale along with other Satchmo-centric items. If you have any interest in jazz and in Armstrong, this is a must-see.

34–56 107th St., Corona, Queens. © **718/478-8274**. www.satchmo.net. $8 adults, $6 seniors, students, and children. Tues–Fri 10am–5pm; Sat–Sun noon–5pm; last tour at 4pm. Subway: 7 to 103rd St.–Corona Plaza. Walk north on 103rd St., turn right on 37th Ave., turn left onto 107th St., and the house is a half-block north of 37th Ave.

P.S. 1 Contemporary Art Center   If you're interested in contemporary art that's too cutting-edge for most museums, don't miss this MoMA affiliate museum. Originally a public school (hence the name), this is the world's largest institution exhibiting contemporary art from America and abroad. You can expect to see a kaleidoscopic array of works from artists ranging from Jack Smith to Julian Schnabel; the museum is particularly well known for large-scale exhibitions by artists such as James Turrell. In 2005 the museum featured a well-received and popular exhibit entitled "Greater New York," featuring works by more than 160 New York–based artists who have come into prominence since the year 2000.

22–25 Jackson Ave. (at 46th Ave.), Long Island City, Queens. © **718/784-2084**. www.ps1.org. Suggested admission $5 adults, $2 seniors and students. Thurs–Mon noon–6pm. Subway: E, V to 23rd St./Ely Ave. (walk 2 blocks south on Jackson Ave. to 46th Ave.); 7 to 45th Rd./Court House Sq. (walk 1 block south on Jackson Ave.).

Queens Museum of Art   One way to see New York in the shortest time (albeit without the street life) is to visit the Panorama, created for the 1939 World's Fair, an enormous building-for-building architectural model of New York City complete with an airplane that takes off from LaGuardia Airport. The 9,335-square-foot Gotham City is the largest model of its kind in the world, with 895,000 individual structures built on a scale of 1 inch=100 feet. A red-white-and-blue ribbon is draped mournfully over the Twin Towers, which still stand in this Big Apple.

Also on permanent display is a collection of Tiffany glass manufactured at Tiffany Studios in Queens between 1893 and 1938. The "Contemporary Currents" series features rotating exhibits focusing on the works of a single artist, often with an international theme (suitable to New York's most diverse borough). History buffs should take note of the museum's NYC Building, which housed the United Nation's General Assembly from 1946 to 1952. Art exhibitions, tours, lectures, films, and performances are part of the program, making this a very strong museum on all fronts.

Next to the Unisphere in Flushing Meadows–Corona Park, Queens. ℭ 718/592-9700. www.queensmuseum.org. Suggested admission $5 adults, $2.50 seniors and students, free for children under 5. Wed–Fri 10am–5pm; Sat–Sun noon–5pm. Subway: 7 to Willets Point/Shea Stadium (follow the yellow signs for the 10-min. walk through the park to the museum, which sits next to the Unisphere).

Socrates Sculpture Park *(Kids*   This former riverside landfill is now the best exhibition space for large-scale outdoor sculpture in the city. No velvet ropes and motion sensors here—interaction with the artwork is encouraged. It's well worth a look, especially on a lovely day. Check the website for the current exhibition schedule—or just let yourself be happily surprised. The park also offers outdoor movie screenings and free tai chi and yoga classes in the summer.

Broadway at Vernon Blvd., Long Island City, Queens. ℭ 718/956-1819. www.socratessculpturepark.org. Free admission. Daily 10am–sunset. Subway: N or W to Broadway; walk 8 blocks along Broadway toward the East River.

11 Spectator Sports

For details on the **New York City Marathon** and the **U.S. Open Tennis Championships,** see the "New York City Calendar of Events," in chapter 3.

BASEBALL   With two baseball teams in town, you can catch a game almost any day from Opening Day in April to the beginning of the playoffs in October. (Don't bother trying to get Subway Series tix, though—they're the hottest seats in town. Ditto for Opening Day or any playoff game.)

Carlos Delgado, Jose Reyes, David Wright, Carlos Beltran, and the rest of the Amazin' **Mets** play at **Shea Stadium** in Queens (subway: 7 to Willets Point/Shea Stadium). Tickets, which are prized at Gold, Silver, Bronze and Platinum levels (based on the team the Mets are playing and the day of the week: i.e., any Yankees game is Platinum; certain early season games are "Value," with deeply discounted tickets) range from $5 to $37 for "Value" games, to $22 to $70 for Platinum games in 2007, with many variations. Trust us, you *do* need a program . . . or to study the seating chart on the team website. For information, call the **Mets Ticket Office** at ℭ 718/507-TIXX or visit **www.mets.com**. Also keep in mind that you can buy game tickets (as well as logo wear and souvenirs, if you want to dress appropriately for the big game) at the **Mets Clubhouse Shop,** which has two midtown Manhattan locations; see p. 336. You'll see the Mets at Shea Stadium through 2008, and in 2009, head across the parking lot to the new stadium, currently under construction.

So the **Yankees** haven't won a World Series in a few years—Manager Joe Torre vows he will fix that! The Yanks play at the House That Ruth Built, otherwise known as

Moments Year-Round Yankee Tour

For a taste of Yankee glory at any time of year, take the **Insider's Tour of Yankee Stadium** (© 718/579-4531). This official tour of the House That Ruth Built will take you onto the field, to Monument Park, and into the dugout. You'll even visit the press box and take a peek inside the clubhouse. The guide peppers the tour with lots of Yankee history and anecdotes as you go. And who knows? You might even spot a certain gorgeous green-eyed multimillionaire shortstop as you make the rounds.

Tours are offered daily at noon except New Year's Day, during Opening Day preparations (usually the 3 weeks prior), and on weekends when the team is at home and weekdays when there is a home day game. Tickets for the 1-hour basic **Classic Tour** are $14 for adults, $7 for kids 14 and under. No reservations are required; all you need to do is show up at the ballpark's press gate just before tour time, but it's still a good idea to call and confirm. Groups of 12 or more require reservations and can book the 80-minute **Champions Tour,** which includes a short film on Yankee history screened in the Adidas Hall of Fame Suite, on a more varied schedule; prices are $20 for adults, $14 for seniors and kids. The **Champions Plus Tour** adds a 15-minute tour of the club level ($25 adults, $17 kids). Check the Yankee website (**www.yankees.com**; click on "Yankee Stadium") for more info.

Yankee Stadium (subway: C, D, 4 to 161st St./Yankee Stadium); NY Waterway (p. 279) offers baseball cruises to games. Call © **800/533-3779** or visit www.nywaterway.com for more info. For single game tickets ($12–$63 in 2007), contact **Ticketmaster** (© **212/307-1212** or 212/307-7171; www.ticketmaster.com) or **Yankee Stadium** *(© 718/293-6000; www.yankees.com). Serious baseball fans check the schedule well in advance for **Old Timers' Day,** usually held in July, when pinstriped stars of years past return to the stadium to take a bow.

At Yankee Stadium, upper-tier box seats (which run about $42), especially those behind home plate, give you a great view of all the action. Upper tier reserve seats are directly behind the box seats and are significantly cheaper ($20). Bleacher seats are even cheaper ($12), and the rowdy commentary from that section's roughneck bleacher creatures is absolutely free. Most of the expensive seats (field boxes) are sold out in advance to season-ticket holders. You can often purchase these very same seats from scalpers, but you'll pay a premium for them. Tickets can be purchased at the team's **clubhouse shop** in Manhattan, at the stadium on the day of the game, and online at http://newyork.yankees.mlb.com; see p. 337. The Yankees will play at original Yankee Stadium through 2008, and are scheduled to open "new" Yankee Stadium (just across the way) for the 2009 season.

Minor-league baseball *(* coexists with the Show in the boroughs, with the **Brooklyn Cyclones,** the New York Mets' A-level farm team, and the **Staten Island Yankees,** the Yanks' junior leaguers. Boasting their very own waterfront stadium, the Cyclones have been a major factor in the revitalization of Coney Island; KeySpan Park sits right off the boardwalk (subway: D, F, N, Q to Stillwell Ave./Coney Island). The SI Yanks also have their own playing field, the Richmond County Bank Ballpark, just a 5-minute walk from the Staten Island Ferry terminal (subway: N, R to Whitehall St.; 4, 5 to Bowling Green; 1 to S. Ferry). What's more, with bargain-basement ticket prices (which topped out at $14 for the Cyclones, $11 for the Yanks in the 2007 season), this is a great way to experience baseball in the city for a fraction of the major-league hassle and cost. Both teams have a rabidly loyal fan base, so it's a good idea to buy your tickets for the June through September season in advance. For the Cyclones, call © **718/449-8497** or visit **www.brooklyncyclones.com**; to reach the SI Yanks, call © **718/720-9200** or go online to **www.siyanks.com**.

BASKETBALL   Though the New Jersey Nets are supposed to be moving to Brooklyn, there are two pro hoops teams that already play in New York at **Madison Square Garden,** Seventh Avenue between 31st and 33rd streets (© **212/465-6741** or www.thegarden.com; **212/307-7171** or www.ticketmaster.com for tickets; subway: A, C, E, 1, 2, 3 to 34th St.), Eddie Curry and the rest of the **New York Knicks** (© **877/NYK-DUNK** or 212/465-JUMP; www.nyknicks.com) are the NBA team from NYC, and their tickets range from $35 to $335. The WNBA's **New York Liberty** (© **212/465-6080;** www.wnba.com/liberty), who electrify fans with their tough defense and scrappy youngsters, occupy MSG from late May through September. Tickets for the Liberty (which celebrated its 10th season in 2006) start at $10 and go up to about $229 for courtside seats behind the benches, with plenty of good seats available ranging from $10 to $30.

ICE HOCKEY   NHL hockey is represented in Manhattan by the **New York Rangers,** who play at Madison Square Garden, Seventh Avenue between 31st and 33rd streets (© **212/465-6741;** www.newyorkrangers.com or www.thegarden.com; subway: A, C, E, 1, 2, 3, to 34th St.). Rangers tickets are hard to get, so plan well ahead; call © **212/307-7171,** or visit www.ticketmaster.com for online orders. Ticket prices range from $27 to $140 and waaaaaaaaaaaay up (for VIP seats).

9

Shopping

For many, shopping is their *raison d'être*—an uncontrollable urge, almost an addiction. What more perfect place than New York to satisfy that urge? No city in the world has the breadth and variety of stores; it's a shopper's paradise.

In this chapter, I've done my best to point out the city's shopping highlights; it's certainly enough to get you started. For much, much more on the New York shopping scene, check out Suzy Gershman's *Born to Shop New York* (Wiley Publishing, Inc.).

1 The Top Shopping Streets & Neighborhoods

Here's a rundown of New York's most interesting shopping areas, with highlights of each to give you a feel for the neighborhood. If location is not given, refer to the store's expanded listing in the appropriate category in "Shopping A to Z," later this chapter.

DOWNTOWN
LOWER MANHATTAN & THE FINANCIAL DISTRICT

South Street Seaport (© **212/732-8257;** subway: 2, 3, 4, 5 to Fulton St.) carries the neighborhood's torch. Familiar names like Abercrombie & Fitch, Ann Taylor, and the Sunglass Hut line Fulton Street, the Seaport's main cobbled drag; several tiers of largely nondescript shops and a large food court fill the levels at Pier 17, a waterfront barge–turned–shopping mall. There's nothing here you can't get anywhere else in Manhattan; come for the historic ambience and the wonderful harbor views. For a store list, visit **www.southstreetseaport.com.**

Century 21, the king of discount department stores, is across the street from the World Trade Center site. Electronics megamart **J&R** is still going strong, now occupying a full city block, with great prices on everything from cameras and computers to CDs and software. Purchase electronics here rather than at the "GOING OUT OF BUSINESS" places in Midtown.

CHINATOWN

Don't expect to find the purchase of a lifetime on Chinatown's crowded streets, but there's some quality browsing. The fish and herbal markets along Canal, Mott, Mulberry, and Elizabeth streets are fun for their bustle and exotica. Dispersed among them (especially along **Canal St.**), you'll find a mind-boggling collection of knockoff sunglasses and watches, backpacks, leather goods, and exotic souvenirs. It's a fun browse, but don't expect quality—and be sure to bargain before you buy. (Also, skip the bootleg CDs, videos, and software—these are stolen goods, and you *will* be disappointed with the product.) Steer clear of electronics like answering machines, radios, and the like, but if you find that you *must* buy, be sure to open the package before you buy.

Tips **Sales Tax**

New York City sales tax is 8.375%, but it is not added to **clothing and footwear items under $110.** If you're visiting from out of state, consider having your purchases shipped directly home to avoid paying sales tax. As with any shipped purchase, be sure to get proper documentation of the sale and keep those receipts handy until the merchandise arrives at your door.

It's a common scam for a sealed box to be offered for sale very cheap, and when you get home you find you've paid for . . . a bunch of newspaper or a brick.

Mott Street, between Pell Street and Chatham Square, boasts the most interesting of Chinatown's off-Canal shopping, with an antiques shop or two dispersed among the tiny storefronts selling blue-and-white Chinese dinnerware. Just around the corner, peek into **Ting's Gift Shop** (18 Doyer St.; © 212/962-1081), one of the oldest operating businesses in Chinatown. Under a vintage pressed-tin ceiling, it sells good-quality Chinese toys, kits, and lanterns.

THE LOWER EAST SIDE

The bargains aren't what they used to be in the **Historic Orchard Street Shopping District**—which basically runs from Houston to Canal along Allen, Orchard, and Ludlow streets, spreading outward along both sides of Delancey Street—but prices on leather bags, shoes, luggage, linens, and fabrics on the bolt are still good. Be aware, though, that the hard sell on Orchard Street can be hard to take. Still, the district is a nice place to discover a part of New York that's disappearing. Come during the week; many stores are Jewish-owned and close Friday afternoon and all day Saturday. Sunday tends to be a madhouse.

The artists and other trendsetters who have been turning this neighborhood into a bastion of hip have also added a cutting edge to its shopping scene in recent years. You'll find a growing—and increasingly upscale—crop of alterna-shops south of Houston and north of Grand Street, between Allen and Clinton streets to the east and west, specializing in up-to-the-minute fashions and edgy club clothes for 20-some-things, plus funky retro furnishings, Japanese toys, and other offbeat items. Before you browse, stop in at the **Lower East Side Visitor Center,** 261 Broome St., between Orchard and Allen streets (© 866/224-0206 or 212/226-9010; subway: F to Delancey St.), for a shopping guide that includes vendors both old-world and new. Or you can preview the list online at **www.lowereastsideny.com.**

SOHO

People love to complain about superfashionable SoHo—it's become too trendy, too tony, too Mall of America. True, **J. Crew** is only one of many big names that have supplanted many of the artists' lofts that used to inhabit its historic buildings. But SoHo is still one of the best shopping 'hoods in the city—and few are more fun to browse. The elegant cast-iron architecture, the cobblestone streets, and the distinct rich-artist vibe: SoHo has a look and feel unlike any other Manhattan neighborhood.

SoHo's shopping grid runs from Broadway west to Sixth Avenue, and Houston Street south to Canal Street. **Broadway** is the most commercial strip, with such recognizable names as **Pottery Barn, Banana Republic, Sephora,** and **A/X Armani Exchange. H&M,** the Swedish department store with cutting-edge fashions sold at very low prices, has two stores that face one another on Broadway. **Bloomingdale's** has opened up a downtown branch on Broadway. **Prada**'s flagship store, also on Broadway, is worth visiting for its spacious, almost soothing design alone (by Dutch architect Rem Koolhaus). A definite highlight is the two-story **Pearl River** Chinese emporium (see "Gifts" in "Shopping A to Z," later in this chapter), which offers everything from silk cheongsam (traditional Chinese high-necked dresses) to teaware.

The big names in avant-garde fashion (see "Clothing" in "Shopping A to Z," later in this chapter) have landed in SoHo, but you'll also find one-of-a-kind boutiques, such as the **Hat Shop,** 120 Thompson St., between Prince and Spring streets (Ⓒ **212/ 219-1445**), a full-service milliner for women that also features plenty of off-the-rack toppers, plus shoe stores galore and high-end home design and housewares boutiques. If you're still hungry for the ultramodern and cutting-edge stop by the **Museum of Modern Art Design Store.** The Midtown museum has an enormous shop in SoHo and it offers the same wonderful chrome and asymmetrical goodies as the original, ranging from pencils to furniture from the museum's collection. There are several not-to-be-missed art galleries along West Broadway and peppered throughout the SoHo area. So if you're looking to expand your collection or just see the work of the next big thing in the art world, be sure to stop by. You can find a full listing of galleries and their hours (most are closed on Mon) at **www.artseensoho.com.**

NOLITA

Not so long ago, **Elizabeth Street** was a quiet adjunct to Little Italy. Today it's one of the hottest shopping strips in the neighborhood known as Nolita. Elizabeth and neighboring **Mott and Mulberry streets** are dotted with an increasing number of shops between Houston Street and the Bowery. It's an easy walk from the Broadway/ Lafayette stop on the F, V line to the neighborhood, since it starts just east of Lafayette Street; you can also take the no. 6 train to Spring Street, or the N, R to Prince Street, and walk east from there.

Nolita is the stepchild of SoHo—meaning don't expect cheap. Its wall-to-wall boutiques are largely the province of shopkeepers specializing in high-quality fashion-forward products. More and more, it's become a beacon of ethnic designs from around the world. **Indomix** (232 Mulberry St.; Ⓒ **212/334-6356; www.indomix.com**) offers beaded tunics and other colorful south-Asian styles by five top designers in India. Texan-born designer and skateboarder **Tracy Feith** (209 Mulberry St.; Ⓒ **212/334-3097**) creates irresistibly pretty slip dresses, skirts, and tops in eye-popping colors and light-as-air Indian silk in his eponymous store on Mulberry Street.

Nolita is also an accessories bonanza; stop in at **Sigerson Morrison (20 Prince St.;** Ⓒ **212/219-3893** for great shoes or **Push** (240 Mulberry St.; Ⓒ **212/965-9699**) for eye-catching jewelry. You'll find more standouts in the listings in "Shopping A to Z," later in this chapter, but just cruising the blocks will do the trick.

THE EAST VILLAGE

The East Village personifies bohemian hip, though many New Yorkers would argue that SoHo's gentrification has engulfed this refuge for alternative purists. The easiest subway access is the no. 6 train to Astor Place, which is just a couple blocks east to the prime hunting grounds.

East 9th Street between Second Avenue and Avenue A is lined with an increasingly smart collection of boutiques, proof that the East Village isn't just for kids anymore. Designers, including **Jill Anderson (331 E. 9th St.;** Ⓒ **212/253-1747**) and **Huminska**

Tips **Additional Sources for Serious Shoppers**

If you're looking for specific items, check the shopping listings at **www.newyork. citysearch.com**, **www.timeoutny.com**, and **www.nymag.com** before you leave home.

For an online guide to sample sales/designer bargains, you can't do better than the free registration site **www.nysale.com**, which will let you in on unadvertised sales taking place throughout the city.

Hard information about current sales, new shops, sample and close-out sales, and special art, craft, and antiques shows is best found in the "Check Out" section of *Time Out New York* or the "Sales & Bargains," "Best Bets," and "Smart City" sections of *New York* magazine. *New York* also runs daily updates of sales at www.nymag.com and *Time Out* publishes a twice-yearly shopping guide that's available on newsstands for about six bucks.

Other Web sources include **www.dailycandy.com**, a daily newsletter highlighting store openings and where to find the day's sales, and **www.girlshop. com**, dedicated to New York insider fashion news. Now Girlshop aficionados have more than just the website: In 2005, the flagship **Girlshop Boutique** opened in the Meat-Packing District (819 Washington St., between Little W. 12th and Gansevoort sts.; ✆ **212/255-4985**).

(315 E. 9th St.; ✆ **212/677-3458**), sell excellent-quality and original fashions for women along here.

If it's strange, illegal, or funky, it's probably available on **St. Marks Place,** which takes over for 8th Street, running east from Third Avenue to Avenue A. This strip is a permanent street market, with countless T-shirt and boho jewelry stands. The height of the action is between Second and Third avenues, which is prime hunting grounds for used-record collectors (see "Music," in "Shopping A to Z," later in this chapter). If you're in search of the harder-edge East Village and feeling a little brave, explore the side streets closer to Avenue A and southward toward the Bowery.

LAFAYETTE STREET FROM SOHO TO NOHO

Lafayette Street has a retail character all its own, distinct from the rest of SoHo. It has grown into something of an Antiques Row, especially strong in furniture. Prices are high, but so is quality. The stretch to stroll is between 8th Street to the north and Spring Street to the south. Take the no. 6 train to Astor Place and work your way south, or get off at Spring Street and walk north, or take the F or V to Broadway-Lafayette and you'll be in the heart of the action. Highlights include **Guéridon,** 37 W. 20th St.; ✆ **212/462-2149;** www.gueridon.com), for sophisticated 20th-century European pieces, mainly French, plus some original designs in the same vein.

GREENWICH VILLAGE

The West Village is great for browsing and gift shopping. Specialty bookstores and record stores, antiques and craft shops, and gourmet food markets dominate. On 8th Street—NYU territory between Broadway and Sixth Avenue—you can find trendy footwear and affordable fashions.

But the biggest shopping boom of late has happened on **Bleecker Street** west of Sixth Avenue. Between Carmine Street and Seventh Avenue, foodies will delight in the strip of boutique food shops, including **Amy's Bread, Wild Edibles,** and **Murray's Cheese.** In between are record stores, guitar shops, and a sprinkling of artsy boutiques. On **Christopher Street** you'll find wonders like **Aedes De Venutas,** a gorgeous little boutique selling fabulous perfumes and scented candles that are difficult to find in the States, and **The Porcelain Room,** 13 Christopher St. (© 212/367-8206), which is located below street level and offers amazing antique and contemporary porcelains that have to be seen to be believed. **The Oscar Wilde Bookshop,** the world's first gay bookstore has been situated on the sleepy eastern end of Christopher Street since 1967. Follow Christopher Street westward where Bleecker becomes boutique alley and one jewel box of a shop follows another. Among them: **Intermix, Olive & Bette, Ralph Lauren, Lulu Guinness,** and **Marc Jacobs.**

Those who really love to browse should also wander **west of Seventh Avenue** and along **Hudson Street,** where charming shops like **House of Cards and Curiosities,** 23 Eighth Ave., between Jane and 12th streets (© 212/675-6178), the Village's own funky take on an old-fashioned nickel-and-dime, are tucked among the brownstones.

CHELSEA/MEAT-PACKING DISTRICT

Almost overnight it seems, west Chelsea has been transformed into the **Chelsea Art District,** where more than 200 galleries have sprouted up in a once-moribund enclave of repair shops and warehouses. The district unofficially stretches from 14th to 29th streets and the West Side Highway and Seventh Avenue, but the high-density area lies between 20th and 26th streets between Tenth and Eleventh avenues.

The Meat-Packing District has also zoomed from quaint to hot (and some say over) in no time, with such big-name designers as **Stella McCartney** (429 W. 14th St.; © 212/255-1556), **Christian Louboutin** (59 Horatio St.; © 212/255-1910), and **Alexander McQueen** (417 W. 14th St.; © 212/645-1797) in residence. **Jeffrey New York,** an offshoot of the Atlanta department store, has pricey designer clothes, an amazing shoe collection, and the friendliest staff in New York.

UNION SQUARE/THE FLATIRON DISTRICT

The hottest shopping/eating/hanging-out neighborhood in the city may be Union Square. The long-forlorn south side of the square is now a mega–shopping area with **Whole Foods, Filene's Basement,** and **DSW (Designer Shoe Warehouse).** Just to the right is a **Virgin Megastore.** On the north side, **Barnes & Noble** is situated in a beautifully restored 1880 cast-iron building. Of course, the beating heart of Union Square is the 4-days-a-week **Greenmarket,** the biggest farmers market in the city.

On Broadway, just a few blocks north of Union Square, is the amazing shopping emporium **ABC Carpet & Home,** where the loft-size floors hold brilliantly decadent

---

Tips Take a Shopping Tour

If you want some help in your shopping and feel a bit intimidated by all the options Manhattan has to offer, you might want to consider taking a shopping tour. **Shop Gotham** (© 212/209-3370; www.shopgotham.com) offers walking tours of SoHo, Fifth Avenue, the Garment Center, and a Big Store tour where you'll hit stores like Macy's, Bloomingdale's, and Century 21 all in 4 hours. Tours range from 2 to 4 hours and from $25 to $85.

displays of furniture, housewares, linens (thread counts off the charts), and tchotchkes of all sizes and shapes.

Upscale retailers who have rediscovered the architectural majesty of **lower Fifth Avenue** include **Banana Republic, Victoria's Secret,** and **Kenneth Cole.** You won't find much that's new along here, but it's a pleasing stretch nonetheless.

When 23rd Street was the epitome of New York uptown fashion more than 100 years ago, the major department stores stretched along **Sixth Avenue** for about a mile from 14th Street up. These elegant stores stood in huge cast-iron buildings that were long ago abandoned and left to rust. In the last several years, however, the area has become the city's discount shopping center, with superstores and off-pricers filling up the renovated spaces: **Filene's Basement, TJ Maxx,** and **Bed Bath & Beyond** are all at 620 Sixth Ave., while **Old Navy** is next door, and **Barnes & Noble** is just a couple of blocks away at Sixth Avenue near 22nd Street.

MIDTOWN
HERALD SQUARE & THE GARMENT DISTRICT
Herald Square—where 34th Street, Sixth Avenue, and Broadway converge—is dominated by **Macy's,** the self-proclaimed world's biggest department store. At Sixth Avenue and 33rd Street is the **Manhattan Mall** (✆ 212/465-0500; www.manhattanmallny.com), home to standards like LensCrafters and RadioShack.

A long block over on Seventh Avenue, not much goes on in the grimy, heavily industrial Garment District. This is, however, where you'll find that quintessential New York experience called the **sample sale** (the box titled "Additional Sources for Serious Shoppers," on p. 308, explains how to find out about upcoming sample sales).

TIMES SQUARE & THE THEATER DISTRICT
You won't find much in the heart of Times Square to entice the serious shopper here, since you can find most of the goods that are sold here back home. Among the best are Richard Branson's rollicking **Virgin Megastore,** and the fabulous **Toys "R" Us** flagship on Broadway and 44th Street, which even has its own full-scale Ferris wheel.

West 47th Street between Fifth and Sixth avenues is the city's famous **Diamond District;** see "Jewelry & Accessories" in "Shopping A to Z," later in this chapter.

You'll also notice a wealth of **electronics stores** throughout the neighborhood, many suspiciously trumpeting GOING OUT OF BUSINESS sales. These guys have been going out of business since the Stone Age. That's the bait-and-switch; pretty soon you've spent too much money for not enough MP3 player. If you want to check out what they have to offer, go in knowing the going price on that PDA or digital camera you're interested in. You can make a good deal if you know exactly what the market is, but these guys will be happy to suck you dry given half a chance. It's better to head downtown to J&R for *real* bargains.

Don't leave the neighborhood just yet. Ninth Avenue, aka Hell's Kitchen (Ninth Ave. to Tenth Ave., between 42nd and 57th sts.), has been undergoing a gentrification and with it has come a wealth of little shops and charming restaurants. One of the more interesting is **Scent Elate** (313 W. 48th St., between Eighth and Ninth aves.; ✆ 212/258-3043). Scent Elate features scented candles, handmade soaps, specialty incenses, essential oils, an array of products produced by local artists, and the legendary Lampe Berger perfume lamps (one of the few places to find them in the city) all in a bright, cozy little shop. One of the things that places this trove above the scores

(*Tips* **When Is It Open?**

Open hours can vary significantly from store to store—even different branches of Gap can keep different schedules depending on location and management. Generally, stores open at 10 or 11am Monday through Saturday, and 7pm is the most common closing hour (although sometimes it's 6pm). Both opening and closing hours tend to get later as you move downtown; stores in the East Village often don't open until 1 or 2pm, and they stay open until 8pm or later.

All of the big department stores are open 7 days a week. However, unlike department stores in suburban malls, most of these stores don't keep a regular 10am-to-9pm schedule. The department stores, and shops along major strips like Fifth Avenue, usually stay open later 1 night a week (often Thurs), although not all shops comply. Sunday hours are usually noon to 5 or 6pm. Most shops are open 7 days a week, but smaller boutiques may close 1 day a week; in addition, some neighborhoods virtually shut down on a particular day—namely the Lower East Side on Saturday, the East Village on Monday, and most of the Financial District for the weekend. But at holiday time, anything goes: Macy's often stays open until midnight for the last couple of weeks before Christmas!

Your best bet is to **call ahead** or print out the schedule from the store website if your heart's set on visiting a particular store.

of other scent emporiums in the city is that the owner, who is almost always on hand, actually selects and tries each product and lends his gregarious manner to helping customers find the scent that's just right. Prices are incredibly reasonable and this little gem (set further back from the sidewalk than the surrounding storefronts) should not be missed. The only thing yummier than the scents at Scent Elate are the cookies at **Ruby et Violette** (457 W. 50th St., between Ninth and Tenth aves.; ✆ **212/582-6720**). Stop in and gorge on some of the over 55 utterly divine chocolate chunk flavors.

If you've still got room for a meal, you're in luck: You're a stone's throw from **Restaurant Row** (46th St. between Eighth and Ninth aves.) where you're sure to be sated, if a bit overwhelmed, by a city block of cuisine from over 11 countries. You might even stop for drinks and a show in one of the many cabaret bars on the street. Find out more at **www.restaurantrownyc.com**.

FIFTH AVENUE & 57TH STREET

The heart of Manhattan retail ranges up Fifth Avenue to 57th Street and across. **Tiffany & Co.**, which has long reigned supreme, sits a stone's throw from **Niketown** and the **NBA Store** and the huge **Louis Vuitton** flagship at the corner of 57th Street and Fifth Avenue. In addition, a good number of mainstream retailers, like **Banana Republic,** have flagships along Fifth, shifting the breadth of higher-end shopping to Madison Avenue north of 59th Street. You will find a number of big-name, big-ticket designers radiating from the crossroads, including **Versace, Chanel, Dior,** and **Cartier.** You'll also find big-name jewelers here, as well as grand old department stores like **Bergdorf Goodman, Henri Bendel,** and **Saks Fifth Avenue,** all Fifth Avenue mainstays that must at least be browsed even if your budget won't allow for more than longing glances at the goods.

Mall with a View

The Shops at Columbus Circle mall, in the Time Warner Center, features not only some of the biggest (and most expensive) names in retail, it also offers shopping with a view of Central Park. Just off the southwest corner of Central Park, the mall is 2 city blocks long and four stories high. But does the picturesque view really matter to the shoppers who set their sights on the goods at retailers like **Williams Sonoma, A/X Armani Exchange, Coach, Hugo Boss, Joseph Abboud, Eileen Fisher, Thomas Pink, Border's Books,** and the massive 59,000-square-foot **Whole Foods Supermarket?** For more information and a complete list of stores, check the mall's website at **www.shopsatcolumbus.com** or call ✆ **212/823-6300.**

UPTOWN

MADISON AVENUE

Madison Avenue from 57th to 79th streets boasts the most expensive retail real estate in the world. Bring lots of plastic. This ultradeluxe strip—particularly in the high 60s—is home to *the* most luxurious designer boutiques, with **Barneys New York** as the anchor. For a sampling of local designers, see "Clothing" in "Shopping A to Z," later in this chapter.

Don't be intimidated by the glamour of this shopper's mile or any of the celebrities you're likely to bump into. There are affordable treasures to be had, like the Ginger Flower room spray at **Shanghai Tang** (714 Madison Ave.; ✆ **212/888-0111**) or a pair of crystal cufflinks at the **Lalique** flagship boutique next door at 712 Madison Ave. (✆ **212/355-6550**).

UPPER WEST SIDE

The Upper West Side's best shopping street is **Columbus Avenue.** Small shops catering to the neighborhood's white-collar mix of young hipsters and families line both sides of the pleasant avenue from 66th Street (where you'll find an excellent branch of **Barnes & Noble**) to about 86th Street. Highlights include **Maxilla & Mandible** for museum-quality natural-science-based gifts and **Harry's Shoes** (see "Museum Stores" and "Shoes" in "Shopping A to Z," later in this chapter), but you won't lack for good browsing along here. **The Shops at Columbus Circle** also offers a world of upscale choices for shopping (see the box "Mall with a View," below).

Boutiques also dot Amsterdam Avenue, but main-drag **Broadway** is most notable for its terrific gourmet edibles at **Zabar's** and **Fairway** markets (see "Edibles" in "Shopping A to Z," later in this chapter).

THE OUTER BOROUGHS

Brooklyn is a shopping destination in its own right, and some of the best and most interesting things can be found in **Williamsburg.** See box "Take the L Train" for more on Willliamsburg.

The other burgeoning area in Brooklyn is **DUMBO** (that's **D**own **U**nder the **M**anhattan **B**ridge **O**verpass), and high-end stores are beginning to move in, including **Jacques Torres Chocolate** (see the sidebar "Chocolate City," later in this chapter).

There is not much fine shopping in any of the other boroughs, with the notable exception of the **Arthur Avenue Retail Market** (see "Edibles" in "Shopping A to Z," later in this chapter) in the Little Italy of the **Bronx.**

Tips **Take the L Train**

Sounds like a good jazzy song title. But really, taking the L train gets you to Williamsburg, Brooklyn and if you want to see what shopping is like on the other side of the East River, this is the place to come. In fact, you may just want to do all your shopping here, the area is becoming that much of a shopping destination. Here are some of Williamsburg's shopping highlights all reachable via the L Train, Bedford Avenue stop.

Beacon's Closet, 88 N. 11th St (btwn Berry St. and Wythe Ave.) © **718/486-0816;** www.beaconscloset.com. This converted warehouse is not only Brooklyn's best vintage clothing and music store, it just may be New York City's as well. You can find women's and men's clothing here, very slightly worn, for under $10; also used CDs and even some vinyl records as well.

Brooklyn Industries, 162 Bedford Ave (at N. 8th St) © **718/486-6464;** www. brooklynindustries.com. There are various outlets of this designer in Brooklyn and even a couple in Manhattan, but you are in Brooklyn, so come to the original source, and find Brooklyn hoodies and sweatshirts along with funky underwear. Here you will find the epitome of urban kitsch to bring back home to the 'burbs or anywhere else outside of Brooklyn.

Earwax, 218 Bedford Ave (at N. 5th St.) © **718/486-3771.** Tower Records might be gone and Virgin is a "megastore", so if you like to peruse your music in an intimate, eclectic setting, come to Earwax. They also have an impressive collection of used CDs and Vinyl.

Mini Mini Market, 218 Bedford Ave (near N. 6th St.) © **718/302-9337;** www. miniminimarket.com. The stock is geared toward girls, especially the inexpensive antique jewelry. The store also features beauty products, hats, bags, and throwback toys.

Noisette, 46B N. 6th St (near Kent St.) © **718/388-5188;** www.noisettenyc. com. Very feminine and *tres Francais* in style, but very Brooklyn in price. What more could a girl ask for? Don't answer that.

2 The Big Department Stores

ABC Carpet & Home 🅐🅐   Shopping ABC has often been compared to taking a fantasy tour of your very rich and very well-traveled ancestor's attic. This two-building emporium is legendary and deserves to be: It's the ultimate home-fashions-and-furnishings department store. On the west side of the street is the stunning 10-floor home emporium. The goods run the gamut from Moroccan mosaic-tile end tables to hand-painted Tuscan pottery to Tiffany-style lamps to distressed bed frames sporting meltingly soft Italian linens to much, much more, all exquisitely displayed. A whole floor of on-the-bolt upholstery fabrics is to die for. These are high-end goods, but sales can produce substantial bargains. The Parlor floor boasts an eclectic collection of beautiful gift items and housewares, and some of the smaller items are quite affordable. Across the street is the multi-floor carpet store, which boasts a stunning collection

Shopping One-Two-Five Street

Maybe it was the arrival of Bill Clinton on the block. Or maybe it's just the latest wave of a Harlem renaissance. Whatever the reason, 125th Street is more vibrant than ever; a true shopping thoroughfare, especially on the blocks between St. Nicholas Avenue and Fifth Avenue. Big chains like **Old Navy, The Children's Store, H&M, The Body Shop, Starbucks,** and **Modell's** have recently set up franchises on 125th. Not everyone is happy with this retail gentrification, believing that Harlem might be losing its identity. But sprinkled among the big names are plenty of stores that represent that unique Harlem character. Hip-hop boutiques like **Jimmy Jazz,** 239 W. 125th St., near Frederick Douglass Boulevard (© 212/663-2827), and **Jersey Man Cap USA,** 112 W. 125th St., between Lenox and Fifth avenues (© 212/222-7942), where you can get anything from a Kangol cap to Girbaud Femme, are mainstays on the Street. Since 1979, the **125th St. Record Shack** at 274 W. 125th St., between Lenox Avenue and Adam Clayton Powell Jr. Boulevard, has been selling jazz, gospel, R&B, doo-wop, and hip-hop, the music usually carrying well out into the already loud street.

At West African importer **African Paradise,** 27 W. 125th St., at Lenox Avenue (© 212/410-5294), you'll find all the supplies you'll need for ancestral worship.

On your shopping tour, you might get hungry—and there is no shortage of places to eat. Skip the usual fast-food options and try the local grub at places like the **M&G Diner,** 383 W. 125th St., at St. Nicholas Avenue (© 212/864-7326), where you'll get some of the best fried chicken in the city (see chapter 7 for more). For coffee, some fine pie, and even a martini, don't miss **Wimp's Southern-Style Bakery, Skye Café and Martini Bar,** 29 W. 125th St., between Fifth and Lenox avenues (© 212/410-2296). For a cultural diversion, stop in at the **Studio Museum in Harlem,** 144 W. 125 St., between Lenox Avenue and Adam Clayton Powell Jr. Boulevard (© 212/864-4500), which also features an interesting gift shop (for more, see chapter 8).

of area rugs. 881 and 888 Broadway (at 19th St.). © 212/473-3000. www.abchome.com. Subway: L, N, R, 4, 5, 6 to 14th St./Union Sq.

Barneys New York 🏵 After financial woes forced the closure of the original Chelsea store a few years back, New York's self-made temple of chic is back on top. While the store focuses on hot-off-the-runway women's wear, its menswear runs the gamut from classic to cutting edge. The fragrance department works hard to offer offbeat and unusual scents as well as the classics. Bring your platinum card, because nothing comes cheap here, although house brands are solidly made and aren't off-the-chart expensive.

Both the downtown (in two locations) and uptown **Barneys Co-Ops** have blossomed into real fashion hot spots, sisterly but separate from the chic Barneys New York Madison Avenue headquarters. At Barneys Co-Op, more downtown-casual fashions for men and women—from such designer names as Diane von Furstenberg, Juicy

Couture, and Rebecca Taylor—set the tone. Prices are more reasonable than at the flagship but not cheap by any means.

Tip: Twice a year, Barneys hosts its famous warehouse sale in Chelsea. Prices are changed daily, but markdowns are 50% to 80% off the original retail prices on all clothing and gifts. So if you are planning a shopping trip to the city, keep your eyes open for when the sales will occur. 660 Madison Ave. (at 61st St.). ⓒ 212/826-8900. www.barneys. com. Subway: N, R to Fifth Ave. Barneys Co-Op: 116 Wooster St. (btwn Prince and Spring sts.). ⓒ 212/965-9964. Subway: N, R to Prince St. 236 W. 18th St. (btwn Seventh and Eighth aves.). ⓒ 212/593-7800. Subway: 1 to 18th St. 2151 Broadway (btwn 75th and 76th sts.). ⓒ 646/335-0978. Subway: 1 to 79th St. Barneys Warehouse: 255 W. 17th St. (btwn Seventh and Eighth aves.). No phone.

Bergdorf Goodman 𝒦𝒦   Bergdorf's is a sybarite's delight. The store is designed on an intimate scale and lacks the kicky nouveau-riche feel of Bendel's. Although the customer base is primarily composed of ladies who lunch and businesswomen with gobs of money but little time for nonsense, fashionistas in the know appreciate Bergdorf's little secret: Sales can garner fantastic bargains, with designer-clothing prices slashed to the bone. Finely tuned designer salons represent both couture powerhouses and downtown darlings. The fifth floor is an open space filled with fashions at more reasonable prices. The jewelry on the main floor and unparalleled gift and tabletop floor are worth a browse alone. The store has two ladies'-shoe departments, one tops for one-stop designer shopping in the $300-and-up range, and the less-expensive fifth-floor salon. Just across the street is **Bergdorf Goodman Man,** a palace of fine men's fashion. 754 Fifth Ave. (at 57th St.). ⓒ 212/753-7300. www.bergdorfgoodman.com. Subway: E, F to Fifth Ave.

Bloomingdale's 𝒦   More accessible than Barneys and more affordable than Saks, Bloomingdale's has a certain New York pizazz. Taking up a whole city block, Bloomie's stocks just about anything you could want, from clothing (both designer and everyday basics) and fragrances to housewares and furniture—not necessarily a good thing, because sometimes it feels too stuffed full of merchandise for comfort. It pays to make a reconnaissance trip to get the overview, then move in for the kill. The main entrance is on Third Avenue, but pop up to street level from the 59th Street station and you'll be right at the Lexington Avenue entrance. A smaller, downtown branch opened in 2004 offering pricier and edgier items. 1000 Third Ave. (Lexington Ave. at 59th St.). ⓒ 212/705-2000. www.bloomingdales.com. Subway: 4, 5, 6 to 59th St. 504 Broadway (at Broome St.). ⓒ 212/729-5900. Subway: N, R to Prince St.

Century 21 (*Value*   Prices here on designer goods are 40% to 70% off what you would pay at a department store or designer boutique. Don't think that $250 Armani blazer is a bargain? Look again at the tag—the retail price is upward of $800. This is the place to find $5 Liz Claiborne tees, $20 Todd Oldham pants, or the $50 Bally loafers you've been dreaming of—not to mention underwear, hosiery, and ties so cheap that they're almost free. Kids' clothes, linens, and housewares are also part of the extensive stock. Expect big crowds and avoid the weekday lunch hour and Saturday if you can help it. 22 Cortlandt St. (btwn Broadway and Church St.). ⓒ 212/227-9092. www. c21stores.com. Subway: 1, 2, 3, 4, 5, M to Fulton St.; A, C to Broadway/Nassau St.; E to Chambers St.

Henri Bendel (*Finds*   This gorgeous Fifth Avenue store is fun to browse. It feels like you're shopping in the townhouse of a slightly offbeat, moneyed lady who doesn't think twice about throwing on a little something by Anna Sui and an outrageously wide-brimmed hat to go out shopping for the day—she's got the panache to pull it off. It's a superstylish, high-ticket collection for ladies with a flair for the funky and frilly—but sales are good, and there are always some one-of-a-kind accessories that make affordable souvenirs (and earn you one of the black-and-white-striped shopping bags, the best in town). The makeup department is always on the cutting edge. The pretty **tearoom** looks out on Fifth Avenue through Lalique windows. 712 Fifth Ave. (btwn 55th and 56th sts.). (C) **212/247-1100.** Subway: N, R to Fifth Ave.

Lord & Taylor Okay, so maybe Lord & Taylor isn't the first place you'd go for a vinyl miniskirt, but this New York institution has an understated, elegant mien. It now operates under the May Company banner but maintains its own sensibility. Long known as an excellent source for women's dresses and coats, L&T stocks all the major labels for men and women, with an emphasis on American designers. Their house-brand clothes (khakis, blazers, turtlenecks, and summer sportswear) are well made and a bargain. Sales, especially around holidays, can be stellar. The store is big enough to have a good selection (especially for petites) but doesn't overwhelm. 424 Fifth Ave. (at 39th St.). (C) **212/391-3344.** www.lordandtaylor.com. Subway: F, V to 42nd St.

Macy's *(Overrated* A four-story sign on the side of the building trumpets MACY'S, THE WORLD'S LARGEST STORE—a hard fact to dispute, since the 10-story behemoth covers an entire city block, dwarfing even Bloomie's on the other side of town. Macy's is a hard place to shop: The size is unmanageable, the service is dreadful, and the incessant din from the crowds on the ground floor alone will kick your migraine into action. But they do sell *everything.* Massive renovation over the past few years has redesigned many departments into more manageable "ministores"—there's a Metropolitan Museum Gift Shop, a Swatch boutique, and cafes and makeup counters on several floors—but the store's one-of-a-kind flair is just a memory now. Still, sales run constantly, holiday or no (1-day sales are popular on Wed and Sat), so bargains are guaranteed. And because so many feel adrift in this retail sea, the store provides personal guides/shoppers at no charge. My advice: Get the floor plan and consult it often to avoid wandering off into the sportswear netherworld. At Christmastime, come as late as you can manage (the store is usually open until midnight in the final shopping days before the holiday). At Herald Sq., W. 34th St., and Broadway. (C) **212/695-4400.** www.macys. com. Subway: B, D, F, N, Q, R, 1, 2, 3 to 34th St.

Saks Fifth Avenue *(★★* There are branches of Saks all over the country now, but this is it: Saks *Fifth Avenue.* No other store better typifies the Big Apple these days than this legendary flagship store, which is well worth your time—and the smaller-than-most size makes it quite manageable. There's something for everyone here. Saks carries a wide range of clothing; departments err on the pricey designer side (stay out of the lingerie department if you're looking for affordable basics), but run the gamut to affordable house-brand basics. The men's department is the finest in the city. The cosmetics and fragrance departments on the main floor are justifiably noteworthy—they carry many hard-to-find and brand-new brands, including Laura Mercier, the Big Apple's own Kiehl's, and more—as are the extensive fine and costume jewelry counters. And the location, right across from Rockefeller Center, makes it a convenient stop for those on the sightseeing circuit. 611 Fifth Ave. (btwn 49th and 50th sts.). (C) **212/753-4000.** www.saksfifthavenue.com. Subway: B, D, F, Q to 47th–50th sts./Rockefeller Center; E, F to Fifth Ave.

Takashimaya *(★ (Finds* This petite branch of Japan's most famous department-store chain exudes an appealingly austere, Japanese-tinged French country charm. Come to

Sale Seasons

These may be obvious to the serious shopper, but for those of us/you less than serious, here are New York's prime sale seasons:

Thanksgiving: Black Friday, or the day after Thanksgiving, is the beginning of the Holiday shopping season. Many stores inaugurate the season with major sales. Stores open ridiculously early and the crowds become more like mobs. Proceed at your own risk.

Pre-Christmas: "Shoppers! Only three X-Boxes left at these amazingly low prices!" You might hear that spiel just before Christmas. Believe it...or don't.

Post-Christmas: With the Christmas returns the day after Christmas, come the markdowns.

Whites: Usually in January, this is a sale of linens...and these days, rarely white.

January Clearance: You'll find the European boutiques advertising clearance around the third week of January.

Valentine's Day: Anything red, chocolaty, or with a heart shape will be advertised "on sale."

President's Day: Late February, usually around the long weekend celebrating Washington (and Lincoln's) birthday. The sales will be mostly for winter clothing.

Memorial Day: Stores hold promotional sales on the last weekend in May.

Fourth of July: Blowout sales on bathing suits and summer attire centered around the long Fourth of July weekend.

Midsummer Clearance: If there is anything summer-related left on the racks after the Fourth of July, you'll find them up until the middle of August.

Back-to-School: Oh, how I hated those three words when I saw them in stores advertising sales for school supplies, furnishings and clothing...while there were still a few weeks left in the summer. Usually in middle August.

Columbus Day: Coats and early fall clothing go on sale on this long weekend usually the second weekend in October.

Election Day: Whatever fall merchandise is hanging around after the Columbus Day sales will be offered at even further reduced prices on Election Day.

see some of the city's most beautiful displays of tableware and boudoir fashions. Paris's most famous florist, Christian Tortu, has a main-floor boutique that's a work of art in its own right. The cosmetics department on the top floor is a must for fans of high-end designer brands looking for something special. The serenely elegant **Tea Box** specializes in delicate bento lunches and beautiful sweets. Aesthetes shouldn't miss this place; it's a wonderful spot for delicate, elegant gifts. 693 Fifth Ave. (btwn 54th and 55th sts.). © 212/350-0100. Subway: E, F to Fifth Ave.

3 Shopping A to Z

ANTIQUES & COLLECTIBLES

Antiques hounds will be dazzled by the bounty that New York has to offer, from Louis XIV settees to vintage DeFranco Family lunchboxes. Be prepared, however—you will pay top dollar for everything.

Traditionalists will love the blocks off **Broadway near 10th and 11th streets,** where the bounty includes Kentshire Galleries (see below); and **East 59th, 60th, and 61st streets** around Second Avenue, not far from the **Manhattan Art and Antiques Center** (1050 Second Ave., between 55th and 56th sts.; ℂ 212/355-4400), where about two dozen high-end dealers line the street and spill over onto surrounding blocks. Fans of midcentury furniture and Americana with a twist should browse **Lafayette Street** in SoHo/NoHo. Just about any dealer you visit will have the current issue of the free *Greyrock Antiques Guide* and/or *Antiques New York,* which will lead you to specialty dealers around the city.

Most called it the 26th Street flea market: The famous **Annex Antiques Fair and Flea Market** (ℂ 212/243-5343; www.hellskitchenfleamarket.com) is an outdoor emporium of nostalgia; you might remember it as filling a few parking lots along Sixth Avenue between 24th and 27th streets on weekends for many years; gentrification in Chelsea has moved the whole shebang uptown, to the (gentrifying) Hell's Kitchen neighborhood, aka "Clinton." It's now on 39th Street, between 9th and 10th avenues on Saturday and Sunday. The assemblage is hit-or-miss—some days you'll find treasures galore, and others it seems like there's nothing but junk. A few quality vendors are almost always on hand, though. The truly dedicated arrive early on Saturday, but the browsing is still good as late as 4pm. Sunday is always best, since there's double the booty on hand. In addition, there's an indoor branch just for antiques on two floors of an indoor garage in Chelsea at 112 W. 25th St., between 5th and 6th aves. It's open Saturday & Sunday from 6:30am to 5pm.

Also check out "Jewelry & Accessories," below.

Alphaville   This gallery specializes in 1940s, 1950s, and 1960s toys and movie posters, all in mint condition and beautifully displayed. Space toys are an emphasis. Well worth a look for nostalgic baby boomers, even if you have no intention of buying. 226 W. Houston St. (btwn Sixth Ave. and Varick St.). ℂ 212/675-6850. www.alphaville.com. Subway: 1 to Houston St.

Chelsea Antiques Building   This 12-floor building houses more than 100 dealers and is open daily. The permanent stalls run the gamut from 18th-century antiques to rare books to early-20th-century radios, jewelry, and toys. Prices are so good that it's known as a dealers' source, and shoppers are the type who love to prowl, touch everything, and sniff out a bargain. 110 W. 25th St. (btwn Sixth and Seventh aves.). ℂ 212/929-0909. Subway: F to 23rd St.

Kentshire Galleries   Still going strong after a half century, this large and lovely gallery is the city's prime stop for 18th- and 19th-century English antiques, ranging from jewelry and tabletop items to formal furnishings. Furniture is displayed in richly appointed rooms that make for great browsing. 37 E. 12th St. (btwn University Place and Broadway). ℂ 212/673-6644. www.kentshire.com. Subway: N, R, L, 4, 5, 6 to 14th St./Union Sq.

Lost City Arts   Lost City features vintage modern furnishings and a quirky selection of accessories (station signs, 3-D photos, and the like), plus their own new midcentury-inspired furniture and accessories, including one inspired by the otherwise forbiddingly expensive custom designs of Machine Age genius Warren MacArthur. A real treat. 18 Cooper Sq. (Third Ave. at 5th St.). (℃ 212/375-0500. www.lostcityarts. com. Subway: N, R to 8th St.

Mood Indigo   This dandy of a shop is the city's top dealer in glassware, dishware, and kitchen accessories from the 1930s through the 1950s. The charming shopkeepers also specialize in Bakelite jewelry and 1939 World's Fair memorabilia and boast a whopping collection of 1950s novelty salt and pepper shakers and even Stork Club cologne (now what could that smell like?). Everything is pristine, so expect to pay accordingly. 181 Prince St. (btwn Sullivan and Thompson sts.). (℃ 212/254-1176. www.moodindigo newyork.com. Subway: C, E to Spring St.; N, R to Prince St.

ART

See the box titled "Art for Art's Sake: The Gallery Scene," on p. 254.

BEAUTY

In addition to the choices below, consider the French beauty superstore **Sephora,** 597 Fifth Ave. (between 48th and 49th sts.; (℃ 212/980-6534; www.sephora.com). There are outlets all over the city, but this Midtown branch is a real beauty.

C. O. Bigelow   Who'd think that a 166-year-old apothecary would carry the city's most eclectic, enjoyable, and international collection of healthy-skin and personal-care products? The goodies run the gamut from Kusco-Murphy hair creams to French Elgydium toothpaste, a bestseller. And now, taking a page from Kiehl's (see below), Bigelow has beautifully packaged its own house-brand line of soaps, salves, essential oils, and beauty treatments. 414 Sixth Ave. (btwn 8th and 9th sts.). (℃ 212/533-2700. www. bigelowchemists.com. Subway: A, C, E, F, V to W. 4th St.

Kiehl's   Kiehl's is more than a store, it's a virtual cult. Models, stockbrokers, foreign visitors, and just about everyone else stop by this always packed, old-time apothecary for its simply packaged, wonderfully formulated products for women and men. Kiehl's now has counters in several department stores (evidence of how they've really moved up in the world), but stop into the original if you can. Love the free samples! 109 Third Ave. (btwn 13th and 14th sts.). (℃ 212/677-3171. www.kiehls.com. Subway: L, N, R, 4, 5, 6 to 14th St./Union Sq.

Ricky's ℱ   This chain of funky drugstores also features a wide range of beauty products. It's a haven for makeup mavens, with multicolored wigs, rainbow-colored lipstick, glitter galore, green nail polish, over 80 kinds of hairbrushes, and even edible undies. Try going into Ricky's and coming out with just a pack of gum. 44 E. 8th St. (at Greene St.). (℃ 212/254-5247. Subway: N, R to 8th St. Also at 466 Sixth Ave. (at 11th St.). (℃ 212/924-3401. Subway: A, C, E, B, D, F to W. 4th St. 112 W. 72nd St. (btwn Columbus Ave. and Broadway). (℃ 212/769-3678. Subway: 1, 2, 3 to 72nd St. 728 Ninth Ave. (at 51st St.). (℃ 212/245-1265. Subway: C, E to 50th St.

Zitomer's ℱℱ   This three-story drugstore is more a mini–department store than a pharmacy. You'll find everything from electronics to pet supplies. But the first floor is where you'll spend most of your time if you're looking for beauty products. They have their own very good line of cosmetics called **Z New York.** Big Apple lip gloss will make a great souvenir; you won't find it in your local Walgreens. 969 Madison Ave. (at 76th St.). (℃ 212/737-2016. www.zitomer.com. Subway: 6 to 77th St.

BOOKS

In addition to the choices below, there are the chains: **Barnes & Noble,** with my favorite outlet opposite Union Square, 33 E. 17th St. (ℂ **212/253-0810;** www.bn. com); and **Borders,** with four stores in Manhattan, including one in the Time Warner Center, 10 Columbus Circle (ℂ **212/823-9775;** www.bordersstores.com).

Argosy Books   Antiquarian-book hounds should check out this stately 77-year-old store, with high ceilings, packed shelves, a quietly intellectual air, and an outstanding collection of rarities, including 18th- and 19th-century prints, maps, and autographs. 116 E. 59th St. (btwn Park and Lexington aves.). ℂ 212/753-4455. www.argosybooks.com. Subway: 4, 5, 6 to 59th St.

Bauman Rare Books   Dealing strictly in highly prized volumes with topics ranging from philosophy and science to children's classics, Bauman is one of the foremost resources for serious collectors willing to spend big money for pristine first editions, ranging from Milton's *Paradise Lost* (1669) to Harper Lee's *To Kill a Mockingbird* (1960), signed by the author. 535 Madison Ave. (btwn 54th and 55th sts.). ℂ 800/99-BAUMAN or 212/751-0011. www.baumanrarebooks.com. Subway: 6 to 51st St. Smaller location at the Waldorf= Astoria Hotel, 301 Park Ave. (btwn 49th and 50th sts.). ℂ 212/759-8300. Subway: 6 to 51st St.

Bluestockings *(Finds*   The self-proclaimed "radical bookstore, fair trade cafe, and activist center in the Lower East Side of Manhattan" packs a lot of literature and activity into its Allen Street storefront (a block south of Houston St.). In addition to books on queer and gender studies, capitalism, feminism, democracy, and liberation, they also carry "good ol' smutty fiction," as well as a variety of independent magazines, journals, and alternative menstrual products (probably the only bookstore in Manhattan so equipped). There's a cafe, so you can buy a cup of tea or free trade coffee before joining the Dyke Knitting Circle or stepping up with your latest poem at an Open Mic. 172 Allen St. (btwn Stanton and Rivington sts.). ℂ 212/777-6028. www.bluestockings.com. Subway: F to Second Ave.; J, M, Z to Essex/Delancey St.

Books of Wonder *(Kids*   You don't have to be a kid to fall in love with this charming bookstore, which served as the model for Meg Ryan's shop in *You've Got Mail.* (Meg even worked here for a spell to train for the role.) Kids will love BOW's story readings; call or check the website for the latest schedule. 18 W. 18th St. (btwn Fifth and Sixth aves.). ℂ 212/989-3270. www.booksofwonder.net. Subway: L, N, R, 4, 5, 6 to 14th St./Union Sq.

Complete Traveller   Whether your destination is Texas or Tibet, you'll find what you need in this, possibly the world's best, travel bookstore. There are travel accessories as well, plus a rare collection of antiquarian travel books whose facts may be outdated but whose writers' perceptions continue to shine. The staff is attentive. 199 Madison Ave. (at 35th St.). ℂ 212/685-9007. www.completetravellerbooks.com. Subway: 6 to 33rd St.

Drama Book Shop *(★*   This store has a resident theater company and in-house performance space. It also hosts discussions, panels, staged readings, and book signings with members of the theater community. Offering thousands of plays, from translations of Greek classics to this season's biggest hits, the shop also sells books, magazines, and newspapers on the craft and business of the performing arts. 250 W. 40th St. (btwn Eighth and Ninth aves.). ℂ 212/944-0595. www.dramabookshop.com. Subway: A, C, E to 42nd St.

Eichler's   *The* Jewish bookstore of New York City, covering everything from cookbooks to Kaballah. The Brooklyn outlet is even bigger and features all manner of Judaica, including silver items, garments, music, gifts, and more. 62 W. 45th St. (btwn Fifth and Sixth aves.). ℂ **877/EICHLERS** or 212/719-1918. www.eichlers.com. Subway: B, D, F, V to 42nd St. Also at 1401 Coney Island Ave. (btwn Avenues J & K). ℂ **888/EICHLERS** or 718/258-7643. Subway: D, Q to Ave. J.

Forbidden Planet   Here is the city's largest collection of sci-fi, comic, and graphic-illustration books. The proudly geeky staff really knows what's what. Great sci-fi-themed toys, too. 840 Broadway (at 13th St.). ℂ **212/473-1576.** Subway: L, N, R, 4, 5, 6 to 14th St./Union Sq.

Housing Works Used Books Cafe *(finds)*   Here's a way to do something good for yourself and others at the same time: Buy your reading material at this spacious yet cozy used-book shop, sporting 45,000 books and records. It's part of Housing Works, a not-for-profit organization that provides housing, services, and advocacy for homeless people living with HIV and AIDS. The collection is terrific and well-organized, with lots of well-priced paperbacks, hardbacks, advance copies, and coffee-table books. There's a cafe in back that serves coffee and tea as well as sandwiches, sweets, and other light bites, plus beer and wine. The bookstore often hosts readings by well-known writers as well as occasional music performances on Wednesday and Thursday evenings; call or check the website for the current listings. 126 Crosby St. (south of Houston St.). ℂ **212/ 334-3324.** www.housingworksubc.com. Subway: B, F, D to Broadway–Lafayette St.; W, R to Prince St.

Hue-Man Bookstore   One of the nation's largest black-owned bookstores, providing the area's largest selection of African-American literature and books. Lines snaked around the block in 2004 when Bill Clinton staged a signing of his memoir. 2319 Frederick Douglass Blvd. (at Eighth Ave.). ℂ **212/665-7400.** www.huemanbookstore.com. Subway: A, B, C, D to 125th St.

Kitchen Arts & Letters   Foodies, take note: Here's the ultimate cook's and food-lover's bookstore. You'll be wowed by the depth of the selection, which includes rare, out-of-print, and foreign-language titles focusing on food and wine. The staff will conduct free searches for hard-to-find titles. The shop is an overstuffed jumble, but if this is your bag, you'll be browsing for hours. 1435 Lexington Ave. (btwn 93rd and 94th sts.). ℂ **212/876-5550.** Subway: 6 to 96th St.

Morningside Bookshop   Right across the street from Columbia University, this is the Upper West Side's best independent bookstore. It's a great place to browse, not only inside, but outside in the remainders bins where you never know what treasures you might find. The store is a favorite with children (and their parents); every Wednesday afternoon there is a sing-a-long by children's entertainer, Danna Banana. For the adults, the store hosts a number of book signings by celebrated authors (many of whom live in the neighborhood). *2915 Broadway (at 14th St)* ℂ **212/222-3350;** www. morningsidebookshop.com. Subway: 1 to 116th St.

Oscar Wilde Bookshop *⊀*   The world's oldest gay and lesbian bookstore was on the brink of extinction a few years ago but has made a strong comeback under new ownership. The nice staff makes browsing in this landmark a pleasure. Recipient of a 2006 Leadership Award from the Publishing Triangle, it's where you'll find the latest literary and popular LGBT work. 15 Christopher St. (btwn Sixth and Seventh aves.). ℂ **212/255-8097.** www.oscarwildebooks.com. Subway: 1 to Christopher St.

Rizzoli   This clubby Italian bookstore is the classiest—and most relaxing—spot in town to browse for visual-art and design books, plus quality fiction, gourmet cookbooks, and other upscale reading. There's a decent selection of foreign-language, music, and dance titles as well. 31 W. 57th St. (btwn Fifth and Sixth aves.). ℂ **212/759-2424.** Subway: N, R to Fifth Ave.

The Scholastic Store *(Kids*   This mammoth store is located at the ground level of the headquarters for children's book publisher Scholastic (which introduced a boy named Harry Potter to America). The 6,200-foot retail space is a veritable interactive playground for kids. Books, toys, and software products feature Scholastic's top-selling brands, from Clifford the Big Red Dog to Captain Underpants. Needless to say, Hogwarts is well represented. A full slate of in-store events, from author signings to craft workshops, also keeps kids busy; check the website or call for the current schedule. 557 Broadway (btwn Prince and Spring sts.). ℂ **212/343-6166.** www.scholastic.com/sohostore. Subway: N, R to Prince St.

Skyline Books *(Value*   A precious holdout from the recent literary shakeout to overtake the city, this wonderful Fourth Avenue book-lover's haven sells rare, used, and hard-to-find books of all types, specializing in art, photography, modern literature, scholarly subjects, Beat literature, first editions, and African-American literature. If you're a devotee of all things literary, dive in and wade through its stacks. 13 W. 18th St. (at Fourth Ave.). ℂ **212/759-5463.** www.skylinebooksnyc.com. Subway: L, N, R, 4, 5, 6 to 14th St./Union Sq.

The Strand *(Value*   Something of a New York legend, The Strand is worth a visit for its staggering "8 miles of books" as well as its extensive inventory of review copies and bargain titles at up to 85% off list price. It's unquestionably the city's best book deal—there's almost nothing marked at list price—and the selection is phenomenal in all categories (there's even a rare-book department on the third floor). Still, you'll work for it: The narrow aisles mean you're always getting bumped; the books are only roughly alphabetized; and there's no air-conditioning in summer. Nevertheless, it's a used-book-lover's paradise. Note that the lower Manhattan location is significantly smaller. 828 Broadway (at 12th St.). ℂ **212/473-1452.** www.strandbooks.com. Subway: L, N, R, 4, 5, 6 to 14th St./Union Sq. Strand Annex: 95 Fulton St. (btwn William and Gold sts.). ℂ **212/732-6070.** Subway: 4, 5, 6 to Fulton St.

Twelfth Street Books *(Value*   Tucked away on West 12th Street between Fifth Avenue and University Place, this cozy little trove offers great used books at amazing prices. Don't miss their small but impressive collection of vinyl records (remember those?) for sale. 11 E. 12th St. ℂ **212/645 4340.** Subway: L, N, R, 4, 5, 6, to 14th St./Union Sq.

Urban Center Books   Housed in an architectural landmark, McKim, Mead & White's 1882 Villard Houses, the Municipal Art Society's bookstore boasts a terrific selection of new books on architecture, urban planning, and landscape design. In the Villard Houses, 457 Madison Ave. (at 51st St.). ℂ **800/352-1880** or 212/935-3595. www.urbancenter books.com. Subway: 6 to 51st St.

CLOTHING
RETAIL FASHIONS
The Top Designers

The legendary locale for the classic designer names has always been Fifth Avenue and 57th Street. There's been some exodus to Madison Avenue (see below), but the opening of the **Gianni Versace** shop at 647 Fifth Ave., between 51st and 52nd streets (ℂ **212/ 317-0224;** www.versace.com), just before the designer's death, heralded a new era of respect for the avenue. Other deluxe designer tenants from Italy's haute couture world are **Prada** (see "For Men & Women," below); **Salvatore Ferragamo,** no. 655, between 52nd and 53rd streets ((C) **212/759-3822;** www.ferragamo.com). Tom Ford's stellar **Gucci** is at Fifth Avenue and 54th Street ((C) **212/826-2600;** www.gucci.com) as well as their Madison Avenue location at 840 Madison Ave. (|tel| **212/717-2619**), while classic **Chanel** is at 15 E. 57th St., between Fifth and Madison avenues ((C) **212/355-5050**), with the freshly hip tartans of **Burberry** just down the block at 9 E. 57th St. ((C) **212/407-7100;** www.burberry.com).

The Upper East Side's Madison Avenue is the heartland of haute couture these days. The biggest names in clean-lined modern design line up along the platinum-coated boulevard; between 59th and 80th streets, you'll find **Calvin Klein, Giorgio Armani, Valentino, Bottega Veneta, Dolce & Gabbana, Emanuel Ungaro, Givenchy, Hermès, Issey Miyake, Krizia, Max Mara, Prada** (see below), **Polo/Ralph Lauren** (see below), **Roberto Cavalli, Versace** (see above), and many more; the density is greatest in the high 60s.

Established avant-garde designers hang out in SoHo. Highlights include **Anna Sui,** 113 Greene St., just south of Prince Street ((C) **212/941-8406;** www.annasui.com), who specializes in boho fashions with a glam edge. **Marc Jacobs,** 163 Mercer St., between Houston and Prince ((C) **212/343-1490;** www.marcjacobs.com), excels at modern takes on classic cuts. Girlish designs are the specialty of **Cynthia Rowley,** 376 Bleecker St., at Perry Street ((C) **212/242-3803; www.cynthiarowley.com**). SoHo has become so designer hot that plenty of established names have moved in, including **Louis Vuitton,** 116 Greene St., between Prince and Spring streets ((C) **212/274-9090;** www.vuitton.com); always-avant **Helmut Lang,** 142 Greene St., near Spring Street ((C) **212/563-0586,** 212/334-2487); **Burberry,** 131 Spring St., between Greene and Wooster streets ((C) **212/925-9300;** www.burberry.com); and, in the same block, **Chanel,** 139 Spring St. ((C) **212/334-0055**).

Talented up-and-comers have set up shop on and around **Bond Street** in NoHo; on **Elizabeth, Mott, and Mulberry streets** in Nolita; along **East 9th Street** in the East Village (see "For Men & Women," below); and on the **Lower East Side,** in the blocks south of Houston Street.

Fashion Flagships

Some New York flagship stores of the major brands are an experience you won't catch in your nearest mall. These stores are display cases for the complete line of fashions, so you'll often find much more to choose from than in your at-home branch. You'll find other locations throughout the city, but these are meant to be the biggest and best. Check out **Ann Taylor** at 645 Madison Ave., at 60th Street ((C) **212/832-2010;** www.anntaylor.com); the **Banana Republic** flagship at Rockefeller Center, 626 Fifth Ave., at 50th Street ((C) **212/974-2350;** www.bananarepublic.com); **Liz Claiborne,** 650 Fifth Ave., at 52nd Street ((C) **212/581-1019;** www.lizclaiborne.com), which carries all of Liz's lines; and **DKNY,** 655 Madison Ave., at 60th Street ((C) **212/223-DKNY;** www.dkny.com). **J. Crew** has a big bi-level SoHo store at 99 Prince St., between Mercer and Greene streets ((C) **212/966-2739;** www.jcrew.com), as well as a large store on Rockefeller Plaza at 50th Street ((C) **212/765-4227**). **Old Navy** has a huge flagship featuring its affordable basics and signature sense of humor at 610 Sixth Ave., at 18th Street ((C) **212/645-0663;** www.oldnavy.com).

For Men & Women

Brooks Brothers   The perfect definition of all that is preppy lies behind this clubby storefront. The label is synonymous with quality, quiet taste, and classic tailoring. The cut of the man's suit is a tad boxy, making it great for the full American body. 346 Madison Ave. (at 44th St.). ℂ 212/682-8800. www.brooksbrothers.com. Subway: S, 4, 5, 6, 7 to 42nd St./ Grand Central. Also at 666 Fifth Ave. (btwn 52nd and 53rd sts.). ℂ 212/261-9440. Subway: 6 to 51st St. 1 Liberty Plaza. ℂ 212/267-2400. Subway: A, C, E to Chambers St.

H&M *(Value* The Swedish super-discounter Hennes & Mauritz has sprouted up all over New York the past 5 years. The loud, bustling stores are mammoth, but the departments are better organized than those at most full-retail department stores. The men's and women's clothing is ultrachic, and the prices are low, low, low. A real fave with teens, in particular. The main Herald Square store carries all lines, including babies, children's, and maternity wear. 1328 Broadway (at 34th St.). ℂ 212/564-9922. www. hm.com. Subway: B, D, F, N, R, V, W to 34th St./Herald Sq. Also at 640 Fifth Ave. (at 51st St.). ℂ 212/ 489-0390. Subway: E, F to Fifth Ave. Smaller location at 558 Broadway (btwn Prince and Spring sts.). ℂ 212/343-0220. Subway: N, R to Prince St.

Jeffrey New York *(★* At the end of a deserted street in the still-industrial Meat-Packing District is this oasis of cutting-edge haute couture. Jeffrey New York caters to the Barneys crowd, but this outpost of the famed Atlanta megaboutique is much more accessible and user-friendly. Great accessories and shoes galore. The collection is mostly geared to women, but there's a notable men's department, too. A worthy schlep for style hounds. 449 W. 14th St. (near Tenth Ave.). ℂ 212/206-1272. Subway: A, C, E, L to 14th St.

Paul Stuart Paul Stuart is a touch more hip and a touch more expensive than Brooks Brothers. Stuart is the classic New York haberdasher—gorgeous fabrics, impeccable tailoring, expensive price tags on everything from suits to weekend wear; there's women's wear, too, but Paul Stuart is more about men. This is a way-of-life store for those who subscribe. Madison Ave. at 45th St. ℂ 212/682-0320. www.paulstuart.com. Subway: 4, 5, 6, 7, S to 42nd St./Grand Central.

Polo/Ralph Lauren Among all the high-ticket designers whose shops line Madison Avenue, Ralph Lauren deserves special mention for the stunning beauty of his flagship store, housed in a landmark Rhinelander mansion. One of New York's first important free-standing American designer shops, it has continued to wear as well as the classics Ralph churns out. Housewares and infants' clothing as well as women's and men's clothes are for sale. The active wear and sporty country looks are at Polo Sport. 867 and 888 Madison Ave. (at 72nd St.). ℂ 212/606-2100. www.ralphlauren.com. Subway: 6 to 68th St.

Prada Few designer labels are more body-conscious, cachet-laden, and downright chic than this sleek Italian line, which reaches beyond clothing to embrace shoes, accessories, and the hippest handbags on the globe (yes, still). SoHo's **Prada Sport** and **Miu Miu** are the destinations for under-30 fashionistas with platinum cards. 841 Madison Ave. (at 70th St.). ℂ 212/327-4200. Subway: 6 to 68th St. **Prada Sport** at 116 Wooster St. (btwn Prince and Spring sts.). ℂ 212/925-2221. Subway: C, E to Spring St. **Miu Miu** at 100 Prince St. (btwn Mercer and Greene sts.). ℂ 212/334-5156. www.miumiu.com. Subway: C, E to Spring St.

Sean John P. Diddy has come a long way from his Harlem roots. In 2004 he opened a flagship on Fifth Avenue and 41st Street featuring his signature hip-hop duds. But the store looks more like a refined library (maybe inspired by the big one across the street—the New York Public Library) than any gangsta club, uptown *or* downtown. Still, if you don't feel like making your way up to 125th Street, you'll find similar street style here in the heart of corporate brand-name Midtown. 475 Fifth Ave. (at 41st St.). ℂ 212/220-2633. Subway: B, D, F, V, 7 to 42nd St.

Seize sur Vingt *(Finds* This Nolita shop custom-tailors Egyptian cotton shirts in bright colors and bold patterns for men and women—perfect for adding a bit of individual flair to your corporate threads. They've also reinvented the bespoke suit in clean, slim, contemporary lines. 243 Elizabeth St. (btwn Houston and Prince sts.). © 212/343-0476. www.16sur20.com. Subway: F, V to Broadway–Lafayette St.; 6 to Spring St.

Ted Baker London This hip Brit import, housed in a store that feels like an old-school country club, is a more-than-welcome addition to the men's clothing options in Manhattan. I like their sloppy-chic button-down shirts, which bring back memories of the post-Beatles British invasion. 107 Grand St. (at Mercer St.). © 212/343-8989. www. tedbaker.co.uk. Subway: J, M, N, R, Z, 6 to Canal St.

Uniqlo *(Value* They call this place "the Japanese Gap"; I see it more like the Asian version of Scandinavian retailer, H&M. Here you'll find hip, "youthful" apparel for men and women at very affordable prices. After a series of "pop-up" stores around the series with Uniqlo's clothes, in late 2006, Uniqlo opened a 36,000-square-foot, tri-level Global flagship store in SoHo. The towering rows of shelves are stocked with cashmere sweaters, brightly colored sweatpants, jeans, and painted t-shirts (some for as little as $5.99). With most of the shelve space vertical, it's easy to browse here and, at these prices, hard to leave the store empty handed. 546 Broadway (between Prince and Spring sts.) © 212/221-9037; www.uniqlo.com. Subway: N,R, to Prince St.

Just Women

Anthropologie Funky, slightly exotic, and affordable wearables and accessories mix with fun gifts, furniture, and home-decorating items. Geared to funky-chic post-collegiate young women who've outgrown Urban Outfitters. 375 W. Broadway (btwn Spring and Broome sts.). © 212/343-7070. www.anthropologie.com. Subway: C, E to Spring St. Also at 85 Fifth Ave. (at 15th St.). © 212/627-5885. Subway: L, N, R, 4, 5, 6 to 14th St./Union Sq.

Eileen Fisher *(((* Making their way around the nation in her own shops and through outlets like Saks and the Garnet Hill catalog, Eileen Fisher's separates are a dream come true for stylish women looking for easy-to-wear classic pieces that transcend the latest fads. She designs fluid clothes in a pleasing neutral palette and uses natural fibers that don't sacrifice comfort for chic. The A-line styles look a bit droopy on shorter women, but otherwise suit all figure types well. The superior quality, fabrics, and style make these clothes worth every penny. The beautifully austere SoHo location is Fisher's prime showcase. The semiannual consolidation sales, in March and August, are a bargain hunter's delight. Note that only the SoHo flagship sells the complete line, including both the petite and women's collections. The closet-size East 9th Street location basically functions as an outlet store, with lots of sale merchandise and seconds on hand. 395 W. Broadway (btwn Spring and Broome sts.). © 212/431-4567. www.eileen fisher.com. Subway: C, E to Spring St. Also at 521 Madison Ave. (at 53rd St.). © 212/759-9888. Subway: 6 to 51st St. 341 Columbus Ave. (near 76th St.). © 212/362-3000. Subway: B, C to 81st St. 1039 Madison Ave. (btwn 79th and 80th sts.). © 212/879-7799. Subway: 6 to 77th St. 314 E. 9th St. (btwn First and Second aves.). © 212/529-5715. Subway: 6 to Astor Place. 166 Fifth Ave. (at 22nd St.). © 212/924-4777. Subway: N, R to 23rd St.

Huminska If you're addicted to colorful, flirty dresses and shapely swirl skirts, make a beeline for this shop. The offerings change with the whims of the designer, but the current collection of dresses seems to be inspired by the 1950s and the wonder that is polka dots. 315 E. 9th St. (btwn First and Second aves.). © 212/677-3458. www.huminska.com. Subway: 6 to Astor Place.

Intermix   The place to dress and accessorize in style, at not-too-expensive prices. The Flatiron location is the original, and remains the best. 125 Fifth Ave. (btwn 19th and 20th sts.). ℭ 212/533-9720. www.intermix-ny.com. Subway: N, R to 23rd St. Also at 210 Columbus Ave. (btwn 69th and 70th sts.). ℭ 212/769-9116. Subway: B, C to 72nd St. 365 Bleecker St. ℭ 212/929-7180. Subway: 1 to Christopher St.

Jill Anderson   Finally, a New York designer who designs affordable clothes for real women to wear for real life—not just for 22-year-old size 2s to match with a pair of Pradas and wear out club-hopping. This narrow, peaceful shop and studio is lined on both sides with Jill's simple, clean-lined designs, which drape beautifully and accentuate a woman's form without clinging. They're wearable for all ages and many figure types. (Her small sizes are small enough to fit petites, and her larges generally fit a full-figured size 14.) Her clothes are feminine without being frilly, retro-reminiscent but completely modern, understated, and utterly stylish. 331 E. 9th St. (btwn First and Second aves.). ℭ 212/253-1747. www.jillanderson.com. Subway: 6 to Astor Place.

Searle   If you're looking for a winter coat or jacket, there aren't many better choices than Searle. But the stores are not only known for their jackets, they also feature great clothes in beautiful colors and fabrics. 156 Fifth Ave. (btwn 20th and 21st sts.). ℭ 212/924-4330. www.searlenyc.com. Subway: N, R to 23rd St. Also at 609 Madison Ave. (at 58th St.). ℭ 212/753-9021. Subway: N, R, 4, 5, 6 to 59th St. 1035 Madison Ave. (at 79th St.). ℭ 212/717-4022. Subway: 6 to 77th St.

Vera Wang   The petite powerhouse is still the hottest name in bridal fashions. Vera dresses scads of top stars (particularly petite ones with great figures) on their big day or for the Oscars in her simple, elegant designs. Vera's studio is open by appointment only, so brides-to-be should call ahead. There's also a Vera Wang salon on the third floor at **Bergdorf's** (p. 315). Ask about the annual warehouse sale, usually held in September. 991 Madison Ave. (at 77th St.). ℭ 212/628-3400. www.verawang.com. Subway: 6 to 77th St. **Bridesmaids' store** at 980 Madison Ave. (btwn 76th and 77th sts., 3rd floor). ℭ 212/628-9898. Subway: 6 to 77th St.

Just Men

Frank Stella   This refined shop sells casually elegant clothes for the well-dressed 21st-century man, including clean-lined blazers, quality knits, and beautifully cut trousers. 440 Columbus Ave. (at 81st St.). ℭ 212/877-5566. Subway: B, C to 81st St. Also at 921 Seventh Ave. (at 58th St.). ℭ 212/957-1600. Subway: A, B, C, D, 1 to 59th St./Columbus Circle.

Paul Smith   This temple of new English fashion is a can't-miss. When it comes to menswear that's at once fashion-forward and undisputedly classic, Paul Smith wins the prize, with jackets, suits, pants, shoes, sportswear, and accessories that are superpricey but worth every cent. 108 Fifth Ave. (at 16th St.). ℭ 212/627-9770. www.paulsmith.co.uk. Subway: F to 14th St.

Saint Laurie Merchant Tailors *(Finds*   Family-owned since 1913, this custom tailor offers a huge selection of fabrics, from Scottish worsted wools to Italian silks, and offers you a selection of styles to choose from. The custom job is about $1,000 for a suit (less when sales are going on), substantially less for a blazer. 22 W. 32nd St. (at Fifth Ave.). ℭ 212/643-1916. www.saintlaurie.com. Subway: 6 to 51st St.

Just Kids

If you need the basics, you'll find branches of **Gap Kids, Baby Gap,** and **The Children's Place** all over town—it's harder to avoid one than to find one. The department stores are also great sources, of course.

Bu & the Duck *(Finds*   This divine shop sells its own unique vintage-inspired clothing and shoes that your kids can really wear. Delightful sock puppets and other vintage-inspired toys are also in the mix. 106 Franklin St. (btwn Church St. and W. Broadway). © 212/431-9226. www.buandtheduck.com. Subway: 1 to Franklin St.

rockstarbaby *(Finds*   Here's the place to clad your kid in the coolest glad rags around. This new line of newborn and infant clothing is a collaboration between rocker Tico Torres (Bon Jovi) and designer Cinzia Spinetti. Despite the pedigree and attitude (how 'bout a bib that says BORN TO ROCK for your favorite newborn?), these are gorgeous, practical, and moderately priced wearables. 298 Elizabeth St. (just north of Houston St.). © 212/226-2771. www.rockstarbaby.com. Subway: 6 to Bleecker St.

Shoofly   Top-quality clothing, footwear, and accessories for kids from newborns through teens. You'll find lots of distinctive stuff here, including imported lines. The shoe selection, in particular, is terrific, and not too pricey. The downtown store also sells toys and infant gifts. 42 Hudson St. (btwn Duane and Thomas sts.). © 212/406-3270. www.shooflynyc.com. Subway: 1, 2, 3 to Chambers St.

Space Kiddets *(Finds*   This sleeper in the Flatiron District has been around for 23 years and features children's clothing in refreshing styles—a cut above chains like The Children's Place. But the prices are also a cut above. Sales are frequent. 46 E. 21st St. (at Broadway). © 212/420-9878. www.spacekiddets.com. Subway: N, R to 23rd St.

Vintage & Consignment Clothing

Allan & Suzi *(Finds*   Make it past the freaky windows and inside you'll find one of the best consignment shops in the city. Allan and Suzi have specialized in gently worn 20th-century designer wear for well over a decade now, and their selection is marvelous. Their extensive vintage and contemporary couture collection—which ranges from conservative Chanel to over-the-top Halston, Mackie, and Versace—is so well priced that it's well within reach of the average shopper looking for something extra-glamorous to wear. 416 Amsterdam Ave. (at 80th St.). © 212/724-7445. Subway: 1 to 79th St.

Michael's *(Value*   This consignment boutique boasts top-drawer designer wear for women—including such names as Chanel, YSL, Prada, Gucci, Richard Tyler, and Escada—at a fraction of the original cost. The bridal salon is an unbeatable find for engaged gals looking for a top-quality dress at an off-the-rack price. 1041 Madison Ave. (btwn 79th and 80th sts., 2nd floor). © 212/737-7273. www.michaelsconsignment.com. Subway: 6 to 77th St.

Screaming Mimi's *(Value*   Think you hate vintage shopping? Think again: Screaming Mimi's is as neat and well organized as any high-priced boutique—yet prices are surprisingly reasonable, especially given the pricey vintage shops that have popped up around the city in recent years. The vintage-housewares department is a wonderful cornucopia of kitsch and includes a selection of New York memorabilia; prices start under $10. 382 Lafayette St. (btwn E. 4th and Great Jones sts.). © 212/677-6464. www.screamingmimis.com. Subway: 6 to Astor Place.

EDIBLES

Arthur Avenue Retail Market *★★*   This colorful, enclosed market opened in the heart of the Bronx's Little Italy in 1940 and is my absolute favorite. The market, like the Bronx, has had its ups and downs but now is thriving. You'll find fresh-produce purveyors like **Biano** fruits and vegetables and **Joe Liberatore's Garden of Plenty,** where I buy the best tomato plants for my terrace. There is **Peter's Market** for homemade sausages and braciole, **Mike's Deli** for freshly made mozzarella and sandwiches, **Café al Mercato** for their amazing broccoli rabe pizza and pasta *fiogoli,* the **Arthur Avenue Baking Company** for loaves of *pane di casa* and Parmesan breadsticks, and even **La Casa Grande Tobacco Company,** where they roll their own cigars. 2344 Arthur Ave., the Bronx. No phone. www.arthuravenuebronx.com. Subway: B, D to Fordham Rd.

Chelsea Market   Located in an old Nabisco factory, this big, dazzling food mall is the city's largest. Come for both raw and ready-to-eat foods, including divinely inspired baked goods and cappuccino from **Amy's Bread;** yummy soups from **Hale and Hearty;** Manhattan's best brownie at **Fat Witch Bakery;** and much more, including the wonderful **Chelsea Wine Vault. Chelsea Market Baskets** is a great place to pick up gifts for home. 75 Ninth Ave. (btwn 15th and 16th sts.). www.chelseamarket.com. Subway: A, C, E to 14th St.; L to Eighth Ave.

Dean & DeLuca   This bright, clean-lined store offers premier quality across the board: In addition to the excellent butcher, fish, cheese, and dessert counters (check out the stunning cakes and the great character cookies) and beautiful fruits and veggies, you'll find a dried-fruit-and-nut bar, a huge coffee-bean selection, a gorgeous cut-flower selection, lots of imported waters and beers in the refrigerator case, and a limited but quality selection of kitchenware in back. A small cafe up front makes a great stop for a cappuccino break from SoHo shopping. 560 Broadway (at Prince St.). ✆ 212/226-6800. www.dean-deluca.com. Subway: N, R to Prince St.

DiPalo's Dairy ✿   Before there was Mario Batali, before Danny Meyer, or Daniel Boulud, there was Louie DiPalo, a true New York food celebrity if there ever was one. But thankfully, Louie won't be hosting any food shows anytime soon. He's too busy behind the counter of his 1910-originated, family-run store putting together packages of the best and hardest to find Italian cheeses around for some of the city's most acclaimed restaurants and chefs. But you don't have to be a chef to enjoy DiPalo's; you just need a little patience—lines can get long and Louie and his staff will take their time with your order. The tiny store is one of the last authentic Italian vestiges in the now tacky and overly gentrified neighborhood of Little Italy. 200 Grand St. (at Mott St.) ✆ 212/226-1033. Subway: B, D to Grand St.

Fairway ✿✿ *Value*   There is no better all-in-one market in Manhattan than Fairway. Here you will find the best and most modestly priced vegetables in the city. Cheeses are top-of-the-line and well organized. The fish counter is excellent and, again, very modestly priced. The second floor of the Broadway store features hard-to-find health foods and a wide array of organic fruits and vegetables. Fairway also carries the gourmet items you might find at Dean & Deluca but at a fraction of the cost. The Harlem store is huge and features a walk-in freezer, complete with down jackets provided for customers' use. 2127 Broadway (btwn 74th and 75th sts.). ✆ 212/595-1888. www.fairwaymarket.com. Subway: 1, 2, 3 to 72nd St. Also at 2328 Twelfth Ave. (at 132nd St.). ✆ 212/234-3883. Subway: 1 to 125th St.

Zabar's ✿   More than any other of New York's gourmet food stores, Zabar's is an institution. This giant deli sells prepared foods, packaged goods from around the world, coffee beans, excellent fresh breads, and much more (no fresh veggies, though). This is the place for lox, and the rice pudding is the best I've ever tasted. You'll also find an excellent—and well-priced—collection of housewares and restaurant-quality cookware on the second floor. Prepare yourself for serious crowds. The attached cafe

Chocolate City

The Big Apple is fast becoming a city consumed by a near-feverish craving for chocolate. Many sweets shops around the city now are turning out homemade chocolates in every variety that are so good, the stores, like four-star restaurants, are destinations in their own right. The best of these can be found just over the Brooklyn Bridge in DUMBO at **Jacques Torres Chocolate** ★★, 66 Water St., Brooklyn (© 718/875-9772; www.mr chocolate.com). Torres, the former celebrated pastry chef at Le Cirque, ventured out on his own a few years ago and opened this mecca to chocolate where your mouth will water as you watch chocolate being made. The variations here are staggering and include chocolate peanut brittle, chocolate-covered corn flakes, champagne truffles, and some of the best hot chocolate you've ever tasted. Take home a tin of the "wicked" hot chocolate, which features allspice, cinnamon, sweet ancho chile peppers, and hot chipotle peppers. Also, the **Jacques Torres Chocolate** chocolate-manufacturing facility, open to the public, is at 350 Hudson St., at King Street, in TriBeCa © **212/ 414-2462.**

In Manhattan, steps from the Metropolitan Museum of Art, is the Madison Avenue incarnation of the Paris import **La Maison du Chocolat,** 1018 Madison Ave., at 78th Street (© **212/744-7117;** www.lamaisonduchocolat. com). This boutique takes its chocolate very seriously. Here you will find possibly the best pure chocolate you've ever tasted. They abhor any bitterness in their chocolate and make it a point to claim that they use nothing stronger than 65% cocoa. Now that's serious chocolate.

One of the oldest chocolate shops in the city is the 1923-established **Li-Lac Chocolates,** 40 Eighth Ave. (at Jane St.; © **866/898-2462** or 212/924-2280; www.li-lacchocolates.com), formerly on Christopher Street, which after 81 years has moved to new digs and now boasts a satellite store in Grand Central Terminal. This West Village shop makes their sweets by hand and whips up its chocolate fudge daily. In fact, they do chocolate fudge like no one else in the city.

Also in the Village is **The Chocolate Bar,** 48 Eighth Ave., between Jane and Horatio streets (© **212/366-1541;** www.chocolatebarnyc.com). Their homemade chocolate bars are worthy of their name. I love the mocha, with its flecks of coffee. For those who worship the cocoa gods, go for the super-dark 72%, so dark and rich you might speak in tongues after a few bites.

---

serves terrific sandwiches and takeout—ideal for a Central Park picnic. 2245 Broadway (at 80th St.). © **212/787-2000.** www.zabars.com. Subway: 1 to 79th St.

COFFEE & TEA

Ito En *Finds*   You want green tea? You want black tea? Herbal tea? White tea? No problem. There are so many varieties of teas here you need a catalog to peruse the selections. Located in a Madison Avenue town house, Ito En is like an art gallery of teas; everything is neatly displayed and there is a calming, serene feel to the store.

There is a *sencha* bar (tea bar) where you can sample some of their teas and get tea advice from the experts working there. They also sell green-tea-dusted chocolate-covered almonds that are an addictive, and very expensive, munchie. 822 Madison Ave. (at 69th St.). ℂ 212/988-7111. www.itoen.com. Subway: 6 to 68th St.

McNulty's Tea & Coffee Company ℛ McNulty's has been around since 1895, making it one of the oldest coffee purveyors in the country. And it still has that old-time feel, with overflowing sacks of coffees and rare teas cluttering the quaint West Village store—and they roast their own coffees right there. The Colombia Supremo is as perfect as it gets, and I can't leave the store without my monthly fix of Italian roast espresso. 109 Christopher St. (btwn Bleecker and Hudson sts.). ℂ 212/242-5351. www.mcnultys.com. Subway: 1 to Christopher St.

SWEETS

Dylan's Candy Bar ℛ Dylan (daughter of Ralph) Lauren is one of the co-owners of this bazaar for sugar addicts. Located across the street from Bloomingdale's, you'll find all the candy classics, such as Necco Wafers, Charleston Chews, and both of my favorite childhood chewing gums, Black Jack and Gold Mine. Dylan's also makes signature chocolates, candy creations, candy spa products like hot-chocolate bath beads, and custom-made ice cream flavors. 1011 Third Ave. (at 60th St.). ℂ 646/735-0078. www.dylanscandybar.com. Subway: 4, 5, 6, N, R to 59th St.

Economy Candy Store While Dylan's is the new generation of candy store, Economy Candy, which has been selling its sweet wares since 1937, in the gentrified Lower East Side across the street from the gleaming Hotel on Rivington (see chapter 6), is a blast from the past. Here, if you are somewhat aged like your author, you will recognize treats from your childhood like Hot Tamales, Bit O'Honey candy, Kosher rock candy, Atomic Fireballs, and Necco Wafers. You'll also find a fine selection of dried fruits and nuts and gourmet chocolate here. A trip to Economy Candy is definitely a trip back in time and worth taking. 108 Rivington St. (btwn Delancey and Norfolk sts.). ℂ 212/254-1531. www.economycandy.com. Subway: F to Delancey St.

Fauchon ℛ *(Finds)* This Parisian chocolatier operates a large, elegant boutique featuring an ultracharming tea salon and sparkling glass cases display a gorgeous array of chocolates and sweet treats flown in daily; the candied fruits are among the most gorgeous foods I've ever seen. Afternoon tea is served daily from noon to 6pm (to 5pm on Sun); you can choose between a two-course tea ($30) or a lovely array of salads, quiches, and so forth. Beautifully packaged candies, biscuits, preserves, and the like make elegant and pretty take-home treats. 442 Park Ave. (at 56th St.). ℂ 212/308-5919. www.fauchon.com. Subway: 4, 5, 6 to 59th St.

ELECTRONICS

The Apple Store ℛ The largest Apple Store opened in early 2006, and hasn't closed yet (it's open 24/7). This glass edifice on Fifth Avenue and 59th St features 18,000-square-feet. Descend a glass staircase or elevator to the store below ground where there is a 46-seat theater and 14 internet connected computers fully loaded with games; a geek's paradise. It's almost impossible to walk by without popping in to see what the fuss is all about. I'm not sure anyone actually buys all the Apple gadgets sold here, but it sure is fun to try out the floor samples. 767 Fifth Ave (at 59th St.) ℂ 212/336-1440; www.apple.com. Subway N, R to Fifth Avenue. Also at 103 Prince St. (at Greene St.). Subway: R to Prince St.

A Taste of New York

Do you want to bring back a *real* New York souvenir—something that evokes the genuine flavor of New York more than an I ♥ NEW YORK T-shirt or an Empire State Building figurine? Give your friends and family some real New York edibles. Possibly the best place to pick up food "souvenirs" is the Lower East Side. This neighborhood, home to so many immigrants over the years, is where a number of traditional New York foods originated. Do you have a friend who craves pickles, pregnant or not? Then venture to **Guss's Pickles** at 85 Orchard St. (☎ **917/701-4000**). Bring home a gallon of half or full sour, a mix of both, or pickled green tomatoes. If you can't lug it back home, have them ship it for you for about $49 a gallon.

If anyone can really explain what a bialy is exactly, I'm all ears. But whatever it really is doesn't matter as long as it tastes good. You'll find the oldest (over 65 years) bialy makers and the best in New York at **Kossar's Bialys,** 367 Grand St., between Norfolk and Essex streets (☎ **212/473-4810**). A dozen go for around $9 and come in different flavors like sesame, poppy, and garlic.

East Houston Street features two New York food-souvenir choices worth bringing home. Start with knishes from the 1910-established **Yonah Schimmel Knishes** at 137 E. Houston St., between First and Second avenues (☎ **212/477-2858**). The choices range from potato to spinach to mushroom; a box of 12 goes for about $34. At 179 E. Houston St., between Allen and Orchard streets, the remarkable **Russ & Daughters** (☎ **212/475-4880;** www.russanddaughters.com) has incomparable smoked fish and nova. A medley of smoked salmon goes for about $70, and, in my humble opinion, is worth every penny.

B&H Photo & Video *Value* Looking for a digital camera at a good price? You won't do any better than B&H, the largest camera store in the country. This camera superstore has everything from lenses to darkroom equipment. If you are a B&H virgin, the store can be somewhat intimidating, but service is helpful. Just follow the signs and they will direct you to whatever you are seeking. (*Note:* B&H is closed Sat.) 420 Ninth Ave. (at 34th St.). ☎ **800/606-6969** or 212/444-5000. www.bhphotovideo.com. Subway: A, C, E to 34th St.

J&R Music & Computer World This block-long Financial District emporium is the city's top discount computer, electronics, small appliance, and office-equipment retailer. The sales staff is knowledgeable but can get pushy if you don't buy at once or know exactly what you want. Don't succumb—take your time and find what you need. Or better yet, peruse the store's copious catalog or extensive website, both of which make advance research, and mail order and comparison-shopping, easy. 23 Park Row (at Ann St., opposite City Hall Park). ☎ **800/806-1115** or 212/238-9000. www.jandr.com. Subway: 2, 3 to Park Place; 4, 5, 6 to Brooklyn Bridge/City Hall.

GIFTS

For first-rate Fifth Avenue gifts, don't forget **Tiffany & Co.,** whose upper level boasts wonderful small gifts, all crafted in signature Tiffany silver or crystal and wrapped in the unmistakable blue box (see "Jewelry & Accessories," below).

For additional suggestions, see "Antiques & Collectibles," earlier in this chapter, and "Home Design & Housewares," below.

auto. If a Lucite tic-tac-toe set sounds like a good idea to you, don't miss this witty Meat-Packing District boutique. The mod and minimalist home accessories and gift items—mostly original designs by Brooklyn-based artists—are both well conceived and good-humored. 805 Washington St. (btwn Gansevoort and Horatio sts.). Ⓒ 212/229-2292. www.thisisauto.com. Subway: A, C, E to 14th St.

Jack Spade Looking for a gift for the man who has everything? Then head to Jack Spade, which specializes in vintage and new "guy toys." The inventory changes constantly, but expect goodies along the lines of vintage phonographs and microscopes, old maps and globes, cool desk accessories, and the like. This shop was launched by the husband of Kate Spade (she of chic handbags and paper-goods fame), so you can expect a smart, upmarket collection. 56 Greene St. (btwn Spring and Broome sts.). Ⓒ 212/625-1820. www.katespade.com. Subway: C, E to Spring St.; N, R to Prince St.

Pearl River (Value Even after moving from tight quarters on Canal Street to a more spacious location, this Chinese mall still overflows with affordable Asian exotica. You need vials of ginseng? They got it. How about a pair of Mandarin-collared silk pajamas or a mah-jongg set? They got it. While you're perusing the goods, enjoy a cup of tea at the cafe and meditate to the sound of the store's bubbling waterfall. 477 Broadway (at Grand St.). Ⓒ 212/431-4770. www.pearlriver.com. Subway: N, R to Canal St.

Steuben Glass This is the flagship store for America's premier manufacturer of fine glass and crystal, said to be the world's purest. The store is gorgeous, and the pieces—which run the gamut from fruit bowls to sculptures—are spectacularly crafted and refract light beautifully. Prices start around $200 for a "hand cooler" (a small collectible, often animal-shaped, that fits in your palm) and run into the five figures. The Corning Gallery, on the lower level, hosts rotating art exhibits. 667 Madison Ave. (at 61st St.). Ⓒ 212/752-1441. www.steuben.com. Subway: N, R to Fifth Ave.

HANDBAGS & LEATHER GOODS

Jutta Neumann (Finds If you stop into this studiolike shop, you're likely to find the artist herself behind the counter, cutting and stitching her geometric, bold-hued leather goods—bags, wallets, boots, and more. Her mules and strappy sandals are also popular. 158 Allen St. (btwn Stanton and Rivington sts.). Ⓒ 212/982-7048. www.juttaneumann-newyork. com. Subway: F to Delancey/Essex sts.

kate spade Kate Spade revolutionized the high-end handbag market with her practical yet chic rectangular handbags, which have seemingly taken over the planet. They come in a wide range of fabrics and sizes, from pretty seersuckers to groovy prints to fashionable flannel to basic black, plus a wide range of solids. The daintier evening line is charming, particularly the grosgrain silks. The line has expanded to include chic baby bags, luggage, sexy shoes, and comfy pajamas. You can also find the signature bags at Saks, Barneys, Bergdorf Goodman, and Bloomingdale's. 454 Broome St. (at Mercer St.). Ⓒ 212/274-1991. www.katespade.com. Subway: N, R to Prince St. **kate spade baby** at 59 Thompson St. (btwn Spring and Broome sts.). Ⓒ 212/965-8654. Subway: C, E to Spring St.

Manhattan Portage Ltd. Store Come here for the hippest nylon and canvas carryalls in town. True to its name, Manhattan Portage manufactures all its bags right in the city, and they're made from hard-wearing materials that can stand up to an urban lifestyle. Popular styles include all-purpose messenger bags, DJ bags, and backpacks (in both standard and nouveau one-shoulder styles) in a range of colors from iridescent yellow to camouflage. Manhattan Portage bags are also sold through other outlets, but

you'll find the most complete selection here. 333 E. 9th St. (btwn First and Second aves.). © 212/
995-5490. Subway: 6 to Astor Place. Also at 301 W. Broadway. © 212/226-4557. Subway: N, R to
Prince St.

HOME DESIGN & HOUSEWARES

Attention, Oriental rug and cilium fans: Dealers line **Broadway** around the queen of
home-furnishings department stores, **ABC Carpet & Home** (see "The Big Department Stores," earlier in this chapter). The second floor of **Zabar's** (see "Edibles," earlier in this chapter) is another excellent source for high-end kitchenware.

Broadway Panhandler   If you're looking for restaurant-quality cookware and
kitchen tools, you've found your place. The best combination of selection, prices, and
service in town. 65 E. 8th St (btwn Broadway and University Pl.). © 212/966-3434. www.broadway
panhandler.com. Subway: N.R, to 8th St.

Fishs Eddy *(R* *(Value*   What a great idea: selling remainders of kitschy, custom-
designed china left over from yesteryear. Ever wanted a dish that *really* says "Blue Plate
Special"? Or how about a mug with the terse logo "Cup o' Joe to Go"? The store is
Browse Heaven, and prices on its American industrial china are low enough. The
store's own designs are equally wonderful, especially its series with the New York skyline. Other items for sale include basic vintage and retro-inspired flatware, heavy
crockery bowls, and classic restaurant-supply glassware that can be hard to find in regular stores, like soda-fountain and pint glasses. 889 Broadway (at 19th St.). © 212/420-9020.
www.fishseddy.com. Subway: L, N, R, 4, 5, 6 to 14th St./Union Sq. St. Also at 1388 Third Ave. (at 79th St.).
© 212/737-2844. Subway: 6 to 77th St.

Frette   This Italian linen maker has taken the hotel world by storm with its silky
cotton sheets and plush terry towels and robes. If you've slept on some and now you
want your own, head to this dedicated boutique or ABC Carpet & Home (p. 313) for
the best selections. Also at Saks, Bloomingdale's, and Bergdorf's. 799 Madison Ave. (btwn
67th and 68th sts.). © 212/988-5221. www.frette.it. Subway: 6 to 68th St.

Jonathan Adler   Anybody who has been reading shelter magazines over the last
couple of years will recognize this hot potter's bold vases and lamps instantly. His style
merges organic shapes, geometric patterns, natural hues, and mod ideas into a one-of-
a-kind style that works in almost any decor—really. Good throw pillows, too. 47 Green
St. (at Broome St.). © 212/941-8950. www.jonathanadler.com. Subway: N, R to Canal St. Also at 1097
Madison Ave. (btwn 83rd and 84th sts.). © 212/722-3410. Subway: 6 to 86th St.

kar'ikter *(Finds*   New York's biggest collection of sleek and playful Alessi housewares
from Italy (including Michael Graves's iconic teakettle with bird whistle), as well as
European animation cells and toys starring Tintin, Babar, and Asterix. 19 Prince St. (btwn
Elizabeth and Mott sts.). © 212/274-1966. www.karikter.com. Subway: 6 to Spring St.

Leader Restaurant Equipment & Supplies *(Value*   The Bowery is the place to
find restaurant-supply-quality kitchenware, and Leader is the best dealer on the block.
This big, bustling, friendly shop is a good source for Chinese and Japanese wares—
chopsticks, rice and noodle bowls, sushi plates, sake cups, and the like. You'll see a lot
of the same styles you'd find at the high-end home stores in SoHo or the Village but
at a fraction of the prices (this is where they buy, too). 191 Bowery (btwn Spring and Delancey
sts.). © 800/666-6888 or 212/677-1982. Subway: 6 to Spring St.

Moss   If you have any interest in modern industrial design, don't miss this sleek,
brightly lit store. All kinds of everyday objects are reinvented by cutting-edge European

designers, from staplers to flatware to shelving units. The products were designed with 21st-century homes in mind, so they're surprisingly utilitarian and space-efficient—not to mention pricey. 146 Greene St. (btwn Houston and Prince sts.). ℭ 212/204-7100. www.mossonline.com. Subway: N, R to Prince St.

Royal Hut   After traveling the globe with her husband, Island Records founder Chris Blackwell, Mary Vinson merged her design degree and her world-travel experience to create her own line of cross-cultural home furnishings. Her own gorgeous line of textiles has been handcrafted by weavers and dyers in Europe, Africa, and Asia. Also expect a stunning collection of dishware, glassware, vessels, and accessories in a riot of Asian- and African-inspired color and texture—ideal for the global home. 328 E. 59th St. (btwn First and Second aves.). ℭ 212/207-3027. www.royalhut.com. Subway: 4, 5, 6 to 59th St.

Terence Conran Shop   Sir Terence Conran rules the London design and restaurant world, and now he's looking to make inroads in America with this bold sleek home shop. It's like an upscale—and, frankly, overpriced—version of IKEA, with lots of sleek contemporary lines, lightweight materials (chrome, blond woods, colorful plastic), and fun twists on standard household goods. Still, he set the tone for affordable contemporary design, and that alone makes this bright, browsable multilevel shop well worth a look. 407 E. 59th St. (at First Ave.). ℭ 212/755-9079. www.conran.com. Subway: 4, 5, 6 to 59th St.

Waterworks   The place to give that most sacred of rooms, the bath, a whole new, luxurious look. Half the store displays top-quality, hard-to-find designer hardware and fixtures, while the other half is dedicated to thick Egyptian terry towels, robes, and bathmats, plus stylish accessories for easy reinvention. 469 Broome St. (at Greene St.). ℭ 212/966-0605. www.waterworks.com. Subway: 6 to Canal St.; N, R to Prince St. Also at 225 E. 57th St. (btwn Second and Third aves.). ℭ 212/371-9266. Subway: 4, 5, 6 to 59th St.

JEWELRY & ACCESSORIES

Every big-name international jewelry merchant has a shop on Fifth Avenue in the 50s: glam Italian jeweler **Bulgari,** 730 Fifth Ave., at 57th Street (ℭ 212/315-9000; www.bulgari.com); royal jeweler **Asprey & Garrard,** no. 725, at 56th Street (ℭ 212/688-1811); ultraglamorous **Harry Winston,** no. 718, also at 56th Street (ℭ 212/245-2000; www.harrywinston.com); **Cartier,** housed in a stunningly restored mansion at 653 Fifth Ave., at 52nd Street (ℭ 212/446-3400; www.cartier.com); and, best of all, **Van Cleef & Arpels,** 744 Fifth Ave., at 57th Street (ℭ 212/644-9500; www.vancleef.com), which also has a boutique at Bergdorf's.

Some of the smaller boutique names are on Madison Avenue in the 60s. **Fred Leighton,** 773 Madison Ave., at 66th Street (ℭ 212/288-1872; www.fredleighton.com), specializes in magnificent estate jewelry.

Boucher *(Finds*   This jewel box of a store sparkles on a gentrifying corner of the Meat-Packing District. Designer Laura Mady and her staff handcraft feminine, nature-inspired necklaces, earrings, and other jewelry using unusual gemstones in organic shapes and freshwater pearls in soft ice cream hues. Affordable, and ideal for dressing up or everyday. 9 Ninth Ave. (near Little W. 12th St., next to Pastis). ℭ 212/206-3775. www.boucherjewelry.com. Subway: A, C, E to 14th St.; L to Eighth Ave.

Doyle & Doyle *(Finds*   Elizabeth Doyle's lovely antiques boutique offers further evidence of the transformation of the Lower East Side from old-world cheap to exceptionally chic. Doyle & Doyle specializes in fine antique and estate jewelry, from the

⟨Value⟩ **The Diamond District**

West 47th Street between Fifth and Sixth avenues is the city's famous Diamond District. Apparently more than 90% of the diamonds sold in the United States come through this neighborhood first, so there are some great deals to be had if you're in the market for a nice rock or a piece of fine jewelry. The street is lined with showrooms; and you'll be wheeling and dealing with the largely Hasidic dealers, who offer quite a juxtaposition to the crowds. For a complete introduction to the district, including smart buying tips, point your Web browser to **www.diamonddistrict.org**. If you're in the market for wedding rings, there's only one place to go: Herman Rotenberg's **1,873 Unusual Wedding Rings**, 4 W. 47th St., booth 86 (ⓒ **800/877-3874** or 212/944-1713; www.unusual weddingrings.com). For semiprecious stones, head 1 block over to the **New York Jewelry Mart**, 26 W. 46th St. (ⓒ **212/575-9701**). Virtually all of these dealers are open Monday through Friday only.

Georgian period to contemporary items. Pieces are all carefully chosen and beautifully displayed. 189 Orchard St. (btwn Houston and Stanton sts.). ⓒ 212/677-9991. www.doyledoyle.com. Subway: F to Second Ave. (exit at the front of the train and walk 1 block east).

Fortunoff ⟨Value⟩   Despite the high-ticket facade, Fortunoff is a good resource for Swatch watches and a nice place to start pricing classic pieces: gold earrings, necklaces, bracelets, and the like. The styles aren't innovative, but the store tries to keep up an image as a discounter, and prices are low. Great for silver and wedding gifts, too. 681 Fifth Ave. (btwn 53rd and 54th sts.). ⓒ **800/FORTUNOFF** or 212/758-6660. www.fortunoff.com. Subway: E, F to Fifth Ave.

Jill Platner ⟨Finds⟩   Platner's Aboriginal- and nature-inspired silver pieces are bold enough to look great on both men and women. Many are strung on brightly colored Tenara (a Gore-Tex-like thread) for a prehistoric-meets-21st century feel. Prices are quite reasonable; it's easy to find a cool pair of earrings or a groovy ring for just a little more than $100. 113 Crosby St. (btwn Houston and Prince sts.). ⓒ **212/324-1298**. www.jillplatner. com. Subway: N, R to Prince St.

Push   Often featuring rough-hewn finishes and asymmetrical gems and stones, Karen Karch's eye-catching jewelry has attracted an A-list clientele to her atmospheric Nolita shop. Six degrees of separation moment: If you buy one of her pieces, you'll take home a work of art from the designer who worked with Ethan Hawke to design Uma Thurman's wedding ring. Wonder whatever became of that ring? 240 Mulberry St. (btwn Prince and Spring sts.). ⓒ 212/965-9699. Subway: 6 to Spring St.

Tiffany & Co.   The most famous jewelry store in New York—and maybe the world—deserves all the kudos. This wonderful multilevel store offers a breathtaking selection of jewelry, signature watches, tableware and stemware, and a handful of surprisingly affordable gift items. The store is so full of tourists that it's easy to browse without having any intention of buying. Believe it or not, it's not hard to find a lovely wearable piece in silver (Tiffany's best color, in my opinion) for around $200. If you do indulge, anything you buy—even a $50 silver bookmark or key chain—comes wrapped in that unmistakable blue box with a white ribbon tied just so. 727 Fifth Ave. (at 57th St.). ⓒ **212/755-8000**. www.tiffany.com. Subway: N, R to Fifth Ave.

Tourneau Time Machine   The snazzy three-floor emporium on East 57th Street is the world's largest watch store, carrying more than 90 brands and 8,000 different styles. The mind-boggling selection runs the gamut from Swatch to Rolex; Swiss Army knives, too. 12 E. 57th St. (btwn Fifth and Madison aves.). ℂ 212/758-7300. www.tourneau.com. Subway: N, R to Fifth Ave. Also at 500 Madison Ave. (at 52nd St.). ℂ 212/758-6098. Subway: 6 to 51st St. 200 W. 34th St. (at Seventh Ave.). ℂ 212/563-6880. Subway: 1, 2, 3 to 34th St. 10 Columbus Circle (The Shops at Columbus Circle). ℂ 212/823-9425. Subway: A, B, C, D, 1 to Columbus Circle.

LOGO STORES

Mets Clubhouse Shop   Stop in for goods galore—baseball caps, T-shirts, posters, Piazza jerseys, '69 Miracle Mets memorabilia, and much more amazin' merchandise. You can buy regular-season game tix here, too. 11 W. 42nd St. (btwn Fifth and Sixth aves.). ℂ 212/768-9534. Subway: B, D, F, V to 42nd St.

The MTV Store   This petite boutique sits streetside, below the MTV studio. There's not much here—but your kids will surely find something they want. *Celebrity Death-match* T-shirt, anyone? Flyers advertising for audience members for MTV shows are sometimes on hand at the register—yet another reason for your teen to drag you in. 1515 Broadway (at 44th St.). ℂ 212/846-5655. Subway: 1, 2, 3, 7, N, R, S to 42nd St./Times Sq.

NBA Store *ℱ*   For all things NBA and WNBA, head to this three-level megastore, a multimedia celebration of pro hoops, complete with a bleacher-seated arena for player appearances and signings. 666 Fifth Ave. (at 52nd St.). ℂ 212/515-6221. www.nbastore. com. Subway: B, D, F, V to 47th–50th sts./Rockefeller Center.

NBC Experience   This mammoth, neon-lit store sits directly across from the *Today* show studio and sells all manner of NBC-themed merchandise, from Matt and Al's favorite mugs to a "You're Fired" T-shirt to a "Fear Factor" 3-D Bug Mug. And yes, there is a clearance department with merch from canceled shows . . . Your kids will enjoy the silly interactive features, like the virtual-reality "Conan O'Brien's Wild Desk Ride," as well as the second-level candy shop. NBC Studio Tours also leave from here; call for details. 30 Rockefeller Plaza (at 49th St.). ℂ 212/664-3700. www.nbcuniversalstore.com. Subway: B, D, F, V to 47th–50th sts./Rockefeller Center.

New York Firefighter's Friend *Finds*   What better way to spend your souvenir budget than by saluting New York's bravest? Here's the place to purchase FDNY logo wear, including T-shirts, sweatshirts, hats, and more. The goods are all top-quality, and a portion of the profits support the widows and children of the 343 firefighter victims lost in the September 11, 2001, terrorist attacks. 263 Lafayette St. (btwn Prince and Spring sts.). ℂ 212/226-3142. www.nyfirestore.com. Subway: 6 to Spring St.

New York 911 *Finds*   Adjacent to Firefighter's Friend (above) is the place to shop for not only NYPD logo wear, but also EMT, FBI, and NYC-coroner gear. The bounty includes shirts, caps, badge pins, patches, logo toys, and much more. (Not all of the products are licensed by the city, however; I suggest trying to stick with those that are.) The store is well stocked and fun to browse, making it a great place to buy souvenirs and gifts for the folks back home. A portion of the proceeds goes to NYPD-related charities. 263 Lafayette St. (btwn Prince and Spring sts.). ℂ 888/723-3907 or 212/219-3907. www.ny911.com. Subway: 6 to Spring St.

Niketown   More multimedia advertorial than sportswear store, Niketown is surprisingly low-key and attractive, with five floors of shoes and athletic wear displayed in Lucite and polished-metal surroundings. "Museum" cases display Sneakers of the

Rich and Famous, and you're assailed by images of celebrity pitchmen and women. No sales or bargains here—plan on paying top dollar for the high-style athletic wear. Somebody's gotta pay for this place! 6 E. 57th St. (btwn Fifth and Madison aves.). © 212/891-6453. www.niketown.com. Subway: N, R to Fifth Ave.

Yankees Clubhouse Shop   For all your Bronx Bombers needs—hats, jerseys, jackets, and so on. Tickets for regular-season home games are also for sale, and there's a limited selection of other New York team jerseys. 245 W. 42nd St. (btwn Seventh and Eighth aves.). © 212/768-9555. Subway: A, C, E to 42nd St./Port Authority. Also at 393 Fifth Ave. (btwn 36th and 37th sts.). © 212/685-4693. Subway: 6 to 33rd St. 110 E. 59th St. (btwn Park and Lexington aves.). © 212/758-7844. Subway: 4, 5, 6 to 59th St. 8 Fulton St. (in the South St. Seaport). © 212/514-7182. Subway: 2, 3, 4, 5 to Fulton St.

MUSEUM STORES

In addition to these standouts, other noteworthy museum shops worth seeking out include the **New York Public Library,** the **Museum for African Art, The Jewish Museum,** and the **American Folk Art Museum** (see chapter 8).

Maxilla & Mandible *(Finds*   This shop is not affiliated with the American Museum of Natural History, but a visit here makes a good adjunct to your trip to the museum (which is around the corner). It may look like a freak shop at first glance, but it's really a fascinating natural-history emporium. Inside you'll find unusual rocks and shells from around the world, luminescent butterflies in display boxes, even surprisingly affordable real fossils containing prehistoric fish and insects that come with details on their history and where they were excavated. There's also a good variety of natural-history-themed toys for the kids. 451 Columbus Ave. (btwn 81st and 82nd sts.). © 212/724-6173. www.maxillaandmandible.com. Subway: B, C to 81st St.

Metropolitan Museum of Art Store   Given the scope of the museum itself, it's no wonder that the gift shop is outstanding. Many treasures from the museum's collection have been reproduced as jewelry, china, and other objets d'art. The range of art books is dizzying, and upstairs is an equally comprehensive selection of posters and inventive children's toys. 1000 Fifth Ave. (at 82nd St.). © 212/570-3894. www.metmuseum.org/store. Subway: 4, 5, 6 to 86th St. Also at Rockefeller Center, 15 W. 49th St. © 212/332-1360. Subway: B, D, F, V to 47th–50th sts./Rockefeller Center. 113 Prince St. (at Greene St.). © 212/614-3000. Subway: N, R to Prince St. On the mezzanine level at Macy's, 34th St. and Sixth Ave. © 212/268-7266. Subway: B, D, F, N, R, Q to 34th St./Herald Sq.

MoMA Design Store   Across the street from the Museum of Modern Art is this terrific shop, whose stock ranges from museum posters and clever toys for kids to fully licensed reproductions of many of the classics of modern design, including free-form Alvar Aalto vases, Frank Lloyd Wright chairs, and Eames recliners. If these high-design items are out of your reach, choose from plenty of more affordable outré home accessories. The SoHo store is equally fabulous. 44 W. 53rd St. (btwn Fifth and Sixth aves.). © 212/767-1050. www.momastore.org. Subway: E, F to Fifth Ave.; B, D, F, Q to 47th–50th sts./Rockefeller Center. Also at 81 Spring St. (at Crosby St.). © 646/613-1367. Subway: 6 to Spring St.

New York Transit Museum Store   Lots of nifty transportation-themed gifts—the cufflinks made out of vintage subway tokens are just great. With all this train stuff, my 4-year-old son could spend hours here. Grand Central Terminal (on the main level, in the shuttle passage next to the Station Masters' office), 42nd St. and Lexington Ave. © 212/878-0106. Subway: 4, 5, 6, 7, S to 42nd St./Grand Central. Also at 1560 Broadway (at 47th St.). © 212/230-4901. Subway: 1 to 50th St. Boerum Place (at Schermerhorn St.), Brooklyn. © 718/694-5100. Subway: 4, 5 to Borough Hall.

MUSIC

AUDIO & VIDEO

Academy Records & CDs   This Flatiron District shop has a cool intellectual air that's more reminiscent of a good used-book store than your average used-record store. Academy is always filled with classical, opera, and jazz junkies perusing the extensive and well-priced collection of used CDs and vinyl. In addition to the extensive classical and jazz collection is a variety of other audiophile favorites, from rare '60s pop songsters to spoken word. 12 W. 18th St. (btwn Fifth and Sixth aves.). ℂ 212/242-3000. www.academy-records.com. Subway: L, N, R, 4, 5, 6 to 14th St./Union Sq.

Colony Music Center ℱ   This long-lived Theater District shop ("since 1948") is housed in the legendary Brill Building, the Tin Pan Alley of 1950s and 1960s pop, where songwriters like Leiber and Stoller and producers like Don Kirshner and Phil Spector crafted the soundtrack for a generation. It's the perfect home for Colony, a nostalgia emporium filled with a pricey but excellent collection of vintage vinyl and new CDs. You'll find a great collection of Broadway scores and cast recordings; decades worth of recordings by pop song stylists both legendary and obscure; the city's best collection of sheet music (including some hard-to-find international stuff); and a great selection of original theater and movie posters. 1619 Broadway (at 49th St.). ℂ 212/265-2050. www.colonymusic.com. Subway: N, R to 49th St.; 1 to 50th St.

Footlight ℱ *(Finds*   If you like Colony (see above), also check out this dreamy collection of vintage vinyl, strong in jazz and pop vocalists, soundtracks, and show tunes. 113 E. 12th St. (btwn Third and Fourth aves.). ℂ 212/533-1572. www.footlight.com. Subway: L, N, R, 4, 5, 6 to 14th St./Union Sq.

Generation Records *(Value*   This tidy little store sells mostly CDs and is an excellent source for "import" live recordings. Originally specializing in hard-core, punk, and heavy metal, the new collection upstairs still has a heavy edge but has since diversified appreciably. Downstairs is a well-organized and well-priced used-CD selection that's not as picked over as most and runs the genre gamut; there's also a good selection of used LPs. Despite the help's tough look, they're actually quite friendly and helpful. 210 Thompson St. (btwn Bleecker and 3rd sts.). ℂ 212/254-1100. Subway: A, B, C, D, E, F, V to W. 4th St.

House of Oldies ℱ   I skipped many a high school class to spend time in this old store searching for doo-wop. I think it was here that I bought a mint "Woo Woo Train," by the Valentines, on Rama Records for less than $5. That same record now probably costs over $60 and you can probably still find it at the House of Oldies. The store has over one million vinyl records in stock in everything from R&B to surf music. If vinyl oldies are your thing, there's no better place. 35 Carmine St. (at Bleecker St.). ℂ 212/243-0500. www.houseofoldies.com. Subway: A, B, C, D, F, V to W. 4th St.

Jazz Record Center   I have a friend from Paris who lives for jazz and this is the first place he hits whenever he visits New York. It's *the* place to find rare and out-of-print jazz records. In addition to the extensive selection of CDs and vinyl (including 78s), videos, books, posters, magazines, photos, and other memorabilia are available. Prices start at $5 for vinyl, $10 for CDs, and soar from there, befitting the rarity of the stock. Owner Frederick Cohen is extremely knowledgeable, so come here if you're trying to track down something obscure. (Cohen does mail-order business as well.) 236 W. 26th St. (btwn Seventh and Eighth aves., 8th floor). ℂ 212/675-4480. www.jazzrecordcenter.com. Subway: 1 to 28th St.

Other Music *(Finds)*   Head to Other Music for the wildest sounds in town. You won't find a major label here. This shop focuses exclusively on small international labels, especially those on the cutting edge. The bizarro runs the gamut from underground Japanese spin doctors to obscure Irish folk; needless to say, the world-music selection is terrific—fascinating and bound to be filled with music you've never heard of. The sales staff really know their stuff, so ask away. 15 E. 4th St. (btwn Broadway and Lafayette St.). ✆ 212/477-8150. www.othermusic.com. Subway: F, V to Broadway–Lafayette St.; 6 to Astor Place.

Virgin Megastore   In the heart of Times Square, this superstore bustles day and night. For the size of it, the selection isn't as wide as you'd think; still, you're likely to find what you're looking for among the two levels of domestic and import CDs. Other pluses are an extensive singles department, a phenomenal number of listening posts, plus a huge video department. There's also a bookstore, a cafe, and a multiplex movie theater, and you can even arrange airfare on Virgin Atlantic with the on-site travel agent. Look for a busy schedule of in-store appearances at both locations. 1540 Broadway (at 45th St.). ✆ 212/921-1020. www.virginmega.com. Subway: N, R, 1, 2, 3, 7 to Times Sq./42nd St. Also at 52 E. 14th St. (at Broadway). ✆ 212/598-4666. Subway: 4, 5, 6, N, R, L to 14th St./Union Sq.

PAPER & STATIONERY

Kate's Paperie *(R)*   Three cheers to Kate's for keeping the art of letter writing alive in our computer age. You could browse for hours among this delightful shop's hand-made stationery and wrap, innovative invitations and thank-yous, imported notebooks, writing tools, and other creative paper products, including cool paper lampshades. Lovely art cards, too—perfect for writing the folks back home—a joy! The SoHo location is best. 561 Broadway (btwn Prince and Spring sts.). ✆ 212/941-9816. www.katespaperie.com. Subway: N, R to Prince St. Also at 8 W. 13th St. (btwn Fifth and Sixth aves.). ✆ 212/633-0570. Subway: F to 14th St. 1282 Third Ave. (btwn 73rd and 74th sts.). ✆ 212/396-3670. Subway: 6 to 77th St. 140 W. 57th St. (btwn Sixth and Seventh aves.). ✆ 212/459-0700. Subway: 1, 2, 3 to 34th St.

SHOES

Designer shoe shops start on **East 57th Street** and amble up **Madison Avenue,** becoming pricier as you move uptown. **SoHo** is an excellent place to search for the latest styles; the streets are overrun with terrific shoe stores. Cheaper copies of the trendiest styles are sold along **8th Street** between Broadway and Sixth Avenue in the Village, which some people call Shoe Row.

Most department stores have two shoe departments—one for designer stuff and one for daily wearables. See "The Top Shopping Streets & Neighborhoods" and "The Big Department Stores," earlier in this chapter. For **Prada** and **Polo/Ralph Laren,** see "Clothing," and for **Niketown,** see "Logo Stores," both earlier in this section.

Camper   This Big Apple outpost features the full line of made-in-Spain Camper footwear for men and women. These are the hippest walking shoes and boots on the planet, hands down—ideal for those with an eye for style and a craving for comfort. 125 Prince St. (at Wooster St.). ✆ 212/358-1842. www.camper.com. Subway: N, R to Prince St.; C, F to Spring St.

Giraudon New York   This French designer makes fashionable, well-made street shoes for hip men and women who want something clean-lined and stylish but not too chunky or trendy. Not cheap, but not overpriced—these shoes last forever. Prices run $115 to $200, and sales are excellent. 152 Eighth Ave. (btwn 17th and 18th sts.). ✆ 212/633-0999. www.giraudonnewyork.com. Subway: A, C, E to 14th St.; L to Eighth Ave.

Harry's Shoes ✩   This shoe store was an Upper West Side institution even before gentrification hit the neighborhood over 20 years ago. They were one of the first shoe stores to carry New Balance in the city and now their selection of brands range from Bruno Magli to retro Keds. With a huge selection of children's brands, Harry's is the place for kids' shoes, which is why you might want to stay away, unless you don't mind parental hysteria during the back-to-school frenzy of late August as well as the presummer camp throngs that descend in late June. 2299 Broadway (at 83rd St.). © 212/874-2035. www.harrys-shoes.com. Subway: 1 to 86th St.

Jimmy Choo   *The* boutique for *sexy* stilettos. The shoe display is gorgeous at this sophisticated three-floor emporium. 645 Fifth Ave. (at 51st St.). © 212/593-0800. www.jimmy choo.com. Subway: E, F to Fifth Ave. Also at 716 Madison Ave. (at 63rd St.). © 212/759-7078. Subway: F, V to Lexington Ave.

Manolo Blahnik   These wildly sexy women's shoes are notorious for their cut and sway and the way they shape the leg. Most famous are the catch-me-if-you-can high heels, but there are plenty of flats and low heels, too. Custom shoes in your own fabric are also a possibility. 31 W. 54th St. (btwn Fifth and Sixth aves.). © 212/582-3007. Subway: E, F to Fifth Ave.

Sacco   These mostly Italian-made women's shoes and wonderful boots combine style with supreme comfort. Good prices and sales, too. 94 Seventh Ave. (btwn 15th and 16th sts.). © 212/675-5180. www.saccoshoes.com. Subway: 1 to 18th St. Also at 14 E. 17th St. (btwn Fifth Ave. and Broadway). © 212/243-2070. Subway: L, N, R, S, 4, 5, 6 to 14th St./Union Sq. 111 Thompson St. (btwn Prince and Spring sts.). © 212/925-8010. Subway: C, E to Spring St. 324 Columbus Ave. (btwn 75th and 76th sts.). © 212/799-5229. Subway: B, C to 81st St. 2355 Broadway (at 86th St.). © 212/ 874-8362. Subway: 1 to 86th St.

Sigerson Morrison *Finds*   Women who love shoes and are willing to pay in the neighborhood of $200 to $300 for something really special should make a beeline for this Nolita shop. These fashion-forward originals wow with their immaculate details, bright color palette, and sexy, strappy retro appeal—worth every penny. You'll also find some of their styles at Bergdorf Goodman and Saks if you don't want to go downtown. Attention, bargain hunters: Check out the January winter and August summer sales; prices drop to less than half of retail as the sales wind down. 28 Prince St. (btwn Mott and Elizabeth sts.). © 212/219-3893. www.sigersonmorrison.com. Subway: B, D, F, Q to Broadway–Lafayette St.; N, R to Prince St.; 6 to Spring St.

SPORTING GOODS

Modell's ✩   I confess, like the annoying ad, I often "gotta go to Mo's." And I have my reasons. The best is the very reasonable prices, especially for sneakers and other footwear. Another is the excellent selection of team apparel; I can get my retro New York Giant football cap at half the price that they sell it at Giants' Stadium. And there are stores in practically every neighborhood, making it very convenient to "go to Mo's." 1293 Broadway (at 33rd St.). © 212/244-4544. www.modells.com. Subway: B, D, F, N, R, V to 34th St. Also at 300 W. 125th St. (at Frederick Douglass Blvd.). © 212/280-9100. Subway: A, B, C, D to 125th St. 51 E. 42nd St. (at Vanderbilt Ave.). © 212/661-4242. Subway: 4, 5, 6, 7, S to Grand Central. 55 Chambers St. (at Broadway). © 212/732-8484. Subway: E to Chambers St.

Paragon Sporting Goods   The emphasis at this excellent all-purpose sporting-goods store—New York's best—is on equipment and athletic wear for virtually every sport, from tennis to biking to mountain climbing. End-of-the-season sales, especially on sneakers and outdoor clothing, bring serious discounts. 867 Broadway (at 18th St.). ℭ **800/ 961-3030** or 212/255-8036. www.paragonsports.com. Subway: L, N, R, 4, 5, 6 to 14th St./Union Sq.

Patagonia   Expensive though it may be, Patagonia deserves kudos for its commitment to producing efficient and eco-friendly sports and adventure wear—fleece pullovers made from recycled plastic soda bottles, shell jackets in ultralight weatherproof materials, and organic cotton T-shirts. 101 Wooster St. (btwn Prince and Spring sts.). ℭ **212/343-1776**. www.patagonia.com. Subway: N, R to Prince St.; C, E to Spring St. Also at 426 Columbus Ave. (btwn 80th and 81st sts.). ℭ **917/441-0011**. Subway: B, C to 81st St.

TOYS
If your kids love to read, don't miss **Books of Wonder** (p. 320). For vintage toys, check out **Alphaville** (p. 318).

American Girl Place ✦   Your princess will never forgive you if you don't take her to this 43,000-square-foot emporium for little girls featuring a cafe, bookstore, and theater. If you come, don't forget to bring her favorite doll so it can get a makeover at the store's own doll salon. Birthday parties at the store are extremely popular, so if you want to plan one for your visit to New York, make sure to book well in advance. 609 Fifth Ave. (at 49th St.). ℭ **800/845-0005** (for reservations) or 212/371-2220. www.americangirl.com. Subway: B, D, F, V to 47th–50th sts./Rockefeller Center.

FAO Schwarz   After closing due to bankruptcy, this venerable toy institution reopened just before Christmas 2004. After eliminating products carried by the big discounters, FAO Schwarz now carries those hard-to-find and oh-so-expensive items like Vespa scooters for older children, mini–luxury cars like Hummers and Jaguars, and serious karaoke machines. There's also a soda fountain where the kids can load up on sugar to fuel their romp through the magical store. The giant piano keys made famous in the movie *Big* thankfully still remain. 767 Fifth Ave. (at 58th St.). ℭ **212/ 644-9400**, ext. 4242. www.faoschwarz.com. Subway: N, R to Fifth Ave.

Kidding Around   This boutique stocks pricey, high-quality toys, many imported from Europe. The emphasis is on the old-fashioned—low-tech goodies like puzzles, rocking horses, and tops. One wall is devoted exclusively to tub toys, windups, and other stocking stuffers. 60 W. 15th St. (btwn Fifth and Sixth aves.). ℭ **212/645-6337**. www.kidding aroundnyc.com. Subway: F to 14th St.

Toys "R" Us   Geoffrey the Giraffe must be mighty pleased with this multilevel, high-tech home. It occupies almost an entire city block in the heart of Times Square, and even boasts its own full-scale Ferris wheel, which kids can ride for free. The huge collection is very well organized, and the store's "ambassadors" are abundant and very helpful; they'll even point you to restaurants and kid-friendly attractions in the neighborhood. Don't miss it if you're traveling with kids. 1514 Broadway (at 44th St.). ℭ **800/869- 7787**. Subway: 1, 2, 3, 7 to 42nd St. Also at 24–30 Union Sq. ℭ **212/674-8697**. Subway: 4, 5, 6, N, R, L, S to 14th St./Union Sq.

WINE & SPIRITS
Acker Merrall & Condit Co.   In business since 1820—which makes Acker America's oldest wine shop—this attractive little store is the Upper West Side's best wine source. There are no bad bottles here. The careful selection is well displayed, with authoritative cards attached to each bin to help you choose. A supremely knowledgeable staff is on hand for additional assistance. 160 W. 72nd St. (btwn Broadway and Columbus Ave.). ℭ **212/787-1700**. www.ackerwines.com. Subway: 1, 2, 3 to 72nd St.

Astor Wines & Spirits *(Value)*   This large store is the source for excellent values on liquor and wine; their stock is deep and diverse. The staff is always willing to recommend a vintage. Astor hosts excellent wine tastings 2 to 3 afternoons a week, often paired with edibles from local restaurants and gourmet shops; call or check the website for the schedule. 399 Lafayette St. (at 4th St). © 212/674-7500. www.astoruncorked.com. Subway: 6 to Astor Place.

Morrell & Company   One of the leading retailers in America boasts a friendly, helpful staff and has a Fine Wine Division that hosts high-profile auctions. Adjacent is the **Morrell Wine Bar & Cafe** (© 212/262-7700; www.morrellwinebar.com), an ideal place to sample the goods. 1 Rockefeller Plaza (at 49th St.). © 212/688-9370. www.morrellwine.com. Subway: B, D, F, V to 47th–50th sts./Rockefeller Center.

Sherry-Lehmann *(★)*   Zagat's has called Sherry-Lehmann "the Rolls-Royce" of wine shops, and the readers of *Decanter* magazine just named it Best Wine Merchant in the United States. Their vast inventory is mind-boggling and includes ritzy gift baskets that make luxurious gifts. Service is excellent and free wine tastings are often offered. Although expensive, this is the place to come if you're looking for a special bottle. 679 Madison Ave. (btwn 61st and 62nd sts.). © 212/838-7500. www.sherry-lehmann.com. Subway: N, R to Lexington Ave.; 4, 5, 6 to 59th St.

Union Square Wines and Spirits *(★) (Finds)*   This small, cozy wine store squeezes in over 4,000 varieties of wines. There are numerous wine tastings throughout the week and recommendations by sommeliers from local restaurants. The store is well located across from the Union Square Greenmarket. If you have loaded up with fresh produce for a picnic, have the very personable clerks pair a wine with your food. 140 Fourth Ave. (at 13th St.). © 212/675-8100. www.unionsquarewines.com. Subway: L, N, R, 4, 5, 6 to 14th St./Union Sq.

10

New York City After Dark

New York's nightlife scene is an embarrassment of riches. There's so much to see and do in this city after the sun goes down that your biggest problem is probably going to be choosing among the many temptations.

There's no way that I can tell you in these pages what's going to be on the calendar while you're in town. For the latest, most comprehensive nightlife listings, from theater and performing arts to live music, and dance-club coverage, *Time Out New York* (www.timeoutny.com) is my favorite weekly source; a new issue hits newsstands every Thursday. The free weekly *Village Voice* (www.villagevoice. com), the city's legendary alterna-paper, is available late Tuesday downtown and early Wednesday in the rest of the city, with even more listings than in the paper copy online at their web site. The arts and entertainment coverage couldn't be more extensive, and just about every live-music venue advertises its shows here.

The *New York Times* (www.nytoday. com) features terrific entertainment coverage, particularly in the two-part Friday "Weekend" section. The cabaret, classical-music, and theater guides are particularly useful. Other great weekly sources are the *New Yorker* (www.newyorker.com), in its "Goings on About Town" section; and *New York* magazine (www.nymag.com, an excellent online source) features the latest happenings in its "The Week" section.

Bar-hoppers should get a hold of the comprehensive *Shecky's New York Bar, Club & Lounge Guide,* printed annually. The website (**www.sheckys.com**) is even more current and offers updated nightlife news at the click of a button.

Another good online bar source is **www.murphguide.com**. This website has all the latest happy-hour information and is a particularly good source if you are seeking out an Irish pub, of which there are many in New York.

NYC/Onstage (© 212/768-1818; www.tdf.org) is a recorded service providing schedules, descriptions, and other details on theater and the performing arts. The bias is toward plays, but NYC/Onstage is a good source for chamber and orchestral music (including all Lincoln Center events), dance, opera, cabaret, and family entertainment.

1 All the City's a Stage: The Theater Scene

Nobody does theater better than New York. No other city—not even London—has a theater scene with so much breadth and depth, with so many wide-open alternatives. Broadway, of course, gets the most ink and the most airplay, and deservedly so. It's where you'll find the big stage productions, from crowd-pleasing warhorses like *The Lion King* to more recent hits like *Jersey Boys.* But today's scene is thriving beyond the bounds of just Broadway—smaller, "alternative" theater has taken hold of the popular imagination, too. With bankable stars onstage, crowds lining up for hot tickets, and hits popular enough to generate major-label cast albums, Off-Broadway isn't just for culture vultures anymore. (And Off-Off-Broadway is the cheapest theater in town, usually well under $20 a ticket.)

I can't tell you precisely what will be on while you're in town, so check the publications listed at the start of this chapter or the websites listed in "Online Sources for Theatergoers & Performing-Arts Fans," below, to get an idea of what you might like to see. Another useful source is the **Broadway Line** (© **888/BROADWAY;** www.live broadway.com), where you can get details and descriptions on current Broadway shows, hear about special offers and discounts, and choose to be transferred to Telecharge or Ticketmaster to buy tickets. The recorded service **NYC/Onstage** (© **212/768-1818;** www.tdf.org) provides the same kind of service for both Broadway and Off-Broadway productions.

Helping to ensure the recent success of the New York theater scene has been the presence of Hollywood stars like Julia Roberts, Harry Connick, Jr., Julianne Moore, Antonio Banderas, Brooke Shields, Kevin Bacon, Liam Neeson, and Dame Judi Dench. But keep in mind that stars' runs are often limited, and tickets tend to sell out fast. If you hear that there's a celeb you'd like to see coming to the New York stage, don't put off your travel and ticket-buying plans. (The box office can tell you how long a star is contracted for a role.)

THE BASICS

The terms **Broadway, Off-Broadway,** and **Off-Off-Broadway** refer to theater size, pay scales, and other arcane details, not location—or, these days, even star wattage. Most of the Broadway theaters are in Times Square, huddled around the thoroughfare the scene is named for, but not directly on it: Instead, you'll find them dotting the side streets that intersect Broadway, mostly in the mid-40s between Sixth and Eighth avenues (44th and 45th sts. in particular) but running north as far as 53rd Street. There's even a Broadway theater outside Times Square: the Vivian Beaumont in Lincoln Center, on the Upper West Side at Broadway and 65th Street.

Off-Broadway, on the other hand, is not so much about location (it has to do with the contract the production has with Actors Equity). Off-Off-Broadway shows tend to be more avant-garde, experimental, and/or nomadic, in smaller theaters, usually with fewer than 100 seats, with fewer performances per week and overall. Off-Broadway productions usually run longer and on the usual 8-a-week performance schedule in slightly larger theaters. These productions are all over town, but there are mini–Theater Districts within Midtown and on the Upper West Side, as well as downtown.

Broadway shows tend to keep pretty regular **schedules.** There are usually eight performances a week: evening shows Tuesday through Saturday, plus matinees on Wednesday, Saturday, and Sunday. Evening shows are usually at 8pm, while matinees are usually at 2pm on Wednesday and Saturday, and 3pm on Sunday, but schedules can vary, especially Off and Off-Off-Broadway. In recent years, especially with shows that are popular with a younger audience, shows sometimes offer more matinees, or earlier curtain times for evening performances. Broadway shows usually start on the dot, or within a few minutes of starting time; if you arrive late, you may have to wait until after the first act to take your seat (and with the plethora of shows without intermission, you may have to watch the whole thing on a monitor in the lobby!)

Ticket prices for Broadway shows vary dramatically. Expect to pay a *lot* for good seats; the high end for any given show is likely to be between $60 and $100 or more (though some shows have recently started charging premium prices for the very best

Theater District Theaters

seats, competing with the licensed ticket brokers). The cheapest end of the price range can be as low as $20 or as high as $50, depending on the theater configuration (or if they offer standing-room or rush tickets). If you're buying tickets at the low end of a wide available range, be aware that you may be buying obstructed-view seats. If all tickets are the same price or the range is small, you can pretty much count on all of the seats being pretty good. Otherwise, price is your barometer. Note that legroom can be tight in these old theaters, and you'll usually get more in the orchestra seats.

Off-Broadway and Off-Off-Broadway shows tend to be cheaper, with tickets often as low as $10 or $15. However, seats for the most established shows and those with star power can command prices as high as $50 to $75.

Don't let price be a deterrent to enjoying the theater. There are ways to pay less if you're willing to make the effort and be flexible, with a few choices at hand as to what you'd like to see. Read on.

TOP TICKET-BUYING TIPS
BEFORE YOU LEAVE HOME

Phone ahead or go online for tickets to the most successful or popular shows as far in advance as you can—in the case of shows like *The Lion King* (yes, even after all these years), it's never too early.

Buying tickets can be simple if the show you want to see isn't sold out. You need only call such general numbers as **Telecharge** (© 212/239-6200; www.telecharge. com), which handles most Broadway and Off-Broadway shows and some concerts, or **Ticketmaster** (© 212/307-4100; www.ticketmaster.com), which also handles Broadway and Off-Broadway shows and most concerts.

Theatre Direct International (TDI) is a ticket broker that sells tickets for select Broadway and Off-Broadway shows—including some of the most popular crowd-pleasers, like *Jersey Boys* and *Wicked!*—directly to individuals and travel agents. Check to see if they have seats to the shows you're interested in by calling © **800/BROAD-WAY** or 212/541-8457; you can also order tickets through TDI via their commercial website, **www.broadway.com**. (Disregard the discounted prices, unless you're buying for a group of 20 or more.) Because there's a minimum service charge of $15 per ticket, you'll definitely do better by trying Ticketmaster or Telecharge first; but because they act as a consolidator, TDI may have tickets left for a specific show even if the major outlets don't.

Another reputable ticket broker is **Keith Prowse & Co.** (© 800/669-8687; www. keithprowse.com). For a list of other licensed ticket brokers recommended by the New York Convention & Visitors Bureau (NYCVB), get a copy of the Official NYC Visitor Kit (see "Visitor Information," in chapter 3, for details). All kinds of ticket brokers list ads in the Sunday *New York Times* and other publications, but don't take the risk. Stick with a licensed broker recommended by the NYCVB.

You may have heard about a new development on the Broadway ticket scene: **Broadway Inner Circle** (© 866/847-8587; www.broadwayinnercircle.com), the ticket agency that, in a supposed effort to circumvent scalpers, has arranged with select in-demand shows to sell select premium seats for prices close to $500 a ticket. If price is no object, you might want to try this service.

If you don't want to pay a service charge, try calling or visiting the **box office** directly. Broadway theaters don't sell tickets over the telephone—the one major exception, the **Roundabout Theatre Company** (© 212/719-1300; www.roundabouttheatre.org), charges a $5-per-ticket "convenience" fee—but a good number of Off-Broadway theaters do.

Also, before you call a broker to snag tickets to a hot show, consider calling the **concierge** at the hotel where you'll be staying. If you've chosen a hotel with a well-connected concierge, he or she may be able to have tickets waiting for you when you check in—for a premium, of course. For more on this, see "When You Arrive," below.

For details on how to obtain advance-purchase theater tickets at a discount, see "Reduced-Price Ticket Deals," below.

Online Sources for Theatergoers & Performing-Arts Fans

Some of your best, most comprehensive, and up-to-date information sources for what's going on about town are in cyberspace.

Three competing commercial sites—**Broadway.com** (www.broadway.com), **Playbill Online** (**www.playbill.com** or www.playbillclub.com), and **TheaterMania** (**www.theatermania.com**)—offer complete information on Broadway and Off-Broadway shows, with links to the ticket-buying agencies once you've selected your show. Each offers an **online theater club** that's free to join and can yield substantial savings—as much as 50%—on advance-purchase theater tickets for select Broadway and Off-Broadway shows. All you have to do is register, and you'll have access to discounts that can range from a few dollars to as much as 50% off regular ticket prices. You can sign up to be notified by e-mail as offers change. By far, I like the *Playbill Club* best; it was the first of the bunch, and its discount offers tend to be the most wide-ranging, often including the best Broadway and Off-Broadway shows. TheaterMania's **TM Insider** is the runner-up; the Broadway.com site wants a bit too much personal information for my taste. Nothing prevents you from signing up with all of them and taking advantage of the best deals.

As an information source for Broadway shows, you can't beat **LiveBroadway.com** (**www.livebroadway.com**), the official website of Broadway, sponsored by the League of American Theatres and Producers. Theater buffs will also enjoy perusing the **Internet Broadway Database** (**www.ibdb.com**), the official archival database for Broadway theater information, past and present.

WHEN YOU ARRIVE

Once you arrive in the city, getting your hands on tickets can take some street smarts—and failing those, cold hard cash. Even if it seems unlikely that seats are available, always **call or visit the box office** before attempting any other route. Single seats are often easiest to obtain, so people willing to sit apart from their companions may find themselves in luck.

You should also try the **Broadway Ticket Center,** run by the League of American Theatres and Producers (the same people behind LiveBroadway.com, above) at the Times Square Information Center, 1560 Broadway, between 46th and 47th streets (open Mon–Sat 10am–6pm; Sun 10am–3pm; hours subject to seasonal changes). They often have tickets available for otherwise sold-out shows, both for advance and same-day purchase, and only charge about $5 extra per ticket.

Even if saving money isn't an issue for you, check the boards at the **TKTS Booth** in Times Square; more on that can be found under "Reduced-Price Ticket Deals," below.

In addition, your **hotel concierge** may be able to arrange tickets for you. These are usually purchased through a broker and a premium will be attached, but they're usually good seats and you can count on them being legitimate. (A $20 tip to the

Kids Take the Stage: Family-Friendly Theater

The family-friendly theater scene is flourishing these days. There's so much going on that it's best to check *New York* magazine, *Time Out New York,* or the Friday *New York Times* for current listings. Besides larger-than-life general-audience Broadway shows, the following offer some dependable kid-targeted entertainment options.

The stunningly renovated **New Victory Theater,** 209 W. 42nd St., between Seventh and Eighth avenues (℃ 646/223-3020; www.newvictory.org), is a full-time family-oriented performing-arts center, and has hosted companies ranging from the Trinity Irish Dance Company to the astounding Flaming Idiots, who juggle everything from fire and swords to beanbag chairs.

The **Paper Bag Players** (℃ 212/663-0390; www.paperbagplayers.org), called "the best children's theater in the country" by *Newsweek,* perform funny tales for children 4 to 9 in a set made from bags and boxes, in winter only, at Hunter College's Sylvia and Danny Kaye Playhouse, 68th Street between Park and Lexington avenues (℃ 212/772-4448). If you can't make it to the Kaye, call the Players to inquire whether they'll be staging other performances about town.

TADA! Youth Theater, 15 W. 28th St., between Fifth Avenue and Broadway (℃ 212/252-1619; www.tadatheater.com), is a terrific youth ensemble that performs musicals and plays with a multi-ethnic perspective for kids, including teens, and their families.

The **Swedish Cottage Marionette Theatre** (℃ 212/988-9093; www.central park.org) puts on marionette shows for kids at its 19th-century Central Park theater throughout the year. Reservations are a must.

The "World Voices Club" of the **New Perspectives Theatre,** 456 W. 37th St. at Tenth Avenue (℃ 212/630-9945; www.newperspectivestheatre.org),

concierge for this service is reasonable—perhaps even more if the tickets are for an extremely hot show. By the time you've paid this tip, you might come out better by contacting a broker or ticket agency yourself.) If you want to deal with a licensed broker directly, **Keith Prowse & Co.** has a local office that accommodates drop-ins at 234 W. 44th St., between Seventh and Eighth avenues, Suite 1000 (℃ **800/223-6108;** open Mon–Sat 9am–8pm; Sun noon–7pm).

If you buy from one of the **scalpers** selling tickets in front of the theater doors, you're taking a risk. They may be perfectly legitimate—a couple from the 'burbs whose companions couldn't make it for the evening, say—but they could be swindlers passing off fakes for big money. It's a risk that's not worth taking.

One preferred **insiders' trick** is to make the rounds of Broadway theaters at about 6pm, when unclaimed house seats are made available to the public. These tickets—reserved for VIPs, friends of the cast, the press, or other hangers-on—offer great locations and are sold at face value.

Also, note that **Monday** is often a good day to cop big-name show tickets. Though most theaters are dark on that day, some of the most sought-after choices aren't. Locals has a different puppet show each month based on fables from different world cultures.

While David Mamet hardly seems like a playwright for the kiddies, the "Atlantic for Kids" series is making a go of it at the **Atlantic Theater Company, 336 W. 20th St.**, between Eighth and Ninth avenues (© **212/645-8015; www.atlantictheater.org**), which Mamet co-founded with Academy Award–nominated actor William H. Macy.

Another excellent troupe that excels at children's theater is the **Vital Theatre Company,** 2162 Broadway, between 76th and 77th streets (© **212/579-0528; www.vitaltheatre.org**); it's well worth seeing what's on.

If you want to introduce your kids to the magic of live opera, check out the "Opera in Brief" program, which runs most Saturdays at 11:30am, at **Amato Opera Theatre** (p. 352). For kid-friendly classical music, see what's on at **Bargemusic** (p. 353), which presents kid-friendly chamber-music concerts throughout their regular season. Look for Young People's Concerts and Kidzone Live!, in which kids get to interact with orchestra members prior to curtain time, at the **New York Philharmonic** (p. 354). Also check to see what's on for the entire family at **Carnegie Hall** (p. 356), which offers family concerts for a bargain-basement ticket price of just $8, plus the CarnegieKids program, which introduces kids ages 3 to 6 to basic musical concepts through a 45-minute music-and-storytelling performance. And don't forget "Jazz for Young People," Wynton Marsalis's stellar family concert series at **Jazz at Lincoln Center** (p. 358) and the new "Jazz for Kids" program at the **Jazz Standard** (p. 367), 116 E. 27th St., between Park and Lexington avenues (© **212/576-2232; www.jazzstandard.net**), which takes place every Sunday afternoon.

are at home on the first night of the workweek, so all the odds are in your favor. Your chances will always be better on weeknights, or for Wednesday matinees, rather than weekends. *Note:* If you're in town especially to see a big star in a show, check to see that said big star is playing all eight shows a week. While most producers' contracts with visiting Hollywood stars (think Julia Roberts or Denzel Washington) require them to play every performance, if it's a vocally demanding role, they may hand the matinees off to their understudies.

REDUCED-PRICE TICKET DEALS

Your best bet is to try before you go. You may be able to purchase **reduced-price theater tickets** in advance over the phone (or in person at the box office) by joining one or more of the online theater clubs. Membership is free and can garner you discounts of up to 50% on select Broadway and Off-Broadway shows. For further details, see "Online Sources for Theatergoers & Performing-Arts Fans," above.

Broadway shows—even blockbusters—sometimes have a limited number of cheaper tickets set aside for students and seniors, and they may even be available at the last

Tips   More Dramatic Venues Worth Seeking Out

When you want a spectacle, there's no place like Broadway: For jukebox musicals, singing green witches and collapsing chandeliers, Broadway is your ticket (and a high-priced one it is, too!). But you can see some amazing work at prices ranging from just-below-Broadway to less than $20 if you know where to look. For Off-Broadway, expect to pay $20 to $65 or so for tickets; Off-Off-Broadway rarely charges more than $20, and you can sometimes get in for $12 or less (so you don't feel as bad leaving at intermission if the show's a stinker!). There are even some theaters that let you see the show for free if you volunteer to usher. (See each company's website for information about how far ahead you should call or email).

Where do you find the hidden gems? The *Village Voice* (which sponsors the annual Obies, or Off-Broadway Awards) is a good source. *Timeout New York* has excellent listings and capsule descriptions for major Off-Broadway productions, as well as a decent listing of Off-Off shows. For more offerings Off-Off-Broadway, check the reviews on **Theatermania.com** (which also lets you purchase tickets and offers regular discounts) and **NYTheatre.com**.

Three resident theaters in New York—**Lincoln Center Theater** (p. 357), the **Roundabout Theatre** (p. 346), and **Manhattan Theatre Club** (www.mtc-nyc. org)—present work in Broadway houses, as well as in smaller venues Off-Broadway. You'll pay Broadway prices (or whatever discount you can get) for the best seats in the big houses, but you can also usually find special, lower prices for students or seniors; or last-minute rush tickets. In their smaller spaces (MTC's Stage II; the Roundabout's Laura Pels Theatre; Lincoln Center's Mitzi Newhouse) you can find good seats for less than $50 to see new plays and revivals by the likes of Terrence McNally and John Patrick Shanley. These theaters often offer extra events like "talkbacks" with the cast and production team, and so on—sometimes free, sometimes for a small charge. Following are a few other notable Off- and Off-Off-Broadway venues, but these are just the tip of the iceberg; check out the sources listed above for many, many more options.

- **Joseph Papp Public Theater** ⟨R⟩, 425 Lafayette St. (© 212/539-8500; www. publictheater.org). Legendary among Off-Broadway theaters, this is the legacy of the late visionary theater producer Joseph Papp. The Public draws top talent to the stage with its groundbreaking stagings of Shakespeare's

minute; call the box office directly to inquire. *Rent* has offered all kinds of bargains to keep younger theatergoers coming.

The best deal in town on same-day tickets for both Broadway and Off-Broadway shows is at the **Times Square Theatre Centre,** better known as the **TKTS** booth run by the nonprofit Theatre Development Fund in the heart of the Theater District. At press time its long-time home at Duffy Square, 47th Street and Broadway was undergoing renovation, and the TKTS booth is temporarily housed across the street outside the New York Marriott Marquis between Broadway and Eighth avenues. The new plays as well as new plays, classical dramas, and solo performances. The Public also hosts New York's best annual alfresco event, **Shakespeare in the Park,** each summer (see the box "Park It! Shakespeare, Music & Other Free Fun," on p. 360). If that's not enough, it's also home to **Joe's Pub** (p. 369).

- **Atlantic Theater Company,** 336 W. 20th St. (btwn Eighth and Ninth aves.). (© **212/645-8015;** www.atlantictheater.org), "produces great plays simply and truthfully, utilizing an artistic ensemble," according to its mission statement. It has recently presented new work by David Mamet, and the musical *Spring Awakening* transferred to Broadway in the spring of 2007, where it won the Tony award for best musical. The Atlantic also accepts volunteer ushers.

- **Signature Theatre Company,** 555 W. 42nd St. (© **212/244-PLAY;** www. signaturetheatre.org), presents season-long explorations of a play-wright's work. You can also volunteer usher here. A corporate grant guaranteed that every seat in the 2007-2008 Charles Mee season (with a "legacy" performance of an Edward Albee play) is available for $20.

- **New York Theater Workshop (NYTW),** 79 E. 4th St. (© **212/460-5475;** www. nytw.org), has been around since 1979, but it was *Rent* that put it on the map. Since the great success of the still-running (and now filmed) musical, several other plays developed by NYTW have gone on to award-winning commercial runs. NYTW specializes in new work, rethought revivals, and collaborations. All Sunday evening performances are $20; there are discounts for students and opportunities to usher.

- **Emerging Artists Theatre (EAT),** © **212/247-2429;** www.eatheatre.org, has been producing new plays Off-Off-Broadway for 14 years and always seems to have something on offer: its fall and spring EATFests of short plays, its award-winning Triple Threat Premieres (three new full-length plays in repertory), and an annual month-long developmental series, which includes programs like One Woman Standing (solo shows), Laugh Out Loud (comedy), Notes on a Page (musicals), and Catch a Cabaret with ticket prices in the $10 range.

—Kathleen Warnock

booth is set to open by the end of 2007. The booth is open 3–8pm for evening performances, 10am–2pm for Wed and Sat matinees, from 11am–8pm on Sun for all performances.

Tickets for that day's performances are usually offered at half price, with a few reduced only 25%, plus a $2.50-per-ticket service charge. Boards outside the ticket windows list available shows; you're unlikely to find the biggest hits, but most other shows turn up. Only cash and traveler's checks are accepted (no credit cards). There's often a huge line, so show up early for the best availability and be prepared to wait—but frankly, the crowd is all part of the fun. If you don't care much what you see and you'd just like to go to a show, you can walk right up to the window later in the day and something's always available.

You can also get same-day tickets to evening shows at the **TKTS Lower Manhattan Theatre Centre,** at South Street Seaport, located at the corner of Front and John streets at 199 Water St. (open Mon–Sat 11am–6pm; subway: 2, 3, 4, 5 to Fulton St.). All the same policies apply. The advantages to coming down here are that the lines are generally shorter, and matinee tickets are available the day before, so you can plan ahead.

Visit **www.tdf.org** or call **NYC/Onstage** at ℂ **212/768-1818** and press "8" for the latest TKTS information.

2 Opera, Classical Music & Dance

While Broadway is the Big Apple's greatest hit, many other performing arts also flourish in this culturally rich and entertainment-hungry town.

In addition to the listings below, see what's happening at **Carnegie Hall** and the **Brooklyn Academy of Music,** two of the most respected—and enjoyable—multifunctional performing-arts venues in the city. The marvelous **92nd Street Y** also regularly hosts events that are worth considering. I've listed the operatic and symphonic companies housed at **Lincoln Center** below; also check the center's full calendar for all offerings. See "Major Concert Halls & Landmark Venues," below.

OPERA

New York has grown into one of the world's major opera centers. The season generally runs September through May, but there's usually something going on at any time of year.

Amato Opera Theatre *(Finds* This cozy, off-the-beaten-track venue functions as a showcase for talented young American singers. The intimate 100-plus-seat house celebrates its 60th season in 2007 amid a rising reputation and increasing ticket sales. The staple is full productions of Italian classics—Verdi's *La Traviata,* Puccini's *Madame Butterfly,* Bizet's *Carmen,* with an occasional Mozart tossed in—at great prices for regular performances ($30, $25 for seniors and kids). Performances, usually held on Saturday and Sunday, now regularly sell out, so it's a good idea to reserve 3 weeks in advance.

Note for adults: On one Saturday a month, "Opera in Brief" offers fully costumed, kid-length versions of the classics interwoven with narration so chaperones have a palatable forum in which to introduce the little ones to opera. At $15 or so per ticket, these matinee performances are wallet-friendly, too. 319 Bowery (at 2nd St.). ℂ **212/228-8200.** www.amato.org. Subway: F to Second Ave.; 6 to Bleecker St.

Metropolitan Opera Tickets can cost a fortune—anywhere from $25 to $295. But for its full productions of the classic repertory and a schedule packed with world-class grand sopranos and tenors, the Metropolitan Opera ranks first in the world. Millions are spent on fabulous stagings, and the venue itself is a wonder of acoustics. Whatever is on the schedule, the quality will be second to none.

To guarantee that its audience understands the words, the Met has outfitted the back of each row of seats with screens for subtitles—translation help for those who want it, minimum intrusion for those who don't. James Levine continues his role as the brilliant and popular conductor of the orchestra. At the Metropolitan Opera House, Lincoln Center, Broadway and 64th St. ℂ **212/362-6000.** www.metopera.org. Subway: 1 to 66th St.

New York City Opera   The New York City Opera is a superb company, with a delightful duality to its approach: It not only attempts to reach a wider audience than the Met with its more "human" scale and significantly lower prices ($32–$115), but it's also committed to adventurous premieres, new operas, the occasional avant-garde work, American musicals *(Porgy and Bess)* and novels *(Of Mice and Men)* presented as fresh, innovative operettas, and even obscure works by mainstream or lesser-known composers. Its mix stretches from the "easy" works of Puccini, Verdi, and Gilbert and Sullivan to the more challenging oeuvres of the likes of Arnold Schönberg and Philip Glass. At the New York State Theater, Lincoln Center, Broadway and 64th St. © 212/870-5570 (information or box office), or 212/307-4100 for Ticketmaster. www.nycopera.com or www.ticketmaster.com. Subway: 1 to 66th St.

New York Gilbert and Sullivan Players   If you're in the mood for lighthearted operetta, try this lively company, which specializes in Gilbert and Sullivan's 19th-century English comic works. Tickets are affordable, usually in the $40-to-$65 range (exact prices for the 2007–08 season were not yet determined at press time). The annual calendar generally runs from October through April and includes four shows a year, with some performances held at **City Center** (p. 355). At Symphony Space, Broadway and 95th St. © 212/864-5400 or 212/769-1000. www.nygasp.org. Subway: 1, 2, 3 to 96th St.

CLASSICAL MUSIC

Bargemusic ✦ *(Finds*   Many thought Olga Bloom peculiar, if not deranged, when she transformed a 40-year-old barge into a chamber-music concert hall. More than 20 years later, Bargemusic is an internationally renowned recital room boasting more than 100 first-rate chamber-music performances a year. Visiting musicians love the chance to play in such an intimate setting, so the roster regularly includes highly respected international musicians as well as local stars like violinist Cynthia Phelps.

There are three shows per week, on Thursday and Friday evenings at 7:30pm and Sunday afternoon at 4pm. The musicians perform on a small stage in a cherry-paneled, fireplace-lit room accommodating 130. The barge may creak a bit and an occasional boat may speed by, but the music rivals what you'll find in almost any other New York concert hall—and the panoramic view through the glass wall behind the stage can't be beat. Neither can the price: Tickets are just $35 ($25 for students), or $40 for performances by larger ensembles. Reserve well in advance. At Fulton Ferry Landing (just south of the Brooklyn Bridge), Brooklyn. © 718/624-2083 or 718/624-4061. www.bargemusic. org. Subway: 2, 3 to Clark St.; A, C to High St.

The Juilliard School *(Value*   During its school year, the nation's premier music-education institution sponsors about 550 performances of the highest quality—at the lowest prices. With most concerts free and $20 as a maximum ticket price, Juilliard is one of New York's greatest cultural bargains. Though most would assume that the school presents only classical-music concerts, Juilliard also offers other music as well as drama, dance, opera, and interdisciplinary works. The best way to find out about the wide array of productions is to call, visit the school's website (click on "Complete Calendar of Events"), or consult the bulletin board in the building's lobby. Note that tickets are sometimes required even for free performances. Watch for master classes and discussions open to the public featuring celebrity guest teachers. 60 Lincoln Center Plaza (Broadway at 65th St.). © 212/799-5000, or 212/721-0965 to charge tickets. www.juilliard.edu. Subway: 1 to 66th St.

Tips Last-Minute Ticket Buying

Most seats at New York Philharmonic performances are sold to subscribers, with just a few left for the rest of us. But there are still ways to get tickets. Periodically, a number of same-day orchestra tickets are made available at the Philharmonic and sold first thing in the morning for $25 a pop (two-ticket maximum). They usually go on sale at 10am weekdays, 1pm Saturday (noon if there's a matinee). And when subscribers can't attend, they may turn their tickets back to the theaters, which then resell them at the last moment. These can be in the most coveted rows of the orchestra. Ticket holders can donate unwanted tickets until curtain time, so tickets that are not available first thing in the morning may become available later in the day. The hopeful form "cancellation lines" 2 hours or more before curtain time for a crack at returned tickets on a first-come, first-served basis. Senior/student/disability rush tickets may be available for $10 (two-ticket max) on concert day, but never at Friday matinees or Saturday evening performances. To check availability for any of these programs at all performances, call Audience Services at ℂ **212/875-5656** before you head to the box office.

Note that Lincoln Center's **Alice Tully Hall** (where the Chamber Music Society performs and other concerts are held), the **Metropolitan Opera**, the **New York City Opera**, and **Carnegie Hall** offer similar last-minute and discount programs (the **New York City Ballet** offers Student Rush tickets only). It makes sense to call the box office first to check on same-day availability before heading to the theater—or, if you're willing to risk coming away empty-handed, be there at opening time for first crack.

New York Philharmonic   Symphony-wise, you'd be hard-pressed to do better than the New York Philharmonic. The country's oldest orchestra is now under the guidance of distinguished conductor Lorin Maazel, formerly of the Bavarian Radio Symphony Orchestra. Don't expect quality to falter one bit. There's a summer season in July, when themed classics brighten the hall, as well as free summer concerts in Central Park that are worth checking into.

Tickets range from $28 to $94; opt for a rush-hour concert or a matinee for the lowest across-the-board prices. If you can afford it—and if the tickets are available—it's well worth it to pay for prime seats. The acoustics of the hall are such that, at the midrange price points, I prefer the second tier (especially the boxes) over the more expensive rear orchestra seats. Go cheap if you have to; you're sure to enjoy the program from any vantage point. At Avery Fisher Hall, Lincoln Center, Broadway at 65th St. ℂ **212/875-5656** for audience services, 212/875-5030 for box office information, or Center Charge at 212/721-6500 for tickets. www.newyorkphilharmonic.org. Subway: 1 to 66th St.

DANCE

In general, dance seasons run September through February and then March through June, but there's almost always something going on. In addition to the major venues and troupes discussed below, some other names to keep in mind are the **Brooklyn Academy of Music,** the **92nd Street Y, Radio City Music Hall,** and **Town Hall** (see "Major Concert Halls & Landmark Venues," below). For particularly innovative works, see what's on at the **Dance Theater Workshop**, in the Bessie Schönberg Theater, 219 W. 19th St., between Seventh and Eighth avenues (© **212/691-6500** or 212/924-0077; www.dtw.org), a first-rate launching pad for nearly a quarter century.

In addition to regular appearances at City Center (below), the **American Ballet Theatre** (www.abt.org) takes up residence at Lincoln Center's Metropolitan Opera House (© **212/477-3030**) for 8 weeks each spring. The same venue also hosts such visiting companies as the Kirov, Royal, and Paris Opéra ballets.

The weekly *Time Out New York,* available on newsstands around town, maintains a section dedicated to dance events around town that's an invaluable resource to fans.

City Center   Modern dance usually takes center stage in this Moorish dome-topped performing-arts palace. The companies of Merce Cunningham, Martha Graham, Paul Taylor, Alvin Ailey, Twyla Tharp, the Dance Theatre of Harlem, and the American Ballet Theatre are often on the calendar. Don't expect cutting edge—but do expect excellence. Sightlines are terrific from all corners, and a new acoustical shell means the sound is pitch-perfect. Ticket prices range from $25 to $100. 131 W. 55th St. (btwn Sixth and Seventh aves.). © **212/247-0430** or 212/581-1212. www.citycenter.org. Subway: F, N, Q, R, W to 57th St.; B, D, E to Seventh Ave.

Joyce Theater   Housed in an old Art Deco movie house, the Joyce has grown into one of the world's greatest modern-dance institutions. You can see everything from Native American ceremonial dance to Maria Benites Teatro Flamenco to the innovative works of Pilobolus to the Martha Graham Dance Company. In residence annually is Eliot Feld's ballet company, Ballet Tech, which WQXR radio's Francis Mason called "better than a whole month of namby-pamby classical ballets." The Joyce has a second space, **Joyce SoHo,** where you can see rising young dancers and experimental works in the intimacy of a 70-seat performance space. In either space, seats go for $35 to $45. 175 Eighth Ave. (at 19th St.). © **212/242-0800**. www.joyce.org. Subway: C, E to 23rd St.; 1 to 18th St. **Joyce SoHo** at 155 Mercer St. (btwn Houston and Prince sts.). © **212/431-9233**. Subway: N, R to Prince St.

New York City Ballet   Highly regarded for its unsurpassed technique, the New York City Ballet is the world's best. The company renders with happy regularity the works of two of America's most important choreographers: George Balanchine, its founder, and Jerome Robbins. Under the direction of Ballet Master in Chief Peter Martins, the troupe continues to expand its repertoire and performs to a wide variety of classical and modern music. The cornerstone of the annual season is the Christmastime production of *The Nutcracker,* for which tickets usually become available in early October. Ticket prices for most events run $28 to $66. At the New York State Theater at Lincoln Center, Broadway at 64th St. © **212/870-5570**. www.nycballet.com. Subway: 1 to 66th St.

3 Major Concert Halls & Landmark Venues

Apollo Theater ⟨ *Moments*   Built in 1914, this legendary Harlem theater launched or abetted the careers of countless musical icons—including Bessie Smith, Billie Holiday, Dinah Washington, Duke Ellington, Ella Fitzgerald, Sarah Vaughan, Count Basie, and Aretha Franklin. And thousands lined the streets in December of 2006 to pay their last respects to the Godfather of Soul on the Apollo stage, the place where he performed some of the greatest shows of all time. This historic venue is in large part responsible for the development and worldwide popularization of black music in America. By the 1970s, it had fallen on hard times, but a 1986 restoration breathed new life into the landmark. In 1992 a major $65-million restoration project was inaugurated and should be completed by 2009. The first phase of that project—refurbishing the terra-cotta facade, a new box office, and a high-tech marquee retaining the original 1940s style and features—was unveiled in late 2005. The theater remains open during the renovations and is still internationally renowned for its African-American acts of all musical genres, from hip-hop acts to Wynton Marsalis's "Jazz for Young People" events. Wednesday's "Amateur Night at the Apollo" is a loud, fun-filled night that draws in young talents from all over the country with high hopes of making it big (a very young Lauryn Hill started out here—and didn't win!). 253 W. 125th St. (btwn Adam Clayton Powell and Frederick Douglass boulevards). ℂ 212/531-5300 or 212/531-5301. www.apollotheater.com. Subway: 1 to 125th St.

Brooklyn Academy of Music *(Finds* BAM is the city's most renowned contemporary-arts institution, presenting cutting-edge theater, opera, dance, and music. Offerings have included historically informed presentations of baroque opera by William Christie and Les Arts Florissants; pop opera from Lou Reed; Marianne Faithfull singing the music of Kurt Weill; dance by Mark Morris and Mikhail Baryshnikov; the Philip Glass ensemble accompanying screenings of *Koyaanisqatsi* and Lugosi's original *Dracula;* the Royal Dramatic Theater of Sweden directed by Ingmar Bergman; and many more experimental works by both renowned and lesser-known international artists as well as visiting companies from all over the world.

Of particular note is the **Next Wave Festival,** September through December, this country's foremost showcase for new experimental works (see the "New York City Calendar of Events," in chapter 3). The **BAM Rose Cinemas** show first-run independent films, and there's free live music every Thursday, Friday, and Saturday night at **BAMcafé,** which can range from atmospheric electronica by cornetist Graham Haynes to radical jazz from the Harold Rubin Trio to the tango band Tanguardia! ($10 food minimum). 30 Lafayette Ave. (off Flatbush Ave.), Brooklyn. ℂ 718/636-4100. www. bam.org. Subway: 2, 3, 4, 5, M, N, Q, R, W to Pacific St./Atlantic Ave.

Carnegie Hall *(ℛℛ* Perhaps the world's most famous performance space (*How* do you get there?), Carnegie Hall offers everything from grand classics to the music of Ravi Shankar. The **Isaac Stern Auditorium,** the 2,804-seat main hall, welcomes visiting orchestras from across the country and the world. Many of the world's premier soloists and ensembles give recitals. The legendary hall is visually and acoustically brilliant; don't miss an opportunity to experience it if there's something on that interests you.

Within the hall, there's also the intimate 268-seat **Weill Recital Hall,** usually used to showcase chamber music and vocal and instrumental recitals. Carnegie Hall has also, after being occupied by a movie theater for 38 years, reclaimed the ornate underground 650-seat **Zankel Concert Hall.** For last-minute ticket-buying tips, see the box on p. 354. 881 Seventh Ave. (at 57th St.). ℂ 212/247-7800. www.carnegiehall.org. Subway: N, Q, R, W to 57th St.

Lincoln Center for the Performing Arts New York is the world's premier performing-arts city, and Lincoln Center is its premier institution. Whenever you're planning an evening's entertainment, check the offerings here which can include opera, dance, symphonies, jazz, theater, film, and more, from the classics to the contemporary. Lincoln Center's many buildings serve as permanent homes to their own companies as well as major stops for world-class performance troupes from around the globe.

Resident companies include the following: The **Chamber Music Society of Lincoln Center** (ℂ 212/875-5788; www.chambermusicsociety.org) performs at Alice Tully Hall or the Daniel and Joanna S. Rose Rehearsal Studio, often in the company of such

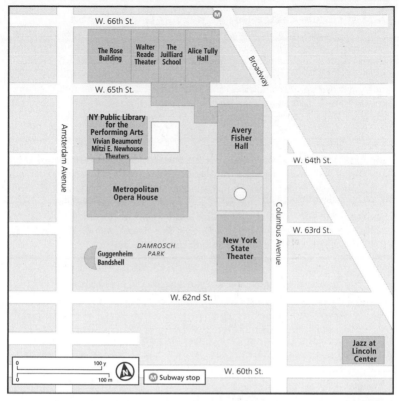

high-caliber guests as Anne Sofie von Otter and Midori. The **Film Society of Lincoln Center** (*℗* **212/875-5600;** www.filmlinc.com) screens a daily schedule of movies at the Walter Reade Theater, and hosts a number of important annual film and video festivals as well as the Reel to Real program for kids, pairing silent screen classics with live performance. **Lincoln Center Theater** (*℗* **212/362-7600;** www.lct.org) consists of the Vivian Beaumont Theater, a modern and comfortable venue with great sightlines that has been home to much good Broadway drama, and the Mitzi E. Newhouse Theater, a well-respected Off-Broadway house that has also boasted numerous theatrical triumphs. Past seasons have included excellent productions of Tom Stoppard's *Arcadia, Carousel* in revival, and the Tony Award–winning *Light in the Piazza.*

For details on the **Metropolitan Opera,** the **New York City Opera,** the **New York City Ballet, The Juilliard School,** the phenomenal **New York Philharmonic,** and the **American Ballet Theatre,** which takes up residence here every spring, see "Opera, Classical Music & Dance," earlier in this chapter.

Most of the companies' **major seasons** run from about September or October to April, May, or June. **Special series** like Great Performers and the new American Songbook, showcasing classic American show tunes, help round out the calendar. Indoor and outdoor events are held in warmer months: Summer kicks off with the **JVC Jazz**

Jazz at Lincoln Center: Not Actually at Lincoln Center

I'm usually a stickler for accuracy, but I'll make an exception for **Jazz at Lincoln Center,** which is not in Lincoln Center, but a few blocks south in the Time Warner Center at Broadway and 60th Street on Columbus Circle ((✆ **212/258-9800;** www.jalc.org). Though the move was slightly downtown, this was definitely a move up. Its complex on the fourth floor of Time Warner's northern tower features two amazing performance spaces, a jazz club, a mini jazz hall of fame, and a 7,000-square-foot atrium with views of Central Park.

The largest of the three venues is the **Rose Theater,** where you might see the Lincoln Center Jazz Orchestra, led by Wynton Marsalis, performing the swing music of Thad Jones. Acoustics are perfect and seating is spacious. The jewel of the Center is the **Allen Room** with its 4,500-square-foot glass backdrop behind the main stage offering glittering views of Central Park and the Manhattan night sky. Hard to believe that what was once played in smoky basements is now presented in venues as spectacular and opulent as these.

Also at Jazz at Lincoln Center is **Dizzy's Club Coca-Cola** ((✆ **212/258-9595;** p. 366), a stylish, intimate jazz club that's open every day.

Festival in June; July sees **Midsummer Night's Swing,** with partner dancing, lessons, and music on the plaza; August's **Mostly Mozart** attracts talents like Alicia de Larrocha and André Watts; **Lincoln Center Festival** celebrates the best of the performing arts; **Lincoln Center Out-of-Doors** is a series of free alfresco music and dance performances; there's also the **New York Film Festival,** and more. Check the "New York City Calendar of Events" section, in chapter 3, or Lincoln Center's website to see what special events will be on while you're in town.

Tickets for all performances at Avery Fisher and Alice Tully halls can be purchased through **CenterCharge** (✆ **212/721-6500**) or online at www.lincolncenter.org (click on "Event Calendar"). Tickets for all Lincoln Center Theater performances can be purchased thorough **Telecharge** (✆ **212/239-6200;** www.telecharge.com). Tickets for New York State Theater productions (New York City Opera and Ballet companies) are available through **Ticketmaster** (✆ **212/307-4100;** www.ticketmaster.com), while tickets for films showing at the Walter Reade Theater can be bought up to 7 days in advance by calling ✆ **212/496-3809.** For last-minute ticket-buying tips, see the box on p. 354.

Lincoln Center is also home to the **New York Public Library for the Performing Arts** (✆ **212/870-1630;** www.nypl.org), which is now reopened after a major renovation.

Offered daily, 1-hour **guided tours** of Lincoln Center tell the story of the great performing-arts complex, and even offer glimpses of rehearsals; call ✆ **212/875-5350.** 70 Lincoln Center Plaza (at Broadway and 64th St.). ✆ **212/546-2656** or 212/875-5456. www.lincoln center.org. Subway: 1 to 66th St.

Madison Square Garden   U2, Springsteen, the Stones, Lauryn Hill, and other monsters of rock and pop regularly fill this 20,000-seat arena, which is also home to pro sports teams like the Knicks, the Rangers, and the Liberty. A cavernous concrete hulk, it's better suited to sports than to concerts, or in-the-round events such as the Ice Capades, Ringling Bros. and Barnum & Bailey Circus, or the International Cat Show. If you end up with seats in the back, you'd better have binoculars.

You'll find far better sightlines at the **Theater at Madison Square Garden,** an amphitheater-style auditorium with 5,600 seats that has also played host to some major pop stars, from the Rolling Stones to Bob Dylan. Watch for annual stagings of *The Wizard of Oz, A Christmas Carol,* and family shows such as *Sesame Street Live.* Newest at MSG is the **Comedy Garden** (www.comedygarden.com), the Garden's own comedy club at the theater, where talent runs the gamut from well-known local comics to Robin Williams and Joan Rivers.

The box office is located at Seventh Avenue and 32nd Street. Or you can purchase tickets through **Ticketmaster** (© 212/307-7171; www.ticketmaster.com). On Seventh Ave. from 31st to 33rd sts. © 212/465-MSG1. www.thegarden.com. Subway: A, C, E, 1, 2, 3 to 34th St.

92nd Street Y Tisch Center for the Arts *Value* This generously endowed community center offers a phenomenal slate of top-rated cultural happenings, from classical to folk to jazz to world music to cabaret to lyric theater and literary readings. Just because it's the Y, don't think this place is small potatoes: Great classical performers— Isaac Stern, Janos Starker, Nadja Salerno-Sonnenberg—give recitals here. In addition, the full concert calendar often includes luminaries such as Max Roach, John Williams, and Judy Collins; Jazz at the Y from Dick Hyman and guests; the long-standing Chamber Music at the Y series; the classical Music from the Jewish Spirit series; and regular cabaret programs. The lectures-and-literary-readings calendar is unparalleled, with featured speakers ranging from James Carville to Ralph Nader to Katie Couric to Erica Jong to Ken Burns to Elie Wiesel to Alan Dershowitz to A. S. Byatt to . . . the list goes on and on. There's a regular schedule of modern dance, too, through the Harkness Dance Project. Best of all, readings and lectures are usually priced between $20 and $30 for nonmembers, dance is usually $20, and concert tickets generally go for $15 to $50—half or a third of what you'd pay at comparable venues. Additionally,

---

Moments **Music Under New York**

The noise of honking horns, car alarms, and sirens are not the only sounds you will hear in your travels around Manhattan. Music is everywhere. In the warm weather, a trumpet player or violinist will set up at a busy corner and play for hours. In the winter musicians head into subway stations, where, legally, they are not allowed to play, but I've rarely seen the law enforced. Many are very good, while others, well, are just trying to make a few bucks. Some of the good ones, who actually audition for the opportunity, perform under a program sponsored by the New York Metropolitan Transit Authority (MTA) called "Music Under New York." If selected, they can perform legally at designated subway stations, including Times Square/42nd Street, 34th Street/Sixth Avenue, 14th Street/Union Square, and 59th Street/Columbus Circle. In the summer there is a Music Under New York festival at Grand Central Station and Bowling Green Park. The variety of music is amazing and the quality is as good as you might see at some of New York's clubs. In subway stations I've heard gospel, blues, Cajun, Dixieland jazz, Andean, Brazilian drumming, rumba, and my favorite, doo-wop, the original sound of the New York subways. So take a few moments before boarding your train and listen to the music. For more information, visit the MTA website (**www.mta.nyc.ny.us/mta/aft/muny.htm**).

Park It! Shakespeare, Music & Other Free Fun

As the weather warms, New York culture comes outdoors to play.

Shakespeare in the Park, a New York institution since 1957, is as much a part of a New York summer as fireworks on the Fourth of July. The outdoor free event at the open-air Delacorte Theater in Central Park was the brainchild of the late Joseph Papp, former director of the Public Theater. Each summer usually features a revival of a Shakespeare play featuring a large company, including at least one or more "names" from film or television. The 2007 slate was set to feature *Romeo and Juliet*. The productions run from June to early September. Depending on the star power, tickets can be quite scarce.

The Delacorte Theater itself, next to Belvedere Castle near 79th Street and West Drive, is a dream—on a starry night, there's no better stage in town. Tickets are distributed at the theater free on a first-come, first-served basis (two per person) at 1pm on the day of the performance. The Delacorte might have 1,881 seats, but each is a hot commodity; whatever the show, people line up next to the theater 2 to 3 hours in advance (even earlier if a big name is involved). You can also pick up same-day tickets between 1 and 3pm at the Public Theater, at 425 Lafayette St. For more information, call the Public Theater at © 212/539-8500 or the Delacorte at © 212/535-4284, or visit www.publictheater.org.

Free concerts by the **New York Philharmonic** and the **Metropolitan Opera** are held beneath the stars on Central Park's Great Lawn and in parks throughout the five boroughs. For schedules, call the Philharmonic at © 212/875-5656 or the Metropolitan Opera at © 212/362-6000. The Philharmonic maintains a

a full calendar of entertainment targeted to the culturally aware in their 20s and 30s—from poetry readings to film screenings to live music, including the debut of a very young Norah Jones—is offered at the Upper West Side community center **Makor.** 1395 Lexington Ave. (at 92nd St.). © 212/415-5500. www.92ndsty.org. Subway: 4, 5, 6 to 86th St.; 6 to 96th St. **Makor:** 35 W. 67th St. © 212/601-1000. www.makor.org. Subway: 1 to 66th St.

Radio City Music Hall   This stunning 6,200-seat Art Deco theater, with interior design by Donald Deskey, opened in 1932, and legendary Radio City continues to be a choice venue, where the theater alone adds a dash of panache to any performance. Star of the Christmas season is the **Radio City Music Hall Christmas Spectacular,** starring the legendary Rockettes. Visiting pop-chart toppers, from Neil Young to the Gipsy Kings, also perform here. Thanks to perfect acoustics and uninterrupted sightlines, there's hardly a bad seat in the house. The theater also hosts dance performances; family entertainment; a number of annual awards shows, such as the Essence Awards, the GQ Man of the Year Awards, and anything MTV is holding in town. 1260 Sixth Ave. (at 50th St.). © 212/247-4777, or 212/307-7171 for Ticketmaster. www.radiocity.com or www.ticket master.com. Subway: B, D, F, V to 49th–50th sts./Rockefeller Center.

Symphony Space *(Finds)*   An eclectic mix of culture can be found at this Upper West Side institution. The variety of shows at the **Peter Jay Sharp Theater** includes music, with series by the World Music Institute as well as classical, rock, and blues;

list of their upcoming gigs at www.newyorkphilharmonic.org; look under "Attend Concerts."

The most active music stage in Central Park, however, is **SummerStage,** at Rumsey Playfield, midpark around 72nd Street. SummerStage has featured everyone from James Brown to Patti Smith; recent offerings have included concerts by Hugh Masekela, the Jon Spencer Blues Explosion, and Marianne Faithfull; "Viva, Verdi!" festival performances by the New York Grand Opera; cabaret nights; and more. The season usually lasts from mid-June to August. While some big-name shows charge admission, tickets aren't usually required but donations are always accepted. Call the hot line at ℂ **212/360-2777** or visit www.summerstage.org.

Beyond Central Park, more free outdoor fun includes the **Bryant Park Summer Film Festival,** held in Bryant Park, just behind the main branch of the New York Public Library, at Sixth Avenue between 41st and 42nd streets. Every Monday night a classic film—think *Dr. Zhivago* or *Viva Las Vegas*—is shown on a large screen under the stars. The lawn is open at 5pm for blankets and picnicking; the movie starts at dusk (about 8 or 9pm). Rain dates are Tuesdays. For the schedule and more information, call ℂ **212/512-5700.**

The calendar of free events heats up throughout the city's parks in summertime. You can find out what's happening by calling the **Parks and Recreation Special Events Hot Line** at ℂ **888/NY-PARKS** or 212/360-3456 or pointing your browser to **www.nycgovparks.org.**

dance, with marathon tributes to choreographers like George Balanchine to original creations of Israeli Zvi Gotheiner; literature, such as the selected shorts series introduced by writers such as Jonathan Lethem, Edwidge Danticat, and Walter Mosely; and family, with performances by folk singer Tom Chapin and the Putuyamo Kids. Adjacent to the Sharp Theater is the **Leonard Nimoy Thalia Theater.** The film-revival house that was known for its quirky sightlines was rescued by none other than Mr. Spock and has now been totally renovated. Though I'm sure it is much more comfortable now, I'll miss having to peer around a pole to watch a movie like *Plan Nine from Outer Space*. 2537 Broadway (at 95th St.). ℂ **212/864-1414.** www.symphonyspace.org. Subway: 1, 2, 3 to 96th St.

Town Hall   This intimate landmark theater—a National Historic Site designed by McKim, Mead & White—is blessed with outstanding acoustics, making it an ideal place to enjoy many kinds of performances, including theater, dance, lectures, drama, comedy, film, and pop and world music. The calendar regularly includes such offerings as American tap and Brazilian tango exhibitions; doo-wop and global rhythms; live tapings of *A Prairie Home Companion* with Garrison Keillor or spoken word from Al Franken; lectures by luminaries such as Marianne Williamson and Frank Gehry; concerts by the likes of David Sanborn or the reunited Blondie; symphony, opera, and ballet companies from around the world; and much more. The grade is extremely steep, so unless Yao Ming sits in front of you, fellow audience members shouldn't block your view. 123 W. 43rd St. (btwn Sixth and Seventh aves.). ℭ **212/840-2824,** or 212/307-4100 for Ticketmaster. www.the-townhall-nyc.org or www.ticketmaster.com. Subway: N, Q, R, S, W, 1, 2, 3, 7 to 42nd St./Times Sq.; B, D, F, V to 42nd St.

4 Live Rock, Jazz, Blues & More

I discuss the top venues, both large and small, below. But there are many more than these, and new ones are popping up all the time. For the latest, be sure to check the publications discussed in the introduction to this chapter as well as the online sources outlined in "Online Sources for Live-Music Fans," below.

LARGER VENUES

For coverage of **Madison Square Garden,** the **Theater at MSG,** and **Town Hall,** see "Major Concert Halls & Landmark Venues," earlier in this chapter.

Beacon Theatre　This pleasing midsize Upper West Side venue—a 1928 Art Deco movie palace with an impressive lobby, stairway, and auditorium seating about 2,700—hosts mainly pop-music performances, usually for the over-30 crowd. Featured acts have ranged from street-smart pop diva Sheryl Crow to a Hall & Oates reunion to a befuddled Beach Boy Brian Wilson to Grateful Dead heirs apparent Phish to not-yet-deads the Allman Brothers (who play an always-sold-out 2- or 3-week gig each spring giving more than a dozen performances). You'll also find such special events as the bodybuilding "Night of Champions" on the mix-and-match calendar. 2124 Broadway (at 74th St.). ℭ **212/496-7070.** Subway: 1, 2, 3 to 72nd St.

Roseland　This old warhorse of a venue, a 1919 ballroom gone to seed, has been under threat of the wrecking ball for years now. Everybody has played at this too-huge-for-its-own-good 2,500-capacity general-admission hall, from Marc Anthony to Fiona Apple to Busta Rhymes to Smashmouth to Rage Against the Machine to Jeff Beck. Recent bands-of-the-moment who have played here include New York's own Yeah Yeah Yeahs and the next-big-Brit-thing Arctic Monkeys. Thankfully, there's also lots of room to steer clear of the pit and still enjoy the show. Advance tickets can be purchased at the **Irving Plaza** box office (p. 363) without the service fee that Ticketmaster charges. Take a moment on your way through the lobby to check out the display cases memorializing Roseland's postwar heyday as the city's premier dance hall. Ballroom dancing still takes place Sunday from 2:30 to 10pm; admission is $10. 239 W. 52nd St. (btwn Broadway and Eighth Ave.). ℭ **212/247-0200,** or 212/307-7171 for Ticketmaster. www.roselandballroom.com. Subway: C, E, 1 to 50th St.

MIDSIZE & MULTIGENRE VENUES

Also see what's on at the stellar **Joe's Pub** (p. 369), a top-flight cabaret that hosts intimate shows by pop acts. Spring 2007 saw the opening of a new venue on the far West Side: the **Highline Ballroom,** at 431 W. 16th St, between 9th and 10th aves., ℭ **212/414-5994;** www.highlineballroom.com. It opened with a series of sold-out shows (it has a capacity of about 700) from acts ranging from Lou Reed to Amy Winehouse and Disco Biscuits.

B.B. King Blues Club & Grill　This 550-seat venue is one of the prime anchors of Times Square's "new" 42nd Street. Despite its name, B.B. King's seldom sticks to the blues; what you're likely to find instead is a bill full of pop, funk, and rock names, mainly

Tips **Ticket-Buying Tips**

Tickets for events at all larger theaters as well as at Hammerstein Ballroom, Roseland, Irving Plaza, B.B. King's, and S.O.B.'s can be purchased through **Ticketmaster** (© 212/307-7171; www.ticketmaster.com).

Advance tickets for an increasing number of shows at smaller venues—including Bowery Ballroom and Mercury Lounge—can be purchased through **Ticketweb** (© 866/468-7619; www.ticketweb.com). Do note, however, that Ticketweb can sell out in advance of actual ticket availability. Just because Ticketweb doesn't have tickets left for an event doesn't mean it's completely sold out, so be sure to check with the venue directly.

Even a sold-out show doesn't mean you're out of luck. There are usually a number of people hanging around at showtime trying to get rid of extra tickets for friends who didn't show, and they're usually happy to pass them off for face value. You'll also see professional scalpers, who often peddle forgeries and are best avoided—it doesn't take a rocket scientist to tell the difference. Be aware, of course, that all forms of resale onsite are illegal.

from the past. The big-ticket talent runs the gamut from George Clinton and the P. Funk All Stars and John Mayall and the Bluesbreakers to Tower of Power to Jimmy Cliff and Delbert McClinton. A few more (relatively) esoteric acts such as Burt Bacharach and surf guitarist Dick Dale take the stage on occasion. Tourist-targeted pricing makes for an expensive night on the town, word is that the food isn't as good as it was in the beginning, and seating policies can be convoluted, but there's no arguing with the quality of the talent. The Sunday gospel lunch is a genuine slice of joy. 237 W. 42nd St. (btwn Seventh and Eighth aves.). © 212/997-4144, or 212/307-7171 for tickets. www.bbkingblues.com. Subway: A, C, E, Q, W, 1, 2, 3, 7 to 42nd St.

Bowery Ballroom   Run by the same people behind the **Mercury Lounge** (see below), the Bowery space is bigger, accommodating a crowd of 500 or so, and even better. The stage is big and raised to allow good sightlines from every corner. The sound couldn't be better, and Art Deco details give the place a sophistication that doesn't come easy to general-admission halls. The balcony has its own bar and seating alcoves. This place is a favorite with alt-rockers like Vic Chesnutt, Travis, Steve Earle, Rinocerose, The Delgados, and Toshi Reagon, as well as more established acts (Neil Finn, Patti Smith, Joan Jett & the Blackhearts), who thrive in an intimate setting. Save on the service charge by buying advance tickets at Mercury's box office. 6 Delancey St. (at Bowery). © 212/533-2111. www.boweryballroom.com. Subway: F to Delancey St.; J, M, Z to Bowery.

The Filmore New York at Irving Plaza   This high-profile midsize music hall is the prime stop for national name rock bands that aren't quite big enough yet (or anymore) to sell out Hammerstein, Roseland, or the Beacon. Think Five for Fighting, the Fels, Jars of Clay, Badly Drawn Boy, the Reverend Horton Heat, the resurrected Television, Kenny Wayne Shepherd, Cowboy Junkies, and Cheap Trick. From time to time, big-name artists also perform—Bob Dylan, Prince, Patti Smith, and A. J. McLean of the Backstreet Boys have all played "secret" shows here. All in all, it's a very nice place to see a show, with a well-elevated stage and lots of open space even on sold-out nights. There's an upstairs balcony that offers unparalleled views, but come early for a spot. 17 Irving Place

Online Sources for Live-Music Fans

These websites are your top online sources for live-music schedules:

- **Clear Channel Entertainment:** www.cc.com
- **Ticketmaster:** www.ticketmaster.com

  Additionally, Web sources **Citysearch (www.citysearch.com)**, *Time Out New York* **(www.timeoutny.com)**, and all of the hard-copy resources (and their corresponding websites) listed at the start of this chapter offer a wealth of live-music listings.

(1 block west of Third Ave. at 15th St.). ℂ **212/777-1224** or 212/777-6800. www.irvingplaza.com. Subway: L, N, Q, R, W, 4, 5, 6 to 14th St./Union Sq.

The Knitting Factory   New York's premier avant-garde music venue has four separate spaces, each showcasing performances ranging from experimental jazz and acoustic folk to spoken-word and poetry readings to out-there multimedia works. Regulars who use the Knitting Factory as their lab of choice include former Lounge Lizard John Lurie; around-the-bend experimentalist John Zorn; guitar gods Vernon Reid, Eliot Sharp, and David Torn; innovative sideman (to Tom Waits and Elvis Costello, among others) Marc Ribot; and Television's Richard Lloyd. (If these names mean nothing to you, chances are good that The Knitting Factory is not for you.) The schedule is peppered with edgy star turns from the likes of Yoko Ono, Taj Mahal, Faith No More's Mike Patton, and Lou Reed. There are often two showtimes a night in the remarkably pleasing main performance space, so it's easy to work a show around other activities. The Old Office Lounge offers an extensive list of microbrews and free live entertainment. 74 Leonard St. (btwn Broadway & Church St.). ℂ **212/219-3132.** www.knitting factory.com. Subway: 1 to Franklin St.

(MOSTLY) ROCK CLUBS

Live music at rock clubs usually begins around 9pm, but check the sources listed at the beginning of this chapter for up-to-date starting times and prices.

In addition to the choices below, rock fans on the hunt for diamonds in the rough might also want to see what's on at folk's legendary **Bitter End,** 147 Bleecker St., between Thompson and LaGuardia streets in the heart of the Village (ℂ **212/673-7030;** www.bitterend.com).

Arlene's Grocery   This casual Lower East Side club boasts a friendly bar and a good sound system; unfortunately, music isn't always free anymore, but the quality of the artists is usually pretty high, and the cover usually tops out at $7. Arlene's Grocery primarily serves as a showcase for hot bands looking for a deal or promoting their self-pressed record. The crowd is an easygoing mix of club-hoppers, rock fans looking for a new fix, and industry scouts looking for new blood. Monday nights host the extremely popular "Hard Rock Karaoke," which is exactly what it sounds like. 95 Stanton St. (btwn Ludlow and Orchard sts.). ℂ **212/995-1652.** www.arlenesgrocery.net. Subway: F to Second Ave.

The Baggot Inn *(Value)*   This easygoing pub has become one of the best showcases in the city for unknown acts, especially if you like quality acoustic and folk-rock music. Blues, Irish music, poetry, acoustic jams, and open-mic nights also regularly pop up on the calendar. The cover is always bargain-priced; happy hour until 7pm and nightly drink specials round out the entertainment value. 82 W. 3rd St. (btwn Thompson and Sullivan sts., below the Boston Comedy Club). ℭ 212/477-0622. www.thebaggotinn.com. Cover free–$5. Subway: A, C, E, F, or V to W. 4th St.

Mercury Lounge   The Merc is everything a top-notch live-music venue should be: unpretentious, extremely civilized, and outfitted with a killer sound system. The rooms themselves are nothing special: a front bar and an intimate back-room performance space with a low stage and a few tables along the wall. The calendar is filled with a mix of accomplished local rockers and national acts like Fat Possum, the Mekons, and Sleepy Jackson. The crowd is grown-up and easygoing. The only downside is that it's consistently packed thanks to the high quality of the entertainment and all-around pleasing nature of the experience. 217 E. Houston St. (at Essex St./Ave. A). ℭ 212/260-4700. www.mercuryloungenyc.com. Subway: F to Second Ave.

Rodeo Bar *Value*   Here's New York's oldest—and finest—honky-tonk. Hike up your Wranglers and head those Fryes inside, where you'll find longhorns on the walls, peanut shells underfoot, first-class margaritas at the bar, and Tex-Mex on the menu. But this place is really about the music: urban-tinged country, foot-stompin' bluegrass, swinging rockabilly, Southern-flavored rock. Bigger names like Brian Setzer and up-and-comers on the tour circuit like Hank Williams III occasionally grace the stage, but regular acts like the Dixieland Swingers, the Flying Neutrinos, cowpunk goddess Rosie Flores, and the good-time BBQ Bob and the Spareribs usually supply free music, keeping the urban cowboys plenty happy. A 10-gallon hat full o' fun. It's happy hour until 7pm; the music starts around 10pm nightly and goes till at least 3am. 375 Third Ave. (at 27th St.). ℭ 212/683-6500. www.rodeobar.com. Subway: 6 to 28th St.

JAZZ, BLUES, LATIN & WORLD MUSIC

Be aware that a night at a top-flight jazz club can be expensive. Cover charges can vary dramatically—from as little as $10 to as high as $65, depending on who's taking the stage—and there is likely to be an additional two-drink minimum (or a dinner requirement if you choose an early show). Call ahead so you know what you're getting into; reservations are also an excellent idea at top spots.

For those of you who like your jazz with an edge, see what's on at **The Knitting Factory** (p. 364). Swingsters should consider **Swing 46** (p. 387). Weekends at **Carnegie Club** (p. 381) are ideal for Sinatra fans looking to relive the moment.

Despite its name, **B.B. King Blues Club & Grill** extends well beyond the blues genre to embrace over-the-hill acts of just about any ilk, from Morris Day and the Time to Blue Oyster Cult. Still, the venerable bluesman does take the stage from time to time, so you might want to see what's on; turn to p. 362.

You might also consider **Jazz at the Kitano**, in the mezzanine of the Kitano Hotel, 66 Park Ave., at 38th Street (ℭ 212/885-7119; www.kitano.com), for some first-rate jazz in a casual, comfortable setting. **The Kitchen,** 512 W. 19th St., between Tenth and Eleventh avenues (ℭ 212/255-5793; www.thekitchen.org), has a full slate of live music and performance art. In association with the 92nd Street Y, **Makor** (p. 360) offers a similarly eclectic mix, as does **Joe's Pub** (p. 369), which adds a cabaret spin.

There's also world-beat jazz every Friday and Saturday from 5 to 8pm in the rotunda at the **Guggenheim Museum;** see chapter 8. And don't forget **Jazz at Lincoln Center,** the nation's premier forum for the traditional and developing jazz canon; see p. 358.

Some of the bars mentioned later in this chapter also have occasional live music. For an eclectic mix of jazz, Latin, and R&B, **Creole** (p. 385) in East Harlem offers a full schedule.

Bill's Place *★★ (Moments*　Imagine hearing great live jazz in your living room. That's about as close as what you will experience at the very intimate and special Bill's Place. Bill is Bill Saxton, a jazz saxophonist extraordinaire and a Harlem legend. Saxton was a Friday night regular for many years at **St. Nick's Pub** (p. 368) and has played at clubs all over Harlem and downtown. In late 2005 he opened his own club in the parlor level of a brownstone on West 133rd Street. In the 1920s, 133rd Street between Lenox and Seventh Avenue, with a number of speakeasies and jazz joints up and down the block, was the original "swing street"; a 17-year-old Billie Holliday was discovered singing in a club on 133rd Street, and the block was the model that West 52nd emulated and tried to imitate in the 1940s and 1950s. So it's appropriate that Saxton's place is on this historic block—the jazz heard here is also the real deal. There are no frills at Bill's Place: Come into the parlor, find a seat—there aren't many, so reservations are a must—and groove to Saxton's pure bop sound. Alcohol is not served, but soft drinks are available and you can bring your own bottle. Open on Friday and Saturday only. On Friday Saxton and his quartet perform while Saturday is reserved for legends and emerging talent. 148 W. 133rd St. (btwn Lenox and Seventh aves.). *©* **917/837-6540.** Subway: 3 to 135th St.

Birdland　This legendary club abandoned its distant uptown roost in 1996 for a more convenient Midtown nest, where it has established itself once again as one of the city's premier jazz spots. While the legend of Parker, Monk, Gillespie, and other bebop pioneers still holds sway, this isn't a crowded, smoky joint of yesteryear. The big room is spacious, comfy, and classy, with an excellent sound system and a top-notch talent roster any night of the week. Expect lots of accomplished big bands and jazz trios, plus occasional appearances by stars like Oscar Peterson and Dave Brubeck. You can't go wrong with the regular Sunday night show, starring Chico O'Farrell's smokin' Afro-Cuban Jazz Big Band. At press time, Tuesday was the domain of the Duke Ellington Orchestra, led by Duke's grandson Paul Ellington every other week. 315 W. 44th St. (btwn Eighth and Ninth aves.). *©* **212/581-3080.** www.birdlandjazz.com. Subway: A, C, E to 42nd St.

Blue Note　The Blue Note has attracted some of the biggest names in jazz to its intimate setting. Those who've played here include just about everyone of note: Dave Brubeck, Ray Charles, B. B. King, Manhattan Transfer, Dr. John, George Duke, Chick Corea, David Sanborn, Arturo Sandoval, Gato Barbieri, and the superb Ahmad Jamal. The sound system is excellent, and every seat in the house has a sightline to the stage. However, in recent years, the hard edge that once was the Blue Note has faded. Softer, smoother jazz is the domain now, so if that's your thing, enjoy. *But be warned:* Prices are astronomical. There are two shows per night, and dinner is served. 131 W. 3rd St. (at Sixth Ave.). *©* **212/475-8592.** www.bluenote.net. Subway: A, B, C, D, E, F, V to W. 4th St.

Dizzy's Club Coca-Cola *★*　This beautiful, cozy new jazz club is part of the Jazz at Lincoln Center complex in the Time Warner Center on Columbus Circle. Acoustics and sightlines are excellent and, though not nearly as dramatic as the window in the complex's Allen Room, there is a window behind the stage with views of Central Park and the city. The club attracts an interesting mix of both up-and-coming and established bands. Every Monday the club features the Upstarts, a student showcase from local

Jazz in the Afternoon

I personally like my jazz in the evenings or the wee, wee hours, if I'm ever awake for them. But I like jazz enough to dig it in the afternoon as well. And in Harlem, you can get your jazz pretty much all day and night thanks to the emergence in 2006 of **Ez's Woodshed,** 2236 Adam Clayton Powell Blvd, between 131st and 132nd sts. (© 212/283-5299; www.bigapplejazz. com/ezswoodshed). At Ez's the gigs begin every day at 2 until 5pm and then again from 5:30 until 8pm. Thursday through Saturday, Ez's has nighttime sets from 8:30 until 11pm. Ez's features up and coming talent, but if you are lucky you just might be there when local talents like Bill Saxton or Eric Reed stop by and sit in a set or two. There is never a cover or minimum, but there is a "suggested donation" of $10 to $15 dollars to keep the music flowing.

schools including Juilliard and the Manhattan School of Music. My only complaint is the high $30 cover every day of the week—even for the Upstarts. Time Warner Center, 60th St. and Broadway. © 212/258-9595. www.jalc.org. Subway: A, B, C, D, 1 to Columbus Circle.

Iridium   This well-respected and snazzily designed jazz club has relocated from its longtime perch across from Lincoln Center to an even better heart-of-the-Theater-District location. Everything else remains the same, including the accomplished talent and big-name acts that always take the stage. Like the Energizer bunny, Les Paul keeps on going, still playing every Monday night, while the very popular Mingus Big Band makes Iridium their home each Tuesday. Other top-notch performers who often appear include Jackie McLean, Mose Allison, McCoy Tyner, and saxophonist Houston Person. A full, rather sophisticated dinner menu is served. 1650 Broadway (at 51st St.). © 212/582-2121. www.iridiumjazzclub.com. Subway: 1 to 50th St.

Jazz at the Cajun   This cozy, rather casual New Orleans–themed supper club is the best venue in town for genuine prewar big band and Dixieland jazz—think Jelly Roll Morton, Scott Joplin, early Duke. The fanatical crowd comes from all walks of life, united in their love of the old-school. The place jumps no matter what top-notch crew takes the stage. The food is affordable and just fine; be sure to reserve in advance. 129 Eighth Ave. (btwn 16th and 17th sts.). © 212/691-6174. www.jazzatthecajun.com. Subway: A, C, E to 14th St.; L to Eighth Ave.

Jazz Standard   Kudos to the Jazz Standard, where both the food and music meet all expectations. Boasting a sophisticated retro-speakeasy vibe, the Jazz Standard is one of the city's largest jazz clubs, with well-spaced tables seating 150 and a reasonable $15 to $25 cover. The rule is straightforward, mainstream jazz by new and established musicians, including such stars as Branford Marsalis. On Sunday afternoons the club features a Jazz for Kids program. A limited menu from Danny Meyer's barbecue joint, **Blue Smoke** (p. 193), upstairs, is available. Jazz, blues, and barbecue—hard to go wrong with that. 116 E. 27th St. (btwn Park Ave. South and Lexington Ave.). © 212/576-2232. www. jazzstandard.net. Subway: 6 to 28th St.

Lenox Lounge   This beautifully renovated classic is a symbol of Harlem's current renaissance. The intimate, Art Deco–cool back room—complete with zebra stripes on the walls and built-in banquettes—hosts top-flight live jazz vocalists, trios, and quartets for a crowd that comes to listen and be wowed. Blues and R&B are the province of Thursday. The cover never goes higher than $15, which makes Lenox Lounge a good value to boot. There's a warm, cozy, and immensely popular bar up front. Good soul food is served. Well worth the trip uptown for those who want a genuine Harlem jazz experience. 288 Malcolm X Blvd. (Lenox Ave.; btwn 124th and 125th sts.). © 212/427-0253. www.lenoxlounge.com. Subway: 2, 3 to 125th St.

St. Nick's Pub 𝒦 (Finds)   As unpretentious a club as you'll find, St. Nick's in Harlem's Sugar Hill district is the real deal, with live entertainment every night and never a cover. On Tuesday it's Oldies but Goodies provided by Sexy Charles and Poetry on the Hill, hosted by Chance & Lilah; all the other nights are devoted to jazz, straight up and rarely with a chaser. 773 St. Nicholas Ave. (at 149th St.). © 212/283-9728. Subway: A, C, D, B to 145th St.

Smoke 𝒦𝒦 (Value)   A superstar in the New York jazz scene and the best place to hear it on the Upper West Side, Smoke is a welcome throwback to the informal, intimate clubs of the past—the kind of place that on most nights you can just walk in and experience solid jazz. And though it seats only 65, for no more than a $30 cover, Smoke still manages to attract big names like the Steve Turre Quartet, Ron Carter, Eddie Henderson, and John Hicks. Sunday through Thursday there is no cover. On Sundays, the club features Latin jazz; every Tuesday, I get to hear my favorite Hammond organ grooves with Mike LeDonne. There are three sets nightly and a very popular happy hour. 2751 Broadway (btwn 105th and 106th sts.). © 212/864-6662. www.smokejazz.com. Subway: 1 to 103rd St.

S.O.B.'s   If you like your music hot, hot, hot, visit S.O.B.'s, the city's top world-music venue, specializing in Brazilian, Caribbean, and Latin sounds. The packed house dances and sings along nightly to calypso, samba, mambo, African drums, reggae, or other global grooves, united in the high-energy, feel-good vibe. Bookings include top-flight performers from around the globe; Astrud Gilberto, Mighty Sparrow, King Sunny Ade, Eddie Palmieri, Buckwheat Zydeco, Beausoleil, and Baaba Maal are only a few of the names who have graced this lively stage. The room's Tropicana Club style has island pizazz that carries through to the Caribbean-influenced cooking and extensive tropical-drinks menu. This place is so popular that it's an excellent idea to book in advance, especially if you'd like table seating. Monday is dedicated to Latin sounds, Tuesday to reggae, Friday features a late-night French Caribbean dance party, while Saturday is reserved for samba. 204 Varick St. (at Houston St.). © 212/243-4940. www.sobs.com. Subway: 1 to Houston St.

Uptown Jazz Lounge at Minton's Playhouse 𝒦 (Finds)   The big neon sign on 118th Street remains intact and is a cultural landmark. The 1948-mural behind the stage of a woman sleeping off a drunk while four musicians jam by her side looks as fresh as it ever did even after a 30-year hiatus while Minton's Playhouse was shuttered. In 2006 the club, where Miles Davis, Charlie Christian, Dizzy Gillespie, Coleman Hawkins, and house pianist, Thelonius Monk once reigned, reopened. The look is sparse; a few archive photos cover the burnt orange walls and hard-backed chairs and formica-topped tables are scattered around the small room. But who cares? The music is straight ahead jazz and the clientele is old school Harlem along with curious European and Japanese tourists. At press time, Patience Higgins and the Sugar Hill

Quartet hold court every Wednesday, while Thursday headlines vocalist Gerald Hayes and the Qualified Gents. No cover Monday through Thursday. 208 W. 118th St (between St. Nicholas Ave. and Adam Clayton Powell Blvd.) ℭ 212/864-8346. www.uptownatmintons.com. Subway: B, C to 116th St.

The Village Vanguard ⓐⓐ   What CBGB was to rock, The Village Vanguard is to jazz. One look at the photos on the walls will show you who's been through since 1935, from Coltrane, Miles, and Monk to recent appearances by Bill Charlap and Roy Hargrove. Expect a mix of established names and high-quality local talent, including the Vanguard's own jazz orchestra on Monday nights. The sound is great, but sightlines aren't, so come early for a front table. If you are looking for serious jazz, this is the place. 178 Seventh Ave. South (just below 11th St.). ℭ 212/255-4037. www.villagevanguard.net. Subway: 1, 2, 3 to 14th St.

5 Cabaret

An evening spent at a sophisticated cabaret just might be the quintessential New York night on the town. It isn't cheap: Covers can range from $10 to $60, depending on the showroom and the act, and also require two-drink or dinner-check minimums. Always reserve ahead, and get the complete lowdown when you do.

Cafe Carlyle ⓐ   Cabaret doesn't get any better than this. This is where the late, great Bobby Short, held court for over 35 years. The club still attracts rarefied talents like Betty Buckley and Barbara Cook. The room is intimate and as swanky as they come. Expect a high tab—admission is $65 to $75 with a $30 per-person minimum; with dinner, two people could easily spend $300—but if you're looking for the best of the best, look no further. Value-minded cabaret fans can save by reserving standing room (which usually results in a spot at the bar) for just $35. On most Mondays, Woody Allen joins the Eddy Davis New Orleans Jazz Band on clarinet to swing Dixie-style ($85 cover). At the Carlyle Hotel, 35 East 76th St. (at Madison Ave.). ℭ 212/744-1600. Closed July–Aug. Subway: 6 to 77th St.

Feinstein's at The Regency ⓕⓘⓝ⓭⓼   This intimate and elegant cabaret-style night-club is the first from Grammy-winning song impresario Michael Feinstein. Cover charges can soar, but you can count on a memorable night of first-quality dining and song, and no other cabaret merges old-school cool and hipster appeal so well. Recent high-wattage talent has included Keely Smith, Patti LuPone, and the man himself. Call ahead to reserve; you can also purchase tickets through Ticketmaster. At the Regency Hotel, 540 Park Ave. (at 61st St.). ℭ 212/339-4095, or 212/307-4100 for Ticketmaster. www.feinsteins attheregency.com or www.ticketmaster.com. Subway: 4, 5, 6 to 59th St.

Joe's Pub   Joe's Pub isn't exactly your daddy's cabaret. Still, this beautiful—and hugely popular—cabaret and supper club, named for the legendary Joseph Papp, is everything a New York cabaret should be. The multilevel space serves up an American menu and top-notch entertainment from a more eclectic mix of talent than you'll find on any other cabaret calendar. The sophisticated crowd comes for music and spoken word that ranges from operatic diva Diamanda Galas to solo shows from Broadway stars like Daphne Rubin-Vega *(Les Miserables)* and Tom Wopat *(Annie Get Your Gun)* to first-class pop from husband-and-wife singer/songwriters Michael Penn and Aimee Mann to modern rumba masters Los Munequitos de Matanzas. There's always jazz on the calendar, and don't be surprised if Broadway actors show up on off nights to exercise their substantial chops. DJs take over during the late-night hours. At the Joseph Papp Public Theater, 425 Lafayette St. (btwn Astor Place and 4th St.). (C) 212/539-8777, or Telecharge at 212/239-6200 (for advance tickets). www.joespub.com. Subway: 6 to Astor Place.

The Oak Room   Recently refurbished to recall its glory days, the Oak Room is one of the city's most intimate, elegant, and sophisticated spots for cabaret. Headliners include such first-rate talents as Andrea Marcovicci, Steve Ross, Dave Frishberg, the marvelous Julie Wilson, and cool-cat jazz guitarist John Pizzarelli, plus occasional lesser names that are destined for greatness. At the Algonquin Hotel, 59 W. 44th St. (btwn Fifth and Sixth aves.). (C) 212/840-6800. Closed July–Aug. Subway: B, D, F, V to 42nd St.

6 Stand-Up Comedy

Cover charges are generally in the $8-to-$20 range, with all-star Carolines going as high as $30 on occasion. Many clubs also have a two-drink minimum. Be sure to ask about the night's cover when you make reservations, which are strongly recommended, *especially* on weekends.

You might also see who's taking the stage at Madison Square Garden's laugh-a-minute offshoot, **Comedy Garden** (p. 359), where even Robin Williams books in to hone his stand-up chops every once in a while.

With the addition of **Comix**, 353 W. 14th St (at Ninth Ave; (C) 212/524-2500; www.comixny.com), the hip Meat-Packing district got its own comedy club, which mixes headliners like Caroline Rhea and Alex Borstein (from "The Family Guy" and "MadTV") with "Fresh Meat" shows introducing up-and-coming talent, and regular nights like the Wendy Williams Comedy Experience every Wednesday.

Carolines on Broadway   Caroline Hirsch presents today's hottest headliners in her upscale Theater District showroom, which doesn't have a bad seat in the house. You're bound to recognize at least one or two of the established names and hot up-and-comers on the bill in any given week, like Dave Chapelle, Janeane Garofalo, Colin Quinn, Bill Bellamy, Kathy Griffin, Robert Wuhl, Jimmie Walker ("Dyn-o-mite!"), Pauly Shore, or Jay Mohr. Monday is usually New Talent Night, while HOT97 radio hosts up-and-coming black comedians on select Tuesdays. 1626 Broadway (btwn 49th and 50th sts.). (C) 212/757-4100. www.carolines.com. Subway: N, R to 49th St.; 1 to 50th St.

Comedy Cellar *(Finds)*   This intimate subterranean club is the venue of choice for stand-up fans in the know, thanks to the best, most consistently impressive lineups in the business. I'll always love the Comedy Cellar for introducing an uproariously funny unknown comic named Ray Romano to me some years back. 117 MacDougal St. (btwn Bleecker and W. 3rd sts.). (C) 212/254-3480. www.comedycellar.com. Subway: A, B, C, D, E, F, V to W. 4th St. (use 3rd St. exit).

Dangerfield's   Dangerfield's is the nightclub version of the comedy club, with a mature crowd and a straight-outta-Vegas atmosphere. The comedians are all veterans of the comedy-club and late-night talk-show circuit. 1118 First Ave. (btwn 61st and 62nd sts.). (C) 212/593-1650. www.dangerfieldscomedyclub.com. Subway: N, R to Lexington Ave.; 4, 5, 6 to 59th St.

Gotham Comedy Club *(Finds)*   Here's the city's trendiest, most comfortable, and most sophisticated comedy club. The young talent—Tom Rhodes, Sue Costello, Mitch Fatel, Lewis Black of the *Daily Show*—is red hot. Jerry Seinfeld has also been exercising his chops here of late. Look for theme nights like "Comedy Salsa" and "A

Very Jewish Christmas." Tuesday is set aside for new talent. 208 W. 23rd St. (btwn Seventh and Eighth aves.). © 212/367-9000. www.gothamcomedyclub.com. Subway: F, N, R to 23rd St.

Stand-Up New York   The Upper West Side's premier stand-up comedy club hosts some of the brightest young comics in the business, plus frequent drop-ins like Dennis Leary, Caroline Rhea, Robin Williams, and Mr. Upper West Side himself, Jerry Seinfeld. 236 W. 78th St. (at Broadway). © 212/595-0850. www.standupny.com. Subway: 1 to 79th St.

Upright Citizens Brigade Theatre *(Value*   You've seen their twisted, highly original sketch comedy on Comedy Central—now you can see the Upright Citizens Brigade, New York's premier alternative comedy troupe, live. The best of the nonstop hilarity is *ASSSSCAT 3000,* the troupe's extremely popular long-form improv show, which often sells out in advance. The company has supplied a few members of the Not-Ready-for-Prime-Time Players in recent years, including Amy Poehler. Reservations are a must and tickets are a cheap 8 bucks or less. 307 W. 26th St. (btwn Eighth and Ninth aves.). © 212/366-9176. www.ucbtheatre.com. Tickets $8 or less. Subway: 1 to 23rd St.

7 Bars & Cocktail Lounges

Remember: Smoking is prohibited in bars but allowed in outdoor spaces.

TRIBECA

Bubble Lounge   From the first cork that popped, this wine bar dedicated to the bubbly was an effervescent hit. More than 300 champagnes and sparkling wines are served in this glamorous living-room setting, more than 30 of them by the glass, to pair with caviar, foie gras, cheese, and sweets. No jeans, sneakers, or baseball caps. There's live bluesy jazz on Monday and Tuesday. 228 W. Broadway (btwn Franklin and White sts.). © 212/431-3433. www.bubblelounge.com. Subway: 1 to Franklin St.

Church Lounge   The big, superstylish Larry Bogdanow–designed atrium-lobby bar and restaurant at the **Tribeca Grand Hotel** (p. 114) is a great place to enjoy a top-flight cocktail and rub elbows with the neighborhood's chic locals (which include just about anybody who has business with Miramax). Dress well and call ahead to see what's on tap that evening if you want to experience the height of the action—around 11pm. 2 Sixth Ave. (at White and Church sts.). © 212/519-6600. Subway: 1 to Franklin St.; A, C, E to Canal St.

Walker's *(Finds*   Walker's is an old holdout from prefabulous TriBeCa. It's got some charm, with a tin ceiling, a long wooden bar, oldies on the sound system, and cozy tables where you can dine on good, affordable meat-and-potatoes fare. Don't get fancy with your drink orders; stick with Guinness or one of the other drafts. 16 N. Moore St. (at Varick St.). © 212/941-0142. Subway: 1 to Franklin St.

CHINATOWN

Double Happiness *(Finds*   The only indicator to the subterranean entrance is a vertical WATCH YOUR STEP sign. Once through the door, you'll find a beautifully designed speak-easyish lounge with artistic nods to the neighborhood throughout, plus a wonderfully low-key vibe. The space is large, but a low ceiling and intimate nooks add a hint of romance. The fabulous food is from the upstairs restaurant, Wyanoka, so this is a great place to satisfy the munchies, too. Don't miss the green-tea martini, an inspired house creation. 173 Mott St. (btwn Grand and Broome sts.). © 212/941-1282. Subway: 6 to Spring St.

Author! Author! Where to Hear Spoken Word

Readings can be some of the most inexpensive and entertaining events in New York City. There are several venues dedicated to presenting spoken word, and popular series are presented in venues ranging from bars to bookstores. Many readings are free; others charge a small cover; and except for the top names, you'll rarely see a charge over $10.

The best sources for finding out who's reading include the "Books" section of *Time Out New York,* which spotlights top readings in its "Don't Miss" section.

To find out which author (or celebrity who's had a book ghost-written) is reading at a NYC Barnes & Noble (there's *always* a major author in town), go to www.barnesandnoble.com and click on "Meet the Writers."

Who are you likely to see at these venues? Everyone from bestselling authors (Candace Bushnell, Tom Wolfe, Norman Mailer), to spoken-word artists (Reg E. Gaines, Alix Olson) to whoever's just scribbled a poem on the back of an envelope at an open-mic event.

Below are some of the top venues/series in town:

- **The Unterberg Poetry Center** at the 92nd Street YMHA (92nd St. at Lexington Ave.; ℂ **212/415-5740;** www.92y.org; subway: 4, 5, 6 to 96th St.). The 92nd Street Y has had all the heavy hitters in its lineup since 1939. In addition to talks and readings by the world's top poets, novelists, playwrights, and critics, the Y also offers "Biographers & Brunch" and "Critics & Brunch." Tickets are usually in the $20 range. The readings are in a 917-seat auditorium, which does on occasion sell out.

- **Nuyorican Poets Café** (236 E. 3rd St., btwn aves. B and C; ℂ **212/505-8183;** www.nuyorican.org; subway: F or V to Second Ave.). For over 30 years, the Nuyorican, brainchild of Miguel Algarin, who still runs it, has presented poetry, drama, music, and film. The raucous, popular **Poetry Slams** (the cafe fields a championship Slam Team) present poetry as a sport: Aspiring stars show up and throw down their work in front of an audience and panel of judges, who score them on the quality of the work and presentation. The Friday slams begin around 10pm (cover charge $7) and feature an invited slam poet. Slam Opens are held most Wednesdays (also a $7 cover). The storefront bar gets crowded quickly, so get there early on Slam nights.

- **Bowery Poetry Club,** 308 Bowery (at 1st St., btwn Houston and Bleeker sts.). (ℂ **212/614-0505;** www.bowerypoetry.com; subway: F or V to Second Ave.). "Poetry Czar" (as anointed by the *Village Voice*) Bob Holman opened his "Home for Poetry" in an 1850 building on (you guessed it) the Bowery. It's open all day for snacks, coffee, and that writer essential, hanging out; a two-for-one happy hour at the bar precedes each evening's festivities. Poetry and fiction readings, open mics, monologues, words with music, and all manner of other spoken word is presented from about 5:30pm each night, with covers ranging from free to $6. National and rising stars on the poetry/spoken-word scene show up here. The space can hold up to 200 people.

- **KGB,** 85 E. 4th St. (btwn Second and Third aves.). (© **212/505-3360;** www. kgbbar.com; subway: F or V to Second Ave.; 6 to Astor Place). This second-floor bar (it's not wheelchair-accessible) in an old East Village brownstone was once a Ukrainian social club and is decorated with vintage Communist memorabilia. There's never a cover (but you are urged to refresh your drink often) for the readings held almost every night of the week (check the website) starting at around 7pm. It's a tiny bar, holding perhaps 40 to 50 comfortably, and double that or more for a "hot" reader (think Adam Rapp, Eileen Myles, A. M. Homes), with "nights" curated by individual writers for poetry, science fiction, and other genres.

FESTIVALS & EVENTS

- **The *New Yorker*** magazine (**http://festival.newyorker.com**) has gone into the readings business with its "New Yorker Festival" in early October. You'll pay dearly (up to $30) for the privilege of seeing, say Sherman Alexie or R. Crumb read from or talk about their work at one of several venues, but the events almost always sell out. There are also free events and book signings scheduled throughout the festival.

- Every New Year's Day, the **Poetry Project at St. Mark's Church,** 131 E. 10th St. (© **212/674-0910;** www.poetryproject.com; subway: N, R, W to Union Sq.; 6 to Astor Place), presents a marathon poetry reading starting around 2pm, and running till . . . whenever. Poets and performers ranging from Patti Smith to Eric Bogosian, Maggie Estep, Tuli Kupferberg, and many (many) more read to welcome in the new year and raise money for the Poetry Projects' readings, workshops, and other programs. Tickets run about $20.

- **Symphony Space,** 2537 Broadway, at 95th St. (© **212/864-5400;** www. symphonyspace.org; subway: 1, 2, 3, to 96th St.; B, C to 96th St.) is the home of both **Selected Shorts** (Oct–Dec) and **Bloomsday on Broadway.** In Selected Shorts, modern and classic short stories are read by professional actors, ranging from the likes of Blair Brown, Cynthia Nixon, Eli Wallach, and John Shea, in the Peter Jay Sharpe Theater (which seats 760). Authors whose work you might hear include John Cheever, Truman Capote, and Woody Allen. Tickets range from $21 to $25, with discounts for students and seniors. And each June 16 (the day Leopold Bloom took his stroll around Dublin in 1904 in James Joyce's *Ulysses*) an ensemble cast of actors and avid Joyceans do a marathon reading from the masterwork. Its tickets ($20 adults, $17 students and seniors) are usually sold out well in advance.

Drinking with Ghosts

The ghosts are everywhere in New York. You might find them in the silent halls of some of the city's greatest structures. Or maybe wandering through narrow downtown streets. But for me, the best place to find the ghosts is in a few of the city's more aged drinking establishments.

Three of the oldest bars in town are a good place to start when seeking out the ghosts. **Pete's Tavern** (129 E. 18th St., at Irving Place; ✆ **212/473-7676**) claims to be the city's oldest continuing operating establishment. Warm up at Pete's on a cold winter night and after a few frothy Guinesses, you might think you see writer O. Henry, a regular at Pete's over a hundred years ago, sitting alone and unkempt in a booth, sipping his beer in between paragraphs of his famous 1906-written Christmas tale *Gift of the Magi*.

From Pete's you might want to venture to the West Village and the **White Horse Tavern** (567 Hudson St., at 11th St.; ✆ **212/243-9260**). At this 1880s pub, through the maze of frat boys chugging pints, you might see a desolate figure, head on table from snoring, empty shot glasses in front of him. Could that be the ghost of Dylan Thomas, author of *A Child's Christmas in Wales* and White Horse regular who took his last sip at the legendary tavern in 1953? Or is it just another drunken yuppie?

McSorley's Old Ale House (15 E. 7th St., between Second and Third aves.; ✆ **212/473-9148**) is over 140 years old and, while Pete's is the oldest tavern in New York, McSorley's claims to be the oldest "saloon." Could someone please explain the difference? Not that it matters to a ghost. Here, if you can avoid the busloads of Greeks (not from Greece) who come to pay respects to their shrine, and visit on, say, a quiet hot afternoon, you might think you see a tall, well-dressed man sitting at the bar taking notes, nursing an 8-ounce mug of ale. Could that be the ghost of *New Yorker* magazine writer Joseph Mitchell, author of *Joe Gould's Secret*? And are those notes for his 1943 book, *McSorley's Wonderful Saloon?* Well go up and ask him—before he disappears.

A bit further uptown, just a few blocks north of Union Square, is the 1892-established **Old Town Bar & Restaurant** (45 E. 18th St., between Broadway and Park Ave. South; ✆ **212/529-6732**). You might recognize the tin ceiling from the *Late Night with David Letterman* opening; the Old Town has been the set for many movies and television shows, but it's never been gussied up for the cameras—the Old Town is the real deal. There are no celebrity ghosts to speak of at the Old Town, but whenever I come here, I see one. This ghost is familiar only to me. He is cramped into a table with a group of friends, a pint and one of the Old Town's very good hamburgers in front of him. He is talking animatedly—a young man with big dreams. He looks confident and happy—as happy as a ghost could possibly look. But then I look in the mirror at my own reflection and the ghost disappears. He always does.

Winnie's   I usually abhor karaoke bars, but I make an exception for Winnie's. Maybe it's because I'm a sucker for Asian pop tunes or perhaps it's the "Hawaiian Punch," a sickly sweet drink that, after a couple, will have you crooning in Cantonese. Even if you don't partake in the Chinatown version of *American Idol,* you will enjoy others as they drunkenly embarrass themselves in the spotlight. 104 Bayard St. (btwn Baxter and Mulberry sts.). ℂ 212/732-2384. Subway: J, M, N, Q, R, Z, 6 to Canal St.

THE LOWER EAST SIDE

Barramundi   This lounge has a friendly staff, and a settled-in feel in a neighborhood overrun by hipster copycats. Come on a weeknight to snare a table in the little corner of heaven out back. A fireplace makes Barramundi almost as appealing on cool nights. 67 Clinton St. (btwn Stanton and Rivington sts.). ℂ 212/529-6900. Subway: F to Delancey St.

SOHO

Ear Inn *(Value*   There are many debates about which is the oldest bar in New York, and with its 1870s origins, Ear Inn is a serious contender for that crown. In superchic SoHo, this pub is a welcome cranky relief. They pull an excellent draft of Guinness and make a surprisingly good margarita as well. On Saturday afternoon the poetry readings just might make you cry into your beer. In warm weather, tables are set up outside within exhaust distance of the nearby UPS depot. *Note:* Respect the no-cellphone policy or suffer the consequences. 326 Spring St. (btwn Greenwich and Washington sts.). ℂ 212/226-9060. Subway: C, E to Spring St.

MercBar   Notable for its long tenure in the fickle world of beautiful-people bars, the upscale MercBar has mellowed nicely. The decor bespeaks civilized rusticity with warm woods, a canoe over the bar, copper-top tables, and butter-leather banquettes— think SoHo goes to Yosemite. The European martini (Stoli raspberry and Chambord) is divine. Look carefully, because there's no sign. 151 Mercer St. (btwn Prince and Houston sts.). ℂ 212/966-2727. www.mercbar.com. Subway: N, R to Prince St.

Pegu Club *(*&*&*   Mixologist and owner Audrey Saunders, formerly of Bemelman's Bar in the Carlyle Hotel, makes magic with cocktails. In 2005 she opened her own little downtown gathering spot where she can even better showcase her immense talents. The cocktails here change seasonally and will astound you with their creativity. It helps that the staff uses fresh squeezed juices, homemade ginger beer and the largest assortment of bitters you will find anywhere. You know you are in serious cocktail heaven when your drinks are served with liquid condiments; your Pisco Punch needs a bit more sugar, you can squeeze a dropperful in. Or your Gin-Gin Mule just doesn't pack the citrus tang you would like, add a dash of lime. Unless it's salty peanuts or pretzels, I usually disdain bar food, but for the Pegu Club's amazing Diver scallop miniburgers and addictive smoked trout deviled eggs, I will happily make an exception. 77 W. Houston St. 2nd Floor (at W. Broadway). ℂ 212/473-PEGU. www.peguclub.com. Subway: A, B, C, D, E, F, V to W. 4th St.

Puck Fair *(Finds*   This gleaming pub looks as if it could have been lifted wholesale out of an equally stylish corner of London and plunked down on this side of the pond. It's genuine through and through, but a young crowd and a hip soundtrack make it feel fresh rather than old-man-neighborhoody (like Fanelli's). Twenty beers are on tap (including Guinness, of course). If you can snare a table, the petite mezzanine makes a great spot to sit down and dig into the surprisingly good pub grub. 298 Lafayette St. (just south of Houston St.). ℂ 212/431-1200. Subway: F to Broadway–Lafayette St.

Cocktails Alfresco (Who's Al Fresco?)

One of my favorite moments in the movie *The Producers* is when Max Bia-lystock (played by Zero Mostel) tries to woo Leo Bloom (Gene Wilder) into helping him carry out his theater scam. Bialystock tells Bloom that he will treat him to dinner and they will dine "alfresco." The next shot is Bialystock buying a hot dog for Bloom from a street vendor near Central Park.

But food and drink always *do* taste better alfresco. Here are some of my favorite places for cocktails out of doors.

The outdoor space at rowdy **Jeremy's Ale House,** 228 Front St. (© **212/964-3537;** www.jeremysalehouse.com), near the South Street Seaport, is no fairy tale, but it does have one of the best views of the Brooklyn Bridge. Maybe that's because the bar is practically under the bridge (on the Man-hattan side). Jeremy's is so close to the river you may think you smell the sea, but what you really smell is an endless supply of calamari and clams siz-zling in the deep fryers and gallons of Coors beer, which are served in 32-ounce Styrofoam cups.

Some of the best outdoor drinking can be found at a few select hotels. The best of the best, way downtown at the southern tip of Manhattan, is the **Rise Bar** 🏵 at the Ritz-Carlton New York, Battery Park, 2 West St., just north of Battery Place (© **212/344-0800**). Located on the 14th floor of the hotel, the bar boasts incomparable views of Lady Liberty and busy New York Harbor from the massive waterfront terrace.

For the more trendy set, where the eye candy is not just the spectacular views, take the elevator up to the top of the Hotel Gansevoort, 18 Ninth Ave., at 13th Street (© **212/206-6700**) to **Plunge,** where the you can gaze out at New Jersey, inhale the chlorine fumes from the hotel's pool (which only guests can use), all the while sipping pricey cocktails. A few blocks north at the Maritime Hotel, 363 W. 16th St., at Ninth Avenue, the scene on the roof at **Cabanas** (© **212/242-4300**) is like something out of Hollywood. In fact, you'll probably recognize a few Hollywood denizens sunning them-selves with colorful drinks, umbrella stirrers and all, balanced on their abnormally firm abs. Uptown, in the heart of Midtown, the **Pen-Top Bar** at the classic grande dame the Peninsula Hotel, 700 Fifth Ave., at 55th Street (© **212/956-2888**), offers views of the glittering neighboring spires and the bustle of Fifth Avenue below that are not only calming but romantic, if that is actually possible.

One of my favorite parks is Riverside Park (see chapter 8), and two of the reasons why I love this park are the **79th Street Boat Basin Café,** 79th Street at the Hudson River (© **212/496-5542;** www.boatbasincafe.com), where you can sip a drink and watch the boats bob on the river as the sun sets, and **Hurley's Hudson Beach Café,** Riverside Park and 103rd Street (© **917/370-3448**), where beach volleyball games and stunning sunsets are the enter-tainment, marred only by the constant automobile buzz of the nearby West Side Highway.

THE EAST VILLAGE & NOHO

Don't forget to visit **McSorley's Old Ale House** (see p. 374, "Drinking with Ghosts).

dba *(Finds)*   dba has completely bucked the loungey trend that has taken over the city, instead remaining firmly and resolutely an unpretentious neighborhood bar. It's a beer- and scotch-lover's paradise, with a massive drink menu on giant chalkboards. Owner Ray Deter specializes in British-style cask-conditioned ales (the kind that you pump by hand) and stocks a phenomenal collection of single-malt scotches. Ray has enclosed the back garden, transforming it into a cozy East Village beer garden. Excellent jukebox, too. During the 2006 World Cup, they had a big sign out front "Footy on the Telly All Day!" Look for daily specials like Sunday Bloody Marys with free lox and bagels from Russ & Daughters. 41 First Ave. (btwn 2nd and 3rd sts.). ☎ 212/475-5097. www.drinkgoodstuff.com. Subway: F to Second Ave.

KGB Bar   This former Ukrainian social club still boasts its Soviet-themed decor, but it now draws creative types who like the low-key boho vibe. There's also free entertainment almost every night, thanks to KGB's excellent, eclectic reading series, where a talented pack of up-and-coming and established writers read their prose in various genres (fiction, science fiction, poetry, and so on) to a receptive crowd starting at 7pm. (The readings are usually over by 9pm, if you don't like literature with your beer). Past readers have included playwright Tina Howe *(Painting Churches),* Janice Erlbaum *(Girlbomb),* and Dave King *(The Ha-Ha).* 85 E. 4th St. (btwn Second and Third aves.). ☎ 212/505-3360. www.kgbbar.com. Subway: 6 to Astor Place.

Temple Bar   One of the first comers to New York's lounge scene, Temple Bar is still a gorgeous Deco hangout, with a long L-shaped bar leading to a lovely seating area with velvet drapes, backlighting, and Sinatra crooning in the background. Cocktails don't get any better than the classic martini (with just a kiss of vermouth) or the smooth-as-peignoir-silk Manhattan (Johnnie Walker Black, sweet vermouth, bitters). Bring a date—and feel free to invite me along. Look for the petroglyph-like lizards on the otherwise-unmarked facade. 332 Lafayette St. (just north of Houston St., on the west side of the street). ☎ 212/925-4242. Subway: 6 to Bleecker St.

Tom & Jerry's (288 Bar)   Here's an extremely pleasing neighborhood bar minus the grunge factor that usually plagues such joints. The place has an authentic local vibe, and the youngish, artsy crowd is unpretentious and chatty. The beer selection is very good and the mixed drinks are better than average. Flea-market hounds will enjoy the vintage collection of "Tom & Jerry" punchbowl sets behind the bar, and creative types will enjoy the rotating collection of works from local artists, which changes monthly. There's no sign, but you'll spy the action through the plate-glass window on the east side of Elizabeth Street just north of Houston. 288 Elizabeth St. ☎ 212/260-5045. Subway: 6 to Bleecker St.

Zum Schneider *(Finds)*   You know New York has just about everything when you can find an authentic indoor German beer garden in Alphabet City. With long tables and bench seating, this is a fun place for a group. There are more than a dozen varieties of German beer on tap here, and all are served in sturdy steins. To complement those hearty beers, you can sample equally hearty German fare such as Bavarian blood sausage and rolled beef filled with pickle, bacon, and mustard. If that seems a bit much, you can just munch on the homemade pretzels. 107 Ave. C (at 7th St.). ☎ 212/598-1098. www.zumschneider.com. Subway: F to Second Ave.; L to First Ave.

GREENWICH VILLAGE & THE MEAT-PACKING DISTRICT

While in the West Village, visit the historic **White Horse Tavern** (see the sidebar, "Drinking with Ghosts," on p. 374).

Bowlmor/Pressure ⊛ Supercool Bowlmor isn't your daddy's bowling alley: DJs spin, martinis flow, candy-colored balls knock down Day-Glo pins, and strikes and spares are automatically tallied into the wee hours. Bowlmor is a blast. Once you're finished with your 10-pin—or while you're waiting for your lane—head upstairs to the rooftop lounge, **Pressure,** housed in a 16,000-square-foot inflated bubble and boasting designer-mod furnishings, a cocktail menu that includes a luscious chocolate martini (infused with Godiva chocolate liqueur), a fleet of pool tables, and always-on movie screens adding an arty-party flair. 110 University Place (btwn 12th and 13th sts.). © 212/ 255-8188 (Bowlmor) or 212/352-1161 (Pressure). www.bowlmor.com or www.pressurenyc.com. Subway: 4, 5, 6, L, N, R to 14th St./Union Sq.

Chumley's   Many bars in New York date their beginnings to Prohibition, but Chumley's still has that speakeasy feel. The crowd doesn't date back nearly as far, however. Come to warm yourself by the fire and indulge in a once-forbidden pleasure: beer. There is a good selection of on-taps and microbrews. The door is unmarked, with a metal grille on the small window; another entrance is at 58 Barrow St., which takes you in through a back courtyard. After a construction accident closed the place in the spring of 2007, the tough old legend announced that it would be reopening in the fall. 86 Bedford St. (at Barrow St.). © 212/675-4449. Subway: 1 to Christopher St.

Employee's Only ⊛ Don't let the palm reader in the doorway of the non-descript exterior of this bar fool you; though if she reads your palm, I can guarantee she will predict that you will very soon savor a tantalizing beverage. Employees Only goes to great lengths to recreate a 1920's speakeasy with a tin ceiling and bartenders in period costume. But who needs gimmicks when the cocktails are as good as they are here? The employees here have been well trained and drinks are done painstakingly and made with the freshest ingredients and top label liquors. The daiquiri I tried was so good, Hemingway would be proud. In fact, it's called the Hemingway Daiquiri. The Ginger Smash, a concoction of muddled ginger root, fresh cranberries, Beefeater Wet and Apple Liquor sounds like a disaster, but the disparate ingredients surprisingly form a classic cocktail. There is a full menu available, but skip the entrees and order a few of the very good appetizers to accompany your drinks, the best being the very ample Serbian charcuterie platter. 510 Hudson St. (btwn Christopher and W. 10th sts.) © 212/ 242-3021. www.employeesonlynyc.com. Subway: 1 to Christopher St.

Hudson Bar & Books   This former gentlemen's club maintains a similar appeal as an elegant bar. Among the draws are cool jazz, a copper-topped marble bar, good lighting, comfortable seating, and an extensive—and expensive—champagne, cocktails, cognacs, and malts menu. Pleasantly, the crowd comprises more at-home locals than preening tourists. A great date place. 636 Hudson St. (btwn Horatio and Jane sts.). © 212/ 229-2642. Subway: A, C, E to 14th St.; L to Eighth Ave.

CHELSEA

Bongo *(Value)*   This casual, comfortable mid-(20th)century-modern lounge is the place to come for cocktails that are well made and a great value considering their bathtub size. Don't miss the French martini, made with Vox vodka and Lillet—yum! Even better: Bongo boasts a full raw-bar—a half-dozen varieties of oysters, cherrystones, and littlenecks, even lobster and caviar—and an excellent lobster roll. The crowd is

Late-Night Bites

I have fond, but now distant, memories of barhopping until the early hours, rounded off by a meal in one of Chinatown's 24-hour restaurants only to emerge as the sun was rising the next day. Throughout the city, but especially downtown, are some great late-night eats. Here's a sampling:

Open until 4am nightly, **Blue Ribbon**, 97 Sullivan St., between Prince and Spring streets in SoHo (✆ **212/274-0404**), is where the city's top chefs come to unwind after they close their own kitchens. Thanks to a top-drawer oyster bar and excellent comfort food, this cozy bistro is always packed, so expect a wait.

Other great choices for after-hours eats include the funky Francophile diner **Florent** (69 Gansevoort St., ✆ **212/989-5779**; www.restaurantflorent.com), in the Meat-Packing District. TriBeCa has **The Odeon** (p. 166), an attractive and affordable Art Deco bistro that's one of the top after-hours eateries in town. In the East Village, head to **Veselka** (p. 176), a comfortable and appealing diner offering eastern European fare at rock-bottom prices; **Katz's Delicatessen** (p. 170) for first-class Jewish deli eats Friday and Saturday until 2:30am. In Chinatown, many restaurants are open late or even all night, but don't miss **Wo Hop** (p. 174), open 24 hours, for really, really late-night dining.

In the Theater District feast on first-class pastrami and cheesecake until 3:45am at **Carnegie Deli** (p. 199), until 2am at the **Stage Deli** (p. 199).

hip but, not too trendy. Come early if you want to have space to sit and eat. 299 Tenth Ave. (btwn 27th and 28th sts.). ✆ 212/947-3654. Subway: C, E to 23rd St.

Kanvas   Apropos to its location, just a stone's throw from west Chelsea's clutch of cutting-edge art galleries, this sleek Chelsea lounge doubles as an art gallery, so it makes a great place to commune with an artsy crowd. It's a plush designer space, with a classic, long wood bar up front, cozy banquettes in back, and artwork that rotates monthly. The martini menu boasts two dozen, including a mint chocolate-chip version. Monday through Wednesday, $20 pitchers of mojitos and sangria are the draw. 219 Ninth Ave. (btwn 23rd and 24th sts.). ✆ 212/727-2616. Subway: C, E to 23rd St.

Serena   Done in deep, sexy reds, Serena is as hip as can be—I've even spotted mixmaster Moby here. It's relatively unpretentious considering its hot-spot status; still, dress the part if you want to make it past the doorman, especially on weekends. The crowd is young and pretty, and the schizophrenic music mix is a blast—think Fatboy Slim meets ABBA meets Foghat, and you'll get the picture. In the basement level of the Hotel Chelsea, 222 W. 23rd St. (btwn Seventh and Eighth aves.). ✆ 212/255-4646. Subway: C, E, 1 to 23rd St.

THE FLATIRON DISTRICT, UNION SQUARE & GRAMERCY PARK

Two of the city's oldest bars are in the Flatiron District, **Old Town Bar & Restaurant** and **Pete's Tavern.** See the sidebar "Drinking with Ghosts," on p. 374, for more.

Dusk *(Finds*   This casual, artsy lounge is a great choice for a cocktail. There's a fab mirrored mosaic wall, cozy banquettes, a friendly bar serving affordable drinks, a pool

The New York Dive Experience

Not all of New York nightlife means bars and clubs with cover charges, expensive cocktails, elegant finger food, beautiful people, and velvet ropes to keep you waiting in the cold. There are places that you should be rewarded for braving; old dark places where the drinks are cheap and the characters colorful. These are the dive bars and they are just as New York as their hot, trendy counterparts. Here are some of my favorites; swing by one of them for a real New York experience.

Jimmy's Corner, 140 W. 44th St., between Broadway and Sixth Avenue (© **212/221-9510**). Owned by a former boxing trainer, Jimmy's is a tough-guy's joint that has been around for more than 30 years and survived the Disney-fication of Times Square. Pictures of boxers adorn the walls, and the jukebox plays lots of R&B and '70s disco. In the pre–smoking ban days, the smoke would get so thick in Jimmy's you needed night goggles to see through the haze. Beer is cheap and drinks aren't fancy. Skip the theme bars and restaurants in the area and go for an after-theater pop at Jimmy's instead.

Rudy's Bar & Grill, 627 Ninth Ave., between 44th and 45th streets (© 212/ 974-9169). This Hell's Kitchen establishment is no secret; its happy hour is legendary and the small place is usually packed with slackers sucking up cheap beer, including the house brand, Rudy's Red, a weak brew served in a huge plastic cup for $3. My advice is to get here before happy hour, grab a seat on one of the few broken banquettes, and keep your eyes open for the hot-dog guy who gives out free hot dogs. You'll need one to balance out a bucket of Rudy's Red. In the summer, Rudy's opens its cement garden for drinks "alfresco."

table, and mostly U.K. tunes—from drum-and-bass to Super Furry Animals to Blur to Enya—on the sound system. Expect an easygoing, youngish crowd that stays relaxed and unpretentious into the evening. No sign, but look for the three blue lights attached to a dark storefront. 147 W. 24th St. (btwn Sixth and Seventh aves.). © 212/924-4490. Subway: F to 23rd St.

Rose Bar ⊛ I usually abhor bars that are "scenes"; where you need to be on a list to gain entry. But what Ian Schrager and artist Julian Schabel have created in the Gramercy Park Hotel makes going through the various humiliations it might take to get in almost worth it. The space is spectacular with rose-colored velvet chairs, original Warhols and Schnabels on the walls, a wood-burning fireplace, a red and white tile floor, and a billiards table you will be very intimidated to even approach. But sit on one of those plush chairs, sip your $20 cocktail, enjoy the flawless sound system commandeered by various top name DJs and for a few moments you might forget that you really don't belong in this swanky, celebrity-laden environment. Reservations (and they are hard to get) are mandatory after 10pm and security is tight. 2 Lexington Ave (btwn 20th and 21st sts.). © 212/920-3300. Subway: 6 to 23rd St.

Subway Inn, 143 E. 60th St., at Lexington Avenue (© **212/223-8929**). My all-time favorite dive, the Subway has been around for over 60 years and I believe some of the regulars have been on their stools the whole time. The red neon sign beckons from outside while inside, no matter what time of day, it's midnight dark. The bartender is ancient and until recently served Schaeffer on tap. The demise of Schaeffer was troubling, but thankfully, not much else has changed. The booths are still wobbly and the models of Godzilla and E.T. along with assorted other dusty junk continue to decorate the shelves behind the bar. The last time I visited, I was barred from entering the men's room by police who were shaking down one of the regulars during a drug bust. You might find workers from the upscale stores in the neighborhood and writers searching for "material" slumming at the Subway, but this joint remains the pinnacle of divedom.

Tap a Keg, 2731 Broadway, between 103rd and 104th streets (© **212/749-1734**). This dog-friendly establishment earned itself permanent Hall of Fame dive status when, on a recent visit, one of man's best friend found the middle of the bar's floor as the perfect spot to leave a hearty mound of affection that remained untouched by both the dog's clueless owner and the bar's unconcerned bartender. Tap a Keg claims to be a "Hell of a Joint" And now there is no doubt of that. If allowing free reign to dogs doesn't bother you, then you'll certainly enjoy the 7-hour happy hour with pints for about $3 and the regular gathering of wizened, disheveled characters.

TIMES SQUARE & MIDTOWN WEST

Don't forget those dives—you can find **Jimmy's Corner** and **Rudy's Bar & Grill** in the neighborhood (see the box "The New York Dive Experience," above).

Carnegie Club *(Finds* Like sister lounge **The Campbell Apartment** (p. 382), this swellegant lounge is another architecturally magnificent space, with soaring ceilings and an intimate mezzanine, plus a grand stone fireplace—a Gothic mood warmed up with plush, contemporary furnishings and a romantic vibe. "Weekends with Sinatra" stars Cary Hoffman and the Stan Rubin Orchestra in a wonderfully evocative—and surprisingly exact—cabaret show featuring the music of Frank Sinatra (two shows nightly on Sat; cover $30, plus $15 minimum). There's also live swing on Friday. Reservations are recommended on live-music nights. 156 W. 56th St. (btwn Sixth and Seventh aves.). © **212/957-9676.** Subway: F, Q to 57th St.

Hudson Bar Outfitted like a futuristic canteen, Hudson Bar, in the Hudson Hotel, glows from below with an underlit floor, while the low ceiling wears a Crayola-like fresco by Francesco Clemente. In between you'll find a tony, older-than-you'd-expect crowd. The one-of-a-kind cocktail menu is terrific. Enter at street level, on the Ninth

Avenue side of the hotel's main entrance; dress well to avoid attitude. 356 W. 58th St. (btwn Eighth and Ninth aves.). ℭ 212/554-6000. Subway: A, B, C, D, 1 to 59th St./Columbus Circle.

Mickey Mantle's *Kids*   Before Mickey Mantle's opened years ago, I was walking past the restaurant, peered into the window, and there was my boyhood idol, the Mick, sitting at the bar by himself. Through the window I waved—and he waved back. It made my day. And though the food's not very good and the drinks are over-priced, I still have a soft spot for Mickey Mantle's and always will. With plenty of Yankee memorabilia on the walls and sports on all the televisions, it's an ideal place to watch a game, but stick with the basics: beer and burgers. 42 Central Park South (btwn Fifth and Sixth aves.). ℭ 212/688-7777. www.theswearingens.com/mick/mmrest.htm. Subway: F to 57th St.

Morrell Wine Bar & Cafe   One of the leading wine purveyors in America (p. 342) has created the ideal place to sample the first-rate collection of vintages in comfort. Situated at the heart of Rockefeller Center, just across the alley from the plaza, the bi-level space is contemporary and comfortable and attended by an extremely knowledgeable waitstaff. In addition to the extensive bar and lounge space, a nice New American menu is also served. Make reservations for dinner. 1 Rockefeller Plaza (at 49th St.). ℭ 212/262-7700. www.morrellwinebar.com. Subway: B, D, F, V to 47th–50th sts./Rockefeller Center.

Rainbow Room   Skip eating here, but come to this legendary bar, sip a too-expensive cocktail, and soak in the ambience, views, and live piano music. No jeans or sneakers, please. There's a cover for drinks and dancing on select Fridays and Saturdays, but you can stop by to have a drink (in appropriate attire) without a cover other times. 30 Rockefeller Plaza (entrance on 49th St., btwn Fifth and Sixth aves., 64th floor). ℭ 212/632-5100. www.rainbowroom.com. Subway: B, D, F, V to 47th–50th sts./Rockefeller Center.

Russian Samovar ℛ   Yes it's a restaurant with Russian food, but the main attraction of this Theater District legend is the vodka. There are over 20 flavors of house-infused vodkas including dill, garlic, ginger, tarragon and, host and impresario Roman Kaplan's favorite, cranberry-lemon. Despite what it might do to you and how it will affect the plans you might have the next 24 hours, it's difficult to resist sampling many of them while listening to standards played by the house pianist. You might want to soften the bite of the vodka with a few appetizers like the Royal Fish Platter, a selection of smoked fish and a little caviar. Do not make this a pre-theater stop—you'll never make it to your show. 256 W. 52nd St. (btwn Eighth Ave. and Broadway). ℭ 212/757-0168. www.russiansamovar.com. Subway: 1 to 50th St.

MIDTOWN EAST & MURRAY HILL

The Campbell Apartment   This swank lounge on the mezzanine level at Grand Central Terminal has been created out of the former business office of prewar businessman John W. Campbell, who transformed the space into a pre-Renaissance palace worthy of a Medici. The high-ceilinged room has been restored to its full Florentine glory, and serves wines and champagnes by the glass, single-malt scotches, and haute noshies to a well-heeled commuting crowd. Try to snag a seat in the little-used upstairs room if you want some quiet. Call ahead before heading over, as the space tends to be closed for private parties on a rather frequent basis. No sneakers, baseball caps, athletic wear, or ripped jeans. In Grand Central Terminal, 15 Vanderbilt Ave. ℭ 212/953-0409. Subway: S, 4, 5, 6, 7 to 42nd St./Grand Central.

The Ginger Man   The big bait at this upscale beer bar is the 66 gleaming tap handles lining the wood-and-brass bar, dispensing everything from Sierra Nevada and

Checking into Hotel Bars

A hotel bar should provide comfort and hospitality to the out-of-town visitor. It should be the kind of place where you can unwind after a day of seeing the sights, have a leisurely drink before heading out to dinner or a show, or enjoy a quiet nightcap before retiring. When the bar becomes a nighttime destination unto itself, and hotel guests have to fight their way through a throng of locals just to get a drink, well, I'd say that hotel bar has defeated its purpose. Thankfully, New York has plenty of hotel bars that draw outsiders but keep their own guests happy, too. Here are my top picks:

Bemelmans Bar, in the Carlyle Hotel, 35 E. 76th St., at Madison Avenue (© 212/744-1600). This is my choice as New York's best hotel bar. It has everything you want in a hotel bar: white-coated service; lush seating with many dark romantic corners to sink into; a nice mix of locals and guests; and incredible cocktails, like the Old Cuban, a *mojito* topped with champagne. The bar is named after children's-book illustrator Ludwig Bemelmans, who created the *Madeline* books after he painted the whimsical mural here.

Bull and Bear, in the Waldorf=Astoria, 301 Park Ave., between 49th and 50th streets (© 212/872-4900). The Bull and Bear is like a gentlemen's pub, with brass-studded red leather chairs, a waistcoated staff, and a grand troika-shaped mahogany bar polished to a high sheen at the center of the room. Still, it's plenty comfy for casual drinkers. Ask Oscar, who's been here for more than 30 years, or one of the other accomplished bartenders to blend you a classic cocktail like The Bronx, a combination of gin, orange juice, and fresh pineapple juice. An ideal place to kick back after a hard day of sightseeing.

King Cole Bar, in the St. Regis, 2 E. 55th St., at Fifth Avenue (© 212/753-4500). The birthplace of the Bloody Mary, this theatrical spot may just be New York's most historic hotel bar. The Maxfield Parrish mural alone is worth the price of a classic cocktail (ask the bartender to tell you about the "hidden" meaning of the painting). The one drawback is the bar's small size; after-work hours and holiday times, the bar is jammed.

Oak Room at the Algonquin, in the Algonquin Hotel, 59 W. 44th St., between Fifth and Sixth avenues (© 212/840-6800). The splendid oak-paneled lobby of this venerable literati-favored hotel is the comfiest and most welcoming in the city, made to linger over pre- or post-theater cocktails. You'll feel the spirit of Dorothy Parker and the Algonquin Round Table that pervades the room. Try the Matilda, a light, refreshing blend of orange juice, Absolut Mandarin, triple sec, and champagne, named after the Algonquin's legendary feline in residence.

Hoegaarden to cask-conditioned ales. The cavernous space has a clubby feel. The Cohiba fumes were ripe here before the smoking ban but the new nonsmoking laws have not stopped the crowds from coming to this popular Murray Hill hangout. 11 E. 36th St. (btwn Fifth and Madison aves.). © 212/532-3740. Subway: 6 to 33rd St.

Monkey Bar   This legendary bar and restaurant has experienced quite a resurgence since Carrie and Mr. Big hooked up here on *Sex and the City.* It definitely deserved the attention: The swanky space is dolled up like a Hollywood supper club from the 1930s, the drinks are faultless, and the legendary monkey murals alone are worth a look. Skip the dining room and head directly to the piano bar for the ultimate Monkey Bar experience. At the Hotel Elysée, 60 E. 54th St. (btwn Madison and Park aves.). © 212/838-2600. Subway: 6 to 51st St.

Under the Volcano *Finds*   If you've been shopping crowded Macy's or braving the lines at the Empire State Building and want (need?) a drink, one of the few choices in the area, but a good one, is this Mexican-themed tequila bar. The decor is Mexican folk with Frida Kahlo undertones throughout, but the main attractions are the 16 varieties of tequila and the very smooth, subtly potent margaritas. The bar also features an excellent selection of aged rums. 12 E. 36th St. (btwn Fifth and Madison aves.). © 212/213-0093. Subway: B, D, F, N, R to 34th St.

Villard Bar & Lounge   This decadent two-floor lounge is a sumptuous place to celebrate over a cocktail and enjoy the McKim, Mead & White architecture of the Villard Houses. Word is the sage-and-pineapple martini is a real treat. Dress well to fit in with the Prada-suited, Manolo-heeled crowd. In the New York Palace Hotel, 24 E. 51st St. (at Madison Ave.). © 212/303-7757. Subway: E to Fifth Ave.; 6 to 51st St.

UPPER WEST SIDE

All State Cafe *Finds*   This subterranean pub is one of Manhattan's undiscovered treasures—the quintessential neighborhood "snugger." It's easy to miss from the street, and the regulars like it that way. The All State attracts a grown-up neighborhood crowd drawn in by the casual ambience, the great burgers, and an outstanding jukebox. If you're lucky, you'll get the round table by the fire. 250 W. 72nd St. (btwn Broadway and West End Ave.). © 212/874-1883. Subway: 1, 2, 3 to 72nd St.

Dublin House   For years, like a welcoming beacon, the Dublin House's neon harp has blinked invitingly. This very old pub is a no-frills Irish saloon and the perfect spot for a drink after visiting the nearby Museum of Natural History or Central Park. There's a long, narrow barroom up front and a bigger room in the back that's good for groups. Original wood veneer detail remains, adding to the pub's charm. The Guinness is cheap and drawn perfectly by the very able and sometimes crusty bartenders. Best enjoyed in the late afternoon or early evening when the regulars populate the bar. Stay away on weekend nights and St. Patrick's Day when the place is overrun with amateurs: frat boys and sorority girls on pub crawls. 225 W. 79th St. (btwn Broadway and Amsterdam Ave.). © 212/874-9528. Subway: 1 to 79th St.

UPPER EAST SIDE

Elaine's   *The Big Chill* claimed that Elaine's was over and done with way back when. They were dreaming. Glittering literati still come here for dinner and book parties. Look for regulars such as Woody Allen and other A-list types. If you can't get a table, you can always scan the room from the bar up front. 1703 Second Ave. (btwn 88th and 89th sts.). © 212/534-8103. Subway: 4, 5, 6 to 86th St.

Great Hall Balcony Bar *Moments*   One of Manhattan's best cocktail bars is only open on Friday and Saturday—and only from 4 to 8:30pm. The Metropolitan Museum of Art transforms the lobby's mezzanine into a cocktail-and-classical-music lounge twice weekly, offering a marvelous only-in–New York experience. The music is usually provided by a piano and string quartet. You'll have to pay the $10 admission, but the galleries are open until 9pm. At the Metropolitan Museum of Art, Fifth Ave. at 82nd St. ℰ 212/535-7710. www.metmuseum.org. Subway: 4, 5, 6 to 86th St.

HARLEM

Creole Tucked away in El Barrio (also known as east Harlem) is a relatively new and welcome addition to the uptown music scene. Creole is an intimate bar/restaurant that features top-notch jazz, Latin, R&B, and on Sunday, gospel. Sit at the bar or enjoy the music while chowing down on very good Southern/Cajun specialties—the gumbo might be the best in the city. Entertainment begins at 8:30pm, but you might want to venture in a little early for Creole's fun happy hour from 5 to 7pm. 2167 Third Ave. (at 118th St.). ℰ 212/876-8838. www.creolenyc.com. Subway: 6 to 116th St.

The Den ℰ *Finds* For not only the most creative cocktails north of 96th Street, but also the most imaginative drink names in all of Manhattan, come uptown to the fun, funky Den. Here you can sip concoctions like the "Pimp Slap," "Sex in the Inner City," "Bahama Baby Mama Drama," and the "Harlem Ice Tea," while watching a blaxploitation flick off the bar/restaurant's brick wall. Don't ask me what's in the drinks, just know that they are colorful, sweet, and very potent. On Saturday the brick wall is the screen for kung fu movies, while on Wednesday it's live old- and new-school R&B. To fortify yourself from those drinks, sample The Den's kitchen creations like the "Not ya mama's chicken and waffles," "Bruce LeeRoy's popcorn shrimp," "Mississippi Burnin' wings," or a "soul roll," The Den's take on sushi stuffed with, not raw fish, but BBQ pulled pork. 2150 Fifth Ave. (btwn 131st and 132nd sts.). ℰ 212/234-3045. www. thedenharlem.com. Subway: 3 to 135th St.

OUTER BOROUGHS

Bohemian Beer Hall & Garden ℰ At one time there were over 800 outdoor German beer gardens in New York. All are now gone except this lone Astoria survivor. A number of European, in particular, excellent Czech beers are available to drink under the stars on a balmy night from late spring to autumn. If you are hungry, there are Eastern European specialties like pork schnitzel and Hungarian goulash to accompany your beer. The Garden features live jazz every Thursday and if you are a member of the Bohemian Benevolent Society of Astoria, you get ten percent off on food. Just something to think about. And even when the garden isn't open, you can still get the hearty Bohemian food (and beer) indoors year-round. 29-19 24th Avenue, Astoria, Queens (btwn 29th & 31st sts.). ℰ 718/274-4925. www.bohemianhall.com. Subway: N/W to Astoria Blvd.

Pete's Candy Store This former candy store is Williamsburg's best place for live entertainment and games. The bar up front features the famous bi-weekly "spelling bee" held every other Monday, bingo on Tuesdays, a Quizz-Off on Wednesdays, and Scrabble on Saturdays. If games are not your thing, there is live music every night featuring some of New York's most promising up-and-coming rock bands. 709 Lorimer St (btwn Richardson and Frost sts.), Williamsburg, Brooklyn. ℰ 718/322-3770. www.petescandystore.com. Subway: L to Lorimer St.

8 Dance Clubs & Party Scenes

Nothing in New York nightlife is as mutable as the club scene. In this world, hot spots don't even get 15 minutes of fame—their time in the limelight is usually more like a commercial break.

First things first: Finding and going to the latest hot spot is not worth agonizing over. Clubbers spend their lives obsessing over the scene. My rule of thumb is that if I know about a place, it must not be hip anymore. Even if I could tell you where the hippest club kids hang out today, they'll have moved on by the time you arrive in town.

"Clubs" as actual, physical spaces don't mean much anymore. The hungry-for-nightlife crowd now follows events of certain party "producers" who switch venues and times each week. A number of bars and lounges listed in the previous section host "club" scenes on various nights of the week.

The tracking game is best left to the perennial party crowd who knows the guy at the door (who lets them in for free) and someone at the bar (who comps them drinks). You're not likely to get that well connected in your weeklong vacation. Just find someplace you like, and enjoy the crowd that enjoys it with you.

I've concentrated on a wide variety of club scenes below, from performance-artsy to perennially popular discos, most of which are generally easy to make your way into. You can find listings for the most current hot spots and movable parties in the **publications and online sources** listed at the start of this chapter. Additional online sources that might score you discount admissions to select clubs include **www.promony.com**. You can also check **www.sheckys.com** for VIP guest list access.

No matter what, **always call ahead,** because schedules change constantly and can do so at the last minute. Even better: You also may be able to put your name on a guest list that will save you a few bucks at the door.

New York nightlife starts late. With the exception of places that have scheduled performances, clubs stay almost empty until about 11pm. Don't depend on plastic—bring cash, and plan on dropping a wad at most places. Cover charges run anywhere from $7 to $30, and often get more expensive as the night wears on.

Avalon   Housed in the former church where dance-club legend Limelight once reigned supreme, the interior has been updated with VIP balconies that overlook the dance floor. Off the dance floor are many small rooms for commingling, if you are tired of dancing. 47 W. 20th St. (at Sixth Ave.). ✆ 212/807-7780. Subway: F to 23rd St.

Baktun   This club has been hot, hot, hot since the word go. Sleek Baktun was conceived in 2000 as a multimedia lounge, and as such incorporates avant-garde video projections (shown on a clever double-sided video screen) into its raging dance parties, as well as live cybercasts. The music tends toward electronica, with some live acts in the mix. At press time, Saturday's Direct Drive was the key drum 'n' bass party in town. 418 W. 14th St. (btwn Ninth Ave. and Washington St.). ✆ 212/206-1590. www.baktun.com. Subway: A, C, E, L to 14th St./Eighth Ave.

Black   Formerly known as Exit, this space has been called the "supermall of nightclubs," and for good reason—it covers 45,000 square feet and is able to accommodate more than 5,000 partiers. Any velvet-rope scene is pure posturing. The main floor is a mammoth atrium with a DJ booth—usually housing the top talent of the moment spinning tunes—suspended above. The space was made for crazy carnival acts like Antigravity, a bizarre clubland take on the Flying Wallendas. Upstairs is a warren of ultraplush VIP rooms, each with its own DJ. With a capacity this big, expect clubgoers of all stripes to show up on any given night. 610 W. 56th St. (btwn Eleventh and Twelfth aves.). ✆ 212/582-8282. www.exitnyc.com. Subway: A, B, C, D, 1 to 59th St./Columbus Circle.

Bungalow 8   This is the ultimate in dance-club extravagance. Here drinks might cost as much as a week at your hotel. All the cutthroat tactics learned on *The Apprentice* or

Survivor might not help to gain entry to this palace. 515 W. 27th St. (btwn Tenth and Eleventh aves.). ℭ **212/629-3333.** Subway: C, E to 23rd St.

Cafe Wha? You'll find a carefree crowd dancing in the aisles of this casual basement club just about any night of the week. From Wednesday through Sunday, the stage features the house's own Wha Band, which does an excellent job of cranking out crowd-pleasing covers of familiar rock-'n'-roll hits from the '70s, '80s, and '90s. Monday night is the hugely popular Brazilian Dance Party, while Tuesday night is Classic Funk Night. Expect to be surrounded by lots of Jersey kids and out-of-towners on the weekends, but so what? Reservations are a good idea. The cover runs from free to $10. 115 MacDougal St. (btwn Bleecker and W. 3rd sts.). ℭ **212/254-3706.** www.cafewha.com. Subway: A, B, C, D, E, F, V to W. 4th St.

Cain At Cain the theme is Africa—South Africa to be specific. The front door, if you gain entry, has elephant-trunk handles, there are zebra hides everywhere, and the big game is celebrity-spotting. The DJ's spin energetic house music to keep the hordes moving, but you might be better off sampling one of the club's excellent cocktails in the "premium seating lounge." God knows what it takes to get a seat there. 544 W. 27th St. (btwn 10th & 11th aves.). ℭ **212/947-8000.** Subway: C, E to 23rd St.

Cielo At Cielo you'll find the best sound system of any small club in New York. House is big here and they regularly bring in some of the best DJs from around the globe. The renowned Louis Vega is the DJ on Wednesday. There's a sunken dance floor and an authentic, glittering disco ball rotating above. What more could you want? 18 Little W. 12th St. (btwn Ninth Ave. and Washington St.). ℭ **212/645-5700.** www.cieloclub. com. Subway: A, C, E, to 14th St.; L to 8th Ave.

Club Shelter House-heads flock to this old-school disco. The big draw is the "Saturday Night Shelter Party," when late 1980s house music takes over. The crowd is racially and sexually diverse and dress is not fancy; wear whatever is comfortable for doing some heavy sweating on the dance floor. 20 W. 39th St. (btwn Fifth and Sixth aves.). ℭ **212/719-4479.** www.clubshelter.com. Subway: B, D, F, Q, V, 7 to 42nd St.

Don Hill's This long-lived, eccentric, divey club draws a heavily integrated gay-lesbian/straight crowd that comes for rock, glam, and punk some nights, campy parties on others. Röck Cändy is a fun neo-glam resurrection on Wednesday nights, featuring live hair-metal bands (for whom there is still a scene in New York). Drinks are affordable. 511 Greenwich St. (at Spring St.). ℭ **212/334-1390.** www.donhills.com. Subway: 1 to Canal St.

Pacha No, you are not on exotic Ibiza, but in Hell's Kitchen, New York. But enter Pacha and wade through the club's four levels, marvel at the palm trees, ogle discreetly the bikini-clad go go girls dancing in the red-lit showers and you'll for a few hours be transported somewhere a little less hellish than Hell's Kitchen. 618 W. 46th St (btwn 11th Ave and the West Side Hwy.). ℭ **212/209-7500.** www.pachany.com. Subway: A, C, E, 7 to 42nd St.

Swing 46 *Finds* Swing is a nightly affair at this Theater District jazz and supper club (supper not required). Music is live nightly except Monday, when a DJ takes over, and runs the gamut from big band to boogie-woogie to jump blues. Do not miss Vince Giordano and His Nighthawks if they're on the bill, especially if sharp-dressed Casey McGill is singing and strumming his ukulele, too. The Harlem Renaissance Orchestra is another great choice. Even first-timers can join in the fun, as free swing lessons are offered Wednesday through Saturday at 9:15pm. No jeans or sneakers. 349 W. 46th St. (btwn Eighth and Ninth aves.). ℭ **212/262-9554.** www.swing46.com. Subway: C, E to 50th St.

13 *Value*   This little lounge is a great place to dance the night away. It's stylish but unpretentious, with a steady roster of fun weekly parties. Sunday night's Britpop fest Shout! lives on, as popular as ever—and with no cover, to boot. The rest of the week runs the gamut from '70s and '80s New Wave and glam nights to progressive house and trance to poetry slams and performance art. If there's a cover, it's usually $5, occasionally $7 or $10. Happy hour offers two-for-one drinks (and no cover) from 4 to 8pm. 35 E. 13th St. (btwn Broadway and University Place), 2nd floor. ℭ 212/979-6677. www.bar13. com. Subway: 4, 5, 6, L, N, R, Q, W to 14th St./Union Sq.

9 The Gay & Lesbian Scene

To get a thorough, up-to-date take on what's happening in gay and lesbian nightlife, pick up copies of *HX* (www.hx.com), *Gay City News* (www.gaycitynews.com), the *New York Blade* (www.nyblade.com), *GONYC* (www.gomag.com) or *Next*. They're available for free in bars and clubs all around town or at the **Lesbian and Gay Community Center,** at 208 W. 13th St., between Seventh and Eighth avenues (ℭ 212/620-7310; www.gaycenter.org). The interdisciplinary weekly *Time Out New York* boasts a terrific gay and lesbian section that some consider the city's best source; another great source is the legendary free weekly *Village Voice.* Or try **Metro Source NY** (www.metrosource.com) a bi-monthy magazine which features an extensive entertainment section. Always remember that asking people in one bar can lead you to discover another that fits your tastes.

These days, many bars, clubs, cabarets, and cocktail lounges are neither gay nor straight but a bit of both, either catering to a mixed crowd or to varying orientations on different nights. In addition to the choices below, most of the clubs listed in "Dance Clubs & Party Scenes," above, cater to a gay crowd, some predominantly so.

Barracuda   Chelsea is central to gay life—and gay bars. This trendy, loungey place is a continuing favorite, regularly voted "Best Bar" by *HX* readers, while *Paper* singles out the hunky bartenders. There's a sexy bar for cruising out front and a comfy lounge in back. Look for the regular drag shows. 275 W. 22nd St. (btwn Seventh and Eighth aves.). ℭ 212/645-8613. Subway: C, E, 1 to 23rd St.

Boiler Room   This down-to-earth East Village bar is everybody's favorite gay dive. Despite the mixed guy-girl crowd, it's a serious cruising scene for well-sculpted beautiful boys and a perfectly fine hangout for those who'd rather play pool. 86 E. 4th St. (btwn First and Second aves.). ℭ 212/254-7536. Subway: F to Second Ave.

Brandy's Piano Bar   Though gay, this intimate, old-school piano bar attracts a mixed crowd for the friendly atmosphere and nightly entertainment. The talented waitstaff does most of the singing while waiting for their big break, but enthusiastic patrons regularly join in. 235 E. 84th St. (btwn Second and Third aves.). ℭ 212/650-1944. Subway: 4, 5, 6 to 86th St.

The Cock *Finds*   This gleefully seedy East Village joint is the most envelope-pushing gay club in town. A self-proclaimed "rock and sleaze fag bar," it's dedicated to good-natured depravity. Head elsewhere if you're the retiring type. 29 Second Ave. (btwn 1st and 2nd sts.). ℭ 212/777-6254. Subway: F, V to Second Ave.

Duplex Cabaret   The heart of the gay cabaret and piano-bar scene. Expect a high camp factor and lots of good-natured fun that runs the gamut from mini-musicals to

Cattyshack is a little ol' place where we can get together . . .

Head over to Park Slope (aka "Dyke Slope") NYC's favorite lesbian bar, **Cattyshack** (249 Fourth Ave., between Carroll and President sts.; © **718/230-5740**; www.cattyshackbklyn.com; take the R train to Union St. or F train to Fourth Ave./9th St.).

Brooke Webster, proprietor of the late, legendary Meow Mix, which succumbed to the rising rents and gentrification of the Lower East Side, took her party across the Manhattan Bridge to a much larger space that has quickly become a favorite hangout for NYC lesbians and their friends. The two-level club offers several kinds of ambience, ranging from casual pool playing, beer sipping, TV watching downstairs to upstairs dance parties where DJs play all genres of music, frequently featuring go-go girls.

Theme nights are popular, with regularly scheduled trivia contests, karaoke, and (of course) *The L Word* viewing parties and events.

On Sunday there's all-you-can-eat pizza and beer during football season (and after). And in good weather, everyone heads for the back patio, where a weekly barbecue/beer bust (with vegetarian selections!) draws crowds all summer long.

drag revues to stand-up comedy. 61 Christopher St. (at Seventh Ave.). © **212/255-5438**. Subway: 1 to Christopher St.

Henrietta Hudson   This friendly and extremely popular women's bar/lounge is known for drawing in an attractive, upmarket lipstick lesbian crowd that comes for the great jukebox and videos as well as the pleasingly-low-key atmosphere. There's a $5-to-$7 cover when DJs spin tunes on Friday and Saturday and when live bands are in the house on Sunday. 438–444 Hudson St. (at Morton St.). © **212/924-3347**. www.henrietta hudsons.com. Subway: 1 to Houston St.

Splash/SBNY   Beautiful bartenders, video screens playing campy scenes, New York's best drag queens—Splash has it all. Theme nights are a big deal. The best is Musical Mondays, dedicated to Broadway video clips and music. Musical Mondays' singalongs are such a blast that they draw a crossover gay/straight crowd as well as such Broadway faves like Nathan Lane and the cast of *Mamma Mia!* 50 W. 17th St. (btwn Fifth and Sixth aves.). © **212/691-0073**. www.splashbar.com. Subway: F, V to 14th St.; 4, 5, 6, L, N, R, Q, W to 14th St./Union Sq.

Stonewall Bar   The spot where it all started. A mixed gay and lesbian crowd—old and young, beautiful, and great personalities—makes this an easy place to begin. At least pop in to relive a defining moment in queer history. 53 Christopher St. (east of Seventh Ave.). © **212/463-0950**. Subway: 1 to Christopher St.

View Bar *(Finds)*   Up front is a very attractive and comfortable lounge, in back is a pool room with the name-worthy view, and throughout you'll find friendly bartenders, affordable drinks, and Kenneth Cole–dressed boys who could pass on either side of bi. A welcome addition to the scene. 232 Eighth Ave. (btwn 21st and 22nd sts.). © **212/929-2243**. Subway: C, E to 23rd St.

Index

See also Accommodations and Restaurant indexes, below.

A Guide for Every Type of Traveler

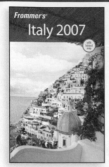

Frommer's Complete Guides

For those who value complete coverage, candid advice, and lots of choices in all price ranges.

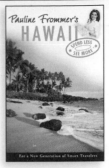

Pauline Frommer's Guides

For those who want to experience a culture, meet locals, and save money along the way.

MTV Guides

For hip, youthful travelers who want a fresh perspective on today's hottest cities and destinations.

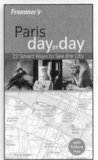

Day by Day Guides

For leisure or business travelers who want to organize their time to get the most out of a trip.

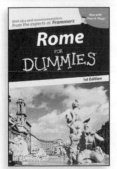

Frommer's With Kids Guides

For families traveling with children ages 2 to 14 seeking kid-friendly hotels, restaurants, and activities.

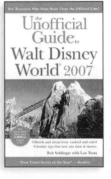

Unofficial Guides

For honeymooners, families, business travelers, and others who value no-nonsense, *Consumer Reports*–style advice.

For Dummies Travel Guides

For curious, independent travelers looking for a fun and easy way to plan a trip.

Visit Frommers.com

Now you know.